Honda ANF125 Innova
Service and Repair Manual
by Matthew Coombs

Models covered
ANF125 Innova 2003 to 2006
ANF125i Innova 2007 to 2012

(4926-256)

© Haynes Publishing 2012

ABCDE
FGHIJ
KLMNO
PQRST

A book in the Haynes Service and Repair Manual Series

All rights reserved. No part of this book may be reproduced or transmitted in any form or by any means, electronic or mechanical, including photocopying, recording or by any information storage or retrieval system, without permission in writing from the copyright holder.

ISBN: **978 1 84425 926 7**

British Library Cataloguing in Publication Data
A catalogue record for this book is available from the British Library

Printed in the USA

Haynes Publishing
Sparkford, Yeovil, Somerset BA22 7JJ, England

Haynes North America, Inc
861 Lawrence Drive, Newbury Park, California 91320, USA

Haynes Publishing Nordiska AB
Box 1504, 751 45 Uppsala, Sweden

Contents

LIVING WITH YOUR HONDA INNOVA

Introduction

The Birth of a Dream	Page	0•4
Acknowledgements	Page	0•8
About this manual	Page	0•8
Model development	Page	0•9
Bike Spec	Page	0•9
Identification numbers	Page	0•10
Buying spare parts	Page	0•11
Safety first!	Page	0•12

Pre-ride checks

Engine oil level	Page	0•13
Suspension and steering	Page	0•13
Front brake fluid level	Page	0•14
Tyres	Page	0•15
Legal and safety checks	Page	0•15

MAINTENANCE

Routine maintenance and servicing

Specifications	Page	1•2
Lubricants and fluids	Page	1•2
Maintenance and service schedule	Page	1•3
Component locations	Page	1•4
Maintenance and service procedures	Page	1•6

Contents

REPAIRS AND OVERHAUL

Engine, transmission and associated systems

Engine, clutches and transmission	Page	**2•1**
Carburettor fuel system and exhaust	Page	**3A•1**
Fuel injection system and exhaust	Page	**3B•1**
Ignition system	Page	**4•1**

Chassis components

Frame and suspension	Page	**5•1**
Brakes, wheels and final drive	Page	**6•1**
Bodywork	Page	**7•1**

Electrical system   Page **8•1**

Wiring diagrams   Page **8•29**

REFERENCE

Tools and Workshop Tips	Page	**REF•2**
Security	Page	**REF•20**
Lubricants and fluids	Page	**REF•23**
Conversion factors	Page	**REF•26**
MOT Test Checks	Page	**REF•27**
Storage	Page	**REF•32**
Fault Finding	Page	**REF•35**
Technical Terms Explained	Page	**REF•44**

Index   Page **REF•48**

Introduction

The Birth of a Dream

by Julian Ryder

There is no better example of the Japanese post-war industrial miracle than Honda. Like other companies which have become household names, it started with one man's vision. In this case the man was the 40-year old Soichiro Honda who had sold his piston-ring manufacturing business to Toyota in 1945 and was happily spending the proceeds on prolonged parties for his friends. However, the difficulties of getting around in the chaos of post-war Japan irked Honda, so when he came across a job lot of generator engines he realised that here was a way of getting people mobile again at low cost.

A 12 by 18-foot shack in Hamamatsu became his first bike factory, fitting the generator motors into pushbikes. Before long he'd used up all 500 generator motors and started manufacturing his own engine, known as the 'chimney', either because of the elongated cylinder head or the smoky exhaust or perhaps both. The chimney made all of half a horsepower from its 50 cc engine but it was a major success and became the Honda A-type.

Less than two years after he'd set up in Hamamatsu, Soichiro Honda founded the Honda Motor Company in September 1948. By then, the A-type had been developed into the 90 cc B-type engine, which Mr Honda decided deserved its own chassis not a bicycle frame. Honda was about to become Japan's first post-war manufacturer of complete motorcycles. In August 1949 the first prototype was ready. With an output of three horsepower, the 98 cc D-type was still a simple two-stroke but it had a two-speed transmission and most importantly a pressed steel frame with telescopic forks and hard tail rear end. The frame was almost triangular in profile with the top rail going in a straight line from the massively braced steering head to the rear axle. Legend has it that after the D-type's first tests the entire workforce went for a drink to celebrate and try and think of a name for the bike. One man broke one of those silences you get when people are thinking, exclaiming 'This is like a dream!' 'That's it!' shouted Honda, and so the Honda Dream was christened.

> 'This is like a dream!'
> 'That's it'
> shouted Honda

Mr Honda was a brilliant, intuitive engineer and designer but he did not bother himself with the marketing side of his business. With hindsight, it is possible to see that employing Takeo Fujisawa who would both sort out the home market and plan the eventual expansion into overseas markets was a masterstroke. He arrived in October 1949 and in 1950 was made Sales Director. Another vital new name was Kiyoshi Kawashima, who along with Honda himself, designed the company's first four-stroke after Kawashima had told them that the four-stroke opposition to Honda's two-strokes sounded nicer and therefore sold better. The result of that statement was the overhead-valve 148 cc E-type which first ran in July 1951 just two months after the first drawings were made. Kawashima was made a director of the Honda Company at 34 years old.

The E-type was a massive success, over 32,000 were made in 1953 alone, a feat of mass-production that was astounding by the

Honda C70 and C90 OHV-engined models

Introduction 0•5

standards of the day given the relative complexity of the machine. But Honda's lifelong pursuit of technical innovation sometimes distracted him from commercial reality. Fujisawa pointed out that they were in danger of ignoring their core business, the motorised bicycles that still formed Japan's main means of transport. In May 1952 the F-type Cub appeared, another two-stroke despite the top men's reservations. You could buy a complete machine or just the motor to attach to your own bicycle. The result was certainly distinctive, a white fuel tank with a circular profile went just below and behind the saddle on the left of the bike, and the motor with its horizontal cylinder and bright red cover just below the rear axle on the same side of the bike. This was the machine that turned Honda into the biggest bike maker in Japan with 70% of the market for bolt-on bicycle motors, the F-type was also the first Honda to be exported. Next came the machine that would turn Honda into the biggest motorcycle manufacturer in the world.

The C100 Super Cub was a typically audacious piece of Honda engineering and marketing. For the first time, but not the last, Honda invented a completely new type of motorcycle, although the term 'scooterette' was coined to describe the new bike which had many of the characteristics of a scooter but the large wheels, and therefore stability, of a motorcycle. The first one was sold in August 1958, fifteen years later over nine-million of them were on the roads of the world. If ever a machine can be said to have brought mobility to the masses it is the Super Cub. If you add in the electric starter that was added for the C102 model of 1961, the design of the Super Cub has remained substantially unchanged ever since, testament to how right Honda got it first time. The Super Cub made Honda the world's biggest manufacturer after just two years of production.

The CB250N Super Dream became a favorite with UK learner riders of the late seventies and early eighties

Honda's export drive started in earnest in 1957 when Britain and Holland got their first bikes, America got just two bikes the next year. By 1962 Honda had half the American market with 65,000 sales. But Soichiro Honda had already travelled abroad to Europe and the USA, making a special

The GL1000 introduced in 1975, was the first in Honda's line of GoldWings

0•6 Introduction

Carl Fogarty in action at the Suzuka 8 Hour on the RC45

An early CB750 Four

point of going to the Isle of Man TT, then the most important race in the GP calendar. He realised that no matter how advanced his products were, only racing success would convince overseas markets for whom 'Made in Japan' still meant cheap and nasty. It took five years from Soichiro Honda's first visit to the Island before his bikes were ready for the TT. In 1959 the factory entered five riders in the 125 class. They did not have a massive impact on the event being benevolently regarded as a curiosity, but sixth, seventh and eighth were good enough for the team prize. The bikes were off the pace but they were well engineered and very reliable.

The TT was the only time the West saw the Hondas in '59, but they came back for more the following year with the first of a generation of bikes which shaped the future of motorcycling – the double-overhead-cam four-cylinder 250. It was fast and reliable – it revved to 14,000 rpm – but didn't handle anywhere near as well as the opposition. However, Honda had now signed up non-Japanese riders to lead their challenge. The first win didn't come until 1962 (Aussie Tom Phillis in the Spanish 125 GP) and was followed up with a world-shaking performance at the TT. Twenty-one year old Mike Hailwood won both 125 and 250 cc TTs and Hondas filled the top five positions in both races. Soichiro Honda's master plan was starting to come to fruition, Hailwood and Honda won the 1961 250 cc World Championship. Next year Honda won three titles. The other Japanese factories fought back and inspired Honda to produce some of the most fascinating racers ever seen: the awesome six-cylinder 250, the five-cylinder 125, and the 500 four with which the immortal Hailwood battled Agostini and the MV Agusta.

When Honda pulled out of racing in '67 they had won sixteen rider's titles, eighteen manufacturer's titles, and 137 GPs, including 18 TTs, and introduced the concept of the modern works team to motorcycle racing. Sales success followed racing victory as Soichiro Honda had predicted, but only because the products advanced as rapidly as the racing machinery. The Hondas that came to Britain in the early '60s were incredibly sophisticated. They had overhead cams where the British bikes had pushrods, they had electric starters when the Brits relied on the kickstart, they had 12V electrics when even the biggest British bike used a 6V system. There seemed no end to the technical wizardry. It wasn't that the technology itself was so amazing but just like that first E-type, it was the fact that Honda could mass-produce it more reliably than the lower-tech competition that was so astonishing.

When in 1968 the first four-cylinder CB750 road bike arrived the world of motorcycling changed for ever, they even had to invent a new word for it, 'Superbike'. Honda raced again with the CB750 at Daytona and won the

Introduction

World Endurance title with a prototype DOHC version that became the CB900 roadster. There was the six-cylinder CBX, the CX500T – the world's first turbocharged production bike, they invented the full-dress tourer with the GoldWing, and came back to GPs with the revolutionary oval-pistoned NR500 four-stroke, a much-misunderstood bike that was more a rolling experimental laboratory than a racer. Just to show their versatility Honda also came up with the weird CX500 shaft-drive V-twin, a rugged workhorse that powered a new industry, the courier companies that oiled the wheels of commerce in London and other big cities.

It was true, though, that Mr Honda was not keen on two-strokes – early motocross engines had to be explained away to him as lawnmower motors! However, in 1982 Honda raced the NS500, an agile three-cylinder lightweight against the big four-cylinder opposition in 500 GPs. The bike won in its first year and in '83 took the world title for Freddie Spencer. In four-stroke racing the V4 layout took over from the straight four, dominating TT, F1 and Endurance championships with the RVF750, the nearest thing ever built to a Formula 1 car on wheels. And when Superbike arrived Honda were ready with the RC30. On the roads the VFR V4 became an instant classic while the CBR600 invented another new class of bike on its way to becoming a best-seller. The V4 road bikes had problems to start with but the VFR750 sold world-wide over its lifetime while the VFR400 became a massive commercial success and cult bike in Japan. The original RC30 won the first two World Superbike Championships is 1988 and '89, but Honda had to wait until 1997 to win it again with the RC45, the last of the V4 roadsters. In Grands Prix, the NSR500 V4 two-stroke superseded the NS triple and became the benchmark racing machine of the '90s. Mick Doohan secured his place in history by winning five World Championships in consecutive years on it.

In yet another example of Honda inventing a new class of motorcycle, they came up with the astounding CBR900RR FireBlade, a bike with the punch of a 1000 cc motor in a package the size and weight of a 750. It became a cult bike as well as a best seller, and with judicious redesigns continues to give much more recent designs a run for their money.

When it became apparent that the high-tech V4 motor of the RC45 was too expensive to produce, Honda looked to a V-twin engine to power its flagship for the first time. Typically, the VTR1000 FireStorm was a much more rideable machine than its opposition and once accepted by the market formed the basis of the next generation of Superbike racer, the VTR-SP-1.

One of Mr Honda's mottos was that technology would solve the customers' problems, and no company has embraced

The CX500 – Honda's first V-Twin and a favorite choice of dispatch riders

cutting-edge technology more firmly than Honda. In fact Honda often developed new technology, especially in the fields of materials science and metallurgy. The embodiment of that was the NR750, a bike that was misunderstood nearly as much as the original NR500 racer. This limited-edition technological tour-de-force embodied many of Soichiro Honda's ideals. It used the latest techniques and materials in every component, from the oval piston, 32-valve V4 motor to the titanium coating on the windscreen, it was – as Mr Honda would have wanted – the best it could possibly be. A fitting memorial to the man who has shaped the motorcycle industry and motorcycles as we know them today.

Innova's Heritage

How do you redesign the most successful motorcycle ever made? The Honda Cub in all its incarnations has sold more than 60-million units, and got more people mobile in more parts of the world than any machine before or since has ever done. It is the solid foundation on which not just the Honda company is built but arguably the modern motorcycle industry as well.

It is impossible to over-state the impact

The VFR400R was a cult bike in Japan and a popular grey import in the UK

Introduction

The ANF125-3 **The ANF125i-7**

of the Cub. The vision of Soichiro Honda's business partner Takeo Fujisawa foresaw a new type of machine, neither bike nor scooter, which would be saleable in the West as well as the developing countries of the Far East. Furthermore, Honda would set up subsidiaries to market it, first in the USA and then in European countries. The sheer audacity of this vision in mid-1950s Japan is impossible to overstate.

The engineering genius of Honda-san himself came up with a simple, rugged, reliable but totally fresh design. Motorcycle-size wheels were necessary for the dirt roads of developing countries but Europe and the States liked them too for stability. Like other early Hondas, the Cub got a pressed-steel frame but plastic bodywork, a major break-through in production engineering. The first Cub was sold in 1958, and by 1960 the Suzuka factory built to make it was the biggest in the world. Fujisawa's vision was borne out. The Cub gave the European ride-to-work customer civilised, reliable and affordable transport yet it was tough enough to deal with the rigours of the Third World.

So, how do you follow that? Sensibly, by not changing very much. Even a design as near-perfect as the Cub has to be updated eventually. The objective remained the same though, a bike for all markets. Unsurprisingly, the basic layout stays with the air-cooled OHC motor suspended horizontally below the frame. The new frame is a square-section tubular steel backbone as opposed to pressed steel, and there is more plastic than in earlier models. There is also more attention to styling. After all, youth is just as fashion-conscious in Jakarta and Kuala Lumpur as it is in Milan and London.

Over its life, the Cub had several different capacity engines whereas the new generation started with three: 100, 110 and 125cc. Collectively they are the NF series, often bearing the model names Wave in Asia and Innova in Europe. The 125 usually got all the good stuff – disc front brake, digital instruments – whereas they were options on the smaller models. The hidden high technology is in the engine of the 125; a ceramic-coated piston and roller bearings for the camshaft. It could be argued that the whole of the engine is a very clever piece of design.

How many other air-cooled four-strokes meet the European Community's current Euro-3 emissions legislation?

There are of course other modern refinements, like fuel injection, but the genes of the original Cub are still easily detectable. There is ease of riding with clutchless gearchanges thanks to the centrifugal clutch; the practicality of weather protection and under-seat storage; a fully enclosed drive chain to protect and extend chain life, very low running costs; and above all the ability to run for years no matter what the conditions.

When the first Cub appeared, no one really knew what to call it. It obviously wasn't a scooter, and couldn't really be described as a motorcycle either. Eventually, the phrase 'step-through' was coined, although not widely used in Malaysia. South-east Asia came up with a second name: 'under-bone,' describing the main frame member running between the rider's feet. Can you think of any other family of bikes that has needed two completely new names to describe them? Neither can I. And for the record, the Cub family has now sold over 66-million units.

Acknowledgements

Our thanks are due to Bransons Motorcycles of Yeovil who supplied the scooters featured in the photographs throughout this manual. We would also like to thank NGK Spark Plugs (UK) Ltd for supplying the colour spark plug condition photos, the Avon Tyres for supplying the tyre sidewall illustration and Draper Tools Ltd for some of the workshop tools shown.

Thanks are due to Julian Ryder who wrote the introduction 'The Birth of a Dream' and to Honda (UK) Ltd. who supplied model photographs.

About this Manual

The aim of this manual is to help you get the best value from your scooter. It can do so in several ways. It can help you decide what work must be done, even if you choose to have it done by a dealer; it provides information and procedures for routine maintenance and servicing; and it offers diagnostic and repair procedures to follow when trouble occurs.

We hope you use the manual to tackle the work yourself. For many simpler jobs, doing it yourself may be quicker than arranging an appointment to get the scooter into a dealer and making the trips to leave it and pick it up. More importantly, a lot of money can be saved by avoiding the expense the shop must pass on to you to cover its labour and overhead costs. An added benefit is the sense of satisfaction and accomplishment that you feel after doing the job yourself.

References to the left or right side of the scooter assume you are sitting on the seat, facing forward.

We take great pride in the accuracy of information given in this manual, but manufacturers make alterations and design changes during the production run of machines about which they do not inform us. No liability can be accepted by the authors or publishers for loss, damage or injury caused by any errors in, or omissions from, the information given.

Illegal copying

It is the policy of Haynes Publishing to actively protect its Copyrights and Trade Marks. Legal action will be taken against anyone who unlawfully copies the cover or contents of this Manual. This includes all forms of unauthorised copying including digital, mechanical, and electronic in any form. Authorisation from Haynes Publishing will only be provided expressly and in writing. Illegal copying will also be reported to the appropriate statutory authorities.

Model development and bike spec 0•9

ANF125 2003 to 2006 models

The ANF125 Innova uses a single cylinder air-cooled engine. Drive to the single overhead camshaft, which actuates the two valves via a pair of rocker arms, is by chain from the left-hand end of the crankshaft. Power from the crankshaft is routed to the transmission via a centrifugal clutch on the right-hand end of the crankshaft that drives the primary drive gear, turning the primary driven gear on the back of a wet, multi-plate clutch on the transmission input shaft. A one-way clutch in the centrifugal clutch allows semi-automatic gear changes when the throttle is closed. Drive to the rear wheel is by chain and sprockets. The engine has both electric and kick starters.

A single 18 mm slide carburettor supplies fuel and air to the engine. An electronic ignition system ignites the mixture via a single spark plug. A catalyst is incorporated in the exhaust system, which features a stainless steel silencer.

The frame is made from steel. Front suspension is by oil-damped 26 mm forks. Rear suspension is by twin shock absorbers and a steel swingarm that pivots through the frame.

The front brake system is hydraulic with a twin-piston sliding caliper acting on a conventional disc, and at the rear is a drum brake.

Available in silver, red and two shades of blue in 2003 and 2004, silver, red, blue/silver and black/silver in 2005 and 2006.

ANF125i 2007-on models

Honda's PGM-FI fuel injection system replaces the carburettor for 2007-on models, along with a closed-loop catalyst in the exhaust system.

Styling changes include modifications to the bodywork and new lights and instruments.

Available in silver, red/orange and blue in 2007, along with a black model in 2008 and 2009, white, silver, black and blue in from 2010 onwards.

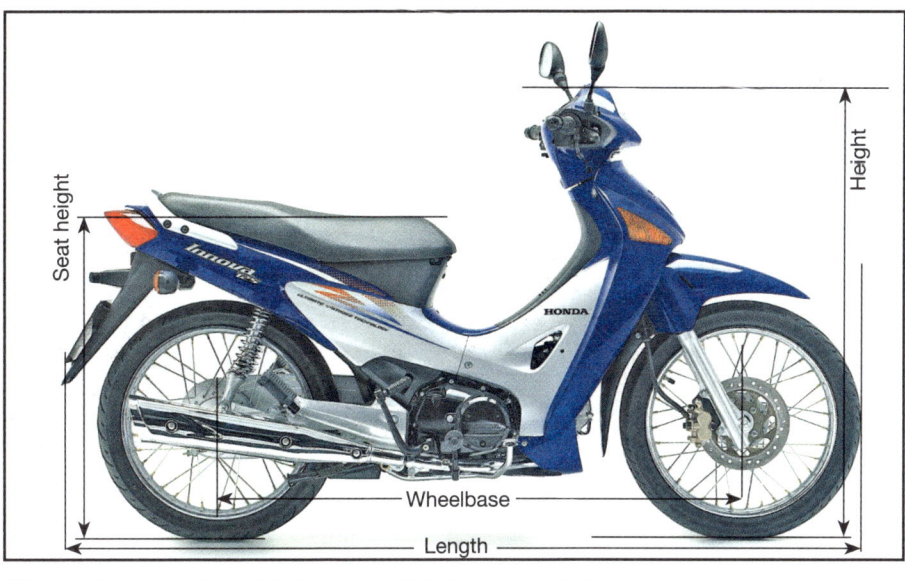

Dimensions and weights

	ANF125 2003 to 2006 (carburettor) models	ANF125i 2007-on (fuel injection) models
Overall length	1890 mm	1896 mm
Overall width	727 mm	727 mm
Overall height	1083 mm	1079 mm
Wheelbase	1240 mm	1240 mm
Seat height	768 mm	778 mm
Ground clearance	145 mm	139 mm
Weight (dry)	99 kg	100 kg
Weight (wet)	104 kg	105 kg
Maximum weight (carrying) capacity	170 kg	170 kg

Engine

Type	Four-stroke, single cylinder
Capacity	124.9 cc
Bore	52.4 mm
Stroke	57.9 mm
Compression ratio	9.3 to 1
Cooling system	Air-cooled
Clutches	Centrifugal and wet multi-plate
Transmission	Four-speed constant mesh
Final drive	Chain and sprockets
Camshaft	SOHC, chain-driven
Fuel system	
2003 to 2006 models	18 mm slide carburettor
2007-on models	22 mm throttle body, single injector
Exhaust system	One-into-one with catalyst
Ignition system	Computer-controlled digital transistorised with electronic advance

Chassis

Frame type	Steel backbone
Rake and Trail	
2003 to 2006 models	26°37', 73.2 mm
2007-on models	26°36', 73.6 mm
Fuel tank capacity	3.7 litres
Front suspension	
Type	26 mm oil-damped telescopic forks
Travel	80.5 mm
Rear suspension	
Type	Twin shock absorber, box-section steel swingarm
Travel (at axle)	81.6 mm
Wheels	17 inch wire spoke
Tyres	
Front	70/100-17MC (40P)
Rear	80/90-17MC (50P)
Front brake	Single 220 mm disc with twin piston sliding caliper
Rear brake	110 mm drum

0•10 Identification numbers

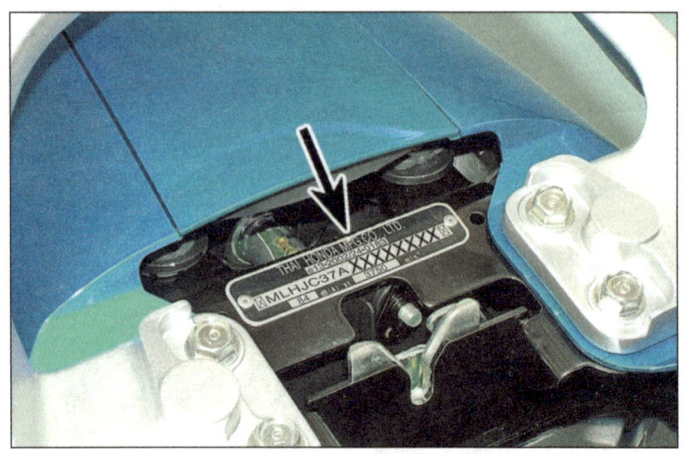

The frame number appears on the VIN plate (arrowed)...

and is also stamped into the frame on the right-hand side of the steering head...

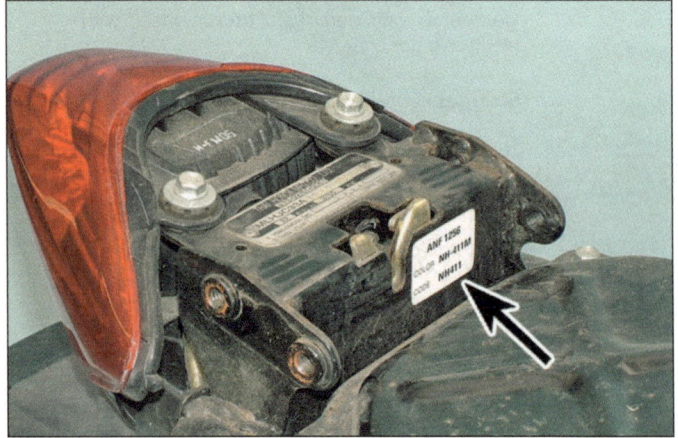

Colour code label (arrowed) is stuck to the frame on carburettor models...

... and to the battery cover on fuel injection models

Identification numbers 0•11

Frame and engine numbers

The frame serial number, or VIN (Vehicle Identification Number) as it is often known, is stamped into the frame on the right-hand side of the steering head, and also appears on the identification (VIN) plate on the back of the frame under the seat. The engine number is stamped into the left-hand side of the crankcase. Both of these numbers should be recorded and kept in a safe place so they can be furnished to law enforcement officials in the event of a theft.

The frame and engine numbers should also be kept in a handy place (such as with your driving licence) so they are always available when purchasing or ordering parts for your scooter.

A colour code label is stuck to the frame at the rear of the fuel tank on carburettor models and on the battery cover in the storage compartment on fuel injection models – this will be needed if ordering colour matched parts, and can be seen by removing the seat.

The procedures in this manual identify models by their production year, or by whether they have a carburettor or fuel injection system – refer to the list below for details. The model code and production year are on the VIN plate.

The engine number is stamped into the left-hand side of the crankcase

Model name	Model code	Production year(s)
ANF125 Innova	ANF125-3	2003 and 2004
ANF125 Innova	ANF125-5 and T5	2005
ANF125 Innova	ANF125-6 and T6	2006
ANF125i Innova	ANF125-7	2007-on

Buying spare parts

When ordering replacement parts, it is essential to identify exactly the model for which the parts are required. While in some cases it is sufficient to identify the machine by its title e.g. 'ANF125i', any modifications made to components mean that it is sometimes necessary to identify the scooter by its year of production, or better still by its frame or engine number prefix.

To be absolutely certain of receiving the correct part, not only is it essential to have the scooter engine or frame number prefix to hand, but it is also useful to take the old part for comparison (where possible). Note that where a modified component has superseded the original, a careful check must be made that there are no related parts which have also been modified and must be used to enable the replacement to be correctly refitted; where such a situation is found, purchase all the necessary parts and fit them, even if this means replacing apparently unworn items.

Purchase replacement parts from an authorised Honda dealer; they are more likely to have the parts in stock or can order them quickly from the importer. Pattern parts may be available for certain components; if used, ensure these are of recognised quality brands which will perform as well as the original.

Expendable items such as lubricants, the spark plug, bearings, bulbs and tyres can usually be obtained at lower prices from accessory shops, motor factors or from specialists advertising in the national motorcycle press.

Safety First!

Professional mechanics are trained in safe working procedures. However enthusiastic you may be about getting on with the job at hand, take the time to ensure that your safety is not put at risk. A moment's lack of attention can result in an accident, as can failure to observe simple precautions.

There will always be new ways of having accidents, and the following is not a comprehensive list of all dangers; it is intended rather to make you aware of the risks and to encourage a safe approach to all work you carry out on your bike.

Asbestos

● Certain friction, insulating, sealing and other products - such as brake pads, clutch linings, gaskets, etc. - contain asbestos. Extreme care must be taken to avoid inhalation of dust from such products since it is hazardous to health. If in doubt, assume that they do contain asbestos.

Fire

● Remember at all times that petrol is highly flammable. Never smoke or have any kind of naked flame around, when working on the vehicle. But the risk does not end there - a spark caused by an electrical short-circuit, by two metal surfaces contacting each other, by careless use of tools, or even by static electricity built up in your body under certain conditions, can ignite petrol vapour, which in a confined space is highly explosive. Never use petrol as a cleaning solvent. Use an approved safety solvent.

● Always disconnect the battery earth terminal before working on any part of the fuel or electrical system, and never risk spilling fuel on to a hot engine or exhaust.

● It is recommended that a fire extinguisher of a type suitable for fuel and electrical fires is kept handy in the garage or workplace at all times. Never try to extinguish a fuel or electrical fire with water.

Fumes

● Certain fumes are highly toxic and can quickly cause unconsciousness and even death if inhaled to any extent. Petrol vapour comes into this category, as do the vapours from certain solvents such as trichloro-ethylene. Any draining or pouring of such volatile fluids should be done in a well ventilated area.

● When using cleaning fluids and solvents, read the instructions carefully. Never use materials from unmarked containers - they may give off poisonous vapours.

● Never run the engine of a motor vehicle in an enclosed space such as a garage. Exhaust fumes contain carbon monoxide which is extremely poisonous; if you need to run the engine, always do so in the open air or at least have the rear of the vehicle outside the workplace.

The battery

● Never cause a spark, or allow a naked light near the vehicle's battery. It will normally be giving off a certain amount of hydrogen gas, which is highly explosive.

● Always disconnect the battery ground (earth) terminal before working on the fuel or electrical systems (except where noted).

● If possible, loosen the filler plugs or cover when charging the battery from an external source. Do not charge at an excessive rate or the battery may burst.

● Take care when topping up, cleaning or carrying the battery. The acid electrolyte, evenwhen diluted, is very corrosive and should not be allowed to contact the eyes or skin. Always wear rubber gloves and goggles or a face shield. If you ever need to prepare electrolyte yourself, always add the acid slowly to the water; never add the water to the acid.

Electricity

● When using an electric power tool, inspection light etc., always ensure that the appliance is correctly connected to its plug and that, where necessary, it is properly grounded (earthed). Do not use such appliances in damp conditions and, again, beware of creating a spark or applying excessive heat in the vicinity of fuel or fuel vapour. Also ensure that the appliances meet national safety standards.

● A severe electric shock can result from touching certain parts of the electrical system, such as the spark plug wires (HT leads), when the engine is running or being cranked, particularly if components are damp or the insulation is defective. Where an electronic ignition system is used, the secondary (HT) voltage is much higher and could prove fatal.

Remember...

✗ **Don't** start the engine without first ascertaining that the transmission is in neutral.

✗ **Don't** suddenly remove the pressure cap from a hot cooling system - cover it with a cloth and release the pressure gradually first, or you may get scalded by escaping coolant.

✗ **Don't** attempt to drain oil until you are sure it has cooled sufficiently to avoid scalding you.

✗ **Don't** grasp any part of the engine or exhaust system without first ascertaining that it is cool enough not to burn you.

✗ **Don't** allow brake fluid or antifreeze to contact the machine's paintwork or plastic components.

✗ **Don't** siphon toxic liquids such as fuel, hydraulic fluid or antifreeze by mouth, or allow them to remain on your skin.

✗ **Don't** inhale dust - it may be injurious to health (see Asbestos heading).

✗ **Don't** allow any spilled oil or grease to remain on the floor - wipe it up right away, before someone slips on it.

✗ **Don't** use ill-fitting spanners or other tools which may slip and cause injury.

✗ **Don't** lift a heavy component which may be beyond your capability - get assistance.

✗ **Don't** rush to finish a job or take unverified short cuts.

✗ **Don't** allow children or animals in or around an unattended vehicle.

✗ **Don't** inflate a tyre above the recommended pressure. Apart from overstressing the carcass, in extreme cases the tyre may blow off forcibly.

✔ **Do** ensure that the machine is supported securely at all times. This is especially important when the machine is blocked up to aid wheel or fork removal.

✔ **Do** take care when attempting to loosen a stubborn nut or bolt. It is generally better to pull on a spanner, rather than push, so that if you slip, you fall away from the machine rather than onto it.

✔ **Do** wear eye protection when using power tools such as drill, sander, bench grinder etc.

✔ **Do** use a barrier cream on your hands prior to undertaking dirty jobs - it will protect your skin from infection as well as making the dirt easier to remove afterwards; but make sure your hands aren't left slippery. Note that long-term contact with used engine oil can be a health hazard.

✔ **Do** keep loose clothing (cuffs, ties etc. and long hair) well out of the way of moving mechanical parts.

✔ **Do** remove rings, wristwatch etc., before working on the vehicle - especially the electrical system.

✔ **Do** keep your work area tidy - it is only too easy to fall over articles left lying around.

✔ **Do** exercise caution when compressing springs for removal or installation. Ensure that the tension is applied and released in a controlled manner, using suitable tools which preclude the possibility of the spring escaping violently.

✔ **Do** ensure that any lifting tackle used has a safe working load rating adequate for the job.

✔ **Do** get someone to check periodically that all is well, when working alone on the vehicle.

✔ **Do** carry out work in a logical sequence and check that everything is correctly assembled and tightened afterwards.

✔ **Do** remember that your vehicle's safety affects that of yourself and others. If in doubt on any point, get professional advice.

● If in spite of following these precautions, you are unfortunate enough to injure yourself, seek medical attention as soon as possible.

Pre-ride checks 0•13

Note: These Pre-ride checks are outlined in your owner's manual and should be performed every time you ride the scooter.

Engine oil level

Before you start:
✔ Support the scooter on the centrestand on level ground.
✔ Start the engine and let it idle for 3 to 5 minutes.
Caution: Do not run the engine in an enclosed space such as a garage or workshop.
✔ Stop the engine and leave it for a few minutes for the oil level to stabilise.

Scooter care:
● If you have to add oil frequently, check the engine joints, oil seals and gaskets for oil leakage. If not, the engine could be burning oil, in which case there will be white smoke coming out of the exhaust (see *Fault Finding*).

The correct oil:
● Engines place great demands on their oil. It is very important that the correct oil for your bike is used.

● Always top up with a good quality motorcycle oil of the specified type and viscosity and do not overfill the engine. Do not use engine oil designed for car use.
Caution: Do not use chemical additives or oils labelled 'ENERGY CONSERVING'.

Oil type	API grade SG or higher, JASO T903 grade: MA
Oil viscosity	SAE 10W30

1 Unscrew the oil filler cap/level dipstick from the right-hand side of the engine.

2 Wipe the dipstick clean.

3 Insert the dipstick so that the cap contacts the engine, but do not screw it in.

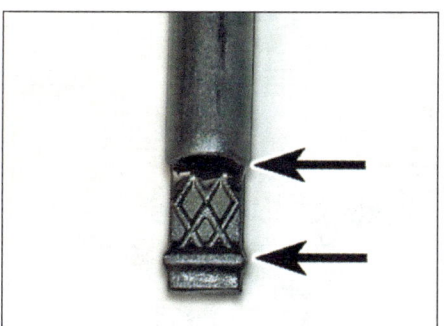
4 Remove the dipstick and check the oil mark – it should lie between the upper and lower level lines (arrowed), i.e. within the cross-hatched area.

5 If the level is on or below the lower line, top up the engine with the recommended grade and type of oil to bring the level almost up to the upper line. Do not overfill.

6 On completion, make sure the O-ring (arrowed) on the underside of the cap is in good condition, clean and properly seated, then smear some oil onto it. Fit the cap and tighten it by hand.

Suspension and steering

● Check that the front and rear suspension operates smoothly without binding.

● Check that the steering moves smoothly from lock-to-lock.

0•14 Pre-ride checks

Front brake fluid level

Before you start:
✔ Support the scooter in an upright position on level ground and turn the handlebars until the brake reservoir is as level as possible.
✔ Make sure you have a supply of DOT 4 brake fluid.
✔ Wrap a rag around the reservoir to ensure that any spillage does not come into contact with painted or plastic surfaces. If any fluid is spilt, wash it off immediately with cold water.

Bike care:
● The fluid in the brake master cylinder reservoir will drop as the brake pads wear. If the fluid level is low check the brake pads for wear (see Chapter 1).
● If the reservoir requires repeated topping-up this is an indication of a fluid leak somewhere in the system, which should be investigated immediately.
● Check for signs of fluid leakage from the brake hoses and components – if found, rectify immediately.
● Check the operation of the front brake before riding the machine. If there is evidence of air in the system (a spongy feel to the lever), bleed the brake as described in Chapter 6.

> **Warning:** Brake fluid can harm your eyes and damage painted surfaces, so use extreme caution when handling and pouring it and cover surrounding surfaces with rag. Do not use fluid that has been standing open for some time, as it absorbs moisture from the air which can cause a dangerous loss of braking effectiveness.

1 On 2003 to 2006 models check the fluid level in the window in the reservoir body – the level must be above the LOWER level line (arrowed).

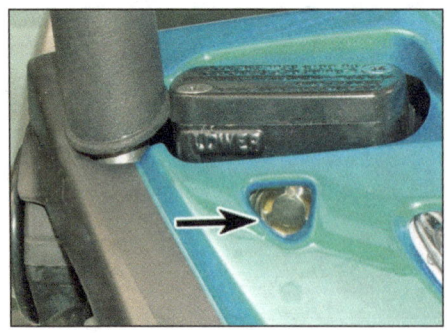
2 On 2007-on models check the fluid level in the window in the reservoir body, via the aperture in the handlebar cover – the level must be above the level shown (arrowed).

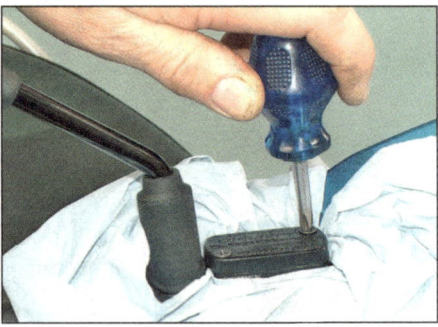
3 If topping up is necessary, undo the reservoir cover screws and remove the cover, diaphragm plate and diaphragm.

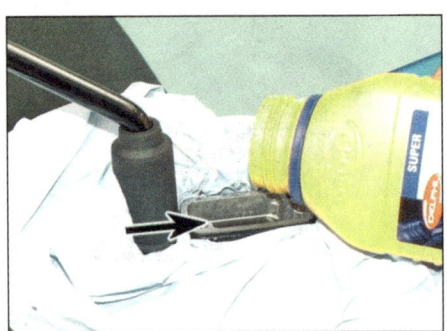
4 Top up with new clean DOT 4 hydraulic fluid, until the level is up to the UPPER line (arrowed) on the inside of the reservoir. Do not overfill and take care to avoid spills (see **Warning** above).

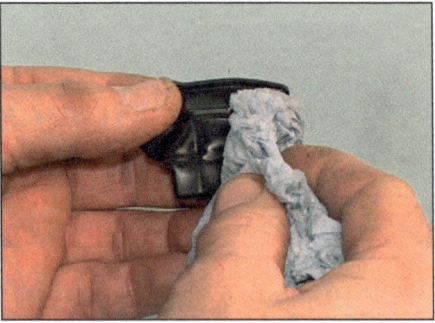
5 Wipe any moisture out of the diaphragm with a tissue.

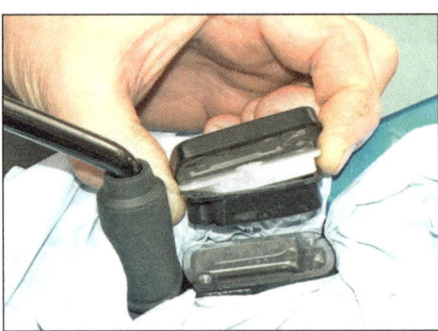
6 Ensure that the diaphragm is correctly seated before fitting the plate and cover. Secure the cover with its screws.

Pre-ride checks

Tyres

Tyre care:
- Check the tyres carefully for cuts, tears, embedded nails or other sharp objects and excessive wear. Operation of the scooter with excessively worn tyres is extremely hazardous, as traction and handling are directly affected.
- Check the condition of the tyre valve and ensure the dust cap is in place.
- Pick out any stones or nails which may have become embedded in the tyre tread. If left, they will eventually penetrate through the casing and inner tube and cause a puncture.
- If tyre damage is apparent, or unexplained loss of pressure is experienced, seek the advice of a tyre fitting specialist without delay.

Tyre tread depth:
- At the time of writing UK law requires that tread depth must be at least 1 mm over 3/4 of the tread breadth all the way around the tyre, with no bald patches. Many riders, however, consider 2 mm tread depth minimum to be a safer limit. Refer to the tyre tread legislation in your country.
- Tyres incorporate wear indicators in the tread. Identify the location marking on the tyre sidewall to locate the indicator bar and replace the tyre if the tread has worn down to the bar.

The correct pressures:
- The tyres must be checked when **cold**, not immediately after riding. Note that low tyre pressures may cause the tyre to slip on the rim or come off. High tyre pressures will cause abnormal tread wear and unsafe handling.
- Use an accurate pressure gauge. Many forecourt gauges are wildly inaccurate. If you buy your own, spend as much as you can justify on a quality gauge.
- Proper air pressure will increase tyre life and provide maximum stability and ride comfort.
- Refer to the table for the correct tyre pressures according to load.

Loading	Front	Rear
Rider only	29 psi (2.0 Bar)	29 psi (2.0 Bar)
Rider with passenger	29 psi (2.0 Bar)	36 psi (2.5 Bar)

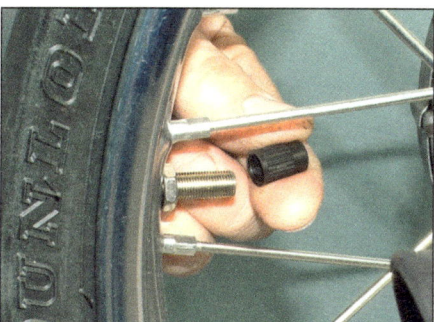

1 Remove the dust cap from the valve and do not forget to fit it after checking the pressure.

2 Check the tyre pressures when the tyres are cold.

3 Measure tread depth at the centre of the tyre using a tread depth gauge.

4 Tyre tread wear indicator bar (A) and its location marking (B – usually an arrow, a triangle or the letters TWI) on the sidewall.

Legal and safety

Lighting and signalling:
- Take a minute to check that the headlight, tail light, brake light, licence plate light, instrument lights and turn signals all work correctly.
- Check that the horn sounds when the switch is operated.
- A working speedometer graduated in mph is a statutory requirement in the UK.

Safety:
- Check that the throttle grip rotates smoothly and snaps shut when released, in all steering positions.
- Check that stand return springs hold the stands securely up when retracted.
- Check that both brakes work correctly when applied and free off when released.
- Make sure the amount of free travel in the toe of the rear brake pedal before the brake takes effect is between 20 and 30 mm. If not, refer to Chapter 1, Section 10, and adjust it.

Fuel:
- This may seem obvious, but check that you have enough fuel to complete your journey. Do not wait until the fuel gauge tells you that the level in the tank is low before filling up.
- If you notice signs of leakage you must rectify the cause immediately.
- Ensure you use the correct grade unleaded petrol, minimum 91 octane (RON).

Notes

Chapter 1
Routine maintenance and servicing

Contents

	Section number
Air filter and crankcase breather	3
Battery	20
Brake fluid level check	see *Pre-ride checks*
Brake pads and shoes	9
Brake system	10
Clutch lifter mechanism	11
Drive chain and sprockets	1
Engine oil, filter and strainer	5
Engine oil level check	see *Pre-ride checks*
Engine wear assessment	see Chapter 2
Fuel system	6
Headlight aim	15

	Section number
Idle speed	8
Nuts and bolts	17
PAIR (pulse secondary air supply) system	19
Spark plug	2
Sidestand, lever pivot and cable lubrication	16
Stands and starter safety circuit	12
Steering head bearings	18
Suspension	13
Throttle and choke cables	7
Tyre checks	see *Pre-ride checks*
Valve clearances	4
Wheels, wheel bearings and tyres	14

Degrees of difficulty

| **Easy**, suitable for novice with little experience  | **Fairly easy**, suitable for beginner with some experience  | **Fairly difficult**, suitable for competent DIY mechanic  | **Difficult**, suitable for experienced DIY mechanic  | **Very difficult**, suitable for expert DIY or professional  |

1•2 Specifications

Engine
Spark plug type
  Standard
    NGK CPR6EA-9
    Denso U20EPR9
  For continuous high speed use
    NGK CPR7EA-9
    Denso U22EPR9
Spark plug electrode gap .... 0.8 to 0.9 mm
Engine idle speed .... 1400 ± 100 rpm
Valve clearances (COLD engine)
  2003 to 2006 (carburettor) models .... 0.05 ± 0.02 mm
  2007-on (fuel injection) models .... 0.10 ± 0.02 mm

Chassis
Drive chain slack
  2003 to 2006 (carburettor) models .... 25 to 35 mm
  2007-on (fuel injection) models .... 30 to 40 mm
Drive chain stretch limit (see text) .... 518 mm
Rear brake pedal freeplay .... 20 to 30 mm
Rear brake drum max ID .... 111.0 mm
Throttle cable freeplay .... 2 to 6 mm
Tyre pressures (cold)
  Rider only .... 29 psi (2.0 Bar) front and rear
  Rider and passenger .... 29 psi (2.0 Bar) front, 36 psi (2.5 Bar) rear

Lubricants and fluids
Engine oil .... SAE 10W30 API grade SG or higher, motorcycle oil, JASO T903 grade: MA
Engine oil capacity
  Oil change .... 0.7 litre
  Following engine overhaul .... 0.9 litre
Brake fluid .... DOT 4
Drive chain .... Aerosol chain lube or SAE 80 or 90 gear oil
Steering head bearings .... Multi-purpose grease with EP2 rating
Bearing seal lips .... Multi-purpose grease
Gearchange lever/rear brake pedal/footrest pivots .... Multi-purpose grease
Stand pivots .... Multi-purpose grease
Throttle twistgrip .... Multi-purpose grease
Front brake lever pivot and piston tip .... Silicone grease
Cables .... Aerosol cable lube

Torque settings
Crankshaft end cap .... 8 Nm
Engine oil drain plug .... 24 Nm
Oil filter cover bolts .... 5 Nm
Rear axle nut .... 59 Nm
Spark plug
  2003 to 2006 (carburettor) models .... 12 Nm
  2007-on (fuel injection) models .... 16 Nm
Steering stem nut .... 74 Nm
Timing inspection cap .... 6 Nm

Maintenance schedule 1•3

Note: *The Pre-ride checks outlined in the owner's manual cover those items which should be inspected before every ride. Also perform the pre-ride inspection at every maintenance interval (in addition to the procedures listed). The intervals listed below are the intervals recommended by the manufacturer for the models covered in this manual.*

Pre-ride
☐ See *'Pre-ride checks'* at the beginning of this manual.

After the initial 600 miles (1000 km)
Note: *This check is usually performed by a Honda dealer after the first 600 miles (1000 km) from new. Thereafter, maintenance is carried out according to the following intervals of the schedule.*

Every 600 miles (1000 km)
☐ Check, adjust, clean and lubricate the drive chain (Section 1)

Every 2500 miles (4000 km) or 6 months
☐ Check the spark plug (Section 2)
☐ Clean the air filter element and crankcase breather (Section 3)
☐ Check and adjust the valve clearances (Section 4)
☐ Change the engine oil (Section 5)
☐ Check the fuel system and hoses (Section 6)
☐ Check and adjust the throttle and choke cables (Section 7)
☐ Check and adjust the engine idle speed – carburettor models (Section 8)
☐ Check the brake pads and shoes for wear (Section 9)
☐ Check the brake system and brake light switch operation (Section 10)
☐ Adjust the clutch (Section 11)
☐ Check the stands and starter safety circuit (Section 12)
☐ Check the front and rear suspension (Section 13)
☐ Check the condition of the wheels, wheel bearings and tyres (Section 14)
☐ Check headlight aim (Section 15)

Every 5000 miles (8000 km) or 12 months
Carry out all the items under the 2500 mile (4000 km) check, plus the following:
☐ Fit a new spark plug (Section 2)
☐ Lubricate the gearchange and brake levers, brake pedal, stand pivots, the throttle cable and where fitted the choke cable (Section 16)
☐ Check the tightness of all nuts, bolts and fasteners (Section 17)

Every 7500 miles (12,000 km) or 18 months
Carry out all the items under the 2500 mile (4000 km) check, plus the following:
☐ Fit a new air filter element (Section 3)
☐ Clean the engine oil filter and strainer (Section 5)
☐ Check and adjust the steering head bearings (Section 18)
☐ Check the PAIR (pulse secondary air injection) system – carburettor models (Section 19)

Every two years
☐ Change the brake fluid (Chapter 6)

Non-scheduled maintenance
☐ Check the battery (Section 20)
☐ Fit a new fuel filter – carburettor models (Section 6)
☐ Clean the fuel strainer – fuel injection models (Section 6)
☐ Fit new fuel system hoses (Section 6)
☐ Fit new brake master cylinder and caliper seals (Section 10)
☐ Fit a new brake hose (Section 10)
☐ Change the front fork oil (Section 13)
☐ Re-grease the swingarm pivot (Section 13)
☐ Re-grease the steering head bearings (Section 18)

1•4 Component locations

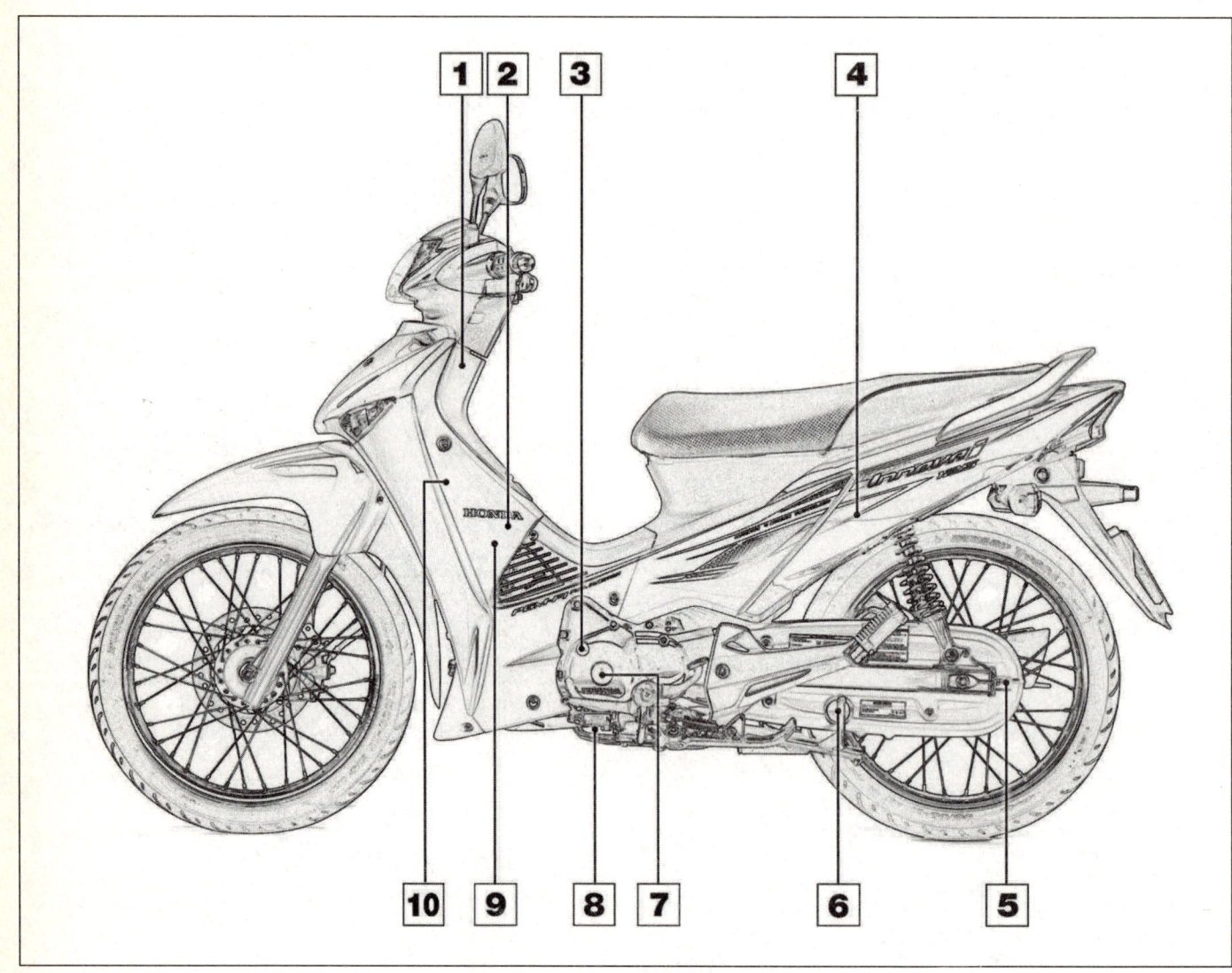

Componenet locations on the left side

1 Steering head bearing adjuster
2 PAIR system air filter (2003 to 2006 models)
3 Timing inspection cap
4 Fuel filter (2003 to 2006 models)
5 Drive chain adjuster
6 Drive chain inspection plug
7 Crankshaft end cap
8 Engine oil drain plug
9 Throttle cable adjuster (2007-on models)
10 Air filter

Component locations 1•5

Component locations on the right side

1. Battery
2. PAIR system control valve (2003 to 2006 models)
3. Idle speed adjuster (2003 to 2006 models)
4. Throttle cable adjuster (2003 to 2006 models)
5. Front brake fluid reservoir
6. Spark plug
7. Engine oil screen
8. Engine oil centrifugal filter
9. Clutch adjuster
10. Engine oil filler/dipstick
11. Rear brake light switch
12. Rear brake pedal freeplay adjuster
13. Drive chain adjuster

1•6 Routine maintenance and servicing

1 This Chapter is designed to help the home mechanic maintain his/her motorcycle for safety, economy, long life and peak performance.
2 Deciding where to start or plug into the routine maintenance schedule depends on several factors. If your motorcycle has been maintained according to the warranty standards and has just come out of warranty, start routine maintenance as it coincides with the next mileage or calendar interval. If you have owned the machine for some time but have never performed any maintenance on it, start at the nearest interval and include some additional procedures to ensure that nothing important is overlooked. If you have just had a major engine overhaul, then start the maintenance routine from the beginning. If you have a used machine and have no knowledge of its history or maintenance record, combine all the checks into one large service initially and then settle into the specified maintenance schedule.
3 Before beginning any maintenance or repair, the machine should be cleaned thoroughly. Cleaning will help ensure that dirt does not contaminate the engine and will allow you to detect wear and damage that could otherwise easily go unnoticed.
4 Certain maintenance information is sometimes printed on labels attached to the motorcycle. If the information on the labels differs from that included here, use the information on the label.

---

1 Drive chain and sprockets

1 A neglected drive chain won't last long and will quickly damage the sprockets. Routine chain adjustment and lubrication isn't difficult and will ensure maximum chain and sprocket life.
2 Place the bike on its centrestand and shift the transmission into neutral. Make sure the ignition switch is OFF. Remove the inspection cap from the drive chain case (see illustration). Note that in certain markets a drive chain case is not fitted.

Check chain slack
3 The diameter of the inspection hole in the drive chain case is the same as the specified amount of slack there should be in the drive chain, so the chain should be level with the bottom of the hole at rest and level with the top of the hole when lifted up as far as it goes, using the same reference point on the chain in each case (i.e. the bottom of the link) (see illustration). As the chain stretches with wear, adjustment will periodically be necessary (see below). Since the chain will rarely wear evenly, turn the rear wheel so that another section of chain can be checked – do this several times to check the entire length of chain, and mark the tightest spot.
Caution: Riding the bike with excess slack in the chain could lead to damage.
4 Where neglect of the chain has caused its links to bind and kink, this will effectively shortens the chain's length and makes it tight (see illustration). Refer to Step 13 and thoroughly clean and work free any such links, then highlight them with a marker pen or paint. Take the bike for a ride.
5 After the bike has been ridden, repeat the measurement for slack in the highlighted area. If the chain has kinked again and is still tight, replace it with a new one (see Chapter 6). A rusty, kinked or worn chain will damage the sprockets and can damage transmission bearings. If in any doubt as to the condition of a chain, it is far better to fit a new one than risk damage to other components and possibly yourself.
6 Check the entire length of the chain for damaged rollers and loose links and pins, and replace it with a new one if necessary. **Note: Never install a new chain on old sprockets, and never use the old chain if you install new sprockets – replace the chain and sprockets as a set.**

Adjust chain slack
7 Position the bike so that the tightest spot of the chain is at the inspection hole. Support the bike on the centrestand.

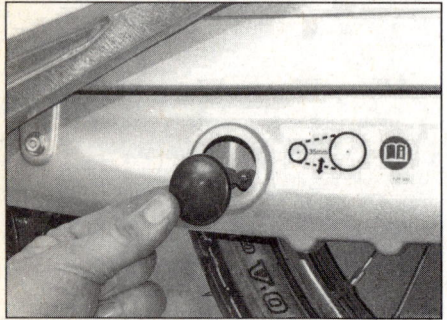
1.2 Remove the cap

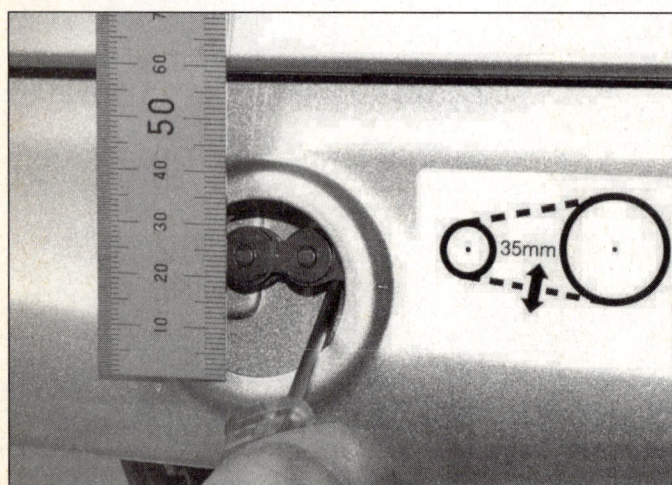
1.3 Chain slack should allow movement between the top and bottom of the hole – no less and no more

1.4 Neglect has caused the links in this chain to kink

Routine maintenance and servicing 1•7

1.8 Slacken the axle nut (arrowed)

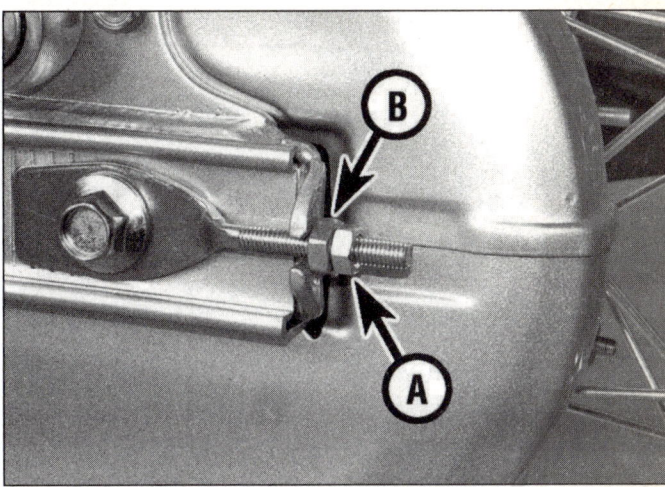

1.9a Slacken the locknut (A) on each side, then turn each adjuster nut (B) by an equal amount . . .

8 Slacken the rear axle nut **(see illustration)**.
9 Slacken the locknut on the adjuster on each side of the swingarm, then turn the adjuster nut as required **(see illustration)** – to reduce chain slack turn the adjuster nut on each side evenly clockwise until the amount of freeplay is correct. Following adjustment, check that the front edge of each chain adjuster aligns with the same index line on each side of the swingarm **(see illustration)**. It is important the alignment is the same on each side otherwise the rear wheel will be out of alignment with the front. Also make sure that the front face of each adjuster nut is butted against the end of the swingarm. If there is a difference in the positions, adjust one of them so that its position is exactly the same as the other. Check the chain freeplay again and readjust if necessary.
10 To increase chain slack turn the adjuster nut on each side of the swingarm evenly anti-clockwise, then push the wheel forwards in the swingarm until the nut butts the end of the swingarm, then apply the same principles given in Step 9 for checking alignment.
11 When adjustment is complete, counter-hold the adjuster nuts to prevent them turning and tighten the locknuts against them. Tighten the axle nut to the torque setting specified at the beginning of the Chapter. Recheck the adjustment as above, then spin the wheel to make sure it runs freely.

Clean and lubricate the chain

12 Remove the drive chain case (see Chapter 6, Section 16).
13 If required, wash the chain using a dedicated aerosol cleaner, or in paraffin (kerosene) or a suitable non-flammable or high flash-point solvent, using a soft brush to work any dirt out if necessary. Wipe the cleaner off the chain and allow it to dry. If the chain is excessively dirty remove it from the machine and allow it to soak in the paraffin or solvent (see Chapter 6).
14 The best time to lubricate the chain is after the motorcycle has been ridden. When the chain is warm, the lubricant will penetrate the joints between the sideplates better than when cold. **Note:** *Honda specifies SAE 80 to SAE 90 gear oil or an aerosol chain lube.* Apply the lubricant to the area where the sideplates overlap – not the middle of the rollers **(see illustration)**.

> **HAYNES HINT** *Apply the lubricant to the top of the lower chain run, so centrifugal force will work the oil into the chain when the bike is moving. After applying the lubricant, let it soak in a few minutes before wiping off any excess.*

> ⚠ **Warning: Take care not to get any lubricant on the rear tyre. Clean off excess lube using a suitable solvent or dedicated brake cleaner before riding the machine.**

1.9b . . . then check the alignment marks as described

1.14 Apply the lubricant to the overlapping sections of the sideplates

1•8 Routine maintenance and servicing

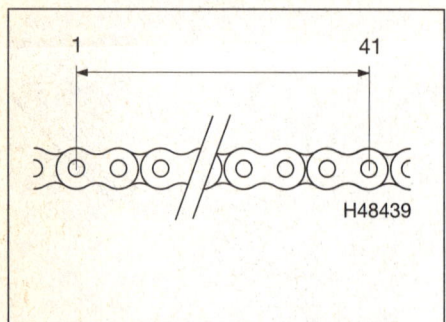

1.16 Measure a 40 link (41 pin) section

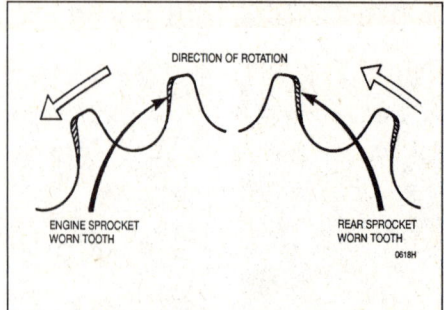

1.19 Check the sprocket teeth for wear in the areas shown

Check chain stretch

15 Remove the drive chain case (see Chapter 6, Section 16).
16 Adjust the chain as described in Steps 8 and 9 until all slack is taken up, but not so much that the chain is taut. Measure a 40 link section along the bottom run of the chain as shown (see illustration). Rotate the rear wheel so that several sections of the chain can be measured, then calculate the average and compare it to the stretch limit specified at the beginning of the Chapter. If the chain stretch measurement exceeds the service limit it must be replaced with a new one (see Chapter 6).
17 If the chain is good, reset the adjusters so that there is the correct amount of freeplay (see Steps 9 to 11).
Caution: Never fit a new chain onto old sprockets, and never use the old chain if you fit new sprockets – replace the chain and sprockets as a set.

Check sprocket wear

18 Remove the drive chain case and the front sprocket cover (see Chapter 6, Section 16).
19 Check the teeth on the front sprocket and the rear sprocket for wear (see illustration). If the sprocket teeth are worn excessively, replace the chain and both sprockets with a new set (see Chapter 6).
20 Check that the sprocket fasteners are tight (refer to Chapter 6 Specifications for torque settings).
21 Inspect the drive chain slider on the front of the swingarm for excessive wear and damage and replace it with a new one if necessary (see Chapter 5).

2 Spark plug

1 You'll need a spark plug socket of 16 mm hex to remove the plug – a suitable one is supplied in the Scooter's tool kit.
2 For best access and to avoid the possibility of damage remove the bottom cover and the front cover on the right-hand side (see Chapter 7).
3 Pull the cap off the spark plug (see illustration).
4 Clean the area around the base of the spark plug to prevent any dirt falling into the engine.
5 Using either the plug removing tool supplied in the toolkit or a suitable spark plug socket, unscrew and remove the plug from the cylinder head (see illustration).
6 Check the condition of the electrodes, referring to the spark plug reading chart on the inside rear cover of this manual if signs of contamination are evident.
7 Clean the plug with a soft wire brush. Examine the tips of the electrodes; if a tip has rounded off, the plug is worn. Measure the gap between the two electrodes using a feeler gauge or a wire type gauge (see illustration). The gap should be as given in the Specifications at the beginning of this chapter; if necessary adjust the gap by bending the side electrode (see illustration).
8 Check the threads, the washer and the ceramic insulator body for cracks and other damage.
9 If the plug is worn or damaged, or if any deposits cannot be cleaned off, replace the plug with a new one. If in any doubt as to the condition of the plug replace it with a new one – the expense is minimal.
10 At the prescribed interval, whatever the condition of the existing spark plug, remove the plug as described above and install a new one.
11 Thread the plug into the cylinder head until the washer seats (see illustration). Since the cylinder head is made of aluminium, which is soft and easily damaged, thread the plug as far as possible by hand. Once the plug is finger-tight, the job can be finished with the

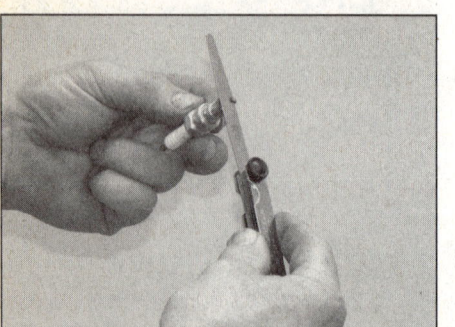

2.3 Pull the cap off the spark plug

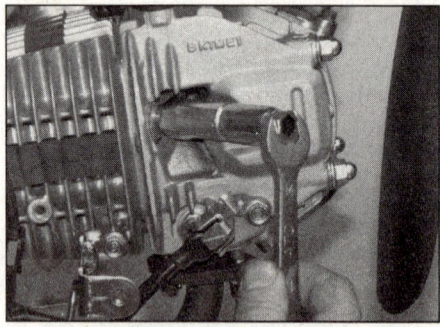

2.5 Unscrew and remove the plug

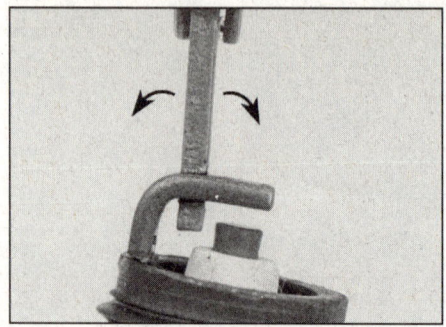

2.7a Using a feeler gauge to measure the spark plug electrode gap

2.7b Adjusting the gap using the fitting provided on the tool

2.11 Thread the plug into the head by hand to prevent cross-threading

Routine maintenance and servicing 1•9

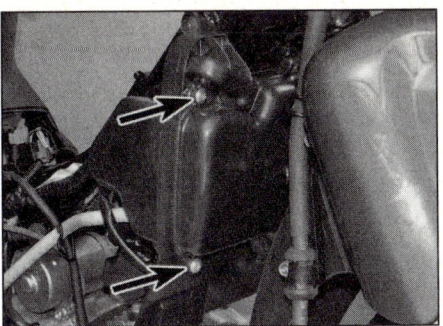
3.2a Undo the screws (arrowed) . . .

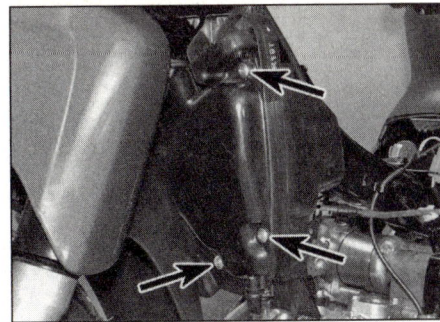
3.2b . . . on each side . . .

3.2c . . . and remove the cover . . .

tool supplied or a socket drive **(see illustration 2.5)**. If a new plug is being installed, tighten it by 1/2 a turn after the washer has seated. If the old plug is being reused, tighten it by 1/8 to 1/4 turn after the washer has seated, or if a torque wrench can be applied, tighten the spark plug to the torque setting specified at the beginning of the Chapter. Otherwise tighten it according the instructions on the box. Do not over-tighten it.

12 Fit the spark plug cap, making sure it locates correctly onto the plug **(see illustration 2.3)**. Install the bodywork if removed (see Chapter 7).

 *A stripped plug thread in the cylinder head can be repaired with a Heli-Coil insert – see 'Tools and Workshop Tips' in the Reference section.*

3 Air filter and crankcase breather

Air filter

Caution: If the machine is continually ridden in wet or dusty conditions, the filter should be cleaned more frequently.

Cleaning

1 Remove the front cover on each side (see Chapter 7).
2 Undo the five screws securing the air filter cover **(see illustrations)**. Remove the cover **(see illustration)**.
3 Remove the filter element, noting how it fits **(see illustration)**.
4 Tap the filter element on a hard surface to dislodge any dirt from the folds on the front, then check for anything stuck between them **(see illustration)**. Use compressed air to clear the element, directing the air in the opposite way to normal flow, i.e. from the back **(see illustration)**. Do not use any solvents or cleaning agents on the element.
5 Wipe any residue from the bottom of the cover and housing and empty the drain collectors if necessary **(see illustrations)**.
6 Check the condition of each sealing ring, one in the cover and one in the housing **(see illustration)**. Replace them with new ones if necessary. Make sure they are correctly seated.
7 Fit the filter element into the housing, making sure it is properly seated, then fit the cover and secure it with its screws **(see illustrations 3.3 and 3.2c, b and a)**. Install the front covers (see Chapter 7).

3.3 . . . and the filter element

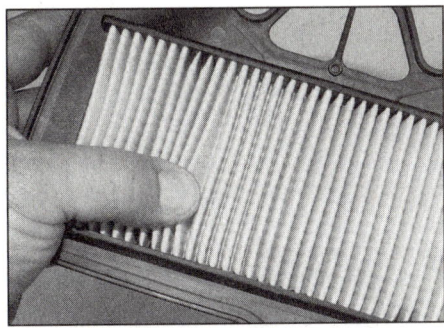
3.4a Check for and remove anything trapped in the folds

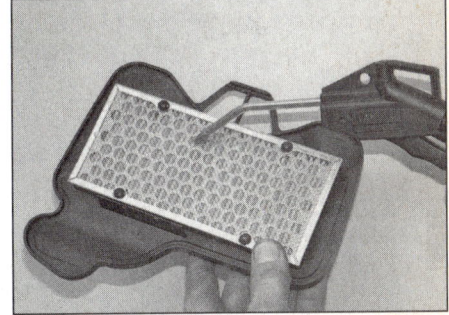
3.4b Direct the air in the opposite direction of normal flow

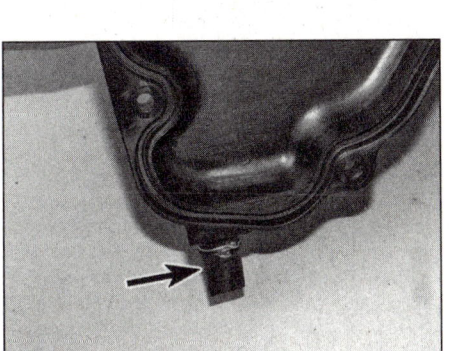
3.5a Drain and clean the collector (arrowed) in the cover . . .

3.5b . . . and the housing

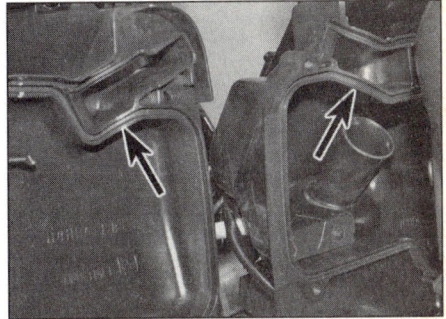
3.6 Check the sealing rings (arrowed)

1•10 Routine maintenance and servicing

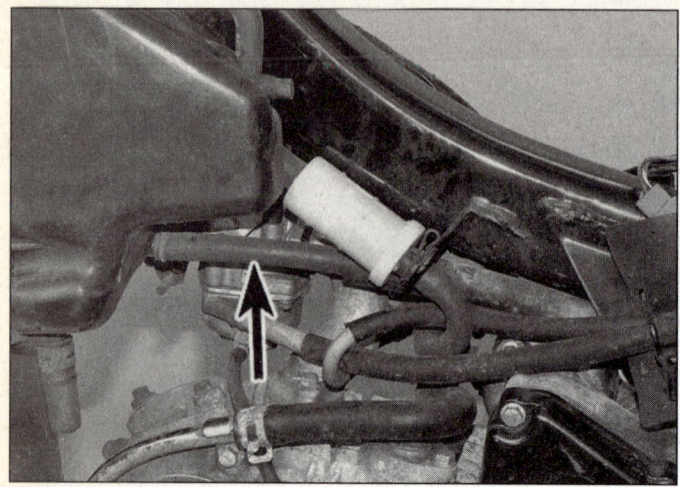

3.9a Crankcase breather hose (arrowed) – carburettor models

3.9b Crankcase breather hose (arrowed) – fuel injection models

Renewal

8 At the prescribed interval remove the filter element (Steps 1 to 3) and replace it with a new one whatever its apparent condition.

Crankcase breather

Caution: If the machine is continually ridden in wet conditions or at full throttle, the crankcase breather should be drained more frequently.

9 Check the condition of the crankcase breather hose between the right-hand side of the engine and the back of the air filter housing **(see illustrations)**. Check for cracks, splits and hardening and fit a new hose if necessary. Make sure the hose is secure on its union at each end.

10 Locate the crankcase breather drain tube on the underside of the air filter housing and check it for deposits **(see illustration 3.5b)**. If any are evident release the clamp, remove the tube and allow any deposits to drain into a rag. Clean the tube and the bottom of the housing, then fit the tube and secure it with the clamp.

4 Valve clearances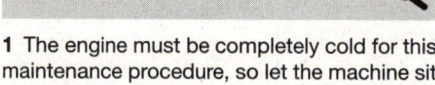

1 The engine must be completely cold for this maintenance procedure, so let the machine sit overnight before beginning.

2 Remove the front cover on each side (see Chapter 7). Remove the spark plug (see Section 2).

3 Unscrew the timing inspection cap and the crankshaft end cap **(see illustration)**. Remove the O-ring from each cap – new ones must be used.

4 Unscrew the valve cover bolts and remove the covers from the cylinder head **(see illustration)**. If they are stuck, do not try to lever them off with a screwdriver. Tap them gently around the sides with a rubber hammer or block of wood to dislodge them. Remove the O-ring from each cover – new ones must be used.

5 The valve clearances are checked with the piston at top dead centre (TDC) on its compression stroke, when both valves are closed and a small clearance can be felt between each rocker arm and valve stem. Turn the engine anti-clockwise using a socket on the alternator rotor nut until the line next to the T mark on the rim of the rotor aligns with the static timing mark, which is a notch in the inspection hole rim **(see illustrations)**. Now check for some freeplay in each rocker arm. If you cannot feel freeplay in each arm rotate the engine anti-clockwise one full turn (360°), and check again.

6 With the engine in this position, check the clearance of each valve by inserting a

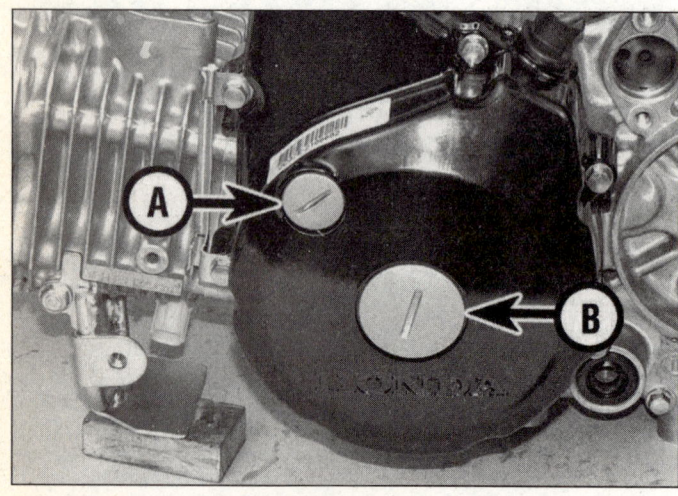

4.3 Remove the timing inspection cap (A) and the crankshaft end cap (B)

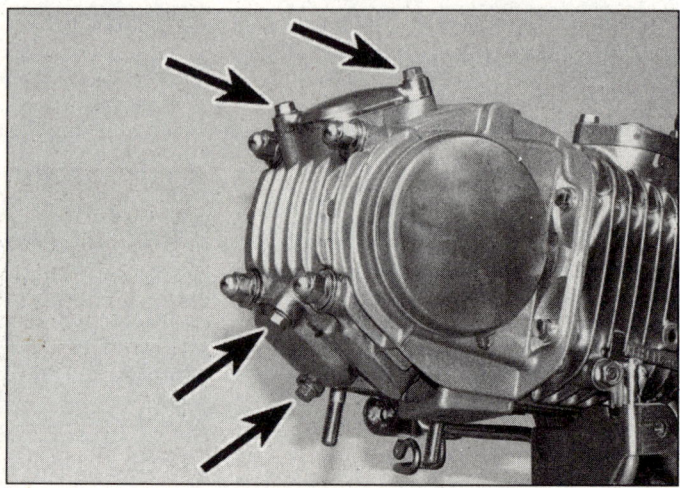

4.4 Unscrew the bolts (arrowed) and remove the covers

Routine maintenance and servicing 1•11

4.5a Turn the engine anti-clockwise using the nut . . .

4.5b . . . until the line next to the T mark aligns with the notch (arrowed)

4.6 Insert the feeler gauge between the base of the adjuster on the arm and the top of the valve stem as shown

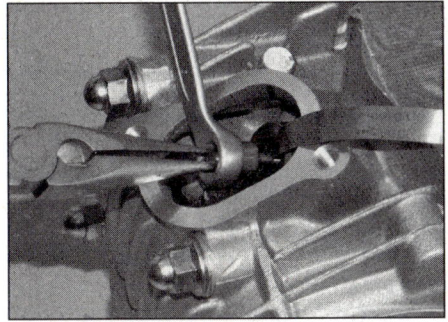

4.7 Slacken the locknut then turn the adjuster using a screwdriver until the gap is correct

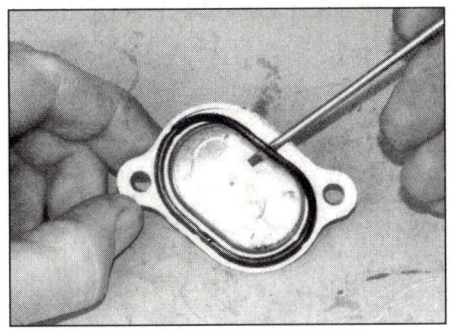

4.8a Fit a new O-ring into the groove . . .

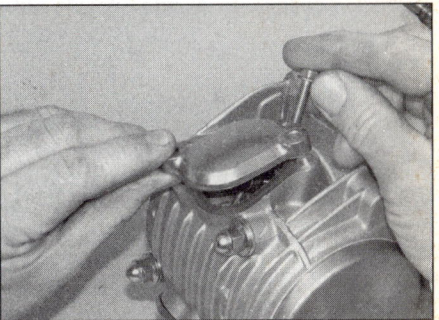

4.8b . . . then fit the cover, making sure the O-ring stays in place

feeler gauge of the same thickness as the correct valve clearance for your model (see Specifications) in the gap between the rocker arm and the valve stem **(see illustration)**. The intake valve is on the top of the cylinder head and the exhaust valve is on the bottom. The gauge should be a firm sliding fit – you should feel a slight drag when you pull the gauge out.

7 If the gap (clearance) is either too wide or too narrow, slacken the locknut on the adjuster in the rocker arm and turn the adjuster as required until the gap is as specified and the feeler gauge is a sliding fit, then hold the adjuster still and tighten the locknut **(see illustration)**. Recheck the clearance after tightening the locknut.

8 Fit a new O-ring smeared with oil into the groove in each valve cover **(see illustration)**. Clean the threads of the cover bolts – if corrosion was evident lightly smear the threads with oil. Fit the covers and tighten the bolts **(see illustration)**.

9 Install the spark plug (Section 2).

10 Fit new O-rings smeared with oil onto the timing inspection and crankshaft end caps **(see illustration)**. Smear the cap threads with oil, and tighten them to the torque settings specified at the beginning of the Chapter.

11 Install the front covers (see Chapter 7).

12 On completion, check and adjust the idle speed – carburettor models only (see Section 8).

5 Engine oil, filter and strainer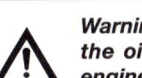

⚠️ **Warning:** *Be careful when draining the oil, as the exhaust pipe, the engine, and the oil itself can cause severe burns. To avoid getting oil over your hands it is best to wear some disposable latex or nitrile gloves, cheaply available from most chemists and hardware stores.*

Oil change

1 Consistent routine oil changes are the single most important maintenance procedure you can perform. The oil not only lubricates the internal parts of the engine, transmission and clutch, but it also acts as a coolant, a cleaner, a sealant, and a protector. Because of these demands, the oil takes a terrific amount of abuse and should be replaced as specified with new oil of the recommended grade and type.

2 Before changing the oil, warm up the engine so the oil will drain easily. Place the bike on its centrestand on level ground. The oil drain plug is on the underside of the engine at the front.

3 Position a clean drain tray below the engine. Unscrew the oil filler cap from the clutch cover to vent the crankcase and to act as a reminder that there is no oil in the engine **(see illustration)**.

4.10 Fit the caps using new O-rings and smear them and their threads with oil

5.3 Unscrew the oil filler cap to act as a vent . . .

1•12 Routine maintenance and servicing

5.4a ... then unscrew the oil drain plug ...

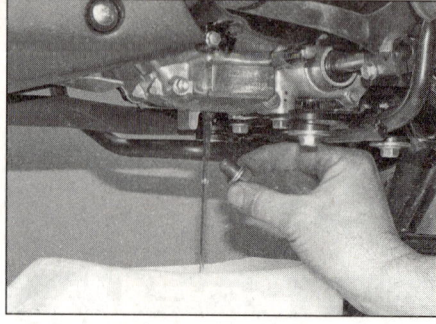

5.4b ... and allow the oil to completely drain

5.4c The sealing washer may need to be cut off

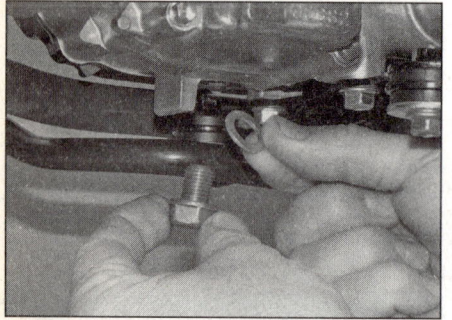

5.5 Fit the drain plug using a new sealing washer and tighten it to the specified torque

4 Unscrew the oil drain plug and allow the oil to flow into the drain tray **(see illustrations)**. Check the condition of the sealing washer on the drain plug and replace it with a new one if it is damaged or worn – it is highly advisable to use a new one whatever the condition of the old one. You may have to cut the old one off **(see illustration)**.

5 When the oil has completely drained, fit the plug into the engine, preferably using a new sealing washer, and tighten it to the torque setting specified at the beginning of the Chapter **(see illustration)**. Do not overtighten it as the threads in the engine are easily damaged.

6 At every third oil change clean the filter and strainer before putting the new oil in.

7 Refill the engine to the proper level using the recommended type and amount of oil (see *Specifications*). The oil level should lie between the upper and lower level lines on the dipstick (see *Pre-ride checks*). Check the condition of the O-ring on the filler cap and replace it with a new one if it is damaged or worn. Install the filler cap **(see illustration 5.3)**.

8 Start the engine and let it run for two or three minutes. Shut it off, wait a few minutes, then check the oil level. If necessary, add more oil to bring the level close to the upper line, but do not go above it.

9 Check around the drain plug for leaks. If a leak is evident and a new washer was not used, you will have to drain the oil again and fit a new washer. If a new washer was used then make sure the plug is tightened to the correct torque setting using a torque wrench. If one is not available tighten the plug a little more but take great care not to overtighten it and strip the threads – if in doubt ask a dealer to check using a torque wrench.

10 The old oil drained from the engine cannot be re-used and should be disposed of properly. Check with your local refuse disposal company, disposal facility or environmental agency to see whether they will accept the used oil for recycling. Don't pour used oil into drains or onto the ground.

 **Haynes Hint**: *Check the old oil carefully – if it is very metallic coloured, then the engine is experiencing wear from break-in (new engine) or from insufficient lubrication. If there are flakes or chips of metal in the oil, then something is drastically wrong internally and the engine will have to be disassembled for inspection and repair. If there are pieces of fibre-like material in the oil, the clutch is experiencing excessive wear and should be checked.*

Oil filter and strainer

Note: *This engine has a centrifugal oil filter rather than a conventional disposable mesh filter.*

11 Drain the engine oil (see Steps 2 to 5).
12 Remove the clutch cover (see Chapter 2).
13 Unscrew the oil filter cover bolts and remove the cover and the gasket **(see illustration)**.
14 Clean the cover and the recessed section of the primary drive plate using a lint-free cloth **(see illustration)**.

5.13 Unscrew the bolts (arrowed) and remove the cover

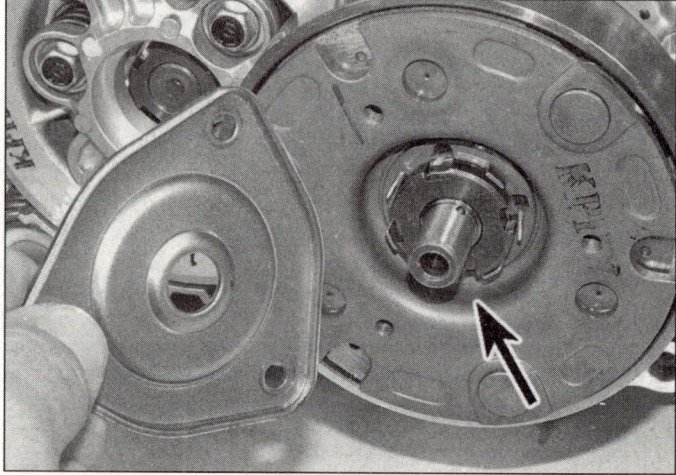

5.14 Clean the inside of the cover and the recessed area (arrowed)

Routine maintenance and servicing 1•13

15 Clean the threads of the bolts, then apply some fresh threadlock to the upper 4 mm of threads, leaving the bottom 1.6 mm clear as shown **(see illustration)**. Fit the cover using a new gasket and tighten the bolts to the torque setting specified at the beginning of the Chapter **(see illustration)**.
16 Withdraw the strainer from its slot in the bottom of the engine, noting which way round it fits **(see illustration)**.
17 Wash the strainer in solvent making sure all debris is removed from the mesh. Check the mesh for holes and damage and replace it with a new one if necessary.
18 Coat the rubber rim of the strainer with clean oil, then slide it into the grooves in its chamber, making sure the thinner edge goes in first **(see illustration)**.
19 Install the clutch cover (see Chapter 2). Refill the engine with oil (see Steps 7 to 10).

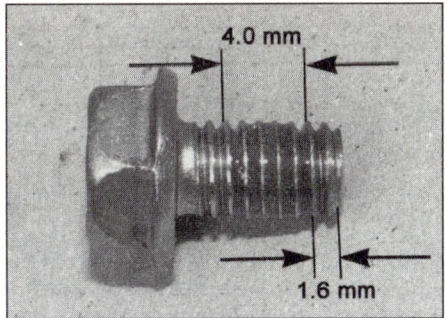
5.15a Apply the threadlock as described

5.15b Fit the cover using a new gasket

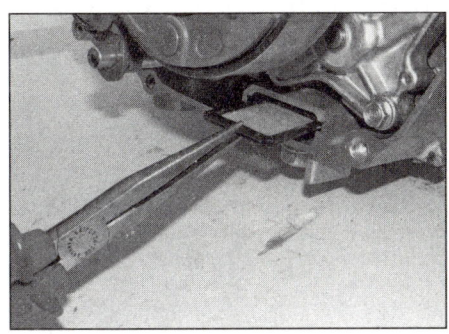
5.16 Withdraw the strainer and clean it

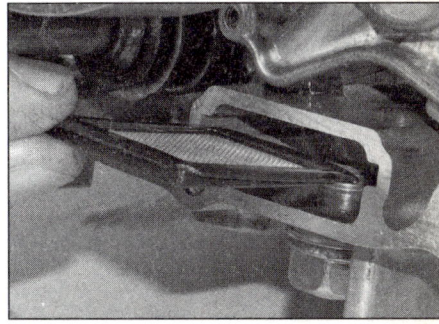
5.18 The thin edge goes in first

Note: *It is illegal and anti-social to dump oil down the drain. To find the location of your local oil recycling bank in the UK, call 08708 506 506 or visit www.oilbankline.org.uk*

6 Fuel system

⚠️ **Warning:** *Petrol is extremely flammable, so take extra precautions when you work on any part of the fuel system. Don't smoke or allow open flames or bare light bulbs near the work area, and don't work in a garage where a natural gas-type appliance is present. If you spill any fuel on your skin, rinse it off immediately with soap and water. When you perform any kind of work on the fuel system, wear safety glasses and have a fire extinguisher suitable for a Class B type fire (flammable liquids) on hand.*

2003 to 2006 (carburettor) models

1 Remove the front covers and the body cover (see Chapter 7).
2 Check the fuel hoses between the tank and the carburettor via the fuel filter and tap for signs of leakage, deterioration or damage **(see illustrations)**. Replace the hoses with new ones if cracked or deteriorated. Make sure that each hose is secure on its union at each end.
3 Check around the filler cap and the fuel level sensor retainer in the top of the fuel tank – fit a new seal onto the filler cap if there is evidence of leakage from around it, and if there is evidence of leakage from the sensor remove it and replace its seal with a new one (see Chapter 3A).
4 If there is evidence of leakage from around

6.2a Check the fuel hoses (arrowed) . . .

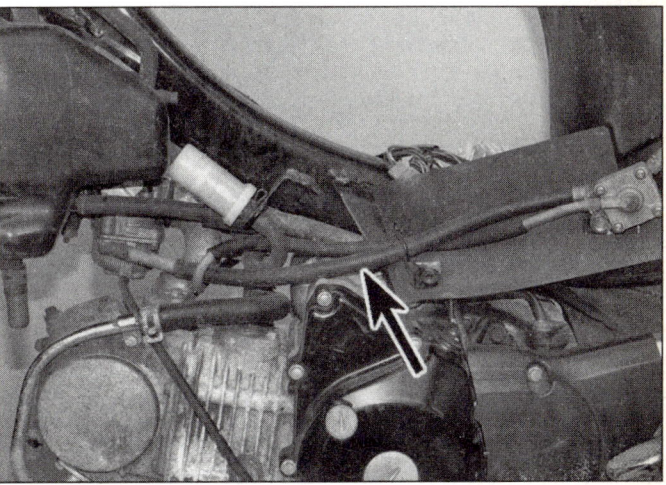
6.2b . . . between the tank and the carburettor

1•14 Routine maintenance and servicing

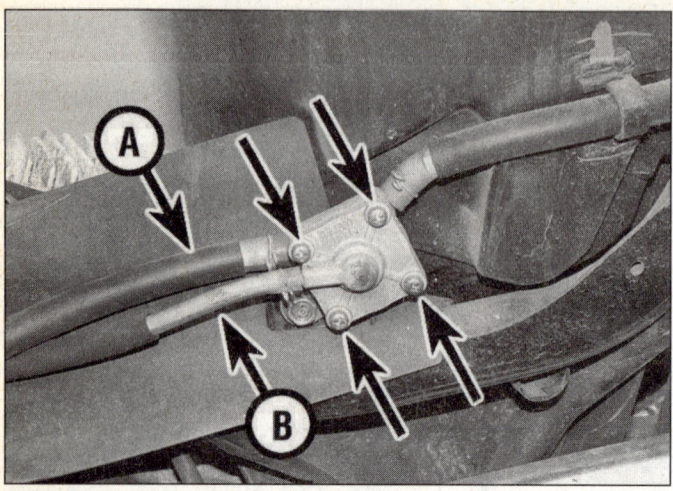

6.4 Check the fuel valve screws (arrowed) are tight. Fuel hose (A), vacuum hose (B)

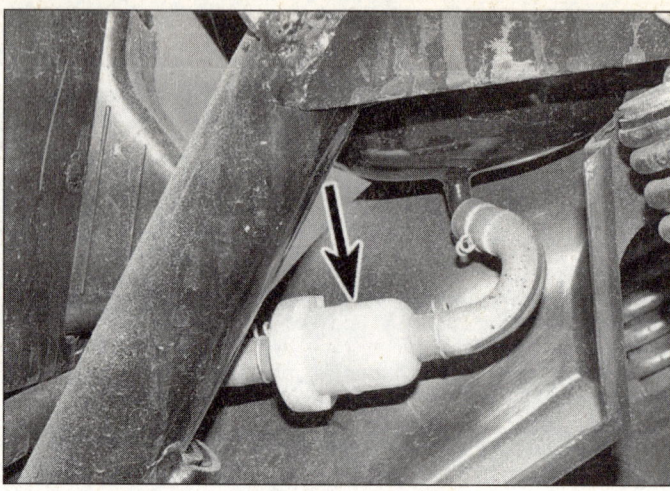

6.6 Fuel filter (arrowed)

the fuel valve, tighten the screws **(see illustration)**. If leakage persists replace the valve with a new one (see Chapter 3A).

5 The fuel valve is vacuum operated and should be closed when the engine is not running. Disconnect the fuel hose (the upper hose) from the valve to check that the valve inside is not leaking **(see illustration 6.4)**. If so, fit a new valve (see Chapter 3A). Make sure the vacuum hose is secure on its union at each end, and check for cracks and deterioration. Replace it with a new one if necessary.

6 Replacement of the fuel filter is advised after a particularly high mileage has been covered or if fuel starvation is suspected (see Chapter 3A). The filter is fitted in the hose between the tank and the tap **(see illustration)**.

7 If the carburettor gaskets are leaking, the carburettor should be disassembled and rebuilt using new gaskets and seals (see Chapter 3A).

8 If fuel starvation is suspected, and if there is a suction on the fuel filler cap caused by a vacuum inside the tank as fuel is used, the vent in the fuel cap is blocked. You could try to clear the vent, but it is best to fit a new cap.

9 If the fuel gauge is believed to be faulty, check the operation of the gauge and sensor (see Chapter 3A).

2007-on (fuel injection) models

10 Remove the front covers and the body cover (see Chapter 7). Remove the fuel pump cover **(see illustration)**.

11 Check the fuel tank and the fuel hose between it and the throttle body for signs of leakage, deterioration or damage **(see illustrations)**. Make sure that the hose is secure on its union at each end. Replace the fuel hose with a new one if it is cracked or deteriorated, referring to the relevant Sections in Chapter 3B for details on how to detach it from the pump and throttle body.

12 Check around the filler cap in the top of the fuel tank – fit a new seal onto the filler cap if there is evidence of leakage from around it.

13 Check around the pump retainer in the top of the fuel tank – if there is evidence of leakage from around it, remove the pump and replace its seal with a new one (see Chapter 3B).

14 If fuel starvation is suspected, and if there is a suction on the fuel filler cap caused by a vacuum inside the tank as fuel is used, the vent in the fuel cap is blocked. You could try to clear the vent, but it is best to fit a new cap. Next check the strainer on the pump is not blocked, then check the operation of the pump itself (see Chapter 3B). The pump also has an integral filter. The filter and strainer are not available separately.

15 If the fuel gauge is believed to be faulty, check the operation of the gauge and sensor (see Chapter 3B).

7 Throttle and choke cables

Throttle cable

1 Ensure the throttle twistgrip rotates easily from fully closed to fully open with the handlebars turned at various angles, and that the twistgrip returns automatically to the fully closed position when released.

2 If the throttle sticks, this is probably due to a cable fault. Disconnect the cable at the twistgrip end (see Chapter 3A for carburettor models or 3B for fuel injection models) and lubricate it (see Section 16).

3 With the cable disconnected, make sure the throttle twistgrip rotates freely on the handlebar – dirt combined with a lack of lubrication can cause the action to be stiff. If necessary, undo the handlebar end-weight screw and remove the end-weight, then slide the twistgrip off

6.10 Unscrew the bolts (arrowed) and remove the cover

6.11a Check the fuel hose (arrowed) between the tank . . .

6.11b . . . and the throttle body

Routine maintenance and servicing 1•15

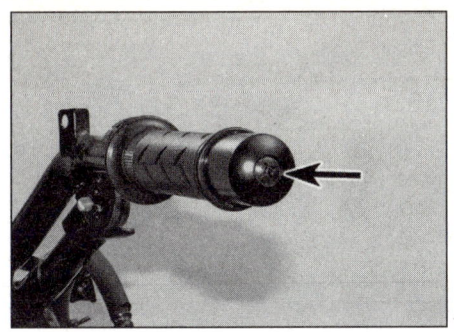

7.3 End-weight screw (arrowed)

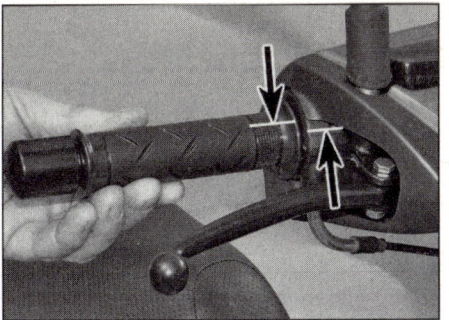

7.5 Throttle cable freeplay is measured in terms of free twistgrip rotation

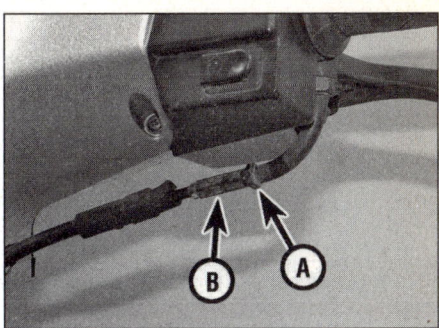

7.6 Slacken the adjuster locknut (A) and turn the adjuster (B) as required

the handlebar **(see illustration)**. Clean any old grease from the bar and the inside of the tube. Smear multi-purpose grease onto the bar, then refit the twistgrip. When fitting the end-weight, align the boss with the cut-out on the inner weight inside the handlebar. Clean the threads of the screw, then apply a suitable non-permanent thread locking compound, hold the weight and tighten the screw.

4 If the throttle action is still stiff, remove the front cover on the right-hand side on carburettor models and on both sides on fuel injection models to access the cable and check for a trapped or damaged section. If required, follow the procedure in Chapter 3A or 3B and install a new cable. Note that in very rare cases the fault could lie in the carburettor or throttle body.

5 With the throttle operating smoothly, check for a small amount of freeplay in the cable, measured in terms of the amount of twistgrip rotation before the throttle opens, and compare the amount to the Specifications at the beginning of this Chapter **(see illustration)**.

6 If there is insufficient or excessive freeplay on carburettor models, pull back the boot on the cable adjuster at the twistgrip end **(see illustration)**. Loosen the locknut on the adjuster, then turn it until the specified amount of freeplay is evident. Tighten the locknut. If the adjuster has reached its limit of adjustment, or the freeplay cannot be set correctly, replace the cable with a new one (see Chapter 3A).

7 If there is insufficient or excessive freeplay on fuel injection models, remove the front covers (see Chapter 7). Loosen the locknut securing the lower end of the cable in the throttle body bracket then turn the adjuster hex as required, keeping the cable pulled up so the lower nut remains captive in the bracket, until the freeplay is correct, and tighten the locknut **(see illustration)**. If the freeplay cannot be set correctly replace the cable with a new one (see Chapter 3B).

8 Start the engine and check the idle speed. If the idle speed is too high, this could be due to incorrect adjustment of the cable. Loosen the locknut and turn the adjuster in – if the idle speed falls as you do, there is insufficient freeplay in the cable. Reset the adjuster (see Step 6 or 7). Turn the handlebars from side to side and check that the idle speed does not change as you do. If it does, the throttle cable is routed incorrectly. Rectify the problem before riding the scooter.

Choke cable (carburettor models)

9 With the engine off, make sure the choke lever moves smoothly and freely.
10 If it is stiff or stuck, this is probably due to a cable fault. Disconnect the cable from the lever (see Chapter 3A) and lubricate it (see Section 16).
11 If the choke is still stiff or stuck remove the front covers to access the cable and check for a trapped or damaged section. If required, follow the procedure in Chapter 3A and install a new cable. Also check the action of the choke valve in the carburettor – it should open smoothly and freely and return under spring pressure.

8 Idle speed

Carburettor models

1 The idle speed (engine running with the throttle twistgrip closed) should be checked and adjusted when it is obviously too high or too low. Before adjusting the idle speed, make sure the throttle cable is correctly adjusted, the spark plug is in good condition with the correct gap, the air filter is clean, and the valve clearances are correct, referring to the relevant Sections in this Chapter.

2 The engine should be at normal operating temperature, which is usually reached after 10 to 15 minutes of stop-and-go riding. Support the machine on its centrestand and make sure it is in neutral.

> ⚠ **Warning: Do not allow exhaust gases to build up in the work area; either perform the check outside or use an exhaust gas extraction system**

3 The idle speed adjuster is a screw located on the right-hand side of the carburettor – it is the front one of the two screws, with the spring behind it **(see illustration)** (the other is the pilot mixture screw and should not be turned). The screw can be turned using a flat-bladed screwdriver inserted in the hole in the front cover **(see illustration)**. With the engine running, turn the screw until the engine idles at the speed specified at the beginning of the Chapter – turn the screw clockwise to increase idle speed, and anti-clockwise to

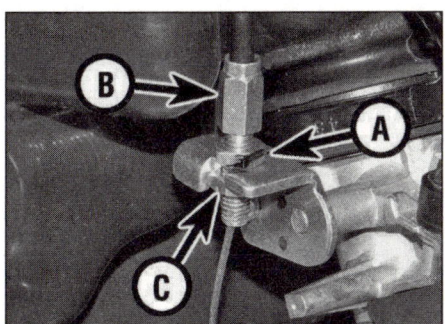

7.7 Throttle cable adjuster locknut (A), adjuster (B) and lower nut (C)

8.3a Idle speed adjuster (arrowed) . . .

8.3b . . . can be turned using a screwdriver inserted in the hole (arrowed)

1•16 routine maintenance and servicing

8.5 Check the intake duct bolts (arrowed) are tight

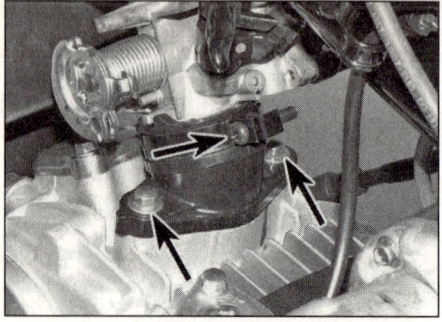

8.8 Check the intake duct clamp screw and flange bolts (arrowed) are tight

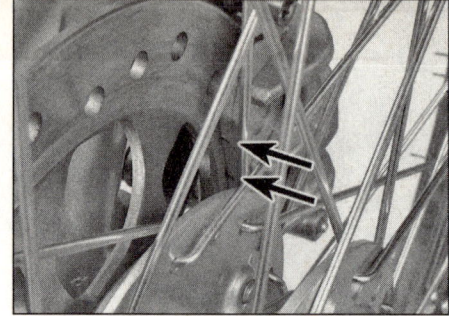

9.1 Front brake pad grooves (arrowed)

decrease it. As no tachometer is fitted you will have to judge the correct idle speed according to what is normal. If you are unsure as to what the correct speed should be take the scooter to a Honda dealer.
4 Snap the throttle open and shut a few times, then recheck the idle speed. If necessary, repeat the adjustment procedure.
5 If a smooth, steady idle can't be achieved, and all the items listed in Step 1 have been checked, there could be an air leak in the intake duct between the carburettor and the cylinder head – check the flange bolts are tight, and if necessary fit new O-rings between the carburettor and the duct, and/or a new gasket between the duct and the head **(see illustration)**. There could also be a problem with the fuel/air mixture screw or the float chamber on the carburettor (see Chapter 3A).
6 If the idle speed has been adjusted, recheck the throttle cable freeplay.

Fuel injection models

7 The idle speed is controlled electronically by the idle air control valve and is not adjustable.
8 If the idle speed is not correct, or the engine is difficult to start and/or does not idle smoothly, there could be an air leak in the intake duct between the throttle body and the cylinder head – remove the front covers (see Chapter 7), and check the duct clamp screw and flange bolts are tight **(see illustration)**, and if necessary fit a new O-ring between the duct and the head. Otherwise refer to Chapter 3B, Section 11 and check the idle air control valve.

9 Brake pads and shoes

Front disc brake pad wear check

1 Each brake pad has grooves in the face of the friction material which act as wear indicators **(see illustration)**. The grooves should be plainly visible by looking at the edges of the friction material from the best vantage point, but note that an accumulation of road dirt and brake dust could make them difficult to see.
2 If the grooves aren't visible, then the amount of friction material remaining should be, and it will be obvious when the pads need replacing. Honda do not specify a minimum thickness for the friction material, but anything less than 1 mm should be considered worn. **Note:** *Some after-market pads may use different indicators to those on the original equipment.*
3 If the pads are worn to the bottom of the groove or there is little friction material remaining, they must be replaced with new ones, though it is advisable to fit new pads before they become this worn.
4 If the pads are dirty or if you are in doubt as to the amount of friction material remaining, remove them for inspection (see Chapter 6). If the pads are excessively worn, check the brake disc (see Chapter 6).

Rear drum brake shoe and drum wear check

5 Make sure the amount of rear brake pedal freeplay is correct (see Section 10, Step 16).
6 Apply the rear brake and check the position of the wear indicator on the top of the brake arm in relation to the triangular mark on the casing **(see illustration)**. As the brake shoes wear and the freeplay is adjusted to compensate, the wear indicator moves closer to the wear limit mark on the casing. If the indicator has reached the mark replace the brake shoes with new ones (see Chapter 6).
7 With the wheel removed check the condition of the drum surface, and measure its internal diameter **(see illustrations)**. If it has worn to or beyond the service limit specified replace the wheel with a new one.

10 Brake system

1 A routine check of the brake system will ensure that any problems are discovered and remedied before the rider's safety is jeopardised. Remove the front handlebar cover (see Chapter 7).
2 Make sure all brake fasteners, including the reservoir cover screws, brake hose banjo bolts and caliper mounting bolts, are tight.

Front brake system

3 Make sure the brake light comes on when the front brake lever is pulled in. If not, first

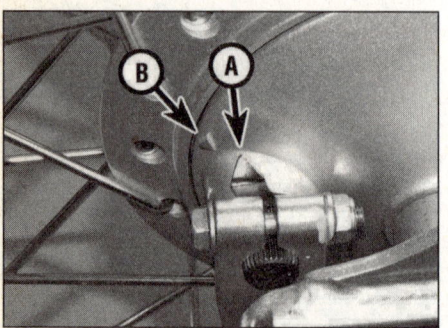

9.6 If the indicator (A) aligns with the mark (B) the shoes need replacing

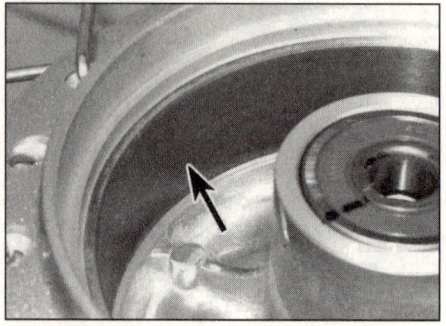

9.7a Check the condition of the lining . . .

9.7b . . . and measure the internal diameter of the drum

Routine maintenance and servicing 1•17

10.9 Twist and flex the hose to check for cracks and deterioration

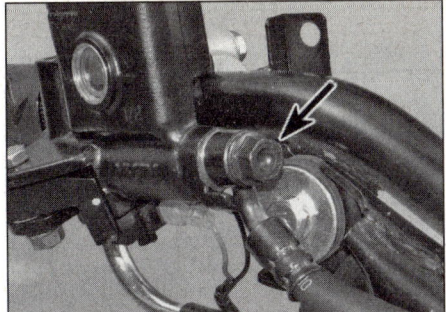

10.11a Check the banjo bolt and union at the master cylinder . . .

10.11b . . . and at the caliper

check the bulb (see Chapter 8). The switch, mounted on the underside of the master cylinder, is not adjustable. If it fails to operate properly, check it (see Chapter 8).
4 Check the brake lever for looseness, rough action, excessive play and other damage. Replace any worn or damaged parts with new ones (see Chapter 5).
5 Clean and lubricate the lever pivot at the specified interval or whenever necessary to reduce wear and ensure safe and trouble-free operation (see Section 16).
6 If the lever action is spongy (i.e. the lever does not come up hard and can travel all the way to the handlebar, first check the fluid level (see *Pre-ride checks*), then bleed the brake (see Chapter 6).

Brake fluid

7 The fluid level in the master cylinder reservoir(s) should be checked before riding the machine (see *Pre-ride checks*).
8 Brake fluid will degrade over a period of time. Honda recommends that it should be changed every 2 years, or whenever the master cylinder or caliper is overhauled or replaced. Refer to the brake bleeding and fluid change section in Chapter 6.

Brake hose

9 Twist and flex the hose while looking for cracks, bulges and seeping fluid **(see illustration)**. Check extra carefully where the hose connects to the banjo fittings as this is a common area for hose failure. If deterioration

is noticed replace the hose with a new one (see Chapter 6).
10 Inspect the banjo fittings – if they are rusted, cracked or damaged, fit a new hose.
11 Inspect the banjo union connections on the master cylinder and caliper for leaking fluid **(see illustrations)**. Check the bolts are tightened to the correct torque setting (see Chapter 6). If they leak when tightened, unscrew the banjo bolt and fit new sealing washers, then bleed the brake (see Chapter 6).

Brake caliper and master cylinder seals

12 Check the brake master cylinder and caliper for signs of leaking fluid.
13 Brake system seals will deteriorate over a period of time and lose their effectiveness. Old master cylinder seals will cause sticky operation of the brake lever and/or fluid to leak; old caliper seals will cause the pistons to stick or fluid to leak. The seals should be replaced with new ones if defects are evident – rebuild kits are available (see Chapter 6).

Rear brake system

14 Make sure the brake light comes on when the rear brake pedal is pressed and just before the rear brake takes effect. The switch is mounted behind the front of the footrest bracket on the right-hand side. If adjustment is necessary, hold the switch and turn the adjuster ring on the switch body until the brake light is activated when required **(see

illustration)**. If the brake light comes on too late or not at all, turn the ring clockwise (when looked at from the top) so the switch threads out of the bracket. If the brake light comes on too soon or is permanently on, turn the ring anti-clockwise so the switch threads into the bracket. If the switch doesn't operate the brake light, first check the bulb, then check the switch (see Chapter 8).
15 Check the brake pedal for looseness, rough action, excessive play and other damage. Clean and lubricate the lever pivot at the specified interval or whenever necessary to reduce wear and ensure safe and trouble-free operation (see Section 16).

Brake pedal freeplay

16 Check the amount of freeplay in the pedal, measured in terms of the amount of travel in the toe of the pedal before the brake comes on **(see illustration)**; it should be as specified at the beginning of the Chapter. If not adjust it by turning the adjuster nut on the rear end of the brake rod as required until the freeplay is correct – to reduce freeplay in the lever, turn the nut clockwise; to increase freeplay, turn the nut anti-clockwise **(see illustration)**. Make sure the nut is set so its cut-out seats around the pivot piece in the arm. After adjustment turn the rear wheel and check that there is no brake drag.

Brake cam

18 To check the operation of the brake cam, first slacken the adjuster nut **(see illustration 10.16b)**.

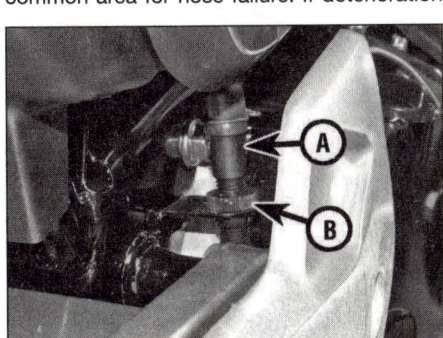

10.14 Hold the rear brake light switch body (A) and turn the adjuster ring (B) as required

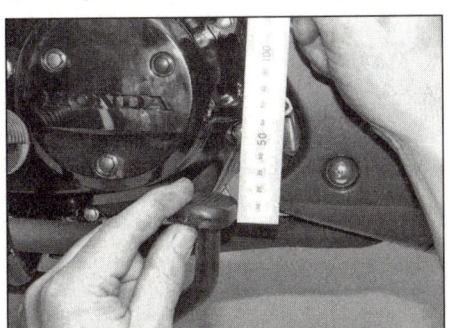

10.16a Check the amount of free pedal travel . . .

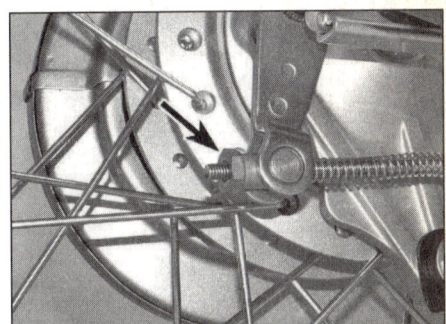

10.16b . . . and adjust as required by turning the nut

1•18 Routine maintenance and servicing

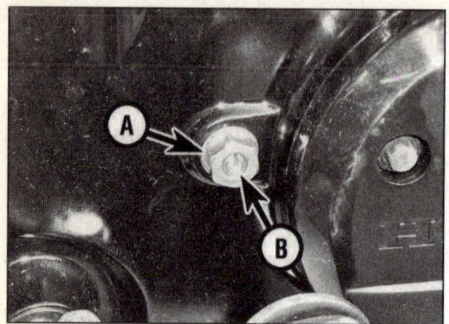

11.2 Clutch adjuster locknut (A) and screw (B)

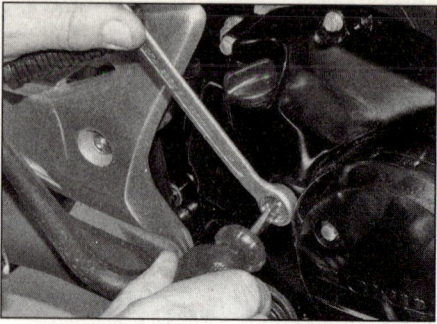

11.3 Counter-hold the screw when tightening the locknut

19 Apply the brake using hand pressure on the arm and ensure that it moves smoothly and freely and returns to the rest position when it is released. If the brake arm is binding in the backplate, follow the procedure in Chapter 6 to remove the brake shoes and inspect the brake cam and the springs on the brake shoes.

20 Apply some copper grease to the bearing surfaces of the cam and its shaft before reassembly. Adjust the freeplay on completion (see Step 16).
Caution: Do not apply too much grease otherwise there is a risk of it contaminating the brake drum and shoe linings.

11 Clutch lifter mechanism

1 Support the machine on its centrestand and make sure it is in neutral.
2 Slacken the locknut on the clutch adjuster in the clutch cover **(see illustration)**.
3 Using a screwdriver turn the adjuster screw one full turn clockwise. Next turn it slowly anti-clockwise until resistance is just felt. Finally turn it clockwise 1/8 turn. Hold the screw and tighten the locknut **(see illustration)**.

12 Stands and starter safety circuit

1 Check the stand springs for damage and distortion **(see illustrations)**. The springs must be capable of retracting the stand fully and holding it retracted when the motorcycle is in use. If a spring is sagged or broken it must be replaced with a new one.
2 Lubricate the stand pivots at the specified interval (see Section 16). Check the tightness of the sidestand pivot bolt and nut.
3 Check the stands and their mounts for bends and cracks. Stands can often be repaired by welding.
4 Check the operation of the starter safety circuit as follows:
● Support the machine on its centrestand and make sure it is in neutral. Retract the sidestand and start the engine. Select first gear. Extend the sidestand. The engine should stop as the sidestand is extended.
● Make sure the engine is in neutral and the sidestand is down, then start the engine. Select first gear. The engine should cut out.
● Check that when the sidestand is down the engine can only be started if the transmission is in neutral.
5 If the circuit does not operate as described, check the sidestand switch and gear position switch, and the circuit wiring between them (see Chapter 8).

13 Suspension

1 The suspension components must be maintained in top operating condition to ensure rider safety. Loose, worn or damaged suspension parts decrease the scooter's stability and control.

Front suspension

2 While standing alongside the scooter, apply the front brake and push on the handlebars to compress the suspension several times **(see illustration)**. See if it moves up-and-down smoothly without binding. If binding is felt, the suspension should be disassembled and inspected (see Chapter 5).
3 Inspect the area around the dust seal for signs of oil leaks **(see illustration)**. If corrosion due to the ingress of water is evident, the seals must be replaced with new ones (see Chapter 5).
4 If oil is leaking, the oil seal has failed and the fork leg must be dismantled and a new seal fitted (see Chapter 5).
5 The chromed finish on the forks is prone to corrosion and pitting, so it is advisable to keep them as clean as possible and to spray them regularly with a rust inhibitor, otherwise the seals will not last long. If corrosion and pitting is evident, tackle it as early as possible to prevent it getting worse, and if necessary replace the fork inner tubes with new ones, or have them re-chromed by a specialist (hard chrome must be used).
6 Check the tightness of the fork clamp bolts.

Rear suspension

7 With the aid of an assistant to support the scooter, compress the rear suspension several

12.1a Check the sidestand springs . . .

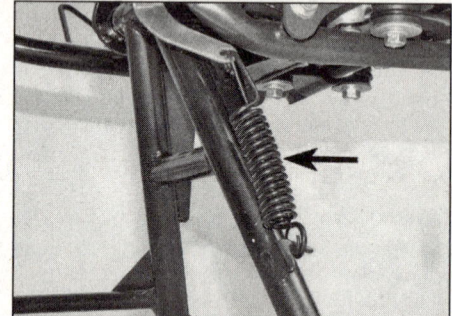

12.1b . . . and the centrestand springs as described

13.2 Compress and release the front suspension

13.3 Check the seal (arrowed) and tube for damage and signs of oil leakage

Routine maintenance and servicing 1•19

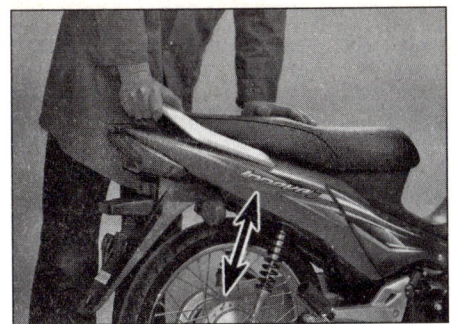

13.7 Compress and release the rear suspension

13.8 Check the rod (arrowed) for leaks and corrosion

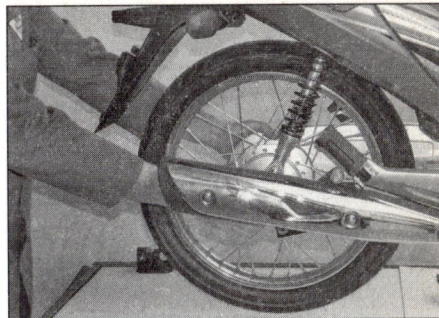

13.9 Checking for play in the swingarm bushes

times **(see illustration)**. It should move up and down freely without binding. If any binding is felt, the worn or faulty component must be identified. The problem could be due to either the shock absorbers or the swingarm pivot.

8 Inspect the rear shock absorbers for fluid leaks and corrosion on the damper rod **(see illustration)**. Check that the upper and lower shock mounting bolts and nuts are tight – refer to the torque setting specified at the beginning of Chapter 5. If a shock is faulty both shocks should be replaced as a pair (see Chapter 5).

9 Support the scooter on its centrestand so that the rear wheel is off the ground. Grab the swingarm and rock it from side-to-side – there should be no discernible movement at the rear **(see illustration)**. If there's a little movement or a slight clicking can be heard, inspect the tightness of the swingarm and shock absorber mounting bolts and nuts, referring to the torque settings specified at the beginning of Chapter 5, and re-check for movement.

10 Next, grasp the top of the rear wheel and pull it upwards – there should be no discernible freeplay before the shock absorbers begin to compress. Any freeplay felt in either check indicates worn bushes in the shock absorbers or swingarm. The worn components must be identified and replaced with new ones (see Chapter 5). Bushes are available for the shock absorbers, but not the swingarm.

11 To make an accurate assessment of the swingarm bushes, remove the rear wheel and the shock absorbers (see Chapters 6 and 5). Grasp the rear of the swingarm with one hand and place your other hand at the junction of the swingarm and the frame. Try to move the rear of the swingarm from side-to-side. Any wear (play) in the bushes should be felt as movement between the swingarm and the frame at the front. If there is any play the swingarm will be felt to move forward and backward at the front (not from side-to-side). If there is any play in the swingarm remove it for inspection (see Chapter 5). If the bushes are worn a new swingarm must be fitted as the bushes are not available separately.

Front fork oil change

12 Although there is no set interval for changing the fork oil, note that the oil will degrade over a period of time and lose its damping qualities. Refer to Chapter 5 for details of front fork removal, oil draining and refilling. The forks do not need to be completely disassembled to change the oil.

Rear suspension lubrication

13 Although there is no set interval, the swingarm pivot bolt should be removed, cleaned and re-greased periodically as necessary (see Chapter 5).

14 Wheels, wheel bearings and tyres

Wire spoke wheels

1 Visually check the spokes for damage and corrosion. A broken or bent spoke must be replaced with a new one immediately because the load taken by it will be transferred to adjacent spokes which may in turn fail. Check the tension in each spoke by tapping each one lightly with a screwdriver and noting the sound produced – each should make the same sound of the correct pitch. Properly tensioned spokes will make a sharp pinging sound, loose ones will produce a lower pitch dull sound and tight ones will be higher pitched. If a spoke needs adjustment turn the adjuster at the rim using a spoke adjustment tool or an open-ended spanner **(see illustration)**.

2 Unevenly tensioned spokes will promote rim misalignment – refer to information on wheel runout in Chapter 6 and seek the advice of a Honda dealer or wheel building specialist if the wheel hub needs repositioning, which it may well do if many spokes are unevenly tensioned. Check front and rear wheel alignment as described in Chapter 6. Check that any wheel balance weights are fixed firmly to the wheel rim. If you suspect that a weight has fallen off, have the wheel rebalanced by a motorcycle tyre specialist.

Wheel bearings

3 Wheel bearings will wear over a considerable mileage and should be checked periodically to avoid handling problems.

4 Support the bike on the centrestand. When checking the front wheel bearings turn the handlebars to full lock on one side so you have something to push against. Check for any play in the bearings by pushing and pulling the wheel against the hub **(see illustration)**. Also rotate the wheel and check that it turns smoothly and without any grating noises.

5 If any play is detected in the hub, or if the wheel does not rotate smoothly (and this is not due to brake or transmission drag), remove the wheel and inspect the bearings for wear or damage (see Chapter 6).

Tyres

6 Check the tyre condition and tread depth thoroughly – see *Pre-ride checks*.

7 Check that the directional arrow on the tyre sidewall is pointing in the normal direction of wheel rotation.

8 Check the valve rubber for signs of damage or deterioration and have it replaced if necessary by a tyre specialist.

14.1 Adjusting the spokes using a multi-sized spoke tool

14.4 Checking for play in the rear wheel bearings

1•20 Routine maintenance and servicing

14.10 The top of the cap doubles as a valve core tool

15.2 Slacken the bolt (arrowed) and pivot the headlight as required

9 Make sure the valve stem cap is in place and tight. Check the valve for signs of damage.

10 If tyre deflation occurs and it is not due to a slow puncture the valve core may be loose or it could be leaking past the seal – remove the cap and make sure the core is tight. Some valve caps double as a tool for the valve core **(see illustration)** – these caps are available in bike and automotive accessory dealers. Alternatively special tools are available, or a tool can be made quite easily by cutting a slot into the threaded end of a bolt using a hacksaw – the bolt must fit inside the valve housing and the slot must be deep enough to locate around the flat sides of the core and grip it. If the core leaks when tight fit a new one. A smear of spit or soapy water across the top of the valve will indicate if it is leaking – the leak will show as bubbles.

15 Headlight aim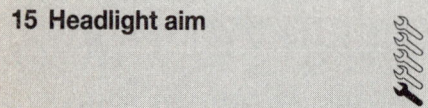

Note: *An improperly adjusted headlight may cause problems for oncoming traffic or provide poor, unsafe illumination of the road ahead. Before adjusting the headlight aim, be sure to consult with local traffic laws and regulations – for UK models refer to MOT Test Checks in the Reference section.*

1 The headlight beam can adjusted vertically. Before making any adjustment, check that the tyre pressures are correct. Make any adjustments to the headlight aim with the scooter on level ground, with the fuel tank half full and with an assistant sitting on the seat. If the bike is usually ridden with a passenger on the back, have a second assistant to do this.

2 Adjustment is made by slackening the bolt on the underside of the headlight, then pivoting the headlight up or down as required, and tightening the bolt **(see illustration)**.

16 Stand, lever pivot and cable lubrication

1 Since the controls, cables and various other components of a motorcycle are exposed to the elements, they should be checked and lubricated periodically to ensure safe and trouble-free operation.

Pivot points

2 The footrest, front brake lever, rear brake pedal, gearchange lever and stand pivots should be lubricated frequently. In order for the lubricant to be applied where it will do the most good, the component should be disassembled and all old lubricant and dirt cleaned off (see Chapter 5). The lubricant recommended by Honda for each application is listed at the beginning of the Chapter. If an aerosol lubricant is being used, it can be applied to the pivot joint gaps and will usually work its way into the areas where friction occurs, so less disassembly of the component is needed (however it is always better to do so and clean off all corrosion, dirt and old lubricant first). If motor oil or light grease is being used, apply it sparingly as it may attract dirt (which could cause the controls to bind or wear at an accelerated rate). The centrestand pivot has a grease nipple, so if you have a grease gun you can apply fresh grease in this way.

Cables

Special tool: *A cable lubricating adapter is necessary for this procedure* **(see illustration 16.3c)**.

3 To lubricate the cables, disconnect the relevant cable at its upper end, then lubricate it with a pressure adapter and aerosol lubricant **(see illustrations)**. See Chapter 3A or 3B for throttle and choke cable removal procedure.

17 Nuts and bolts

1 Since vibration tends to loosen fasteners, all nuts, bolts, screws, etc. should be periodically checked for proper tightness.

2 Pay particular attention to the following:
   Spark plug
   Carburettor/throttle body clamps and
      intake duct bolts
   Engine oil drain plug
   Sidestand pivot nut and bolt
   Engine mounting nuts/bolts
   Suspension nuts/bolts
   Wheel axle nuts
   Handlebar bolts
   Brake caliper mounting bolts (front brake)
   Brake hose banjo bolts (front brake)
   Exhaust system bolts/nuts

3 If a torque wrench is available, use it along with the torque specifications given at the beginning of each Chapter.

18 Steering head bearings

Check

1 The steering head bearings consist of ball bearings which run in races at the top and

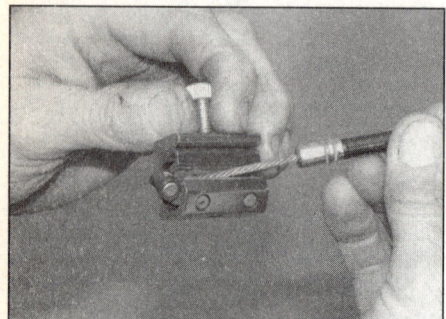

16.3a Fit the cable into the adapter . . .

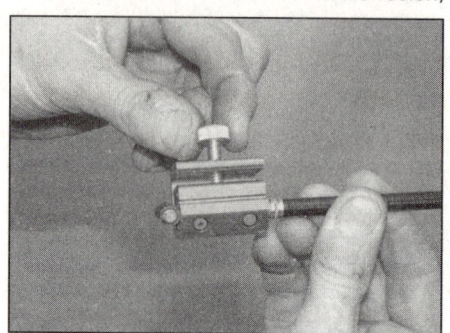

16.3b . . . and tighten the screw to seal it in . . .

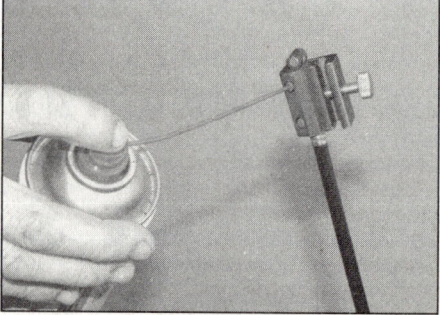

16.3c . . . then apply the lubricant using the nozzle provided inserted in the hole in the adapter

Routine maintenance and servicing 1•21

18.5 Checking for play in the steering head bearings

18.9 Slacken the steering stem nut

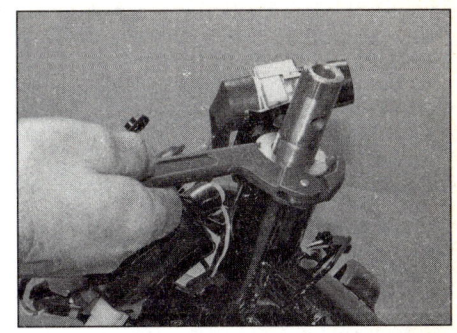

18.10 Using a C-spanner to adjust the head bearings

bottom of the steering head. The races can become dented or rough during normal use and the balls will gradually wear. In extreme cases, worn or loose steering head bearings can cause steering wobble – a condition that is potentially dangerous.

2 Support the scooter on its centrestand. Have an assistant push down on the rear or place a support under the engine or footrest bracket (not under the exhaust) so the front wheel is off the ground.

3 Point the front wheel straight-ahead and slowly turn the handlebars from side-to-side. Any dents or roughness in the bearing races will be felt and the bars will not move smoothly and freely. If the bearings are damaged they must be replaced with new ones (see Chapter 5).

4 Again point the wheel straight-ahead, and tap the front of the wheel to one side. The wheel should 'fall' under its own weight to the limit of its lock, indicating that the bearings are not too tight (take into account the restriction that the brake hose, cables and wiring may have). Check for similar movement to the other side.

5 Next, grasp the bottom of the forks and try to move them forwards and backwards **(see illustration)**. Any freeplay in the steering head bearings will be felt as front-to-rear movement of the steering stem. If play is felt in the bearings, follow the procedure described below to adjust them.

> **Haynes hint** – Make sure you are not mistaking any movement between the bike and stand, or between the stand and the ground, for freeplay in the bearings. Do not pull and push the forks too hard – a gentle movement is all that is needed.

6 Over a period of time the grease in the bearings will harden or may be washed out. Follow the procedure in Chapter 5 to disassemble the steering head and re-grease the bearings. If the bearing balls and races are damaged they must be replaced with new ones.

Adjustment

7 Remove the top cover and the handlebar covers, and to prevent the possibility of damage the front cover on each side (see Chapter 7).

8 Remove the handlebars and handlebar support post (see Chapter 5).

9 Slacken the steering stem nut **(see illustration)**.

10 Turn the adjuster nut using a C-spanner located in one of the notches, either clockwise to tighten the head bearings or anti-clockwise to loosen them, and only moving it a small amount at a time **(see illustration)**. After each small adjustment recheck the freeplay as described in steps 2 to 5, before making further adjustments. The object is to set the adjuster nut so that the bearings are under a very light loading, just enough to remove any freeplay, but not so much that the steering does not move freely from side-to-side as described in the check procedure above.

11 Tighten the steering stem nut, to the torque setting specified at the beginning of the Chapter if you have a deep enough socket.

12 Re-check the bearing adjustment as described in steps 2 to 5 and re-adjust if necessary.

13 Install the handlebars and covers (see Chapters 5 and 7).

Lubrication

14 Over a considerable time the grease in the bearings will be dispersed or will harden allowing the ingress of dirt and water.

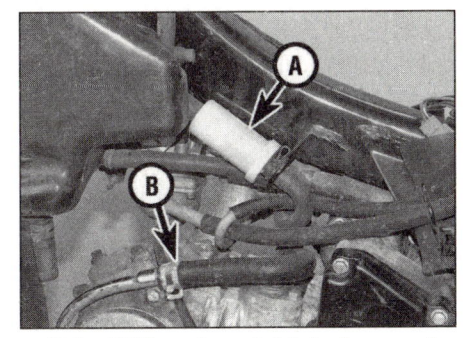

15 The steering head should be disassembled periodically and the bearings cleaned and re-greased (see Chapter 5, Sections 7 and 8).

19 PAIR (Pulse secondary air supply) system

1 On 2003 to 2006 (carburettor) models, to reduce the amount of unburned hydrocarbons released in the exhaust gases, a pulse secondary air supply (PAIR) system is fitted. The system consists of an air intake hose that draws air in via a filter connected to the control valve, containing a diaphragm valve and a reed valve, connected to the exhaust port via an air supply hose and pipe and air passage through the cylinder head **(see illustrations)**. The control valve is actuated by a vacuum sourced from the intake duct between the carburettor and the cylinder head.

2 Under normal running conditions, the PAIR control valve is open allowing filtered air to be drawn through it and the reed valve and cylinder head passage and into the exhaust port. The air mixes with the exhaust gases, causing any unburned particles of the fuel in the mixture to be burnt in the exhaust port/pipes. This process changes a considerable amount of hydrocarbons and carbon monoxide into relatively harmless carbon dioxide and water. The reed valve is fitted to prevent the flow of exhaust gases back through the control valve. When the throttle is closed on over-run the vacuum created in the intake duct acts on the diaphragm valve to

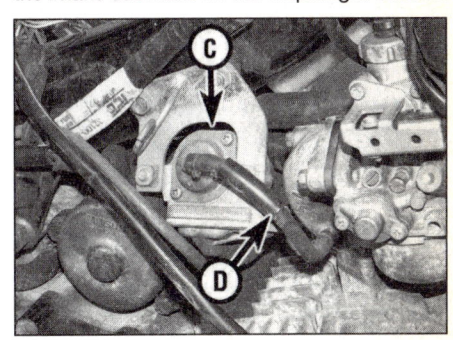

19.1a PAIR system air intake hose and filter (A), air supply hose/pipe (B) . . .

19.1b . . . control valve (C) and vacuum hose (D)

1•22 Routine maintenance and servicing

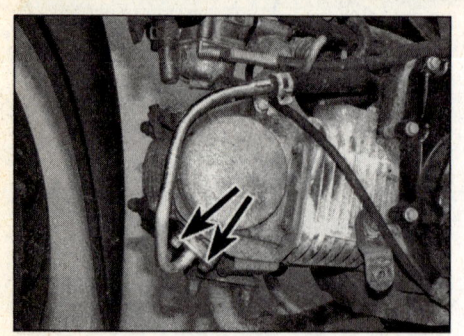

19.3 Check the bolts (arrowed) are tight

close the air passage and prevent popping in the exhaust.

3 The system is not adjustable and requires little maintenance. Check that the hoses are not kinked or pinched, are in good condition and are securely connected at each end – remove the front covers (see Chapter 7) for access. Replace any hoses that are cracked, split or generally deteriorated with new ones. Make sure the pipe flange bolts to the cylinder head are tight **(see illustration)**.

4 Check the air filter for dirt and debris and replace it with a new one if airflow through it is impaired – note the directional arrow which must point in the direction of air flow.

5 Refer to Chapter 3A for further information on the system and for functional checks if it is believed to be faulty.

20 Battery

Caution: Be extremely careful when handling or working around the battery. The electrolyte is very caustic and an explosive gas (hydrogen) is given off when the battery is charging.

1 All models covered in this manual are fitted with a sealed MF (maintenance free) battery. **Note:** *Do not attempt to remove the battery caps to check the electrolyte level or battery specific gravity. Removal will damage the caps, resulting in electrolyte leakage and battery damage.*

2 All that should be done is to check that the terminals are clean and tight and that the casing is not damaged or leaking. See Chapter 8 for further details.

3 If the machine is not in regular use, disconnect the battery, and give it a refresher charge every month to six weeks (see Chapter 8).

4 The state of charge of the battery can be assessed by measuring its open-circuit voltage (see Chapter 8).

Chapter 2
Engine, clutch and transmission

Contents

	Section number		Section number
Alternator	see Chapter 8	Gear position switch	see Chapter 8
Cam chain tensioner	7	Gearchange mechanism	21
Camshaft and rocker arms	8	General information	1
Cam chain, tensioner blade and guide blade	9	Idle speed check and adjustment	see Chapter 1
Clutch assemblies removal and installation	17	Kickstart mechanism	22
Centrifugal clutch – overhaul	18	Oil change	see Chapter 1
Clutch (multi-plate) – overhaul	19	Oil level check	see Pre-ride checks
Clutch lifter/brake mechanism	20	Oil pump	23
Clutch cover	16	Oil filter and strainer cleaning	see Chapter 1
Clutch check	see Chapter 1	Piston	13
Component access	2	Piston rings	14
Crankcases and bearings	25	Running-in procedure	30
Crankcase separation and reassembly	24	Selector drum and forks	29
Crankshaft and connecting rod	26	Spark plug	see Chapter 1
Cylinder block	12	Starter clutch and gears	15
Cylinder head removal and installation	10	Starter motor	see Chapter 8
Cylinder head and valve overhaul	11	Transmission shafts overhaul	28
Engine disassembly and reassembly general information	5	Transmission shafts removal and installation	27
Engine removal and installation	4	Valve clearance check and adjustment	see Chapter 1
Engine wear assessment	3	Valve covers	6

Degrees of difficulty

Easy, suitable for novice with little experience	Fairly easy, suitable for beginner with some experience	Fairly difficult, suitable for competent DIY mechanic	Difficult, suitable for experienced DIY mechanic	Very difficult, suitable for expert DIY or professional

Specifications

General
Type	Four-stroke, single cylinder
Capacity	124.9 cc
Bore	52.4 mm
Stroke	57.9 mm
Compression ratio	9.3 to 1
Cooling system	Air-cooled
Camshaft	SOHC, chain-driven
Clutches	Centrifugal and wet multi-plate
Transmission	Four-speed constant mesh
Final drive	Chain and sprockets

Cylinder head
Cylinder compression
  2003 to 2006 (carburettor) models . . . . 171 psi (12 Bar) @ 600 rpm
  2007-on (fuel injection) models . . . . 183 psi (12.9 Bar) @ 600 rpm
Warpage (max) . . . . 0.05 mm

Camshaft and rockers
Intake lobe height
  2003 to 2006 (carburettor) models
    Standard . . . . 32.347 to 32.447 mm
    Service limit (min) . . . . 31.94 mm
  2007-on (fuel injection) models
    Standard . . . . 32.312 to 32.552 mm
    Service limit (min) . . . . 32.0 mm
Exhaust lobe height
  2003 to 2006 (carburettor) models
    Standard . . . . 32.191 to 32.291 mm
    Service limit (min) . . . . 31.79 mm
  2007-on (fuel injection) models
    Standard . . . . 32.155 to 32.395 mm
    Service limit (min) . . . . 31.8 mm
Rocker arm bore diameter
  Standard . . . . 10.000 to 10.015 mm
  Service limit (min) . . . . 10.10 mm
Rocker arm shaft diameter
  Standard . . . . 9.972 to 9.987 mm
  Service limit (min) . . . . 9.91 mm
Rocker arm-to-shaft clearance
  Standard . . . . 0.013 to 0.043 mm
  Service limit (min) . . . . 0.044 mm

Valves, guides and springs
Valve clearances . . . . see Chapter 1
Stem diameter
  Intake valve
    Standard . . . . 4.975 to 4.990 mm
    Service limit (min) . . . . 4.965 mm
  Exhaust valve
    Standard . . . . 4.955 to 4.970 mm
    Service limit (min) . . . . 4.945 mm
Guide bore diameter – intake and exhaust valves
  Standard . . . . 5.000 to 5.012 mm
  Service limit (max) . . . . 5.03 mm
Stem-to-guide clearance
  Intake valve
    Standard . . . . 0.010 to 0.037 mm
    Service limit . . . . 0.065 mm
  Exhaust valve
    Standard . . . . 0.030 to 0.057 mm
    Service limit . . . . 0.085 mm
Seat width – intake and exhaust valves
  Standard . . . . 1.0 mm
  Service limit (max) . . . . 1.6 mm
Valve spring free length – intake and exhaust valves
  Standard . . . . 37.62 mm
  Service limit (min) . . . . 35.8 mm

Cylinder bore
Bore
  Standard . . . . 52.405 to 52.415 mm
  Service limit (max) . . . . 52.445 mm
Warpage (max) . . . . 0.05 mm
Ovality (out-of-round) (max) . . . . 0.010 mm
Taper (max) . . . . 0.010 mm

Piston

Piston diameter (measured 10 mm up from skirt, at 90° to piston pin axis)
  2003 to 2006 (carburettor) models
    Standard.. 52.362 to 52.400 mm
    Service limit (min)..................................... 52.292 mm
  2007-on (fuel injection) models
    Standard.. 52.370 to 52.390 mm
    Service limit (min)..................................... 51.67 mm
Piston-to-bore clearance
  2003 to 2006 (carburettor) models
    Standard.. 0.005 to 0.054 mm
    Service limit (min)..................................... 0.159 mm*
  2007-on (fuel injection) models
    Standard.. 0.015 to 0.045 mm
    Service limit (min)..................................... 0.10 mm*
Piston pin diameter
  Standard... 12.994 to 13.000 mm
  Service limit (min).. 12.98 mm
Piston pin bore diameter in piston
  Standard... 13.002 to 13.008 mm
  Service limit (max)....................................... 13.03 mm
Piston pin-to-piston pin bore clearance
  Standard... 0.002 to 0.014 mm
  Service limit .... 0.075 mm

*If the piston-to-bore clearance exceeds the service limit, the cylinder can be rebored – Honda supply +0.25, +0.5, +0.75 and +1.00 oversize pistons and rings. Following rebore, the piston-to-bore clearance must be as standard for a normal piston.

Piston rings

Ring end gap (installed)
  Top and second rings
    Standard.. 0.10 to 0.30 mm
    Service limit (max).................................... 0.50 mm
  Oil ring side-rail
    Standard.. 0.20 to 0.70 mm
    Service limit (max).................................... 1.1 mm
Ring-to-groove clearance
  Top ring
    2003 to 2006 (carburettor) models
      Standard.. 0.030 to 0.065 mm
      Service limit (max)................................ 0.10 mm
    2007-on (fuel injection) models
      Standard.. 0.015 to 0.050 mm
      Service limit (max)................................ 0.09 mm
  Second ring
    Standard.. 0.015 to 0.050 mm
    Service limit (max).................................... 0.09 mm

Oil pump

Inner rotor tip-to-outer rotor clearance (max)................... 0.20 mm
Outer rotor-to-body clearance
  Standard... 0.15 to 0.21 mm
  Service limit (max)....................................... 0.26 mm
Rotor end-float
  Standard... 0.03 to 0.09 mm
  Service limit (max)....................................... 0.15 mm

Connecting rod

Small-end internal diameter
  Standard... 13.016 to 13.034 mm
  Service limit (max)....................................... 13.06 mm
Small-end-to-piston pin clearance
  Standard... 0.016 to 0.040 mm
  Service limit (max)....................................... 0.07 mm
Big-end side clearance
  Standard... 0.10 to 0.35 mm
  Service limit (max)....................................... 0.60 mm
Big-end radial clearance
  Standard... 0.008 mm
  Service limit (max)....................................... 0.05 mm

2•4 Engine, clutch and transmission

Crankshaft
Runout (max) .... 0.10 mm

Starter clutch
Starter driven gear hub OD – 2007-on models
   Standard .... 45.660 to 45.673 mm
   Service limit (min) .... 45.20 mm
Starter driven gear hub OD – 2003 to 2006 models .... not available

Centrifugal clutch
Clutch drum ID
   Standard .... 104.0 to 104.2 mm
   Service limit (max) .... 104.3 mm
Clutch weight lining thickness
   Standard .... 1.5 mm
   Service limit (min) .... 1.0 mm
One-way clutch roller OD
   Standard .... 4.990 to 5.000 mm
   Service limit (min) .... 4.97 mm
One-way clutch housing ID
   Standard .... 42.00 to 42.02 mm
   Service limit (max) .... 42.04 mm
Primary drive gear ID
   Standard .... 21.030 to 21.058 mm
   Service limit (max) .... 21.11 mm
Crankshaft OD at primary drive gear
   Standard .... 20.967 to 20.980 mm
   Service limit (min) .... 20.92 mm
Clutch brake lining thickness
   Standard .... 3.35 mm
   Service limit (min) .... 2.5 mm

Clutch (multi-plate)
Friction plates 4
Plain plates 3
Friction plate thickness
   Standard .... 2.5 to 2.7 mm
   Service limit (min) .... 2.2 mm
Plain plate warpage (max) .... 0.20 mm
Spring free length
   Standard .... 27.4 mm
   Service limit (min) .... 26.8 mm
Clutch housing ID
   Standard .... 23.000 to 23.021 mm
   Service limit (max) .... 23.07 mm
Clutch guide OD
   Standard .... 22.959 to 22.980 mm
   Service limit (min) .... 22.94 mm
Clutch guide ID
   Standard .... 16.991 to 17.009 mm
   Service limit (max) .... 17.049 mm
Input shaft OD at clutch guide
   Standard .... 16.966 to 16.984 mm
   Service limit (min) .... 16.87 mm

Selector drum and forks
Selector fork end thickness
   Standard .... 4.93 to 5.00 mm
   Service limit (min) .... 4.9 mm
Selector fork bore ID
   Standard .... 10.000 to 10.018 mm
   Service limit (max) .... 10.07 mm
Selector fork shaft OD
   Standard .... 9.986 to 9.995 mm
   Service limit (min) .... 9.93 mm

Selector drum and forks (continued)

Selector drum right-hand journal OD	
Standard	27.959 to 27.980 mm
Service limit (min)	
2003 to 2006 (carburettor) models	27.94 mm
2007-on (fuel injection) models	27.80 mm
Selector drum left-hand journal OD	
Standard	23.959 to 23.980 mm
Service limit (min)	
2003 to 2006 (carburettor) models	23.94 mm
2007-on (fuel injection) models	23.80 mm
Selector drum bore ID in right-hand crankcase	
Standard	28.000 to 28.021 mm
Service limit (max)	28.10 mm
Selector drum bore ID in left-hand crankcase	
Standard	24.000 to 24.033 mm
Service limit (max)	24.10 mm

Kickstart

Pinion ID	
Standard	20.000 to 20.021 mm
Service limit (max)	20.08 mm
Shaft OD	
Standard	19.959 to 19.980 mm
Service limit (min)	19.94 mm

Transmission

Gear ratios (no. of teeth)	
Primary reduction	3.350 to 1 (67/20)
Final reduction	2.500 to 1 (35/14)
1st gear	2.500 to 1 (35/14)
2nd gear	1.550 to 1 (31/20)
3rd gear	1.150 to 1 (23/20)
4th gear	0.923 to 1 (24/26)
Input shaft 2nd and 3rd gears ID	
Standard	17.000 to 17.018 mm
Service limit (max)	17.04 mm
Input shaft OD at 3rd gear point	
Standard	16.966 to 16.984 mm
Service limit (min)	16.95 mm
Input shaft-to-gear clearance at 3rd gear point	
Standard	0.016 to 0.052 mm
Service limit (max)	0.09 mm
Output shaft 1st gear ID	
Standard	18.000 to 18.018 mm
Service limit (max)	18.04 mm
Output shaft 4th gear ID	
Standard	20.000 to 20.021 mm
Service limit (max)	20.04 mm
Output shaft 1st gear bush OD	
Standard	17.966 to 17.984 mm
Service limit (min)	17.94 mm
Output shaft 1st gear-to-bush clearance	
Standard	0.016 to 0.052 mm
Service limit (max)	0.10 mm
Output shaft 1st gear bush ID	
Standard	15.000 to 15.018 mm
Service limit (max)	15.04 mm
Output shaft OD at 1st gear bush point	
Standard	14.966 to 14.984 mm
Service limit (min)	14.95 mm
Output shaft-to-bush clearance at 1st gear bush point	
Standard	0.016 to 0.052 mm
Service limit (max)	0.09 mm

2•6 Engine, clutch and transmission

Torque settings

Camshaft sprocket bolts	9 Nm
Camshaft sprocket cover bolt	10 Nm
Centrifugal clutch nut	64 Nm
Clutch lifter plate bolts	12 Nm
Clutch nut	64 Nm
Crankcase bolts (see Section 24)	12 Nm
Crankshaft end cap	8 Nm
Cylinder head nuts	24 Nm
Decompression plunger bolt	10 Nm
Engine mounting bolt nuts	59 Nm
Engine oil temperature (EOT) sensor	14 Nm
Intake duct bolts to cylinder head	12 Nm
Oil pump cover bolts	5 Nm
Oil filter cover bolts	5 Nm
Selector drum cam plate holder bolt	10 Nm
Starter clutch bolts	
2003 to 2006 models	30 Nm
2007-on models	16 Nm
Stopper arm bolt	12 Nm
Timing inspection cap	6 Nm

1 General information

The engine/transmission unit is an air-cooled single cylinder of unit construction. The two valves are operated by rocker arms actuated by a single overhead camshaft which is chain driven off the left-hand end of the crankshaft. The crankcase divides vertically.

The crankcase incorporates a wet sump, pressure-fed lubrication system which uses a single rotor trochoidal oil pump that is gear-driven off the right-hand end of the crankshaft. Oil is cleaned by a strainer in the bottom of the crankcase and a centrifugal filter on the right-hand end of the crankshaft.

The alternator is on the left-hand end of the crankshaft. The ignition timing triggers are on the outside of the alternator rotor, and the pulse generator coil is mounted in the alternator cover along with the stator.

Power from the crankshaft is routed to the transmission via a centrifugal clutch on the right-hand end of the crankshaft that drives the primary drive gear, turning the primary driven gear on the back of a wet, multi-plate clutch on the transmission input shaft. A one-way clutch in the centrifugal clutch allows semi-automatic gear changes when the throttle is closed. The transmission is a four-speed constant-mesh unit. Final drive to the rear wheel is by chain and sprockets.

The engine has both electric and kick starters.

2 Component access

Operations possible with the engine in the frame

The components and assemblies listed below can be removed without having to remove the engine from the frame. If however, a number of areas require attention at the same time, removal of the engine is recommended.

Cam chain, tensioner and blades
Camshaft and rockers
Cylinder head and valves
Cylinder block and piston
Alternator and starter clutch
Centrifugal, one-way and wet multi-plate clutches
Gearchange mechanism
Oil pump, centrifugal filter and oil strainer
Starter motor
Kickstart mechanism return spring and retainer

Operations requiring engine removal

It is necessary to remove the engine from the frame to gain access to the following components.

Crankshaft, connecting rod and bearings
Transmission shafts and bearings
Selector drum and forks
Kickstart mechanism shaft and gears

3 Engine wear assessment

Cylinder compression test

Special tool: *A compression gauge is required to perform this test.*

1 Poor engine performance may be caused by leaking valves, incorrect valve clearances, a leaking head gasket, or worn piston, piston rings or cylinder wall. A cylinder compression check will highlight these conditions and can also indicate the presence of excessive carbon deposits in the cylinder head.

2 The only tools required are a compression gauge (there are two types, one with a threaded adapter to fit the spark plug hole in the cylinder head, the other has a rubber seal which is pressed into the spark plug hole to create a seal – the threaded adapter type is preferable – you'll need to use a 10 mm thread size adapter), and a spark plug socket with 16 mm hex. Depending on the outcome of the initial test, a squirt-type oil can may also be needed.

3 Make sure the valve clearances are correctly set (see Chapter 1) and that the cylinder head nuts and bolts are tightened to the correct torque settings (see Section 10).

4 Run the engine until it is at normal operating temperature. Remove the spark plug (see Chapter 1). Fit the plug back into the plug cap and earth the plug against the engine away from the plug hole – if the plug is not earthed the ignition system could be damaged.

5 Thread the gauge adapter into the spark plug hole **(see illustration)** – if the rubber cone type is used keep the gauge pressed onto the hole throughout the test to maintain a good seal.

6 With the ignition switch ON, the throttle held fully open and the spark plug earthed, turn the engine over on the starter motor until

3.5 Thread the gauge hose into the spark plug hole

Engine, clutch and transmission 2•7

3.6a Hold the throttle fully open and turn the engine over . . .

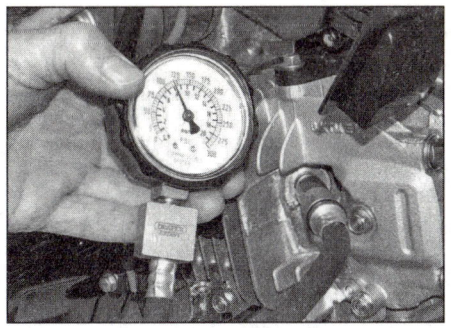

3.6b . . . until the reading on the gauge has stabilised

the gauge reading has built up and stabilised **(see illustrations)**.

7 Compare the reading on the gauge to the cylinder compression figure specified at the beginning of the Chapter (under Cylinder head).

8 If the reading is low, it could be due to a worn cylinder bore, piston or rings, failure of the head gasket, or worn valve seats. To determine which is the cause, pour a small quantity of engine oil into the spark plug hole to seal the rings, then repeat the compression test. If the figures are noticeably higher the cause is worn cylinder, piston or rings. If there is no change the cause is a leaking head gasket or worn valve seats.

9 If the reading is high there could be a build-up of carbon deposits in the combustion chamber although this is unlikely. Remove the cylinder head and scrape all deposits off the piston and the cylinder head.

Leak-down (cylinder leakage) test

10 A leak down or 'cylinder leakage' test is similar to a compression test in that it tells you how well a cylinder is sealing, but it does so by testing how much pressure is lost through leakage, as opposed to how much pressure is created through compression. Many professionals prefer a leak test to a compression test as it more accurately pin-points the cause of the problem before any disassembly is done, as it is easy to tell where the leakage is occurring. Generally however the required equipment is more expensive than for a compression test and a source of compressed air is essential. If you think a test is needed take the scooter to a suitably equipped dealer or workshop. If you decide to purchase your own equipment follow the manufacturer's instructions.

11 A leakage test can also be used in conjunction with a compression test to diagnose other kinds of problems, such as a faulty valve train component, incorrect valve timing, faulty ignition or fuel delivery problems.

4 Engine removal and installation

Caution: The engine weighs approximately 25 kg (54 lbs). Enlist the aid of an assistant to help manoeuvre the engine if you doubt your ability to do so safely.

Removal

1 Support the bike on its centrestand, making sure it is on level ground. Work can be made easier by raising the bike to a suitable working height on an hydraulic ramp or a suitable platform. Make sure the scooter is secure and will not topple over, and tie the front brake lever to the handlebar to prevent it rolling forwards.

2 Remove the front covers and the body cover(s) (see Chapter 7).

3 If the engine is dirty, particularly around its mountings, wash it thoroughly. This will make work much easier and rule out the possibility of caked on lumps of dirt falling into some vital component. At this stage it is a good idea get a digital camera and take lots of pictures of the routing of all the cables, wiring and hoses, and the positions of small brackets and wiring clamps, to avoid error and confusion on reassembly.

4 Drain the engine oil (see Chapter 1).

5 Disconnect the negative (–ve) lead from the battery (see Chapter 8).

6 Remove the exhaust system (see Chapter 3B).

7 Pull the spark plug cap off the plug and secure it clear of the engine **(see illustration)**.

8 On 2003 to 2006 (carburettor) models detach the PAIR air hose from the pipe **(see illustration)**.

9 On 2007-on (fuel injection) models free the engine oil temperature (EOT) sensor wiring from its clamps and disconnect the wiring connector **(see illustrations)**. Secure it clear, noting its routing. Unscrew the oxygen sensor wiring cap holder bolt and remove the holder **(see illustration)**. Pull the cap off the sensor

4.7 Pull the cap off the spark plug

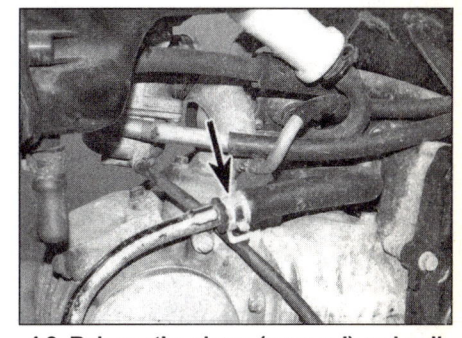

4.8 Release the clamp (arrowed) and pull the hose off the pipe

4.9a Free the wire from its guides (arrowed) . . .

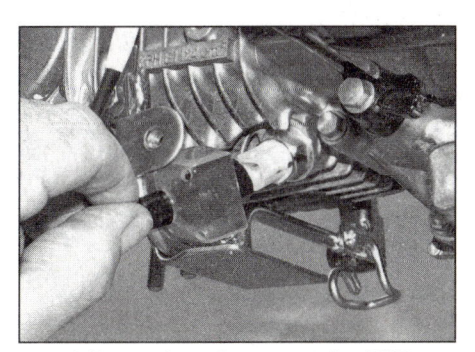

4.9b . . . then disconnect the EOT connector

4.9c Unscrew the bolt (arrowed) and remove the holder . . .

2•8 Engine, clutch and transmission

4.9d ... then free the wiring from the guides (arrowed) ...

4.9e ... and disconnect the oxygen sensor connector

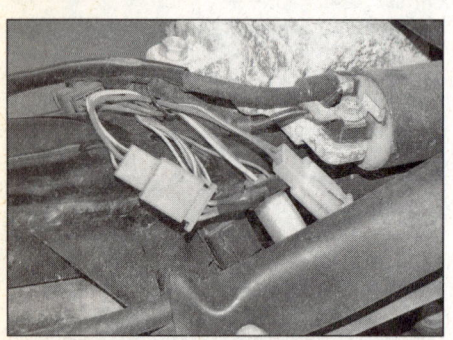

4.10a On carburettor models lift the rubber sheet to access the wiring connectors

(see illustration). Free the wiring from its clamps and secure it clear, noting its routing (see illustration).

10 Disconnect the gear position switch wiring connector, the speed sensor wiring connector, the sidestand switch wiring connector, and the alternator and crankshaft position sensor wiring connector(s) (see illustrations). Release the sidestand switch wiring from its clamps and feed it down to the switch, noting its routing.

11 Unscrew the cylinder head intake duct bolts (see illustrations).

12 Disconnect the crankcase breather hose (see illustrations).

13 If required, remove the starter motor (see Chapter 8). If you want to leave the starter motor in situ, pull back the rubber cover on its terminal, then unscrew the nut and disconnect the lead (see illustration) – spray it with some penetrating fluid first if it is corroded. Also unscrew the mounting bolt securing the earth lead and detach the lead (see illustration).

14 Remove the rider's footrest assembly and the footrest/sidestand bracket with the stand attached to it, the passenger footrest brackets,

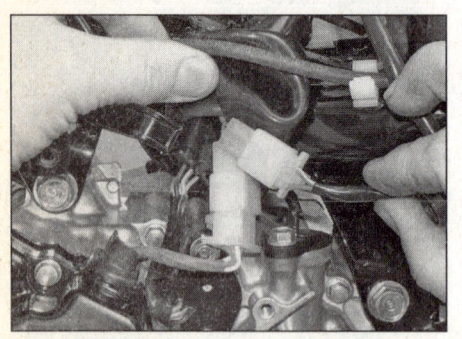

4.10b On fuel injection models the connectors are inside a rubber boot

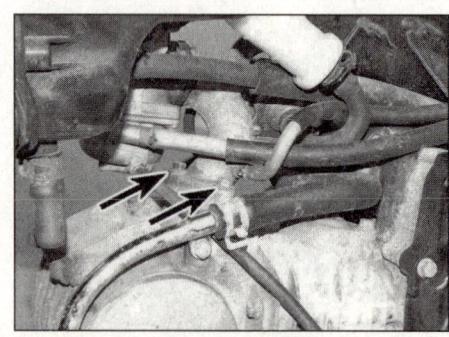

4.11a Intake duct bolts (arrowed) – carburettor models

4.11b Intake duct bolts (arrowed) – fuel injection models

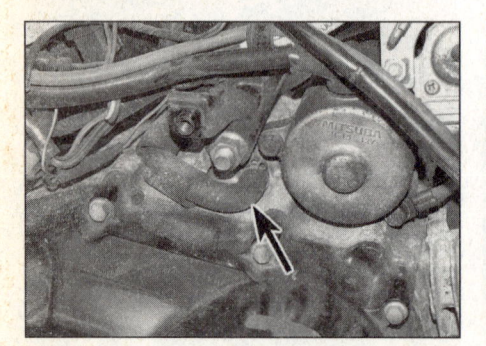

4.12a Crankcase breather hose (arrowed) – carburettor models

4.12b Crankcase breather hose (arrowed) – fuel injection models

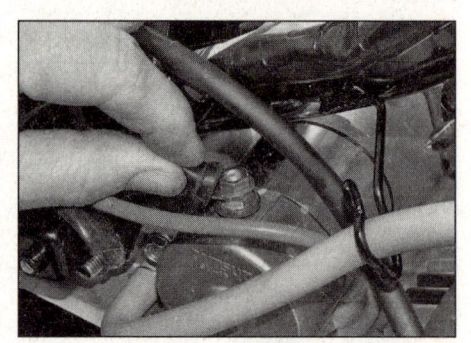

4.13a Detach the lead from the starter motor terminal ...

Engine, clutch and transmission 2•9

4.13b . . . and the mounting bolt

4.16 Support the engine on a jack

the gearchange lever, and the kickstart lever – refer to Chapter 5 for details.

15 Remove the front sprocket (see Chapter 6). Lay the drive chain against the front of the swingarm.

16 Position an hydraulic or mechanical jack under the engine with a block of wood between them **(see illustration)**. Make sure the jack is centrally positioned so the engine will not topple in any direction when the last mounting bolt is removed. Raise the jack to take the weight of the engine, but make sure it is not lifting the bike and taking the weight of that as well. The idea is to support the engine so that there is no pressure on any of the mounting bolts once they have been slackened, so they can be easily withdrawn. Note that it may be necessary to alter the position of the jack as some of the bolts are removed to relieve the stress transferred to the other bolts.

17 Unscrew the nuts on the right-hand ends of the engine mounting bolts **(see illustration)**.
18 Withdraw the front mounting bolt from the left **(see illustration)**.
19 Check that the engine is properly supported by the jack. Withdraw the upper and lower rear mounting bolts from the left **(see illustrations)**.
20 The engine can now be removed (see **Caution** above). Check that all wiring, cables and hoses are free and clear, then carefully lower the jack, making sure the intake duct detaches from the cylinder head, and manoeuvre the engine clear. Remove the intake duct gasket (carburetor models) or O-ring (fuel injection models) and plug the engine intake with clean rag.

Installation

Note: *It is advised to smear copper grease onto the engine mounting bolt shafts, not the threads, to prevent the possibility of them seizing in the engine or frame due to corrosion.*

21 Fit a new gasket (carburetor models) or O-ring (fuel injection models) onto the intake duct flange – a smear of grease will help to

4.17 Engine mounting bolt nuts (arrowed)

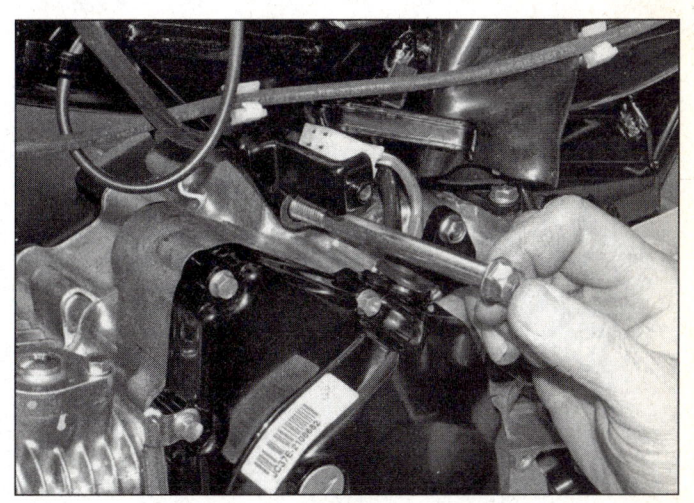

4.18 Withdraw the front mounting bolt

4.19a Withdraw the upper rear bolt . . .

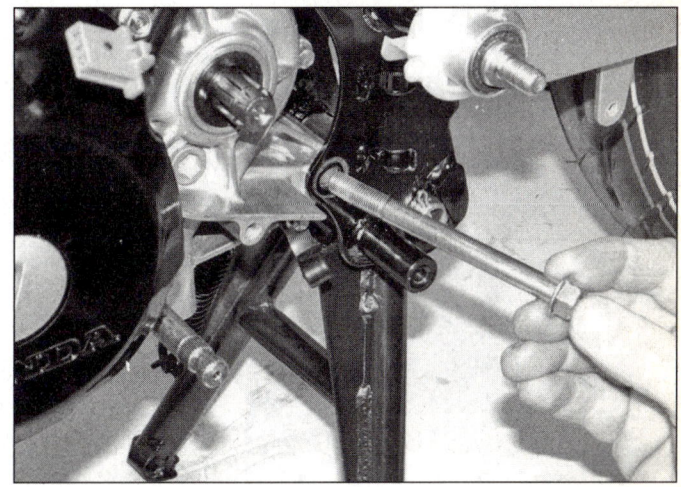

4.19b . . . then the lower rear bolt, and remove the engine

2•10 Engine, clutch and transmission

stick it in place. Remove the rag from the intake on the cylinder head.
22 Manoeuvre the engine into position on the jack **(see illustration 4.16)**. Raise the engine to align all the mounting bolt holes, making sure that all cables and wiring are correctly routed and do not get trapped. Note that it may be necessary to adjust the jack as the bolts are installed to realign the other bolt holes.
23 Install the mounting bolts from the left-hand side, then fit their nuts and tighten them finger-tight **(see illustrations 4.19b and a, 4.18 and 4.17)**.
24 First tighten the upper rear mounting bolt nut to the torque setting specified at the beginning of the Chapter. Next tighten the lower rear mounting bolt nut to the specified torque. Finally tighten the front mounting bolt nut to the specified torque.
25 Remove the jack from under the engine.
26 The remainder of the installation procedure is the reverse of removal, noting the following points:
- Tighten the intake duct bolts to the cylinder head to the specified torque.
- Refer to the procedures and torque settings in Chapter 5 when installing the footrest and sidestand assemblies and the gearchange and kickstart levers.
- Use a new gasket on the exhaust pipe.
- Make sure all wires, cables and hoses are correctly routed and connected, and secured by any clips or ties.
- On 2007-on (fuel injection) models make sure the oxygen sensor wiring cap clicks into place. Fit the holder and bolt, aligning the hole in the holder with the locating pin.
- Refill the engine with oil to the correct level (see Chapter 1 and *Pre-ride checks*).
- Adjust the throttle cable freeplay.
- Adjust the drive chain (see Chapter 1).
- Start the engine and check that there are no oil leaks.

5 Engine disassembly and reassembly general information

1 Before beginning the engine overhaul, read through the related procedures to familiarise yourself with the scope and requirements of the job. Overhauling an engine is not all that difficult, but it is time consuming. Check on the availability of parts and make sure that any necessary special tools are obtained in advance.
2 Most work can be done with a decent set of typical workshop hand tools, although a number of precision measuring tools are required for inspecting parts to determine if they are worn.
3 To ensure maximum life and minimum trouble from a rebuilt engine, everything must be assembled with care in a spotlessly clean environment.

Disassembly

4 Before disassembling the engine, thoroughly clean and degrease its external surfaces. This will prevent contamination of the engine internals, and will also make the job a lot easier and cleaner. A high flash-point solvent, such as paraffin (kerosene) can be used, or better still, a proprietary engine degreaser such as Gunk. Use old paintbrushes and toothbrushes to work the solvent into the various recesses of the casings. Take care to exclude solvent or water from the electrical components and intake and exhaust ports.

⚠ **Warning: The use of petrol (gasoline) as a cleaning agent should be avoided because of the risk of fire.**

5 When clean and dry, position the engine on the workbench, leaving suitable clear area for working. Gather a selection of small containers, plastic bags and some labels so that parts can be grouped together in an easily identifiable manner. Also get some paper and a pen and a digital camera so that notes and pictures can be taken if required. You will also need a supply of clean rag, which should be as absorbent as possible.
6 Before commencing work, read through the appropriate section so that some idea of the necessary procedure can be gained. When removing components note that great force is seldom required, unless specified (checking the specified torque setting of the particular bolt being removed will indicate how tight it is, and therefore how much force should be needed). In many cases, a component's reluctance to be removed is indicative of an incorrect approach or removal method – if in any doubt, re-check with the text.
7 When disassembling the engine, keep 'mated' parts (valve components, rockers and shafts, etc) that have been in contact with each other during engine operation together. These 'mated' parts must be refitted together.
8 A complete engine stripdown should be done in the following general order with reference to the appropriate Sections.
Remove the starter motor (see Chapter 8)
Remove the cylinder head
Remove the cylinder block and piston
Remove the alternator and starter clutch (see Chapter 8)
Remove the cam chain and blades
Remove the clutches
Remove the gearchange mechanism
Remove the oil pump
Separate the crankcase halves
Remove the kickstart shaft and gears
Remove the selector drum and forks
Remove the transmission shafts
Remove the crankshaft

Reassembly

9 Reassembly is accomplished by reversing the general disassembly sequence.

6 Valve covers

Note: *The valve covers can be removed with the engine in the frame. If the engine has been removed, ignore the steps which do not apply.*

Removal

1 Remove the front cover on each side (see Chapter 7).
2 Unscrew the valve cover bolts and remove the covers from the cylinder head **(see illustration)**. If they are stuck, do not try to lever them off with a screwdriver. Tap them gently around the sides with a rubber hammer or block of wood to dislodge them. Remove the O-ring from each cover – new ones must be used.

Installation

3 Fit a new O-ring smeared with oil into the groove in each valve cover **(see illustration)**. Clean the threads of the cap bolts – if corrosion was evident lightly smear the threads with oil. Fit the covers and tighten the bolts **(see illustration)**.
4 Install the front covers (see Chapter 7).

6.2 Unscrew the bolts (arrowed) and remove the covers

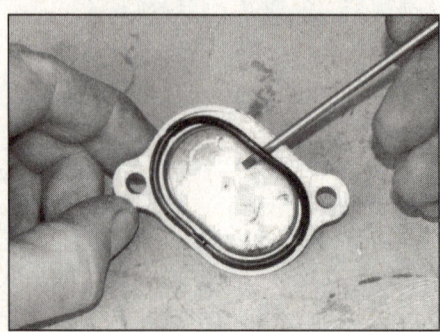

6.3a Make sure the O-ring locates in the groove . . .

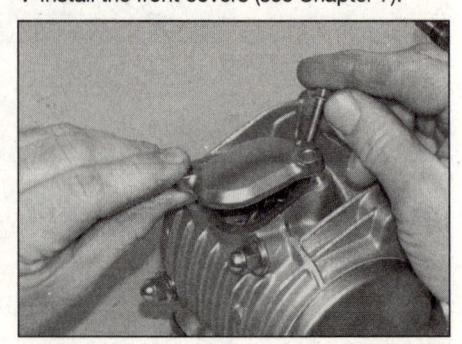

6.3b . . . and stays in place when fitting the cover

Engine, clutch and transmission 2•11

7.2 Undo the cap screw and remove the O-ring (arrowed)

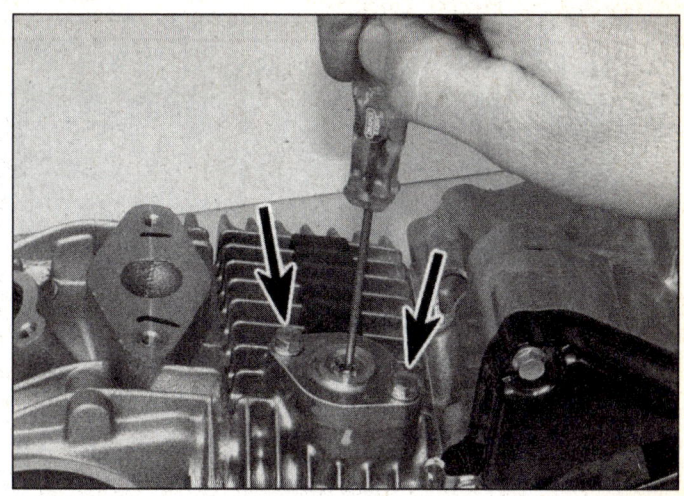

7.3a Slacken the mounting bolts (arrowed) slightly then insert the screwdriver, retract the plunger, ...

7 Cam chain tensioner

Note: *The cam chain tensioner can be removed with the engine in the frame. If the engine has been removed, ignore the steps which do not apply.*

Removal

1 Remove the front covers (see Chapter 7).
2 Undo the tensioner cap screw and remove the O-ring **(see illustration)**.
3 Slacken the tensioner mounting bolts slightly **(see illustration)**. Insert a small flat-bladed screwdriver in the end of the tensioner so that it engages the slotted plunger **(see illustration)**. Turn the screwdriver clockwise until the plunger is fully retracted and hold it in this position, then unscrew the tensioner mounting bolts and withdraw the tensioner from the engine **(see illustration)**. Release the screwdriver – the plunger will spring back out, but can be easily reset on installation.
4 Discard the gasket and O-ring as new ones must be used on installation. Do not attempt to dismantle the tensioner.

7.3b ... unscrew the mounting bolts ...

Inspection

5 Check that the plunger moves smoothly when wound into the tensioner and springs back out freely when released **(see illustration)**. Make sure the plunger cannot be pushed into the body **(see illustration)**.

Installation

6 Make sure the tensioner and cylinder block surfaces are clean and dry. Lay a new gasket onto the cylinder block **(see illustration 7.3c)**. Insert a small flat-bladed screwdriver in the end of the tensioner so that it engages the slotted plunger then turn the screwdriver clockwise

7.3c ... and remove the tensioner and its gasket

until the plunger is fully retracted and hold it in this position **(see illustration 7.5a)**. Fit the tensioner and tighten its mounting bolts **(see illustrations 7.3c and b)**. Release and remove the screwdriver – as you release it your should hear the tensioner plunger move out.
7 Fit a new O-ring smeared with clean oil onto the tensioner, then fit the cap screw and tighten it **(see illustration 7.3a)**.
8 Install the front covers (see Chapter 7).

8 Camshaft and rocker arms

Note: *The camshaft and rockers can be removed with the engine in the frame, or if preferred you can remove the cylinder head first (Section 10), then remove the camshaft and rocker arms from it on the bench. Stuff clean rag into the cam chain tunnel to prevent anything dropping into the engine.*

Removal

1 Remove the front cover on each side.
2 Remove the spark plug (see Chapter 1).
3 Remove the valve covers (see Section 6).
4 Unscrew the camshaft sprocket cover bolt, noting the sealing washer, and remove the

7.5a Wind the plunger in and make sure it springs back out when released

7.5b Make sure you cannot push the plunger in

2•12 Engine, clutch and transmission

8.4 Unscrew the bolt and remove the sprocket cover

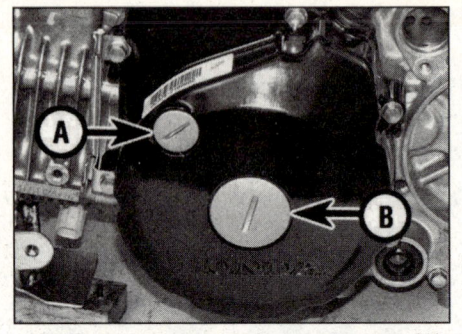

8.5 Remove the timing inspection cap (A) and the crankshaft end cap (B)

8.6a Turn the engine anti-clockwise using the nut . . .

cover **(see illustration)**. A new sealing washer and cover gasket must be used.

5 Unscrew the timing inspection cap and the crankshaft end cap **(see illustration)**. Remove the O-ring from each cap – new ones must be used.

6 The engine must be turned so that the piston is at TDC (top dead centre) on its compression stroke. Turn the engine anti-clockwise using a socket on the alternator rotor nut until the line next to the T mark on the rim of the rotor aligns with the static timing mark, which is a notch in the inspection hole rim, and the 'O' mark on the sprocket faces forwards and aligns with the index mark on the head **(see illustrations)**. There should now be some freeplay in each rocker arm (i.e. they are not contacting the valve stem). If the 'O' mark faces back, rotate the engine anti-clockwise one full turn (360°) until the line next to the T mark again aligns with the static timing mark, at which point the 'O' mark will face forwards.

7 Remove the cam chain tensioner (see Section 7).

8 Counter-hold the alternator rotor nut and slacken the cam chain sprocket bolts **(see illustration)**. Remove the bolts and slip the sprocket off the end of the camshaft and disengage it from the chain **(see illustration)**. Remove the sprocket locating dowel – do not drop it in the engine **(see illustration)**. Prevent the chain from slipping down its tunnel by securing it with a piece of wire.

9 Unscrew the retainer plate bolt and remove the plate **(see illustration)**.

10 Mark each rocker arm and shaft according to its location in the holder so they can be installed in their original position. Hold the rocker arm and draw the shaft out, rotating it as you do to ease removal **(see illustrations 8.23b and a)**. Slide the rocker back onto its shaft to prevent mixing up – both rocker arms are identical and are therefore interchangeable, though the shafts are different.

11 Withdraw the camshaft from the head **(see illustration 8.22)**. While the camshaft is out do not rotate the crankshaft – the chain may drop down and bind between the crankshaft and case, which could damage these components.

12 Place a rag over the cylinder head.

Inspection

13 Check the bearing on each end of the camshaft – they must run smoothly, quietly and freely, and there should be no excessive play between the inner and outer races, or between the inner race and the camshaft, or between the outer race and the bearing

8.6b . . . until the line next to the T mark aligns with the notch (arrowed) . . .

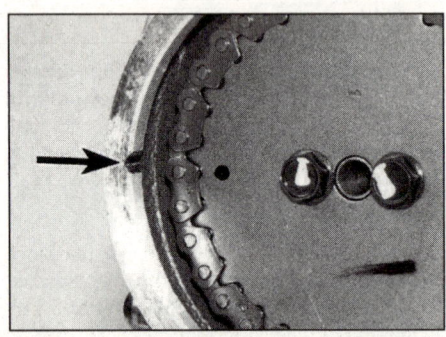

8.6c . . . and the camshaft mark aligns as shown

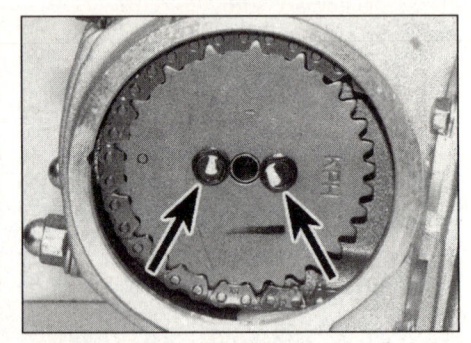

8.8a Unscrew the bolts (arrowed) . . .

8.8b . . . and remove the sprocket . . .

8.8c . . . and its locating dowel

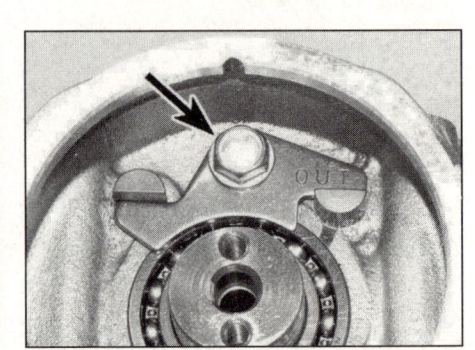

8.9 Unscrew the bolt (arrowed) and remove the plate

Engine, clutch and transmission 2•13

8.13 Check the bearings (arrowed) as described

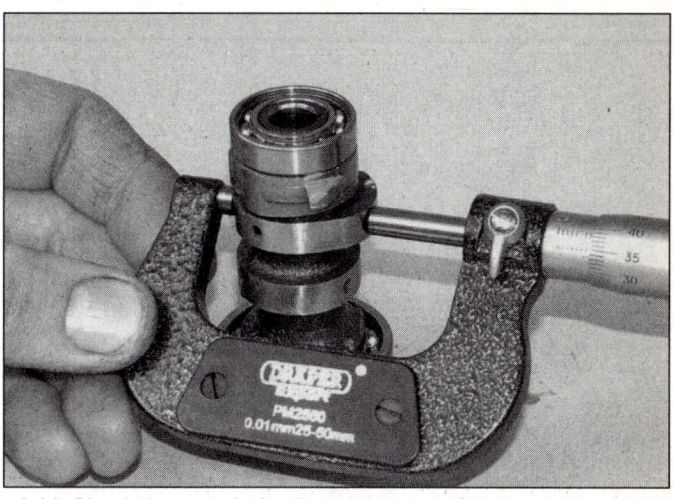

8.14 Check the camshaft lobes and measure their height with a micrometer

housings in the head **(see illustration)**. If not, replace the camshaft with a new one – it comes fitted with bearings, and the bearings are not available separately. Check that the bearing housings in the head are neither worn nor damaged.

14 Check the camshaft lobes for heat discoloration (blue appearance), score marks, chipped areas, flat spots and spalling. Measure the height of each lobe with a micrometer **(see illustration)** and compare the results to the minimum height listed in this Chapter's Specifications. If damage is noted or wear is excessive, the camshaft must be replaced with a new one.

15 Make sure the decompression cam can turn in one direction only (anti-clockwise when looked at from the right-hand end of the shaft) **(see illustration)**. If it turns in both directions or not at all, replace the camshaft with a new one. Make sure the decompression plunger in the head moves in and out smoothly against the spring **(see illustration)**. If required unscrew the plunger bolt and remove the sealing washer, spring and plunger **(see illustrations)**. Clean the components, check for wear and damage and replace with new ones as required. Lubricate the plunger and spring before fitting them. Fit the bolt with a new sealing washer and tighten it to the torque setting specified at the beginning of the Chapter.

HAYNES HINT *Refer to Tools and Workshop Tips in the Reference section for details of how to read a micrometer.*

16 Check the rocker arm rollers for wear and make sure they turn smoothly and freely **(see illustration)**. Check the bottom of each clearance adjuster and the top of each valve stem for wear and damage **(see illustration)**. If damage is noted or wear is excessive, the

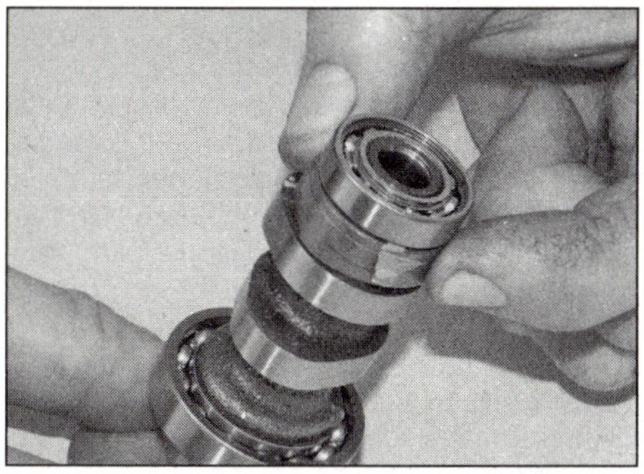

8.15a Check the decompression cam . . .

8.15b . . . and the plunger in the head

8.15c Unscrew the bolt . . .

8.15d . . . and remove the plunger and spring

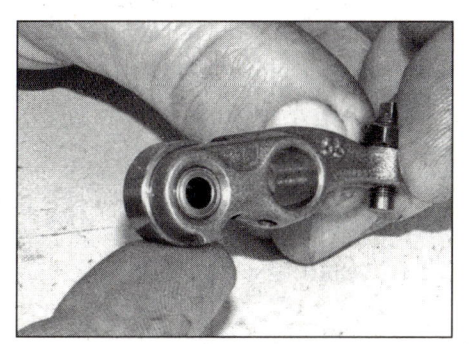

8.16a Check the rollers . . .

8.16b . . . and the bottom of each adjuster

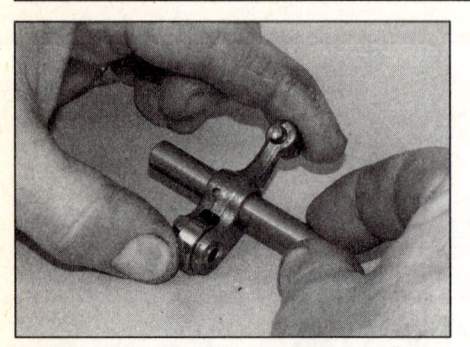

2•14 Engine, clutch and transmission

8.17a Check for freeplay between each arm and its shaft

8.17b Measure the internal diameter of each bore and the external diameter of each shaft

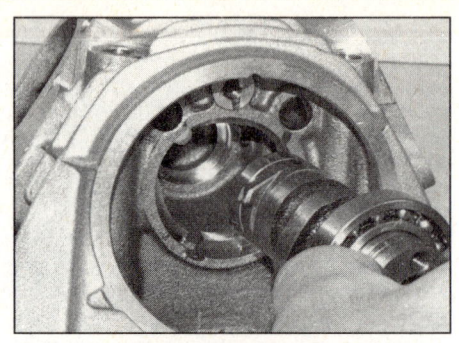

8.22 Align the camshaft as described and slide it into the head

rocker arms, camshaft and valves must be replaced with new ones as required.
17 Check the rocker arm bores and shafts for heat discoloration (blue appearance), score marks, chipped areas, flat spots and spalling. Check for freeplay between each rocker arm and its shaft **(see illustration)**. The arms should move freely with a light fit but no appreciable freeplay. Measure the internal diameter of the arm bores and the corresponding diameter of the shaft, and calculate the clearance between them **(see illustration)**. Replace the arms and/or shafts with new ones as required if the clearance exceeds the limit specified. Check that the rocker shaft holes in the cylinder head are neither worn nor damaged.
18 Except in cases of oil starvation, the cam chain should wear very little. If the chain has stretched excessively, which makes it difficult to maintain proper tension, or if it is stiff or the links are binding or kinking, replace it with a new one (Section 9).
19 Check the sprocket for wear, cracks and other damage, and replace it with a new one if necessary. If the sprocket is worn, the cam chain is also worn, and so probably is the sprocket on the crankshaft. If severe wear is apparent, the entire engine should be disassembled for inspection.
20 Inspect the cam chain guide and tensioner blade (see Section 9).

Installation

21 Remove all old gasket from the sprocket cover and cylinder head mating surfaces.
22 Lubricate the camshaft bearings and lobes and the decompression cam with clean engine oil. Slide the camshaft into the head, making sure the decompression cam clears the plunger, and position the lobes pointing down into the head, towards the piston **(see illustration)**.
23 Lubricate each rocker shaft and arm with clean engine oil. Position each rocker arm in its location in the head, making sure the adjuster is above the valve stem and the roller locates against the camshaft lobes, and slide its shaft through **(see illustrations)** – the longer shaft goes on the exhaust side.
24 Align the shaft ends as shown then fit the retainer plate with the OUT mark facing out and tighten the bolt **(see illustrations)**.
25 Check that the line next to the T mark on the alternator rotor aligns with the notch in the inspection hole rim **(see illustration 8.6b)**. Turn the camshaft so that the lobes point away from the rocker arms and the bolt holes are aligned with the retainer plate bolt head.
26 Fit the locating dowel into the end of the camshaft **(see illustration 8.8c)**. Engage the cam chain sprocket with the chain, making sure the crankshaft does not rotate, that the bottom run of the chain between the sprockets is tight and that any slack is in the top run so it will be taken up by the tensioner, that the 'O' mark is facing out and to the front in line with the index mark, and fit the sprocket onto the camshaft, locating it over the dowel and aligning the bolt holes **(see illustration 8.8b)**.
27 Fit the cam chain sprocket bolts and tighten them to the specified torque setting, counter-holding the alternator rotor nut **(see illustration)**.
28 Use a piece of wooden dowel or other suitable tool to press on the cam chain

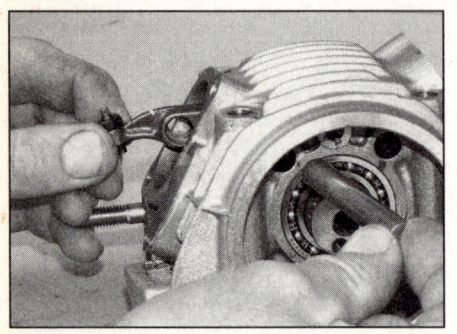

8.23a Fit the exhaust side rocker arm with the long shaft . . .

8.23b . . . and the intake side arm with the short shaft

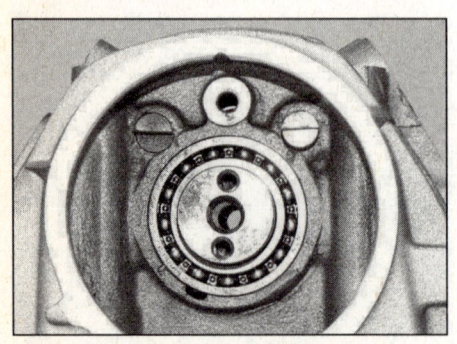

8.24a Align the shaft ends as shown . . .

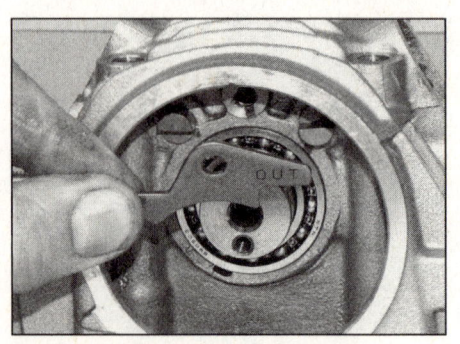

8.24b . . . then fit the plate

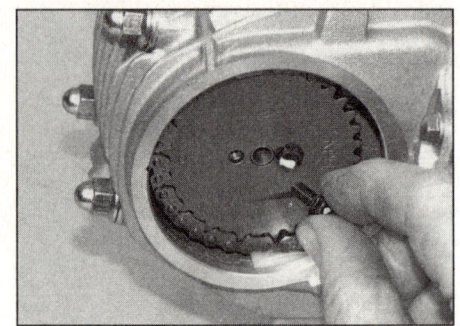

8.27 Fit the sprocket bolts and tighten them

Engine, clutch and transmission 2•15

8.31a Fit a new gasket onto the cover ...

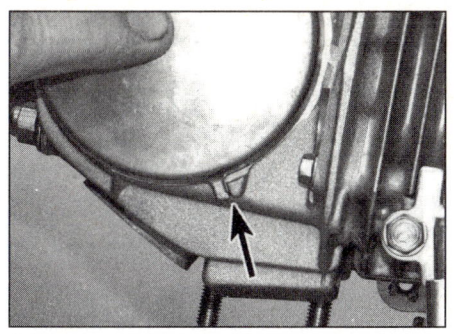

8.31b ... then locate the cover, butting the tab against the lug as shown ...

8.31c ... and secure it with the bolt, using a new sealing washer

tensioner blade via the tensioner bore in the cylinder block to ensure that any slack in the cam chain is taken up and transferred to the rear run of the chain. At this point check that all the timing marks are still in **exact** alignment as described in Step 6 **(see illustrations 8.6b and c)**. Note that it is easy to be slightly out (one tooth on the sprocket) without the marks appearing drastically out of alignment. If the marks are out unscrew the sprocket's bolts and slide the sprocket off the camshaft, then disengage it from the chain. Move the camshaft and/or crankshaft round as required, then fit the sprocket back into the chain and onto the camshaft, and check the marks again. With everything correctly aligned, tighten the bolts to the torque setting specified at the beginning of the Chapter.
Caution: If the marks are not aligned exactly as described, the valve timing will be incorrect and the valves may strike the piston, causing extensive damage to the engine.
29 Install the cam chain tensioner (see Section 7).
30 Turn the engine anti-clockwise through two full turns and check again that all the timing marks still align (see Step 6) **(see illustrations 8.6a, b and c)**. Check the valve clearances and adjust them if necessary (see Chapter 1).
31 Fit the sprocket cover using a new gasket and the bolt using a new sealing washer, and tighten the bolt to the specified torque **(see illustrations)**.
32 Fit new O-rings smeared with oil onto the timing inspection and crankshaft end caps **(see illustration)**. Smear the cap threads with oil, and tighten them to the torque settings specified at the beginning of the Chapter.
33 Install the valve covers (see Section 6). Install the spark plug (see Chapter 1). Install the front covers (see Chapter 7).

9 Cam chain, tensioner blade and guide blade

Note: *The cam chain and its blades can be removed with the engine in the frame.*

Removal
Cam chain

1 Remove the camshaft sprocket (see Section 8, Steps 1 to 8).
2 Remove the alternator rotor and starter clutch (see Chapter 8).
3 Unscrew the retainer plate bolt and remove the plate, spring and plunger **(see illustrations)**.
4 Draw the cam chain off the crankshaft sprocket and out of the engine **(see illustration)**.

8.32 Fit the caps using new O-rings and smear them and the threads with oil

9.3a Unscrew the bolt and remove the plate ...

9.3b ... and the plunger and spring

9.4 Removing the cam chain

2•16 Engine, clutch and transmission

9.7a Unscrew the bolt and remove the plate...

9.7b ...then draw the blade off and out

9.9 Draw the guide blade out, noting how it locates

Tensioner blade

5 Remove the cylinder head (see Section 10).
6 Remove the alternator rotor and starter clutch (see Chapter 8).
7 Unscrew the retainer plate bolt and remove the plate, then slide the blade off its pivot and draw it out of the top of the cylinder block **(see illustrations)**.

Guide blade

8 Remove the cylinder head (see Section 10).
9 Draw the guide blade out of the top of the cylinder block, noting how it locates **(see illustration)**.

Inspection

Cam chain

10 Check the chain for binding, kinks and any obvious damage and replace it with a new one if necessary. Check the camshaft and crankshaft sprocket teeth for wear and replace the cam chain, camshaft sprocket and crankshaft sprocket with a new set if necessary – the drive sprocket on the crankshaft is pressed on (see Section 25). Note the alignment of the sprocket – a tooth must align exactly with the slot for the alternator rotor Woodruff key.

Tensioner and guide blades

11 Check the sliding surface and edges of the blades for excessive wear, deep grooves, cracking and other obvious damage, and replace them with new ones if necessary.

Installation

12 Installation of the sprocket, chain and blades is the reverse of removal. Make sure the bottom of the guide blade sits in its seat and the lugs near its top locate in the cut-outs in the cylinder block **(see illustrations)**. Lubricate the chain and the tensioner blade pivot with clean oil, and make sure the retainer plate locates over the end of the pivot **(see illustration)**. Lubricate the plunger and spring with oil. Refer to Section 8, Steps 25-on to fit the camshaft sprocket.

9.12a Make sure the bottom of the guide blade locates in its seat...

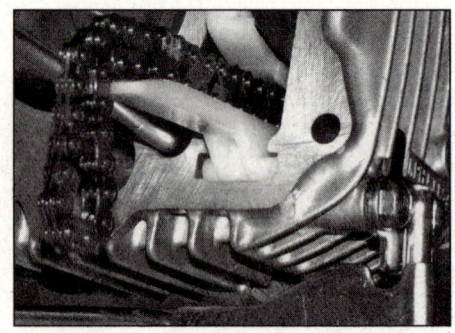

9.12b ...and the lugs locate in the cut-outs

9.12c Make sure the hole in the retainer locates over the end of the pivot

10 Cylinder head

Note: *The cylinder head can be removed with the engine in the frame. If the engine has been removed ignore the steps that do not apply.*

Removal

1 On 2003 to 2006 (carburettor) models detach the PAIR air hose from the pipe **(see illustration 4.8)**. If required unscrew the pipe flange and retaining bolts and detach the pipe **(see illustration)**. Remove the gasket – a new one must be used.

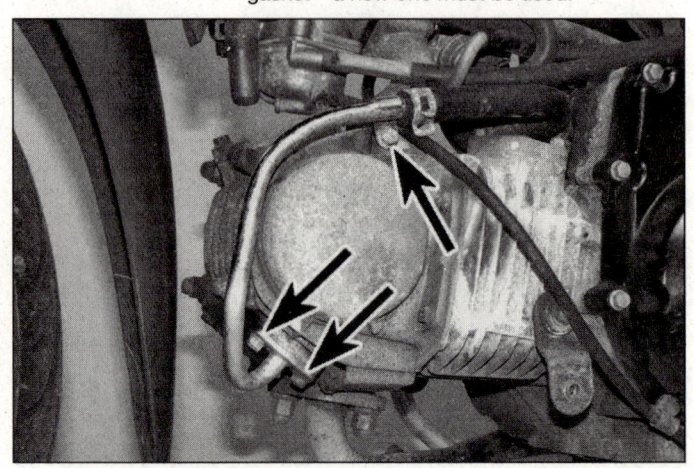

10.1 Unscrew the bolts (arrowed) and remove the pipe

Engine, clutch and transmission 2•17

10.6 Cylinder head bolts (A), cylinder head nuts (B)

10.8 Carefully pull the head off the block

2 On 2007-on (fuel injection) models unscrew the oxygen sensor wiring cap holder bolt and remove the holder **(see illustration 4.9c)**. Pull the cap off the sensor **(see illustration 4.9e)**.
3 Remove the exhaust system (see Chapter 3B).
4 Remove the camshaft sprocket (see Section 8, Steps 1 to 8). If required also remove the camshaft and rocker arms, and the decompression plunger (see Section 8, Steps 9 to 11 and 15).
5 Unscrew the cylinder head intake duct bolts **(see illustration 4.11a or b)**.
6 Unscrew and remove the two bolts on the side of the head **(see illustration)**.
7 Unscrew the cylinder head nuts 1/4 a turn at a time in a criss-cross pattern until they are all loose, then remove them, and remove the washers **(see illustration 10.15)**. Discard the washers as new ones should be used.
8 Pull the cylinder head off the block **(see illustration)**. Do not let the chain fall into the engine – lay it over the front of the block and secure it with a piece of wire. If the head is stuck, tap around the joint faces with a soft-faced mallet. Do not attempt to free it by inserting a screwdriver between the head and block mating surfaces – you'll damage them.
9 Remove the cylinder head gasket and discard it as a new one must be used **(see illustration 10.13)**. If they are loose, remove the dowels from the cylinder block or the underside of the cylinder head.
10 Check the cylinder head gasket and the mating surfaces on the cylinder head and cylinder block for signs of leakage, which could indicate warpage. Refer to Section 11 and check the cylinder head gasket surface for warpage.
11 Clean all traces of old gasket material from the cylinder head and cylinder block. If a scraper is used, take care not to scratch or gouge the soft aluminium. Be careful not to let any of the gasket material fall into the cylinder bore or cam chain tunnel. Remove the intake duct gasket (carburetor models) or O-ring (fuel injection models) and cover the engine with clean rag.

Installation

12 Make sure the cam chain guide blade is correctly seated **(see illustrations 9.12a and b)**. Fit a new gasket or O-ring onto the intake duct flange – a smear of grease will help to stick it in place. If removed, fit the dowels into the cylinder block **(see illustration 10.13)**.
13 Ensure both cylinder head and cylinder block mating surfaces are clean. Lay the new head gasket over the studs, the cam chain and blades and onto the block, locating it over the dowels and making sure all the holes are correctly aligned **(see illustration)**. Never re-use the old gasket.

14 Carefully fit the cylinder head over the studs and onto the block, feeding the cam chain up through the tunnel as you do, and making sure it locates correctly onto the dowels **(see illustration 10.8)**. Secure the chain in place with a piece of wire to prevent it slipping back down.
15 Fit new sealing washers over the studs – the copper washer goes over the bottom right stud **(see illustration)**. Fit the nuts and tighten them finger-tight. Now tighten the nuts evenly and a little at a time in a criss-cross sequence and several stages to the torque setting specified at the beginning of the Chapter.
16 Fit the two side bolts and tighten them **(see illustration)**.
17 Fit the intake duct bolts and tighten to the specified torque **(see illustration 4.11a or b)**.
18 Install the decompression plunger, camshaft and rocker arms and camshaft sprocket as required according to removal procedure (see Section 8).
19 Install the exhaust system (see Chapter 3B).
20 On 2003 to 2006 (carburettor) models if detached fit the PAIR pipe onto the head using a new gasket and tighten the bolts **(see illustration 10.1)**. Connect the hose to the pipe and secure it with the clamp **(see illustration 4.8)**.
21 On 2007-on (fuel injection) models fit the

10.13 Fit the dowels (arrowed) then lay the new gasket on the block

10.15 Fit the new sealing washers with the copper one bottom right

10.16 Fit the side bolts

2•18 Engine, clutch and transmission

11.6a Compressing the valve springs using a valve spring compressor

11.6b Make sure the compressor locates correctly both on the top of the spring retainer . . .

11.6c . . . and on the bottom of the valve

oxygen sensor wiring cap, making sure it clicks into place **(see illustration 4.9e)**. Fit the holder and bolt, aligning the hole in the holder with the locating pin **(see illustration 4.9c)**.

11 Cylinder head and valve overhaul

1 Because of the complex nature of this job and the special tools and equipment required, most owners leave servicing of the valves, valve seats and valve guides to a professional. However, you can make an initial assessment of whether the valves are seating correctly, and therefore sealing, by pouring a small amount of solvent into each of the valve ports.

11.7a Remove the collets . . .

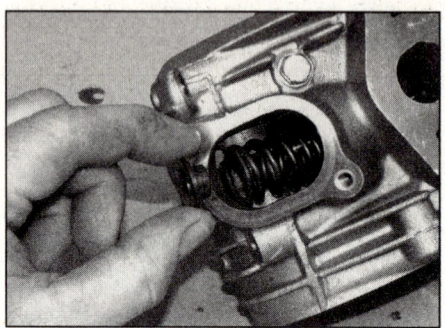

11.7b . . . the spring retainer and the spring . . .

11.7c . . . and the valve

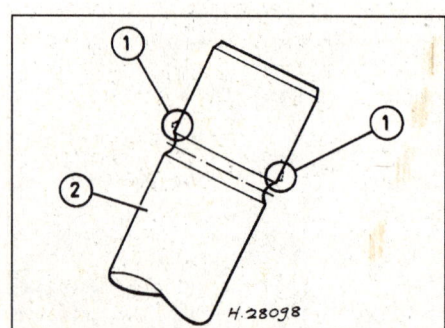

11.7d If the valve stem (2) won't pull through the guide, deburr the area (1) above the collet groove

If the solvent leaks past any valve into the combustion chamber area the valve is not seating correctly and sealing.
2 With the correct tools (a valve spring compressor is essential – make sure it is suitable for motorcycle work), you can also remove the valves and associated components from the cylinder head, clean them and check them for wear to assess the extent of the work needed, and, unless seat cutting or guide replacement is required, grind in the valves and reassemble them in the head.
3 A dealer service department or specialist can replace the guides and re-cut the valve seats if they are damaged or show excessive wear.
4 After the valve service has been performed, be sure to clean the head very thoroughly before installation to remove any metal particles or abrasive grit that may still be present from the valve service operations. Use compressed air, if available, to blow out all the holes and passages.

Disassembly

5 Before proceeding, arrange to label and store the valves along with their related components in such a way that they can be returned to their original locations without getting mixed up. Labelled plastic bags or a plastic container with two compartments are ideal.
6 Compress the valve spring on the first valve with a spring compressor, making sure it is correctly located onto each end of the valve assembly **(see illustration)**. On the top of the valve the adaptor needs to be about the same size as the spring retainer – if it is too small it will be difficult to remove and install the collets **(see illustration)**. On the underside of the head make sure the plate (where fitted) on the compressor only contacts the valve and not the soft aluminium of the head **(see illustration)** – if the plate is too big for the valve, use a spacer between them. Do not compress the spring any more than is absolutely necessary.
7 Remove the collets, using a magnet or a screwdriver with a dab of grease on it **(see illustration)**. Carefully release the valve spring compressor and remove the spring retainer, noting which way up it fits, the spring and the valve **(see illustrations)**. If the valve binds in the guide and won't pull through, push it back into the head and deburr the area around the collet groove with a very fine file or whetstone **(see illustration)**.
8 Pull the valve stem seal off the top of the valve guide with pliers and discard it (the old seals should never be re-used), then remove the spring seats noting which way up they fit **(see illustrations)**.
9 Repeat the procedure for the other valve. Remember to keep the parts for each valve together so they can be reinstalled in the same location.
10 Clean the cylinder head with solvent and dry it thoroughly. Compressed air will speed the drying process and ensure that all holes

Engine, clutch and transmission 2•19

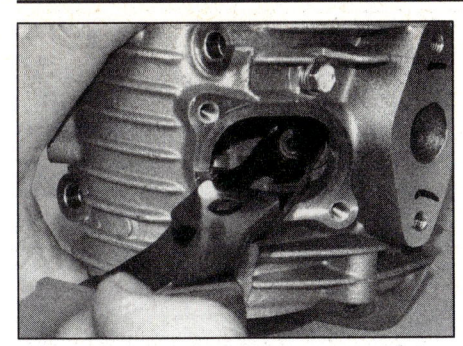

11.8a Pull the seal off the valve stem . . .

11.8b . . . then remove the upper and lower spring seats

11.15 Check the valve seat and measure the width

and recessed areas are clean. **Note:** *Do not use a wire brush mounted in a drill motor to clean the combustion chamber as the head material is soft and may be scratched or eroded away by the wire brush.*

11 Clean the valve springs, collets, retainers and spring seats with solvent and dry them thoroughly. Do the parts from one valve at a time so that no mixing of parts between valves occurs.

12 Scrape off any deposits that may have formed on the valve, then use a motorised wire brush to remove deposits from the valve heads and stems. Again, make sure the valves do not get mixed up.

Inspection

13 Inspect the head very carefully for cracks and other damage. If cracks are found, a new head is required.

14 Using a precision straight-edge and a feeler gauge set to the warpage limit listed in the specifications at the beginning of the Chapter, check the head gasket mating surface for warpage. Take six measurements, one along each side and two diagonally across. If the head is warped beyond the limit specified at the beginning of this Chapter, consult a Honda dealer or take it to a specialist repair shop for an opinion, though be prepared to have to buy a new one.

15 Examine the valve seats in the combustion chamber and their related surface on the valve. If they are pitted, cracked or burned, the head will require work beyond the scope of the home mechanic. Measure the valve seat width and compare it to this Chapter's Specifications **(see illustration)**. If it exceeds the service limit, or if it varies around its circumference, overhaul is required.

16 Working on one valve and guide at a time, measure the valve stem diameter **(see illustration)**. Clean the valve's guide using a guide reamer to remove any carbon build-up – insert the reamer from the top of the head on 2003 to 2006 models and from the underside on 2007-on models, and in both cases turn it clockwise only. Now measure the inside diameter of the guide (at both ends and in the centre of the guide) with a small bore gauge, then measure the gauge with a micrometer **(see illustration)**. Measure the guide at the ends and at the centre to determine if they are worn in a bell-mouth pattern (more wear at the ends). Subtract the stem diameter from the valve guide diameter to obtain the valve stem-to-guide clearance. If the stem-to-guide clearance is greater than listed in this Chapter's Specifications, replace whichever component is beyond its specification limits with a new one – take the head to a specialist for valve guide replacement. If the valve guide is within specifications, but is worn unevenly, it should be replaced with a new one. Repeat for the other valve.

17 Carefully inspect the valve face, stem and collet groove area for cracks, pits and burned spots.

18 Rotate the valve and check for any obvious indication that it is bent, in which case it must be replaced with a new one. Check the end of the stem for pitting and excessive wear. The presence of any of the above conditions indicates the need for valve servicing.

19 Check the end of the valve spring for wear and pitting. Measure the spring free length and compare it to the specifications **(see illustration)**. If a spring is shorter than specified it has sagged and must be replaced with a new one. Also place the spring upright on a flat surface and check it for bend by placing a ruler against it, or alternatively lay it against a set square. If the bend is excessive, it must be replaced with a new one.

20 Check the spring seats, retainer and collets for obvious wear and cracks. Any questionable parts should not be re-used, as extensive damage will occur in the event of failure during engine operation.

21 If the inspection indicates that no overhaul work is required, the valve components can be reinstalled in the head.

Reassembly

22 Unless a valve service has been performed, before installing the valves in the head they should be ground in (lapped) to ensure a positive seal between the valves and seats. This procedure requires coarse and fine valve grinding compound and a valve grinding tool (either hand-held or drill driven – note that some drill-driven tools specify using only

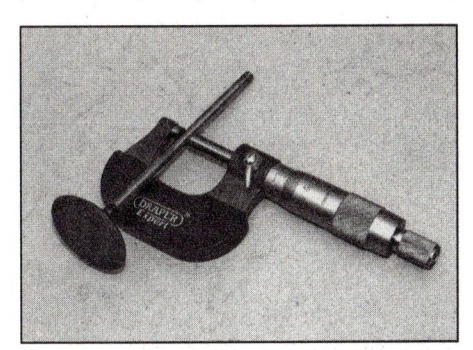

11.16a Measure the valve stem diameter with a micrometer

11.16b Measure the valve guide with a small bore gauge, then measure the bore gauge with a micrometer

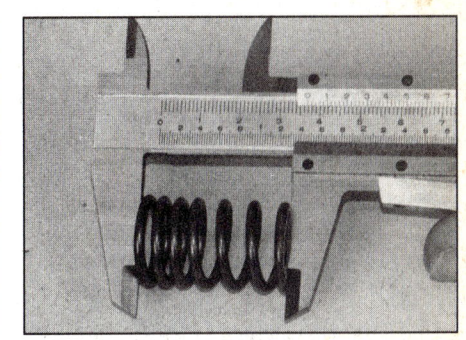

11.19 Measure the free length of the valve springs and check them for bend

2•20 Engine, clutch and transmission

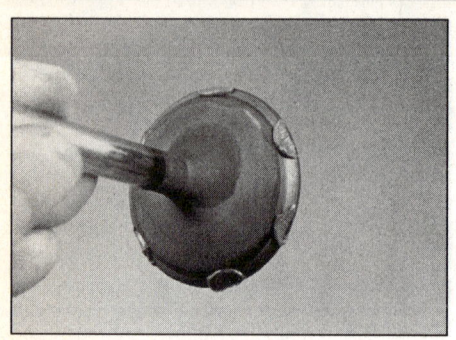

11.23 Apply a few dabs of grinding paste

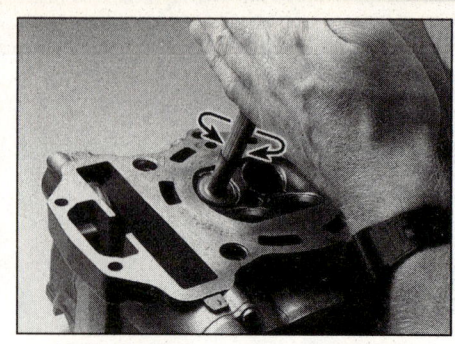

11.24 Grind the valves as described

11.27 Fit the lower (plain) and upper (shouldered) spring seats

a fine grinding compound). If a grinding tool is not available, a piece of rubber or plastic hose can be slipped over the valve stem (after the valve has been installed in the guide) and used to turn the valve.

23 Apply a small amount of coarse grinding compound to the valve face **(see illustration)**. Smear some clean engine oil onto the valve stem, then slip the valve into the guide **(see illustration 11.29)**. **Note:** *Make sure each valve is installed in its correct guide and be careful not to get any grinding compound on the valve stem.*

24 Attach the grinding tool to the valve and rotate the tool between the palms of your hands **(see illustration)**. Use a back-and-forth motion (as though rubbing your hands together) rather than a circular motion (i.e. so that the valve rotates alternately clockwise and anti-clockwise rather than in one direction only). If a motorised tool is being used, take note of the correct drive speed for it – if your drill runs too fast and is not variable, use a hand tool instead. Lift the valve off the seat and turn it at regular intervals to distribute the grinding compound properly. Continue the grinding procedure until the valve face and seat contact area is of uniform width, and unbroken around the entire circumference **(see illustration 11.15)**.

25 Carefully remove the valve and wipe off all traces of grinding compound, making sure none gets in the guide. Use solvent to clean the valve and wipe the seat area thoroughly with a solvent soaked cloth.

26 Repeat the procedure with fine valve grinding compound, then use solvent to clean the valve and flush the guide, and wipe the seat area thoroughly with a solvent soaked cloth. Repeat the entire procedure for the other valve. On completion thoroughly clean the entire head again, then blow through all passages with compressed air. Make sure all traces of the grinding compound have been removed before assembling the head.

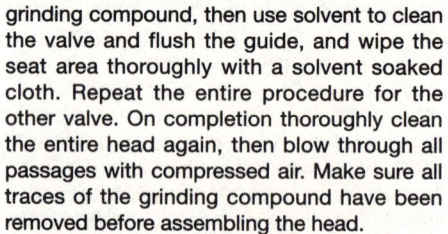

27 Working on one valve at a time, lay the lower spring seat in the cylinder head, then fit the upper spring seat with its shouldered side facing up **(see illustration)**.

28 Fit a new valve stem seal onto the guide, using finger pressure, a stem seal fitting tool or an appropriate size deep socket, to push the seal squarely onto the end of the valve guide until it is felt to clip into place **(see illustrations)**.

29 Coat the valve stem with clean oil, then slide it into its guide, rotating it slowly to avoid damaging the seal **(see illustration)**. Check that the valve moves up-and-down freely in the guide.

30 Next, install the spring, with the closer-wound coils facing down into the cylinder head **(see illustration)**. Fit the spring retainer, with its shouldered side facing down so that it fits into the top of the spring **(see illustration)**.

31 Apply a small amount of grease to the collets to help hold them in place. Compress the valve spring just enough to slip the collets

11.28a Fit a new valve stem seal ...

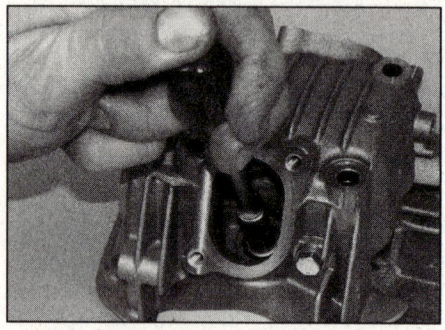

11.28b ... and press it squarely into place

11.29 Rotate the valve as you slide it in

11.30a Fit the spring, closer wound coils first ...

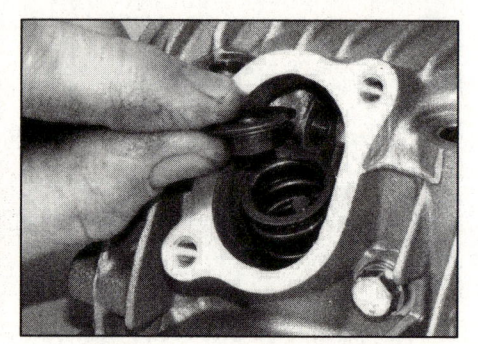

11.30b ... then fit the retainer

Engine, clutch and transmission 2•21

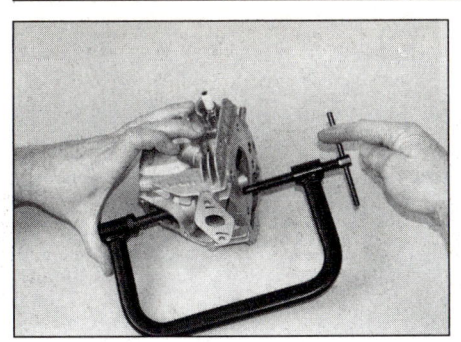

11.31a Compress the spring . . .

11.31b . . . and locate each collet in its groove in the top of the valve stem

11.31c Make sure the collets are correctly locked

into place **(see illustration)**. Locate each collet in turn into the groove in the valve stem using a screwdriver with a dab of grease on it **(see illustration)**. Carefully release the compressor, making sure the collets seat and lock in the retaining groove **(see illustration)**.
32 Repeat the procedure for the other valve.
33 Support the cylinder head on blocks so the valves can't contact the work surface, then tap the end of each valve stem lightly to seat the collets in their grooves **(see illustration)**.

> **HAYNES HiNT** Check for proper sealing of the valves by pouring a small amount of solvent into each of the valve ports. If the solvent leaks past any valve into the combustion chamber the valve grinding operation on that valve should be repeated.

34 After the cylinder head, camshaft and rockers have been installed, check the valve clearances and adjust as required (see Chapter 1).

12 Cylinder block

Note: *The cylinder block can be removed with the engine in the frame.*

Removal

1 Remove the cylinder head (see Section 10).
2 Draw the cam chain guide blade out of the top of the block, noting how it locates **(see illustration 9.9)**.
3 If required remove the front cover bracket(s), secured by a bolt on each side **(see illustration)** – on 2003 to 2006 models note the collars fitted in the rubber grommets. Replace the grommets with new ones if cracked, hardened or deformed.
4 On 2007-on models disconnect the engine oil temperature (EOT) sensor wiring connector **(see illustration 4.9b)**. If required have a rag ready to catch any oil and unscrew and remove the sensor – a new sealing washer will be needed.
5 Pull the cylinder block off the crankcase, supporting the piston so the connecting rod does not knock against the engine, and pass the cam chain down through the tunnel **(see illustration)**. Do not let the chain slip into the engine – lay it over the front and secure it with a piece of wire. If the block is stuck, tap around the joint faces with a soft-faced mallet. Do not attempt to free it by inserting a screwdriver between the block and crankcase mating surfaces – you'll damage them.
6 Remove the base gasket and discard it as a new one must be used. If they are loose, remove the dowels from the crankcase or the underside of the cylinder block **(see illustration 12.17)**.
7 Stuff some clean rag into the cam chain tunnel and around the connecting rod to protect and support it and the piston and to prevent anything falling into the engine.
8 If required remove the cooling fin damping rubbers.
9 Clean all traces of old gasket material from the cylinder block and crankcase. If a scraper is used, take care not to scratch or gouge the soft aluminium. Be careful not to let any of the gasket material fall into the engine.

Inspection

Note: *Do not attempt to separate the cylinder liner from the cylinder block.*
10 Check the cylinder walls carefully for scratches and score marks.
11 Using a precision straight-edge and a feeler gauge set to the warpage limit listed in the specifications at the beginning of the Chapter, check the block top surface for warpage. Take six measurements, one along each side and two diagonally across. If the block is warped beyond the limit specified at the beginning of this Chapter, consult a Honda dealer or take it to a specialist repair shop for an opinion, though be prepared to have to buy a new one.
12 Using a telescoping bore gauge and a micrometer, check the dimensions of the cylinder to assess the amount of wear, taper and ovality. Measure near the top (but below the level of the top piston ring at TDC), centre and bottom (but above the level of the oil ring at BDC) of the bore, both parallel to and

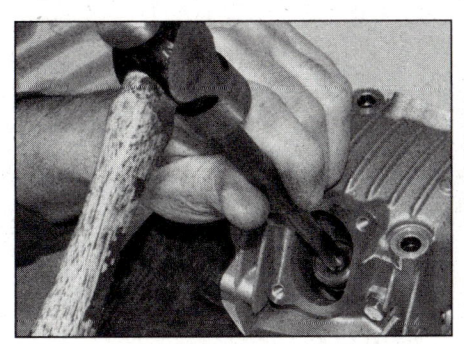

11.33 Seat the collets as described

12.3 Unscrew the bolt (arrowed) on each side and remove the bracket(s)

12.5 Carefully lift the block up off the crankcase

2•22 Engine, clutch and transmission

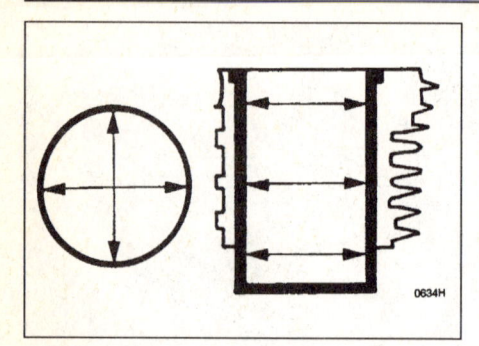

12.12a Measure the cylinder bore in the directions shown . . .

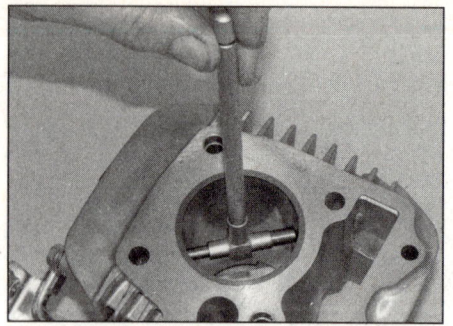

12.12b . . . using a telescoping gauge, then measure the gauge with a micrometer

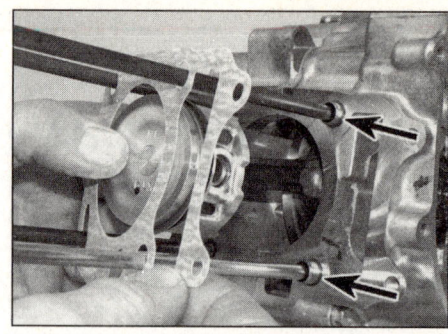

12.17 Lay the new gasket over the dowels (arrowed) and onto the crankcase

across the crankshaft axis (see illustrations). Compare the results to the specifications at the beginning of the Chapter. If the cylinder is worn, oval or tapered beyond the service limit it can be re-bored – oversize (+0.25, +0.5, +0.75 and +1.00) sets of pistons and rings are available. Note that the person carrying out the re-bore must be aware of the piston-to-bore clearance (see Specifications).
13 If the precision measuring tools are not available, take the cylinder block to a Honda dealer or specialist motorcycle repair shop for assessment and advice.

Installation

14 Check that the mating surfaces of the cylinder block and crankcase are free from oil or pieces of old gasket.
15 Check that all the studs are tight in the crankcase. If any are loose, or need to be replaced with new ones, remove them, noting that there are three different types – the two with part nos. 90031 fit on the right-hand side, no. 90032 is the bottom stud on the left and 90033 the top. Clean their threads and smear them with clean engine oil. Fit them into the crankcase with the marked end at the top, and tighten them using a stud tool, or by threading two nuts onto the top of the stud and tightening them together so they are locked on the stud, then tighten the stud by turning the upper of the two nuts (see *Tools and Workshop Tips* at the end of this manual).
16 If removed, fit the dowels over the studs and into the crankcase and push them firmly home (see illustration 12.17).
17 Remove the rags from around the piston and the cam chain tunnel, taking care not to let the connecting rod fall against the rim of the crankcase, and lay the new base gasket in place, locating it over the dowels (see illustration). The gasket can only fit one way, so if all the holes do not line up properly it is the wrong way round. Never re-use the old gasket.
18 Ensure the piston ring end gaps are positioned correctly before fitting the cylinder block (see Section 14) (see illustration 14.11). If possible, have an assistant to support the cylinder block while the piston rings are fed into the bore.
19 Rotate the crankshaft so that the piston is at its highest point (top dead centre). It is useful to place a support under the piston so that it remains at TDC while the block is fitted so the crankshaft does not turn. Lubricate the cylinder bore, piston and piston rings with clean engine oil.
20 Carefully slide the block over the studs and onto the piston until the crown fits into the bore, holding the underside of the piston, and making sure it enters the bore squarely and does not get cocked sideways (see illustration). Feed the cam chain up the tunnel and slip a piece of wire through it to prevent it falling back into the engine. Keep the chain taut to prevent it becoming disengaged from the crankshaft sprocket.
21 Carefully compress and feed each ring into the bore as the cylinder is lowered (see illustration). If necessary, use a soft mallet to gently tap the cylinder down, but do not use force if it appears to be stuck as the piston and/or rings will be damaged.
22 When the piston and rings are correctly located in the bore, remove the support if used then press the cylinder block down onto the base gasket, making sure the dowels locate.
23 Hold the block down and turn the crankshaft to check that everything moves as it should.
24 On 2007-on models, if removed fit the EOT sensor with a new sealing washer and tighten it to the torque setting specified at the beginning of the Chapter. Connect the EOT sensor wiring connector (see illustration 4.9b).
25 If removed fit the front cover bracket(s), secured by a bolt on each side (see illustration 12.3) – on 2003 to 2006 models make sure the collars are fitted in the rubber grommets.
26 Install the cam chain guide blade, making

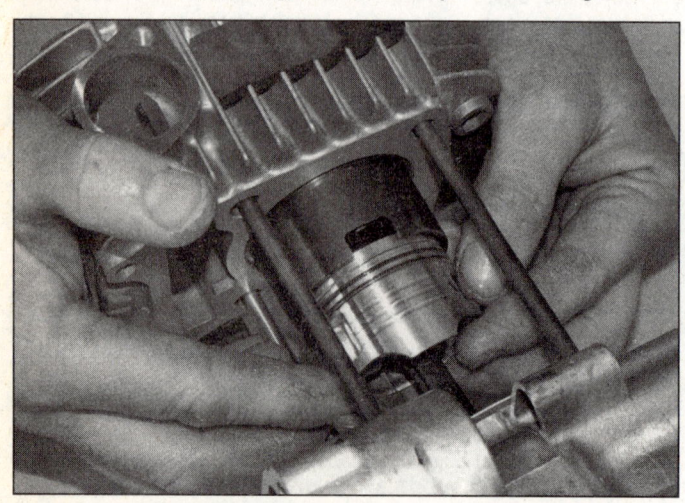

12.20 Slide the block onto the piston . . .

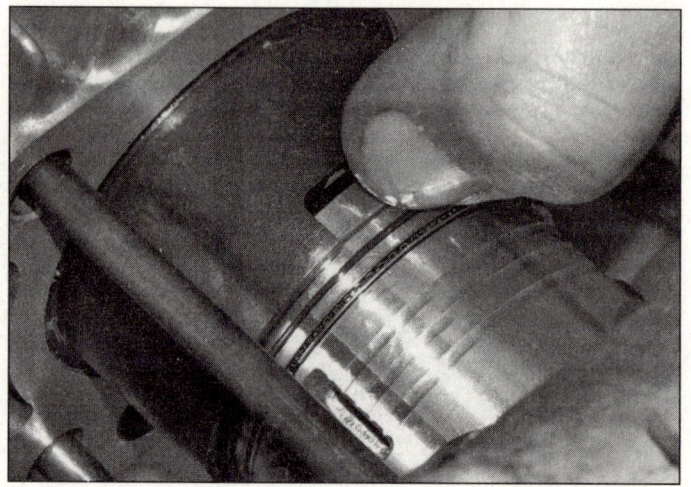

12.21 . . . and carefully feed each ring into the bore

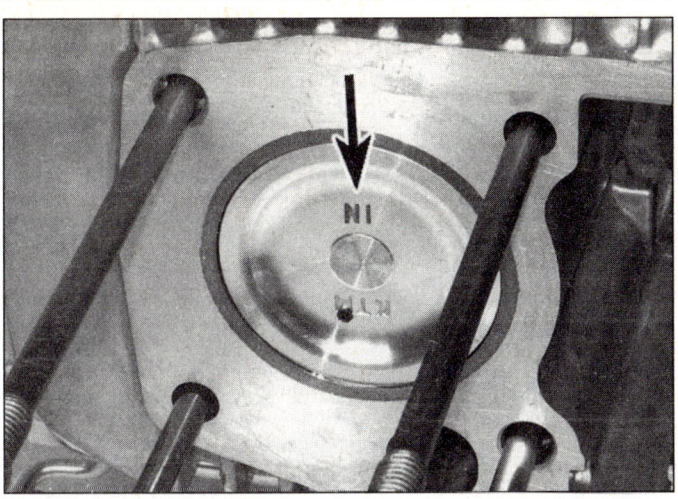

Engine, clutch and transmission 2•23

13.1 Note the 'IN' mark (arrowed) on the intake side of the piston

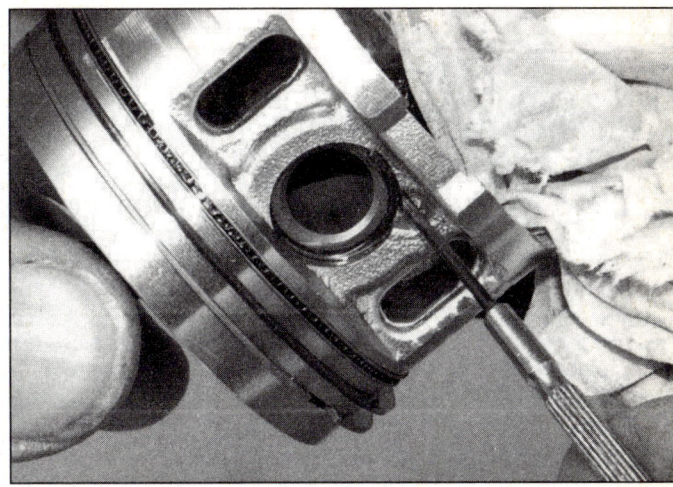

13.3a Prise out the circlip using a suitable tool in the notch . . .

sure the bottom of the blade sits in its seat and the lugs near its top locate in the cut-outs in the cylinder block **(see illustrations 9.12a and b)**.
27 Install the cylinder head (see Section 10).

13 Piston

Note: *The piston can be removed with the engine in the frame.*

Removal

1 Note that the piston crown is marked IN (though the mark is likely to be invisible until the piston is cleaned) and this mark faces the intake side of the cylinder **(see illustration)**.
2 Remove the cylinder block (see Section 12). Check that the hole into the cam chain tunnel is completely blocked with rag.
3 Carefully prise out the circlip on one side of the piston using needle-nose pliers or a small flat-bladed screwdriver inserted into the notch **(see illustration)**. Push the piston pin out from the other side to free the piston from the connecting rod **(see illustration)**. If required remove the other circlip. New circlips must be used.

> **HAYNES HiNT**
> *If a piston pin is a tight fit in the piston bosses, heat the piston using a heat gun – this will expand the alloy piston sufficiently to release its grip on the pin. If the piston pin is particularly stubborn, extract it using a drawbolt tool, but be careful to protect the piston's working surfaces.*

4 Using your thumbs or a piston ring removal and installation tool, carefully remove the rings from the piston **(see illustrations 14.10, 14.9, 14.6c, b and a)**. Do not nick or gouge the piston in the process. Carefully note which way up each ring fits and in which groove as they must be installed in their original positions if being re-used. The middle and top rings are identifiable by their different colours and profiles, and each is marked with the letters RS at one end to denote the upper surface **(see illustration 14.8)**.
5 Scrape all traces of carbon from the top of the piston. A hand-held wire brush or a piece of fine emery cloth can be used once most of the deposits have been scraped away. Do not, under any circumstances, use a wire brush mounted in a drill motor to remove deposits from the piston; the piston material is soft and will be eroded away by the wire brush.
6 Use a piston ring groove cleaning tool to remove any carbon deposits from the ring grooves. If a tool is not available, a piece broken off an old ring will do the job. Be very careful to remove only the carbon deposits. Do not remove any metal and do not nick or gouge the sides of the ring grooves.
7 Once the deposits have been removed, clean the piston with solvent and dry it thoroughly. Make sure the oil return holes below the oil ring groove are clear.

Inspection

8 Carefully inspect the piston for cracks around the skirt, at the pin bosses and at the ring lands. Normal piston wear appears as even, vertical wear on the thrust surfaces. If the skirt is scored or scuffed, the engine may have been suffering from overheating and/or abnormal combustion, which caused excessively high operating temperatures. Also check that the circlip grooves are not damaged.
9 Although unlikely, a hole in the top of the piston or burned areas around the edge of the piston crown, indicate that pre-ignition or knocking under load have occurred. If you find evidence of any problems the cause must be corrected or the damage will occur again (see *Fault Finding* in the *Reference* section).
10 Measure the piston ring-to-groove clearance by laying each piston ring in its groove and slipping a feeler gauge in beside it **(see illustration)**. Make sure you have the correct ring for the groove (see Step 4). Check the clearance at three or four locations around the groove. If the clearance is greater than specified, replace both the piston and rings as a set. If new rings are being used, measure the clearance using the new rings. If the clearance is greater than that specified, the piston is worn and must be replaced with a new one.
11 Check the piston-to-bore clearance by measuring the bore (see Section 12), then measure the piston 10 mm up from the bottom

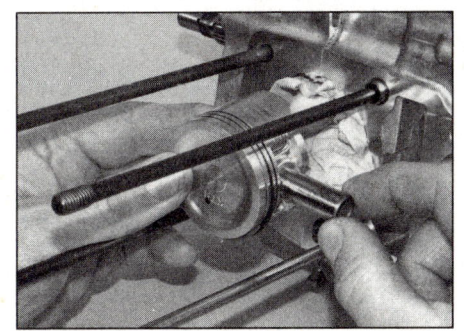

13.3b . . . then push out the pin and separate the piston from the rod

13.10 Measure the piston ring-to-groove clearance with a feeler gauge

2•24 Engine, clutch and transmission

13.11 Measure the piston diameter with a micrometer at the specified distance from the bottom of the skirt

13.12a Fit the pin into the piston and check for any freeplay

of the skirt and at 90° to the piston pin axis **(see illustration)**. Refer to the Specifications at the beginning of the Chapter and subtract the piston diameter from the bore diameter to obtain the clearance. If it is greater than the specified figure, the piston must be replaced with a new one (assuming the bore itself is within limits).

12 Apply clean engine oil to the piston pin, insert it into the piston and check for any freeplay between the two **(see illustration)**. Measure the pin external diameter at each end and the pin bore in the piston **(see illustration)**. Calculate the difference to obtain the piston pin-to-piston pin bore clearance. Compare the result to the specifications at the beginning of the Chapter. If the clearance is greater than specified, replace the components that are worn beyond their specified limits. Repeat the check and measurements between the middle of the pin and the connecting rod small-end **(see illustrations)**.

Installation

13 Inspect and install the piston rings (see Section 14).
14 Lubricate the piston pin, the piston pin bore and the connecting rod small-end bore with clean engine oil.
15 When fitting the piston onto the connecting rod make sure the IN mark on the piston crown faces the intake side (top) of the engine **(see illustration 13.1)**.
16 If removed fit a *new* circlip into one side of the piston (do not re-use old circlips). Line up the piston on the connecting rod and insert the piston pin from the other side **(see illustration 13.3b)**. Secure the pin with the other *new* circlip **(see illustration)**. When fitting the circlips, compress them only just enough to

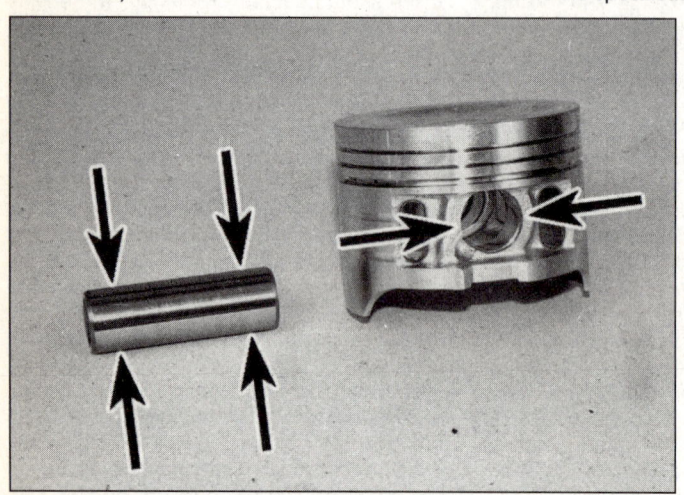

13.12b Measure the external diameter of each end of the pin and the internal diameter of the bore in the piston on each side

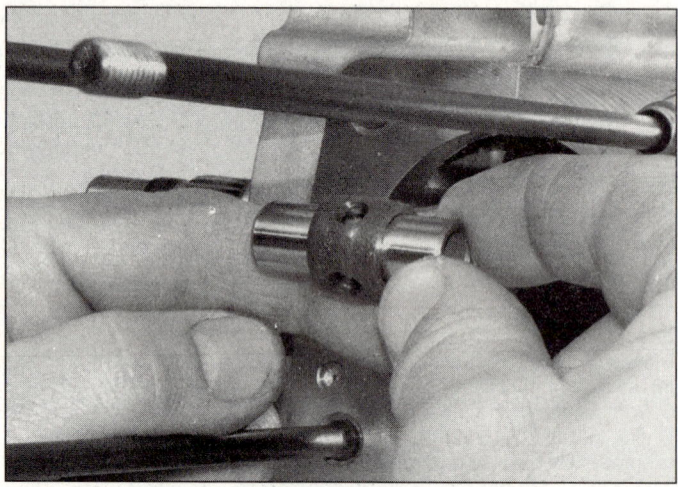

13.12c Fit the pin into the connecting rod and check for any freeplay

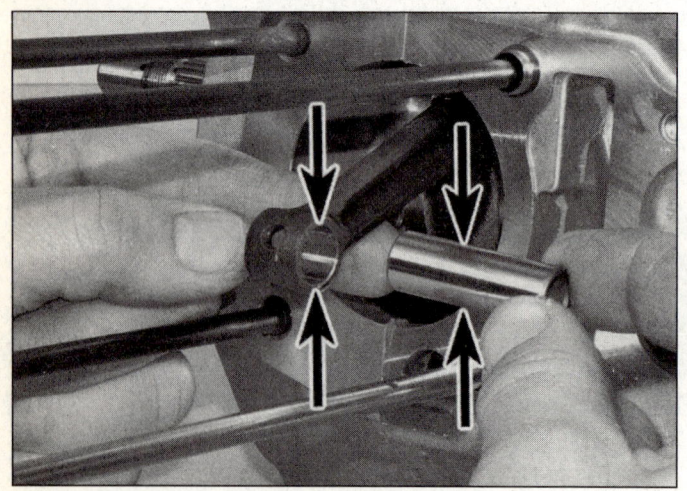

13.12d Measure the external diameter of the middle of the pin and the internal diameter of the connecting rod

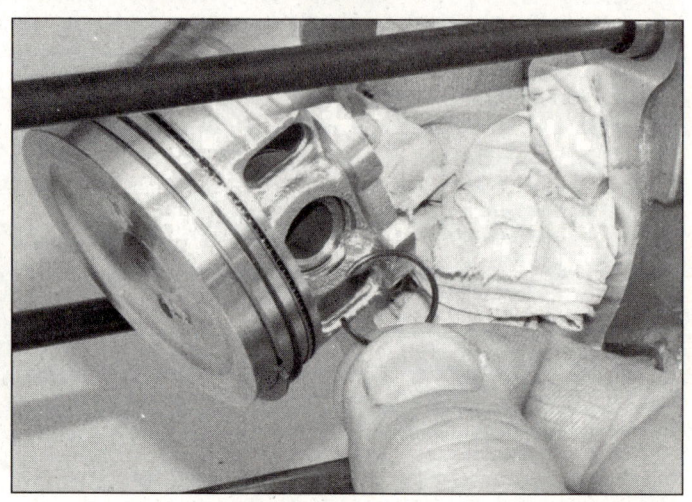

13.16 Use new circlips and make sure they locate correctly

Engine, clutch and transmission 2•25

fit them in the piston, and make sure they are properly seated in their grooves with the open end away from the removal notch.
17 Install the cylinder block (see Section 12).

14 Piston rings

Inspection

1 It is good practice to replace the piston rings with new ones when an engine is being overhauled. Before installing the new rings, check the end gaps with the rings installed in the bore, as follows.
2 Insert the top ring into the bottom of the bore and square it up with the bore walls by pushing it in with the top of the piston **(see illustrations)**. The ring should be about 20 mm below the bottom edge of the bore. Slip a feeler gauge between the ends of the ring and compare the measurement to the specifications at the beginning of the Chapter **(see illustration)**.
3 If the gap is larger or smaller than specified, double check to make sure that you have the correct ring before proceeding; excess end gap is not critical unless it exceeds the service limit.
4 If the service limit is exceeded with new rings, check the bore for wear (see Section 12). If the gap is too small, the ring ends may come in contact with each other during

14.2a Fit the ring in its bore . . .

engine operation, which can cause serious damage.
5 Repeat the procedure for the middle ring and the oil control ring side-rails, but not the expander ring.

Installation

6 Install the oil control ring (lowest on the piston) first. It is composed of three separate components, namely the expander and the upper and lower side-rails. Slip the expander into the groove, making sure the ends don't overlap, then fit the lower side-rail **(see illustrations)**. Do not use a piston ring installation tool on the side-rails as they may be damaged. Instead, place one end of the side-rail into the groove between the expander and the ring land. Hold it firmly in place and slide a finger around the piston while pushing the rail into the groove. Next, fit the upper

14.2b . . . and set it square using the piston . . .

side-rail in the same manner **(see illustration)**. Check that the ends of the expander have not overlapped.
7 After the three oil ring components have been installed, check to make sure that both the upper and lower side-rails can be turned smoothly in the ring groove.
8 Identify which of the two compression rings is the middle and which is the top by their different colours and profiles, and note the letters RS at one end of each ring that denotes its upper side **(see illustration and 14.11)**.
9 Install the second (middle) ring next. Make sure that the identification letters near the end gap are facing up. Fit the ring into the middle groove in the piston **(see illustration)**. Do not expand the ring any more than is necessary to slide it into place. To avoid breaking the ring, use a piston ring installation tool.

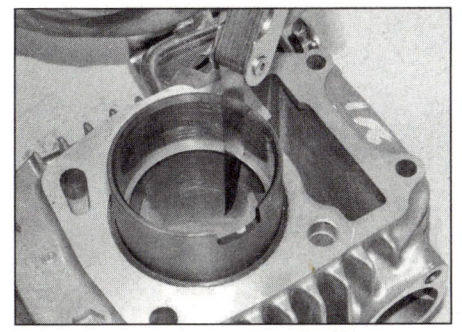

14.2c . . . then measure the end gap using a feeler gauge

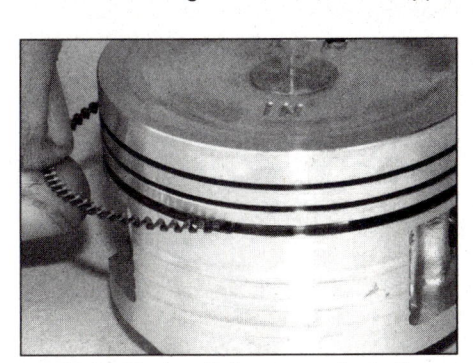

14.6a Fit the oil ring expander in its groove . . .

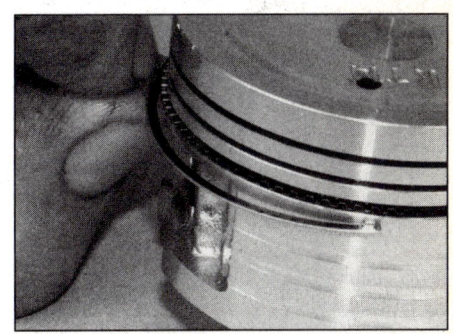

14.6b . . . then fit the lower side rail . . .

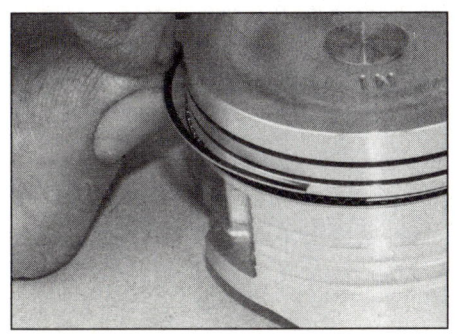

14.6c . . . and the upper side rail on each side of it

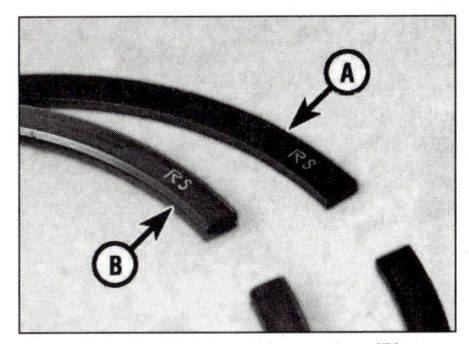

14.8 Middle ring (A), top ring (B)

14.9 Install the middle ring . . .

2•26 Engine, clutch and transmission

14.10 ... and the top ring as described

10 Finally, install the top ring in the same manner into the top groove in the piston **(see illustration)**. Make sure the identification letters near the end gap are facing up, or that the wider section of the angled inner rim is at the bottom.

11 Once the rings are correctly installed, check they move freely without snagging and stagger their end gaps as shown **(see illustration)**.

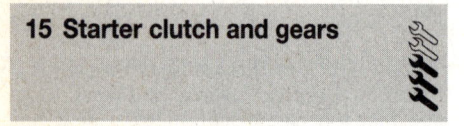

15 Starter clutch and gears

Note: *The starter clutch can be removed with the engine in the frame.*

Check

1 The operation of the starter clutch can be checked while it is in situ. Remove the starter motor (see Chapter 8). Check that the idle/reduction gear is able to rotate freely clockwise as you look at it via the starter motor aperture, but locks when rotated anti-clockwise **(see illustration)**. If not, the starter clutch is faulty and should be removed for inspection.

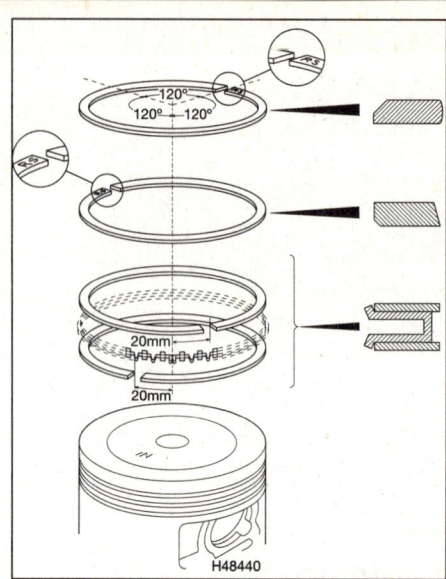

Removal

2 Remove the alternator rotor (see Chapter 8) – the starter clutch is bolted to the back of it.
3 If the starter driven gear did not come away with the rotor, slide it off the crankshaft, followed by the needle bearing **(see illustrations 15.11b and a)**.

Inspection

4 If separated on removal fit the starter driven gear into the starter clutch, rotating it anti-clockwise as you do **(see illustration 15.5)**. With the alternator face down on a workbench, check that the starter driven gear rotates freely anti-clockwise and locks against the clutch when turned clockwise **(see illustration)**. If it doesn't, the starter clutch should be dismantled for further investigation.

5 Withdraw the starter driven gear from the starter clutch, rotating it anti-clockwise as you do **(see illustration)**.

6 Check the condition of the surfaces on the driven gear hub and the rollers in the clutch **(see illustration)**. On 2007-on models, measure the outside diameter of the hub and check that it has not worn beyond the service limit specified. If the hub is worn, damaged, marked or flattened at any point replace the driven gear with a new one.

7 Remove the rollers and springs from the clutch, noting how they fit **(see illustration)**. Check the condition of the rollers, and springs. If the rollers are worn, damaged, marked or flattened, or the springs have sagged or distorted, replace the clutch assembly with a new one – the rollers and springs are not available separately.

8 To remove the starter clutch assembly, hold the alternator rotor using a holding strap and unscrew the three bolts (2003 to 2006 models) or six bolts (2007-on models) inside the rotor **(see illustration)**. Install the new assembly in

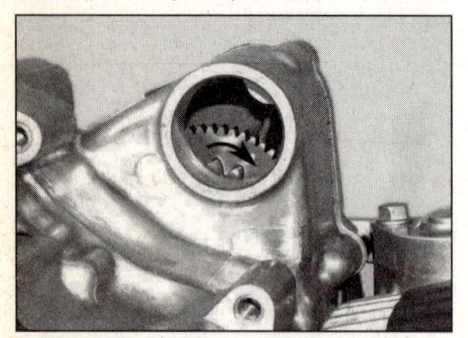

14.11 Piston ring installation details - stagger the ring end gaps as shown

15.1 Check the operation of the clutch as described

15.4 Check the operation of the clutch as described

15.5 Withdraw the driven gear

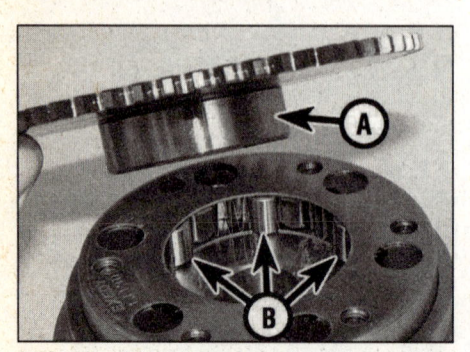

15.6 Check the driven gear hub (A) and the rollers (B)

15.7 Remove the rollers and springs from their housings

15.8 The starter clutch is secured by bolts (arrowed)

Engine, clutch and transmission 2•27

15.9 Check the bearing and bearing surfaces for wear

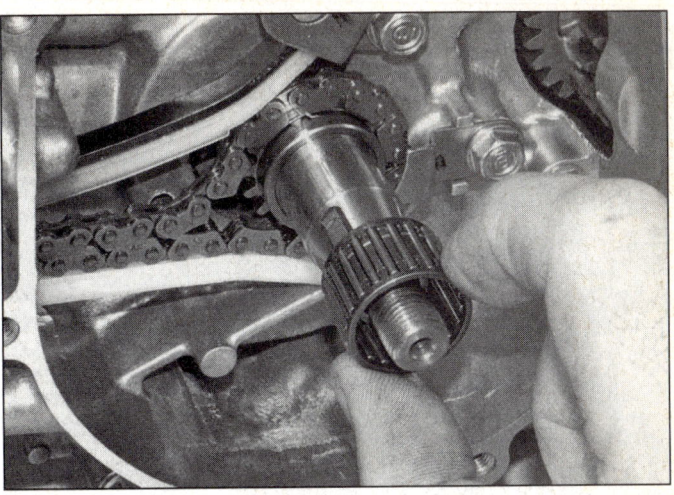

15.11a Slide the needle bearing . . .

a reverse sequence. Clean the threads of the bolts and apply a suitable non-permanent thread locking compound, and tighten them to the torque setting specified at the beginning of the Chapter for your model. Apply clean engine oil to the rollers, then fit the springs and rollers into the clutch.

9 Check the needle bearing and its bearing surfaces on the crankshaft and in the driven gear hub **(see illustration)**. If the bearing is worn replace it with a new one. If there is damage to the surface on the crankshaft, fit a new one.

10 Check the teeth of the idle/reduction gear and the corresponding teeth of the starter driven gear and starter motor drive shaft. Replace the gears and/or starter motor if worn or chipped teeth are discovered on related gears. Also check the idle/reduction gear shaft for damage, and check that the gear is not a loose fit on it. Check the shaft ends and the bores they run in for wear.

Installation

11 Lubricate the needle bearing with clean engine oil and slide it onto the crankshaft **(see illustration)**. Slide the starter driven gear onto the bearing **(see illustration)**. Lubricate the outer surface of the driven gear hub with oil.

12 Install the alternator rotor (see Chapter 8).

16 Clutch cover

Note: *The clutch cover can be removed with the engine in the frame. If the engine has been removed, ignore the steps which don't apply.*

1 Remove the front cover on the right-hand side (see Chapter 7).
2 Remove the rider's footrest assembly and kickstart lever (see Chapter 5).
3 Drain the engine oil (see Chapter 1).
4 Remove the exhaust system (see Chapter 3B).
5 Working evenly in a criss-cross pattern, unscrew the clutch cover bolts, noting the wiring guides on 2007-on models **(see illustration)**. Remove the cover, pushing down on the rear brake pedal for clearance as required, and being prepared to catch any residual oil.

15.11b . . . and the driven gear onto the shaft

6 Remove the gasket and discard it **(see illustration 16.14a)**. Remove the two dowels from either the cover or the crankcase if they are loose.

Inspection

7 Remove the oil jet from the cover or crankcase, noting which way round it fits, clean with solvent and blow through with compressed air **(see illustration)**. Clean the

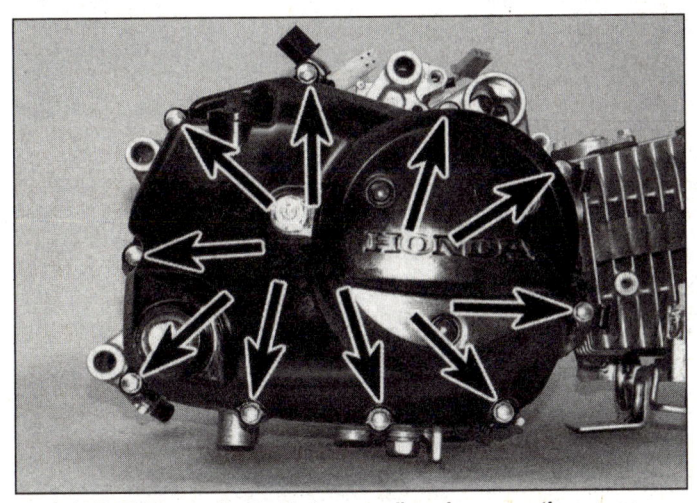

16.5 Unscrew the bolts (arrowed) and remove the cover

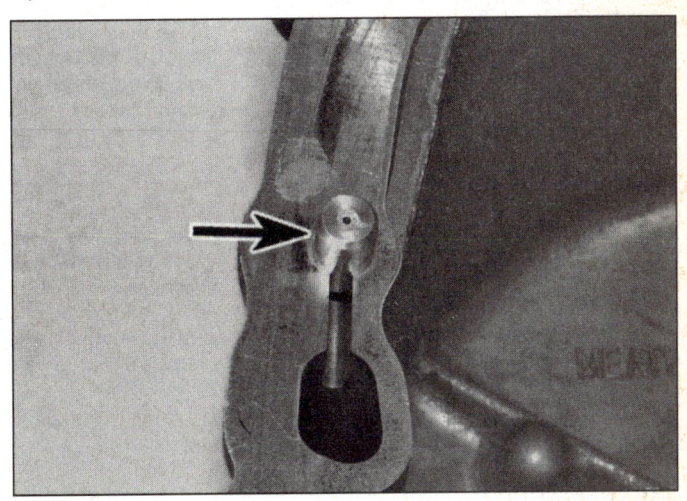

16.7 Remove the oil jet (arrowed) and clean it and the oil passage

2•28 Engine, clutch and transmission

16.9 Check the bearing (arrowed)

16.11a Lever the old seal out . . .

16.11b . . . and press the new one in

16.14a Locate the new gasket over the dowels (arrowed) . . .

16.14b . . . then fit the cover

cover, removing all traces of gasket from it and the crankcase. Clean the oil passage to the bearing with solvent and blow through with compressed air. Fit the jet back into its bore in the cover with the small end of the hole facing out.

8 Refer to Section 20 for the clutch lifter adjuster plate in the cover.

9 Check that the ball bearing runs smoothly and is a tight fit in the cover **(see illustration)**. Check the inner race and the end of the crankshaft for signs of scoring. To remove the bearing use an expanding extractor located behind the inner race and attached to a slide-hammer, then have an assistant hold

16.14c On 2007-on models make sure the wiring guides (arrowed) are correctly fitted

the cover down on some clean rag and jar the bearing out. Heat the bearing housing using a hot air gun to ease removal if necessary. Drive the new bearing in, with the sealed side facing into the cover, until it seats using a suitable driver or socket seated on the outer race.

10 On 2003 to 2006 models similarly check the needle bearing for the gearchange shaft, removing it in the same way if required. The new bearing should be pressed in rather than driven in, to avoid damaging the cage.

11 Clean and check the kickstart shaft oil seal. The seal can be replaced by levering the old one out with a seal hook or screwdriver and pressing the new one in **(see illustrations)**.

Installation

12 Make sure the crankcase and clutch cover surfaces are clean, and wipe over them with solvent. The ball lifter and spring on the clutch are easily dislodged when installing the cover, so to make it easier put the bike on its sidestand if the engine is in the frame, and if the engine is out of the frame seat it on its left side.

13 Apply some oil to the crankshaft bearing and to the gearchange shaft bearing or journal, according to model. Lubricate the kickstart shaft oil seal lips with grease.

14 Make sure the oil jet is correctly fitted **(see**

illustration 16.7). Fit the two dowels into the crankcase if removed. Place a new gasket on the crankcase, locating it over the dowels **(see illustration)**. Fit the cover, taking care not to damage the oil seal lips, and locating the shaft ends in the bearings and the cover on the dowels **(see illustration)**. Fit all the bolts finger-tight, not forgetting the wiring guides on 2007-on models, then tighten them evenly and a little at a time in a criss-cross pattern **(see illustration)**.

15 Adjust the clutch lifter mechanism (see Chapter 1).

16 Install the exhaust system, kickstart lever and footrest assembly (see Chapter 3B and 5).

17 Fill the engine with the correct amount and type of oil (see Chapter 1 and *Pre-ride checks*). Install the front cover (see Chapter 7).

17 Clutch assemblies removal and installation

Note 1: The clutches can be removed with the engine in the frame.
Note 2: The centrifugal clutch plate/weight assembly can be removed from the drum for

Engine, clutch and transmission 2•29

17.0 The Honda double-ended peg spanner

17.3 Unscrew the bolts (arrowed) and remove the cover

17.4a Bend the tab out of the notch

17.4b Locate the pegs of a holding tool in the slots . . .

17.4c . . . and slacken the nut

HAYNES HiNT

A peg spanner can be made by cutting castellations into a socket of the correct size using a hacksaw – for the centrifugal clutch nut use a 22 mm socket, and for the multi-plate clutch nut use an 18 mm socket.

inspection of its components and replacement of the shoes without having to first remove the complete clutch assemblies – refer to Steps 1 to 5 and 15 to 19 only.

Special tools: *To remove the clutch nuts, a peg spanner (available from Honda, part No. 07716-0020100) is required* **(see illustration).** *This tool is double-ended and has both sizes required. Alternatively peg spanners can be made by cutting castellations into old sockets* **(see Tool Tip).**

Removal

1 Remove the clutch cover (see Section 16).
2 Remove the clutch lifter/brake mechanism components (see Section 20).
3 Unscrew the oil filter cover bolts and remove the cover and the gasket **(see illustration)**.

4 Bend the tab(s) of the centrifugal clutch nut lockwasher out of the notch(es) in the nut. Counter-hold the centrifugal clutch plate using the Honda service tool (Pt. No. 07725-0030000) or the pegged side of a commercially available clutch holding tool as shown, and slacken the nut using the peg spanner **(see illustrations)**. Unscrew the nut and remove the washer and lockwasher **(see illustrations 16.16b and a)**. Check the condition of the lockwasher tabs and replace the washer with a new one if necessary – Honda specify to use a new one.
5 If required, for example if you are just checking the centrifugal clutch shoes and drum and not removing the complete assemblies, remove the centrifugal clutch plate/weight assembly from the drum now,

turning it clockwise as you draw it out **(see illustration)**.
6 Remove the bearing from the clutch lifter plate **(see illustration)**.
7 Lock the primary drive and driven gears together where they mesh on the underside, using either a gear locking tool (part No. 07724-0010200), a suitable piece of aluminium or copper (DO NOT use steel) as shown, or a large aluminium or copper washer, or a stout piece of rag suitably wedged **(see illustration)**. With the gears locked slacken

17.5 Remove the centrifugal clutch plate/weight assembly from the drum

17.6 Remove the bearing

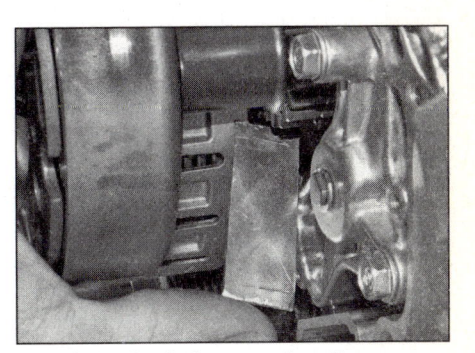

17.7a Lock the gears together as described . . .

2•30 Engine, clutch and transmission

17.7b . . . and slacken the nut

17.8 Draw the complete clutch assemblies off the shafts

the clutch nut using the peg spanner **(see illustration)**. Unscrew the nut and remove the washer, then remove the locking tool.
8 Draw the clutch assemblies off the shafts together **(see illustration)**.
9 If the clutch guide is still on the shaft slide it off **(see illustration 17.11b)** – if it isn't there it will be in the clutch housing **(see illustration 19.2c)**. Slide the spacer off the shaft **(see illustration 17.11a)**.
10 Refer to Sections 18 and 19 for disassembly, inspection and reassembly of the clutches, and to Section 20 for the lifter/brake mechanism.

Installation

11 Make sure all components are clean. Smear the spacer and clutch guide inside and out with clean engine oil, then slide them onto the shaft **(see illustrations)**. Smear the exposed section of the crankshaft with molybdenum disulphide oil (a 50/50 mixture of molybdenum disulphide grease and clean engine oil).
12 The primary drive gear has an offset sprung sub-gear to reduce backlash – turn the sub-gear slightly against the spring until the tooth with the cut-away and paint mark on the sub-gear aligns with the tooth with the cut-away on the main gear, and hold it there **(see illustration)**. Place the clutch assemblies together so the primary drive and driven gears are engaged, and slide the clutches onto the shafts **(see illustration 17.8)**.
13 Fit the clutch nut washer, then apply oil to the threads and seating face of the clutch nut and thread it onto the shaft **(see illustration)**. Using the method employed on removal to lock the primary drive and driven gears, but locating the tool where the teeth mesh at the top, and the tool to fit the nut (see Step 7), tighten the nut to the torque setting specified at the beginning of the Chapter **(see illustrations)**.

17.11a Slide the spacer . . .

17.11b . . . and the guide onto the shaft

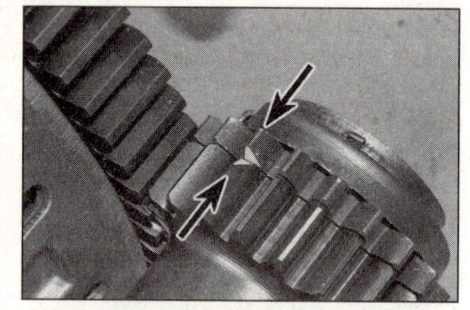

17.12 Align the cut-away drive gear and sub-gear teeth as described and engage them with the driven gear

17.13a Fit the washer and the nut . . .

17.13b . . . then lock the gears . . .

17.13c . . . and tighten the nut to the specified torque

Engine, clutch and transmission 2•31

17.16a Locate the tab (arrowed) in the slot

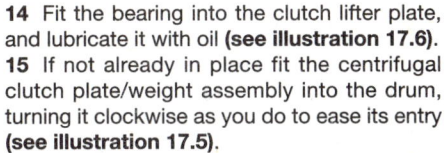

17.16b Fit the washer and the nut . . .

17.16c . . . then tighten the nut to the specified torque

14 Fit the bearing into the clutch lifter plate, and lubricate it with oil **(see illustration 17.6)**.
15 If not already in place fit the centrifugal clutch plate/weight assembly into the drum, turning it clockwise as you do to ease its entry **(see illustration 17.5)**.
16 Fit a new lockwasher, locating the single inward facing tab into the slot in the plate **(see illustration)**. Fit the washer with the OUTSIDE mark facing out **(see illustration)**. Apply oil to the threads and seating face of the centrifugal clutch nut and thread it onto the shaft. Using the method employed on removal to hold the plate and the tool to fit the nut (see Step 4), tighten the nut to the torque setting specified at the beginning of the Chapter **(see illustration)**. Check that one of the lockwasher tabs aligns exactly with one of the notches in the nut **(see illustration)** – if none align, tighten the nut further until the closest

17.16d Check the alignment of a tab with a notch . . .

17.16e . . . then bend the tab into it

tab aligns with its notch. Bend the tab into the notch to lock the nut **(see illustration)**.
17 Clean the threads of the oil filter cover bolts, then apply some fresh threadlock to the upper 4 mm of threads, leaving the bottom 1.6 mm clear as shown **(see illustration)**. Fit the cover using a new gasket and tighten the bolts to the torque setting specified at the beginning of the Chapter **(see illustration)**.
18 Install the clutch lifter/brake mechanism components (see Section 20).
19 Install the clutch cover (see Section 16).

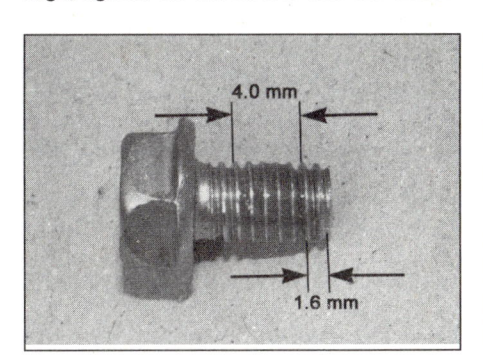

17.17a Apply threadlock as shown . . .

17.17b . . . and fit the cover using a new gasket

18 Centrifugal clutch – overhaul

Note: *The centrifugal clutch plate/weight assembly can be removed from the drum for inspection of its components and replacement of the shoes without having to first remove the complete clutch assemblies – refer to Section 17, Steps 1 to 5 only.*

Inspection and disassembly

1 Remove the clutch assemblies (Section 17). Before taking the centrifugal clutch apart check that it turns freely clockwise and locks against the one-way clutch rollers when you turn it anti-clockwise **(see illustration)**. If not, there is a problem with the one-way clutch components. Remove the plate/weight assembly **(see illustration)**.
2 Remove the circlip securing the one-way clutch, then remove the washer (see

18.1a Check the operation of the clutch as described

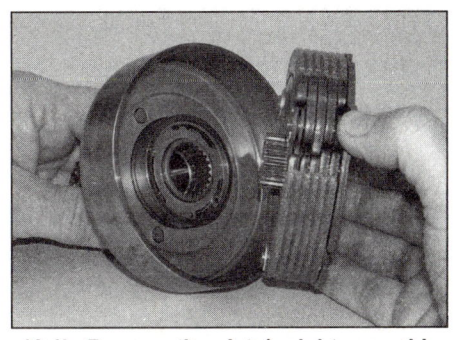

18.1b Remove the plate/weight assembly from the drum

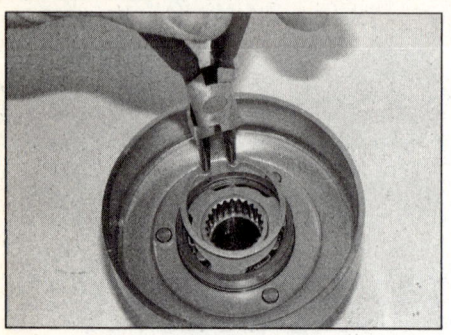

2•32 Engine, clutch and transmission

18.2a Release the circlip...

18.2b ...and remove the washer...

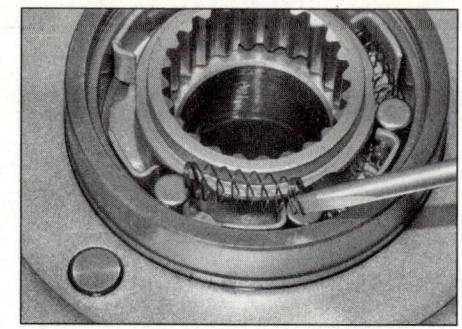

18.2c ...the springs and rollers...

18.2d ...and the one-way clutch body

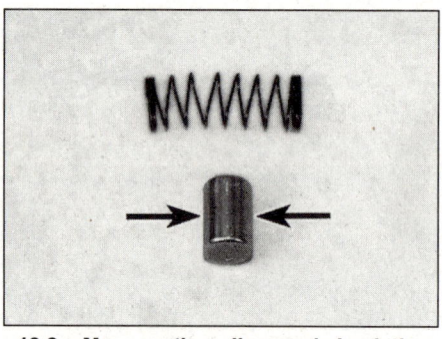

18.2e Measure the rollers and check the springs

18.2f Measure the clutch housing

illustrations). Remove the rollers and springs, noting how they fit **(see illustration)**. Remove the one-way clutch body and check it for damage **(see illustration)**. Check the rollers

and housing for scoring, flat spots and other damage. Measure the diameter of each roller and replace them with new ones if beyond the limit specified at the beginning of the

Chapter **(see illustration)**. Check the springs for sagging and distortion. Measure the inside diameter of the clutch housing and replace the drum with a new one if worn beyond its limit **(see illustration)**.

3 Measure the amount of friction lining on each clutch weight and replace them with new ones if worn to the limit **(see illustration)**. Measure the inside diameter of the clutch drum and replace it with a new one if worn beyond its limit **(see illustration)**. To remove the weights remove the E-clips, side plate, friction spring and spring seat, then lever the weights up off their posts, moving from one to the other and levering them up evenly and a little at a time, and when free detach the springs **(see illustrations)**. Remove the rubber dampers and check them for damage and deterioration **(see illustration)**.

18.3a Measure the friction material on each shoe...

18.3b ...and the drum

18.3c Prise out the E-clips...

18.3d ...and remove the side plate...

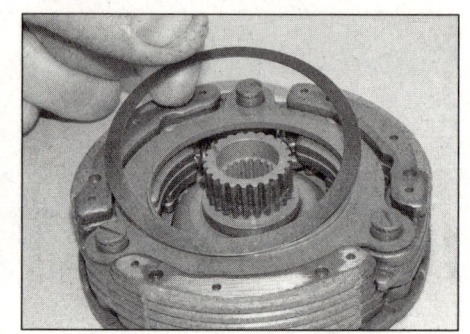

18.3e ...the friction spring...

Engine, clutch and transmission 2•33

18.3f . . . and the spring seat

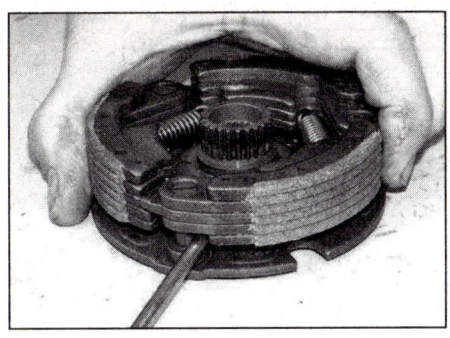

18.3g Evenly lever the weights up off their posts . . .

18.3h . . . then unhook the springs

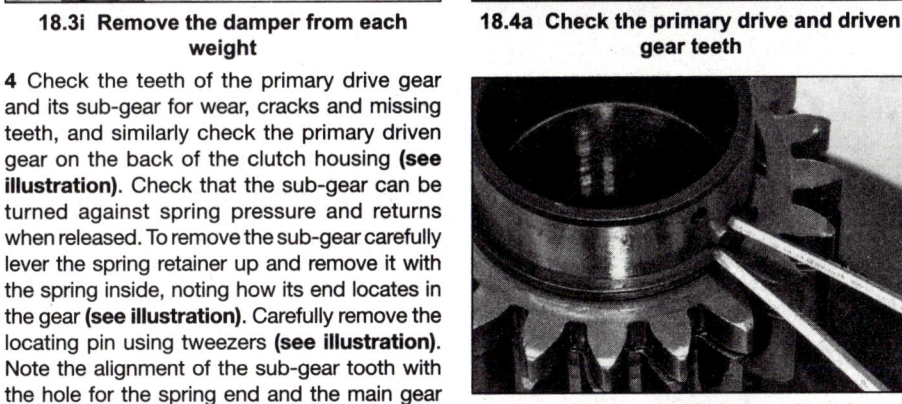

18.3i Remove the damper from each weight

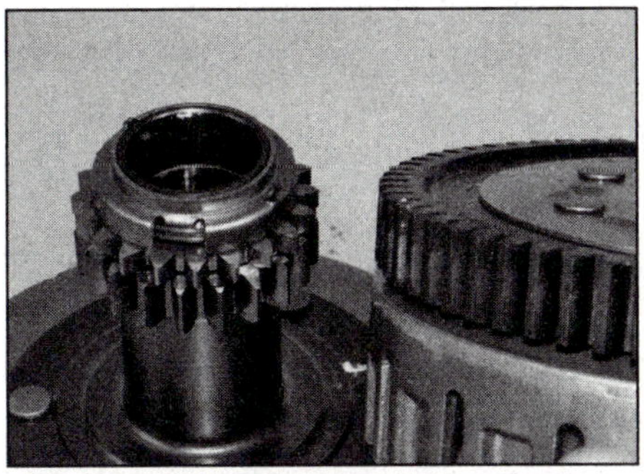

18.4a Check the primary drive and driven gear teeth

18.4b Carefully lever the retainer off

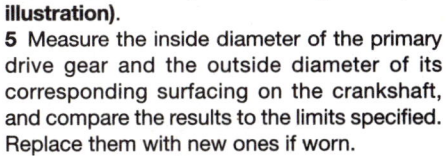

4 Check the teeth of the primary drive gear and its sub-gear for wear, cracks and missing teeth, and similarly check the primary driven gear on the back of the clutch housing **(see illustration)**. Check that the sub-gear can be turned against spring pressure and returns when released. To remove the sub-gear carefully lever the spring retainer up and remove it with the spring inside, noting how its end locates in the gear **(see illustration)**. Carefully remove the locating pin using tweezers **(see illustration)**. Note the alignment of the sub-gear tooth with the hole for the spring end and the main gear tooth with a cut-away. Release the snap-ring from its groove and lift the sub-gear off **(see illustration)**.

5 Measure the inside diameter of the primary drive gear and the outside diameter of its corresponding surfacing on the crankshaft, and compare the results to the limits specified. Replace them with new ones if worn.

18.4c Remove the locating pin using tweezers

Reassembly

6 Fit the sub-gear onto the primary drive gear, aligning the sub-gear tooth with a hole and the main gear tooth with a cut-away **(see illustration)**. Secure the gear with the snap-ring, making sure it seats in its groove

18.4d Release the snap-ring and remove the sub-gear

(see illustration). Smear a dab of grease into the locating pin hole. Fit the locating pin with its narrow end going into the hole **(see illustration 18.4c)**. Make sure the spring is correctly seated in the retainer **(see illustration)**. Fit the retainer, locating the

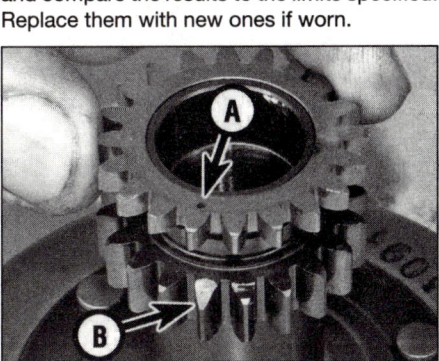

18.6a Align the hole (A) with the cut-away tooth (B)

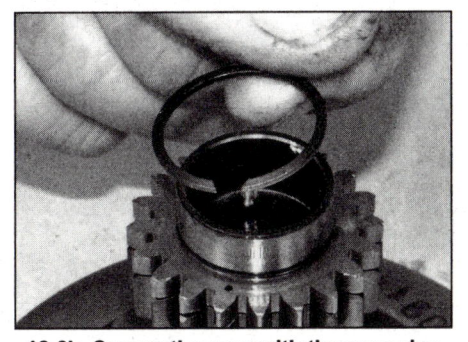

18.6b Secure the gear with the snap-ring

18.6c Make sure the spring is correctly seated

2•34 Engine, clutch and transmission

18.6d Locate the spring end in the hole . . .

18.6e . . . and the indent over the pin

18.6f The assembled sub-gear should be as shown

18.7a Fit the dampers onto their posts

18.7b Fit the weights . . .

spring end into the hole in the sub-gear, then turn the retainer and locate the indent in its rim over the locating pin, and press down until the retainer clicks into place **(see illustrations)**.

7 Fit the rubber dampers onto the plate **(see illustration)**. Lubricate the weight pivot posts on the plate with a smear of oil. Fit the weights onto the posts and pivot them across so the slots slide over the dampers **(see illustration)**. Connect the springs **(see illustration)**. Fit the spring seat, spring and side plate **(see illustrations 18.3f, e and d)**. Press the side plate down and fit the E-clips into their grooves in the posts, aligning their ends as shown **(see illustrations)**.

8 Lubricate the one-way clutch housing and body with clean oil. Fit the body into the housing **(see illustration 18.2d)**. Lubricate the rollers. Fit the rollers and springs into their housings **(see illustration 18.2c)**. Fit the washer and secure the assembly with the circlip, making sure it seats in the groove **(see illustrations 18.2b and a)**. Refer to Step 1 and check the one-way clutch.

9 Install the clutch assemblies (Section 17).

19 Clutch (multi-plate) – overhaul

18.7c . . . then push them onto the dampers so they locate in the slots . . .

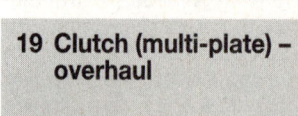

18.7d . . . and hook up the springs . . .

Disassembly

1 Remove the clutch assemblies (Section 17). Have an assistant hold the clutch, or hold it

18.7e . . . as shown

18.7f Fit each E-clip into its groove . . .

18.7g . . . and align the open end as shown

Engine, clutch and transmission 2•35

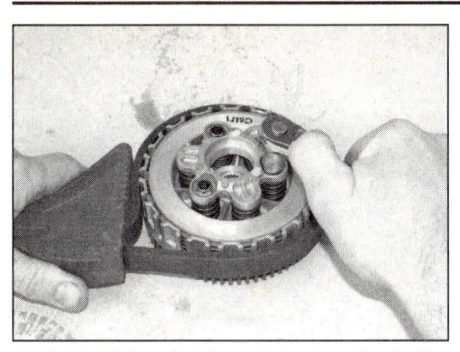

19.1 Hold the clutch and slacken the bolts

19.2a Lift the clutch plate assembly out ...

19.2b ... and remove the washer ...

yourself using a rotor strap, and working in a criss-cross pattern gradually slacken the clutch lifter plate bolts until pressure is released **(see illustration)**.

2 Grab hold of the lifter plate and draw the clutch plate assembly out of the clutch housing, noting how the friction plate tabs locate **(see illustration)**. Remove the washer from the clutch housing **(see illustration)**. If the clutch guide didn't stay on the shaft remove it from the housing **(see illustration)**.

3 Remove the bolts, lifter plate and springs **(see illustrations)**. Place the clutch centre face down and remove the pressure plate from the back **(see illustration)**.

4 Remove the clutch friction and plain plates, noting how they fit and keeping them in order **(see illustrations 19.12b and a)**.

Inspection

5 After an extended period of service the clutch friction plates will wear and promote clutch slip. Measure the thickness of each friction plate using a Vernier calliper **(see illustration)**. If any plate has worn to or beyond the service limit specified at the beginning of the Chapter, or if any of the plates smell burnt or are glazed, the friction plates must be replaced with a new set.

6 The plain plates should not show any signs of excess heating (bluing). Check for warpage using a flat surface and feeler gauges **(see illustration)**. If any plate exceeds the maximum warpage specified, or shows signs

19.2c ... and the guide if there

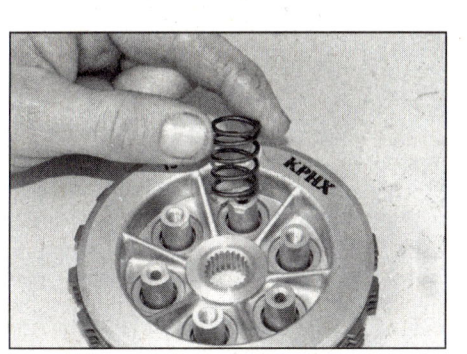

19.3b ... and the springs

of bluing, all plain plates must be replaced with a new set.

7 Measure the free length of each clutch

19.3a Unscrew the bolts and remove the lifter plate ...

19.3c Turn the assembly over and remove the pressure plate

spring **(see illustration)**. Place each spring upright on a flat surface and check it for bend by placing a ruler against it, or alternatively lay

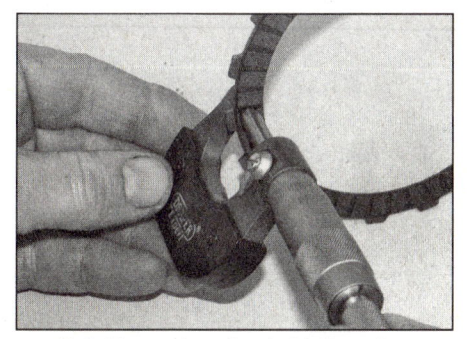

19.5 Measuring clutch friction plate thickness

19.6 Check the plain plates for warpage

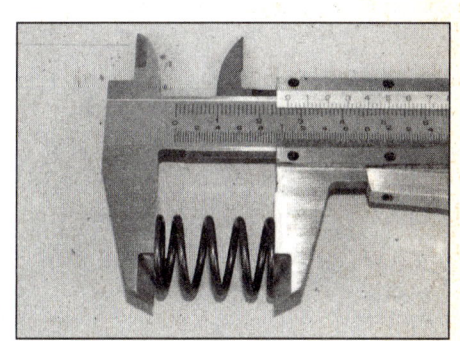

19.7 Measure the free length of the clutch springs and check them for bend

2•36 Engine, clutch and transmission

19.8a Check the friction plate tabs and housing slots . . .

19.8b . . . and the plain plate teeth and centre slots as described

19.9 Check the bearing surfaces on the bush (A), the guide (B) and the shaft

19.10 Check the lifter plate and its bearing

it against a set square. If any spring is below the minimum free length specified or if the bend in any spring is excessive, replace all the springs as a set.

8 Inspect the friction plate tabs and the clutch housing slots for burrs and indentations on the edges **(see illustration)**. Similarly check for wear between the inner teeth of the plain plates and the slots in the clutch centre **(see illustration)**. Wear of this nature will cause clutch drag and slow disengagement during gear changes as the plates will snag when the pressure plate is lifted. With care a small amount of wear can be corrected by dressing with a fine file, but if this is excessive the worn components should be replaced with new ones.

9 Inspect the bearing surfaces of the clutch housing bush and on the clutch guide and input shaft **(see illustration)**. Measure the internal diameter of the bush, the external and internal diameters of the guide and the external diameter of the input shaft where the guide sits, and compare the results to the specifications at the beginning of the Chapter. If there are any signs of wear, pitting or other damage the affected parts must be replaced with new ones.

10 Check the lifter plate and its bearing for signs of wear or damage and roughness **(see illustration)**. Check that the bearing outer race is a good fit in the centre of the lifter, and that the inner race rotates freely without any rough spots. Refer to Section 20 for all other lifter mechanism components. Replace any parts necessary with new ones.

11 Check the teeth of the primary driven gear on the back of the clutch housing and the corresponding teeth of the primary drive gear on the centrifugal clutch drum (see Section 18) **(see illustration 18.4a)**.

Reassembly

12 Place the clutch centre outer face down on the bench. Coat each clutch plate with engine oil, then build up the plates in the housing, starting with a friction plate, then a plain plate, alternating friction and plain plates until all are installed, and aligning the friction plate tabs **(see illustrations)**.

19.12a Fit a friction plate first . . .

19.12b . . . then fit a plain plate and so on . . .

Engine, clutch and transmission 2•37

19.13 ... then fit the pressure plate, aligning the marks and making sure the castellations engage

19.15a Grease the washer and place it on the clutch housing

19.15b Slide the clutch assembly onto the guide to align everything ...

19.15c ... then tighten the bolts to the specified torque

13 Fit the pressure plate into the back of the pack, aligning the mark on the plate with that on the clutch centre, and making sure its castellations locate in the teeth of the inner plain plate **(see illustration)**. Turn the pack over and check there is no gap between the pressure plate and the upper friction plate – if there is, it means the pressure plate has not located properly.

14 Fit the clutch springs and the lifter plate, then tighten the bolts just enough to keep the assembly held together, but so the friction plates are just free enough to move **(see illustrations 19.3b and a)**. Make sure the friction plate tabs are aligned.

15 Fit the washer into the clutch housing, using some dabs of grease to stick it in place **(see illustration)**. Fit the clutch plate assembly into the clutch housing, locating the friction plate tabs in the slots **(see illustration 19.2a)**. Slide the spacer and clutch guide onto the transmission shaft **(see illustrations 17.11a and b)**. Slide the clutch assembly onto the shaft and over the guide **(see illustration)**

– this aligns the washer, clutch housing and clutch centre (if the assembly won't slide on the washer has probably slipped out of place between the housing and the centre). Hold the clutch and tighten the lifter plate bolts evenly and a little at a time in a criss-cross sequence to the torque setting specified at the beginning of the Chapter **(see illustration)**.

16 Slide the assembly off the shaft and remove the guide and spacer.

17 Install the clutch assemblies (Section 17).

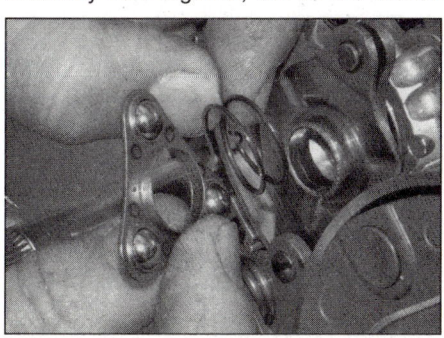

20 Clutch lifter/brake mechanism

Note: *The clutch lifter/brake mechanism can be removed with the engine in the frame.*

Removal

1 Remove the clutch cover (see Section 16).
2 Remove the ball lifter and spring from the cam plate **(see illustration)**.
3 Remove the clutch brake/lever assembly from the gearchange shaft, noting its alignment with the shaft and how it locates over the post on the cam plate **(see illustration)**.

20.2 Remove the ball lifter and spring ...

20.3 ... the brake/lever assembly ...

2•38 Engine, clutch and transmission

4 Remove the lifter cam plate from the clutch **(see illustration)**.

Inspection

5 Check the surface of the clutch lifter adjuster plate in the clutch cover, the ball lifter, balls, spring and the cam plate for distortion, wear and damage **(see illustration)**.

6 If required unscrew the nut on the adjuster bolt in the clutch cover and remove the washer and O-ring, then draw the lifter and adjuster bolt out of the cover **(see illustrations)**. Discard the O-ring – a new one must be used. Thread the bolt out of the plate **(see illustration)**. Replace any worn or damaged components with new ones. Reassemble the plate on the adjuster bolt and fit it into the cover, locating the peg in the hole. Fit a new O-ring smeared with oil over the outer end of the bolt and into the gap between it and the cover **(see illustration)**. Fit the washer and the nut, but do not fully tighten it as the mechanism must be adjusted after installing the cover **(see illustration)**.

7 Check the brake lever assembly for damage. Make sure the brake moves smoothly around its post and returns under pressure of the spring **(see illustration)**. Measure the amount of friction material on the brake shoe and replace the brake with a new one if it has worn to the limit specified **(see illustration)**. To remove the brake from the lever, release the E-clip and remove the washer, then draw the brake and spring off the post on the lever, noting how the spring seats around the lug **(see illustration)**. Check the spring for damage and distortion, and replace it with a new one if necessary. Fit the spring onto the brake with its ends on each side of the lug. Fit the brake and spring onto the lever, seating the spring around the lug.

20.4 . . . and the cam plate

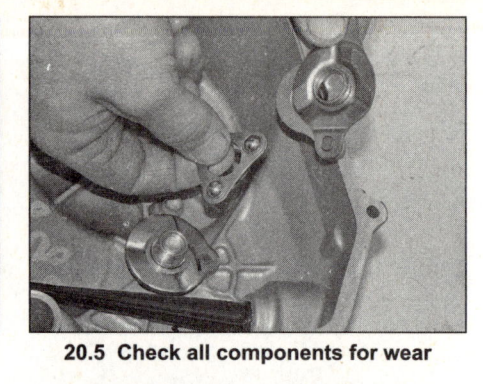

20.5 Check all components for wear

20.6a Hold the screw and undo the nut

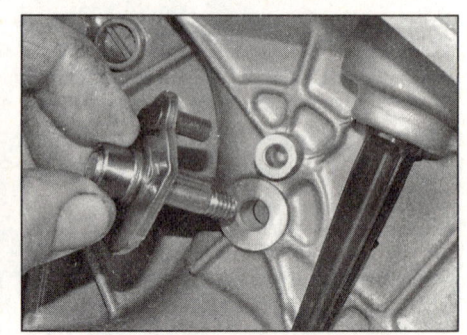

20.6b Draw the lifter/adjuster out

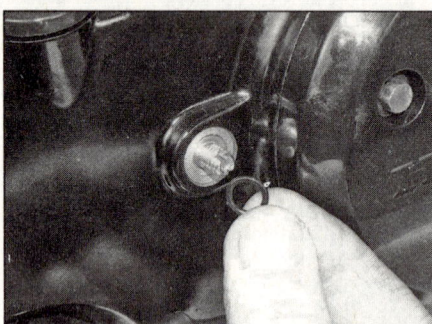

Installation

8 Fit the lifter cam plate onto the lifter bearing **(see illustration 20.4)**.

9 Fit the clutch brake/lever assembly onto the gearchange shaft, aligning the punch mark on

20.6c If required thread the adjuster bolt out of the plate

20.6d Use a new O-ring

20.6e Fit the washer and lightly tighten the nut only

20.7a Check the action of the brake

20.7b Measure the amount of brake friction material

20.7c Remove the E-clip (arrowed) to free the brake

Engine, clutch and transmission 2•39

20.9 Align the punch mark on the lever with the line on the shaft

21.4 Push the arm down and withdraw the shaft/arm assembly, noting how it fits

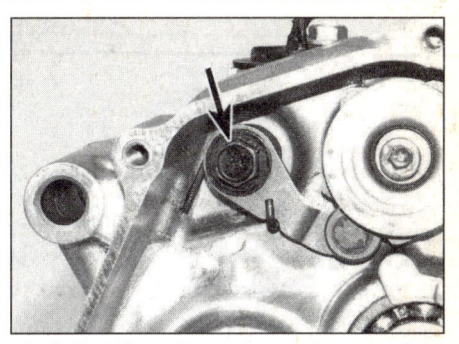

21.5 Note how the spring ends and roller locate, then unscrew the bolt (arrowed) and remove the arm

the lever with the index line on the shaft **(see illustration)**, and locating it over the post on the cam plate **(see illustration 20.3)**.
10 Fit the spring onto the ball lifter, then fit them onto the lifter cam plate **(see illustration 20.2)**.
11 Install the clutch cover (see Section 16).

21 Gearchange mechanism

Note: *The gearchange mechanism can be removed with the engine in the frame.*

Removal

1 Make sure the transmission is in neutral. Remove the clutch cover and clutch assemblies (see Sections 16 and 17).
2 Remove the gearchange lever (see Chapter 5).
3 Wrap a single layer of thin insulating tape around the gearchange shaft splines to protect the oil seal lips as the shaft is removed.
4 Note how the gearchange shaft centralising spring ends fit on each side of the locating pin in the casing, and how the pawls on the selector arm locate onto the pins on the end of the selector drum behind the cam plate. Grasp the end of the shaft, then push the selector arm down until it clears the cam plate and withdraw the shaft/arm assembly **(see illustration)**.

5 Note how the stopper arm spring ends locate and how the roller on the arm locates in the neutral detent on the selector drum cam, then unscrew the stopper arm bolt and remove the arm with the washer and spring, noting how they fit **(see illustration)**.
6 If the crankcases are being separated or otherwise required, unscrew the cam plate holder bolt **(see illustration)** – the drum will turn initially but then come against a stop, allowing the bolt to unscrew. Remove the holder, noting that there are five small pins pressed into the cam plate behind it – they should not be loose but take care just in case **(see illustration)**. Remove the cam plate, noting there are two pins that locate the plate on the end of the selector drum –

they should stay in the end of the drum, but again take care that they could drop out **(see illustration)**. Remove them from the drum for safekeeping **(see illustration)**.

Inspection

7 Check the selector arm for cracks, distortion and wear of its pawls, and check for any corresponding wear on the pins on the selector drum cam plate **(see illustration)**. Also check the stopper arm roller and the detents in the cam plate for any wear or damage, and make sure the roller turns freely **(see illustration)**. Replace any components that are worn or damaged with new ones – the selector arm can be slid off the shaft after removing

21.6a Unscrew the bolt (arrowed) and remove the holder . . .

21.6b . . . the cam plate . . .

21.6c . . . and the locating pins

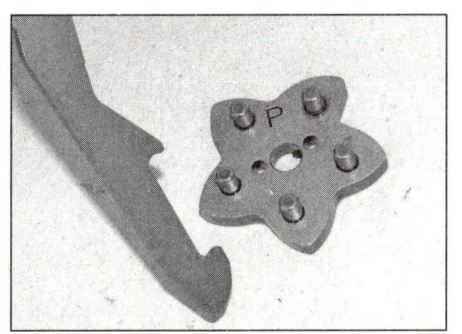

21.7a Check the selector arm pawls and cam plate pins . . .

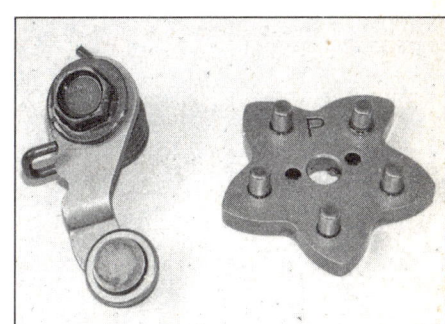

21.7b . . . and the stopper arm roller and cam plate detents

2•40 Engine, clutch and transmission

21.7c Slide the centralising spring (arrowed) off, followed by the arm

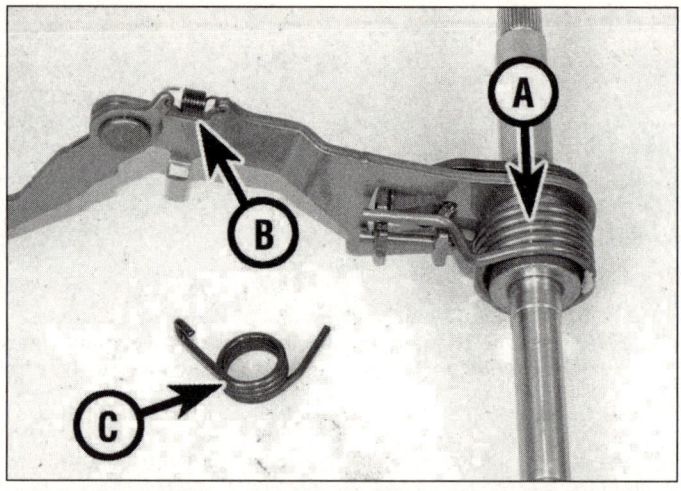

21.8a Centralising spring (A), selector arm spring (B), stopper arm spring (C)

the centralising spring **(see illustration)**. If required (and not already done), refer to Step 6 for removal of the cam plate, and to Step 10 for installation.

8 Inspect the shaft centralising spring, the selector arm spring and the stopper arm return spring for fatigue, wear or damage **(see illustration)**. If any is found, they must be replaced with new ones. To replace the shaft spring, slide it off the end of the shaft, noting how its ends locate **(see illustration 21.7c)**. Fit the new spring, locating the ends on each side of the tabs **(see illustration)**. To replace the selector arm spring simply unhook its ends. Also check that the centralising spring locating pin in the crankcase is securely tightened. If it is loose, remove it and apply a non-permanent thread locking compound to its threads, then tighten it.

9 Check the gearchange shaft is straight and look for damage to the splines. If the shaft is bent you can attempt to straighten it, but if the splines are damaged the shaft must be replaced with a new one. Also check the condition of the shaft oil seal in the left-hand side of the crankcase. If it is damaged, deteriorated or shows signs of leakage it must be replaced with a new one, but note that it is a good idea to fit a new one whatever its apparent condition – lever out the old seal with a seal hook or screwdriver. Press or drive the new seal squarely into place using your fingers, a seal driver or suitable socket **(see illustration)**.

Installation

10 If removed, fit the cam plate locating pins into the end of the selector drum **(see illustration 21.6c)**. Locate the cam plate onto the pins **(see illustration 21.6b)**. Clean the threads of the cam plate bolt and apply a suitable non-permanent thread locking compound. Fit the bolt into the holder, locate them on the cam plate and tighten the bolt to the torque setting specified at the beginning of the Chapter **(see illustration)**.

11 Clean the threads of the stopper arm bolt. Fit the bolt through the stopper arm, then fit the washer **(see illustration)**. Apply a suitable non-permanent thread locking compound to the bolt. Fit the stopper arm spring onto its post with the curved end outermost and the inner end against the back of the crankcase. Install the arm, locating the roller onto the neutral detent on the selector drum and making sure the spring ends are positioned correctly **(see illustration 21.5)**. Tighten the bolt to the torque setting specified at the beginning of the Chapter.

12 Check that the shaft centralising spring is properly positioned **(see illustration 21.8b)**. Apply some grease to the lips of the gearchange shaft oil seal in the left-hand side of the crankcase. Slide the shaft into place and push it all the way through the case until the splined end comes out the other side, and push the selector arm down so it fits behind the cam plate **(see illustration 21.4)**. Locate the selector arm pawls onto the pins on the selector drum and the centralising spring ends onto each side of the locating pin in the crankcase.

21.8b Make sure the spring ends locate correctly

21.9 Lever out the seal and press a new one into place

21.10 Apply threadlock and fit the bolt with the holder

21.11 Locate the spring then fit the bolt with the arm and the washer on it

Engine, clutch and transmission 2•41

21.13 This is how it should all be positioned

13 Check that all components are correctly positioned (see illustration).
14 Install the clutches (see Section 17). Install the gearchange lever (see Chapter 5).

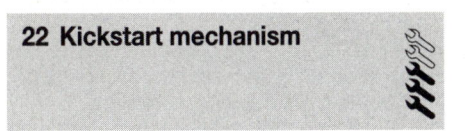

22 Kickstart mechanism

Note: *The kickstart mechanism return spring and retainer can be removed with the engine in the frame. To remove the shaft and gears the engine must be removed and the crankcases separated.*

Return spring removal

1 Remove the clutch cover (see Section 16).
2 Carefully unhook the spring end from its rest on the crankcase and allow it relax, then remove the spring, noting how its other end locates against the retainer.

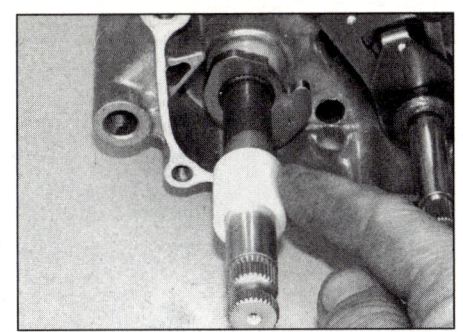

22.3a Slide off the outer sleeve . . .

3 Remove the outer sleeve (see illustration). Note the position of the retainer, then slide it off the shaft, followed by the inner sleeve (see illustration).

Shaft and gear removal

4 Remove the engine and separate the crankcase halves (see Section 24).
5 Grasp the inner end of the shaft and draw it out of the crankcase (see illustration).
6 The thrust washer on the inner end of the shaft has a slightly out-of round section on its inner rim that locates in a groove in the shaft. To remove the washer slip one or two flat-bladed screwdrivers behind it and lever it up so it is forced out of the groove and off the end of the shaft (see illustration).
7 Release the outer circlip then slide the ratchet pinion off (see illustrations). Release the inner circlip then slide the thrust washer and idle pinion off (see illustrations).

22.3b . . . the retainer . . .

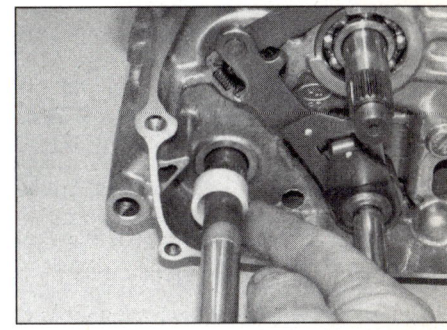

22.3c . . . and the inner sleeve

Inspection

8 Clean all the components in solvent.
9 Check the teeth on each pinion and the helical splines between the ratchet pinion and the shaft for wear and damage (see illustration).

22.5 Lift the shaft out of the crankcase

22.6 Remove the washer as described

22.7a Release the circlip . . .

22.7b . . . and remove the ratchet pinion

22.7c Expand the circlip then push it along the shaft using the gear

22.9 Check the teeth and splines for wear and damage

2•42 Engine, clutch and transmission

22.13a Fit the pinion . . .

22.13b . . . and the thrust washer . . .

22.13c . . . and secure them with the circlip

10 Check the return spring and friction spring (around the ratchet pinion) for deformation, wear and damage and replace them with new ones if necessary.

11 Check the shaft, the sleeves and the shaft bore in each crankcase half for wear. Check the shaft is straight. Measure the internal diameter of the idle gear and outside diameter of the section of shaft it runs on, and replace either with a new one if worn beyond the limit specified.

12 Check the circlips and washers for deformation. If the circlips distorted on removal or did not feel tight replace them with new ones – it is a good idea to fit new ones whatever the apparent condition of the old.

Gear and shaft installation

13 Lubricate the shaft helical splines and where the idle pinion runs with oil. Slide the idle pinion on with its toothed face towards the inner end of the shaft **(see illustration)**. Slide the thrust washer on **(see illustration)**. Fit the circlip with is chamfered side facing the thrust washer, making sure it locates in the groove **(see illustration)** – when installing the circlips, do not expand its ends any further than is necessary, and make sure the ends are against rather than between the splines as shown **(see illustration 22.14c)**.

14 If removed fit the friction spring into the groove in the ratchet pinion. Slide the pinion on with its toothed face towards that of the idle pinion. Fit the circlip with is chamfered side facing the pinion, making sure it locates in the groove **(see illustrations)**.

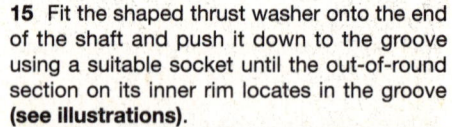

15 Fit the shaped thrust washer onto the end of the shaft and push it down to the groove using a suitable socket until the out-of-round section on its inner rim locates in the groove **(see illustrations)**.

16 Slide the shaft into the crankcase **(see illustration 22.5)** and seat the friction spring loop in the cut-out **(see illustration)**.

17 Assemble the crankcase halves (see Section 24).

Return spring installation

18 Smear some oil over the shaft splines and inside the sleeves. Slide the inner sleeve onto the shaft **(see illustration 22.3c)**. Slide the retainer onto the splines with the OUT mark facing out **(see illustration 22.3b)**, butting its lower edge against the stop on the crankcase

22.14a Fit the ratchet pinion . . .

22.14b . . . and the circlip . . .

22.14c . . . making sure it locates correctly

22.15a Fit the washer onto the end of the shaft . . .

22.15b . . . and push it down to the groove using a socket

22.16 Locate the friction spring loop as shown

Engine, clutch and transmission 2•43

22.18 Make sure the retainer is aligned so it butts against the crankcase

23.2a Unscrew the bolts . . .

23.2b . . . and remove the pump

(see illustration). Slide the outer sleeve on (see illustration 22.3a).
19 Slide the spring on with its ends innermost, and hook the inward facing end onto the retainer. Grasp the other end with pliers and wind the spring round so you can locate the end on its rest on the crankcase.
20 Install the clutch cover (see Section 16).

23 Oil pump

Note: *The oil pump can be removed with the engine in the frame. If the engine has been removed, ignore the steps which don't apply.*

Removal

1 Remove the clutch cover (see Section 16).
2 Unscrew the three bolts and remove the pump from the crankcase (see illustrations).
3 If required slide the oil pump drive gear off the crankshaft and remove the locating pin (see illustration).

Inspection

Note: *When removing the rotors from the oil pump, keep them the right way up so they can be fitted the same way in reassembly to ensure that mated surfaces continue to run together.*
4 Remove the E-clip from the outer end of the shaft (see illustration). Lift the gear and draw the shaft out of the pump (see illustration).

Remove the drive pin and slide the gear off the shaft (see illustration).
5 Remove the dowels, then unscrew the bolts and remove the cover (see illustration). Remove the inner and outer rotors, noting which way round they fit (see illustration).
6 Clean all the components in solvent.
7 Inspect the pump body and rotors for scoring and wear. If any damage, scoring or uneven or excessive wear is evident, replace the components with new ones.
8 Fit the inner and outer rotors into the pump body the same way as noted on removal (see illustration 23.5b). Fit the shaft into the inner rotor, aligning the flats. Measure the clearance between the inner rotor tip and the outer rotor with a feeler gauge and compare it to the service limit listed in the specifications at the beginning

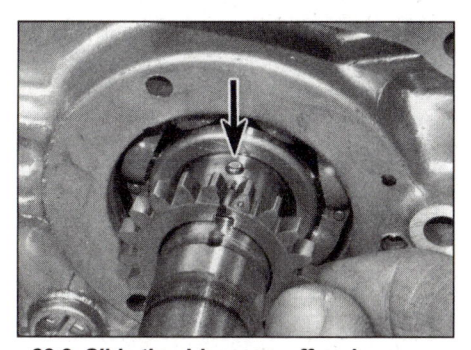

23.3 Slide the drive gear off and remove the drive pin (arrowed)

23.4a Remove the E-clip . . .

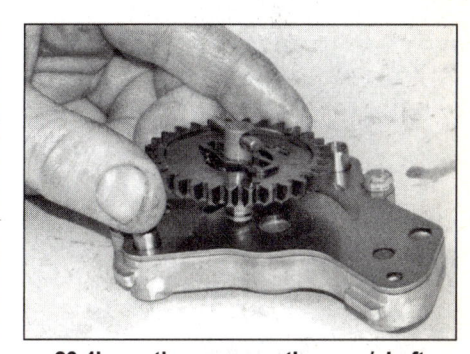

23.4b . . . then remove the gear/shaft assembly

23.4c Slide the gear down the shaft to remove the drive pin

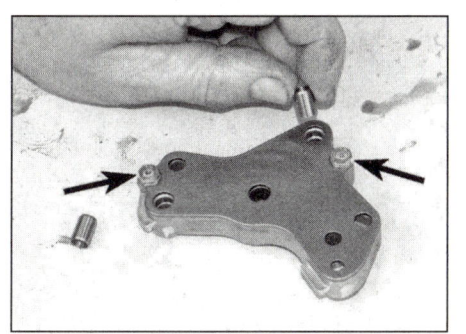

23.5a Remove the dowels then unscrew the bolts (arrowed) and remove the cover . . .

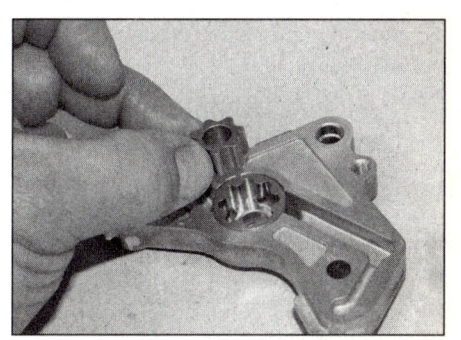

23.5b . . . and the rotors

2•44 Engine, clutch and transmission

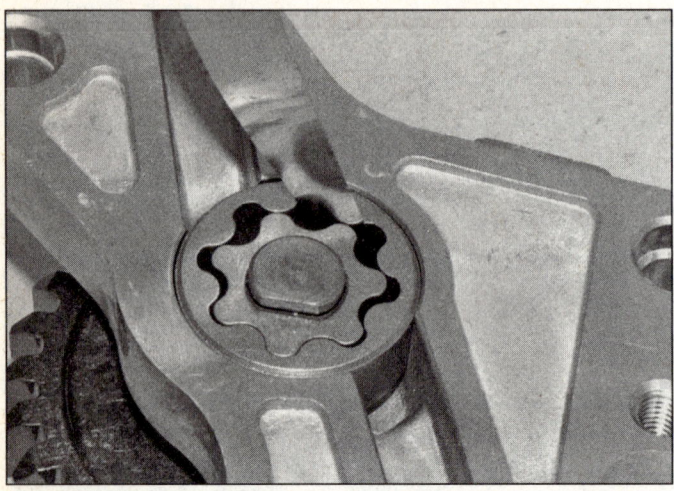

23.8 Measure the inner rotor tip-to-outer rotor clearance as shown (inner cover shown removed for clarity)

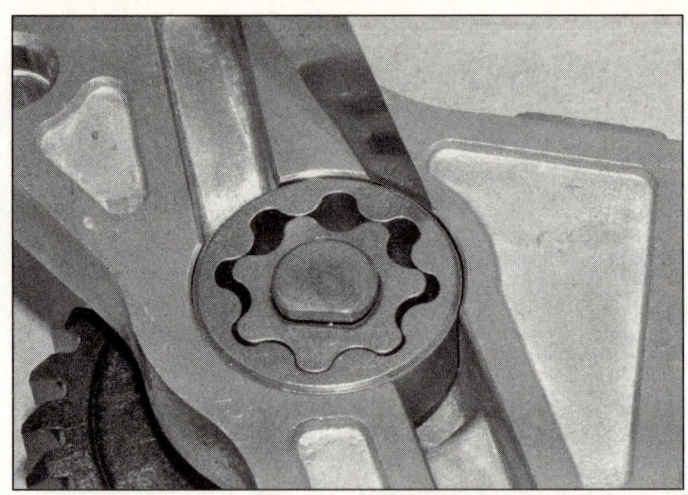

23.9 Measure the outer rotor-to-body clearance as shown

of the Chapter **(see illustration)**. If the clearance measured is greater than the maximum listed, replace the rotors with new ones.

9 Measure the clearance between the outer rotor and the pump body with a feeler gauge and compare it to the maximum clearance listed in the specifications at the beginning of the Chapter **(see illustration)**. If the clearance measured is greater than the maximum listed, replace the outer rotor and pump body with new ones.

10 Remove the shaft. Lay a straight-edge across the rotors and the pump body and, using a feeler gauge, measure the rotor end-float (the gap between the rotors and the straight-edge **(see illustration)**. If the clearance measured is greater than the maximum listed, replace the rotors and pump body with new ones.

11 Check the pump drive and driven gears, shaft and drive pin for wear or damage, and replace them with new ones if necessary.

12 If the pump is good, make sure all the components are clean and dry, then lubricate them with new engine oil.

13 Fit the outer and inner rotors into the pump body the same way as noted on removal **(see illustration 23.5b)**.

14 Fit the locating dowels then fit the cover onto the pump body **(see illustrations)**. Fit the bolts and tighten them to the torque setting specified at the beginning of the Chapter **(see illustration)**.

15 Fit the gear and drive pin onto the shaft, locating the pin ends into the cut-outs in the gear **(see illustration 23.4c)**. Slide the drive shaft through the pump, aligning the flats between the shaft and inner rotor **(see illustration)**. Fit the E-clip into its groove in the outer end of the shaft **(see illustration)**.

16 Fill the pump with oil. Rotate the pump shaft by hand and check it turns the rotors smoothly and freely.

23.10 Measure rotor end-float as shown

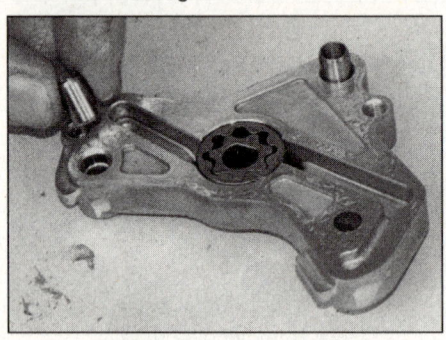

23.14a Fit the dowels . . .

23.14b . . . then the cover . . .

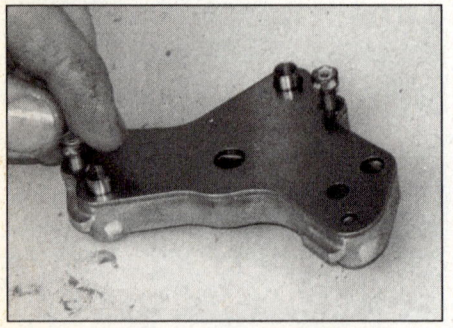

23.14c . . . and the bolts

23.15a Slide the shaft through . . .

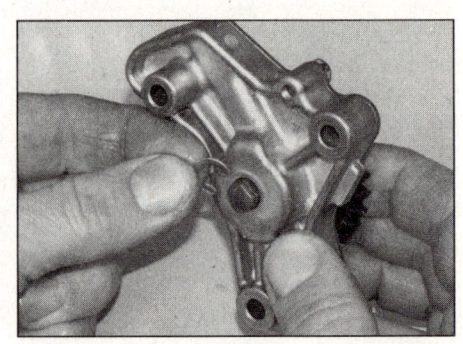

23.15b . . . and secure it with the E-clip

Engine, clutch and transmission 2•45

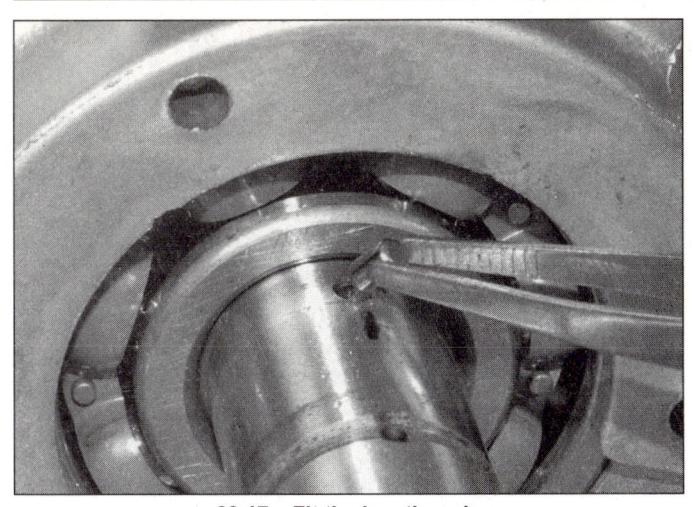

23.17a Fit the locating pin

23.17b ... then locate the cut-out in the gear over it

Installation

17 If removed fit the drive gear locating pin into the crankshaft, then slide the gear on, seating its cut-out over the pin **(see illustrations)**.
18 Fit the pump, making sure the dowels locate in the crankcase, and the gears engage correctly, then fit the bolts and tighten them **(see illustrations 23.2b and a)**.
19 Install the clutch cover (see Section 16).

24 Crankcase separation and reassembly

Note: *To separate the crankcase halves, the engine must be removed from the frame.*

Separation

1 To access the crankshaft and connecting rod assembly, kickstart shaft, transmission shafts, selector drum and forks, and their bearings, the crankcase must be split into its two halves.
2 Before the crankcases can be separated the following components must be removed:
  Starter motor (Chapter 8)
  Gear position switch, plunger and spring
    (Chapter 8)
  Speed sensor (Chapter 8)
  Cylinder head (Section 10)
  Cam chain and blades (Section 9)
  Cylinder block (Section 12)
  Piston (Section 13)
  Alternator and starter clutch gears
    (Chapter 8)
  Clutch cover and oil jet (Section 16)
  Clutch assemblies (Section 17)
  Gearchange mechanism (Section 21)
  Kickstart return spring and retainer
    (Section 22)
  Oil pump and its drive gear (Section 23)
  Oil strainer (Chapter 1)
3 Place the engine on its right-hand side, laying it on wooden blocks so the shaft ends are clear of the bench.

4 Unscrew the eleven crankcase bolts evenly, a little at a time and in a criss-cross sequence until they are finger-tight, then remove them, noting the wiring guide secured by the lower rear bolt **(see illustration)**.
5 Carefully lift the left crankcase half off the right half, using a soft-faced hammer to tap around the joint to initially separate the halves if necessary **(see illustration)**. **Note:** *If the halves do not separate easily, make sure all fasteners have been removed. Do not try and separate the halves by levering against the crankcase mating surfaces as they are easily scored and will leak oil in the future if damaged.* The left-hand crankcase half will come away leaving the crankshaft, transmission shafts, kickstart shaft and selector drum and forks in the right-hand half.
6 Remove the two locating dowels from the crankcase if they are loose (they could be in either half) **(see illustration 24.11)**.
7 Refer to Sections 25 to 29 for the removal and installation of the components housed within the crankcases.

24.4 Crankcase bolts (arrowed) – note the wiring guide (A)

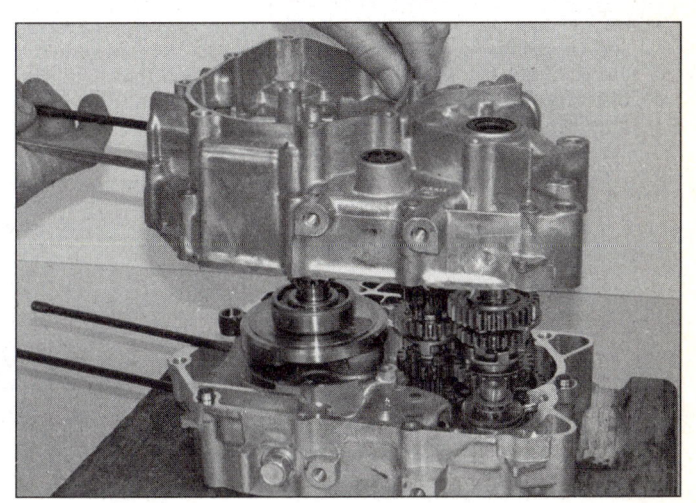

24.5 Carefully separate the crankcase halves

2•46 Engine, clutch and transmission

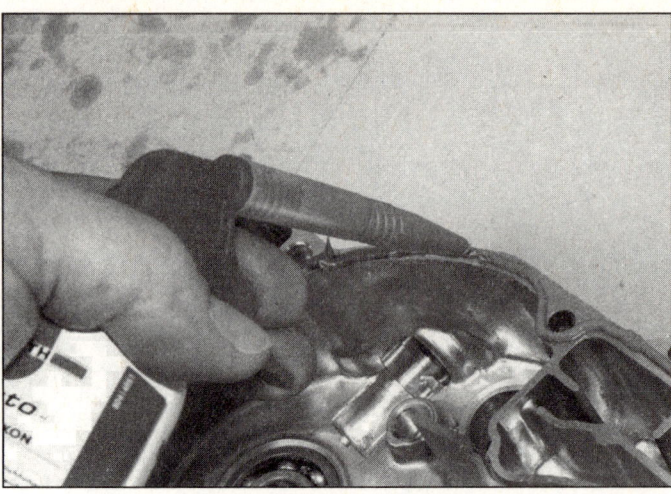

24.11 Make sure the dowels (arrowed) are fitted

24.12a Apply the sealant . . .

Reassembly

8 Remove all traces of sealant from the crankcase mating surfaces. Clean the threads of all the crankcase bolts.
9 Ensure that all components and their bearings are in place in the right-hand crankcase half, and that all bearings and new oil seals are in the left-hand half (see Section 21 for the gearchange shaft oil seal and Section 27 for the transmission output shaft seal).
10 Generously lubricate the crankshaft and transmission shaft bearings and gears and the selector fork shafts and fork ends and the tracks in the selector drum and the kickstart shaft end and pinions with clean engine oil. Now wipe over the mating surfaces of both crankcase halves using a clean rag soaked in high flash-point solvent to remove all traces of oil.
11 If removed, fit the two locating dowels into the right-hand crankcase half **(see illustration)**.
12 Apply a small amount of suitable sealant (Three-Bond 1215 or equivalent RTV sealant – ask your dealer) to the mating surface of the left-hand crankcase half as shown, avoiding the oil passage in the top of the crankcase **(see illustrations)**.
Caution: Apply the sealant only to the mating surfaces. Do not apply an excessive amount as it will ooze out when the case halves are assembled and may obstruct oil passages. Do not apply the sealant close to any of the oil passages.
13 Check again that all components are in position **(see illustration 24.11)**. Carefully fit the left-hand crankcase half down onto the right-hand crankcase half, making sure the shaft ends and dowels all locate correctly **(see illustration 24.5)**.
14 Check that the left-hand crankcase half is correctly seated.
Caution: The crankcase halves should fit together without being forced. If the casings are not correctly seated, remove the left-hand crankcase half and investigate the problem. Do not attempt to pull them together using the crankcase bolts as the casing will crack and be ruined.
15 Install the crankcase bolts, not forgetting the wiring guide with the lower rear bolt **(see illustration and 24.4)**. Secure the bolts finger-tight at first, then tighten them evenly and a little at a time in a criss-cross sequence in three stages – no torque setting is specified, but bolts of that size should tightened to 12 Nm.
16 With all crankcase fasteners tightened, check that the crankshaft and transmission shafts rotate smoothly and easily. Check that the transmission shafts rotate freely and independently in neutral, then rotate the selector drum by hand and select each gear in turn whilst rotating the input shaft. If there are any signs of undue stiffness, tight or rough spots, or of any other problem, the fault must be rectified before proceeding further.
17 Install all other removed assemblies in a reverse of the sequence given in Step 2.

25 Crankcases and bearings

Crankcases

1 After the crankcases have been separated, remove the kickstart shaft, the crankshaft, the selector drum and forks and the transmission shafts, referring to the relevant Sections of this Chapter.
2 Clean the crankcases thoroughly with new solvent and dry them with compressed air. Blow out all oil passages with compressed air.
3 Remove all traces of old sealant from the mating surfaces. Clean up minor damage to the surfaces with a fine sharpening stone or grindstone.
Caution: Be very careful not to nick or gouge the crankcase mating surfaces or oil leaks will result. Check both crankcase halves very carefully for cracks and other damage.
4 Small cracks or holes in aluminium castings can be repaired with an epoxy resin adhesive as a temporary measure or with one of the low temperature welding kits. Permanent repairs can only be done by TIG (tungsten inert gas or heli-arc) welding, and only a specialist in this process is in a position to advise on the economy or practical aspect of such a repair. If any damage is found that can't be repaired, replace the crankcase halves as a set.
5 Damaged threads can be economically reclaimed using a diamond section wire insert, for example of the Heli-Coil type (though there are other makes), which are easily fitted after drilling and re-tapping the affected thread.

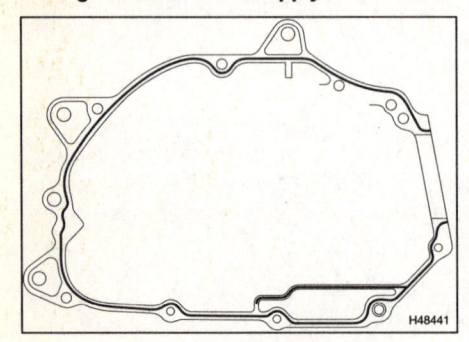

24.12b . . . to the area shown

24.15 Do not forget the wiring guide

Engine, clutch and transmission 2•47

6 Sheared studs or screws can usually be removed with extractors, which consist of a tapered, left-hand thread screw of very hard steel. These are inserted into a pre-drilled hole in the stud, and usually succeed in dislodging the most stubborn stud or screw. If a stud has sheared above its bore line, it can be removed using a conventional stud extractor which avoids the need for drilling.

> **HAYNES HiNT**: *Haynes Hint: Refer to Tools and Workshop Tips for details of installing a thread insert and using screw extractors.*

7 Install all components and assemblies, referring to the relevant Sections of this and the other Chapters, before reassembling the crankcase halves.

Bearing information

8 The crankshaft and transmission shaft bearings should all be replaced with new ones as part of a complete engine overhaul, or individually as required due to wear or failure.

9 Bearing failure occurs mainly because of lack of lubrication, the presence of dirt or other foreign particles, overloading the engine, break-up of one or more of the bearing components due to fatigue, or corrosion. Regardless of the cause of bearing failure, it must be corrected before the engine is reassembled to prevent it from happening again.

10 The bearings should rotate smoothly, freely and quietly, there should be no rough spots, and there should be no excessive play between the inner and outer races, or between the inner race and the shaft it fits on, or between the outer race and its housing in the crankcase.

11 Dirt and other foreign particles get into the engine in a variety of ways. They may be left in the engine during assembly or they may pass through filters or breathers, then get into the oil and from there into the bearings. Metal chips from machining operations and normal engine wear are often present. Abrasives are sometimes left in engine components after reconditioning operations, especially when parts are not thoroughly cleaned using the proper cleaning methods. The best prevention for this cause of bearing failure is to clean all parts thoroughly and keep everything spotlessly clean during engine reassembly. Regular oil changes are also recommended.

12 Lack of lubrication or lubrication breakdown has a number of interrelated causes. Excessive heat (which thins the oil), overloading and oil leakage all contribute to lubrication breakdown. Blocked oil passages will starve a bearing of lubrication and destroy it.

13 Riding habits can have a definite effect on bearing life. Full throttle low, speed operation, or labouring the engine, puts very high loads on bearings. Short trip riding leads to corrosion of bearings, as insufficient engine heat is produced to drive off the condensed water and corrosive gases produced. These products collect in the engine oil, forming acid and sludge. As the oil is carried to the engine bearings, the acid attacks and corrodes the bearing material.

14 Incorrect bearing installation during engine assembly will lead to bearing failure as well. To avoid bearing problems, clean all parts thoroughly before reassembly, and lubricate the new bearings with clean engine oil during installation.

Bearing removal and installation

Note: *If the correct bearing removal and installation tools are not available take the crankcases and crankshaft to a Honda dealer for removal and installation of the bearings – do not risk damaging either the cases or the crankshaft.*

Crankshaft (main) bearings

15 If the crankshaft (main) bearings have failed, excessive rumbling and vibration will be felt when the engine is running.

16 Separate the crankcase halves (Section 24) and remove the crankshaft (Section 26).

17 To remove the right-hand main bearing from the crankcase, heat the bearing housing with a hot air gun, then tap the bearing out from the outside of the crankcase using a bearing driver or a suitable socket. If the bearing is on the crankshaft remove it using an external bearing puller as for the left-hand bearing (Step 19).

18 Smear the outside of the new bearing with clean oil and fit it with its marked side towards the inside of the engine, then heat the housing again and drive the bearing squarely in until it seats using a driver or socket that bears only on the outer race.

19 To remove the left-hand main bearing from the crankshaft, use an external bearing puller as shown to first pull the camshaft sprocket off, and then to pull the bearing off **(see illustration)**.

20 Smear the inside of the new bearing with clean oil and fit it with its marked side towards the crankshaft, then heat the bearing inner race and drive the bearing squarely on until it seats using a tubular driver that bears only on the inner race. Next drive the cam chain sprocket on in the same way, on 2003 to 2006 models making sure it is the correct way round with the sprocket teeth on the inside, on all models aligning the tip of a tooth exactly with the centre line of the slot for the alternator rotor Woodruff key, and on 2007-on models making sure it is set precisely so the distance from the outside of the left-hand crank web to the outer rim of the sprocket is 36.4 ± 1.5 mm as shown **(see illustrations)**.

Connecting rod (big-end) bearing

21 If the connecting rod (big-end) bearing has failed, there will be a pronounced knocking noise when the engine is running, particularly under load and increasing with engine speed. Refer to Section 26, Step 6 for checks that can be made.

22 The bearing is available as part of a kit containing a new connecting rod and crankpin, but the work required to separate the crankshaft webs requires special equipment and a degree of skill and accuracy. Compare the cost of a complete new built-up crankshaft unit against the cost of the connecting rod kit plus that of having to disassemble then reassemble the crankshaft components before making a decision, and bear in mind the new crankshaft will come with a new left-hand main bearing and camshaft sprocket fitted. If you do fit a new crankshaft you should also fit a new right-hand main bearing, which comes separately (Steps 17 and 18).

Transmission shaft bearings

23 If the transmission bearings have failed, excessive rumbling and vibration will be felt when the engine is running.

24 Separate the crankcase halves (Section 24) and remove the transmission shafts and the output shaft oil seal (Section 27).

25 Unscrew the bolts securing the input shaft

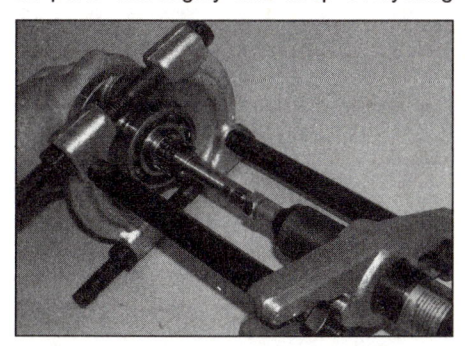

25.19 Using a puller to remove the bearing from a crankshaft

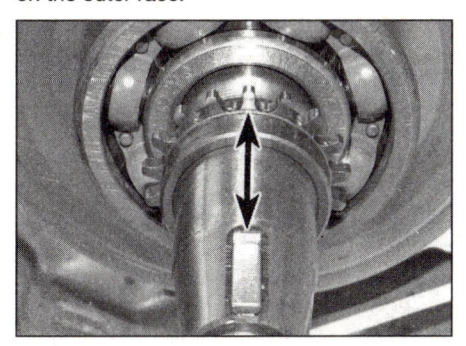

25.20a A tooth must align exactly with the Woodruff key . . .

25.20b . . . and on 2007-on models the distance shown must be exactly as given

2•48 Engine, clutch and transmission

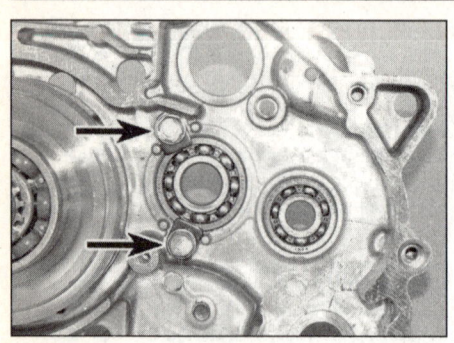

25.25 Unscrew the bolts (arrowed) and remove the plate

25.26 Drive the bearing out from the outside

25.27a Locate the end of the puller behind the bearing . . .

25.27b . . . and use the slide-hammer to jar it out

25.28 Drive the bearing in from the inside until it seats

bearing retainer plates on the inside of the right-hand crankcase **(see illustration)**.

26 To remove the input and output shaft bearings from the right-hand crankcase and the output shaft bearing from the left-hand crankcase, heat the bearing housing with a hot air gun, then tap the bearing out from the outside of the crankcase using a bearing driver or a suitable socket **(see illustration)**.

27 To remove the input shaft bearing from the left-hand crankcase, an expanding knife-edge bearing puller with slide-hammer attachment is required. Heat the bearing housing with a hot air gun, then fit the expanding end of the puller behind the bearing, then turn the puller to expand it and lock it **(see illustration)**. Attach the slide-hammer to the puller, then hold the crankcase firmly down and operate the slide-hammer to jar the bearing out **(see illustration)**.

28 Smear the outside of the new bearing with clean oil and fit it with its marked side towards the inside of the engine, then heat the housing again and drive the bearing squarely in until it seats using a driver or socket that bears only on the outer race **(see illustration)**.

29 Clean the threads of the bearing retainer plate bolts. Apply a suitable non-permanent thread locking compound, then fit the plates and tighten the bolts **(see illustration 25.25)**.

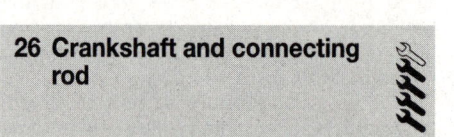

26 Crankshaft and connecting rod

Note: *To remove the crankshaft the engine must be removed from the frame and the crankcase halves separated. Note that some*

26.4 Measure the big-end side clearance using a feeler gauge

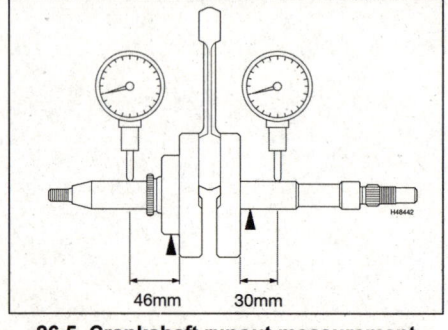

26.5 Crankshaft runout measurement points

of the inspection checks can be made with the crankshaft still in the crankcase.

Removal

1 Remove the engine from the frame (see Section 4) and separate the crankcase halves (see Section 24).

2 The crankshaft needs to be pressed out of the right-hand crankcase using an hydraulic press. DO NOT be tempted to strike the end of the crankshaft – you could bend it. Whenever the crankshaft is removed the right-hand main bearing (which should stay in the crankcase but could come away on the shaft) must be replaced with a new one – see Section 25 for details. As special tools are also required to draw the crankshaft into the crankcase on installation (see Step 10) it is probably best to take the complete crankshaft/right-hand crankcase assembly to a dealer or specialist and get them to perform the operation, including removing and fitting the new bearing.

Inspection

3 Clean the crankshaft with solvent. If available, blow the crank dry with compressed air. Check the camshaft sprocket and the shaft splines for wear or damage. If any of the sprocket teeth are excessively worn, chipped or broken, refer to Section 25, Steps 19 and 20 and replace it with a new one. If the splines are worn or damaged the crankshaft must be replaced with a new one.

4 Measure the connecting rod side clearance (the gap between the connecting rod big-end and the crankshaft web) with a feeler gauge **(see illustration)**. If the clearance is greater than the service limit listed in this Chapter's Specifications, replace the crankshaft with a new one.

5 Place the crankshaft on V-blocks and check for runout in the positions shown and at each end using a dial gauge **(see illustration)**. Compare the reading to the maximum specified at the beginning of the Chapter. If the runout exceeds the limit, the crankshaft must be replaced with a new one.

6 Hold the crankshaft still and check for any radial (up and down) play in the big-end

Engine, clutch and transmission 2•49

26.6 Check for any radial play in the big-end bearing

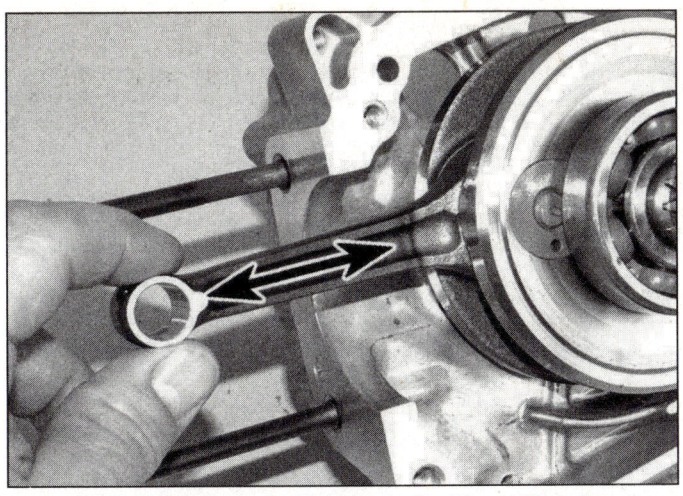

27.3 Lift the transmission shafts out together

bearing by pushing and pulling the rod against the crank **(see illustration)**. If a dial gauge is available measure the amount of radial play and compare the reading to the maximum specified at the beginning of the Chapter. If the play exceeds the limit, the bearing is worn and a new connecting rod kit must be fitted, or the complete crankshaft must be replaced with a new one – see Section 25, Step 22 for more information.
7 Refer to Section 13 and check the connecting rod small-end and piston pin for wear.
8 Have the rod checked for twist and bend by a Honda dealer if you are in doubt about its straightness.
9 Refer to Section 25 and check the crankshaft (main) bearings.

Installation

10 The crankshaft needs to be drawn into the new main bearing in the right-hand crankcase using a special tool, Honda part No. 07JMF-KW70100. This tool supports the thrust through the inner race of the main bearing so

the bearing is not damaged. If the tool or its exact equivalent is not available, or cannot be fabricated, have the crankshaft installed by a dealer equipped with the tool. If doing the job yourself, make sure that as you draw the crankshaft in the connecting rod is correctly aligned with the crankcase mouth – if it contacts the crankcase it will get bent.
11 Check that the crankshaft rotates freely and easily.
12 Reassemble the crankcase halves (see Section 24).

27 Transmission shafts removal and installation

Note: *To remove the transmission shafts the engine must be removed from the frame and the crankcases separated.*

Removal

1 Remove the engine from the frame and separate the crankcase halves (see Section 24).

2 Remove the selector drum and forks (see Section 29).
3 Grasp the input shaft and output shaft together and lift both shafts out of the crankcase **(see illustrations)**. If the shafts are stuck, use a soft-faced hammer and gently tap on their ends.
4 Prise the output shaft oil seal out of the left-hand crankcase using a seal hook or screwdriver **(see illustration)**. Discard the seal as a new one must be used.
5 If necessary, the transmission shafts can be disassembled and inspected for wear or damage (see Section 28).
6 Refer to Section 25 and check the transmission shaft bearings.

Installation

7 Press or drive a new output shaft oil seal into the left-hand crankcase, setting it flush with the surface **(see illustration)**. Lubricate its lips with oil.
8 Join the shafts together on the bench so their related gears are engaged. Grasp the shafts together and fit them into the right-hand

27.4 Remove and discard the oil seal

27.7 Press the new seal into place so it is flush with the rim

2•50 Engine, clutch and transmission

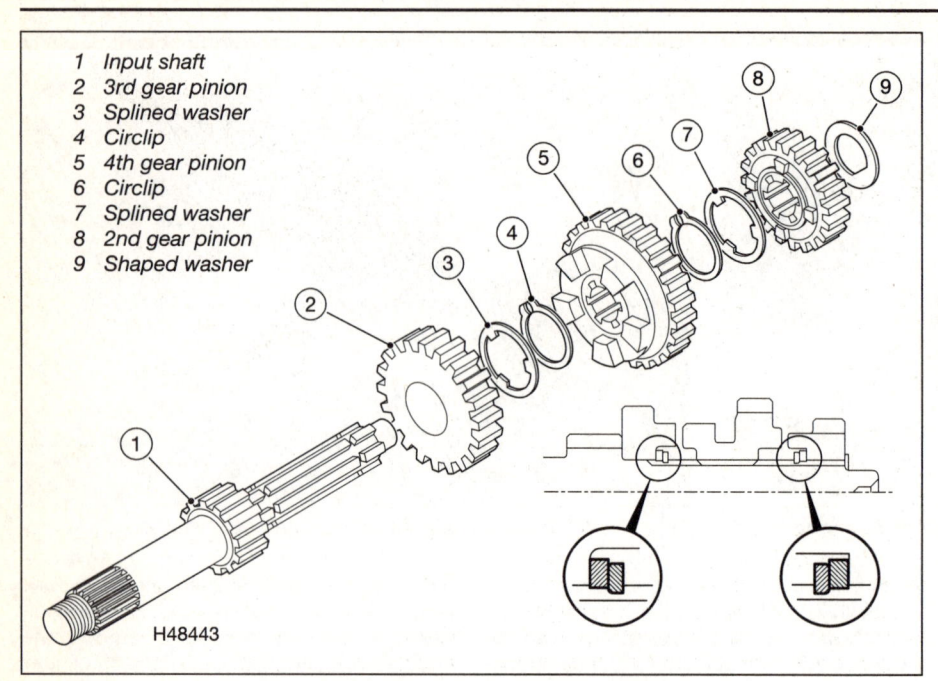

28.1a Transmission input shaft components

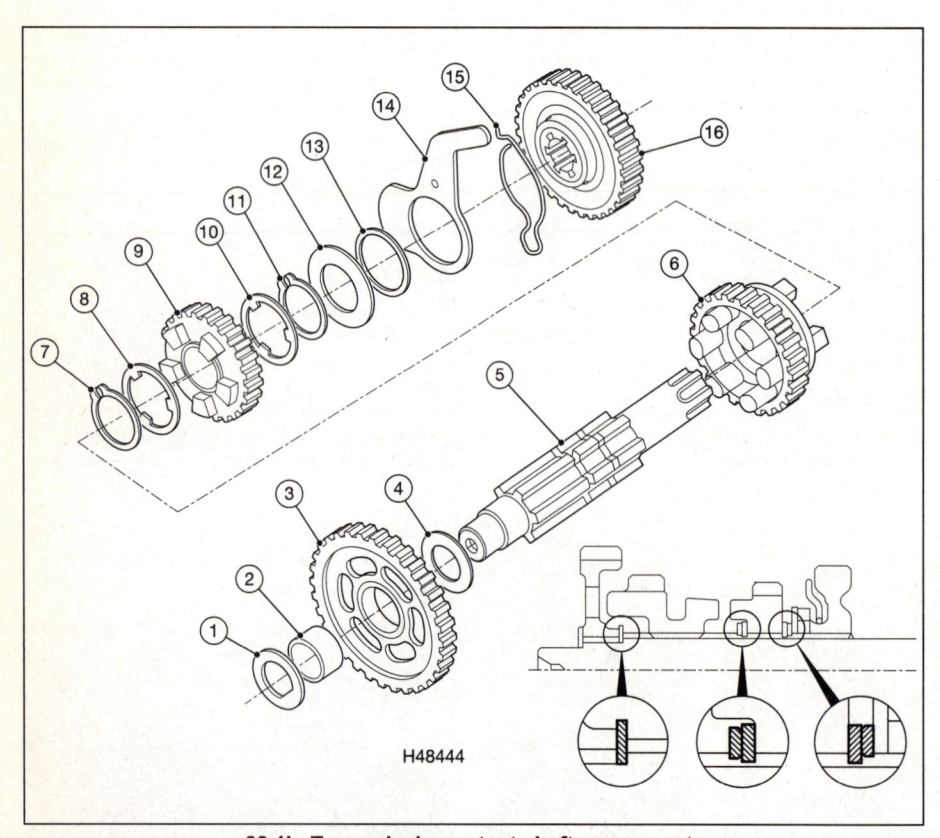

1 Input shaft
2 3rd gear pinion
3 Splined washer
4 Circlip
5 4th gear pinion
6 Circlip
7 Splined washer
8 2nd gear pinion
9 Shaped washer

28.1b Transmission output shaft components

1 Shaped washer	7 Circlip	12 Thrust washer
2 1st gear pinion bush	8 Splined washer	13 Collar
3 1st gear pinion	9 4th gear pinion	14 Locking arm
4 Thrust washer	10 Splined washer	15 Friction spring
5 Output shaft	11 Circlip	16 2nd gear pinion
6 3rd gear pinion		

crankcase, locating the shaft ends in the bearings **(see illustration 27.3)**.
9 Make sure both transmission shafts are correctly seated and their related pinions are correctly engaged.
10 Install the selector drum and forks (see Section 29).
11 Position the gears in the neutral position and check the shafts are free to rotate easily and independently (i.e. the input shaft can turn whilst the output shaft is held stationary) before proceeding further. Also check that each gear can be selected by turning the input shaft with one hand and the selector drum with the other.
12 Reassemble the crankcase halves (see Section 24).

28 Transmission shafts overhaul

1 Remove the transmission shafts from the crankcase (see Section 27). Always disassemble the transmission shafts separately to avoid mixing up the components **(see illustrations)**.

Input shaft

Disassembly

2 The thrust washer on the left-hand end of the shaft has a slightly out-of-round section on its inner rim that locates in a groove in the shaft. To remove the washer slip one or two flat-bladed screwdrivers behind the 2nd gear pinion and lever it up so the washer is forced out of the groove and off the end of the shaft **(see illustration)**. Slide the 2nd gear pinion off the left-hand end of the shaft, followed by the splined washer **(see illustrations 28.16b and a)**.
3 Remove the circlip then slide the 4th gear pinion off the shaft **(see illustrations 28.15b and a)**.
4 Remove the circlip then slide the splined washer and the 3rd gear pinion off the shaft **(see illustrations 28.14c, b and a)**.

HAYNES HINT

When disassembling the transmission shafts, place the parts on a long rod or thread a wire through them to keep them in order and facing the proper direction.

Engine, clutch and transmission 2•51

28.2 Use a screwdriver to lever the washer out of the groove

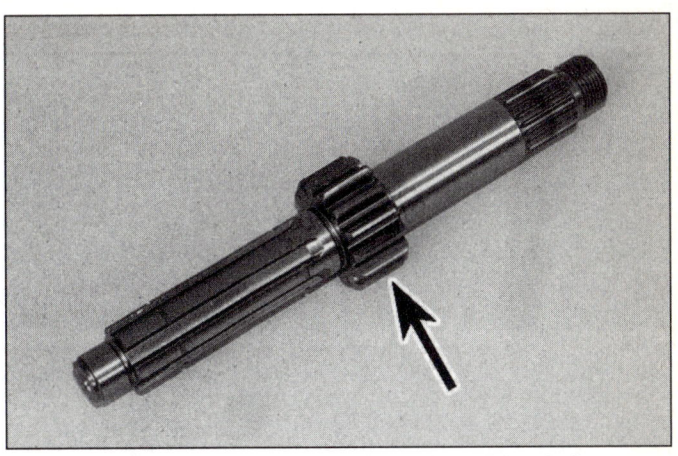

28.5 1st gear pinion (arrowed) is part of the shaft

5 The 1st gear pinion is integral with the shaft **(see illustration)**.

Inspection

6 Wash all of the components in clean solvent and dry them off.

7 Check the gear teeth for cracking, chipping, pitting and other obvious wear or damage. Any pinion that is damaged as such must be replaced with a new one.

8 Inspect the dogs and the dog holes in the gears for cracks, chips, and excessive wear especially in the form of rounded edges. Make sure mating gears engage properly. Replace the paired gears as a set if necessary.

9 Check for signs of scoring or bluing on the pinions, bush (output shaft) and shaft. This could be caused by overheating due to inadequate lubrication. Check that all the oil holes and passages are clear. Replace any damaged parts.

10 Check that each pinion moves freely on the shaft or its bush but without undue freeplay. On the output shaft check that the 1st gear pinion bush moves freely on the shaft but without undue freeplay. If the necessary equipment is available the individual components for which dimensions are given in the Specifications at the beginning of this Chapter can be measured to assess the extent of wear.

11 The shaft is unlikely to sustain damage unless the engine has seized, placing an unusually high loading on the transmission, or the machine has covered a very high mileage. Check the surface of the shaft, especially where a pinion turns on it, and replace the shaft if it has scored or picked up, or if there are any cracks. Damage of any kind can only be cured by replacement.

12 Check the washers and circlips and replace any that are bent or appear weakened or worn. Use new ones if in any doubt. Note that it is good practice to use new circlips when overhauling gearshafts.

Reassembly

13 During reassembly, apply molybdenum disulphide oil (a 50/50 mixture of molybdenum disulphide grease and clean engine oil) to the mating surfaces of the shaft and pinions. When installing the circlips, do not expand their ends any further than is necessary. Install the stamped circlips and washers so that their chamfered side faces away from the thrust side.

14 Slide the 3rd gear pinion onto the shaft with its dogs facing away from the integral 1st gear **(see illustration)**. Slide the splined washer onto the shaft, then fit the circlip, making sure that it locates correctly in the groove in the shaft **(see illustrations)**.

15 Slide the 4th gear pinion onto the shaft with the selector fork groove facing the 3rd gear pinion **(see illustration)**. Fit the circlip,

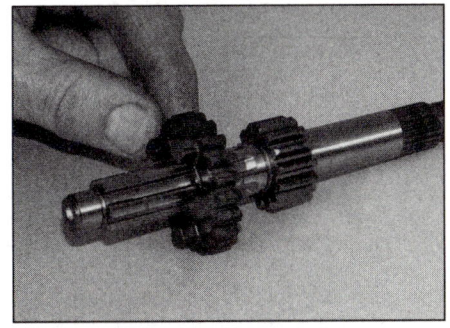

28.14a Slide the 3rd gear pinion . . .

28.14b . . . and the splined washer onto the shaft . . .

28.14c . . . and secure them with the circlip . . .

28.14d . . . making sure it locates properly in its groove

28.15a Slide the 4th gear pinion onto the shaft . . .

2•52 Engine, clutch and transmission

28.15b . . . and secure it with the circlip . . .

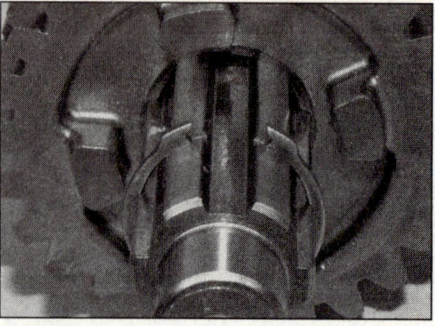

28.15c . . . making sure it locates properly in its groove

28.16a Slide the splined washer . . .

28.16b . . . and the 2nd gear pinion onto the shaft

28.17a Fit the shaped washer . . .

28.17b . . . and use a socket to push it into the groove

making sure it is locates correctly in its groove in the shaft **(see illustrations)**.

16 Slide the splined washer onto the shaft, followed by the 2nd gear pinion, with its dogs face the 4th gear pinion **(see illustrations)**.

17 Fit the shaped thrust washer onto the end of the shaft and drift it down to the groove using a suitable socket until the out-of-round section on its inner rim locates in the groove **(see illustrations)**.

18 Check that all components have been correctly installed **(see illustration)**.

Output shaft

Disassembly

19 Slide the 2nd gear pinion/selector drum locking arm assembly off the left-hand end of the shaft, followed by the thrust washer **(see illustrations 28.29b and a)**. Remove the collar

fitted in the arm **(see illustration 28.28b)**. If required unhook the spring end and remove the arm **(see illustration 28.28a)**. If required slip the spring off the pinion.

20 The thrust washer on the right-hand end of the shaft has a slightly out-of round section on its inner rim that locates in a groove in the shaft. To remove the washer slip one or two flat-bladed screwdrivers behind the 1st gear pinion and lever it up so the washer is forced out of the groove and off the end of the shaft **(see illustration)**. Slide the 1st gear pinion, its bush, the thrust washer and the 3rd gear pinion off the right-hand end of the shaft **(see illustrations 28.26b and a, and 28.25b and a)**.

21 Remove the circlip and slide the splined washer, the 4th gear pinion and the splined washer off the shaft **(see illustrations 28.24e, d, c, and b)**. The circlip can

stay on the shaft, but remove it if required **(see illustration 28.24a)**.

Inspection

22 Refer to Steps 6 to 12 above.

Reassembly

23 During reassembly, apply molybdenum disulphide oil (a 50/50 mixture of molybdenum disulphide grease and clean engine oil) to the mating surfaces of the shaft, pinions and bush. When installing the circlips, do not expand the ends any further than is necessary. Install the stamped circlips and washers so that their chamfered side faces away from the thrust side.

24 If removed fit the circlip into its groove in the shaft, making sure it locates correctly **(see illustration)**. Slide the splined washer onto the right-hand end of the shaft, followed by the 4th gear pinion, with its dogs facing away from the

28.18 The complete input shaft should be as shown

28.20 Use a screwdriver to lever the washer out of the groove

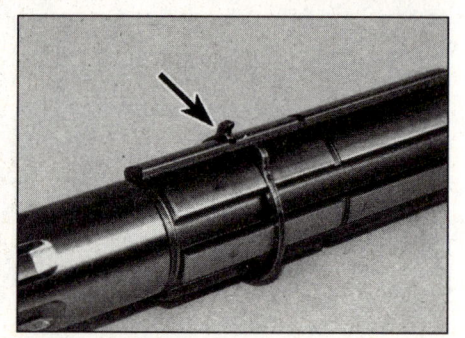

28.24a Fit the circlip (arrowed) if removed

Engine, clutch and transmission 2•53

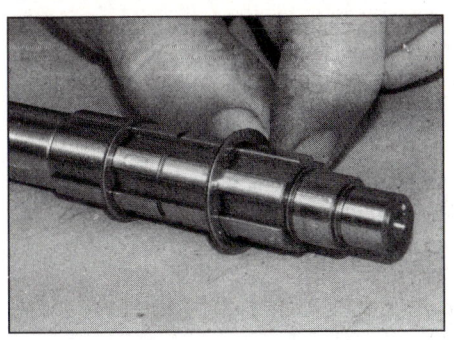

28.24b Slide the splined washer . . .

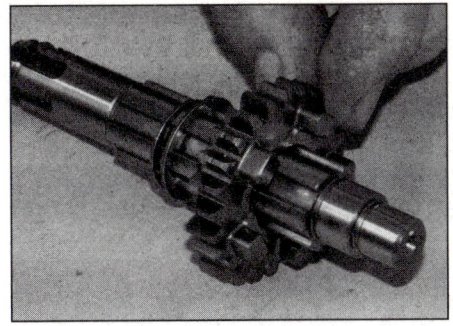

28.24c . . . and the 4th gear pinion onto the shaft

28.24d Slide the splined washer onto the shaft . . .

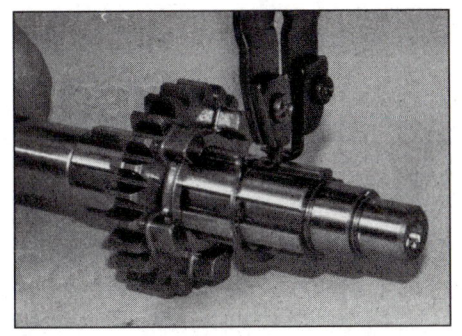

28.24e . . . and secure it with the circlip . . .

28.24f . . . making sure it locates in the groove

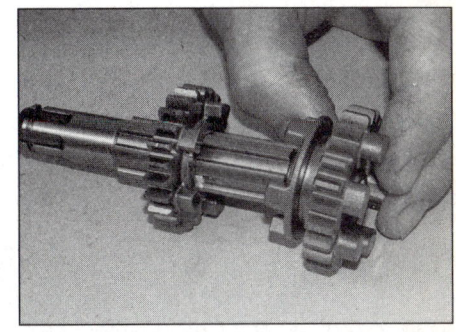

28.25a Slide the 3rd gear pinion . . .

washer **(see illustrations)**. Slide the splined washer on, then fit the circlip, making sure it locates correctly in the groove **(see illustration)**.
25 Slide the 3rd gear pinion onto the shaft, with its selector fork groove facing the 4th gear pinion, then fit the thrust washer **(see illustrations)**.
26 Slide the 1st gear pinion bush onto the shaft, then slide the 1st gear pinion onto the bush with its shaped side facing the 3rd gear pinion **(see illustrations)**.
27 Fit the shaped thrust washer onto the end of the shaft and push it down to the groove using a suitable socket until the out-of-round section on its inner rim locates in the groove **(see illustration and 28.17b)**.

28.25b . . . and the thrust washer onto the shaft

28.26a Slide the bush onto the shaft. . .

28.26b . . . and the 1st gear pinion onto the bush

28.27 Fit the shaped washer and push it down to the groove

2•54 Engine, clutch and transmission

28 If removed fit the friction spring into the groove in the 2nd gear pinion. Fit the arm, hooking the spring end into the hole (see illustration). Fit the collar into the arm (see illustration).
29 Slide the thrust washer onto the left-hand end of the shaft (see illustration). Slide the arm/2nd gear pinion assembly onto the left-hand end of the shaft with the arm facing the thrust washer (see illustration).
30 Check that all components have been correctly installed (see illustration).

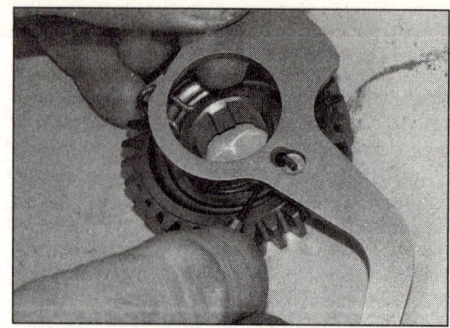

29 Selector drum and forks

Note: *To remove the selector drum and forks the engine must be removed from the frame and the crankcases separated.*

Removal

1 Remove the engine (see Section 4) and separate the crankcase halves (see Section 24).
2 Pivot the selector drum locking arm out of its groove in the selector drum and clear of the forks (see illustration 29.16).
3 Before removing the selector forks, note that the right-hand fork is marked R and the left-hand fork L, with the marks facing the left-hand side of the engine.
4 Support the selector forks and withdraw the shaft from the casing (see illustration). Pivot each fork out of its groove in the selector drum.
5 Withdraw the selector drum from the

28.28a Fit the arm as shown, hooking the spring end into the hole

28.28b Fit the collar into the middle of the arm

28.29a Slide the thrust washer on . . .

28.29b . . . followed by the arm/2nd gear pinion

28.30 The assembled output shaft should be as shown

29.4 Withdraw the shaft and move the forks aside . . .

Engine, clutch and transmission 2•55

29.5 ... then remove the selector drum

29.6 Check the fit of each fork in its pinion ...

crankcase (see illustration). Slide each fork out of its pinion and remove them (see illustrations 29.12b and a). Once removed, slide the forks back onto the shaft to keep them in the correct order and way round.

Inspection

6 Inspect the selector forks for any signs of wear or damage, especially around the fork ends where they engage with the groove in the pinion. Check that each fork fits correctly in its pinion groove (see illustration). Check closely to see if the forks are bent. If the forks are in any way damaged they must be replaced with new ones.

7 Measure the thickness of the fork ends and compare the readings to the specifications (see illustration). Replace the forks with new ones if they are worn beyond their specifications.

8 Check that the forks fit correctly on the shaft (see illustration). They should move freely with a light fit but no appreciable freeplay. Measure the internal diameter of the fork bores and the corresponding diameter of

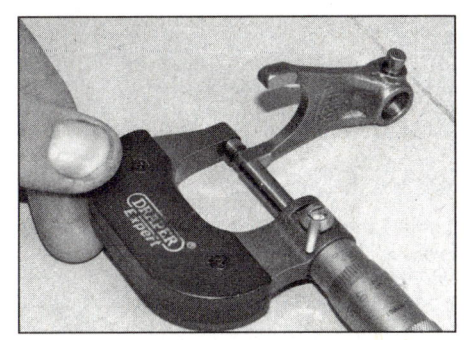

29.7 ... and measure the fork end thickness

the fork shaft. Replace the forks and/or shaft with new ones if they are worn beyond their specifications. Check that the fork shaft holes in the casing are neither worn nor damaged.

9 Check the selector fork shaft is straight by rolling it along a flat surface. A bent rod will cause difficulty in selecting gears and make the gearchange action heavy. Replace the shaft with a new one if it is bent.

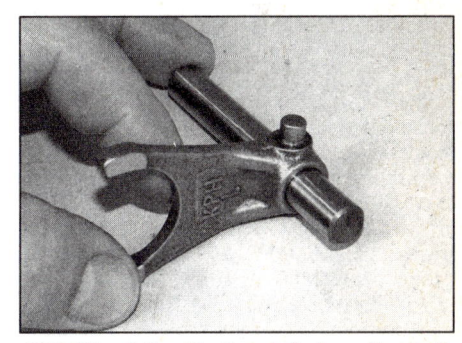

29.8 Check the fit of each fork on its shaft

10 Inspect the selector drum grooves and selector fork guide pins for signs of wear or damage (see illustration). If either component shows signs of wear or damage the fork(s) and drum must be replaced with new ones.

11 Check that the selector drum rotates freely in each crankcase half and has no sign of freeplay between it and the casing (see illustration). Measure the diameter of the each

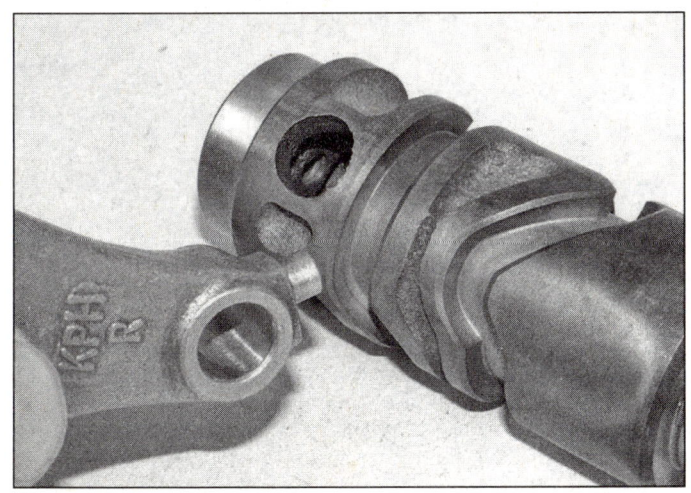

29.10 Check the guide pins and their grooves in the drum

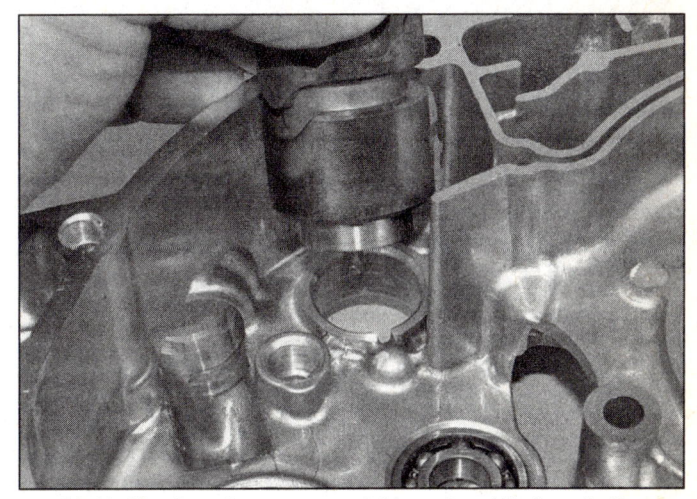

29.11 Check and measure each journal and its bore in the crankcase

2•56 Engine, clutch and transmission

29.12a Locate the R fork in its pinion . . .

29.12b . . . then locate the L fork

journal and the corresponding internal diameter of the bore in each crankcase. Replace the drum and/or crankcases with new ones if they are worn beyond their specifications.

Installation

12 Lubricate each fork with oil. Locate the fork marked R into the groove in the 3rd gear pinion in the output shaft with the R facing up **(see illustration)**. Locate the fork marked L into the groove in the 4th gear pinion in the input shaft with the L facing up **(see illustration)**.
13 Lubricate the selector drum ends with clean engine oil. Slide the selector drum into position in the crankcase **(see illustration 28.5)**. Rotate it so that the slot for the selector drum locking arm will align with the arm **(see illustration 29.16)**.
14 Pivot each fork round to locate its guide pin in its groove in the selector drum.

15 Lubricate the selector fork shaft with oil. With both forks located in the drum and aligned slide the shaft through each and into its bore in the crankcase **(see illustration)**.
16 Pivot the selector drum locking arm into its groove **(see illustration)**.
17 Reassemble the crankcase halves (see Section 24).

30 Running-in procedure

1 Make sure the engine oil level is correct (see *Pre-ride checks*). Make sure there is fuel in the tank.
2 Start the engine and allow it to run at a moderately fast idle until it reaches operating temperature.

⚠️ **Warning: If the oil pressure warning light doesn't go off, or it comes on while the engine is running, stop the engine immediately.**

3 If a lubrication failure is suspected, stop the engine immediately and try to find the cause. If an engine is run without oil, even for a short period of time, severe damage will occur.
4 Check carefully that there are no oil leaks and make sure the transmission and controls, especially the brakes, function properly before road testing the machine.
5 Treat the machine gently for the first few miles to make sure oil has circulated throughout the engine and any new parts installed have started to seat.
6 Even greater care is necessary if a new piston and rings or a new cylinder has been fitted, and the bike will have to be run in as when new. This means greater use of the transmission and a restraining hand on the throttle until at least 300 miles (500 km) have been covered. There's no point in keeping to any set speed limit – the main idea is to keep from labouring the engine and to gradually increase performance up to the 300 miles (500 km) mark. Experience is the best guide, since it's easy to tell when an engine is running freely.
7 Upon completion of the road test, and after the engine has cooled down completely, recheck the valve clearances (see Chapter 1) and check the engine oil level (see *Pre-ride checks*).

29.15 Locate each fork guide pin in its groove in the drum and slide the shaft through

29.16 Swing the locking arm into the groove in the drum

Chapter 3A
Carburettor fuel system and exhaust

Contents

	Section number
Air filter	see Chapter 1
Air filter housing	5
Carburettor heater and thermo switch	15
Carburettor overhaul	8
Carburettor removal and installation	7
Exhaust system	11
Float height check	9
Fuel gauge and level sensor	13
Fuel system checks	see Chapter 1
Fuel filter	2

	Section number
Fuel tank	4
Fuel valve	3
General information and precautions	1
Idle fuel/air mixture adjustment	6
Idle speed	see Chapter 1
Pulse secondary air (PAIR) system	12
Throttle and choke cable check and adjustment	see Chapter 1
Throttle and choke cables	10
Throttle switch	14

Degrees of difficulty

Easy, suitable for novice with little experience	Fairly easy, suitable for beginner with some experience	Fairly difficult, suitable for competent DIY mechanic	Difficult, suitable for experienced DIY mechanic	Very difficult, suitable for expert DIY or professional

Specifications

Fuel
Grade	Unleaded. Minimum 91 RON (Research Octane Number)
Fuel tank capacity	3.7 litres

Carburettor
Type	Slide
ID number	APBF4A
Pilot screw initial setting (see text)	1 5/8 turns out
Float height	11.7 mm
Idle speed	1400 ± 100 rpm
Pilot jet	35
Main jet	#75A

Carburettor heater
Resistance	8.3 to 13.4 ohms

Fuel level sensor
Sensor resistance
FULL position	5 to 7 ohms
EMPTY position	204 to 210 ohms

PAIR system
Control valve vacuum	470 mmHg (63 kPa)

Torque settings
Carburettor intake duct bolts	12 Nm
Exhaust downpipe nuts	27 Nm

3A•2 Carburettor fuel system and exhaust

1 General information and precautions

Models from 2003 to 2006 are fitted with a carburettor. Later models have a fuel injection system and are covered in Chapter 3B.

The fuel system consists of the fuel tank, fuel filter, fuel valve, carburettor, fuel hoses and control cables.

The fuel filter is fitted in the fuel hose between the tank and the valve. The fuel valve is automatic in operation and is opened by engine vacuum.

For cold starting, a choke lever on the handlebar connected by a cable to the carburettor opens and closes the choke valve. There is an electric heater controlled by a thermo switch screwed into the carburettor body. A throttle switch sends throttle opening information to the ECU.

Air is drawn into the carburettor via an air filter which is housed under the steering head.

Precautions

⚠ **Warning:** *Petrol (gasoline) is extremely flammable, so take extra pre-cautions when you work on any part of the fuel system. Always disconnect the battery (see Chapter 8). Don't smoke or allow open flames or bare light bulbs near the work area, and don't work in a garage where a natural gas-type appliance is present. If you spill any fuel on your skin, rinse it off immediately with soap and water. When you perform any kind of work on the fuel system, wear safety glasses and have a fire extinguisher suitable for a class B type fire (flammable liquids) on hand.*

Always perform service procedures in a well-ventilated area to prevent a build-up of fumes.

Never work in a building containing a gas appliance with a pilot light, or any other form of naked flame. Ensure that there are no naked light bulbs or any sources of flame or sparks nearby.

Do not smoke (or allow anyone else to smoke) while in the vicinity of petrol (gasoline) or of components containing it. Remember the possible presence of vapour from these sources and move well clear before smoking.

Check all electrical equipment belonging to the house, garage or workshop where work is being undertaken (see the Safety first! section of this manual). Remember that certain electrical appliances such as drills, cutters etc. create sparks in the normal course of operation and must not be used near petrol (gasoline) or any component containing it. Again, remember the possible presence of fumes before using electrical equipment.

Always mop up any spilt fuel and safely dispose of the rag used.

Any stored fuel that is drained off during servicing work must be kept in sealed containers that are suitable for holding petrol (gasoline), and clearly marked as such; the containers themselves should be kept in a safe place.

Read the Safety first! section of this manual carefully before starting work.

2 Fuel filter

⚠ **Warning:** *Refer to the precautions given in Section 1 before starting work.*

Check

1 The filter is located under the left-hand side of the fuel tank – remove the body cover (see Chapter 7).
2 Visually inspect the filter for signs of dirt and sediment inside **(see illustration)**. If required remove and drain the filter, then inspect again. You may be able to swill out any dirt and sediment using some clean fuel, but replace the filter with a new one if necessary, or if you are in any doubt over its condition.
3 Make sure the fuel hoses are in good condition.

Removal

4 Remove the body cover (see Chapter 7). Have some rag and a container suitable for holding fuel.
5 If a hose clamp is available, fit it onto the hose from the tank to the filter, then detach the hose from the filter and drain the fuel from the filter and hoses into the container **(see illustration 2.2)**.
6 If a hose clamp is not available you will have to drain the tank – make sure your container is large enough for the amount of fuel inside. Unscrew the tank filler cap and rest it on the filler rim. Detach the fuel inlet hose from the fuel valve and drain the fuel from the tank, filter and hoses into the container **(see illustration)**. When all the fuel has drained fit the hose back onto the valve and secure it with the clamp.
7 Detach the hoses from the filter and remove it **(see illustration 2.2)**.

Installation

8 Connect the filter to the hoses, making sure the arrow on the filter points in the direction of fuel flow, and the hoses are pushed fully on **(see illustration 2.2)**. Secure the hoses with their clamps, using new ones if they have weakened or deformed.
9 Release the hose clamp or fill the tank with the drained fuel, and check for leaks at the hose connections.
10 Install the body cover (see Chapter 7).

3 Fuel valve

⚠ **Warning:** *Refer to the precautions given in Section 1 before starting work.*

Check

1 The fuel valve is located on the left-hand side of the storage compartment – remove the body cover (see Chapter 7).
2 The valve is automatic, opened by a vacuum created when the engine is running acting on a diaphragm inside the valve. If the valve is faulty, it must be replaced with a new one – it is a sealed unit for which no individual components are available. The most likely problem is a hole or split in the valve diaphragm. Before fitting a new valve make sure the filter isn't blocked (Section 2).
3 To check the valve, remove the body cover (see Chapter 7). Detach the fuel hose from the carburettor and place the open end in a small container **(see illustration)**. Detach the vacuum hose from the intake duct; apply a

2.2 Fuel filter (arrowed)

2.6 To drain the tank detach the fuel valve inlet hose (arrowed)

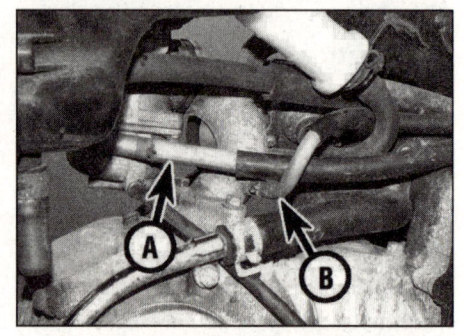

3.3 Detach the fuel hose (A) and the vacuum hose (B)

Carburettor fuel system and exhaust 3A•3

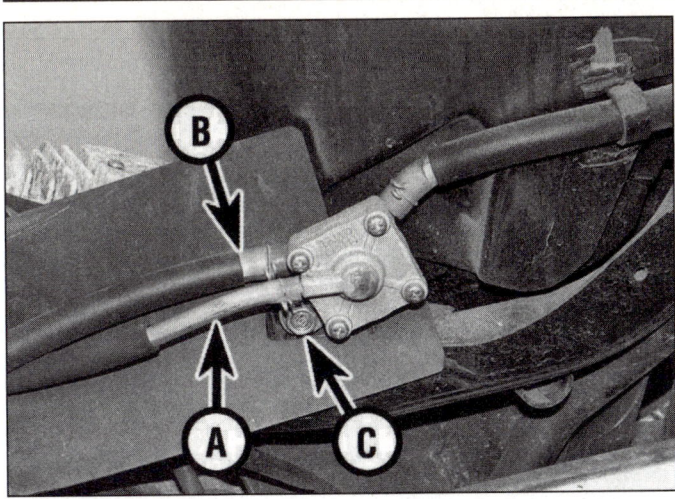

3.8 Vacuum hose (A), fuel outlet hose (B), fuel valve bolt (C)

4.2 Storage box right-hand bolt

vacuum to it using a vacuum pump, or suck on the hose end (first make sure it is clean). Fuel should flow from the valve and into the container – if it doesn't, the diaphragm is probably split.

4 Before fitting a new valve, check that the vacuum hose is securely attached, and that there are no splits or cracks in it. If in doubt, attach a spare hose to the vacuum union on the valve and again apply a vacuum. If fuel still does not flow, remove the valve and fit a new one.

Removal

5 Remove the body cover (see Chapter 7). Have some rag and a container suitable for holding fuel.
6 If a hose clamp is available, fit it onto the inlet hose close to the valve, then detach the hose from the valve and drain the fuel from the valve and hose into the container **(see illustration 2.6)**.
7 If a hose clamp is not available you will have to drain the tank – make sure your container is large enough for the amount of fuel inside. Unscrew the tank filler cap and rest it on the filler rim. Detach the inlet hose from the fuel valve and drain the fuel from the tank filter and hoses into the container **(see illustration 2.6)**.
8 Detach the vacuum hose and outlet hose from the valve **(see illustration)**.
9 Unscrew the bolt and remove the valve **(see illustration 3.8)**.

Installation

10 Fit the fuel valve and tighten the bolt.
11 Fit the fuel and vacuum hoses onto their respective unions, making sure they are pushed fully on. Secure the hoses with their clamps, using new ones if they have weakened or deformed.
12 Release the hose clamp or fill the tank with the drained fuel, and check for leaks at the hose connections.
13 Install the body cover (see Chapter 7).

4 Fuel tank

Removal

1 Remove the storage compartment (see Chapter 7).
2 Trace the wiring from the sensor and disconnect it at the connector **(see illustration 13.9b)**. Unscrew the bolt securing the right-hand side of the storage box **(see illustration)**. Free the wiring from any ties or guides and feed it back to the sensor, noting its routing, and lifting the box for clearance.
3 Next drain the tank – have some rag and a container suitable and large enough for holding the amount of fuel in the tank. Unscrew the tank filler cap and rest it on the filler rim. Detach the fuel inlet hose from the fuel valve and drain the fuel from the tank, filter and hoses into the container **(see illustration 2.6)**. When all the fuel has drained fit the hose back onto the valve and secure it with the clamp.
4 Detach the hose from the tank **(see illustration 2.2)**.
5 Unscrew the bolts, one on each corner, and carefully lift the tank out.

Installation

6 Installation is the reverse of removal. Secure the hose with the clamp, using a new one if it has weakened or deformed. Make sure the wiring is correctly routed. Fill the tank with the drained fuel, and check for leaks at the hose connections.

5 Air filter housing

1 Remove the air filter (see Chapter 1).
2 Detach the crankcase breather hose from its union on the rear of the housing **(see illustration)**.
3 Slacken the clamp securing the air duct to the carburettor **(see illustration)**.
4 Unscrew the bolt on each side at the

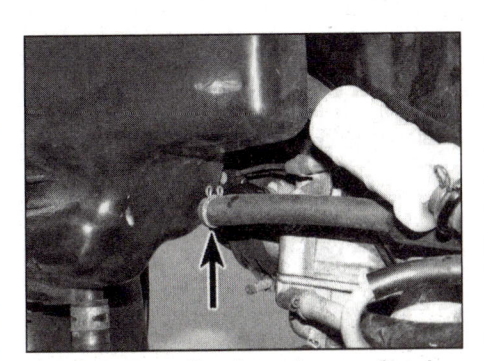

5.2 Release the clamp (arrowed) and detach the hose

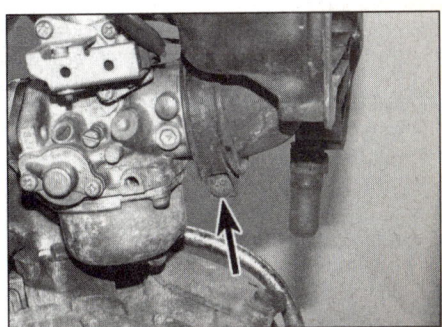

5.3 Slacken the clamp screw (arrowed)

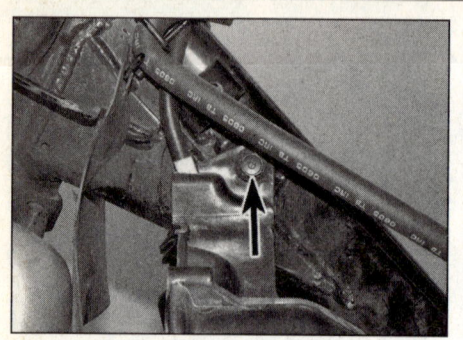

3A•4 Carburettor fuel system and exhaust

5.4a Unscrew the bolt (arrowed) on each side . . .

5.4b . . . and remove the housing

top and manoeuvre the housing out **(see illustrations)**.

5 Installation is the reverse of removal.

6 Idle fuel/air mixture adjustment

⚠️ *Warning: Adjustment of the pilot screw is made with the engine running. Do not run the scooter in an enclosed space.*

Special tool: *To perform this procedure, you'll need an auxiliary tachometer and vacuum pump.*

1 Idle fuel/air mixture is set using the pilot air screw **(see illustration 8.14)**. Adjustment is not normally necessary and should only be performed if the engine is running roughly, stalls continually, or if the pilot screw has been turned during a carburettor overhaul, or a new pilot screw has been fitted. Before adjusting the pilot screw make sure the spark plug is clean and in good condition with the correct gap, the air filter is clean, the fuel, air and vacuum hoses are all in good condition and secure at each end, and the carburettor clamps are tight and the ducts in good condition so there are no air leaks, and the intake duct bolts are tight, and the valve clearances and idle speed are correct – refer to Chapter 1.

2 To perform this procedure accurately you need to connect a tachometer capable of accurately reading changes in engine speed of 50 rpm. Some electrical multimeters have a tachometer function and adapter lead. Connect the tachometer, following the manufacturer's instructions.

3 Take the bike for a ride so it is at normal working temperature. Remove the front cover on the right-hand side (see Chapter 7).

4 With the engine off, screw the pilot screw in until it seats lightly, then back it out the number of turns specified at the beginning of this Chapter.

5 Disconnect the PAIR vacuum hose from the intake duct and plug the union on the duct. Connect the hose to a vacuum pump and apply 470 mmHg (63 kPa) of vacuum.

6 Start the engine and check the idle speed, adjusting if necessary (see Chapter 1). With the engine running, turn the pilot screw slowly in (clockwise) and out (anti-clockwise) until the highest idle speed is achieved. Open the throttle lightly a few times. Re-adjust the idle speed.

7 Now turn the pilot screw out until idle speed drops by 100 rpm. Finally turn the screw in one full turn.

8 Disconnect the pump from the vacuum hose, remove the plug and connect the hose to the intake duct. Re-adjust the idle speed.

9 If it is not possible to achieve a satisfactory idle speed after adjusting the pilot screw, take the machine to a scooter dealer and have the fuel/air mixture adjusted with the aid of an exhaust gas analyser. Also bear in mind that it is possible the problem is not down to the fuel system – ignition system causes should also be considered.

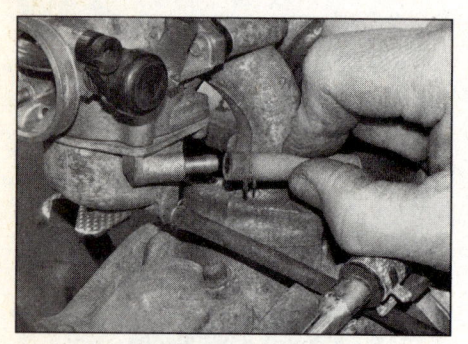

7 Carburettor removal and installation

⚠️ *Warning: Refer to the precautions given in Section 1 before starting work.*

Removal

1 Remove the front cover on each side (see Chapter 7).

2 Remove the air filter housing (Section 5).

3 Detach the throttle cable from the throttle valve and the choke cable from the pulley (Section 10).

4 Loosen the drain screw on the bottom of the carburettor and drain the fuel into a suitable container via the drain hose. Tighten the screw.

5 Have some rag to hand to catch the residual fuel in the fuel hose. Release the clamp and detach the hose from its union **(see illustration)**. Detach the drain hose and breather hose **(see illustrations)**.

6 Disconnect the carburettor heater wiring connectors **(see illustration)**.

7.5a Detach the fuel hose . . .

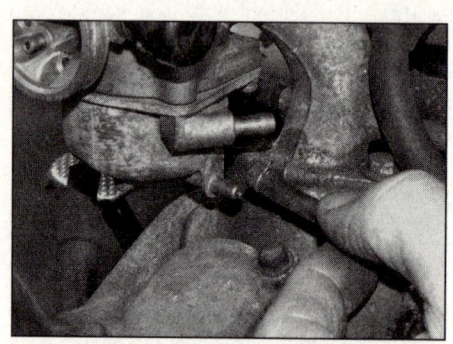

7.5b . . . the drain hose . . .

7.5c . . . and the breather hose

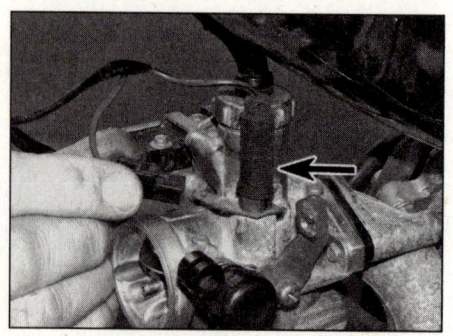

7.6 Disconnect the heater wiring connectors . . .

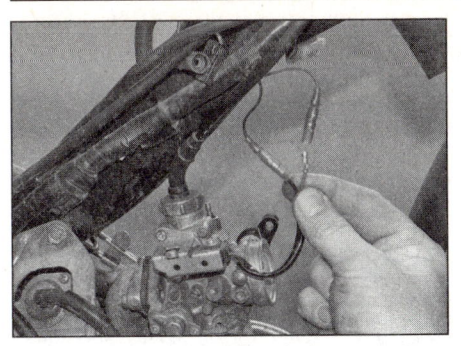

Carburettor fuel system and exhaust 3A•5

7.7 . . . and the throttle switch connectors

7.8a Unscrew the bolts (arrowed) . . .

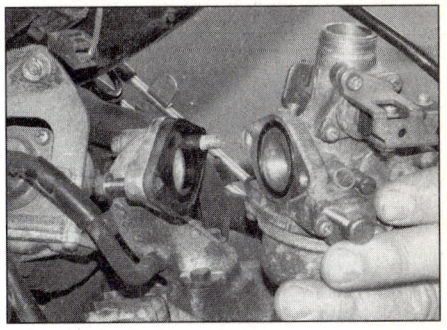

7.8b . . . and remove the carburettor . . .

7 Disconnect the throttle switch wiring connectors **(see illustration)**.
8 Unscrew the bolts securing the carburettor to the intake duct **(see illustration)**. Manoeuvre the carburettor out, then remove the insulator that sits between the carburettor and the duct **(see illustrations)**. Remove the O-rings – new ones must be used **(see illustration)**.
Caution: Stuff clean rag into the intake duct removing the carburettor to prevent anything from falling inside.

Installation

9 Installation is the reverse of removal, noting the following:
- Make sure the drain screw on the bottom of the carburettor is tight.
- Fit a new O-ring into the groove in both the carburettor flange and the insulator **(see illustration 7.8d)**. Fit the insulator with the O-ring facing the intake duct and the rib at the top **(see illustration 7.8c)**, then fit the carburettor onto the insulator and insert and tighten the bolts **(see illustration 7.8b)**.
- Make sure all hoses and wiring are correctly routed and secured and not trapped or kinked.
- Refer to Section 10 to connect the throttle cable and fit the throttle valve, and to connect the choke cable. Check the throttle cable adjustment (see Chapter 1).
- Check the idle speed and adjust as necessary (see Chapter 1).

8 Carburettor overhaul

⚠ **Warning: Refer to the precautions given in Section 1 before proceeding.**

General information

1 Poor engine performance, difficult starting, stalling, flooding and backfiring are all signs that carburettor maintenance may be required.
2 Keep in mind that many so-called carburettor problems can often be traced to other faults in the fuel system, faults within the engine, or faults in the ignition system. Try to establish for certain that the carburettor is

7.8c . . . and the insulator

in need of maintenance before beginning a major overhaul.
3 Check the fuel valve and filter, the fuel and vacuum hoses, the intake duct joints, the air filter, the spark plug and the ignition system before assuming that a carburettor overhaul is required.
4 Most carburettor problems are caused by dirt particles, varnish and other deposits which build up in and eventually block the fuel jets and air passages inside the carburettor. Also, in time, gaskets and O-rings deteriorate and cause fuel and air leaks which lead to poor performance.
5 When overhauling the carburettor, disassemble it completely and clean the parts thoroughly with a carburettor cleaning solvent. If available, blow through the fuel jets and air passages with compressed air to ensure they are clear. Once the cleaning process is complete, reassemble the carburettor using new gaskets and O-rings – a kit is available that contains all the necessary parts.

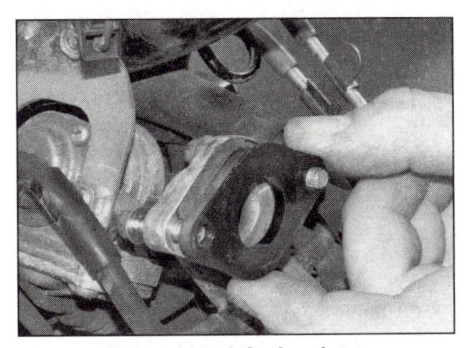

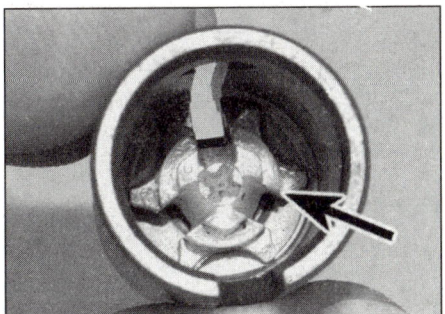

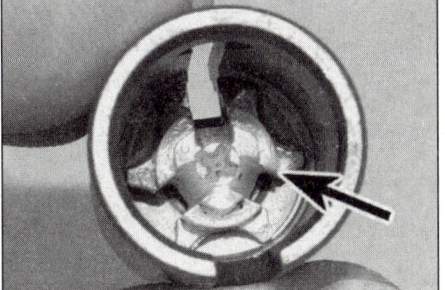

8.9a Release the needle retainer (arrowed) . . .

7.8d Remove the O-rings (arrowed)

6 Before disassembling the carburettor, make sure you have the correct carburettor gasket set, some carburettor cleaner, a supply of clean rags, some means of blowing out the carburettor passages and a clean place to work.

Disassembly

7 Remove the carburettor (see Section 7). Take care when removing components to note their exact locations and any springs or O-rings that may be fitted.
8 Remove the throttle switch (see Section 14), and if required the heater (Section 15).
9 Using a Phillips screwdriver push down lightly on the needle retainer in the throttle valve and turn it 90° anti-clockwise, then lift out the retainer, noting the spring fitted underneath **(see illustration)**. Push the needle up from the bottom of the valve and withdraw it from the top **(see illustration)**.
10 Undo the screws securing the float

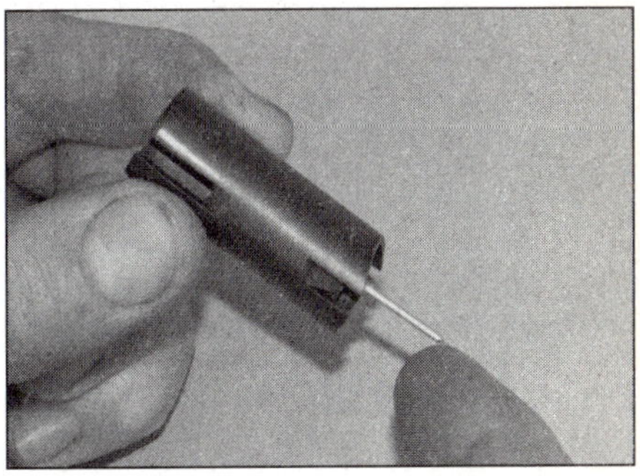

8.9b . . . and remove the needle from the piston

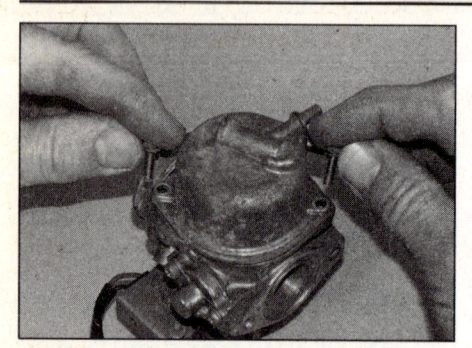

3A•6 Carburettor fuel system and exhaust

8.10 Undo the screws and remove the float chamber

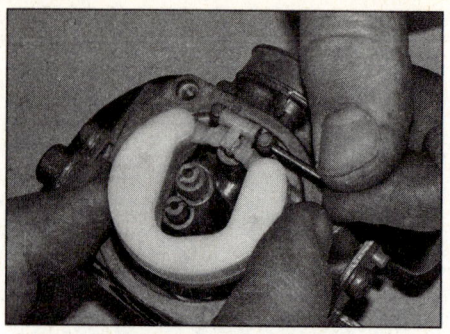

8.11 Withdraw the pin and remove the float

8.12a Unscrew the pilot jet . . .

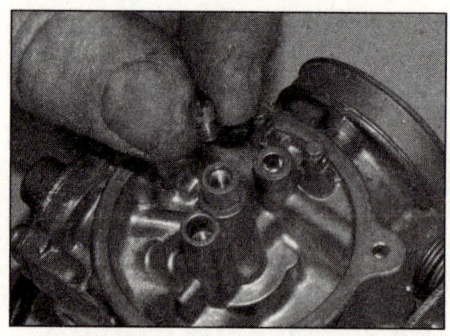

8.12b . . . the main jet . . .

chamber to the base of the carburettor and remove it **(see illustration)**. Remove the sealing ring – a new one must be used.

11 Withdraw the float pin and remove the float **(see illustration)** – if necessary, displace the pin using a small punch or a nail. Remove the float needle valve, noting how it fits **(see illustration 8.29a)**.

12 Unscrew the pilot jet **(see illustrations)**. Unscrew the main jet, which threads into the base of the needle jet holder **(see illustration)**. Unscrew the holder, and remove the needle jet **(see illustrations)** – if it doesn't come out with the holder push its top down from inside the venturi and it should drop down.

13 Undo the air cut-off valve screws and remove the cover, spring, diaphragm, and O-ring **(see illustration)**.

14 The pilot screw can be removed if required, but note that its setting will be disturbed (see *Haynes Hint*). Unscrew and remove the pilot screw along with its spring, washer and O-ring **(see illustration)**.

> **HAYNES HINT** To record the pilot screw's current setting, mark a line between the screw and the carburettor, then turn the screw in until it seats lightly, counting the number of turns necessary to achieve this, then unscrew it fully. On installation, turn the screw in until it seats, then back it out the number of turns you've recorded, using the alignment marks for the precise position.

Cleaning

15 Use carburettor cleaning solvent to loosen and dissolve the varnish and other deposits on and in the jets, on the carburettor body and in the float chamber **(see illustration)** – use a nylon-bristled brush to remove the stubborn deposits. Dry the components with compressed air. **Note:** *Avoid soaking the carburettor body in solvent if any O-ring seals remain inside.*

16 If available, use compressed air to blow out all the fuel jets and the air passages in the carburettor body, not forgetting the passages in the carburettor intake **(see illustration)**.

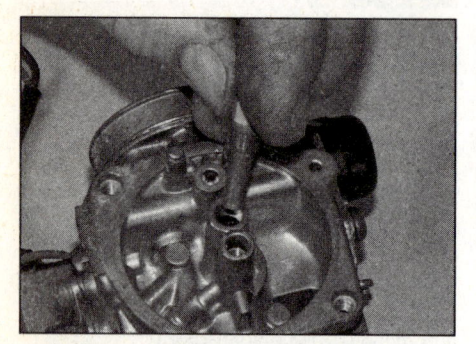

8.12c . . . and the main jet holder . . .

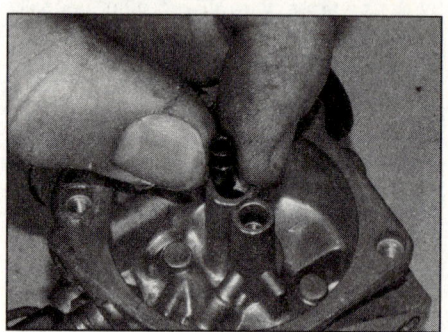

8.12d . . . and remove the needle jet

8.13 Undo the screws (arrowed) and remove the air cut-off valve components

8.14 Pilot screw (arrowed)

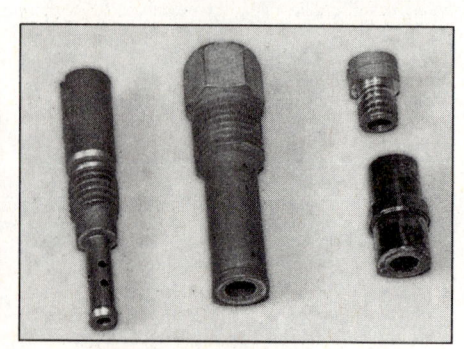

8.15 Clean the jets . . .

8.16 . . . and air passages

Carburettor fuel system and exhaust 3A•7

8.19 Check the throttle valve and its bore

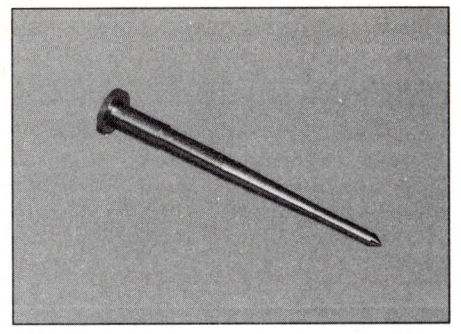

8.20 Check the needle is straight and not worn

8.21 Check the needle valve tip is not worn

Caution: *Never clean the jets or passages with a piece of wire as they will be enlarged, causing the fuel and air metering rates to be upset.*

Inspection

17 If removed, check the tapered portion of the pilot screw and the spring for wear or damage and replace them with new ones if necessary.
18 Check the carburettor body, float chamber and top cap for cracks, distorted sealing surfaces and other damage. If any defects are found, replace the faulty component, although replacement of the entire carburettor may be necessary.
19 Insert the throttle valve in the carburettor body and check that it moves up-and-down smoothly in its bore **(see illustration)**. Check the surface of the valve for wear. If it's worn or scored excessively or doesn't move smoothly, replace it with a new one.
20 Check the needle is straight by rolling it on a flat surface such as a piece of glass **(see illustration)**. Fit a new needle if it is bent or if the tip is worn.
21 Inspect the tip of the float needle valve **(see illustration)**. If it has grooves or scratches in it, or is in any way worn, it must be replaced with a new one. If the valve seat is damaged a new carburettor body will have to be fitted.
22 Check the float for damage. This will usually be apparent by the presence of fuel inside the float. If the float is damaged, replace it with a new one.
23 Inspect the air cut-off valve diaphragm for splits, holes and general deterioration. Holding it up to a light will help to reveal problems of this nature. Also check the spring for distortion.
24 Operate the choke arm to make sure the butterfly valve opens and closes smoothly **(see illustration)**. If it doesn't, and thorough cleaning makes no difference, fit a new carburettor.

Reassembly

Note: *When reassembling the carburettor, be sure to use new O-rings and seals. Do not overtighten the carburettor jets and screws as they are easily damaged.*

25 If removed, fit the pilot screw, spring, washer and O-ring, and screw in until it seats lightly **(see illustration 8.14)**. If you are fitting the original screw and are happy with the previous setting turn the screw out the number of turns noted on removal and align the marks (see **Haynes Hint**). If a new pilot screw is fitted, or if you want to make sure the previous setting was correct, turn it out the number of turns specified at the beginning of this Chapter for the initial setting, and after assembling and installing the carburettor refer to Section 6 and adjust the idle fuel/air mixture.
26 Fit a new O-ring onto the air cut-off valve air passage **(see illustration)**. Fit the diaphragm, locating the needle in the hole, then fit the spring and the cover and tighten the screws **(see illustrations)**.
27 Fit the needle jet if removed, with its larger internal diameter end going in first **(see illustration 8.12d)** – make sure the top of the jet is visible in the venturi. Fit the needle jet holder, then screw the main jet into the bottom of it **(see illustrations 8.12c and b)**.
28 Fit the pilot jet **(see illustration 8.12a)**.
29 Slide the float needle valve into its seat on

8.24 Check the action of the choke arm and valve

8.26a Fit a new O-ring (arrowed)

8.26b Fit the diaphragm ...

8.26c ... the spring and the cover...

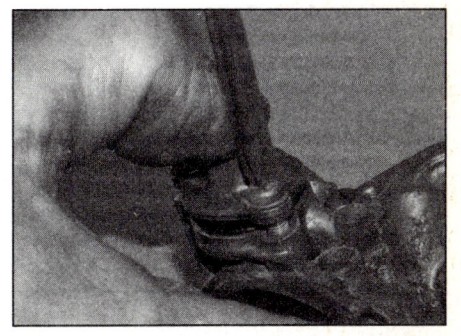

8.26d ... then push the cover down and tighten the screws

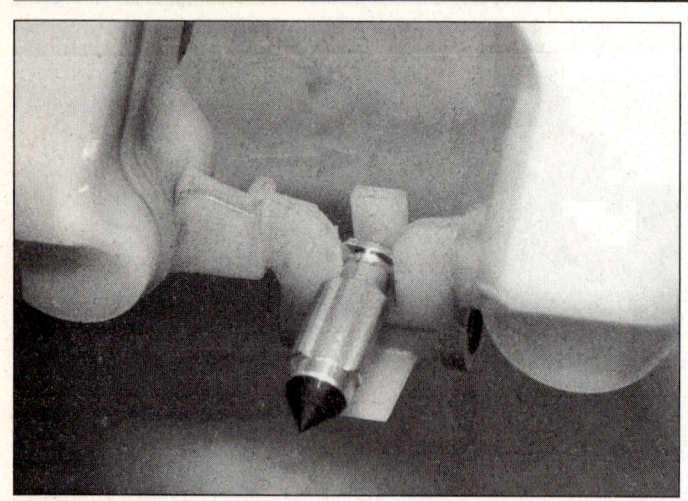

3A•8 Carburettor fuel system and exhaust

8.29a Fit the needle valve onto the float . . .

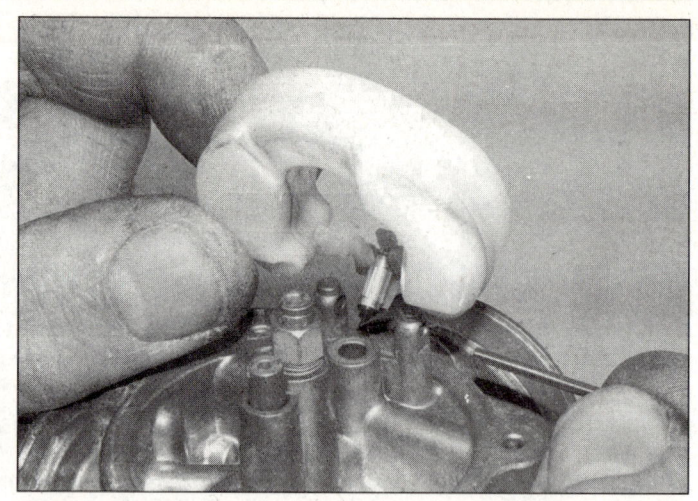

8.29b . . . then position them in the float chamber and insert the pin

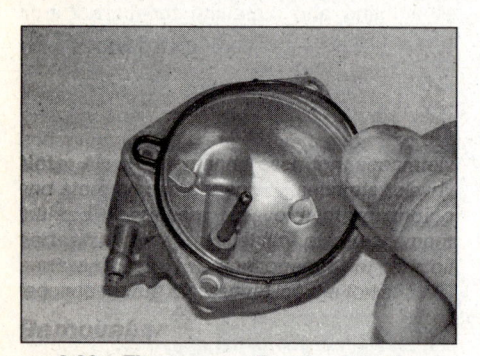

8.30a Fit a new sealing ring into the groove . . .

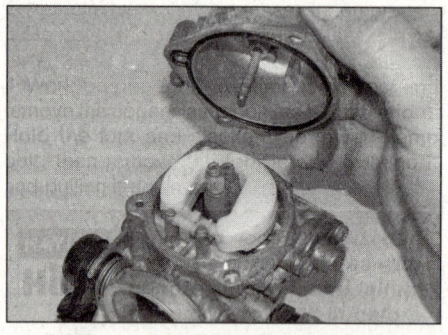

8.30b . . . then fit the float chamber

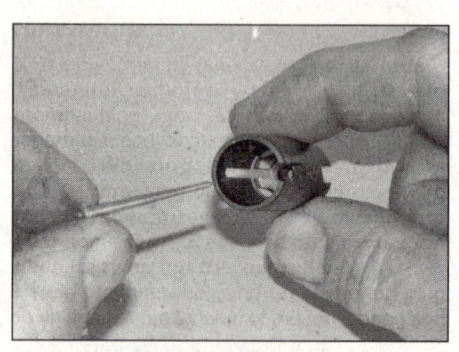

8.31a Fit the needle

the float **(see illustration)**. Position the float assembly in the carburettor, making sure the needle valve enters its seat, and fit the pin **(see illustration)**. Check the float height (see Section 9).

30 Fit a new sealing ring onto the float chamber, making sure it is seated properly in its groove, then fit the chamber onto the carburettor and tighten the screws **(see illustrations)**.

31 Insert the needle into the throttle valve **(see illustration)**. Fit the spring, then fit needle retainer, aligning its tabs correctly, then pressing down lightly on it and turning it 90° clockwise to lock it in place **(see illustrations)**.

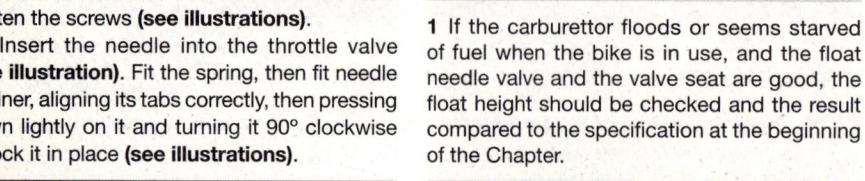

32 If removed, fit the heater and throttle switch (see Sections 15 and 14).
33 Install the carburettor (see Section 7).

9 Float height check

1 If the carburettor floods or seems starved of fuel when the bike is in use, and the float needle valve and the valve seat are good, the float height should be checked and the result compared to the specification at the beginning of the Chapter.

2 If not already done, remove the carburettor (see Section 7).
3 Undo the screws securing the float chamber to the base of the carburettor and remove it **(see illustration 8.10)**. Discard the sealing ring as a new one must be used.
4 Turn the carburettor on its side so that the float needle valve is just resting against the valve seat and measure the distance between the float chamber mating face and the bottom of the float **(see illustration)**.
5 Compare the result with the specified measurement.

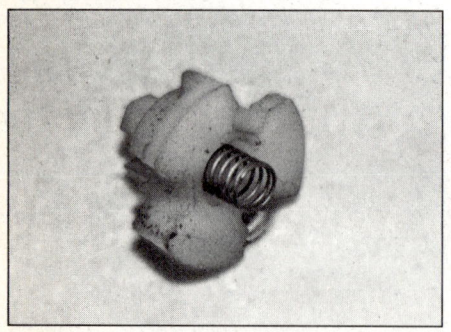

8.31b Make sure the spring is in place . . .

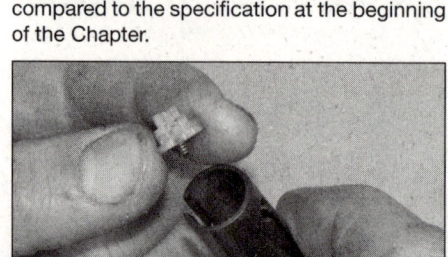

8.31c . . . then fit the retainer

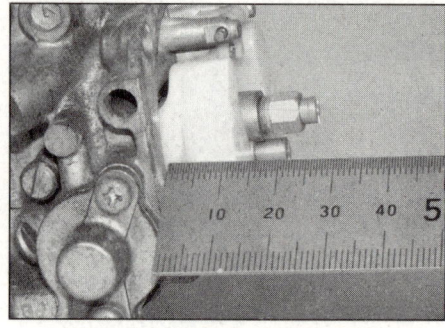

9.4 Checking the float height

Carburettor fuel system and exhaust 3A•9

10.2a Unscrew the cap . . .

10.2b . . . and draw the valve out

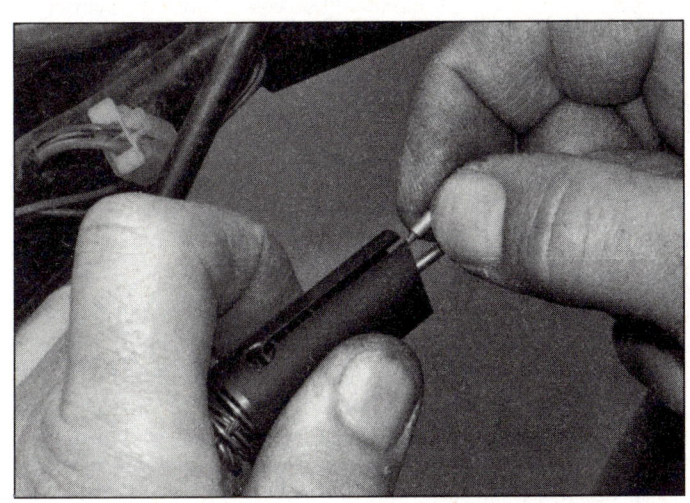

10.2c Slip the cable out and remove the valve and the spring . . .

10.2d . . . then draw the cable out of the cap

6 If the float height is incorrect, fit a new float – the height is not adjustable.
7 Fit a new sealing ring onto the float chamber, making sure it is seated properly in its groove, then fit the chamber onto the carburettor and tighten the screws **(see illustrations 8.30a and b)**.

10 Throttle and choke cables

⚠ *Warning: Refer to the precautions given in Section 1 before proceeding.*

Throttle cable

Removal

1 Remove the handlebar covers and the front cover on the right-hand side (see Chapter 7).
2 Undo the carburettor top cap and draw the throttle valve out **(see illustrations)**. Push the valve up against the spring and slip the cable end out of its slot **(see illustration)**. Draw the valve and the spring off the cable, then draw the cable out of the top **(see illustrations)**. Check the condition of the cap sealing ring and replace it with a new one if necessary – it is included in the overhaul kit if you are overhauling the carburettor, but otherwise is only available with a new cap.
3 Draw the cable out, noting its routing through the guides and the hole in the rear handlebar cover **(see illustration)**.
4 Unscrew the cable elbow nut from the throttle pulley housing **(see illustration)**. Undo the housing screw and pivot the top half up

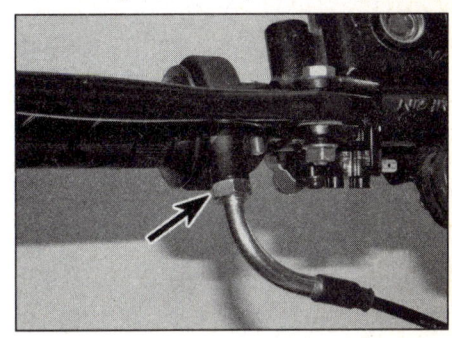

10.3 Note the routing of the cable

10.4a Unscrew the nut (arrowed) . . .

3A•10 Carburettor fuel system and exhaust

10.4b ... then undo the housing screw (arrowed) and detach the housing

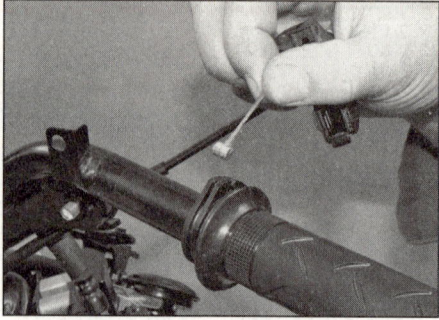

10.4c Free the cable end ...

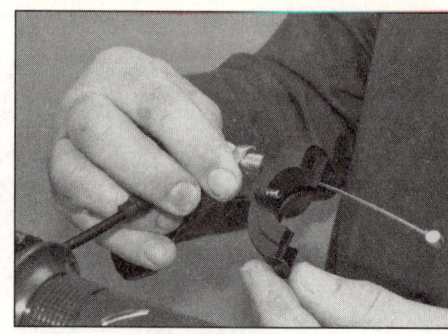

10.4d ... then thread the housing off the cable

and off **(see illustration)**. Detach the housing and free the cable end from the pulley, then thread the housing off the cable elbow and draw the cable out **(see illustrations)**.

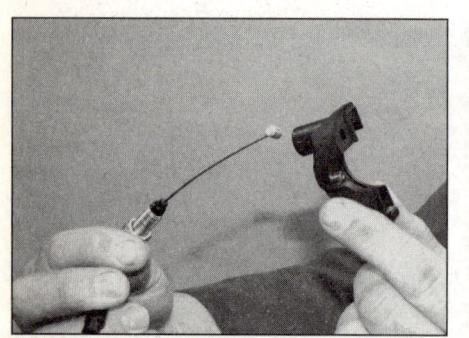

Installation

5 Thread the throttle pulley housing onto the upper end of the cable elbow without it becoming tight – the elbow must stay loose so that it aligns itself **(see illustration)**. Lubricate the cable end with multi-purpose grease and fit it into the throttle pulley **(see illustration 10.4c)**. Assemble the housing halves onto the handlebar, making sure the pin in the bottom half locates in the hole, then fit the screw **(see illustrations)**.

6 Feed the cable through to the carburettor, making sure it is correctly routed through the rear handlebar cover and the guides **(see illustration 10.3)**. The cable must not interfere with any other component and should not be kinked or bent sharply. Now tighten the cable elbow nut on the housing **(see illustration 10.4a)**.

7 Lubricate the cable end with multi-purpose grease, fit it through the cap and seat the rubber boot **(see illustration)**. Fit the spring and the valve over the cable, then push the valve up against the spring and slip the cable end into its slot **(see illustrations)**.

8 Fit the valve into the carburettor, aligning the cut-out in its base with the idle speed adjuster screw **(see illustration)** – when the valve contacts the throttle switch plunger gently push it down so the plunger moves in. Make sure the spring is correctly seated at each end, then thread the cap on **(see illustration 10.2a)**.

9 Operate the throttle to check that it opens and closes freely, and check the amount of freeplay (see Chapter 1).

10 Turn the handlebars back-and-forth to make sure the cable doesn't cause the steering to bind.

11 Start the engine and check the idle speed

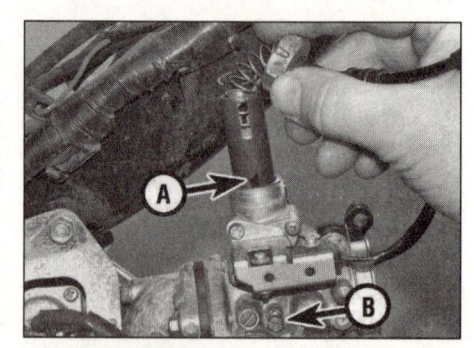

10.5a Fit the cable through and thread the housing onto it

10.5b Locate the pin on the bottom half in the hole ...

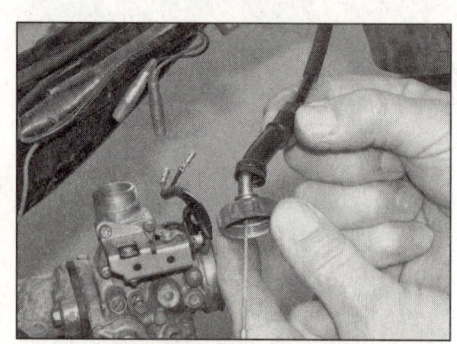

10.5c ... then hook the top half on and pivot it down onto the handlebar

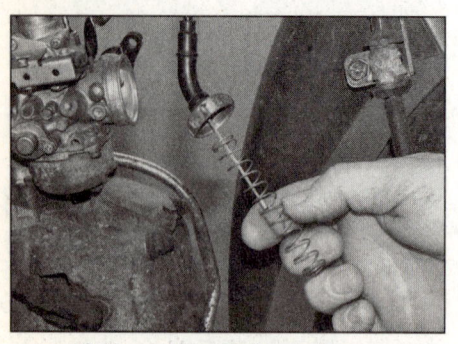

10.7a Fit the cable into the cap ...

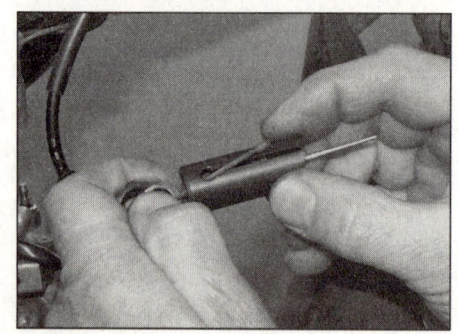

10.7b ... then fit the spring ...

10.7c ... and the valve

10.8 Align the cut-out (A) with the idle speed adjuster (B)

Carburettor fuel system and exhaust 3A•11

(see Chapter 1). Check that the idle speed does not rise as the handlebars are turned. If it does, the throttle cable is routed incorrectly. Correct the problem before riding the scooter.
12 Install the covers (see Chapter 7).

Choke cable

Removal

13 Remove the front handlebar cover and the front covers (see Chapter 7).
14 Remove the air filter housing (Section 5).
15 Release the cable from its holder on the carburettor and detach the end from the pulley **(see illustrations)**.
16 Draw the cable out, noting its routing, and freeing it from any guides.
17 Draw the cable out of the holder on the handlebar and detach the end from the choke lever **(see illustrations)**.

Installation

18 Lubricate the cable end with multi-purpose grease and fit it into the choke lever **(see illustration 10.17b)**. Align the cable with the slot in the holder and fit it in **(see illustration 10.17a)**.
19 Feed the cable through to the carburettor, making sure it is correctly routed. The cable must not interfere with any other component and should not be kinked or bent sharply.
20 Lubricate the cable end with multi-purpose grease and fit it into the pulley **(see illustration 10.15b)**. Locate the cable in its holder **(see illustration 10.15a)**.
21 Operate the choke lever to check that it opens and closes freely.
22 Turn the handlebars back-and-forth to make sure the cable doesn't cause the steering to bind.
23 Install the air filter housing (Section 5).
24 Start the engine and check that the idle speed does not change as the handlebars are turned. If it does, the choke cable is routed incorrectly. Correct the problem before riding the scooter.
25 Install the covers (see Chapter 7).

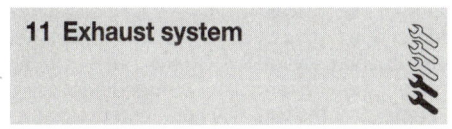

11 Exhaust system

The procedure for removing and installing the exhaust system on carburettor models is the same as on fuel injection models – refer to Chapter 3B for details.

12 Pulse secondary air (PAIR) system

General information

1 To reduce the amount of unburned hydrocarbons released in the exhaust gases, a pulse secondary air (PAIR) system is fitted. The system consists of the control valve that contains a vacuum-operated diaphragm valve and a reed valve, and the hoses, one supplying filtered air to the valve, one supplying a vacuum to the diaphragm, and one passing the air from the valve to the cylinder head.
2 Under normal running conditions, the diaphragm valve is open allowing air to be drawn into the air supply hose, which contains a filter, through the reed valve, air outlet hose/pipe and cylinder head passage and into the exhaust port. The air mixes with the exhaust gases, causing any unburned particles of the fuel in the mixture to be burnt in the exhaust port/pipes. This process changes a considerable amount of hydrocarbons and carbon monoxide into relatively harmless carbon dioxide and water. The reed valve is fitted to prevent the flow of exhaust gases back up the cylinder head passage and into the control valve. When the throttle is closed the vacuum created in the intake duct, linked to the control valve by a hose, acts on the diaphragm and closes the valve, cutting off the air supply and preventing exhaust popping on over-run. **Note:** *If popping occurs even though the PAIR system is working properly, check the air cut-off valve on the carburettor (Section 8).*

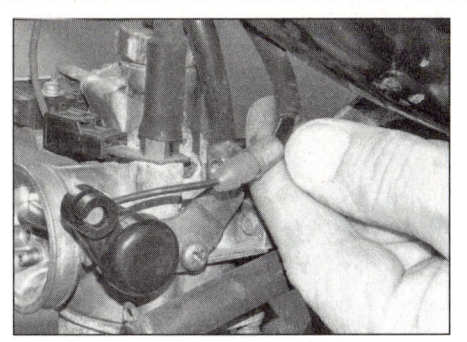

Testing

3 Remove the front cover on each side (see Chapter 7).
4 Make sure the air filter in the air intake hose is not blocked and is clean and replace it with a new one if necessary **(see illustration)**. Check the condition of all the hoses, looking for cracks, splits and hardening, and replace them with new ones as required **(see illustration)**. Make sure the hose clamps have not weakened or deformed.

Diaphragm valve

5 Make sure the intake end of the air supply

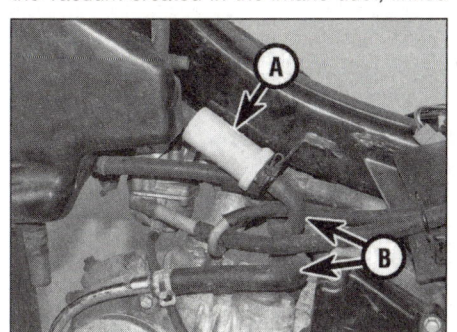

10.15a Release the cable from its holder . . .

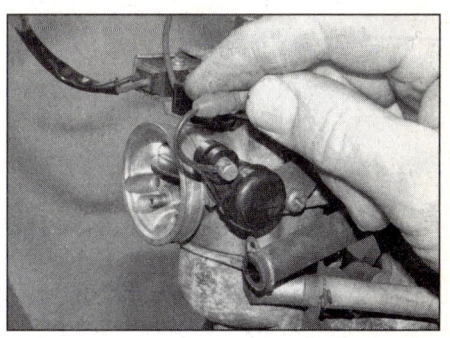

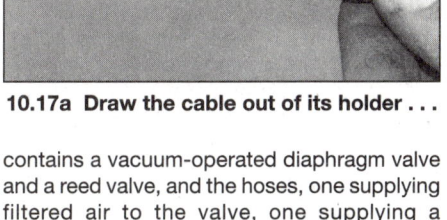

10.15b . . . then detach the end

10.17a Draw the cable out of its holder . . .

10.17b . . . then detach the end

12.4a Check the filter (A), the air hoses (B) . . .

12.4b . . . and the vacuum hose (arrowed)

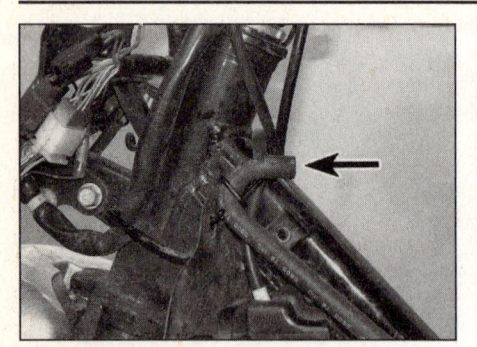

3A•12 Carburettor fuel system and exhaust

12.5 Clean the end of the hose (arrowed) and blow down it as described

12.9 PAIR control valve bracket bolts (arrowed)

12.10 The reed valve housing is on the underside

hose is clean **(see illustration)**. Check the operation of the valve by blowing into the hose – air should flow through the valve hose. Now disconnect the vacuum hose from its union on the intake duct **(see illustration 12.4b)** and apply a vacuum to it (Honda say 470 mmHg (63 kPa) using a vacuum pump) and repeat the check – no air should now flow through the valve, and the vacuum should be held constant and not bleed, if it is functioning correctly. Replace the valve with a new one if faulty.

Reed valve

6 Make sure the intake end of the air supply hose is clean **(see illustration 12.5)**. Check the operation of the valve by blowing into and sucking on the hose end. Air should flow through the hose only when blown into it and not when sucked back up. If this is not the case the reed valve is faulty, though it is worth removing it and cleaning off any carbon deposits, and checking the reed and the seal (see Step 10).

Removal and installation

7 Remove the front cover on each side (See Chapter 7).
8 Release the clamps and detach the hoses from the control valve, noting which fits where **(see illustrations 12.4a and b)**.
9 Unscrew the bracket bolts and remove the valve **(see illustration)**. If required separate the valve from its bracket.
10 If required unscrew the bolts securing the reed valve cover and remove the cover

(see illustration). Remove the reed valve, noting which way around it fits. Check for carbon deposits and scrape and wipe clean. Check the reed valve seal for damage and deformation. Make sure the reed seats correctly and lifts off its seat when pushed lightly. Replace the control valve with a new one if necessary – individual components are not available.
11 If required unscrew the bolts securing the air pipe to the cylinder head and detach it **(see illustration)**. Discard the gasket – a new one must be used. Check the pipe for damage. Make sure the pipe and head mating surfaces are clean and not scored.
12 Installation is the reverse of removal. Make sure the hoses are pushed fully onto their unions and secured by their clamps. If the pipe has been removed fit it using a new gasket, and fit all three bolts loosely before tightening any of them, and then tighten the bracket bolt before the flange bolts.

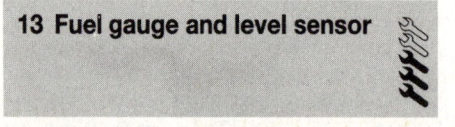

13 Fuel gauge and level sensor

Check

Note: *Refer to electrical system fault finding in Section 2 of Chapter 8 and to the wiring diagram for your model at the end of Chapter 8.*

1 The circuit consists of the level sensor mounted in the top of the fuel tank and the gauge mounted in the instrument cluster. When the ignition is switched on all segments of the gauge should come on temporarily before showing the actual level – this serves as an indication that the gauge is functioning correctly. If the instruments malfunction check the instrument cluster power supply and earth (see Chapter 8).
2 Remove the sensor (Steps 8 to 10).
3 Check that no fuel has entered the float due to a leak, and check that the arm moves up and down smoothly.
4 Connect the probes of an ohmmeter to the terminals on the sensor connector. Move the arm up and down and check the resistance of the sensor in both the FULL and EMPTY positions **(see illustrations)**. If the readings are not as specified at the beginning of the Chapter, replace the sensor with a new one.
5 Connect the sensor to its wiring connector. Turn the ignition on and move the arm up and down – the gauge should show all segments with the arm fully raised, and only the E segment (which should flash) with the arm in its lowest position. Turn the ignition off and disconnect the sensor.
6 If the gauge does not respond as described, remove the handlebar front cover (see Chapter 7). Check the wiring between the sensor connector and the gauge connector on the back of the instrument cluster for continuity, and check for continuity to earth in the green wire at each connector, referring to electrical system testing and the wiring diagram in Chapter 8. If the wiring is good and the power

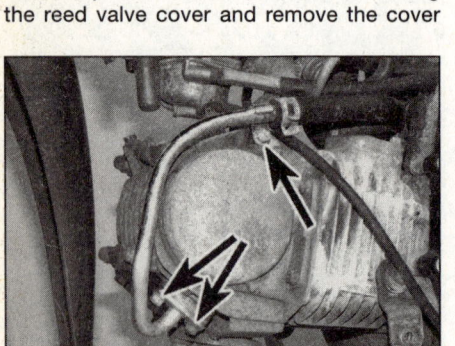

12.11 Air pipe bolts (arrowed)

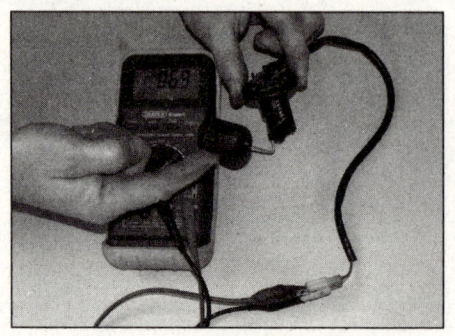

13.4a Check the resistance in the FULL position . . .

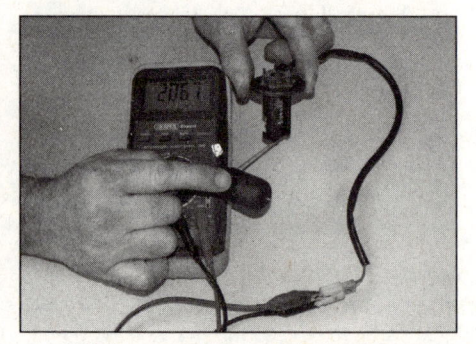

13.4b . . . and the empty position

Carburettor fuel system and exhaust 3A•13

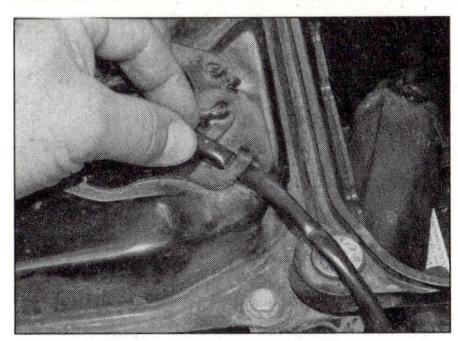

13.9a Free the wiring from the guide

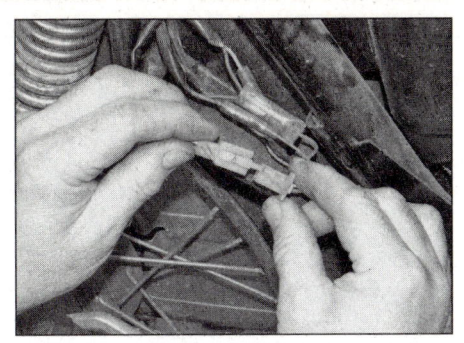

13.9b Disconnect the wiring connector...

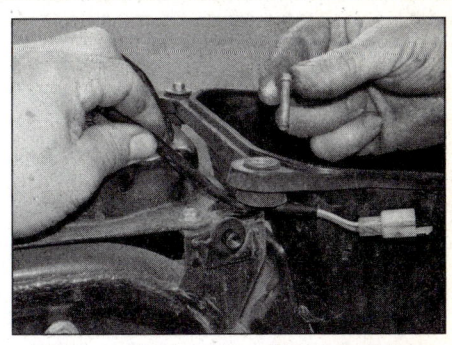

13.9c ...then unscrew the storage box bolt and lift the box to allow the wiring to be drawn up

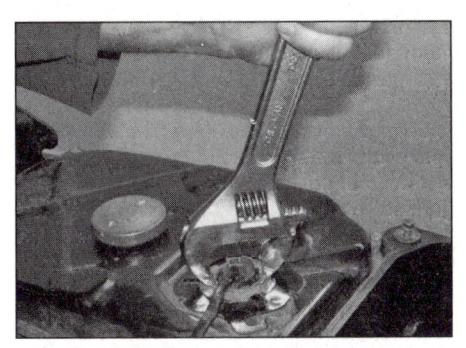

13.10a Turn and remove the retainer...

13.10b ...and remove the sensor

13.11a Fit a new sealing ring

supply to the instrument cluster is good, the instrument board is faulty (see Chapter 8).

Replacement

⚠️ **Warning: Refer to the precautions given in Section 1 before starting work.**

7 The fuel gauge is part of the instrument cluster and is covered in Chapter 8.
8 To replace the sensor, remove the body cover (see Chapter 7).
9 Free the wiring from the guide **(see illustration)**. Trace the wiring from the sensor and disconnect it at the connector **(see illustration)**. Unscrew the bolt securing the right-hand side of the storage box, then draw the wiring up to the sensor, noting its routing and lifting the box for clearance **(see illustration)**.
10 Turn the sensor retainer anti-clockwise using a suitable tool and remove it, noting how it locates **(see illustration)**. Carefully manoeuvre the sensor out of the tank, taking care not to snag the float arm **(see illustration)**. Remove the sealing-ring – a new one must be used.
11 Fit a new sealing-ring onto the tank **(see illustration)**. Fit the sensor into the tank, aligning the wiring with the guide and locating the squared section over the tab **(see illustration)**. Fit the retainer so that the marks on it and the tank will be aligned and turn it clockwise to lock it **(see illustrations)**. Reconnect the wiring.
12 Install the body cover (see Chapter 7).

14 Throttle switch

Check

Note: *Refer to electrical system fault finding in Section 2 of Chapter 8 and to the wiring diagram for your model at the end of Chapter 8.*

1 Remove the front cover on the right-hand side (see Chapter 7).
2 Disconnect the switch wiring connectors **(see illustration 7.7)**.
3 Connect the probes of a multimeter set to test continuity or resistance to the terminals on the switch side of the connectors **(see**

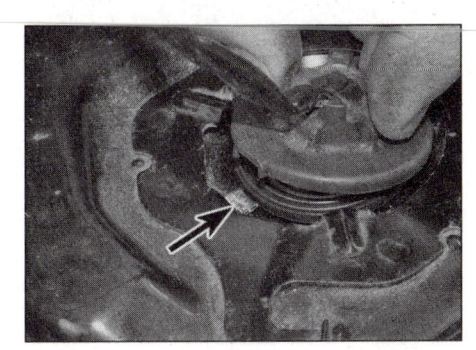

13.11b Align the wiring and seat the squared section over the tab (arrowed)

13.11c Fit the retainer...

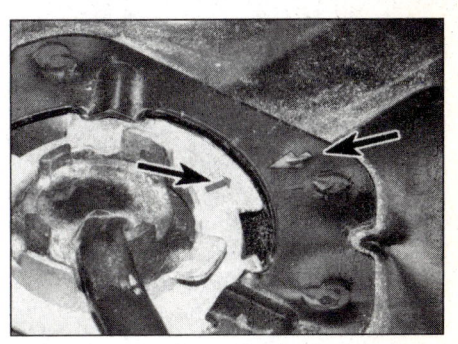

13.11d ...so the marks (arrowed) align

3A•14 Carburettor fuel system and exhaust

14.3 Connect a meter to the switch connectors

14.4 Check the switch plunger

14.7 Undo the screws (arrowed) and remove the switch

illustration). Slowly open the throttle while watching the meter. With the throttle closed and until the throttle is about half open there should be continuity or zero resistance. Between half-throttle and full throttle there should be no continuity or infinite resistance.

4 If the switch does not perform as described remove it (see below). Check that the plunger moves in freely and out under spring pressure **(see illustration)**. Repeat the continuity test, moving the plunger by hand, and replace the switch with a new one if it fails the test. If the switch appears to work, undo the carburettor top cap and draw the throttle valve out and check it where it bears on the throttle valve **(see illustrations 10.2a and b)**.

Replacement

⚠️ *Warning: Refer to the precautions given in Section 1 before starting work.*

5 Remove the front cover on the right-hand side (see Chapter 7).
6 Disconnect the switch wiring connectors **(see illustration 7.7)**.
7 Undo the screws and remove the switch **(see illustration)**. Remove the sealing ring – a new one must be fitted.
8 Fit the new sealing ring into its groove in the carburettor **(see illustration)**.
9 Fit the switch, aligning the plunger with the hole, and tighten the screws **(see illustration)**. Reconnect the wiring. Check the switch (Step 3).
10 Install the front cover.

15 Carburettor heater and thermo switch

Check

Note: Refer to electrical system fault finding in Section 2 of Chapter 8 and to the wiring diagram for your model at the end of Chapter 8.

1 Remove the front cover on the right-hand side (see Chapter 7).
2 Check the connectors to the heater itself on the carburettor are secure **(see illustration 7.6)**.
3 Disconnect the heater sub-loom wiring connector – it is a white 2-pin connector in amongst the wiring and cables on the top of the air filter housing on the right-hand side **(see illustration)**. Connect the probes of a multimeter set to test resistance to the terminals on the heater side of the connector and the check the resistance is as specified at the beginning of the Chapter. If not, check the wiring from the connector to the heater for continuity. If the wiring is good, the heater is faulty.
4 Disconnect the thermo switch wiring connector **(see illustration 15.3)**. Connect the positive probe of a voltmeter to the black wire terminal in the loom side of the connector and the negative (-) probe to a good earth. Turn the ignition ON – there should be battery voltage. If there is, check for continuity in the brown/black wire to the heater wiring connector. If there was no voltage check the black wire for a break.
5 If the wiring is good connect the probes of a continuity tester to the terminals in the thermo switch side of the black connector. The switch should be on, so the meter should show continuity, at anything up to about 20°C, at which point it should switch off (no continuity). You can use a hair dryer to raise the temperature if necessary, otherwise test it at different times according to ambient temperature. Replace the switch with a new one if it does not perform as described.

Replacement

⚠️ *Warning: Refer to the precautions given in Section 1 before starting work.*

6 To remove the heater, remove the air filter housing (see Section 5). Disconnect the wiring connectors, then unscrew the switch, noting the earth terminal **(see illustration 7.6)**.
7 To remove the thermo switch remove the front cover on the right-hand side (see Chapter 7). Disconnect the wiring connector, then release the switch from the loom **(see illustration 15.3)**.
8 Installation is the reverse of removal.

14.8 Fit a new sealing ring . . .

14.9 . . . then fit the switch

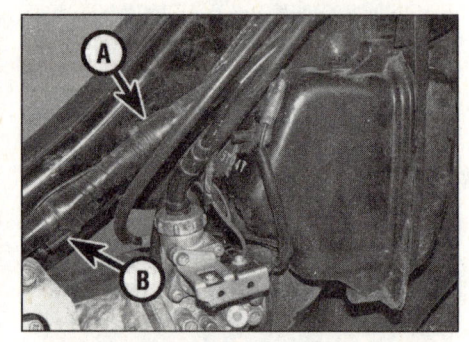

15.3 The heater loom connector (not shown), the thermo switch (A) and its connector (B)

Chapter 3B
Fuel injection system and exhaust

Contents

	Section number
Air filter	see Chapter 1
Air filter housing	5
Catalytic converter	15
Electronic control unit (ECU)	see Chapter 4
Exhaust system	13
Fuel gauge and level sensor	14
Fuel injection system description	7
Fuel injection system fault diagnosis	8
Fuel injection system sensors	9
Fuel injector	10

	Section number
Fuel pump	4
Fuel pressure check	3
Fuel system checks	see Chapter 1
Fuel tank	2
General information and precautions	1
Idle air control valve (IACV)	11
Idle speed check	see Chapter 1
Throttle body	6
Throttle cable check and adjustment	see Chapter 1
Throttle cable removal and installation	12

Degrees of difficulty

Easy, suitable for novice with little experience	Fairly easy, suitable for beginner with some experience	Fairly difficult, suitable for competent DIY mechanic	Difficult, suitable for experienced DIY mechanic	Very difficult, suitable for expert DIY or professional

Specifications

Fuel
Grade	Unleaded. Minimum 91 RON (Research Octane Number)
Fuel tank capacity	3.7 litres

Fuel injection system
Throttle body ID number	GQR3A
Idle speed	1400 ± 100 rpm
Fuel pressure at specified idle speed	43 psi (3.0 Bar)
Minimum fuel flow rate	14 cc every 10 seconds

Fuel injection system test data
Intake air temperature (IAT) sensor resistance	1.13 to 18.8 K-ohms at 20°C (68°F)
Engine oil temperature (EOT) sensor resistance	
At 20°C (68°F)	2.5 to 2.8 K-ohms
At 100°C (212°F)	210 to 220 ohms
Fuel injector resistance	9 to 12 ohms
Idle air control valve (IACV) resistance	110 to 150 ohms

Fuel level sensor
Sensor resistance
FULL position	5 to 7 ohms
EMPTY position	204 to 210 ohms

Torque settings
Engine oil temperature (EOT) sensor	14 Nm
Exhaust downpipe nuts	27 Nm
Fuel injector holder bolts	5 Nm
Fuel pump nuts	12 Nm
Intake duct bolts	12 Nm
Oxygen sensor	25 Nm
Sensor unit screws	3.4 Nm

3B•2 Fuel injection system and exhaust

1 General information and precautions

General information

Models from 2007-on are fitted with a fuel injection system. Earlier models have a carburettor and are covered in Chapter 3A.

The fuel supply system consists of the fuel tank with internal and integral fuel pump, filter, pressure regulator and level sensor, the fuel hose, the injector, the throttle body, and the throttle cable. Idle speed and fast idle speed for cold starting are set automatically by the electronic control unit (ECU) and the idle air control valve (IACV) on the throttle body. The injector is operated by the ECU using the information obtained from the various sensors it monitors. The sensor unit on the throttle body is an integrated unit containing the manifold absolute pressure (MAP) sensor, intake air temperature (IAT) sensor and throttle position (TP) sensor. Refer to Section 7 for more information on the operation of the fuel injection system.

All models have a fuel gauge incorporated in the instrument cluster, actuated by the level sensor inside the fuel tank.

Note: *Individual engine management system components can be checked but not repaired. If system troubles occur, and the faulty component can be isolated, the only cure for the problem in most cases is to replace the part with a new one. Keep in mind that most electronic parts, once purchased, cannot be returned. To avoid unnecessary expense, make very sure the faulty component has been positively identified before buying a new part.*

Precautions

⚠ **Warning:** *Petrol (gasoline) is extremely flammable, so take extra precautions when you work on any part of the fuel system. Always disconnect the battery (see Chapter 8). Don't smoke or allow open flames or bare light bulbs near the work area, and don't work in a garage where a natural gas-type appliance is present. If you spill any fuel on your skin, rinse it off immediately with soap and water. When you perform any kind of work on the fuel system, wear safety glasses and have a fire extinguisher suitable for a class B type fire (flammable liquids) on hand.*

With the fuel injection system, some residual pressure will remain in the fuel feed hose and injector after the engine has been stopped. Before disconnecting the fuel hose, ensure the ignition is switched OFF and make sure you have some clean rag to catch and mop up the fuel. It is vital that no dirt or debris is allowed to enter any part of the system while a fuel hose is disconnected. Any foreign matter in the fuel system components could result in injector damage or malfunction. Ensure the ignition is switched OFF before disconnecting or reconnecting any fuel injection system wiring connector. If a connector is disconnected or reconnected with the ignition switched ON, the engine control unit (ECU) may be damaged.

Always perform service procedures in a well-ventilated area to prevent a build-up of fumes.

Never work in a building containing a gas appliance with a pilot light, or any other form of naked flame. Ensure that there are no naked light bulbs or any sources of flame or sparks nearby.

Do not smoke (or allow anyone else to smoke) while in the vicinity of petrol (gasoline) or of components containing it. Remember the possible presence of vapour from these sources and move well clear before smoking.

Check all electrical equipment belonging to the house, garage or workshop where work is being undertaken (see the *Safety first!* section of this manual). Remember that certain electrical appliances such as drills, cutters etc, create sparks in the normal course of operation and must not be used near petrol (gasoline) or any component containing it. Again, remember the possible presence of fumes before using electrical equipment.

Always mop up any spilt fuel and safely dispose of the rag used.

Any stored fuel that is drained off during servicing work must be kept in sealed containers that are suitable for holding petrol (gasoline), and clearly marked as such; the containers themselves should be kept in a safe place. Note that this last point applies equally to the fuel tank if it is removed from the machine; also remember to keep its filler cap closed at all times.

Read the *Safety first!* section of this manual carefully before starting work.

2 Fuel tank

1 Remove the storage compartment (see Chapter 7).
2 Remove the fuel pump cover – the right-hand bolt also secures the front-right of the tank **(see illustration)**. Disconnect the fuel pump wiring connector and release the wire from the clamp **(see illustration)**. Refer to Section 4 and either remove the pump, or just detach the fuel hose from it (Step 9).
3 If required drain the tank into a suitable container using a siphon pump inserted in the filler hole.
4 Unscrew the bolts and carefully lift the tank out **(see illustration)**.
5 Installation is the reverse of removal. Refer to Section 4, Step 14 and connect the fuel hose to the pump using a new retainer.

3 Fuel pressure check

⚠ **Warning:** *Refer to the precautions given in Section 1 before starting work.*

Note: *A pressure gauge is required for this check. Honda specify the use of their gauge (Pt. No. 07406-0040004) along with an adapter (Pt No. 07ZAJ-S5A0111) and hoses (Pt. Nos. 07ZAJ-S5A0120, -0130 and -0150), that fit between the fuel hose and the fuel pump.*

1 Disconnect the battery negative (–) lead (see Chapter 8).
2 Remove the fuel pump cover **(see illustration 2.2a)**.
3 Refer to Section 4, Step 9 and detach the fuel hose from the pump. Fit the gauge, hoses and adapter between the fuel hose and fuel pump.

2.2a Unscrew the bolts (arrowed) and remove the cover

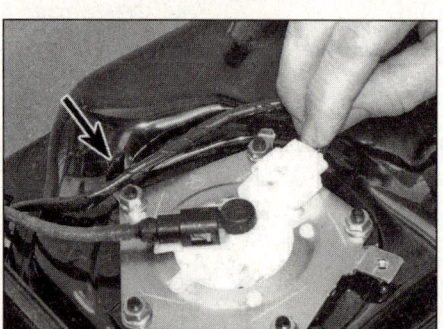

2.2b Disconnect the wiring connector, and if necessary release the clamp (arrowed)

2.4 Fuel tank bolts (arrowed)

Fuel injection system and exhaust 3B•3

4 Reconnect the battery negative (–) lead. Start the engine and allow it to idle. Note the pressure present in the fuel system by reading the gauge, then turn the engine off. Compare the reading obtained to that given in the Specifications.
5 If the fuel pressure is higher than specified, the fuel pump is faulty and must be replaced with a new one.
6 If the fuel pressure is lower than specified, likely causes are.
- Leaking fuel hose – this should be obvious by looking and smelling.
- Blocked fuel strainer – remove the pump and clean the strainer.
- Blocked fuel cap breather – if you hear a hissing sound (air being draw in) when you remove the filler cap, replace the cap with a new one.
- Blocked fuel filter.
- Faulty fuel pump.

If the strainer is clean, the cap is good and there are no leaks evident a new pump assembly must be installed – individual components, including the filter, are not available.
7 On completion, disconnect the battery negative (–) lead again. Disconnect the fuel pressure gauge assembly, being prepared to catch the residual fuel. Refer to Section 4, Step 14 and connect the fuel hose to the pump using a new retainer.
8 Reconnect the battery then start the engine and check that there is no sign of fuel leakage. Install the fuel pump cover.

4 Fuel pump

Warning: Refer to the precautions given in Section 1 before starting work.

Check

1 The fuel pump is fitted into the fuel tank. The fuel pump runs for a few seconds when the ignition is switched ON to pressurise the fuel system, and then cuts out until the engine is started. Check that it does this.
2 If the pump is thought to be faulty, lift the seat and remove the fuel pump cover **(see illustration 2.2a)**.
3 Ensure the ignition is switched OFF then disconnect the fuel pump wiring connector **(see illustration 2.2b)**. Connect the positive (+) lead of a voltmeter to the black/blue wire terminal on the loom side of the connector and the negative (–) lead to the brown wire terminal. Switch the ignition ON whilst noting the reading obtained on the meter.
4 If battery voltage is present for a few seconds, the fuel pump circuit is operating correctly and the fuel pump itself is faulty and must be replaced with a new one.
5 If no reading is obtained, refer to electrical system fault finding and the wiring diagram in Chapter 8 and check the fuel pump circuit wiring for continuity, and make sure all the connectors are free from corrosion and are securely connected. Repair/replace the wiring as necessary and clean the connectors using electrical contact cleaner. If this fails to reveal the fault, check the following components.
- Fuses (see Chapter 8).
- Power relay (see Chapter 8).
- Ignition switch (see Chapter 8).

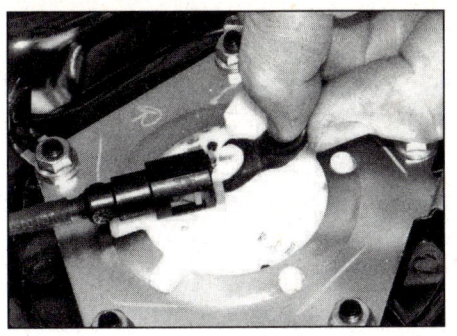

4.9a Pull the rubber tab back and seat the ring around the union

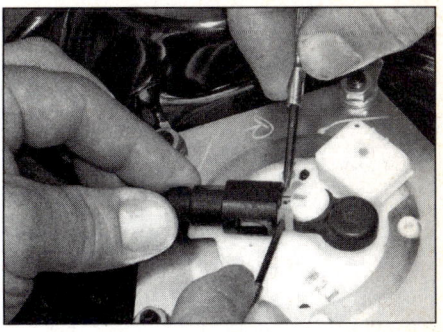

4.9b Press the tabs in and pull the connector off

- Regulator/rectifier (see Chapter 8).
- Engine control unit (ECU) (see Chapter 4).

Removal

6 Disconnect the battery negative (–) terminal (see Chapter 8).
7 Remove the fuel pump cover **(see illustration 2.2a)**.
8 Disconnect the fuel pump wiring connector and release the wire from the clamp **(see illustration 2.2b)**.
9 Lift the rubber tab off the top of the fuel hose union on the fuel pump and pull it away from the hose connector so the ring section is clear of the green retainer, and seat the ring around the top of the union to keep it clear **(see illustration)**. Place some rag around the fuel hose. Press in the tabs on the retainer and draw the connector off the union **(see illustration)**. Remove the retainer from the union **(see illustration)** – Honda specify to use a new one.
10 Unscrew the nuts and remove the pump retaining plate **(see illustration)**. Carefully lift the pump out of the tank, taking care not to snag the level sensor float **(see illustration 4.13b)**. Remove the rubber seal from the pump and discard it – a new one must be used **(see illustration 4.13a)**.
11 The pump comes as a complete assembly and no individual components are available.

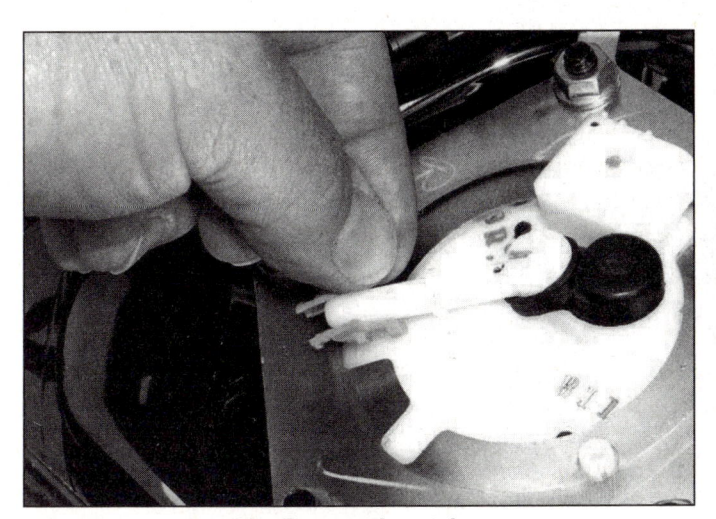

4.9c Remove the retainer

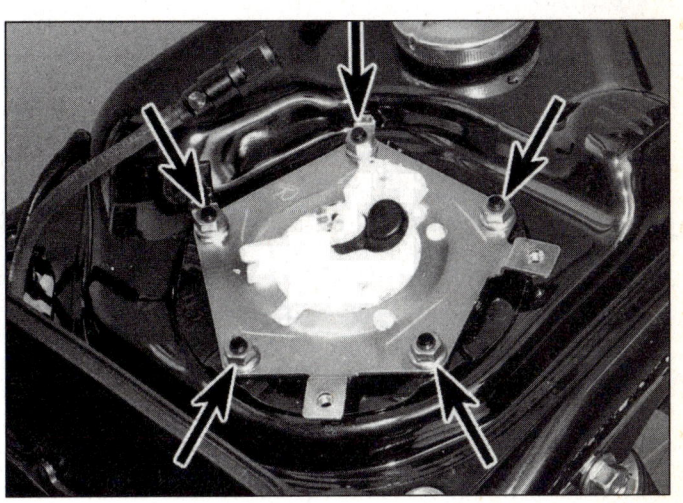

4.10 Retaining plate nuts (arrowed)

3B•4 Fuel injection system and exhaust

4.12 Check the strainer (arrowed)

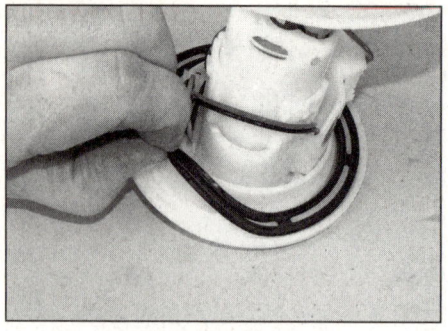

4.13a Fit a new seal . . .

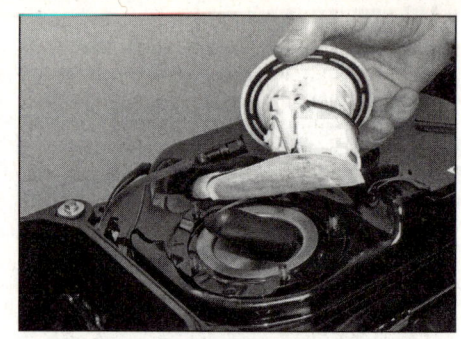

4.13b . . . then insert the pump . . .

4.13c . . . and align the hose union with the triangle (arrowed)

4.13d Locate the plate

4.14a Relocate the rubber ring as shown

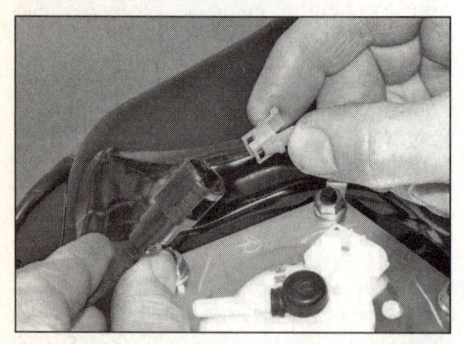

4.14b Fit a new retainer into the connector

4.14c Push the connector onto the union

Installation

12 Make sure the fuel strainer is clean **(see illustration)**. Clean the mating surfaces of the pump and the fuel tank.
13 Fit the new rubber seal onto the pump **(see illustration)**. Fit the pump into the tank, aligning the hose union with the triangular mark **(see illustrations)**. Fit the retainer plate **(see illustration)** – align the threaded tabs for the cover correctly **(see illustration 4.10)**. Check that the pump, seal and plate are all evenly seated with the hose union aligned with the triangular mark. Fit the nuts and tighten them finger-tight **(see illustration 4.10)**. Now tighten the nuts evenly and a little at a time in the sequence shown to the torque setting specified at the beginning of the Chapter.
14 Relocate the rubber ring on the union as shown **(see illustration)**. Fit a new hose retainer into the end of the connector, aligning the locking tabs with the holes and making sure it clicks into place **(see illustration)**. Push the connector fully onto the pump union, again until it clicks into place **(see illustration)** – check it is secure by trying to pull it off.
15 Connect the fuel pump wiring connector and secure the wiring in the clamp **(see illustration 2.2b)**.
16 Connect the battery negative (–) terminal (see Chapter 8). Install the pump cover **(see illustration 2.2a)**.

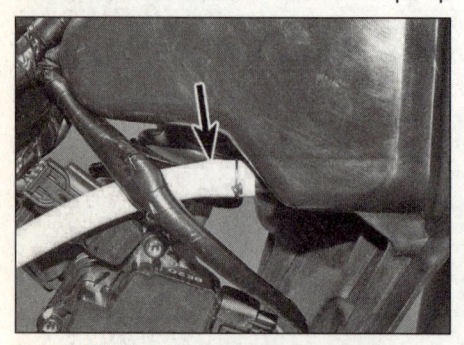

5.2 Detach the hose (arrowed)

5.3 Slacken the clamp screw (arrowed)

5 Air filter housing

1 Remove the air filter (see Chapter 1).
2 Detach the crankcase breather hose from its union on the rear of the housing **(see illustration)**.
3 Slacken the clamp securing the air duct to the throttle body **(see illustration)**.
4 Unscrew the bolt on each side at the

Fuel injection system and exhaust 3B•5

top and manoeuvre the housing out **(see illustrations)**.

5 Installation is the reverse of removal.

6 Throttle body

⚠️ **Warning: Refer to the precautions given in Section 1 before starting work.**

Removal

1 Remove the front cover on each side (see Chapter 7).
2 Disconnect the wiring connectors from the idle air control valve (IACV), the sensor unit and the fuel injector **(see illustrations)**.
3 Undo the throttle cable bracket screw and free the cable end from the pulley **(see illustrations)**.
4 Pull the rubber restrictor tabs so the pegs come out of the fuel hose connector then turn the restrictor so the pegs are clear of the green retainer **(see illustration)**. Place some rag around the fuel hose. Press in the tabs on the retainer and draw the connector off the union **(see illustration)**. Remove the retainer from the union **(see illustration)** – Honda specify to use a new one. Remove the rubber restrictor from the union for safekeeping **(see illustration 6.12b)**.
5 Slacken the clamp screw on the air intake duct **(see illustration 5.3)**.

5.4a Unscrew the bolt (arrowed) on each side – note the routing of the wiring

5.4b Manoeuvre the housing out

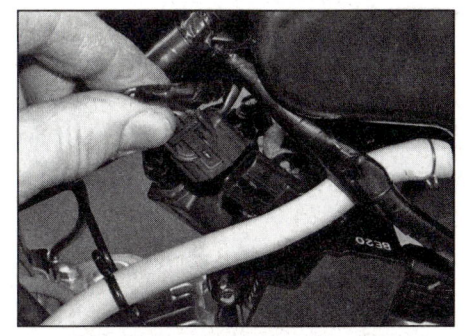

6.2a Disconnect the IACV wiring connector . . .

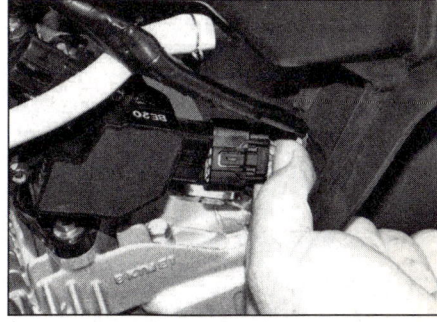

6.2b . . . the sensor unit wiring connector . . .

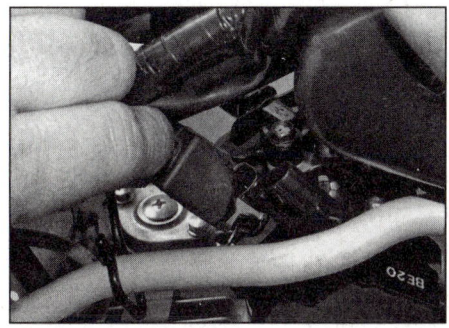

6.2c . . . and the injector wiring connector

6.3a Undo the bracket screw (arrowed) . . .

6.3b . . . and free the cable end

6.4a Pull the rubber tabs away and turn the restrictor

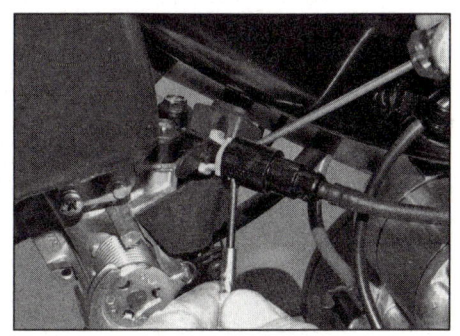

6.4b Press the tabs in and pull the connector off

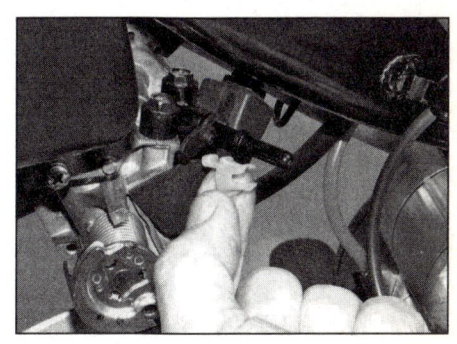

6.4c Remove the retainer

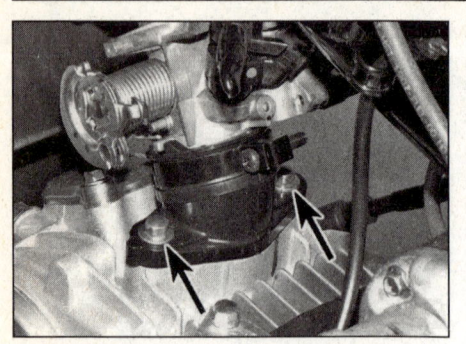

3B•6 Fuel injection system and exhaust

6.6a Unscrew the bolts (arrowed) . . .

6.6b . . . and remove the throttle body

6.9 Fit a new O-ring into the groove

Caution: Do not snap the throttle from fully open to fully closed once the cable has been disconnected because this can lead to engine idle speed problems.

6 Unscrew the intake duct bolts (see illustration). Ease the throttle body assembly out of the air duct and remove it (see illustration). Remove the O-ring from the intake duct flange – a new one must be used.

Caution: Tape over or stuff clean rag into the intake duct after removing the throttle body assembly to prevent anything from falling in.

7 If required slacken the intake duct clamp screw and remove the duct. For removal of the sensor unit, fuel injector, and IACV refer to Sections 9, 10, and 11 respectively. After removing the these components you can blow through all the passages with compressed air – DO NOT poke anything solid into the passages.

Caution: NEVER loosen the white-painted nut or screw on the throttle body.

Installation

8 If the intake duct was removed fit it onto the throttle body, seating its ribs on each side of the tab (see illustration 6.6a). Tighten the clamp screw so the distance between its ends is 6 to 8 mm.

9 Remove the tape/plug from the intake duct. Fit a new O-ring smeared with grease into the groove in the intake duct flange (see illustration).

10 Fit the throttle body assembly into the air duct and onto the head, making sure the O-ring stays in place (see illustration 6.6b). Fit the intake duct bolts and tighten them evenly in stages to the torque setting specified at the beginning of the Chapter (see illustration 6.6a).

11 Tighten the clamp screw on the air intake duct (see illustration 5.3).

12 Fit a new hose retainer into the end of the connector, aligning the locking tabs with the holes and making sure it clicks into place (see illustration). Fit the rubber restrictor and position the tabs horizontally on the union (see illustrations). Push the connector fully onto the union, again until it clicks into place (see illustration) – check it is secure by trying to pull it off.

13 Lubricate the throttle cable end with multi-purpose grease and fit it into the pulley (see illustration 6.3b). Locate the bracket on the throttle body, seating the hole over the peg, and tighten the screw.

14 Reconnect the wiring connectors (see illustrations 6.2c, b and a).

15 Check and adjust throttle cable freeplay (see Chapter 1).

16 Install the front covers (see Chapter 7).

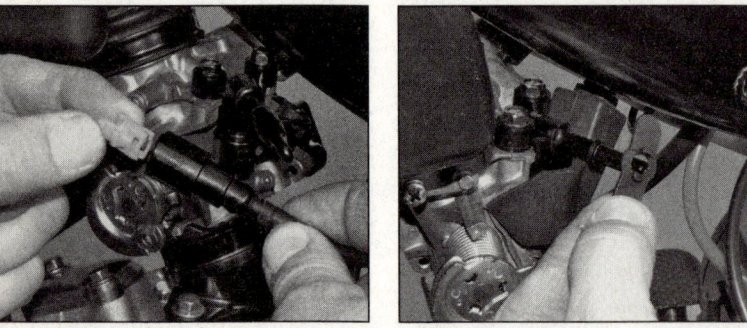

7 Fuel injection system description

1 All models covered in this Chapter are equipped with Honda's programmed fuel injection (PGM-FI) system. It is controlled by an electronic control unit (ECU) that operates both the injection and ignition systems.

2 The ECU monitors signals from the following sensors:

6.12a Fit a new retainer into the connector

6.12b Fit the restrictor onto the union . . .

6.12c . . . and position it as shown

6.12d Push the connector onto the union

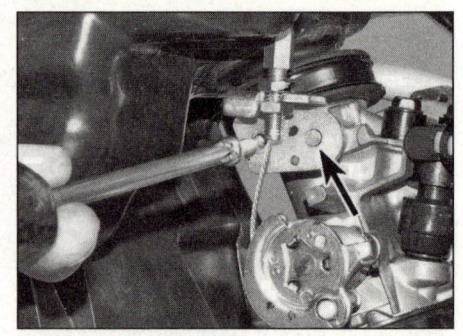

6.13 Locate the hole in the bracket over the peg (arrowed)

Fuel injection system and exhaust 3B•7

8.4a Data link connector (arrowed)

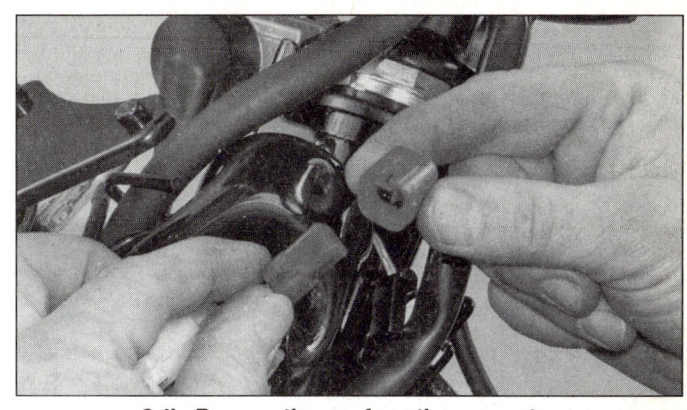

8.4b Remove the cap from the connector

- Throttle position (TP) sensor – informs the ECU of the throttle position, and the rate of throttle opening or closing.
- Engine oil temperature (EOT) sensor – informs the ECU of engine temperature.
- Manifold absolute pressure (MAP) sensor – informs the ECU of the engine load by monitoring the pressure in the throttle body air intake duct.
- Intake air temperature (IAT) sensor – informs the ECU of the temperature of the air entering the throttle body.
- Ignition pulse generator coil – informs the ECU of engine speed and crankshaft position (see Chapter 4).
- Speed sensor – informs the ECU of the road speed of the scooter (see Chapter 8).
- Lean angle sensor – stops the engine if the bike falls over.
- Oxygen sensor – informs the ECU of the oxygen content of the exhaust gases.

3 The manifold absolute pressure (MAP) sensor, intake air temperature (IAT) sensor and throttle position (TP) sensor are all integrated in the sensor unit on the throttle body. All the information from the sensors is analysed by the ECU, and from that it determines the appropriate ignition and fuelling requirements of the engine. The ECU controls the fuel injector by varying its pulse width – the length of time the injector is held open – to provide more or less fuel, as appropriate for cold starting, warm up, idle, cruising, and acceleration.

4 Cold starting and warm up idle speeds are controlled automatically by the ECU and the idle air control valve (IACV).

8 Fuel injection system fault diagnosis

1 When the ignition is switched on the malfunction indicator lamp (MIL) in the instrument cluster will come on for a few seconds, then go out. When the engine is started the fuel injection system automatically performs a self-diagnosis check. If all is good the MIL remains off. If there is an abnormality in any of the readings obtained from any sensor, the ECU enters its back-up mode. If the ECU enters this back-up mode while performing its self-diagnosis check on start-up, when idling or when the sidestand is down the MIL will flash. If it enters this back-up mode while riding the MIL will come on, then will start to flash when the sidestand is lowered with the engine idling. In back-up mode the ECU ignores the abnormal sensor signal, and assumes a pre-programmed value which may, depending on the sensor in question and the fault detected, allow the engine to continue running (albeit at reduced efficiency). Otherwise the engine will stop, or will not be able to be restarted once it has been stopped. In each case the relevant fault code will be stored in the ECU memory. The fault can be identified by reading the fault code or codes as follows.

2 If the engine can be started, place the scooter on its sidestand then start the engine and allow it to idle. Whilst the engine is idling, observe the MIL on the instrument cluster, and go to Step 5.

3 If the engine cannot be started, turn the engine over on the starter motor for more then ten seconds and observe the MIL on the instrument cluster, and go to Step 5.

4 Alternatively, and to check for any stored fault codes even though the MIL has not illuminated, remove the top cover to gain access to the fuel injection system data link connector (DLC), which is a capped red 4-pin connector inside the black rubber boot **(see illustration)**. Ensure the ignition is switched OFF then remove the cap and either fit the Honda DLC short connector (Part No. 070PZ-ZY30100, available at reasonable cost from your dealer), or make your own using suitable connectors and a piece of wire joining them, between the blue and green/black wire terminals in the connector **(see illustration)**. Turn the ignition ON and observe the warning light. If there are stored fault codes, the light will flash – go to Step 5.

5 The light emits long (1.3 second) and short (0.5 second) flashes to give out the fault code. A long flash is used to indicate the first digit of a double digit fault code (i.e. 10 and above). If a single digit fault code is being displayed (i.e. 0 – 9), there will be a number of short flashes equivalent to the code being displayed. For example, two long (1.3 sec) flashes followed by nine short (0.5 sec) flashes indicates the fault code number 29. If there is more than one fault code, there will be a gap before the other codes are revealed, and the codes will be revealed in order, starting with the lowest and finishing with the highest. Once all codes have been revealed, the ECU will continuously run through the code(s) stored in its memory, revealing each one in turn with a short gap between them. The fault codes are shown in the table.

Fault code (No. of flashes)	Symptoms	Possible causes
1	Engine runs normally	Faulty manifold absolute pressure (MAP) sensor or wiring
7	Engine difficult to start at low temperatures	Faulty engine oil temperature (EOT) sensor or wiring
8	Poor throttle response	Faulty throttle position (TP) sensor or wiring
9	Engine runs normally	Faulty intake air temperature (IAT) sensor or wiring
12	Engine does not start	Faulty injector or wiring
21	Engine operates normally	Faulty oxygen sensor or wiring
29	Engine hard to start, stalls, rough idle	Faulty idle air control valve (IACV) or wiring
54	Engine operates normally	Faulty lean angle sensor or wiring

3B•8 Fuel injection system and exhaust

Once all the codes have been revealed, switch off the ignition and (where necessary) remove the tool from the data link connector. Identify the fault using the table above, then refer to Steps 7 and 8 for checking procedures.

6 Once the fault has been identified and corrected, it will be necessary to reset the system by removing the fault code from the ECU memory. To do this, make sure the ignition is switched OFF then fit the Honda DLC short connector or your home-made equivalent (see Step 4). Turn the ignition switch ON. Disconnect the tool from the DLC. When the tool is disconnected the light should come on for about five seconds, during which time the tool must be reconnected. The light should start to flash when it is reconnected, indicating that all fault codes have been erased. Turn off the ignition then remove the tool. Check the light – in some cases it may be necessary to repeat the erasing procedure more than once.

7 While some of the sensors can be checked using home equipment, there are others which can only be tested using the Honda diagnostic system (HDS) tester which can be plugged into the system. If a fault appears, use the diagnostic function and fault code system described above to work out which component is faulty. First ensure that the relevant system wiring connectors are securely connected and free of corrosion – poor connections are the cause of the majority of problems. Also check the wiring itself for any obvious faults or breaks, and use a continuity tester to check the wiring between the component, its connectors and the ECU, referring to electrical system fault finding and the wiring diagram in Chapter 8. It is also possible that a temporary glitch has occurred, which can be checked by clearing the system (Step 6), then starting the engine and checking if the same fault code comes up. Next refer to the relevant Section(s) in this Chapter to see if there are any other specific checks that can be made on that particular component. If this fails to reveal the cause of the problem, the scooter should be taken to a Honda dealer – they will have the tester which should locate the fault quickly and simply.

8 Also ensure that the fault is not due to poor maintenance – i.e. check that the air filter element is clean, that the spark plug is in good condition, that the valve clearances are correctly adjusted, the cylinder compression pressure is correct, and the ignition timing is correct (refer to Chapters 1, 2 and 4). It is also worth removing the sensor(s) in question and checking that the sensing tip or head is clean and not obstructed by anything.

9 Fuel injection system sensors

Caution: Ensure the ignition is switched OFF before disconnecting/reconnecting any fuel injection system wiring connector. If a connector is disconnected/reconnected with the ignition switched ON the ECU could be damaged.

1 If a fault is indicated in any of the system sensors, first check the wiring and connectors between the sensor and the ECU (refer to *Electrical system fault finding* at the beginning of Chapter 8, and to the *Wiring diagram* at the end of it). A continuity test of all wires will locate a break or short in any circuit. Inspect the terminals inside the wiring connectors and ensure they are not loose, bent or corroded. Spray the inside of the connectors with a proprietary electrical terminal cleaner before reconnection.

2 The MAP, TP and IAT sensors are all contained within the sensor unit on the throttle body, and share the same wiring connector and power source. For fault codes 1, 8 and 9, before checking the individual sensor check the power circuit of the sensor unit.

Sensor unit

3 Remove the front cover on the right-hand side (see Chapter 7).

Power circuit check – Fault codes 1, 8 and 9

4 Disconnect the sensor unit wiring connector **(see illustration 6.2b)**.
5 Connect the positive (+) lead of a voltmeter to the yellow/red terminal in the sensor wiring connector, then connect the negative (–) lead to the green/orange wire terminal. Turn the ignition switch ON and check that a voltage of 4.75 to 5.25 volts is present. If the voltage is good, check the output of the relevant sensor. If there is no voltage, check for continuity in each wire to the ECU. If there is no continuity locate the break and repair it. If the wiring is good, the ECU could be faulty.

Removal

6 Disconnect the sensor unit wiring connector **(see illustration 6.2b)**.
7 Undo the screws and remove the sensor **(see illustration)**. Remove the sealing ring – a new one must be used.

Installation

8 Fit a new sealing ring onto the throttle body.
9 Fit the sensor, aligning the TP tab and making sure the sealing ring stays in place, and tighten the screws to the torque setting specified at the beginning of the Chapter.
10 Connect the wiring connector **(see illustration 9.7)**.
11 The throttle valve closed position must now be reset for the TP sensor to work properly. Clear any fault codes – see Section 8, Step 6.
12 Reconnect the tool to the DLC.
13 Disconnect the EOT sensor wiring connector **(see illustration 9.21)**. Short between the two terminals in the EOT sensor wiring connector using an auxiliary wire. Turn the ignition switch ON – the MIL should start to blink slowly (every 1.2 secs) and will do so for ten seconds, during which time you must disconnect the auxiliary wire. With the wire disconnected the MIL should start to blink rapidly (every 0.3 secs), indicating the reset procedure was successful. If the MIL comes on and stays on, repeat the reset procedure.
14 Turn the ignition off. Remove the tool from the DLC and connect the EOT sensor wiring connector.
15 Install the front cover.

Manifold absolute pressure (MAP) sensor – Fault code 1

16 Remove the front cover on the right-hand side (see Chapter 7).

Check

17 First check the power circuit to the sensor unit (Steps 4 and 5).
18 With the connector disconnected and the ignition ON check the voltage between the light green/yellow and green/orange wire terminals of the connector. If there is 4.75 to 5.25 volts, the MAP sensor is faulty. If there is no voltage check for continuity to the ECU in each of the wires. If there is none, trace the fault in the wire and repair it. If all the wiring is good the ECU could be faulty.

Removal and installation

19 See Steps 6 to 15.

Engine oil temperature (EOT) sensor – Fault code 7

20 Remove the front cover on the left-hand side (see Chapter 7).

Check

21 Disconnect the wiring connector from the sensor **(see illustration)**.

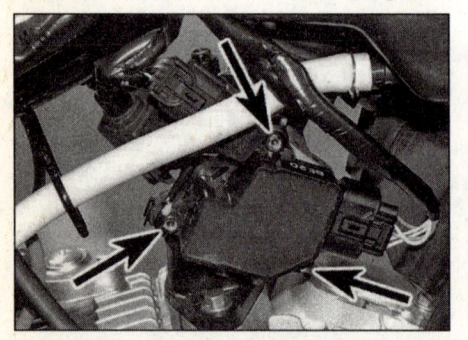

9.7 Sensor unit screws (arrowed)

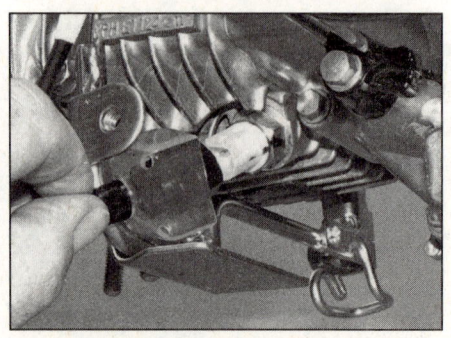

9.21 Disconnect the EOT wiring connector

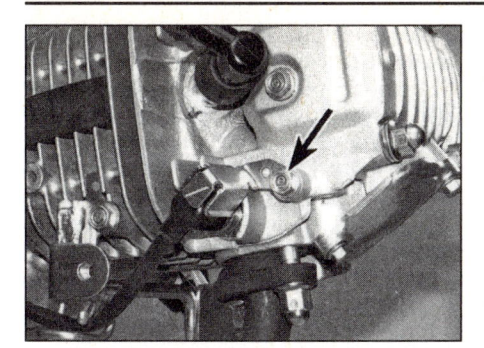

Fuel injection system and exhaust 3B•9

9.42a Unscrew the bolt (arrowed) and remove the cover . . .

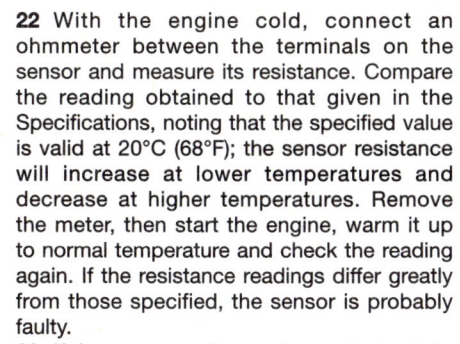

9.42b . . . then pull the connector off

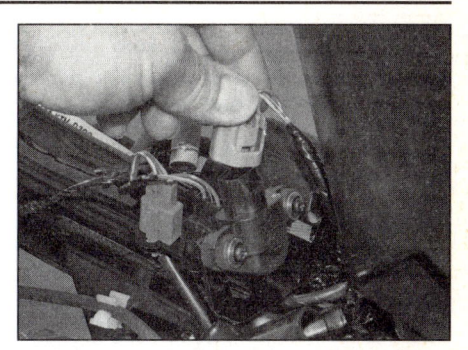

9.46 Disconnect the lean angle sensor wiring connector

22 With the engine cold, connect an ohmmeter between the terminals on the sensor and measure its resistance. Compare the reading obtained to that given in the Specifications, noting that the specified value is valid at 20°C (68°F); the sensor resistance will increase at lower temperatures and decrease at higher temperatures. Remove the meter, then start the engine, warm it up to normal temperature and check the reading again. If the resistance readings differ greatly from those specified, the sensor is probably faulty.

23 If the sensor resistance is good, check its power supply. Connect the positive (+) lead of a voltmeter to the yellow/blue wire terminal in the sensor wiring connector, then connect the negative (–) lead to a good earth. Turn the ignition switch ON and check that a voltage of 4.75 to 5.25 volts is present. If it isn't, check for continuity in the yellow/blue wire to the ECU. If there is no continuity locate the break and repair it. If the wiring is good, the ECU could be faulty. If voltage was present, now connect the negative lead to the green/orange terminal of the connector and check that the same voltage is present. If it isn't, there is a fault in the green/orange wire or the ECU. If there is voltage, the ECU is probably faulty.

Removal

24 Drain the engine oil (see Chapter 1).
25 Disconnect the wiring connector from the sensor **(see illustration 9.21)**.
26 Unscrew the sensor and remove the sealing washer – a new one must be used.

Installation

27 Fit the sensor using a new sealing washer and tighten to the torque setting specified at the beginning of the Chapter.
28 Connect the wiring connector.
29 Fill the engine with oil (see Chapter 1).

Throttle position (TP) sensor – Fault code 8

30 Remove the front cover on the right-hand side (see Chapter 7).

Check

31 First check the power circuit to the sensor unit (Steps 4 and 5).

32 Next check for continuity in the yellow wire to the ECU.
33 If all is good have the sensor output voltage checked by a Honda dealer.

Removal and installation

34 See Steps 6 to 15.

Intake air temperature (IAT) sensor – Fault code 9

35 Remove the front cover on the right-hand side (see Chapter 7).

Check

36 First check the power circuit to the sensor unit (Steps 4 and 5).
37 With the connector disconnected, connect an ohmmeter between the grey/blue and green/orange wire terminals on the sensor and measure its resistance. Compare the reading obtained to that given in the Specifications, noting that the specified value is valid at 20°C (68°F). If the resistance readings differ greatly from those specified, the sensor is probably faulty.
38 With the connector disconnected and the ignition ON check the voltage between the grey/blue and green/orange wire terminals in the connector. If there is 4.75 to 5.25 volts, the IAT sensor is faulty. If there is no voltage check for continuity to the ECU in the each of the wires. If there is none, trace the fault in the wire and repair it. If all the wiring is good the ECU could be faulty.

Removal and installation

39 See Steps 6 to 15.

Oxygen sensor – Fault code 21

40 Remove the front cover on the right-hand side (see Chapter 7).

Check

41 Refer to Step 42 to disconnect the wiring and check for continuity in the wire to the ECU. If all is good reset the system as described in Section 8, Step 6, then start the engine and check if the same fault code comes up. If it does the sensor is probably faulty.

Removal and installation

Note: *The oxygen sensor is delicate and will not work if it is dropped or knocked, or if any cleaning materials are used on it. Ensure the exhaust system is cold before proceeding.*

42 Unscrew the sensor connector cover bolt and remove the cover **(see illustration)**. Pull the connector off the sensor **(see illustration)**.
43 Unscrew and remove the sensor.
44 Installation is the reverse of removal. Tighten the sensor to the torque setting specified at the beginning of the Chapter.

Lean angle sensor – Fault code 54

45 Remove the front body cover (see Chapter 7).

Check

46 Disconnect the sensor wiring connector **(see illustration)**.
47 To check the power input connect the positive (+) lead of a voltmeter to the yellow/red wire terminal in the sensor wiring connector, then connect the negative (–) lead to the green/orange wire. Turn the ignition switch ON and check that a voltage of 4.75 to 5.25 volts is present. If it isn't, check the wiring and connectors to the ECU for continuity. If the wiring is good the ECU could be faulty.
48 If the voltage is good, check for continuity in the red/blue wire to the ECU.
49 If the wiring is all good, displace the sensor **(see illustration 9.51)**, leaving the connector connected. Connect the positive (+) lead of a voltmeter to the red/blue wire terminal in the connector, and the negative (-) lead to a good earth on the frame. Hold the sensor horizontal and switch the ignition ON – there should be 3.6 to 4.4 volts. Slowly tilt the sensor to the left – once the sensor reaches an angle of approximately 60° the voltage should drop to between 0.7 and 1.3 volts. Switch the ignition OFF and return the sensor to the horizontal, then switch the ignition back ON again and repeat the test, this time tilting the sensor to the right – the same voltage readings should be obtained. If not the sensor is faulty.

Removal and installation

50 Disconnect the sensor wiring connector **(see illustration 9.46)**.
51 Undo the screws and remove the sensor

3B•10 Fuel injection system and exhaust

9.51 Lean angle sensor screws (arrowed)

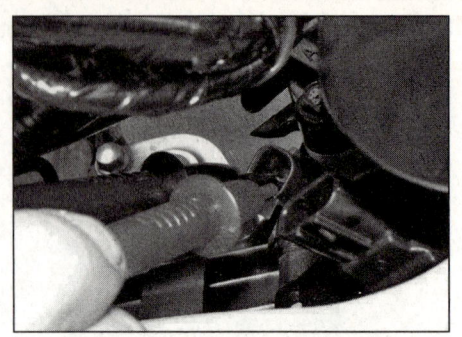

10.3 Checking injector resistance

(see illustration). Note the collars in the mounting grommets.

52 Installation is the reverse of removal. Make sure the collars are in place and the sensor is fitted with its UP mark facing upwards (see illustration 9.51).

10 Fuel injector

⚠ **Warning: Refer to the precautions given in Section 1 before starting work.**

1 Remove the front cover on the left-hand side (see Chapter 7).

Check

2 Disconnect the wiring connector from the injector (see illustration 6.2c) – for best access you may want to disconnect the IACV wiring connector first (see illustration 6.2a).

3 Connect an ohmmeter between the terminals and measure the resistance (see illustration). Compare the reading to that given in the Specifications. If the resistance of the injector differs greatly from that specified a new injector should be fitted.

4 To check the power input connect the positive (+) lead of a voltmeter to the black/blue wire terminal in the injector connector, and connect the negative (–) lead to a good earth. Turn the ignition switch ON and check that battery voltage is present. If it isn't, check the black/blue wire and connectors to the ECU for continuity. If the voltage is good check the pink/green wire for continuity to the ECU. If all is good the ECU could be faulty.

Removal

5 Refer to Section 6, Step 4 and disconnect the fuel hose.

6 Disconnect the wiring connector from the injector (see illustration 6.2c).

7 Clean around the base of the injector to prevent any dirt falling into the throttle body. Unscrew the holder bolts and carefully lift the holder and injector off together (see illustrations). Remove the seal – a new one must be used (see illustration). Cover the throttle body.

8 If required carefully pull the injector out of its holder (see illustration). Remove the O-ring – a new one must be used (see illustration 10.9).

Installation

9 Fit a new O-ring lubricated with clean engine oil into the groove in the injector (see illustration). Fit the injector into the holder aligning it so the socket butts against the tab (see illustration 10.8).

10 Fit a new seal lubricated with clean engine oil onto the injector nozzle (see illustration). Fit the injector assembly into the throttle body aligning the bolt holes (see illustrations 10.7b and a). Tighten the bolts evenly to the torque setting specified at the beginning of the Chapter.

11 Connect the wiring connector(s).

12 Refer to Section 6, Step 12 and connect the fuel hose.

13 Run the engine and check there are no leaks from the injector and that the fuel system is working correctly before fitting the front cover and taking the machine out on the road.

10.7a Unscrew the bolts . . .

10.7b . . . and remove the injector assembly

10.7c Remove the seal

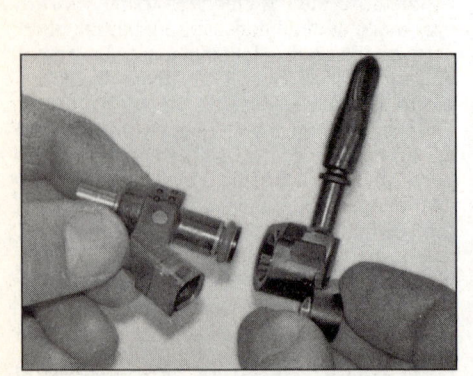

10.8 Pull the injector out of the holder

10.9 Fit a new O-ring

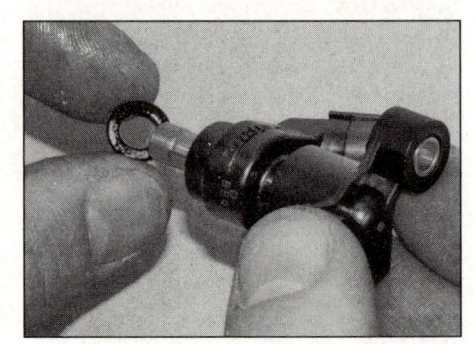

10.10 Fit a new seal

Fuel injection system and exhaust 3B•11

11.10a Undo the screws (arrowed) and remove the plate . . .

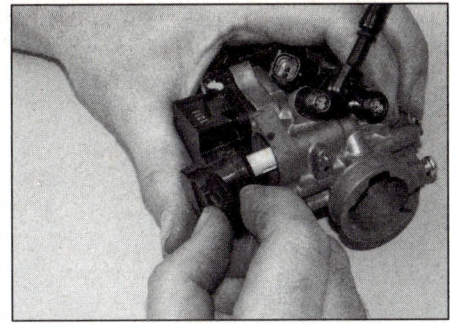

11.10b . . . then draw the valve out

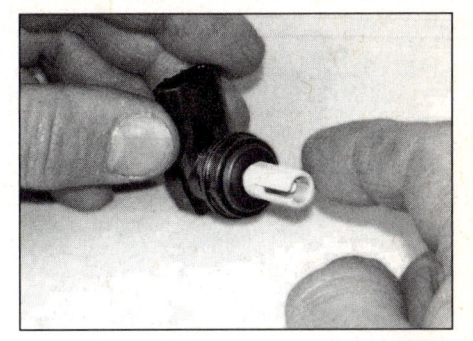

11.11a Turn the valve clockwise until it seats

11 Idle air control valve (IACV)

⚠️ **Warning: Refer to the precautions given in Section 1 before starting work.**

1 Idle speed is controlled automatically by a valve that adjusts a flow of air that by-passes the throttle valve in the throttle body. The valve is actuated by the ECU and adjusts according to information received from the fuel injection system sensors. When the ignition is switched ON the valve self-checks by turning through its range of movement, and should emit a beep – if you are not sure you can remove the valve, reconnect its wiring, turn the ignition ON and visually check. If there is a fault, a fault code should be indicated by the warning light in the instrument cluster (see Sections 7 and 8).

2 If the engine idle speed is not as specified at the beginning of the Chapter, and there is no fault indicated, check the throttle cable freeplay, spark plug, air filter and the valve clearances (see Chapter 1). Also inspect the air and intake ducts for anything loose or cracked that could cause an air leak, causing a weak mixture.

Check

3 Remove the front cover on the right-hand side (see Chapter 7).
4 Disconnect the control valve wiring connector **(see illustration 6.2a)**. Check the connector wires and terminals are secure and clean.
5 Check the resistance of the control valve windings by connecting an ohmmeter first between the black/white and brown/white wire terminals on the valve, and then between the black/yellow and brown/yellow wire terminals. The resistance in each case should be as specified at the beginning of the chapter. If not, replace the valve with a new one.
6 If the valve is good check each wire between the connector and the ECU for continuity. If all is good the ECU could be faulty.

Removal

Note: *The valve is secured by security Torx screws for which a special bit is needed.*
7 Remove the front cover on the right-hand side (see Chapter 7).

11.11b Align the groove with the pin (arrowed)

8 Disconnect the control valve wiring connector **(see illustration 6.2a)**.
9 Clean the area around the valve to prevent any dirt entering the air passages.
10 Undo the valve screws (a security Torx bit is needed) and remove the plate, then draw the valve out **(see illustrations)**. Check the action of the valve by turning it.

Installation

11 Turn the valve clockwise until lightly seated **(see illustration)**. Align the groove in the valve with the pin in its housing, then insert the valve **(see illustration)**. Fit the plate with its longer arm to the rear, turning the valve to align the tab with the rear cut-out, and tighten the screws **(see illustration)**.
12 Connect the wiring connector **(see illustration 6.2a)**. Check the operation of the valve (Step 1) before fitting the front cover.

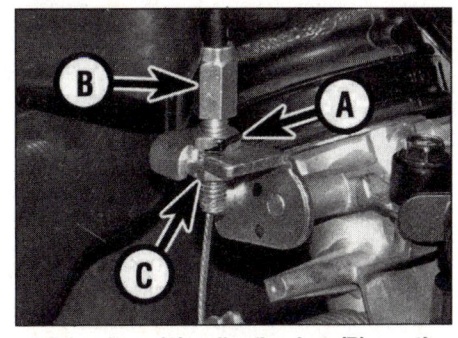

12.2 Locknut (A), adjusting hex (B), captive nut (C)

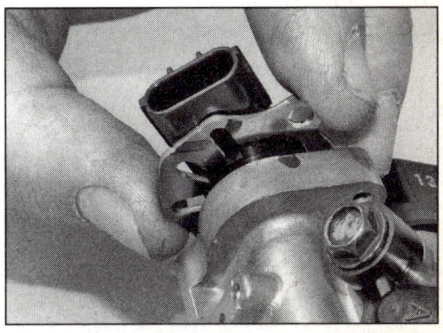

11.11c Align the plate and valve as described and shown

12 Throttle cable

⚠️ **Warning: Refer to the precautions given in Section 1 before proceeding.**

Removal

1 Remove the handlebar covers and the front covers (see Chapter 7).
2 Slacken the locknut securing the cable in its bracket on the throttle body, then unscrew the adjusting hex until the captive nut is free and slip the cable out of the bracket **(see illustration)**. Detach the cable end from the pulley **(see illustration 6.3b)**.
3 Draw the cable out, noting the routing.
4 Unscrew the cable elbow nut from the throttle pulley housing **(see illustration)**. Undo

12.4a Unscrew the nut (arrowed) . . .

3B•12 Fuel injection system and exhaust

12.4b ... then undo the housing screw (arrowed) and detach the housing

12.4c Free the cable end ...

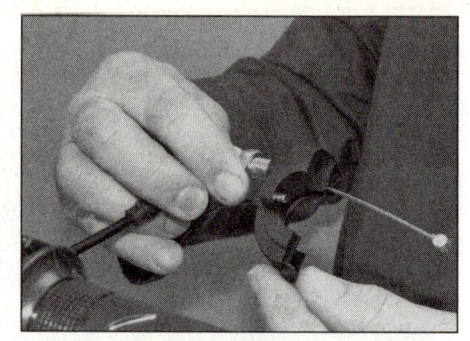

12.4d ... then thread the housing off the cable

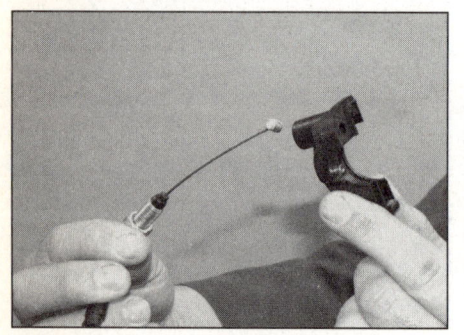

12.5a Fit the cable through and thread the housing onto it

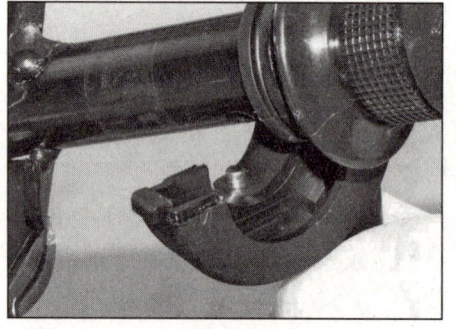

12.5b Locate the pin on the bottom half in the hole ...

12.5c ... then hook the top half on and pivot it down onto the handlebar

the housing screw and pivot the top half up and off **(see illustration)**. Detach the housing and free the cable end from the pulley, then thread the housing off the cable elbow and draw the cable out **(see illustrations)**.

Installation

5 Thread the throttle pulley housing onto the upper end of the cable elbow without it becoming tight – the elbow must stay loose so that it aligns itself **(see illustration)**. Lubricate the cable end with multi-purpose grease and fit it into the throttle pulley **(see illustration 12.4c)**. Assemble the housing halves onto the handlebar, making sure the pin in the bottom half locates in the hole, then fit the screw **(see illustrations)**.

6 Feed the cable through to the throttle body, making sure it is correctly routed. The cable must not interfere with any other component and should not be kinked or bent sharply. Now tighten the cable elbow nut on the housing **(see illustration 12.4a)**.

7 Lubricate the cable end with multi-purpose grease and fit it into the pulley **(see illustration 6.3b)**. Seat the cable in the bracket and pull it up so the lower nut is captive, then turn the adjuster so the freeplay is as specified in Chapter 1 and tighten the locknut onto the bracket **(see illustration 12.2)**.

8 Operate the throttle to check that it opens and closes freely, and double-check the amount of freeplay.

9 Turn the handlebars back-and-forth to make sure the cable doesn't cause the steering to bind.

10 Start the engine and check the idle speed (see Chapter 1). Check that the idle speed does not rise as the handlebars are turned. If it does, the throttle cable is routed incorrectly. Correct the problem before riding the scooter.

11 Install the covers (see Chapter 7).

13 Exhaust system

⚠ *Warning: If the engine has been running the exhaust system will be very hot. Allow the system to cool before carrying out any work.*

Removal

1 Remove the bottom cover (see Chapter 7).
2 Remove the rider's footrest assembly (see Chapter 5).
3 Undo the nuts securing the downpipe to the exhaust port in the head **(see illustration)**.
4 Unscrew the nut and withdraw the bolt securing the silencer **(see illustration)**.
5 Support the exhaust system, unscrew the middle bolt, and manoeuvre the exhaust out, pressing the rear brake pedal down for clearance **(see illustrations)**.

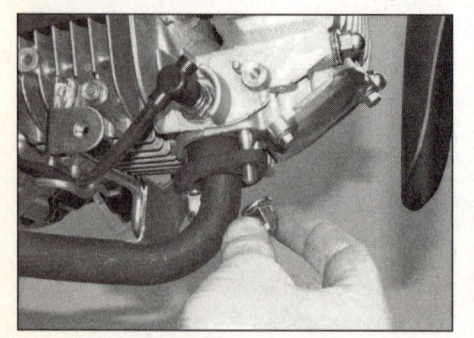

13.3 Undo the nuts

13.4 Unscrew the nut and withdraw the bolt

13.5a Unscrew the bolt (arrowed) ...

Fuel injection system and exhaust 3B•13

13.5b ... and remove the exhaust

13.6 Remove the old gasket

6 Remove the gasket from the exhaust port – a new one must be used **(see illustration)**.
7 If required remove the shields from the exhaust, noting the arrangement of the collars and rubbers with the rear shield, and the washers and spacers with the front one.

> **HAYNES HiNT** *Exhaust system fixings tend to become corroded and seized. It is advisable to spray them with penetrating oil before attempting to loosen them.*

Installation

8 Installation is the reverse of removal, noting the following:
- Clean the exhaust port studs and exhaust mounting bolts and lubricate them with a suitable copper-based grease before reassembly. If the shields have been removed clean and lubricate the screws.
- Clean the jointing surfaces of the exhaust port and the pipe.
- Use a new gasket and fit it into the port, using dabs of grease to hold it in place if necessary **(see illustration)**.

- Leave the nuts and bolts finger-tight until all have been installed, then tighten the exhaust port nuts first, to the torque setting specified at the beginning of the Chapter, then the bolts/nut.
- Run the engine and check that there are no exhaust gas leaks.

14 Fuel gauge and level sensor

Check

1 The circuit consists of the level sensor that is an integral part of the fuel pump and the gauge mounted in the instrument cluster. When the ignition is switched on all segments of the gauge should come on temporarily before showing the actual level – this serves as an indication that the gauge is functioning correctly. If the instruments malfunction check the instrument cluster power supply and earth (see Chapter 8).
2 Remove the fuel pump (Section 4).
3 Check that no fuel has entered the float due to a leak, and check that the arm moves up and down smoothly.
4 Connect the probes of an ohmmeter to the yellow/white and adjacent green wire terminals in the pump as shown **(see illustration)**. Move the arm up and down and check the resistance of the sensor in both the FULL and EMPTY positions **(see illustration)**. If the readings are not as specified at the beginning of the Chapter, replace the sensor with a new one.
5 Connect the sensor to its wiring connector. Turn the ignition on and move the arm up and down – the gauge should show all segments with the arm fully raised, and only the E segment (which should flash) with the arm in its lowest position. Turn the ignition off and disconnect the sensor.
6 If the gauge does not respond as described, remove the handlebar front cover (see Chapter 7). Check the wiring between the fuel pump connector and the gauge connector on the back of the instrument cluster for continuity, and check for continuity to earth in the green wire at each connector, referring to electrical system testing and the wiring diagram in Chapter 8. If the wiring is good and the power supply to the instrument cluster is good, the instrument board is faulty (see Chapter 8).

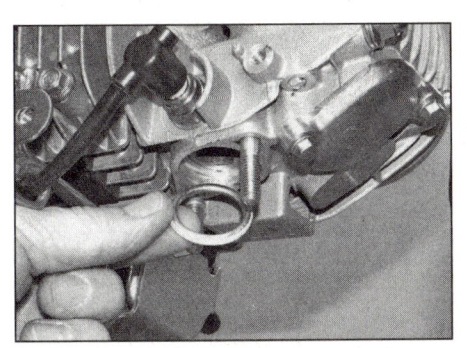

13.8 Fit the new gasket onto the exhaust pipe

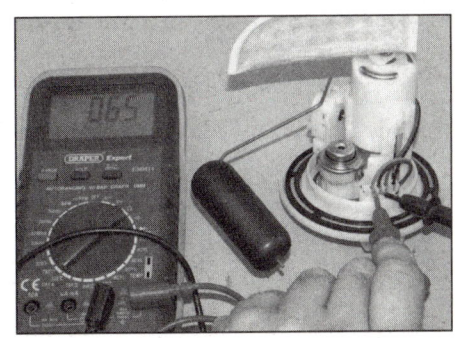

14.4a Connect the meter as shown and check fuel level sensor resistance in the full position ...

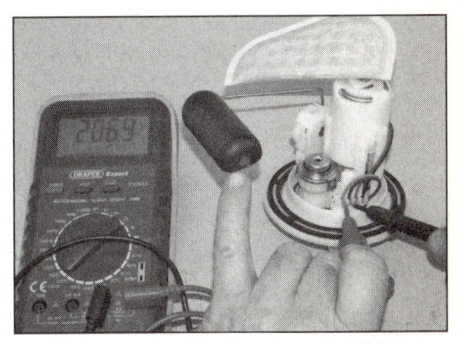

14.4b ... and in the empty position

Replacement

⚠️ **Warning: Refer to the precautions given in Section 1 before starting work.**

7 The fuel gauge is part of the instrument cluster and is covered in Chapter 8.

8 The fuel level sensor is an integral part of the fuel pump assembly and is covered in Section 4.

15 Catalytic converter

General information

1 A catalytic converter is incorporated in the exhaust system to minimise the level of exhaust pollutants released into the atmosphere.

2 The catalytic converter consists of a canister containing a fine mesh impregnated with a catalyst material, over which the hot exhaust gases pass. The catalyst speeds up the oxidation of harmful carbon monoxide, unburned hydrocarbons and soot, effectively reducing the quantity of harmful products released into the atmosphere via the exhaust gases.

3 The catalytic converter is of the closed-loop type with exhaust gas oxygen content information being fed back to the fuel injection system engine control unit (ECU) by the oxygen sensor mounted in the cylinder head.

4 Refer to Section 13 for exhaust system removal and installation, and Section 9 for oxygen sensor removal and installation information.

Precautions

5 The catalytic converter is a reliable and simple device which needs no maintenance in itself, but there are some facts of which an owner should be aware if the converter is to function properly for its full service life.

- DO NOT use leaded or lead replacement petrol (gasoline) – the additives will coat the precious metals, reducing their converting efficiency and will eventually destroy the catalytic converter.
- Always keep the ignition and fuel systems well-maintained in accordance with the manufacturer's schedule – if the fuel/air mixture is suspected of being incorrect have it checked on an exhaust gas analyser.
- If the engine develops a misfire, do not ride the scooter at all (or at least as little as possible) until the fault is cured.
- DO NOT use fuel or engine oil additives – these may contain substances harmful to the catalytic converter.
- DO NOT continue to use the scooter if the engine burns oil to the extent of leaving a visible trail of blue smoke.
- Remember that the catalytic converter and oxygen sensor are FRAGILE – do not strike them with tools during servicing work.

Chapter 4
Ignition system

Contents

	Section number		Section number
Electronic control unit (ECU)	5	Ignition system check	2
General information	1	Pulse generator coil	4
Ignition timing	6	Sidestand switch	see Chapter 8
Ignition coil	3	Spark plug	see Chapter 1
Ignition switch	see Chapter 8		

Degrees of difficulty

Easy, suitable for novice with little experience	**Fairly easy,** suitable for beginner with some experience	**Fairly difficult,** suitable for competent DIY mechanic	**Difficult,** suitable for experienced DIY mechanic	**Very difficult,** suitable for expert DIY or professional

Specifications

General information
Spark plug ..... see Chapter 1

Pulse generator coil
Resistance
   2003 to 2006 (carburettor) models ..... approx. 50 to 200 ohms
   2007-on (fuel injection) models ..... see text
Minimum peak voltage (see text) ..... 0.7 volts

Ignition coil
Primary winding resistance
   2003 to 2006 (carburettor) models ..... approx. 0.2 to 1.0 ohm
   2007-on (fuel injection) models ..... approx. 2.5 ohms
Secondary winding resistance (with plug cap on)
   2003 to 2006 (carburettor) models ..... approx. 12.8 K-ohms
   2007-on (fuel injection) models ..... approx. 14.5 K-ohms
Secondary winding resistance (without plug cap)
   2003 to 2006 (carburettor) models ..... approx. 7.8 K-ohms
   2007-on (fuel injection) models ..... approx. 10 K-ohms
Spark plug cap resistance ..... approx. 4.5 to 5 K-ohms
Minimum peak voltage (see text) ..... 100 volts min

Torque wrench setting
Timing inspection cap ..... 6 Nm

4•2 Ignition system

1 General Information

All models are fitted with a fully transistorised electronic ignition system which, due to its lack of mechanical parts, is totally maintenance-free. The system comprises triggers on the alternator rotor, a pulse generator coil, the electronic control unit (ECU) and the ignition coil (refer to *Wiring Diagrams* at the end of Chapter 8 for details).

The ignition triggers magnetically operate the pulse generator coil as the crankshaft rotates. The pulse generator coil sends signals to the ECU, which then actuates the ignition coil to produce a spark at the plug.

The ECU incorporates an electronic advance system controlled by signals from the ignition triggers and pulse generator coil.

Because of their nature, the individual ignition system components can be checked but not repaired. If ignition system troubles occur, and the faulty component can be isolated, the only cure for the problem is to replace the part with a new one. Keep in mind that most electrical parts, once purchased, cannot be returned. To avoid unnecessary expense, make very sure the faulty component has been positively identified before buying a replacement part.

Note that there is no provision for adjusting the ignition timing.

2 Ignition system check

⚠️ **Warning: The energy levels in electronic systems can be very high. On no account should the ignition be switched on whilst the plug or plug cap is being held. Shocks from the HT circuit can be most unpleasant. Secondly, it is vital that the engine is not turned over or run with the plug cap removed, and that the plug is soundly earthed (grounded) when the system is checked for sparking. The ignition system components can be seriously damaged if the HT circuit becomes isolated.**

1 As no means of adjustment is available, any failure of the system can be traced to failure of a system component or a simple wiring fault. Of the two possibilities, the latter is by far the most likely. In the event of failure, check the system in a logical fashion, as described below.

2 For best access and to avoid the possibility of damage remove the bottom cover and the front cover on the right-hand side (see Chapter 7).

3 Put the scooter on its centrestand. Pull the cap off the spark plug **(see illustration)**. Fit a spare spark plug that is known to be good into the cap and lay the plug against the cylinder head with the threads contacting it. If necessary, hold the spark plug with an insulated tool.

2.3 Pull the cap off the spark plug

⚠️ **Warning: Do not remove the spark plug from the engine to perform this check – atomised fuel being pumped out of the open spark plug hole could ignite, causing severe injury! Make sure the plug is securely held against the engine – if it is not earthed when the engine is turned over, the ECU could be damaged.**

4 Turn the ignition switch ON, and turn the engine over on the starter motor or kickstart. If the system is in good condition a regular, fat blue spark should be seen at the plug electrodes. If the spark appears thin or yellowish, or is non-existent, further investigation is necessary.

5 The ignition system must be able to produce a spark which is capable of jumping a particular size gap – Honda do not give a specification, but a healthy system should produce a spark capable of jumping at least 6 mm. Simple ignition spark gap testing tools are commercially available – follow the manufacturer's instructions **(see illustration)**.

6 If the test results are good the entire ignition system can be considered good.

7 Ignition faults can be divided into two categories, namely those where the ignition system has failed completely, and those which are due to a partial failure. The likely faults are listed below, starting with the most probable source. Work through the list systematically, referring to the subsequent sections for full details of the necessary checks and tests, to electrical system fault finding at the beginning of Chapter 8 and to the *Wiring Diagrams* at the end of it. **Note:** *Before checking the following items ensure that the battery is fully charged and that the fuses are in good condition.*

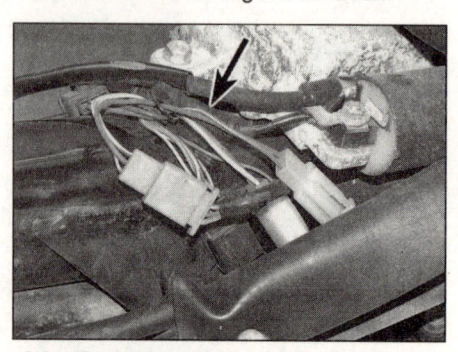

3.3a On 2003 to 2006 models disconnect the wiring connector (arrowed)

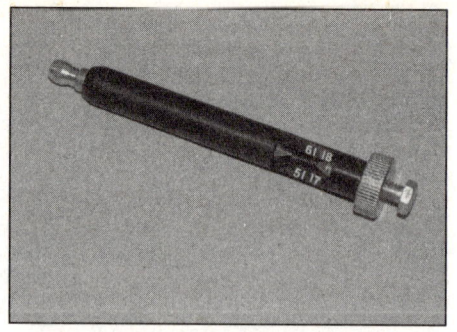

2.5 A typical spark gap testing tool

- Loose, corroded or damaged wiring and connectors, broken or shorted wiring between any of the component parts of the ignition system (see Chapter 8).
- Faulty HT lead or spark plug cap, faulty spark plug, dirty, worn or corroded plug electrodes, or incorrect gap between electrodes.
- Faulty pulse generator coil or damaged trigger(s).
- Faulty ignition coil.
- Faulty ignition switch (see Chapter 8).
- Faulty sidestand switch (see Chapter 8).
- Faulty lean angle sensor (fuel injection models – see Chapter 3B).
- Faulty electronic control unit (ECU).

8 If the above checks don't reveal the cause of the problem, have the ignition system tested by a Honda dealer.

3 Ignition coil

Check

1 On 2003 to 2006 (carburettor) models remove the front and rear centre covers and the front cover on the right-hand side (see Chapter 7). On 2007-on models remove the front body cover (see Chapter 7). Check the coil visually for loose or damaged connectors and terminals, cracks and other damage **(see illustration 3.13 or 3.14)**.

2 Make sure the ignition is off.

3 Disconnect the primary wiring connector(s) **(see illustrations)**. Pull the cap off the spark

3.3b On 2007-on models disconnect the wiring connectors

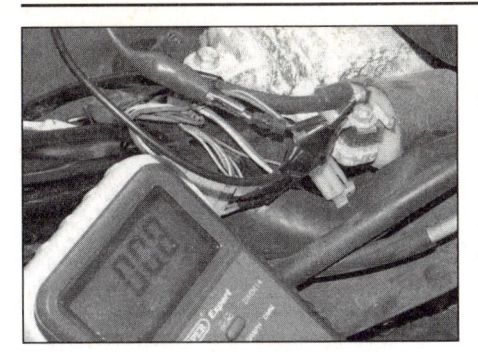

Ignition system 4•3

3.4a Testing the coil primary resistance on 2003 to 2006 models

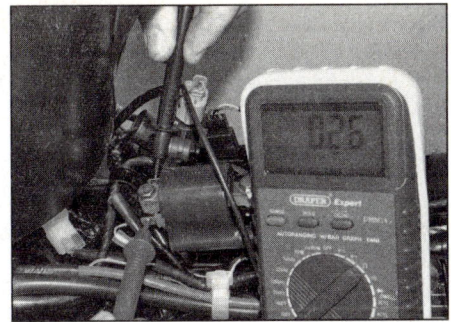

3.4b Testing the coil primary resistance on 2007-on models

3.5 Testing the coil secondary resistance on 2007-on models

plug (see illustration 2.3). Feed the HT lead back to the coil, noting its routing.

4 Set an ohmmeter or multimeter to the ohms x 1 scale. On 2003 to 2006 (carburettor) models measure the resistance between the primary wiring connector and the earth terminal on the coil (see illustration). On 2007-on (fuel injection) models measure the resistance between the primary terminals on the coil (see illustration). This will give a resistance reading of the primary windings of the coil – Honda do not specify a figure, but you should get roughly the figure we measured, given in the specifications at the beginning of the Chapter. The important thing is that you do not get a zero or infinite reading.

5 Now set the meter to the K-ohm scale. Connect one meter probe to the primary wiring connector on 2003 to 2006 (carburettor) models or one of the primary terminals on the coil on 2007-on (fuel injection) models, and insert the other probe in the end of the spark plug cap, making sure the probe is long enough to make contact (see illustration). This will give a resistance reading of the secondary windings of the coil – again Honda do not specify a figure, but you should get roughly the figure we measured, given in the specifications at the beginning of the Chapter. The important thing is that you do not get a zero or infinite reading.

6 If the reading is not as described, unscrew the plug cap from the end of the HT lead, then repeat the test in Step 5, inserting one of the probes into the end of the HT lead (see illustrations). If the result is good measure the resistance of the spark plug cap by connecting the meter probes between the HT lead socket and the spark plug contact (see illustration). The reading should be as specified. If not, replace the spark plug cap with a new one.

7 If the primary and secondary resistance readings obtained are not as described, it is possible that the coil is defective. To confirm this, it must be tested as follows using the specified equipment, or by a Honda dealer. Honda specify their own Imrie diagnostic tester (model 625), or the peak voltage adapter (Pt. No. 07HGJ-0020100) with an aftermarket digital multimeter having an impedance of 10 M-ohm/DCV minimum, for a complete test. If this equipment is available, reconnect the primary wiring connector(s). Connect the cap to a new spark plug and rest the plug on the engine with its threads contacting it. If necessary, hold the spark plug with an insulated tool. Connect the positive (+) lead of the voltmeter and peak voltage adapter arrangement to the primary wire connector on carburettor models, or to the pink/blue wire terminal on fuel injection models, with the wiring connector still connected, and connect the negative (–) lead to a suitable earth (ground) point.

8 Turn the ignition switch ON. Check that there is battery voltage reading on the meter, then turn the engine over on the starter motor and note the peak voltage reading on the meter. Once both readings have been noted, turn the ignition switch off and disconnect the meter.

9 If the peak voltage readings are lower than the specified minimum then a fault is present somewhere else in the ignition system circuit (see Section 2).

10 If the initial and peak voltage readings are as specified and the plug does not spark, then the coil is faulty and must be replaced with a new one.

Removal and installation

11 On 2003 to 2006 (carburettor) models remove the body cover (see Chapter 7). On 2007-on (fuel injection) models remove the rear body cover (see Chapter 7).

12 Disconnect the primary wiring connector(s) (see illustration 3.3a or b). Pull the cap off the spark plug (see illustration 2.3). Feed the HT lead back to the coil, noting its routing.

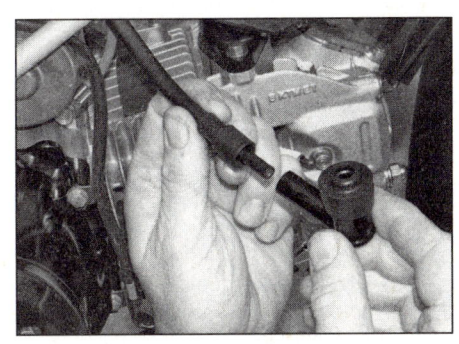

3.6a Unscrew the cap from the lead

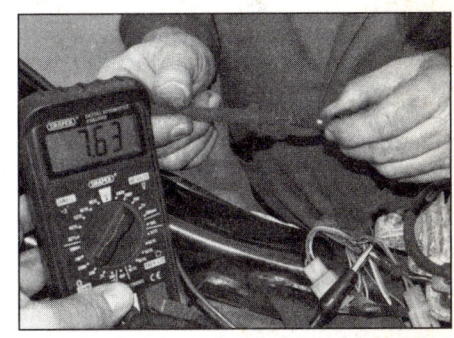

3.6b Testing the coil secondary resistance without the cap on 2003 to 2006 models

3.6c Testing the coil secondary resistance without the cap on 2007-on models

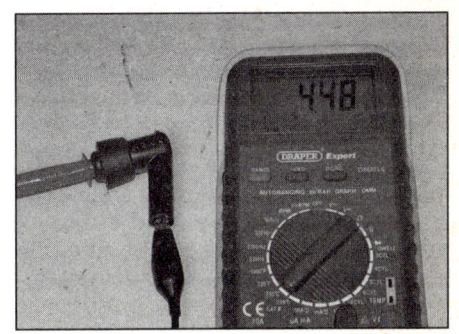

3.6d Measuring the resistance of the spark plug cap

4•4 Ignition system

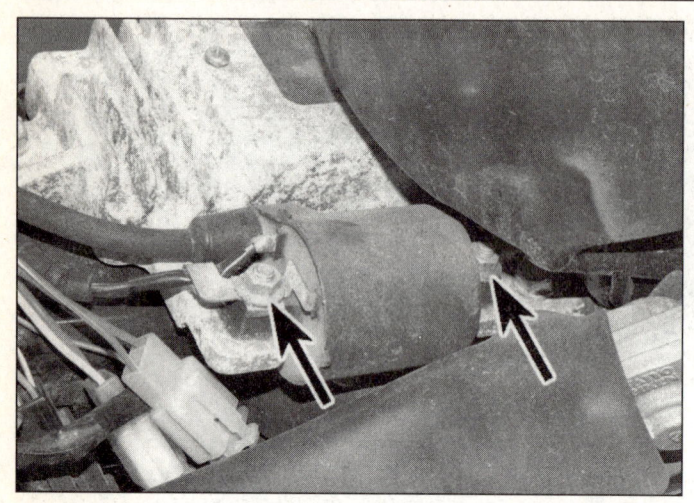

3.13 Coil mounting nuts (arrowed) – 2003 to 2006 models

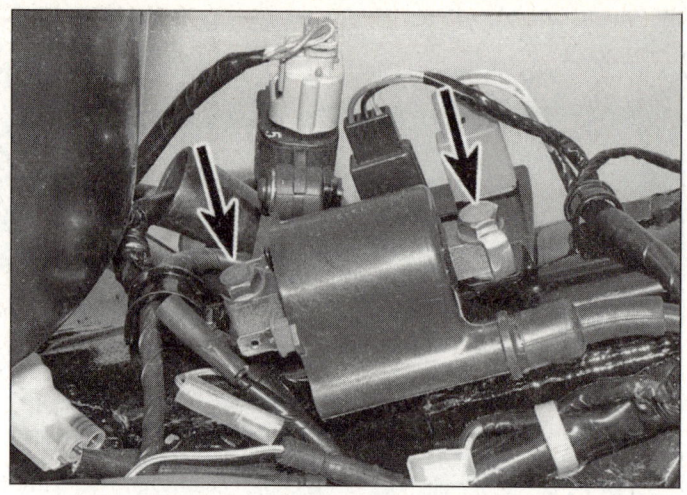

3.14 Coil mounting bolts (arrowed) – 2007-on models

13 On 2003 to 2006 (carburettor) models unscrew the nuts, withdraw the bolts and remove the coil **(see illustration)**.
14 On 2007-on (fuel injection) models unscrew the bolts and remove the coil, noting the spacer on each mount **(see illustration)**.
15 Installation is the reverse of removal.

4 Pulse generator coil

Check

1 On 2003 to 2006 (carburettor) models remove the body cover (see Chapter 7). On 2007-on (fuel injection) models remove the rear body covers (see Chapter 7).
2 Trace the wiring from the top of the alternator cover on the left-hand side of the engine and disconnect it at the single connector with the blue/yellow wire on 2003 to 2006 (carburettor) models, or at the 4-pin connector containing the blue/yellow and white/yellow wires on 2007-on (fuel injection) models **(see illustrations)**.
3 Using a multimeter set to the ohms x 10 scale, measure the resistance between the blue/yellow wire (alternator side of the connector) and ground on 2003 to 2006 (carburettor) models, and the blue/yellow and white/yellow wires in the alternator side of the connector on 2007-on (fuel injection) models. Honda specify a figure (given at the beginning of the Chapter) for 2003 to 2006 (carburettor) models, but not for 2007-on (fuel injection) models. The important thing is that you do not get a zero or infinite reading. If the reading obtained is not as described, it is possible that the coil is defective.
4 To confirm this, it must be tested as described below using the specified equipment and with the connector still connected, or by a Honda dealer. Honda specify their own Imrie diagnostic tester (model 625), or the peak voltage adapter (Pt. No. 07HGJ-0020100) with an aftermarket digital multimeter having an impedance of 10 M-ohm/DCV minimum, for a complete test. If this equipment is available, on 2003 to 2006 (carburettor) models connect the positive (+) lead of the voltmeter and peak voltage adapter arrangement to the blue/yellow wire connector, and the negative (–) lead to a good earth, and on fuel injection models connect the positive (+) lead to the blue/yellow wire terminal in the wiring connector, and the negative (–) lead to the white/yellow wire terminal.
5 Turn the ignition switch ON, turn the engine over on the starter motor and note the peak voltage reading on the meter. If the peak voltage reading is lower than the specified minimum, the pulse generator coil is faulty.
6 If the ignition pulse generator coil functions correctly then the fault must be in the wiring harness to the ECU. Check the wiring for continuity, referring to electrical system fault finding at the beginning of Chapter 8 and to the *Wiring Diagrams* at the end of it. If the wiring is good, the ECU could be faulty.

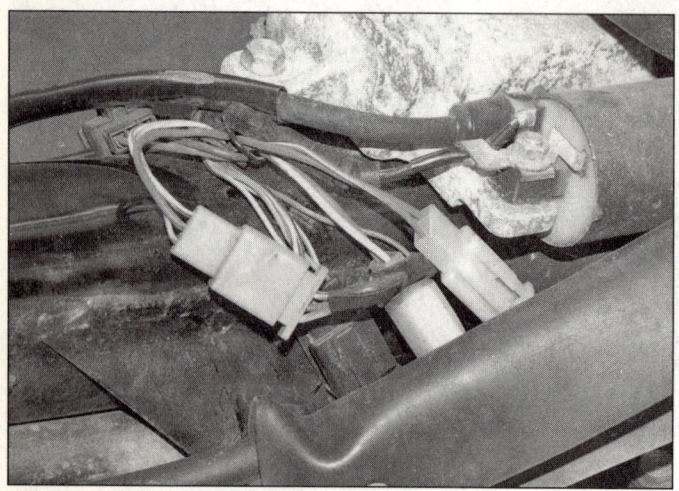

4.2a Look for the connector with the blue/yellow wire on 2003 to 2006 models

4.2b Pulse generator coil (and alternator) wiring connector (arrowed) – 2007-on models

Ignition system 4•5

Removal and installation

7 The pulse generator coil is part of the alternator stator assembly and cannot be replaced separately. Refer to Chapter 8 for removal and installation of the alternator stator assembly.

5 Electronic control unit (ECU)

Check

1 If the tests shown in the preceding or following Sections have failed to isolate the cause of an ignition fault, it is possible that the ECU itself is faulty.

2 No test details on the unit itself are available – the best way to determine whether it is faulty is to substitute it with a known good one, if available. Before condemning the ECU make sure the wiring connectors are secure and the terminals are clean and none of the wires have broken – check them for continuity, referring to the wiring diagrams at the end of Chapter 8. Make sure the ignition is off before disconnecting the wiring connector, and refer below for access.

3 Also make sure the power supply and earth wires are good – with the ignition off disconnect the wiring connector, then check for battery voltage at the red/black wire terminal in the connector on 2003 to 2006 (carburettor) models, or the black/blue wire terminal in the connector on 2007-on (fuel injection) models, with the ignition on. Also check for continuity to earth in the green wire on 2003 to 2006 (carburettor) models and the green and green/black wires on 2007-on (fuel injection) models.

Removal

2003 to 2006 (carburettor) models

4 Make sure the ignition is off.
5 Remove the regulator/rectifier (see Chapter 8).

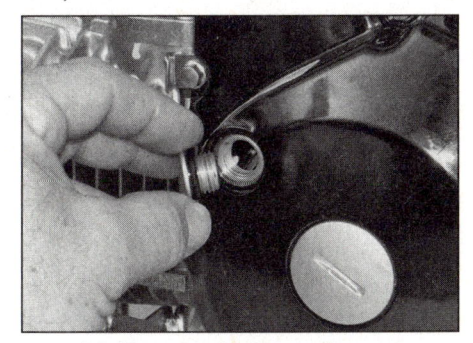

6.4 Unscrew the inspection cap

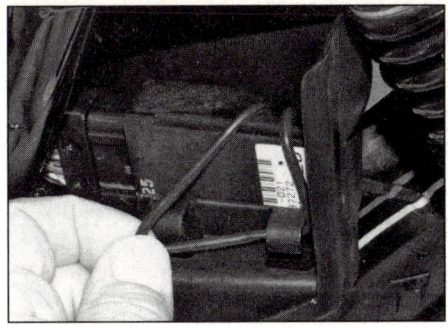

5.9a Release the rubber strap . . .

6 Undo the screws securing the ECU and remove it.

2007-on (fuel injection) models

7 Make sure the ignition is off.
8 Remove the rear body cover (see Chapter 7).
9 Release the rubber strap, displace the ECU and disconnect the wiring connector (see illustrations).

Installation

10 Installation is the reverse of removal. Make sure the wiring is securely re-connected.

6 Ignition timing

General information

1 Since no provision exists for adjusting the ignition timing and since no component is subject to mechanical wear, there is no need for regular checks: only if investigating a fault such as a loss of power or a misfire, should the ignition timing be checked.

2 The ignition timing is checked dynamically (engine running) using a stroboscopic lamp. The inexpensive neon lamps should be adequate in theory, but in practice may produce a pulse of such low intensity that the

6.5 The line next to the F should align with the notch (arrowed)

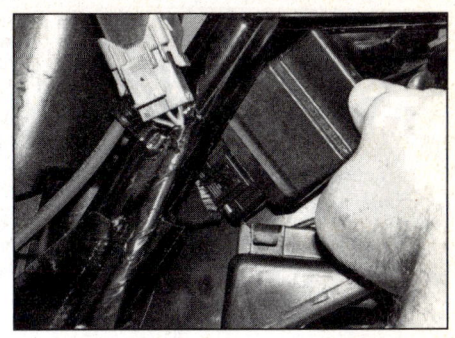

5.9b . . . then displace the ECU and disconnect the wiring connector

timing mark remains indistinct. If possible, one of the more precise xenon tube lamps should be used, powered by an external source of the appropriate voltage. **Note:** *Do not use the scooter's own battery, as an incorrect reading may result from stray impulses within the electrical system.*

Check

3 Warm the engine up to normal operating temperature, then stop it.
4 Unscrew the timing inspection cap from the alternator cover on the left-hand side of the engine (see illustration).
5 The mark on the timing rotor which indicates the firing point at idle speed is a line next to an 'F' (see illustration). The static timing mark with which this should align is the notch in the inspection hole.

> **HAYNES HINT** *The timing marks can be highlighted with white paint to make them more visible under the stroboscope light.*

6 Connect the timing light to the coil HT lead as described in the manufacturer's instructions.
7 Start the engine and aim the light at the inspection hole.
8 With the machine idling at the specified speed, the 'F' mark should align with the static timing mark.
9 Slowly increase the engine speed whilst observing the 'F' mark. The mark should appear to move until it reaches full advance (no identification mark).
10 As already stated, there is no means of adjusting the ignition timing. If the ignition timing is incorrect, or suspected of being incorrect, one of the ignition system components is at fault, and the system must be tested as described in the preceding Sections of this Chapter.
11 Install the timing inspection cap using a new O-ring if required, and smear the O-ring and the cap threads with clean oil. Tighten the cap to the torque setting specified at the beginning of the Chapter.

Notes

Chapter 5
Frame and suspension

Contents

	Section number
Footrests, levers and pedals	4
Frame	2
Front forks	6
General information	1
Handlebars	3
Rear shock absorbers	9

	Section number
Stands	5
Steering head bearing adjustment	see Chapter 1
Steering head bearing overhaul	8
Steering stem	7
Suspension check	see Chapter 1
Swingarm	10

Degrees of difficulty

Easy, suitable for novice with little experience	**Fairly easy,** suitable for beginner with some experience	**Fairly difficult,** suitable for competent DIY mechanic	**Difficult,** suitable for experienced DIY mechanic	**Very difficult,** suitable for expert DIY or professional

Specifications

Front forks
Fork oil type	10W fork oil
Fork oil capacity	70.5 to 72.5 ml per fork
Fork oil level*	76 mm
Fork spring free length	
2003 to 2006 (carburettor) models	
Standard	316.3 mm
Service limit (min)	303.1 mm
2007-on (fuel injection) models	
Standard	328.3 mm
Service limit (min)	321.7 mm
Fork inner tube runout	0.2 mm

*measured from top of fork tube, spring removed and leg fully compressed

Torque settings
Fork clamp bolts	64 Nm
Fork damper rod bolt	20 Nm
Handlebar support post bolt nut	59 Nm
Handlebar bolts	25 Nm
Rear shock absorbers bolt/nut	24 Nm
Sidestand pivot bolt	18 Nm
Sidestand pivot bolt nut	44 Nm
Steering head bearing adjuster nut	
Initial setting	25 Nm
Final setting	
2003 to 2006 models	3 Nm, then 15° anti-clockwise
2007-on models	2.5 Nm, then 15° anti-clockwise
Steering stem nut	74 Nm
Swingarm pivot bolt nut	39 Nm

5•2 Frame and suspension

1 General information

All models have a tubular steel one-piece backbone frame.

Front suspension is by conventional telescopic forks, and is not adjustable.

At the rear, a box-section steel swingarm acts on twin oil damped shock absorbers. The swingarm pivots through the frame.

Ancillary items such as stands and handlebars are covered in this Chapter.

2 Frame

1 The frame should not require attention unless accident damage has occurred. In most cases, fitting a new frame is the only satisfactory remedy for such damage. A few frame specialists have the jigs and other equipment necessary for straightening the frame to the required standard of accuracy, but even then there is no simple way of assessing to what extent the frame may have been over-stressed.

2 After a high mileage, the frame should be examined closely for signs of cracking or splitting at the welded joints. Loose engine mount and suspension bolts can cause ovaling or fracturing of the mounting points. Minor damage can often be repaired by specialist welding, depending on the extent and nature of the damage.

3 Remember that a frame which is out of alignment will cause handling problems. If misalignment is suspected as the result of an accident, it will be necessary to strip the scooter completely so the frame can be thoroughly checked (see Chapter 6 for wheel alignment checks).

3 Handlebars

Removal

1 Remove the top cover and the handlebar covers, and to prevent the possibility of damage also remove the front covers (see Chapter 7).

2 Displace the front brake master cylinder from the handlebars (see Chapter 6). Make sure no strain is placed on the hose. Keep the brake fluid reservoir upright to prevent air entering the system.

3 Undo the handlebar end-weight screws and remove the weights **(see illustration)**.

4 Detach the throttle cable from the twistgrip (see Chapter 3A or 3B). Slide the twistgrip off the end of the handlebar.

5 On 2003 to 2006 (carburettor) models free the choke cable from the lever (see Chapter 3A). If required remove the lever and the cable holder **(see illustration)**.

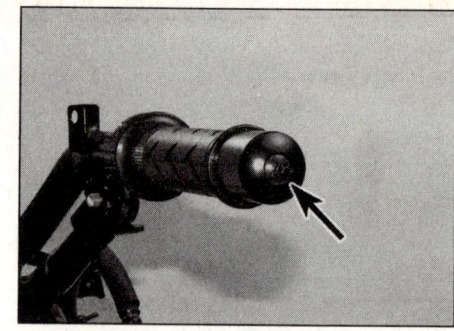

3.3 Handlebar end-weight screw (arrowed)

6 Remove the left-hand grip. It may be possible to pull the grip off the end of the bar, but if necessary cut it off.

7 Unscrew the three bolts, noting the collars, and remove the handlebars **(see illustrations)**.

8 To remove the handlebar support post free the brake hose, cable(s) and wiring from its guides as required. Undo the handlebar bolt nut and remove the spacer, noting which way round it fits **(see illustration)**. Withdraw the bolt with its spacer, then ease the post up off the stem **(see illustrations)**.

Handlebar weights

9 If new handlebars are being installed, you need to transfer the inner weights to the new bars – to do this, reinstall the end-weight and tighten its screw. Squirt some lubricant (such as WD40) into the inner weight retainer

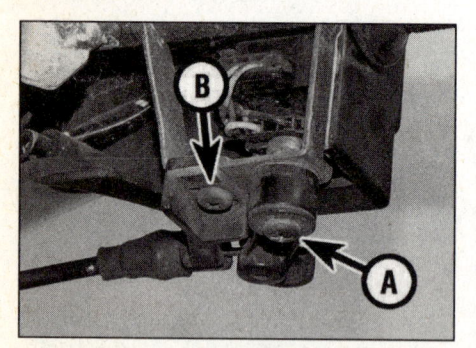

3.5 Choke lever screw (A), cable holder screw (B)

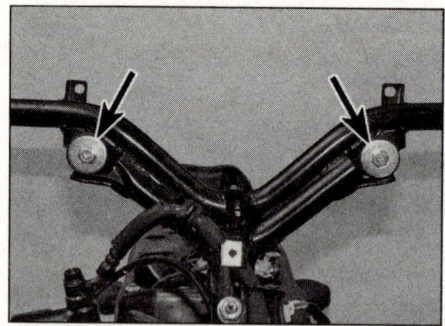

3.7a Unscrew the bolts (arrowed) on the front . . .

3.7b . . . and the bolt (arrowed) on the back

3.8a Unscrew the nut and remove the spacer (arrowed) . . .

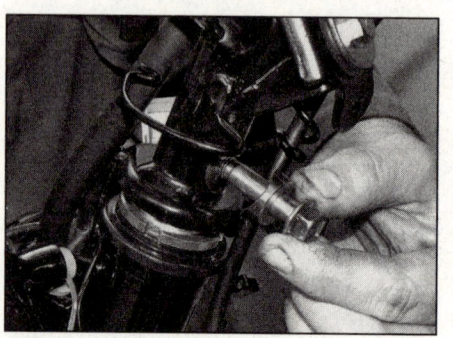

3.8b . . . then withdraw the bolt with its spacer . . .

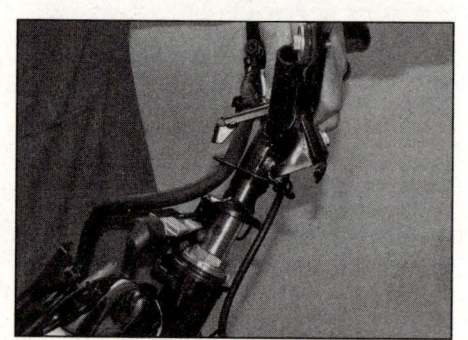

3.8c . . . and lift the support post off

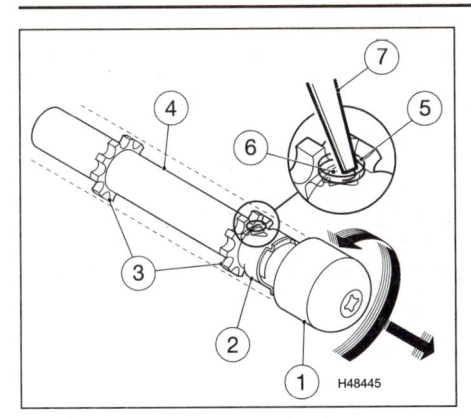

Frame and suspension 5•3

3.9 Removing the handlebar inner weight

1 End-weight
2 Retainer
3 Rubbers
4 Inner weight
5 Hole in handlebar
6 Retainer tab
7 Screwdriver

tab hole, then press down on the tab using a screwdriver and twist and pull the end-weight, drawing the inner weight assembly out **(see illustration)**. Remove the end-weight and discard the retainer as a new one should be used. Check the condition of the rubbers on the inner weight and fit new ones if they are damaged, deformed or deteriorated.

Installation

10 Installation is the reverse of removal, noting the following.
- Make sure the handlebar post bolt spacers are the correct way round with the rounded side against the steering stem **(see illustration 3.8a)**. Tighten the post bolt nut to the torque setting specified at the beginning of this Chapter.
- Make sure the handlebar mount rubbers are in good condition – fit new ones if necessary. Fit the collars and tighten the bolts to the specified torque setting.
- Make sure all cables, hoses and wiring are correctly routed and secured.
- Check the throttle cable adjustment (see Chapter 1).
- Check the operation of the brake and switches before riding the scooter.

4 Footrests, levers and pedals

Footrests and brackets

Removal

1 To remove the rider's footrest assembly, unscrew the four bolts, then press the brake pedal down and manoeuvre the assembly out **(see illustrations)** – to get more clearance if necessary unscrew the brake adjuster nut on the end of the brake rod a few turns **(see illustration 4.12a)**. If required slide the footrest rubbers off. Remove the collars and check the condition of the footrest bar damping rubbers **(see illustration)** – replace them with new ones if damaged, deformed or deteriorated.

2 To remove the footrest assembly/sidestand bracket either disconnect the sidestand switch wiring, remove the switch, or remove the stand from the bracket, as required – refer to Chapter 8 or Section 5. Unscrew the bolts and remove the bracket **(see illustration)**.

3 To remove a passenger footrest, straighten and remove the split pin from the bottom of the footrest pivot pin, collecting the washer, then withdraw the pivot pin and remove the footrest, noting the plate **(see illustration)**. Discard the split pin. If required draw the rubber off the peg.

4 To remove a passenger footrest bracket, unscrew the nut and the bolt and draw the bracket off the swingarm pivot **(see illustrations)**.

4.1a Unscrew the bolts (arrowed) . . .

4.1b . . . then press the brake pedal down and remove the assembly

4.1c Remove the collars and check the rubbers

Installation

5 Installation is the reverse of removal. Apply a small amount of multi-purpose grease to the passenger footrest pivot pins. Use new split pins, and bend the ends round the pivot pin.

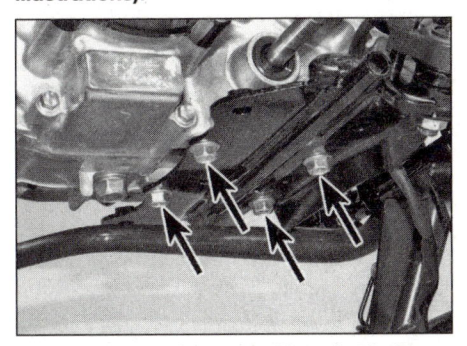

4.2 Footrest/sidestand bracket bolts (arrowed)

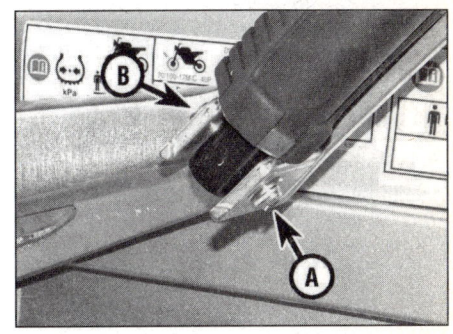

4.3 Remove the split pin (A) and washer then withdraw the pivot pin (B)

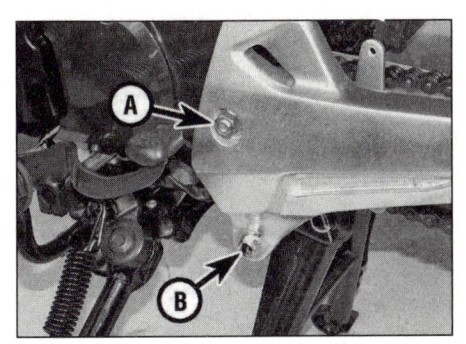

4.4a Unscrew the nut (A) and the bolt (B) . . .

4.4b . . . and draw the bracket off

5•4 Frame and suspension

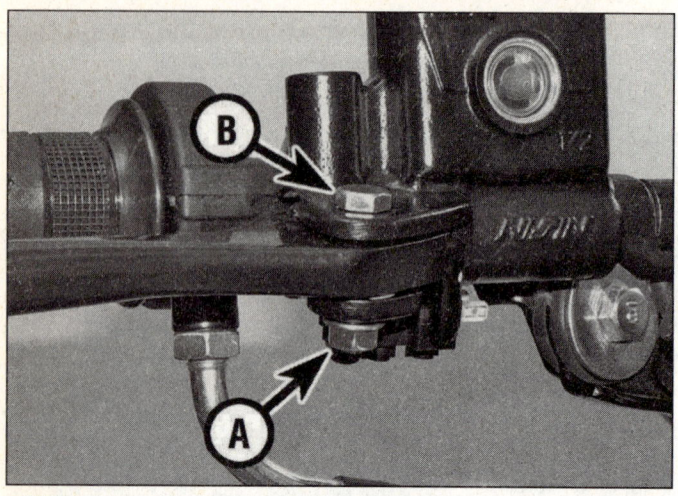

4.7 Unscrew the locknut (A) then unscrew the pivot bolt (B) and remove the lever

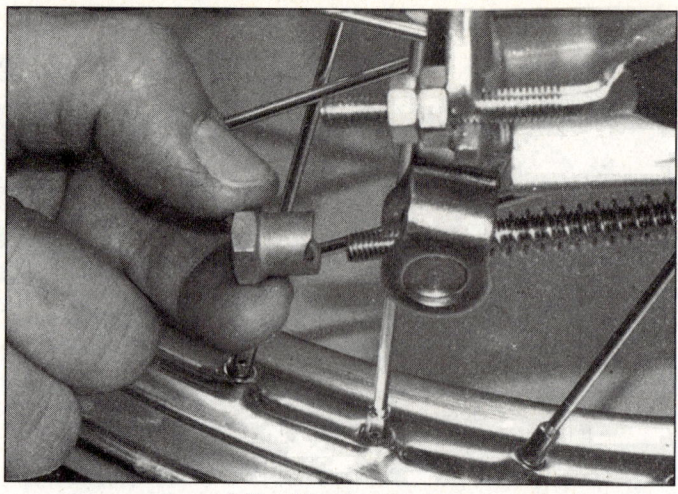

4.12a Unscrew the nut

4.12b Draw the rod out of the arm . . .

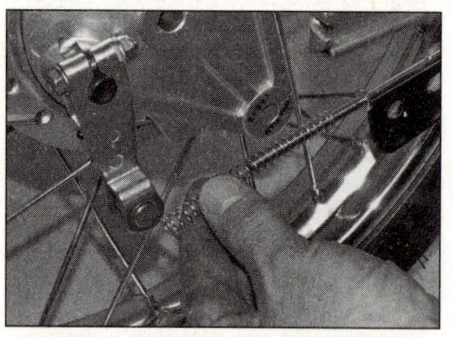

4.12c . . . and remove the spring . . .

4.12d . . . and the trunnion

Brake lever

6 Remove the front handlebar cover (see Chapter 7).
7 Unscrew the lever pivot bolt locknut, then unscrew the pivot bolt and remove the lever **(see illustration)**.
8 Installation is the reverse of removal. Apply a smear of silicone grease to the pivot bolt shank and the contact areas between the lever and its bracket, and to the lever tip that contacts the end of the master cylinder piston. Tighten the pivot bolt lightly, then hold the bolt and tighten the locknut. Check that the lever doesn't bind in its bracket. Make sure the brake functions correctly before riding the scooter.

Brake pedal

Removal

9 Place the bike on its sidestand. Tie the front brake lever on.
10 Remove the right-hand passenger footrest bracket (Step 4).
11 Remove the exhaust system (see Chapter 3B).
12 Unscrew the adjusting nut from the end of the brake rod **(see illustration)**. Push the brake pedal down and the brake arm back and draw the rod out of the trunnion **(see illustration)**. Slide the spring off the rod and the pin out of the arm **(see illustrations)**.
13 Unhook the brake pedal return spring, the brake light switch spring and the centrestand springs **(see illustrations)**. Remove the centrestand spring plate.

4.13a Unhook the pedal return spring . . .

4.13b . . . the switch spring (arrowed) . . .

4.13c . . . and the stand springs (arrowed)

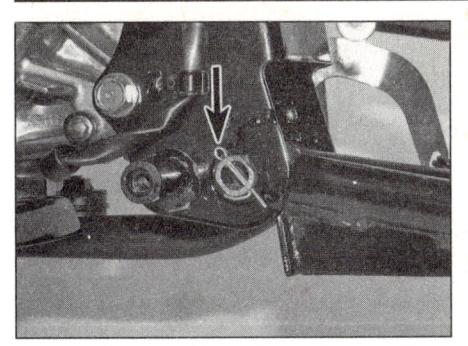

Frame and suspension 5•5

4.14 Remove the split pin (arrowed)

4.17 Make sure the spring plate is correctly positioned

4.18 Note the alignment...

14 Straighten and remove the split pin on the left-hand end of the brake pedal/centrestand pivot (see illustration). Discard the split pin.
15 Grasp the pedal and draw it away bringing the pivot with it, supporting the centrestand as you do. Slide the pedal off the pivot.
16 Straighten and remove the split pin and the washer securing the brake rod in the pedal and detach the rod. Discard the split pin.

Installation

17 Installation is the reverse of removal, noting the following:
- Use a new split pin to secure the brake rod in the pedal and bend its ends around.
- Clean off any old grease and corrosion from the pivot and apply fresh grease to the sliding surfaces.
- Align the flats on the left-hand end of the pivot with those in the frame (see illustration 4.14). Secure the pivot with a new split pin, and bend its ends around as shown.
- Make sure the centrestand spring plate is correctly located (see illustration).
- Make sure the springs are correctly connected (see illustrations 4.13a, b and c).
- Check the operation of the rear brake and the brake light switch (see Chapter 1). Make sure the centrestand is held up by the springs.

Gearchange lever

18 Note the alignment of the slit in the lever clamp with the shaft (see illustration).
19 Unscrew the clamp bolt and draw the lever off the shaft (see illustration).
20 Clean the shaft splines with a wire brush, wipe clean and smear with grease. Align the lever clamp slit with the shaft (see illustration 4.18) and slide the lever on, and secure it with the bolt (see illustration 4.19).

Kickstart lever

21 Mark the alignment of the slit in the lever clamp with the shaft.
22 Unscrew the clamp bolt and draw the lever off the shaft (see illustration).
23 Clean the shaft splines with a wire brush, wipe clean and smear with grease. Align the lever clamp slit with the mark made on

4.19 ... then unscrew the bolt and remove the lever

4.22 Note the alignment then unscrew the bolt and remove the lever

removal and slide the lever on, and secure it with the bolt (see illustration 4.22).

5 Stands

Centrestand

1 Refer to Section 4 and remove the brake pedal – the stand comes away at the same time.

Sidestand

2 Support the scooter on its centrestand.
3 Unscrew the sidestand switch bolt and displace the switch, noting how it locates (see illustration).
4 Unhook the stand springs, noting how they fit (see illustration 5.3).

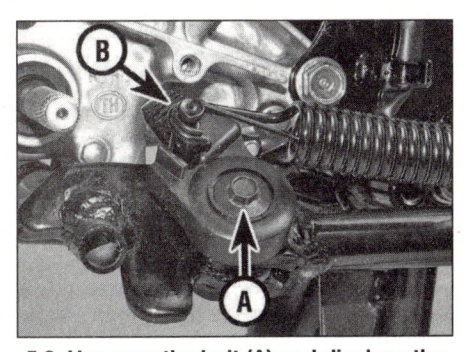

5.3 Unscrew the bolt (A) and displace the switch, then unhook the springs (B)

5 Unscrew the nut on the stand pivot bolt, then unscrew the bolt and remove the stand (see illustration).
6 Installation is the reverse of removal, noting the following:
- Apply grease to the pivot bolt shank.
- Tighten the pivot bolt to the torque setting specified at the beginning of the Chapter, then fit the nut and tighten that to the specified torque.
- Make sure that the springs hold the stand up securely when it is not in use. If necessary, fit new springs.
- Make sure the sidestand switch locates correctly – the pin on the inner side of the switch locates in the hole just below the pivot bolt, and the cut-away in the switch body locates around the spring post.

5.5 Pivot bolt nut (arrowed)

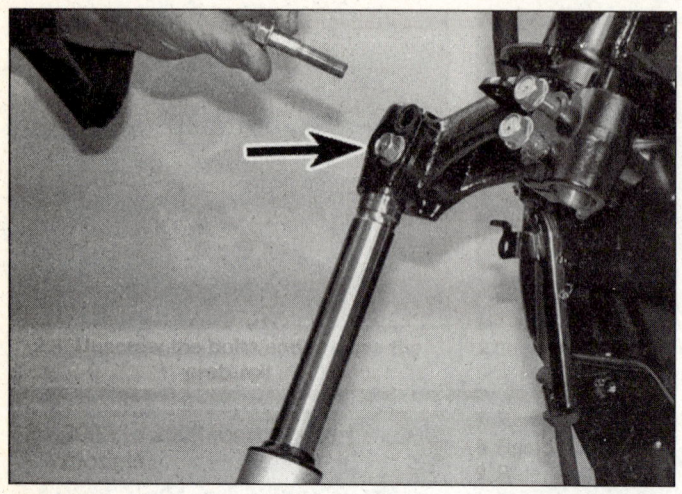

5•6 Frame and suspension

6.4 Remove the upper clamp bolt and slacken the lower one (arrowed) then draw the fork out of the yoke

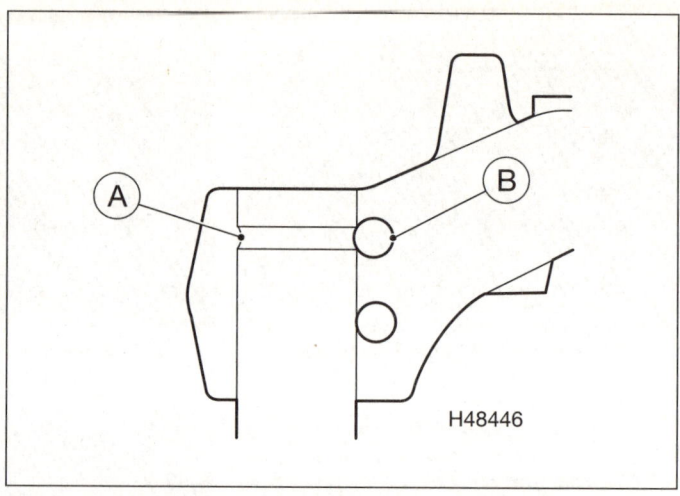

6.6 Cross-section of fork yoke showing fork groove (A) and bolt hole (B) aligned

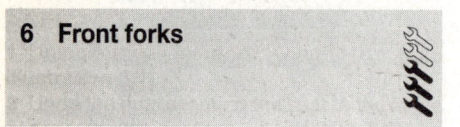

6 Front forks

Note: *Always dismantle each fork separately and store all components in separate, clearly marked containers to avoid interchanging parts. Check the availability of replacement parts and the type and quantity of fork oil required before disassembling the forks.*

Removal

1 Displace the front brake caliper from the fork (see Chapter 6).

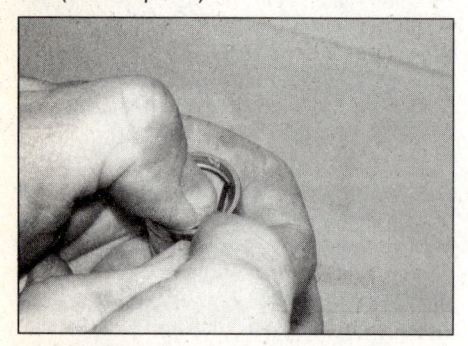

2 Remove the front wheel (see Chapter 6).
3 Remove the front mudguard (see Chapter 7).
4 Work on one fork at a time. Unscrew and remove the upper clamp bolt **(see illustration)**. Hold the fork and slacken the lower clamp bolt, then remove the fork leg by twisting it and pulling it downwards.

> **HAYNES HiNT** *If the fork legs are seized in the yoke, spray the area with penetrating oil and allow time for it to soak in before trying again.*

Installation

5 Remove all traces of corrosion from the fork inner tubes and in the yoke. Install each fork separately.
6 Slide the fork up into the yoke and align the groove in the top of the inner tube with the upper clamp bolt hole in the yoke **(see illustration)**. Insert the bolt and tighten it to the torque setting specified at the beginning of the Chapter. Tighten the lower clamp bolt to the same torque.
7 Install the remaining components in the reverse order of removal. Check the operation of the front forks and brake before riding the scooter.

Oil change

8 Remove the fork (see Steps 1 to 4). Always dismantle each fork separately to avoid interchanging parts. Store all components in separate, clearly marked containers.

> **Warning:** *The fork spring is pressing on the fork top plug with some pressure. It is advisable to wear some form of eye and face protection when carrying out this operation.*

9 Hold the inner tube and press the top plug down against the tension of the fork spring and remove the retaining ring **(see illustration)**. Ease the plug out carefully **(see illustration)**. If you are working by yourself and having trouble doing this, fit the fork back into the yoke and tighten the lower pinch bolt to hold it. If you do this you may want to remove the front cover on one side to give better access (see Chapter 7).
10 Slide the inner tube down into the outer tube and withdraw the spring **(see illustration 6.13)**.
11 Invert the fork over a suitable container and pump it to expel as much oil as possible **(see illustration)**.
12 Slowly pour in the correct quantity of the specified grade of fork oil and carefully pump the fork to distribute the oil evenly **(see illustration)**. Support the fork upright and

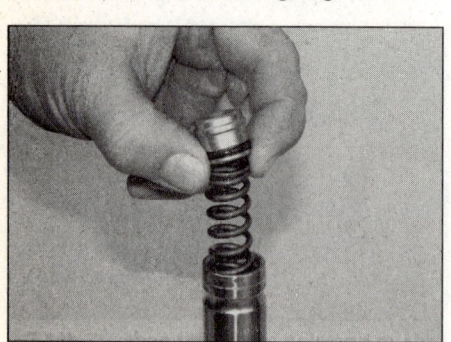

6.9a Press down on the top plug and remove the retaining ring . . .

6.9b . . . then release and remove the plug

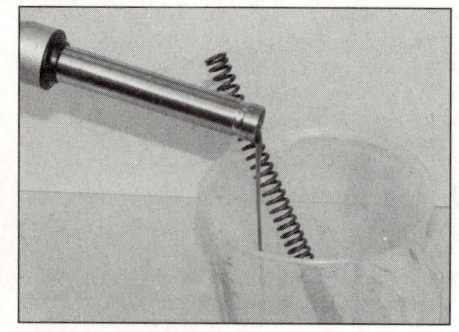

6.11 Invert the fork over a container and tip the oil out

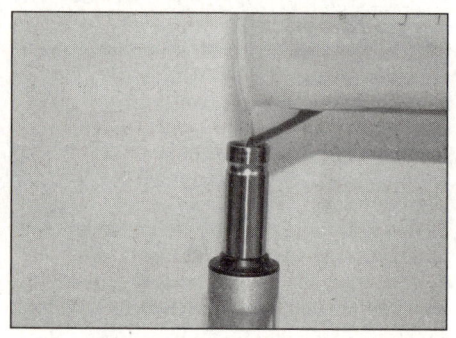

6.12a Pour the oil into the top of the tube and distribute it as described . . .

Frame and suspension 5•7

6.12b ... then measure the level ...

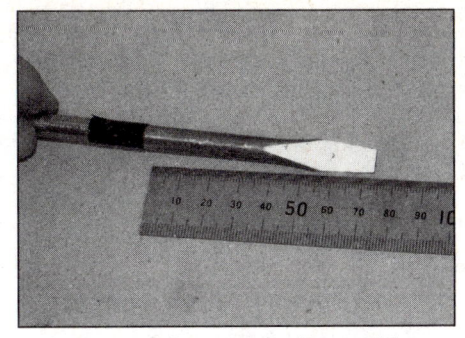

6.12c ... using a marked screwdriver

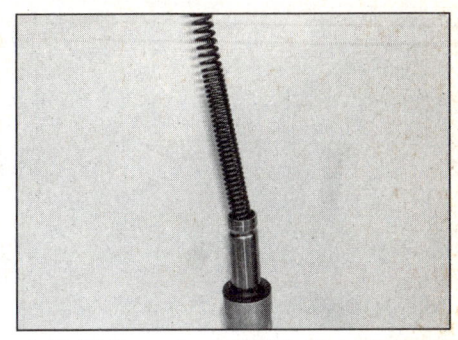

6.13 Fit the spring with the closer-wound coils at the bottom

allow the oil to settle for a few minutes, then measure the oil level from the top of the inner tube with it fully compressed – as the hole is too narrow for a conventional ruler use a rod or screwdriver with some tape on it as an index line, and measure the distance between the tape and the oil on the rod **(see illustrations)**. Add or extract oil as necessary to ensure the level is correct.

13 Pull the inner tube out, then fit the spring with the closer-wound coils at the bottom **(see illustration)**.

14 Check the condition of the O-ring on the fork top plug and fit a new one if necessary **(see illustration)**. Lubricate the O-ring with clean fork oil.

15 Using the same holding method as for removal (Step 9), press the plug down onto the spring until the retaining ring groove is visible, then hold it there and fit the ring **(see illustration)**. Make sure the ring is correctly located in its groove, then slowly release pressure so the plug seats on the underside of the ring.

16 Install the fork (see Steps 5 to 7).

Disassembly

17 Remove the fork (see Steps 1 to 4).

18 Turn the fork upside down and compress it so that the spring exerts maximum pressure on the damper rod head, then loosen the damper rod bolt in the base of the fork outer tube **(see illustration)**.

19 Drain the oil from the fork (see Steps 9 to 11).

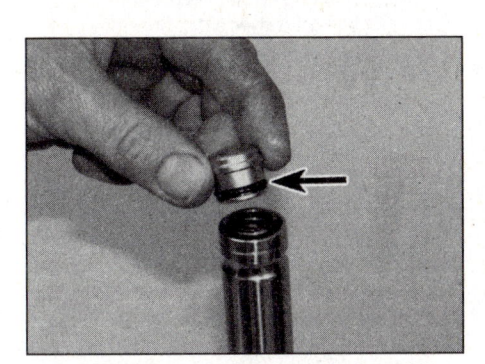

6.14 Check the O-ring (arrowed) and fit a new one if necessary

6.15 Fit the plug then press it down and fit the retaining ring into its groove

6.18 Slacken the damper rod bolt

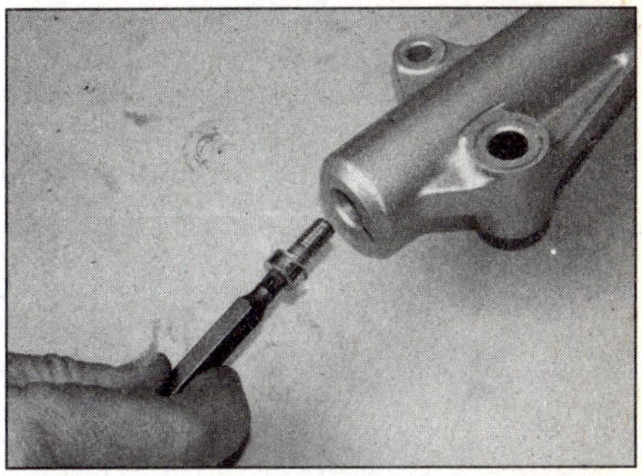

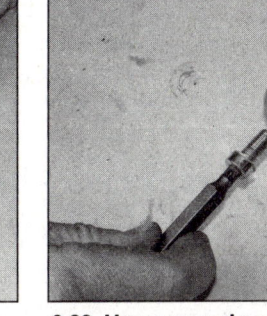

6.20 Unscrew and remove the damper rod bolt

20 Lay the fork flat and unscrew the damper rod bolt **(see illustration)**. Discard the sealing washer as a new one must be used on reassembly.

21 Pull the inner tube and damper rod out of the outer tube **(see illustration)**. Tip the damper rod out of the top of the inner tube **(see illustration)**.

22 Carefully lever the dust seal out of the top of the outer tube **(see illustration)**.

23 Prise out the oil seal retaining clip **(see illustration)**.

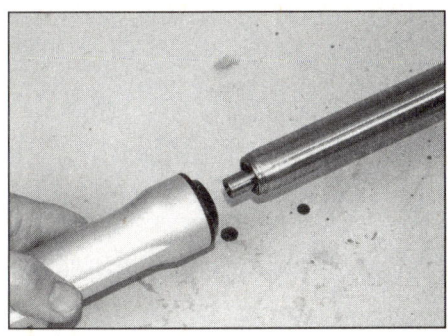

6.21a Draw the inner tube out of the outer tube ...

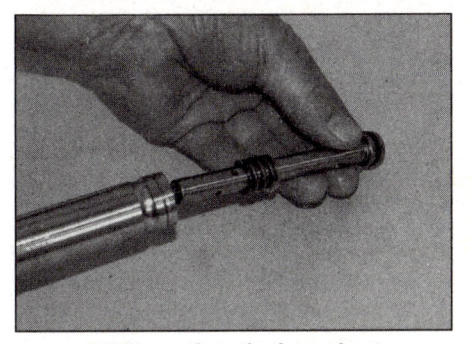

6.21b ... then tip the rod out

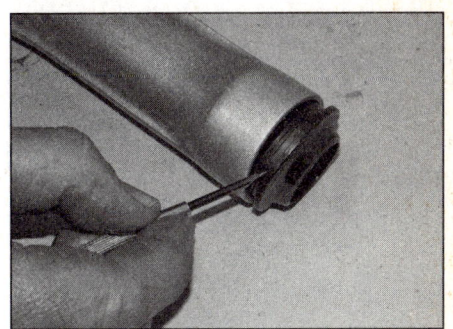

6.22 Prise out the dust seal using a flat-bladed screwdriver

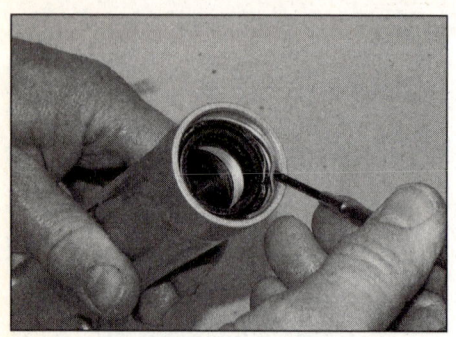

5•8 Frame and suspension

6.23 Prise out the retaining clip using a flat-bladed screwdriver

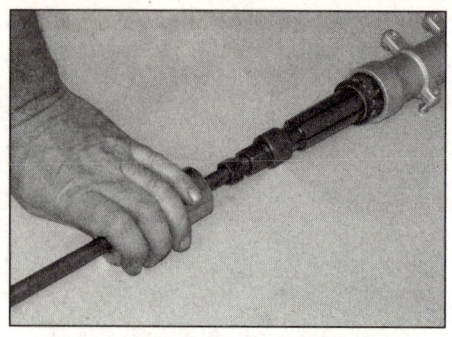

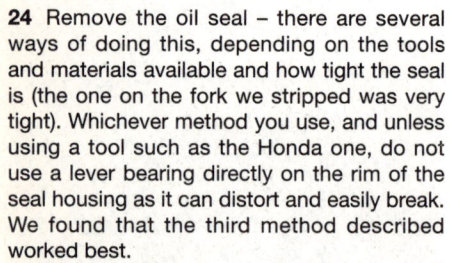

6.24a Locate the puller under the oil seal and jar the seal out using the slide-hammer attachment

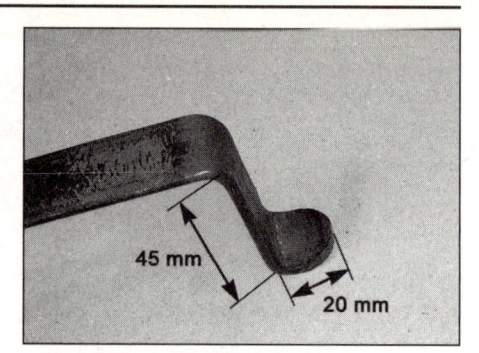

6.24b Bend a piece of steel to the shape shown . . .

24 Remove the oil seal – there are several ways of doing this, depending on the tools and materials available and how tight the seal is (the one on the fork we stripped was very tight). Whichever method you use, and unless using a tool such as the Honda one, do not use a lever bearing directly on the rim of the seal housing as it can distort and easily break. We found that the third method described worked best.
- You can use an internal expanding puller with slide-hammer attachment **(see illustration 6.24a)**.
- You can use a levering tool, such as the Honda tool (part No. 07748-0010001) or its commercially available equivalent, or a home-made version using a suitable piece of steel bent as shown, so that it can be fitted under the seal and a piece of wood can be used to protect the fairly fragile rim of the seal housing **(see illustrations 6.24b and c)**. The dimensions of our tool are given with the illustration, but make yours to suit the piece of wood being used.
- You can curve and flatten the end of a piece of steel rod that is about four inches longer than the fork outer tube, with the curved section being no longer that 20 mm **(see illustration 6.24d)**. Insert the straight end through the seal, down the fork and out the hole in the bottom, then invert the fork and locate the curved end under the rim of the seal, and use a hammer on the straight end to drive the seal out **(see illustrations 6.24e, f and g)**.

25 Discard the oil and dust seals as new ones must be used on reassembly.

Inspection

26 Clean all parts in a suitable solvent and dry them with compressed air, if available.
27 Inspect the fork inner tubes for score marks, pitting or flaking of the chrome finish and excessive or abnormal wear. Check each tube is straight by laying a straight-edge along it. If any bend is evident check the amount of runout using V-blocks and a dial gauge. If either of the tubes is damaged or worn, or the amount of runout exceeds the limit specified at the beginning of the Chapter, replace both inner tubes with new ones.
28 Check the condition of the damper rod and its rebound spring **(see illustration)**. Check the piston ring in the groove in the top of the rod for wear and replace it with a new one if necessary.

6.24c . . . and use it with a piece of wood to lever the seal out

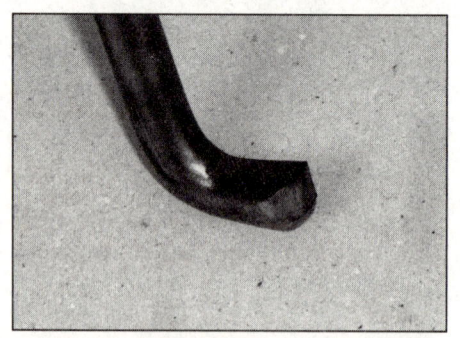

6.24d Curve and shape the end of a piece of rod as shown . . .

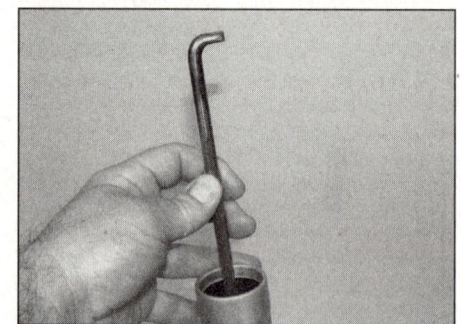

6.24e . . . then insert it in the fork . . .

6.24f . . . locate it under the seal . . . .

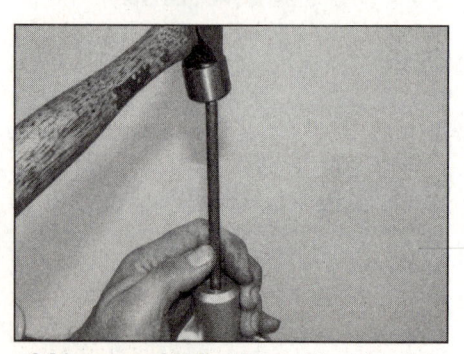

6.24g . . . and strike the end to drive the seal out

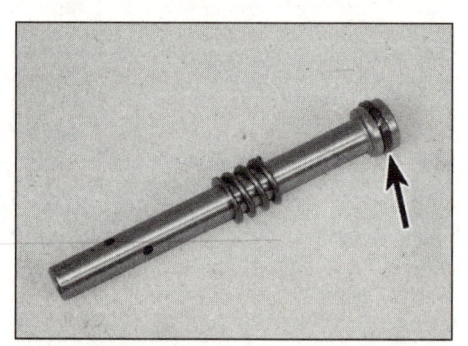

6.28 Check the rod and spring for damage and the ring (arrowed) for wear

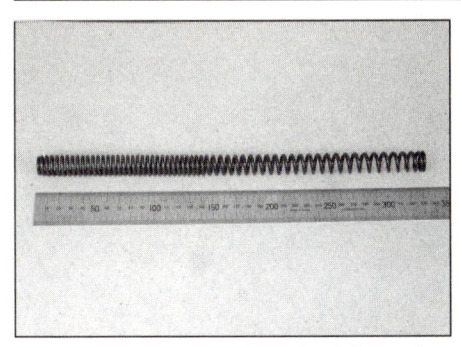

Frame and suspension 5•9

6.29 Measure the free length of the spring

6.30a Fit the oil seal . . .

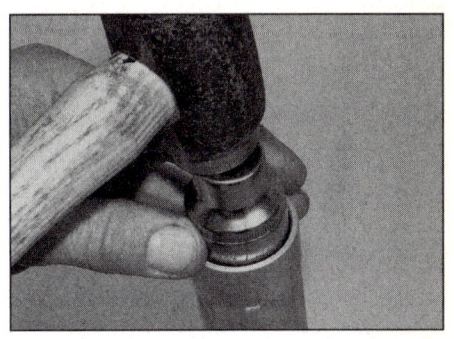

6.30b . . . and drive it into place . . .

29 Inspect the fork springs for cracks, wear and other damage. Over an extended period, the springs will sag – measure the spring free length, and check they are both the same length **(see illustration)**. If one spring is defective, or if the springs have sagged, replace the springs with a new pair.

Reassembly

30 Drive a new oil seal into place in the outer tube, with the marked side facing up, using a driver or suitably-sized socket that bears on the outer edge of the seal only and does not contact the seal housing as the seal is driven in **(see illustrations)** – we found that a thin-walled 27 mm socket worked well, but a thick-walled socket came into contact with the housing, and a 26 mm socket is not wide enough.

31 Fit the retaining clip, making sure it locates correctly in its groove **(see illustration)**.

32 Press the new dust seal into the top of the tube **(see illustration)**. Lubricate the lips of both seals with fork oil **(see illustration)**.

33 If removed fit the rebound spring onto the damper rod, and the piston ring into the groove in its head **(see illustration 6.28)**. Fit the damper rod into the top of the inner tube and slide it down so that it protrudes from the bottom **(see illustration)**.

34 Slide the inner tube fully into the outer tube, taking care not to damage the lips of the seal **(see illustration)**.

35 Clean the threads of the damper rod bolt,

6.30c . . . until the retaining clip groove (arrowed) is fully exposed

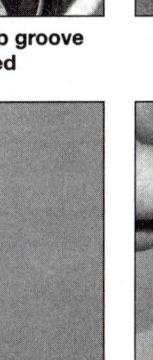

6.31 Fit the seal retaining clip into its groove

6.32a Fit the dust seal . . .

6.32b . . . then lubricate the lips of each seal

then fit a new sealing washer and apply a few drops of a suitable, non-permanent thread-locking compound **(see illustration)**. Thread

the bolt into the bottom of the damper rod via the hole in the bottom of the outer tube and tighten it to the torque setting specified at the

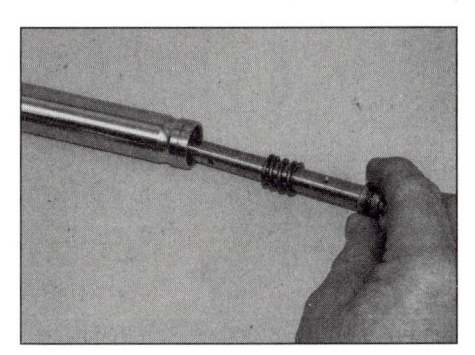

6.33 Fit the damper rod into the inner tube . . .

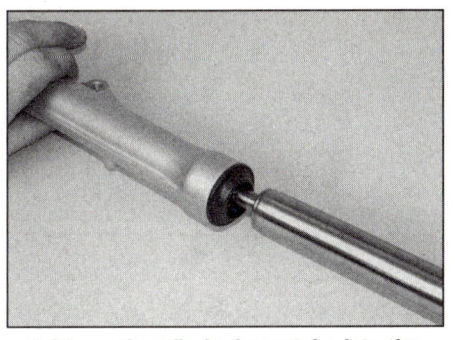

6.34 . . . then fit the inner tube into the outer tube

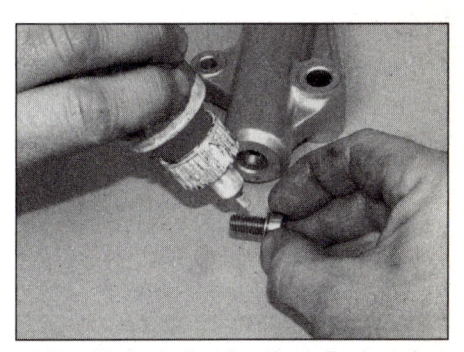

6.35a Fit the bolt using threadlock and a new sealing washer . . .

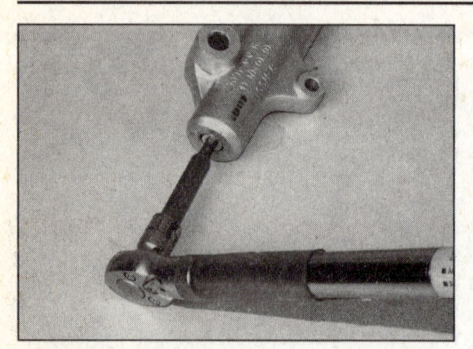

5•10 Frame and suspension

6.35b ... and tighten it to the specified torque

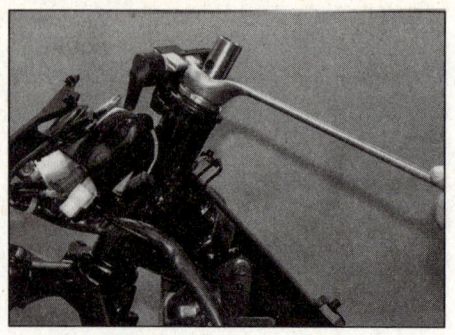

7.4a Unscrew the nut ...

7.4b ... and remove the washer

beginning of the chapter **(see illustration)**. If the damper rotates inside the tube, wait until the fork is fully assembled then hold it with spring pressure as on disassembly.

36 Add the recommended quantity of oil then finish rebuilding the fork – see Steps 12 to 16. Do not forget to tighten the damper rod bolt if necessary.

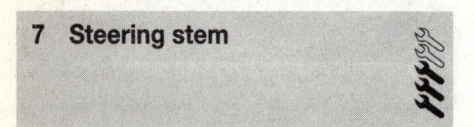

7 Steering stem

Note: *The steering stem uses uncaged ball bearings, which means that unless there is a sufficient amount of grease to hold them in place the ones in the bottom of the steering head could drop out when the steering stem is lowered out of the head. To avoid this get a* container and hold it below the head to catch the balls as you lower the stem.

Removal

1 Remove the handlebar covers and the front cover on each side (see Chapter 7).
2 Remove the front forks (Section 6).
3 Remove the handlebars and handlebar support post (Section 3).
4 Unscrew and remove the steering stem nut, and remove the washer **(see illustrations)**.
5 Slacken the bearing adjuster nut using a C-spanner located in one of the notches if necessary **(see illustration)**.
6 Support the bottom yoke then unscrew and remove the adjuster nut **(see illustration 7.10d)**. Remove the inner race from the top of the steering head **(see illustration 7.10c)**. Collect the bearing balls, using a magnet if available **(see illustration)**.
7 Hold your container (see **Note**) under the steering head, then gently lower the yoke and steering stem out of the frame, catching any balls that drop **(see illustration)**. Remove any balls that have remained stuck in place from the inner race on the bottom of the stem or the outer race in the head as necessary.
8 Wash all traces of old grease from the bearing balls and races using solvent or paraffin, then check them for wear or damage as described in Section 8. **Note:** *Do not attempt to remove the races from the steering head or the steering stem unless they are to be replaced with new ones (see Section 8).*

Installation

9 Smear a liberal quantity of multi-purpose grease onto the bearing races **(see illustrations)**. Stick the bearing balls to the grease on the inner race on the base of the steering stem **(see illustration)**.

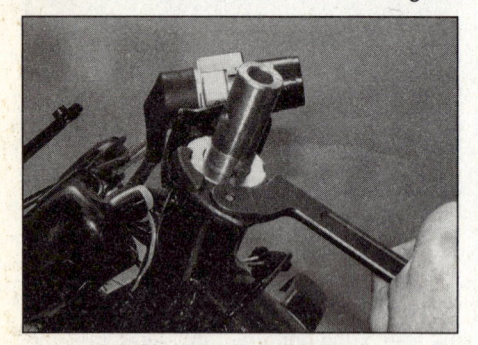

7.5 Slacken the adjuster nut

7.6 Use a magnet to remove the balls

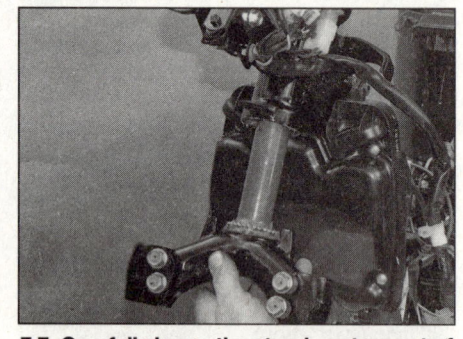

7.7 Carefully lower the steering stem out of the head, being prepared for escaping balls

7.9a Grease the upper race in the head ...

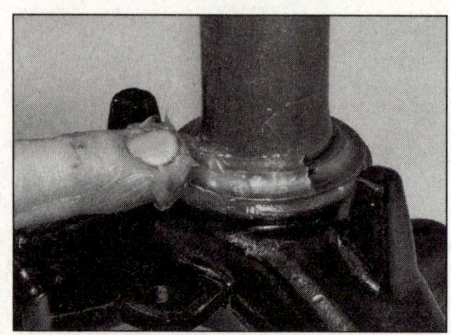

7.9b ... and the lower race

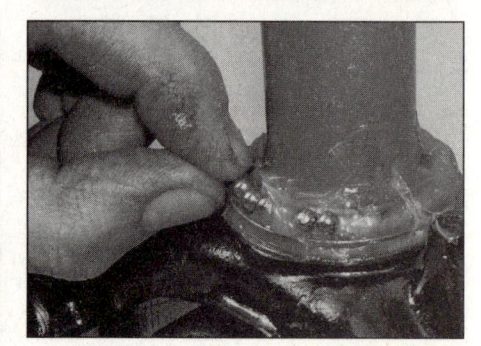

7.9c Stick the balls to the race on the stem

Frame and suspension 5•11

7.10a Carefully seat the stem in the head

7.10b Stick the balls to the outer race . . .

7.10c . . . then fit the inner race . . .

There should be 29 balls for the bottom bearing. Make sure all the balls are pressed against the race to prevent them being dislodged by the opposite race when fitted.

10 Carefully lift the steering stem up through the steering head, making sure all balls stay in place, and when it has located turn it a few times to spread and seat the lower bearing balls, then support it **(see illustration)**. Stick the bearing balls to the grease on the outer race in the top of the steering head **(see illustration)**. There should be 23 balls for the top bearing. Fit the inner race, taking care not to dislodge the balls, and turn it to spread and seat the balls **(see illustration)**. Thread the adjuster nut finger-tight onto the steering stem **(see illustration)**.

11 If the Honda service tool (Part No. 07916-3710101) or a suitable peg spanner and a torque wrench are available, tighten the adjuster nut to the initial torque setting specified at the beginning of the Chapter, then turn the steering stem through its full lock at least five times, then slacken the nut so that it is loose, and then tighten it to the final torque setting specified for your model. Finally turn the nut anti-clockwise 15° (1/24th of a turn). Turn the steering stem from lock-to-lock following adjustment – you will feel some resistance but do not worry, as when the forks and wheel are installed the movement should be free and smooth.

12 If the correct tools are not available, tighten the nut fairly tight using a C-spanner **(see illustration 7.5)** so that the bearings are pre-loaded, but the steering stem is able to move from lock-to-lock, then slacken the nut so that it is loose, and then tighten it very lightly so that any play is just eliminated – the nut must be literally on the point of being loose.

Caution: Take great care not to apply excessive pressure because this will cause premature failure of the bearings.

13 Fit the washer onto the steering stem, locating the tab in the groove **(see illustration 7.4b)**. Fit the steering stem nut and tighten it, to the torque setting specified at the beginning of the Chapter if you have the necessary tools **(see illustration)**.

14 Now install the forks, wheel, handlebars and all remaining components so that their leverage and inertia can be taken into account, then refer to the check and adjustment procedures in Chapter 1 to double-check the bearings.

7.10d . . . and the adjuster

8 Steering head bearing overhaul

Inspection

1 Remove the steering stem (see Section 7).
2 Remove all traces of old grease from the bearings and races and check them for wear or damage.
3 The races should be polished and free from indentations **(see illustration)**. The outer races are in the steering head, the upper inner

7.13 Fit and tighten the steering stem nut

8.3 Check the races for wear and damage

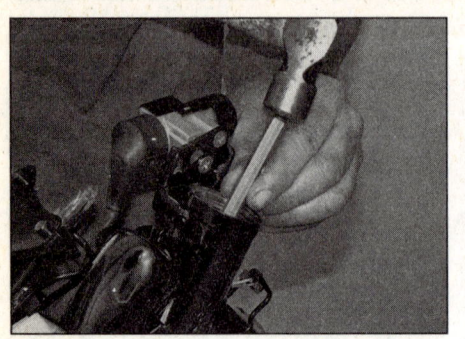

5•12 Frame and suspension

8.6a Drive the bearing races out with a brass drift...

8.6b ...locating it against the exposed rim (arrowed)

race rests on top of the upper bearing balls, and the lower inner race is on the bottom of the steering stem.
4 Inspect the bearing balls for signs of wear, pitting or corrosion.
5 If there are any signs of wear or damage on any of the above components both upper and lower bearing races and balls should be replaced as a set. Only remove the races from the steering head and the stem if new ones are to be fitted – do not re-use them once they have been removed.

Renewal

6 The outer races are an interference fit in the steering head and can be tapped from position using a suitable drift located against the inner rim **(see illustrations)**. Tap firmly and evenly around each race to ensure that it

8.9a Remove the lower bearing race using a cold chisel...

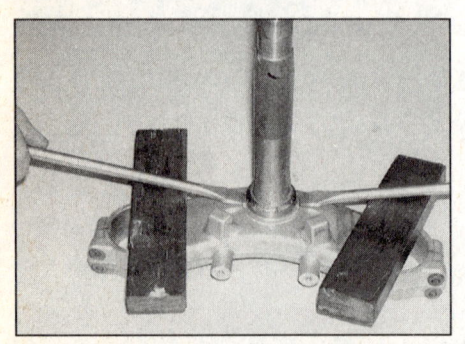

8.9b ...and screwdrivers...

is driven out squarely. You can curve the end of the drift slightly to improve access.
7 Alternatively, the races can be pulled out using a slide-hammer with internal expanding extractor **(see illustration 6.24a)**.
8 The new outer races can be pressed into the frame using a drawbolt arrangement **(see illustration)**, or by using a large diameter tubular drift which bears only on the outer edge of the race – if you do this make sure the scooter is solidly supported as all the force needs to be transmitted to the race. Ensure that the drawbolt washer or drift (as applicable) bears only on the outer edge of the race and does not contact the working surface.

> **HAYNES HiNT** *Installation of new bearing outer races is made much easier if the races are left overnight in the freezer. This causes them to contract slightly making them a looser fit.*

9 To remove the lower inner race from the steering stem, first drive a chisel between the base of the race and the fork yoke **(see illustration)**. Work the chisel around the race to ensure it lifts squarely. Once there is clearance beneath the race, use two levers placed on opposite sides of the race to work it free, using blocks of wood to improve leverage and protect the yoke **(see illustration)**. If the race is firmly in place it can drawn off using a

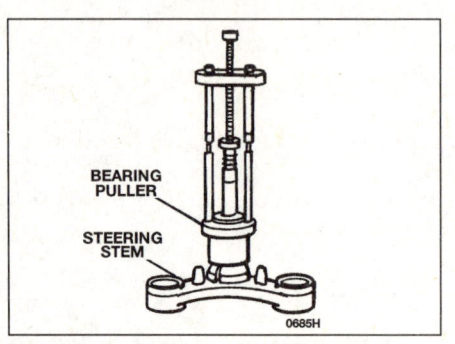

8.9c ...or a puller if necessary

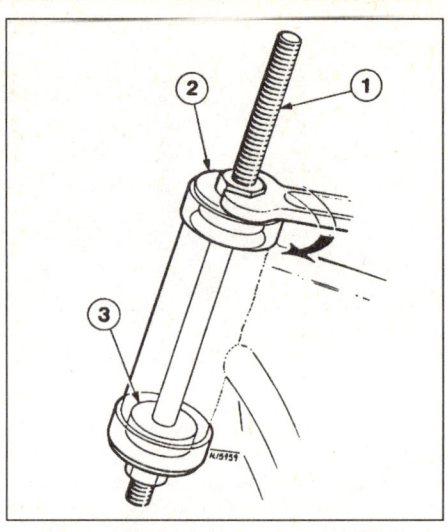

8.8 Drawbolt arrangement for fitting steering stem bearing races

1 Long bolt or threaded bar
2 Thick washer
3 Guide for lower race

puller **(see illustration)**. Remove the dust seal and replace it with a new one.
10 Fit the new lower inner race bearing onto the steering stem. A length of tubing with an internal diameter slightly larger than the steering stem will be needed to tap the new race into position **(see illustration)**. Ensure that the tube bears only on the inner edge of the race and does not contact its working surface.
11 Install the steering stem (see Section 7).

9 Rear shock absorbers

Removal

1 Support the scooter on its centrestand, then position a support under the rear wheel so that the swingarm does not drop when the second shock absorber is removed. Check that the

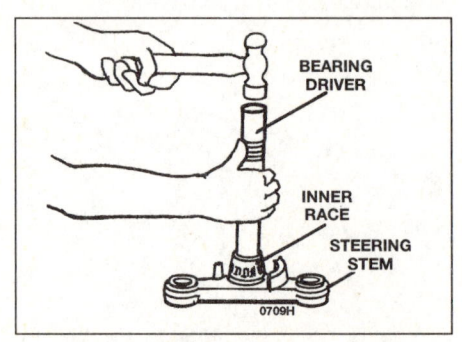

8.10 Drive the new race on using a suitable bearing driver or a length of pipe that bears only against the inner edge

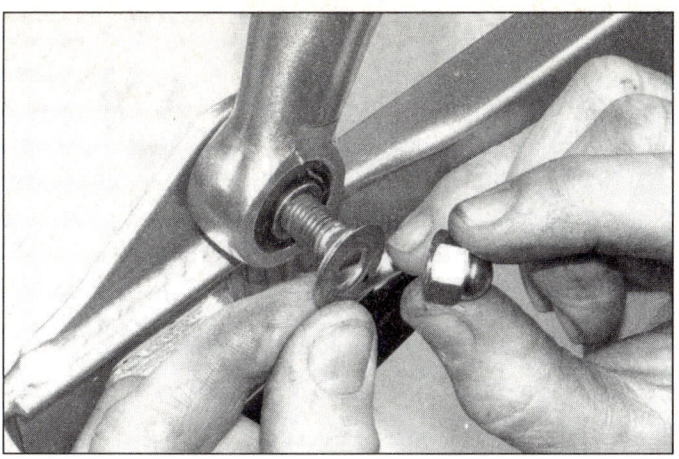

Frame and suspension 5•13

9.3a Unscrew the nut and remove the washer . . .

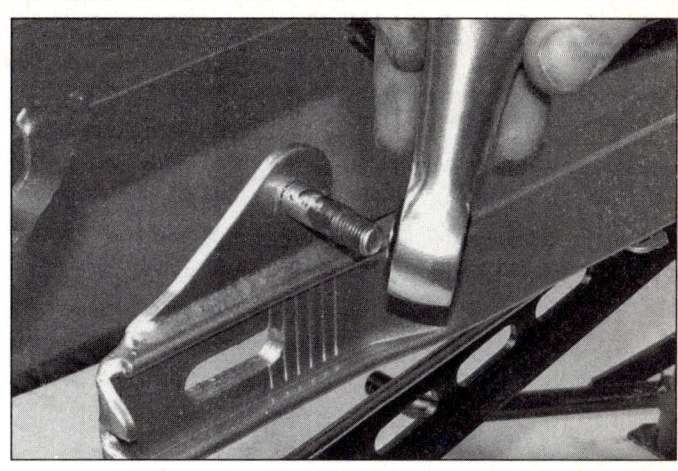

9.3b . . . then draw the shock off the mount

weight of the scooter is off the rear suspension so that the shock is not compressed.

2 On 2003 to 2006 models remove the body cover and on 2007-on models remove the rear body cover (see Chapter 7). On all models remove the exhaust system to access the right-hand shock absorber (see Chapter 3B).

3 Undo the nut and remove the washer securing the bottom of the shock and draw it off its mount **(see illustrations)**.

4 Undo the bolt securing the top and remove the shock absorber **(see illustration)**.

Inspection

5 Inspect the shock absorber for obvious physical damage. Check the coil spring for looseness, cracks or signs of fatigue.

6 Inspect the damper rod for signs of bending, pitting and oil leaks **(see illustration)**.

7 Inspect the bush and metal sleeve in each mount for wear, and replace them with new ones if necessary **(see illustration 9.6)** – they are listed as separate parts. Removal and installation of the bushes is best done using a drawbolt arrangement such as the one shown, which uses a 23 mm socket to rest on the housing and into which the bush is drawn as the nut is turned on the end of the bolt, pushed out by the head of the bolt which must be small enough to pass through the mount **(see illustrations)**. When installing the new bushes replace the socket with a large washer that seats around the rim of the mount, and fit a similar washer under the head of the bolt

so the bush is pushed in flush. Also check the top mount bolt and bolt holes and the bottom mount lug for wear.

8 With the exception of the bushes and mounting hardware, individual components are not available for the shocks. If any parts are worn or damaged, a new shock must be fitted – it is best to replace them as a pair.

Installation

9 Installation is the reverse of removal. Tighten the bolts and nuts to the torque setting specified at the beginning of the Chapter.

10 Swingarm

Removal

1 Remove the exhaust system (see Chapter 3B).

2 Remove the passenger footrest brackets (Section 4).

3 Remove the drive chain case and rear wheel (see Chapter 6).

4 Undo the nut and remove the washer securing the bottom of each shock absorber and draw them off the mounts **(see illustrations 9.3a and b)**.

5 Unscrew the nut on the right-hand end of the swingarm pivot bolt **(see illustration)**.

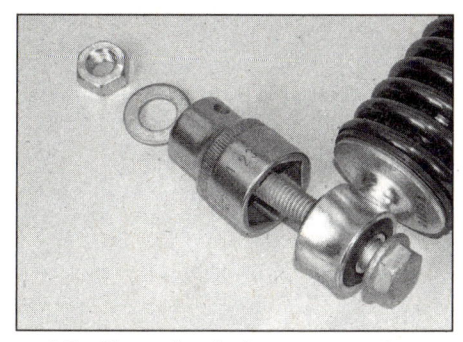

9.4 Unscrew the bolt and remove the shock

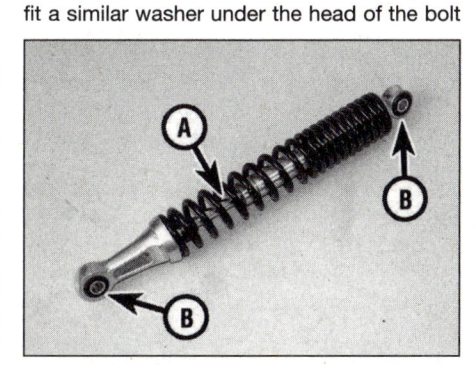

9.6 Check for oil leaks around the rod (A), and check the bushes (B)

9.7a Use a drawbolt arrangement as shown . . .

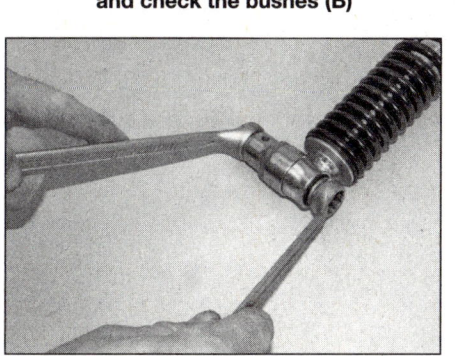

9.7b . . . to remove the bushes

10.5 Unscrew the nut

5•14 Frame and suspension

10.6a Withdraw the pivot bolt . . .

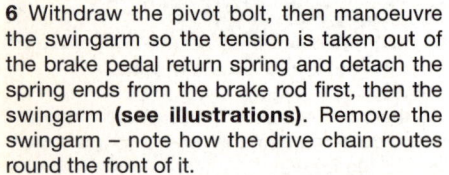

10.6b . . . then move the arm to relax the spring, and unhook it from the rod . . .

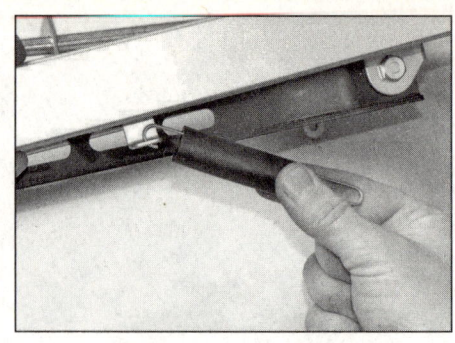

10.6c . . . and swingarm

6 Withdraw the pivot bolt, then manoeuvre the swingarm so the tension is taken out of the brake pedal return spring and detach the spring ends from the brake rod first, then the swingarm **(see illustrations)**. Remove the swingarm – note how the drive chain routes round the front of it.

7 If required remove the chain slider from the swingarm, noting how it locates **(see illustration)**. If it is badly worn or damaged, it should be replaced with a new one.

8 If required on 2007-on models, remove the split pin from the torque arm bolt, then unscrew the nut, remove the washers, withdraw the bolt and remove the arm **(see illustration)**.

Inspection

9 Thoroughly clean the swingarm, removing all traces of dirt, corrosion and grease.
10 Inspect the swingarm closely, looking for obvious signs of wear such as heavy scoring and cracks or distortion due to accident damage.
11 Inspect the bushes in the swingarm pivots for wear or damage **(see illustration)**.

If necessary replace the swingarm with a new one – the bushes are not available separately.
12 Check the swingarm pivot bolt for straightness by rolling it on a flat surface such as a piece of plate glass (first wipe off all old grease and remove any corrosion using steel wool). Replace the pivot bolt with a new one if it is bent.

Installation

13 Clean off all old grease, then lubricate the bushes and the pivot bolt with multi-purpose grease.
14 If removed on 2007-on models, fit the brake torque arm as shown, with the spring washer under the plain washer, using a new split pin and bending its ends round **(see illustration 10.8)**.
15 If removed, fit the chain slider, making sure it locates correctly over the drive chain case lug and the lugs at the front **(see illustration 10.7)**.
16 Offer up the swingarm and connect the brake pedal return spring **(see illustrations 10.6c and b)**. Make sure the drive chain is looped over the front of the swingarm. Slide the pivot bolt through from the left-hand side **(see illustration 10.6a)**.
17 Thread the nut onto the pivot bolt and tighten it finger-tight only at this stage **(see illustration 10.5)**.
18 Fit each shock absorber onto its mount, then fit the washers and tighten the nuts to the torque setting specified at the beginning of the Chapter **(see illustrations 9.3b and a)**.
19 Install the footrest brackets (Section 4).
20 Install the rear wheel and drive chain case (see Chapter 6).
21 Take the scooter off its stand and support it upright – both wheels must be on the ground so the weight of the scooter is taken through the suspension. Tighten the swingarm pivot bolt nut to the specified torque setting. Put the scooter back on its stand.
22 Install the exhaust system (see Chapter 3B).
23 Check and adjust the drive chain slack (see Chapter 1). Check the operation of the rear suspension and brake before taking the machine on the road.

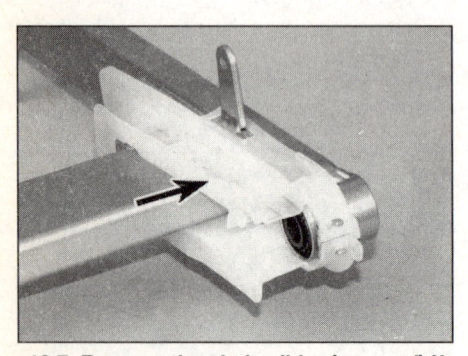

10.7 Remove the chain slider (arrowed) if required

10.8 Remove the split pin (arrowed) and detach the arm as described

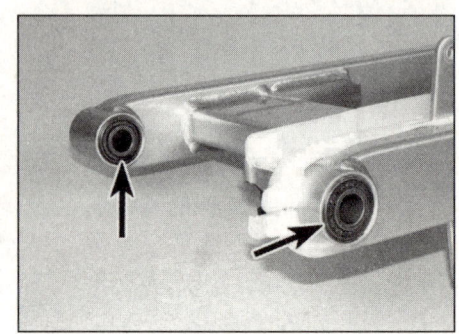

10.11 Check the bushes (arrowed) for wear

Chapter 6
Brakes, wheels and final drive

Contents

	Section number		Section number
Brake fluid level check	see Pre-ride checks	Front wheel	11
Brake hose	6	General information	1
Brake lever and pedal	see Chapter 5	Rear drum brake	8
Brake light switches	see Chapter 8	Rear sprocket coupling/rubber dampers	17
Brake pad and shoe wear check	see Chapter 1	Rear wheel	12
Brake system bleeding and fluid change	7	Sprockets	16
Brake system check	see Chapter 1	Tyres	14
Drive chain	15	Tyre pressure, tread depth and condition	see Pre-ride checks
Drive chain adjustment and lubrication	see Chapter 1	Wheel bearing check	see Chapter 1
Front brake caliper	3	Wheel bearings	13
Front brake disc	4	Wheel alignment check	10
Front brake master cylinder	5	Wheel check	see Chapter 1
Front brake pads	2	Wheel inspection and repair	9

Degrees of difficulty

Easy, suitable for novice with little experience	Fairly easy, suitable for beginner with some experience	Fairly difficult, suitable for competent DIY mechanic	Difficult, suitable for experienced DIY mechanic	Very difficult, suitable for expert DIY or professional

Specifications

Front disc brake
Brake fluid type	DOT 4
Caliper bore ID	
Standard	25.400 to 25.450 mm
Service limit	25.460 mm
Caliper piston OD	
Standard	25.318 to 25.368 mm
Service limit	25.310 mm
Master cylinder bore ID	
Standard	12.700 to 12.743 mm
Service limit	12.755 mm
Master cylinder piston OD	
Standard	12.657 to 12.684 mm
Service limit	12.645 mm
Disc thickness	
Standard	3.8 to 4.2 mm
Service limit (min)	3.5 mm
Disc maximum runout	0.3 mm

Rear drum brake
Drum internal diameter	
Standard	110.0 mm
Service limit	111.0 mm

Wheels
Type	17 inch, steel rim and wire spoke
Maximum wheel runout (front and rear)	
Axial (side-to-side)	2.0 mm
Radial (out-of-round)	2.0 mm
Maximum axle runout (front)	0.20 mm

6•2 Brakes, wheels and final drive

Final drive
Drive chain slack and lubricant . . . . see Chapter 1
Drive chain type
   Size and no. of links . . . . 420, 104 links
   Original equipment fitting . . . . DID 420DX-104RB or RK 420SB-104RJ
Sprocket sizes
   Front (engine) sprocket 14
   Rear (wheel) sprocket 35

Tyres
Tyre pressures . . . . see *Pre-ride checks*
Tyre sizes*
   Front 70/100-17MC (40P)
   Rear 80/90-17MC (50P)
Refer to the owners handbook or the tyre information label on the chaincase (chainguard) for approved tyre brands.

Torque settings
Brake caliper bleed valve . . . . 5 Nm
Brake disc bolts . . . . 42 Nm
Brake hose banjo bolts . . . . 34 Nm
Front axle nut . . . . 59 Nm
Front brake caliper mounting bolts . . . . 30 Nm
Front brake pad retaining pin . . . . 17 Nm
Front sprocket bolts . . . . 12 Nm
Rear axle nut . . . . 59 Nm
Rear sprocket nuts
   2003 to 2006 models . . . . 32 Nm
   2007-on models . . . . 49 Nm
Rear sprocket studs . . . . 20 Nm

1 General information

All models have an hydraulically operated front disc brake, with a twin piston sliding caliper, and a rear drum brake.

The wheels are 17 inch steel-rimmed wire spoked designed for tubed tyres only.

Caution: *Disc brake components rarely require disassembly. Do not disassemble components unless absolutely necessary. If a hydraulic brake hose is loosened or disconnected, the union sealing washers must be replaced with new ones and the system bled upon reassembly. Do not use solvents on internal brake components. Solvents will cause the seals to swell and distort. Use only clean DOT 4 brake fluid for cleaning. Use care when working with brake fluid as it can injure your eyes and it will damage painted surfaces and plastic parts.*

2 Front brake pads

Warning: *The dust created by the brake system is harmful to your health. Never blow it out with compressed air and don't inhale any of it. An approved filtering mask should be worn when working on the brakes.*

Note: *Honda recommend using new caliper mounting bolts. This is because the bolts are pre-treated with a locking compound. If* they are not available it is possible, however, to clean up the old bolts and reinstall them using a suitable non-permanent thread locking compound that is commercially available.

Removal

1 Slacken the pad retaining pin **(see illustration)**.

2 Unscrew the caliper mounting bolts and slide the caliper off the disc **(see illustration)**. Free the brake hose from the mudguard to give more freedom of movement if required **(see illustration 3.2)**.

3 Unscrew and remove the pad pin, then remove the pads, noting how they fit **(see illustrations)**.

2.1 Slacken the pad pin (arrowed)

2.2 Unscrew the bolts (arrowed) and slide the caliper off the disc

2.3a Unscrew the pin . . .

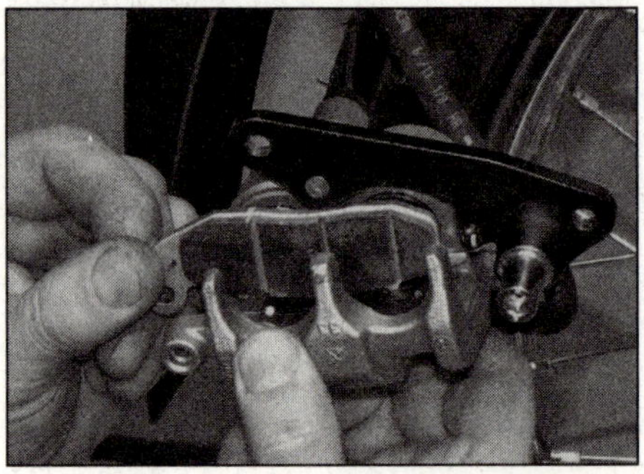

2.3b . . . and remove the pads

Brakes, wheels and final drive 6•3

2.7 Clean the pad pin and fit a new O-ring (arrowed) if necessary

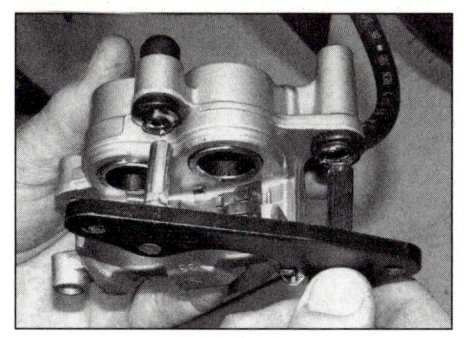

2.8a Slide the caliper off the bracket

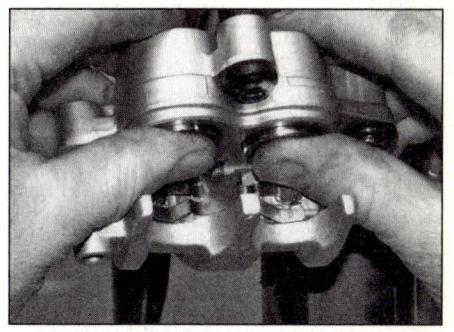

2.8b Push the pistons in using one of the methods described . . .

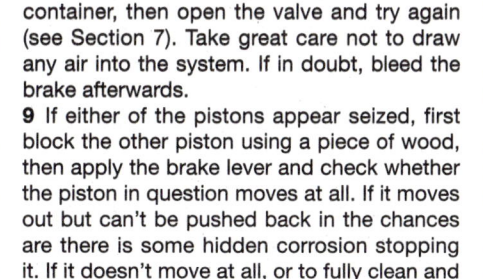

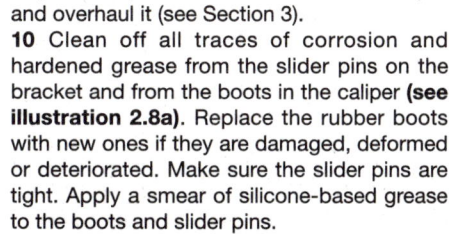

2.8c . . . this shows a proper tool

Inspection

4 Inspect the surface of each pad for contamination and check that the friction material has not worn beyond its service limit (see Chapter 1, Section 9). If either pad is worn down to, or beyond, the service limit wear indicator (i.e. the wear indicator is no longer visible), is fouled with oil or grease, or heavily scored or damaged, fit a set of new pads.
Note: *It is not possible to degrease the friction material; if the pads are contaminated in any way they must be replaced with new ones.*

5 If the pads are in good condition clean them carefully, using a fine wire brush which is completely free of oil and grease to remove all traces of road dirt and corrosion. Using a pointed instrument, dig out any embedded particles of foreign matter. If required, spray with a dedicated brake cleaner to remove any dust.

6 Check the condition of the brake disc (see Section 4).

7 Remove all traces of corrosion from the pad pin and check it for wear and damage. Check the condition of the O-ring on its inner end and replace it with a new one if necessary **(see illustration)**.

8 Slide the caliper off the bracket **(see illustration)**. Clean around the exposed section of each piston to remove any dirt or debris that could cause the seals to be damaged. If new pads are being fitted, now push the pistons all the way back into the caliper to create room for them; if the old pads are still serviceable push the pistons in a little way. To push the pistons back use finger pressure or a piece of wood as leverage, or place the old pads back in the caliper and use a metal bar or a screwdriver inserted between them, or use grips and a piece of wood, with rag or card to protect the caliper body **(see illustration)**. Alternatively obtain a proper piston-pushing tool from a good tool supplier **(see illustration)**. If there is too much brake fluid in the reservoir it may be necessary to remove the master cylinder reservoir cover, plate and diaphragm and siphon some out (see *Pre-ride checks*). If the pistons are difficult to push back, remove the bleed valve cap, then attach a length of clear hose to the valve and place the open end in a suitable container, then open the valve and try again (see Section 7). Take great care not to draw any air into the system. If in doubt, bleed the brake afterwards.

9 If either of the pistons appear seized, first block the other piston using a piece of wood, then apply the brake lever and check whether the piston in question moves at all. If it moves out but can't be pushed back in the chances are there is some hidden corrosion stopping it. If it doesn't move at all, or to fully clean and inspect the pistons, disassemble the caliper and overhaul it (see Section 3).

10 Clean off all traces of corrosion and hardened grease from the slider pins on the bracket and from the boots in the caliper **(see illustration 2.8a)**. Replace the rubber boots with new ones if they are damaged, deformed or deteriorated. Make sure the slider pins are tight. Apply a smear of silicone-based grease to the boots and slider pins.

Installation

11 Make sure the pad spring and guide are correctly located in the caliper and on the bracket respectively **(see illustrations)**. Make sure the sliding surfaces of the guide and the post that the pad ends sit on are clean. Slide the caliper onto the bracket **(see illustration 2.8a)**.

12 Lightly smear the back of the backing material and the pad pin, guide and post with copper-based grease, making sure that none gets on the friction material. Apply a smear of silicone-based grease to the O-ring on the retaining pin **(see illustration 2.7)**.

13 Fit the outer pad into the caliper, making sure its upper end locates correctly against the guide on the bracket **(see illustration 2.3b)**. Fit the inner pad, locating its curved end over the post **(see illustration)**. Press the lower end of each pad up against the spring so the holes for the pad pin align, then

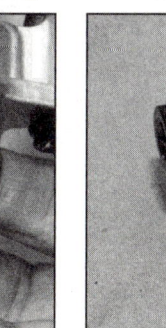

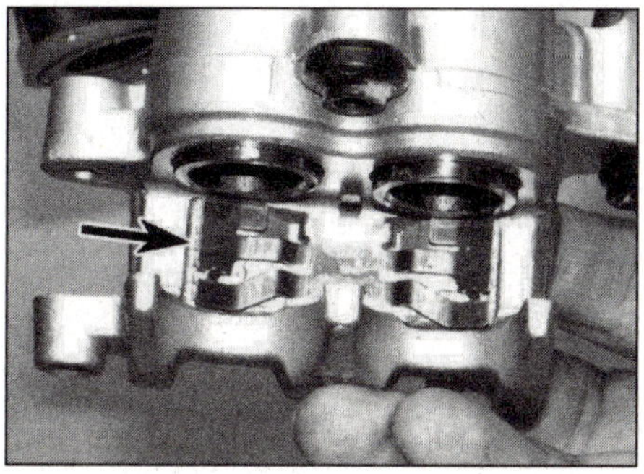

2.11a Make sure the spring (arrowed) . . .

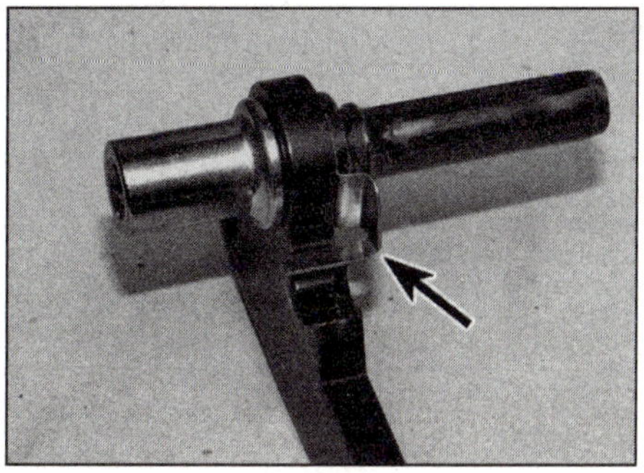

2.11b . . . and guide (arrowed) are correctly fitted

2.13 Make sure the pads locate correctly

6•4 Brakes, wheels and final drive

2.14 Slide the caliper onto the disc and fit the bolts

3.2 Unscrew the bolt (arrowed) to free the hose from the mudguard

3.3a Unscrew the banjo bolt (arrowed) and detach the hose

insert the pin and tighten it finger-tight (see illustration 2.3a).

14 Slide the caliper onto the disc making sure the pads locate correctly on each side **(see illustration)**. Fit the caliper mounting bolts and tighten them to the torque setting specified at the beginning of the Chapter. Fit the brake hose onto the mudguard if displaced **(see illustration 3.2)**.

15 Tighten the pad pin to the torque setting specified at the beginning of this Chapter **(see illustration 2.1)**.

16 Operate the brake lever until the pads contact with the disc. Check the level of fluid in the hydraulic reservoir and top-up if necessary (see *Pre-ride checks*).

17 Check the operation of the front brake before riding the bike.

3 Front brake caliper

⚠️ **Warning:** *If the caliper is in need of an overhaul it is best to drain all old brake fluid from the system, then fill with new fluid after the overhaul (see Section 7). Overhaul of the brake caliper must be done in a spotlessly clean work area to avoid contamination and possible failure of the brake hydraulic system components. Do not, under any circumstances, use petroleum-based solvents to clean brake parts. Use clean DOT 4 brake fluid or dedicated brake cleaner as described. Brake fluid attacks painted finishes and plastics – to prevent damage from spilled fluid, always cover paintwork when working on the braking system, and clean up any spills immediately using brake cleaner.*

Note 1: *If the caliper is being overhauled (usually due to sticking pistons or fluid leaks) read through the entire procedure first and make sure that you have obtained all the new parts required, including some new DOT 4 brake fluid.*

Note 2: *Honda recommend using new caliper mounting bolts. This is because the bolts are pre-treated with a locking compound. If they are not available it is possible, however, to clean up the old bolts and reinstall them using a suitable non-permanent thread locking compound that is commercially available.*

Note 3: *If the caliper is just being displaced from the fork leg and not overhauled, do not operate the brake lever while it is off the disc.*

Removal

1 If the caliper is being overhauled, slacken the brake pad retaining pin **(see illustration 2.1)**. If the caliper is just being displaced from the forks as part of another procedure, the brake pads can be left in place.

2 Free the brake hose from the mudguard to give more freedom of movement if required **(see illustration)**.

3 If the caliper is being completely removed or overhauled, unscrew the brake hose banjo bolt and detach the banjo union, noting its alignment with the caliper **(see illustration)**. If the brake fluid has not been drained seal the banjo unions – a good way of doing this is to place a piece of rubber over each side of the union (we used some rubber blanking caps), and clamp them in place using a spring clamp **(see illustration)**. Discard the sealing washers – new ones must be used.

4 Unscrew the caliper mounting bolts and slide the caliper off the disc **(see illustration 2.2)**. If the caliper is just being displaced, secure it to the scooter with a cable-tie to avoid straining the brake hose.

5 If the caliper is being overhauled, remove the brake pads (see Section 2).

Overhaul

6 Slide the caliper off the bracket **(see illustration 2.8a)**. Clean the exterior of the caliper and bracket with brake system cleaner. Have some clean rag ready to catch any spilled brake fluid. Clean off all traces of corrosion and hardened grease from the slider pins on the bracket and from the rubber boots in the caliper. Replace the rubber boots with new ones if they are damaged, deformed or deteriorated. Make sure each slider pin is tight.

7 Find a piece of wood that fits between the pistons and the arms on the inner side of the caliper. Make sure the bleed valve is tight. Block one piston from moving using the wood, and place some rag over the other piston. Place the caliper piston-down on the bench.

8 Apply compressed air gradually and progressively, starting with a fairly low pressure, to the fluid inlet in the caliper and allow the unblocked piston to ease out of its bore, controlling it with hand pressure and the rag **(see illustrations)**.

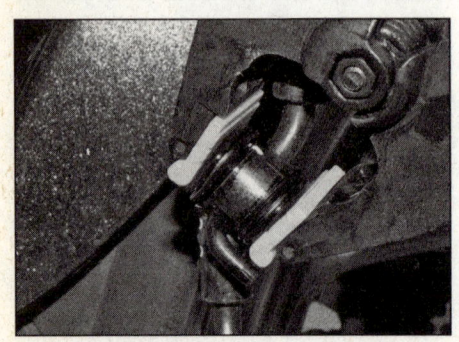

3.3b Seal the banjo union using pieces of rubber and a spring clamp

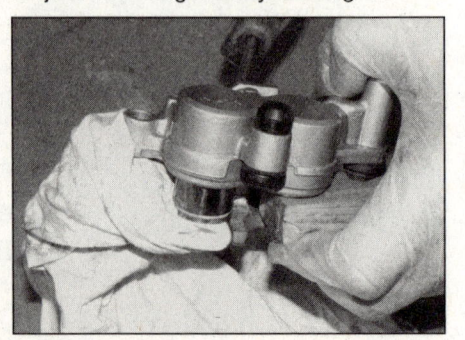

3.8a Apply compressed air to the fluid passage . . .

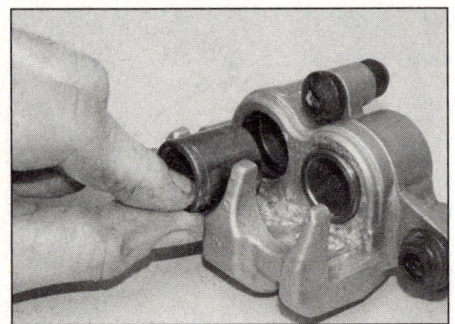

3.8b . . . until the piston is displaced

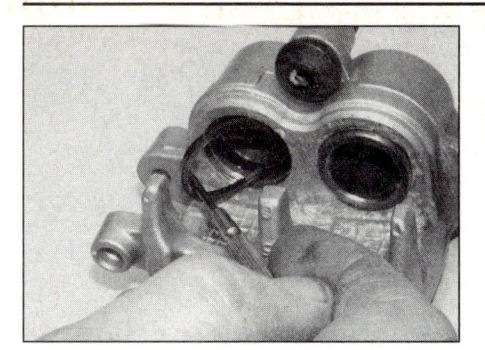

Brakes, wheels and final drive 6•5

3.10 Remove the seals and discard them

3.13a Lubricate the new piston seal with brake fluid . . .

3.13b . . . then fit it into its groove . . .

9 If the piston is stuck in its bore due to corrosion, find a suitable bolt to block the fluid inlet banjo bolt bore and thread it in, then unscrew the bleed valve and apply the air to this in the same way – the narrower bore will allow more air pressure to be applied to the piston as less can escape. Do not try to remove a piston by levering it out or by using pliers or other grips. If the piston has completely seized you may have to replace the caliper with a new one.
10 Remove the dust seal and the piston seal from the piston bore using a soft wooden or plastic tool to avoid scratching the bores (see illustration). Discard the seals as new ones must be fitted.
11 Clean the piston and bore with DOT 4 brake fluid or brake system cleaner. If compressed air is available, blow it through the fluid galleries in the caliper to ensure they are clear (make sure it is filtered and unlubricated).
Caution: Do not, under any circumstances, use a petroleum-based solvent to clean brake parts.
12 Inspect the caliper bore and piston for signs of corrosion, nicks and burrs and loss of plating. If surface defects are present, the pistons and/or the caliper assembly must be replaced with new ones. If the necessary measuring equipment is available, compare the dimensions of the caliper bores and pistons to those specified at the beginning of this Chapter, and obtain new pistons or a new caliper if necessary.
13 Lubricate the new piston seal with clean

brake fluid and fit it into the inner groove in the caliper bore (see illustrations).
14 Lubricate the new dust seal with silicone grease and fit it into the outer groove in the caliper bore (see illustration).
15 Lubricate the piston with clean brake fluid and fit it, closed-end first, into the caliper bore, taking care not to displace the seals (see illustration). Using your thumbs, push the piston all the way in, making sure it enters the bore squarely.
16 Repeat Steps 7 to 15 for the other piston.
17 Apply a smear of silicone-based grease to the boots and slider pins (see illustration 2.8a). Slide the caliper onto the bracket.

Installation

18 If the caliper has not been overhauled, refer to Steps 6 and 17 and clean, check and re-grease the slider pins and boots.
19 If removed, install the brake pads (see Section 2).
20 Slide the caliper onto the brake disc, making sure the pads locate correctly on each side (see illustration 2.14).
21 Fit the caliper mounting bolts and tighten them to the torque setting specified at the beginning of the Chapter. If disturbed, tighten the pad pin to the torque setting specified at the beginning of this Chapter (see illustration 2.1).
22 If removed, connect the brake hose to the caliper, using a new sealing washer on each side of the banjo fitting (see illustration 3.3a). Locate the hose elbow between the lugs on the caliper. Tighten the banjo bolt to the specified torque setting.

23 Fit the brake hose onto the mudguard if displaced (see illustration 3.2).
24 Top up the hydraulic reservoir with DOT 4 brake fluid (see *Pre-ride checks*) and bleed the system as described in Section 7. Check that there are no fluid leaks and test the operation of the brake before riding the scooter.

4 Front brake disc

Inspection

1 Inspect the surface of the disc for score marks and other damage. Light scratches are normal after use and won't affect brake operation, but deep grooves and heavy score marks will reduce braking efficiency and accelerate pad wear. If a disc is badly grooved it must be replaced with a new one.
2 The disc must not be machined or allowed to wear down to a thickness less than the service limit listed in this Chapter's Specifications. The minimum thickness should also be stamped on the disc. Check the thickness of the disc with a Vernier gauge or micrometer and replace it with a new one if necessary (see illustration).
3 To check if the disc is warped, position the scooter on its centrestand with the front wheel raised off the ground and turned to one side. Mount a dial gauge to the fork leg, with the gauge plunger touching the surface of the disc about 10 mm from the outer edge (see

3.14 . . . followed by the new dust seal

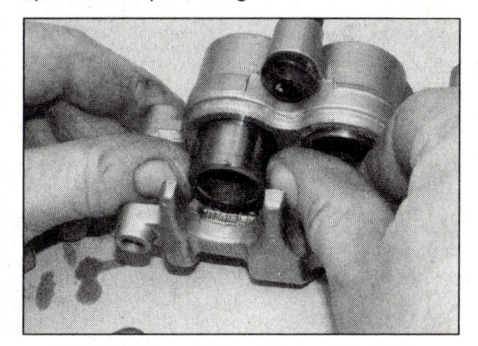

3.15 Fit the piston and push it all the way in

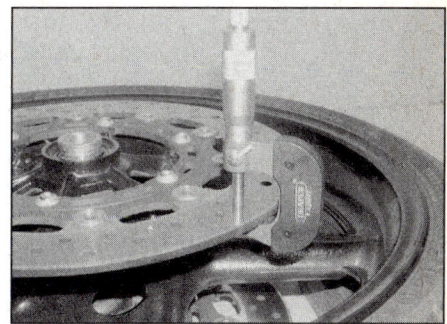

4.2 Measure the thickness of the disc

6•6 Brakes, wheels and final drive

4.3 Checking disc runout with a dial gauge

4.5 The disc is secured by four bolts

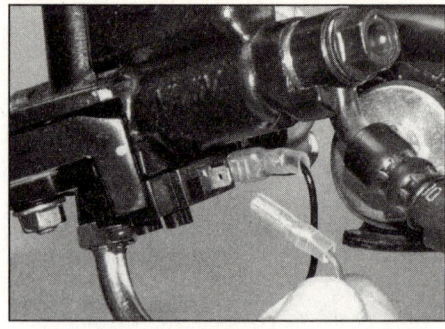

5.2 Disconnect the brake light switch connectors

illustration). Hold the handlebars against the stop then rotate the wheel and watch the gauge needle, comparing the reading with the limit listed in the Specifications at the beginning of this Chapter. If the runout is greater than the service limit, check the wheel bearings for play (see Chapter 1). If the bearings are worn, install new ones (see Section 13) and repeat this check. If the disc runout is still excessive, a new disc will have to be fitted.

Removal

4 Remove the wheel (see Section 11).
Caution: Don't lay the wheel down and allow it to rest on the disc – the disc could become warped. Set the wheel on wood blocks so the wheel rim supports the weight of the wheel.
5 If you are not replacing the disc with a new one, mark the relationship of the disc to the wheel so it can be installed in the same position. Unscrew the disc bolts, loosening them evenly and a little at a time in a criss-cross pattern to avoid distorting the disc, then remove the disc **(see illustration)**.

Installation

Note: *Honda specify to use new disc mounting bolts, which come pre-treated with a thread locking compound. If preferred, clean the old locking compound off the original bolts and apply fresh compound just before fitting them.*
6 Before installing the disc, make sure there is no dirt or corrosion where the disc seats on

the hub. If the disc does not sit flat when it is bolted down, it will appear to be warped when checked or when the front brake is used.
7 Fit the disc on the wheel with its marked side facing out, aligning the previously applied matchmarks (if you're reinstalling the original disc).
8 Fit the mounting bolts (see **Note** above) and tighten them evenly and a little at a time in a criss-cross pattern to the torque setting specified at the beginning of this Chapter. Clean the disc using acetone or brake system cleaner. If a new disc has been installed, remove any protective coating from its working surfaces and fit new brake pads.
9 Install the front wheel (see Section 11).
10 Operate the brake lever several times to bring the pads into contact with the disc. Check the operation of the brake before riding the scooter.

5 Front brake master cylinder

Warning: If the brake master cylinder is in need of an overhaul it is best to drain all old brake fluid from the system, then fill with new fluid after the overhaul (see Section 7). Overhaul must be done in a spotlessly clean work area to avoid contamination and possible failure of the brake hydraulic system components. Do not, under any circumstances, use petroleum-based

solvents to clean brake parts. Use clean DOT 4 brake fluid or dedicated brake cleaner as described. Brake fluid attacks painted finishes and plastics – to prevent damage from spilled fluid, always cover paintwork when working on the braking system, and clean up any spills immediately using brake cleaner.

Note: *If the master cylinder is being overhauled (usually due to sticking or poor action, or fluid leaks) read through the entire procedure first and make sure that you have obtained all the new parts required, including some new DOT 4 brake fluid – a rebuild kit is available that contains the rubber boot, circlip, piston, seal, cup and spring.*

Removal

1 Remove the handlebar covers (see Chapter 7).
2 Disconnect the wiring connectors from the brake light switch **(see illustration)**.
3 If the master cylinder is being overhauled, follow Steps 4 to 9. If the master cylinder is just being displaced, follow this Step only: unscrew the master cylinder clamp bolts and remove the back of the clamp, noting how it fits, then position the master cylinder assembly clear of the handlebar **(see illustration)**. Ensure no strain is placed on the hydraulic hose. Keep the reservoir upright to prevent air entering the system.
4 Unscrew the brake hose banjo bolt and detach the banjo union, noting its alignment with the master cylinder **(see illustration)**. If

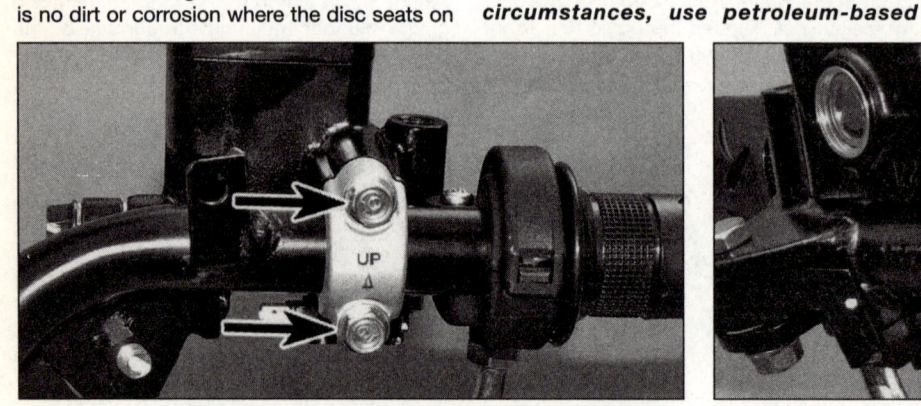

5.3 Unscrew the bolts and remove the master cylinder and its clamp

5.4 Unscrew the banjo bolt (arrowed) and detach the hose – note its alignment

Brakes, wheels and final drive 6•7

the brake fluid has not been drained seal the banjo unions – a good way of doing this is to place a piece of rubber over each side of the union (we used some rubber blanking caps), and clamp them in place using a spring clamp **(see illustration 3.3b)**. Discard the sealing washers – new ones must be used.

5 Remove the brake lever (see Chapter 5).

6 Slacken the reservoir cover screws **(see illustration)**.

7 Unscrew the master cylinder clamp bolts and remove the back of the clamp, noting how it fits, then lift the master cylinder and reservoir away from the handlebar **(see illustration 5.3)**.

8 Remove the reservoir cover, diaphragm plate and diaphragm. Drain the brake fluid from the master cylinder and reservoir into a suitable container. Wipe any remaining fluid out of the reservoir with a clean rag.

9 If required, undo the screw securing the brake light switch to the bottom of the master cylinder and remove the switch **(see illustration 5.2)**.

Overhaul

10 Carefully remove the rubber boot from the master cylinder **(see illustration)**.

11 Depress the piston and use circlip pliers to remove the circlip **(see illustration)**. Slide out the piston assembly and spring, noting how they fit **(see illustration)**. If they are difficult to remove, apply low pressure compressed air to the brake fluid outlet. Lay the parts out in the proper order to prevent confusion during reassembly.

12 Clean the master cylinder bore with clean brake fluid. If compressed air is available, blow it through the fluid galleries to ensure they are clear (make sure the air is filtered and unlubricated).

Caution: Do not, under any circumstances, use a petroleum-based solvent to clean brake parts.

13 Check the master cylinder bore for corrosion, scratches, nicks and score marks. If the necessary measuring equipment is available, compare the dimensions of the piston and bore to those given in the Specifications at the beginning of this Chapter. If damage or wear is evident, the master cylinder must be replaced with a new one. If the master cylinder is in poor condition, then the caliper should be checked as well.

14 The rubber boot, circlip, piston, seal, cup and spring are all included in the master cylinder rebuild kit. Use all of the new parts, regardless of the apparent condition of the old ones.

15 Smear the cup and seal with new brake fluid. If not already assembled fit them into their grooves in the piston so their flared ends will fit into the master cylinder first, according to the layout of the removed assembly **(see illustrations)**.

16 Fit the spring onto the end of the piston, twisting it slightly clockwise to spread the coils if necessary **(see illustration)**.

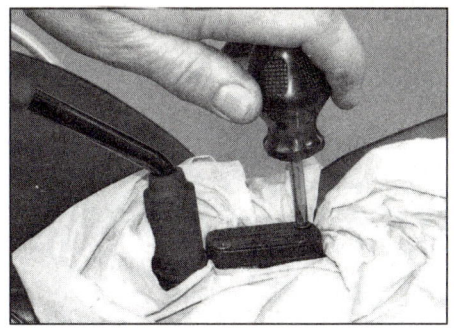

5.6 Slacken the cover screws

5.10 Remove the boot

5.11a Release the circlip . . .

5.11b . . . then draw out the piston assembly and the spring

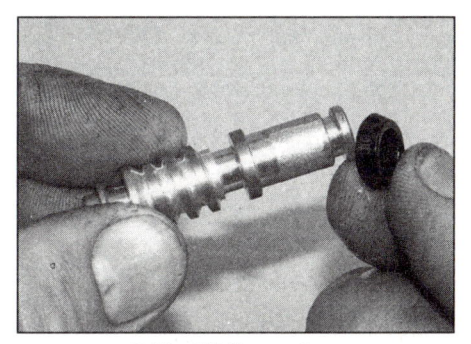

5.15a Fit the seal . . .

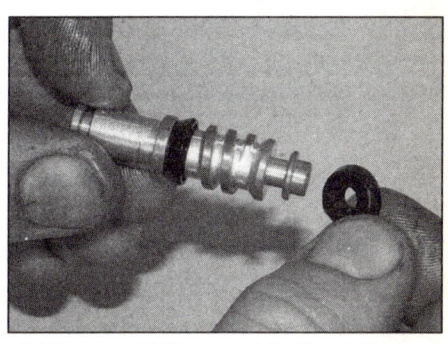

5.15b . . . and the cup onto the piston . . .

5.15c . . . making sure they are as shown

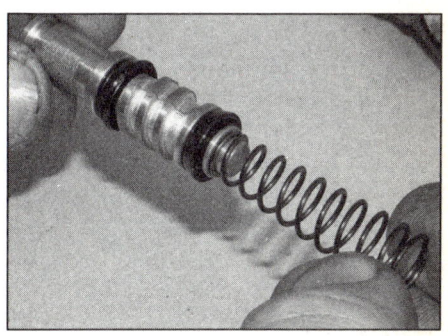

5.16 Fit the spring onto the end of the piston

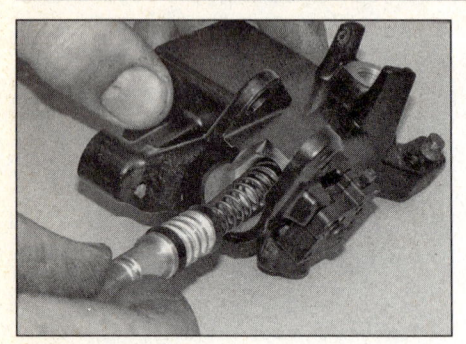

6•8 Brakes, wheels and final drive

5.17a Fit the assembly into the cylinder . . .

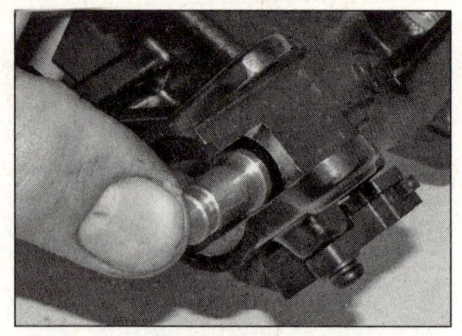

5.17b . . . making sure the lips do not turn inside out

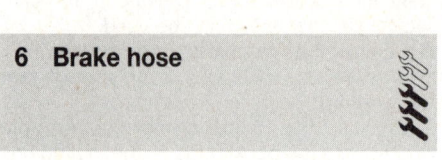

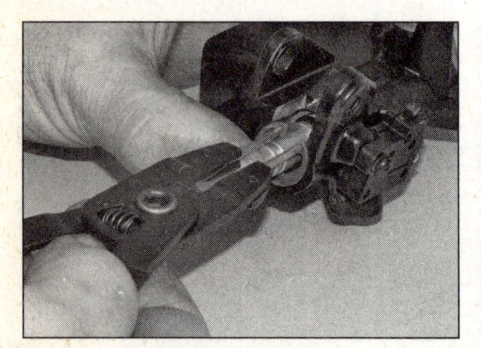

5.17c Fit the circlip . . .

5.17d . . . and push it into its groove

17 Lubricate the piston and the master cylinder bore with new brake fluid and slide the assembly into the master cylinder **(see illustration)**. Make sure the lips on the cup and seal do not turn inside out. Fit the circlip, with its chamfered side facing in, over the end of the piston, then push the piston in to compress the spring and fit the circlip into its groove, making sure it locates correctly **(see illustrations)**.
18 Smear some silicone grease onto the lips and inside of the rubber boot. Fit the rubber boot onto the piston so its outer end lips locate in the groove and press the boot into place in the end of the cylinder **(see illustrations)**.
19 Inspect the reservoir diaphragm and fit a new one if it is damaged or deteriorated.

Installation

20 If removed, fit the brake light switch onto the bottom of the master cylinder, making sure the pin locates in the hole, and tighten the screw.
21 Attach the master cylinder to the handlebar, aligning the clamp joint with the punch mark on the top of the handlebar, then fit the back of the clamp with its UP mark facing up **(see illustration)**. Tighten the upper bolt first, then the lower bolt.
22 Connect the brake light switch wiring **(see illustration 5.2)**.
23 Install the brake lever (see Chapter 5).
24 Connect the brake hose to the master cylinder, aligning it as noted on removal, and using a new sealing washer on each side of the banjo fitting **(see illustration 5.4)**. Tighten the banjo bolt to the torque setting specified at the beginning of this Chapter.
25 Fill the fluid reservoir with new DOT 4 brake fluid (see *Pre-ride checks*). Refer to Section 7 and bleed the air from the system.
26 Install the handlebar covers (see Chapter 7). Check the operation of the brake before riding the scooter.

6 Brake hose

Inspection

1 see Chapter 1, Section 10.

Removal and installation

Caution: Brake fluid attacks painted finishes and plastics – to prevent damage from spilled fluid, always cover paintwork when working on the braking system, and clean up any spills immediately using brake cleaner.
2 Remove the handlebar covers (see Chapter 7).
3 Drain the brake fluid (Section 7).
4 The brake hose has a banjo union on each end. Cover the surrounding area with plenty of rags and be prepared to catch any residual fluid. Unscrew the banjo bolt at each end of the hose, noting the alignment of the union **(see illustrations 3.3a and 5.4)**. Free the hose from any clips or guides and remove it, noting its routing. Discard the sealing washers. **Note:** *Do not operate the brake lever while the brake hose is disconnected.*
5 Position the new hose, making sure it isn't twisted or otherwise strained, and ensure that it is correctly routed through any clips or guides **(see illustration 3.2)** and is clear of all moving components.
6 Check that the fittings align correctly, then install the banjo bolts, using a new sealing washer on each side of each union. Tighten the banjo bolts to the torque setting specified at the beginning of this Chapter.
7 Refill the system with new DOT 4 brake fluid (see Section 7).
8 Check the operation of the brake before riding the scooter.

5.18a Fit the rubber boot . . .

5.18b . . . locating it as shown

5.21 Align the clamp mating surface with the punch mark (arrowed)

Brakes, wheels and final drive 6•9

7 Brake system bleeding and fluid change

Bleeding

1 Bleeding the brake is the process of removing aerated brake fluid from the master cylinder, the hose and the brake caliper. Bleeding is necessary whenever a brake system hydraulic connection is loosened, after a component or hose is replaced with a new one, when the master cylinder or caliper is overhauled, or when there is a spongy feel to the lever and it travels all the way back to the handlebar, and where braking force is less than it should be, and it is not due to any mechanical fault in the system (i.e. a sticking piston in the caliper, or a pad that is not moving as it should due to corrosion, for example on the pad pin). Leaks in the system may also allow air to enter, but leaking brake fluid will reveal their presence and warn you of the need for repair.

2 Brake bleeding is considered by some as a bit of a black art – seasoned professionals sometimes have trouble getting a good firm feel in the brake lever, while a first timer may have no trouble at all. One of the problems is that you are working against natural principles – science dictates that air bubbles in a liquid will rise to the top, but the process entails pumping the brake fluid and any air bubbles it contains down, from the master cylinder at the top to the bleed valve in the caliper at the bottom, so while the fluid is moving down the air bubbles will want to rise. Air bubbles can also get trapped, particularly where there are high points in its path.

3 To bleed the brake using the conventional method, you will need some new DOT 4 brake fluid, a length of clear flexible hose, a small container partially filled with clean brake fluid, some rags, and a spanner to fit the brake caliper bleed valve. Bleeding kits that include the hose, a one-way valve and a container are available relatively cheaply from a good auto store, and simplify the task.

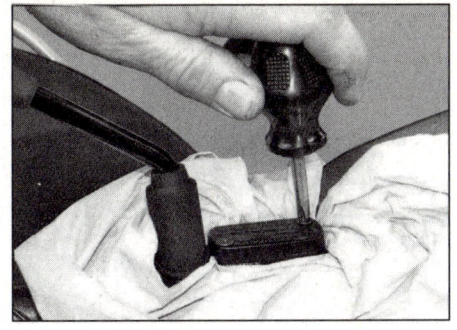

4 Cover painted components to prevent damage in the event that brake fluid is spilled. **Caution: Brake fluid attacks painted finishes and plastics – to prevent damage from spilled fluid, always cover paintwork when working on the braking system, and clean up any spills immediately using brake cleaner.**

5 Remove the reservoir cover, diaphragm plate and diaphragm **(see illustrations)**. Slowly pump the brake lever a few times, until no air bubbles can be seen floating up from the holes in the bottom of the reservoir. This bleeds the air from the master cylinder end of the line. Temporarily refit the reservoir cover.

6 Pull the dust cap off the bleed valve **(see illustrations)**. If using a ring spanner (which is preferable to an open-ended one) fit it onto the valve **(see illustration)**. Attach one end of the hose to the bleed valve and, if not using a kit, submerge the other end in the clean brake fluid in the container **(see illustration)**.

7 Check the fluid level in the reservoir – keep it topped up to the upper level line **(see illustration 7.17)**. Do not allow the level to drop below the bottom of the window during the procedure.

8 Slowly pump the brake lever three or four times, then hold it in and open the bleed valve a quarter turn **(see illustrations)**. When the valve is opened, brake fluid will flow out of the caliper into the clear tubing, and the lever will move toward the handlebar. If there is air in the system there will be air bubbles in the brake fluid coming out of the caliper.

9 Tighten the bleed valve, then release the

7.5a Undo the screws . . .

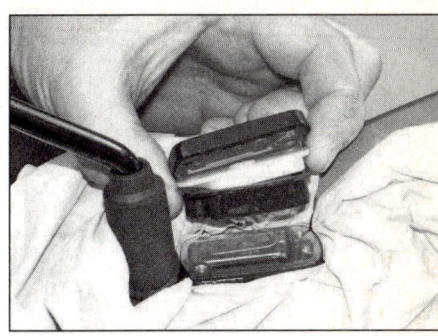

7.5b . . . and remove the cover, diaphragm plate and diaphragm

7.6a Pull the cap off the valve . . .

7.6b . . . then fit a ring spanner . . .

7.6c . . . and the hose

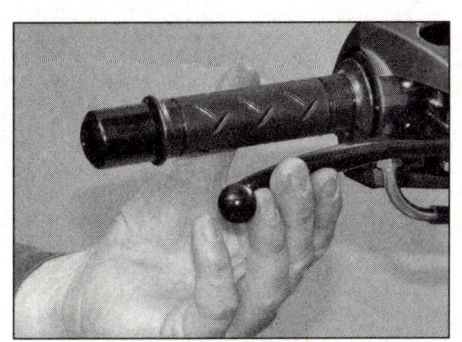

7.8a Hold the brake lever in . . .

7.8b . . . and open the bleed valve ¼ turn

6•10 Brakes, wheels and final drive

7.9 Tighten the valve then release the lever

7.11 Tie the brake lever on

brake lever gradually **(see illustration)**. Repeat the process until no air bubbles are visible in the brake fluid leaving the caliper, and the lever is firm when applied, topping the reservoir up when necessary.

10 If it is not possible to produce a firm feel to the lever, remove the front cover on the right-hand side (see Chapter 7) and look for any high point in the system in which a pocket of air may become trapped. Displace and move the hose so the bubble can be dislodged – tapping it may help. If necessary displace the master cylinder from the handlebar and the caliper from the fork, then free the brake hose from its guides and invert the whole system to dislodge the air and encourage it towards the caliper.

11 If you are still having trouble the fluid may be full of many tiny air bubbles rather than a few big ones. To remedy this apply some pressure to the system by tying the front brake lever lightly back to the handlebar **(see illustration)** – do not apply too much pressure or the cup and seals in the master cylinder and caliper may fail. Let the fluid stabilise for a few hours, after which the tiny bubbles should either have risen to the top in the reservoir, or have formed into one or more big bubbles that can be more easily bled out by repeating the bleeding procedure.

12 If bleeding the system using the conventional tools and methods stated does not give satisfactory results, or if otherwise preferred, you can use a commercially available vacuum-type brake bleeding tool, such as the Mity-vac, following the manufacturer's instructions **(see illustration)**. This type of tool literally sucks the fluid out by creating a vacuum at the bleed valve. Users of such tools often get confused by the amount of air that appears to be in the brake fluid – more often than not this is caused by the vacuum sucking air past the bleed valve threads (air provides less resistance to the vacuum than the brake fluid) where it mixes with the fluid being drawn out. If this is the case the vacuum applied may be too great, or the bleed valve may have been loosened too much. One way to get around this is to remove the bleed valve and thread some PTFE tape around its threads, but note that doing so will be a bit messy, so have some rag to hand.

13 When the system has been successfully bled there should be a good and progressively firm feel as the lever is applied, and the lever should not be able to travel all the way back to the handlebar.

14 On completion remove the equipment used and make sure the bleed valve is tight (to the torque setting specified at the beginning of the Chapter if you have a suitable torque wrench), then fit the dust cap. Top-up the reservoir, then fit the diaphragm, diaphragm plate, and cover **(see illustration 7.5b)**. Check for spilled brake fluid and clean up as required. Check the entire system for fluid leaks.

15 Check the operation of the brake before riding the scooter.

Fluid change

16 Changing the brake fluid is a similar process to bleeding the brakes and requires the same materials plus a suitable tool (such as a syringe, or alternatively lots of absorbent rag or paper) for siphoning the fluid out of the reservoir.

17 Follow Steps 4 and 6, then remove the reservoir cap, diaphragm plate and diaphragm and siphon the old fluid out of the reservoir **(see illustrations 7.5a and b)**. Wipe the reservoir clean. Fill the reservoir with new brake fluid to the upper level line **(see illustration)**. Slowly pump the brake lever three or four times then hold it in and open the bleed valve **(see illustrations 7.8a and b)**. When the valve is opened, brake fluid will flow out of the caliper into the clear tubing, and the lever will move toward the handlebar.

18 Tighten the bleed valve, then release the brake lever gradually **(see illustration 7.9)**. Keep the reservoir topped-up with new fluid at all times or air may enter the system and greatly increase the length of the task. Repeat the process until new fluid can be seen emerging from the caliper bleed valve.

> **HAYNES HINT**: Old brake fluid is invariably much darker in colour than new fluid, making it easy to see when all old fluid has been expelled from the system.

19 On completion remove the equipment used and make sure the bleed valve is tight (to the torque setting specified at the beginning of the Chapter if you have a suitable torque wrench), then fit the dust cap. Top-up the

7.12 This is a vacuum pump used to suck the fluid from the system

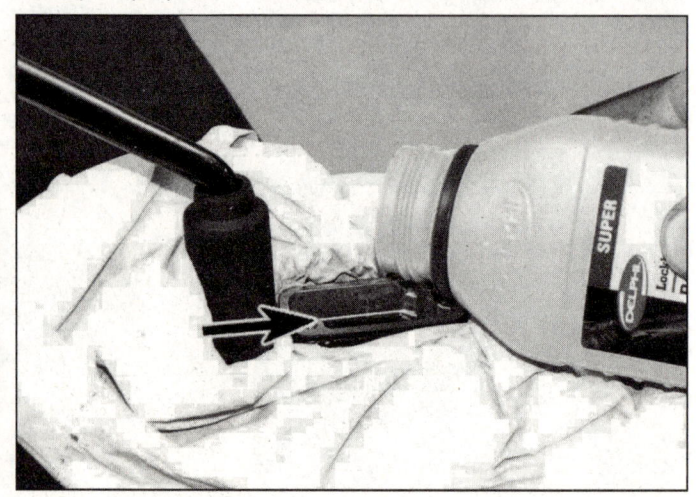

7.17 Fill the reservoir with new fluid (upper level line arrowed)

Brakes, wheels and final drive 6•11

8.3 Check the friction material

8.6a Check the surface of the drum . . .

8.6b . . . and measure the diameter

reservoir, then fit the diaphragm, diaphragm plate, and cover. Check for spilled brake fluid and clean up as required. Check the entire system for fluid leaks.
20 Check the operation of the brake before riding the scooter.

Draining the system for overhaul

21 Draining the brake fluid is again a similar process to bleeding the brakes. The quickest and easiest way is to use a commercially available vacuum-type brake bleeding tool (see Step 12) – follow the manufacturer's instructions. Otherwise follow the procedure described above for changing the fluid, but quite simply do not put any new fluid into the reservoir – the system fills itself with air instead.

8 Rear drum brake

Warning: The dust created by the brake system is harmful to your health. Never blow it out with compressed air and don't inhale any of it. An approved filtering mask should be worn when working on the brakes.

Check

1 Remove the rear wheel (see Section 12).

2 If not already done remove the brake plate from the drum **(see illustration 12.6)**.
3 Inspect the surface of the friction material on each shoe for contamination **(see illustration)**. If either shoe is fouled with oil or grease, or heavily scored or damaged by dirt and debris, both shoes must be replaced with a new set (Steps 11 to 13). Note that it is not possible to degrease the friction material.
4 If the shoes are in good condition clean them carefully, using a fine soft wire brush which is completely free of oil and grease, or some sandpaper, to remove all traces of road dirt and corrosion. Using a pointed instrument, dig out any embedded particles of foreign matter. If the material appears glazed, roughen up the surface using course sandpaper, bearing in mind the **Warning** above.
5 Check the condition of the brake shoe springs and replace them if they appear weak or are obviously deformed or damaged.
6 Clean the brake drum lining using brake cleaner or a rag soaked in solvent. Examine the surface of the lining for cracks, scoring and excessive wear **(see illustration)**. While light scratches are expected, any heavy scoring or cracks will impair braking and there is no satisfactory way of removing them – the wheel should be replaced with a new one. Measure the internal diameter of the drum and replace the wheel with a new one if it has worn below the service limit specified at the beginning of the Chapter **(see illustration)**.
7 Check that the brake cam operates smoothly and to its full limits of travel by operating the lever arm. If the action is stiff or rough (take into account the force of the springs) remove the shoes (Step 11), then unscrew the nut and withdraw the bolt clamping the arm, then lift the arm off the shaft and remove the wear indicator plate **(see illustration)**. Draw the cam out. Remove the felt washer – check its condition and replace it with a new one if necessary. Clean off all traces of old and hardened grease from the cam and the shoe pivot post **(see illustration 8.13)**. If the bearing surfaces of the cam are worn or damaged it should be replaced with a new one. Re-grease the cam, both where it acts on the shoes and turns in the brake plate, and grease the post. Fit the cam into the plate. Apply some gear oil to the felt washer and fit it over the shaft and onto the plate. Fit the indicator plate with the curved end of the pointer towards the plate, aligning the wide splines. Fit the arm, aligning the punch marks **(see illustration)**. Fit the bolt and tighten the nut.
8 Check the brake rod is straight and the spring is in not deformed. Check the brake pedal moves smoothly – refer to Chapter 5 to remove it and lubricate it if necessary.

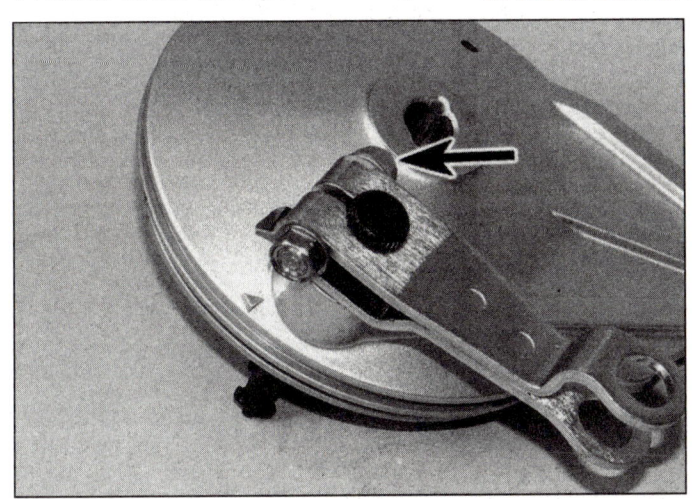

8.7a Unscrew the nut (arrowed), withdraw the bolt and remove the arm and wear indicator plate

8.7b Align the punch marks

6•12 Brakes, wheels and final drive

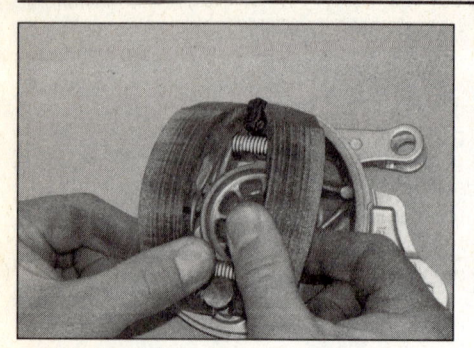

8.11a Fold the shoes up off the plate as shown

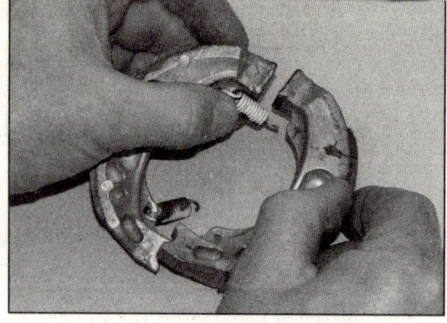

8.11b Unhook the springs

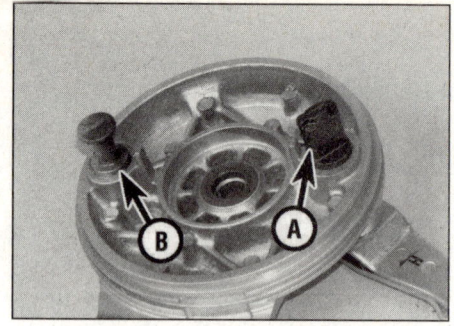

8.13 Grease the cam (A) and the post (B)

Shoe replacement

9 Remove the wheel (see Section 12).
10 If not already done remove the brake plate from the drum **(see illustration 12.7)**.
11 Grasp the outer edge of each shoe and fold them upwards and inwards to form a 'V', noting that they are under the pressure of the springs, then remove them, noting how they locate around the cam and the pivot post **(see illustration)**. Remove the springs from the shoes **(see illustration)**.
12 Check the shoes and the drum as outlined above.
13 Apply some grease to the bearing surfaces on the cam and pivot post **(see illustration)**. Fit the springs onto the shoes **(see illustration 8.11b)** – make sure the shoes are the same way round, with their rounded ends together and their flat ends together. Position the shoes in the V shape and so that the rounded end of each shoe fits around the pivot post and the flat end against the flats on the cam **(see illustration 8.11a)**. Fold the shoes flat, making sure they sit correctly on each side of the pivot and the cam and the springs remain in place. Operate the lever arm to check that the cam and shoes work correctly.
14 Install the wheel (see Section 12). Check the operation of the brake before riding the scooter.

9.2 Check the wheel for radial (out-of-round) runout (A) and axial (side-to-side) runout (B)

9 Wheel inspection and repair

1 To carry out a proper inspection of the wheels, support the scooter on its centrestand so the wheel being inspected is raised off the ground. Clean the wheels thoroughly to remove mud and dirt that may interfere with the inspection procedure or mask defects. Make a general check of the wheels and spokes (see Chapter 1) and also the tyres (see *Pre-ride checks*).
2 Attach a dial gauge to the fork or the swingarm and position its tip against the side of the wheel rim. Spin the wheel slowly and check the axial (side-to-side) runout of the rim **(see illustration)**.
3 In order to accurately check radial (out of round) runout with the dial gauge, remove the wheel from the machine, and the tyre from the wheel. With the axle clamped in a vice and the dial gauge positioned on the top of the rim, the wheel can be rotated to check the runout **(see illustration 9.2)**.
4 An easier, though slightly less accurate, method is to attach a stiff wire pointer to the fork or the swingarm and position the end a fraction of an inch from the wheel rim where the wheel and tyre join. If the wheel is true, the distance from the pointer to the rim will be constant as the wheel is rotated. **Note:** *If wheel runout is excessive, check the wheel bearings very carefully before renewing the wheel.*
5 A wheel building expert can correct excessive wheel runout by adjusting spoke tension, or in severe cases by rebuilding the wheel using a new rim. Check first, that the problem is not being caused by wear in the wheel bearings.

10 Wheel alignment check

1 Misalignment of the wheels due to a bent frame or forks can cause strange and possibly serious handling problems. If the frame or forks are at fault, repair by a specialist or renewal are the only options. Poor wheel alignment can also result from failure to set the drive chain adjusters evenly when adjusting chain slack. Index lines are provided on each face of the swingarm to enable correct wheel alignment to be maintained (see Chapter 1, Section 1).
2 To check wheel alignment you will need an assistant, a length of string or a perfectly straight piece of wood and a ruler. A plumb bob or spirit level for checking that the wheels are vertical will also be required.
3 In order to make a proper check of the wheels it is necessary to support the scooter in an upright position, using an auxiliary stand. First measure the width of both tyres at their widest points. Subtract the smaller measurement from the larger measurement, then divide the difference by two. The result is the amount of offset that should exist between the front and rear tyres on both sides of the machine.
4 If a string is used, have your assistant hold one end of it about halfway between the floor and the rear axle, with the string touching the back edge of the rear tyre sidewall.
5 Run the other end of the string forward and pull it tight so that it is roughly parallel to the floor **(see illustration)**. Slowly bring the string into contact with the front edge of the rear tyre sidewall, then turn the front wheel until it is

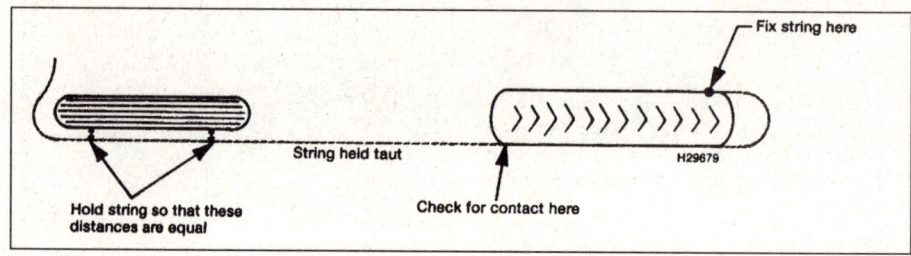

10.5 Wheel alignment check using string

Brakes, wheels and final drive 6•13

parallel with the string. Measure the distance from the front tyre sidewall to the string.
6 Repeat the procedure on the other side of the scooter. The distance from the front tyre sidewall to the string should be equal on both sides.
7 As previously mentioned, a perfectly straight length of wood or metal bar may be substituted for the string **(see illustration)**.
8 If the distance between the string and tyre is greater on one side, or if the rear wheel appears to be out of alignment, have your machine checked by a Honda dealer or frame specialist.
9 If the front-to-back alignment is correct, the wheels still may be out of alignment vertically.
10 Using a plumb bob or spirit level, check the rear wheel to make sure it is vertical. To do this, hold the string of the plumb bob against the tyre upper sidewall and allow the weight to settle just off the floor. If the string touches both the upper and lower tyre sidewalls and is perfectly straight, the wheel is vertical. If it is not, adjust the stand until it is.
11 Once the rear wheel is vertical, check the front wheel in the same manner. If both wheels are not perfectly vertical, the frame and/or major suspension components are bent.

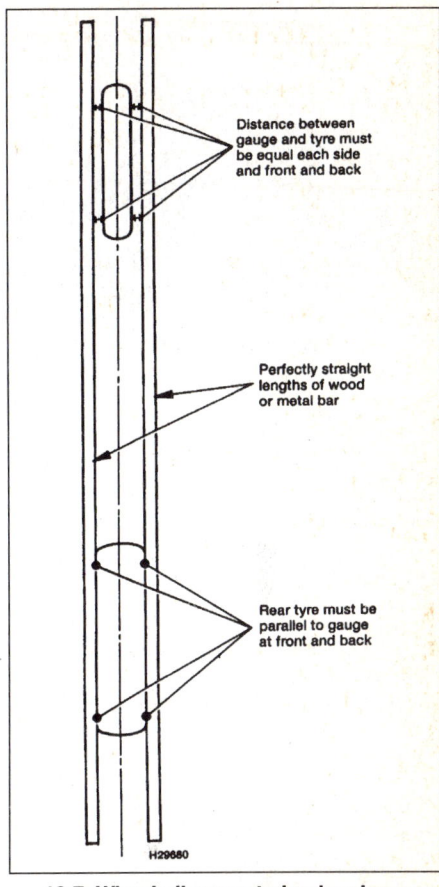

11 Front wheel

Removal

1 Position the bike on its centrestand.
2 If required displace the front brake caliper (Section 3) – it is not necessary to do so, but makes installation of the wheel slightly easier. Support the caliper with a cable tie or a bungee cord so that no strain is placed on the hydraulic hose. There is no need to disconnect the hose from the caliper. **Note**: *Do not operate the front brake lever with the caliper removed.*
3 Where fitted, remove the axle nut cap **(see illustration)**. Slacken the axle nut. Place a support under the engine so the front wheel is off the ground. Make sure the scooter is secure.
4 Unscrew and remove the axle nut **(see illustration)**. Take the weight of the wheel, then withdraw the axle **(see illustration)**. Carefully lower the wheel and draw it forwards.
5 Remove the spacer from each side of the wheel **(see illustration 11.8)**. Clean all old grease off the spacers, axle and bearing seals.
Caution: Don't lay the wheel down and allow it to rest on the disc – it could become warped. Set the wheel on wood blocks so the disc doesn't support the weight of the wheel.
6 Check the axle is straight by rolling it on a flat surface such as a piece of plate glass (first remove any corrosion using steel wool

or a suitable alternative). If the equipment is available, place the axle in V-blocks and check for runout using a dial gauge. If the axle is bent or the runout exceeds the limit specified, replace it with a new one.
7 Check the condition of the grease seals and wheel bearings (see Section 13).

Installation

Note: *If a new tyre has been fitted, make sure the directional arrow on the tyre is pointing in the direction of normal rotation of the wheel.*
8 Apply a smear of grease to the inside of each wheel spacer and to the seal lips. Fit a spacer into each side of the wheel **(see illustration)** – they are the same.
9 Manoeuvre the wheel into position between the forks, making sure the brake disc is on the right-hand side. Apply a thin coat of grease to the axle.
10 Lift the wheel into place, making sure the spacers remain in position, and that if the caliper is in place the disc locates squarely between the pads. Slide the axle through **(see illustration 11.4b)**.
11 Fit the axle nut and tighten it to the torque setting specified at the beginning of the Chapter **(see illustration 11.4a)** – counter-hold the axle head if necessary.
12 Lower the front wheel to the ground. If removed install the brake caliper (Section 3).
13 Apply the front brake a few times to bring the pads back into contact with the disc.
14 Check the operation of the front brake before riding the scooter.

10.7 Wheel alignment check using a straight-edge

11.3 Remove the cap if fitted to access the axle nut (arrowed)

11.4a Unscrew the nut . . .

11.4b . . . then withdraw the axle and remove the wheel

11.8 Fit the wheel spacers into the seals

6•14 Brakes, wheels and final drive

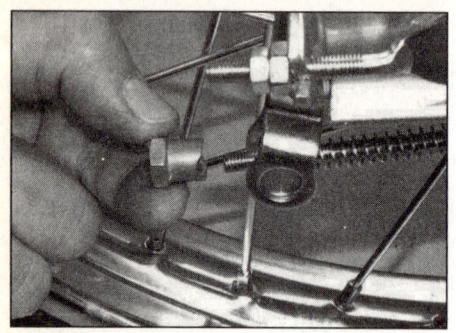

12.2 Thread the nut off the rod

12.3 Remove the split pin (arrowed), unscrew the nut and detach the rod

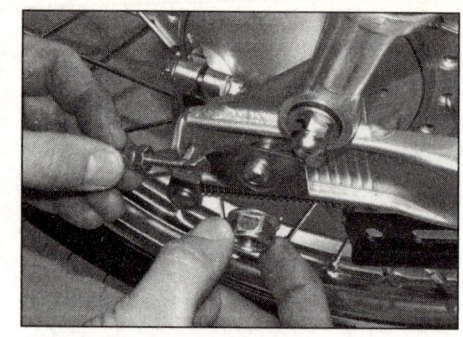

12.4 Unscrew the axle nut and remove the adjuster

12 Rear wheel

Removal

1 Position the scooter on its centrestand so that the rear wheel is off the ground. Remove the drive chain case (Section 16). Create some slack in the chain (see Chapter 1, Section 1).
2 Unscrew the rear brake adjuster nut **(see illustration)**.
3 On 2007-on models remove the split pin from the brake torque arm bolt, then unscrew the nut, remove the washers, and withdraw the bolt **(see illustration)**.
4 Unscrew the axle nut and remove the chain adjuster **(see illustration)**.

5 Take the weight of the wheel, then withdraw the axle with the chain adjuster from the left-hand side and lower the wheel to the ground **(see illustration)**. If the axle is difficult to withdraw, drive it through with a drift, making sure you don't damage the threads. Disengage the chain from the sprocket then draw the wheel back slightly so the brake rod comes out of the arm **(see illustrations)**. Remove the spring from the rod and the trunnion from the arm for safekeeping **(see illustrations)**.
6 Draw the wheel back out of the swingarm and remove the brake plate **(see illustration)**.
7 Remove the spacer from the left-hand side of the wheel **(see illustration 12.11)**. Retrieve the spacer which will have dropped out from between the brake plate in the right-hand side of the wheel and the swingarm **(see illustration 12.15)**.

8 Clean all old grease off the spacers, axle and the seal in the sprocket coupling.
9 Check the axle is straight by rolling it on a flat surface such as a piece of plate glass (if the axle is corroded, first remove any corrosion with steel wool or a suitable alternative). If the equipment is available, place the axle in V-blocks and check the runout using a dial gauge. If the axle is bent replace it with a new one.
10 Check the condition of the wheel bearings (see Section 13).

Installation

Note: *If a new tyre has been fitted, make sure the directional arrow on the tyre is pointing in the direction of normal rotation of the wheel.*

11 Apply a smear of grease to the inside and ends of the wheel spacers, and to the seal lips. Fit the short spacer into the seal in the

12.5a Withdraw the axle and lower the wheel

12.5b Slip the chain off the sprocket

12.5c Move the wheel back so the rod comes out of the arm . . .

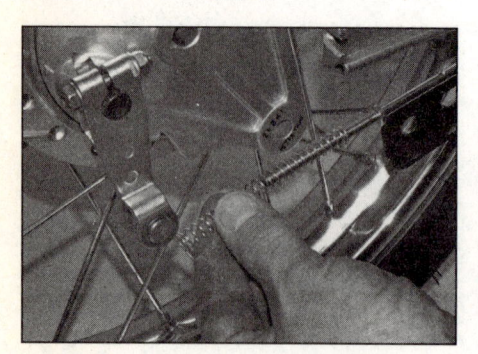

12.5d . . . then remove the spring . . .

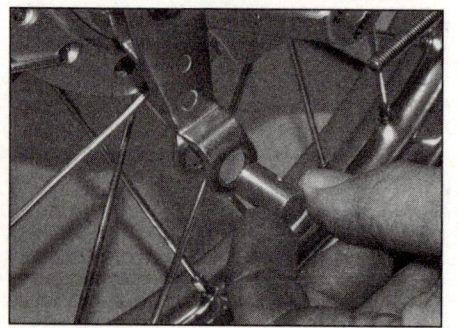

12.5e . . . and the trunnion

12.6 Remove the brake plate from the wheel

Brakes, wheels and final drive 6•15

12.11 Fit the spacer into the seal

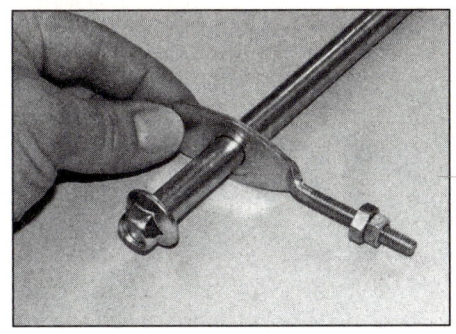

12.14 Make sure the adjuster is the correct way round

12.15 Fit the spacer as you slide the axle through

left-hand side of the wheel **(see illustration)**. Apply a thin coat of grease to the axle.

12 Place the wheel between the ends of the swingarm with the sprocket to the left. Fit the brake plate into the drum **(see illustration 12.6)**.

13 Fit the trunnion into the brake arm and the spring onto the rod, then fit the rod into the trunnion and move the wheel forwards so it stays there **(see illustrations 12.5e, d and c)**.

14 Engage the drive chain with the sprocket **(see illustration 12.5b)**. Slide the left-hand chain adjuster onto the axle as shown **(see illustration)**.

15 Lift the wheel into position, on 2003 to 2006 models locating the brake plate slot over the leg on the swingarm, and slide the axle in from the left, making sure the spacer stays in place **(see illustration 12.5a)**. As you slide the axle through the brake plate fit the long spacer between it and the swingarm, and locate the left-hand chain adjuster in its cut-out in the end of the swingarm **(see illustration)**. Check that everything is correctly aligned, then fit the right-hand chain adjuster, again seating it in the cut-out **(see illustration 12.4)**. Fit the axle nut but leave it loose.

16 On 2007-on models align the torque arm with the brake plate then fit the bolt through from the inside **(see illustration)**. Fit the rubber washer, the plain washer and the nut, and tighten the nut. Fit a new split pin through the hole in the end of the bolt and bend its ends around the bolt **(see illustration)**.

17 Check and adjust the drive chain slack (see Chapter 1). On completion tighten the axle nut to the torque setting specified at the beginning of the Chapter.

18 Thread the adjuster nut onto the brake rod **(see illustration 12.2)**. Check and adjust brake pedal freeplay (see Chapter 1). Check the operation of the rear brake carefully before riding the scooter.

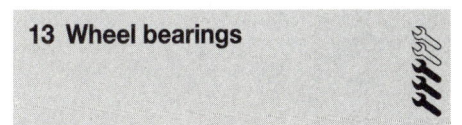

13 Wheel bearings

Caution: *Don't lay the wheel down and allow it to rest on the disc or the sprocket – they could become warped. Set the wheel on wood blocks so the wheel rim supports*

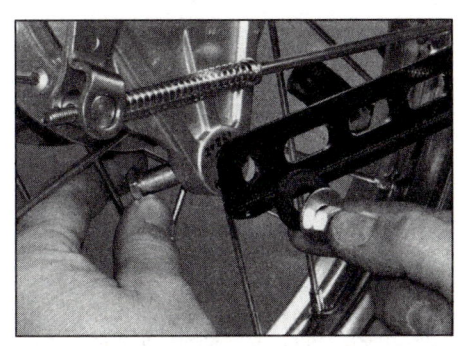

12.16a Fit the bolt from the inside, then fit the rubber washer, plain washer and nut onto the bolt

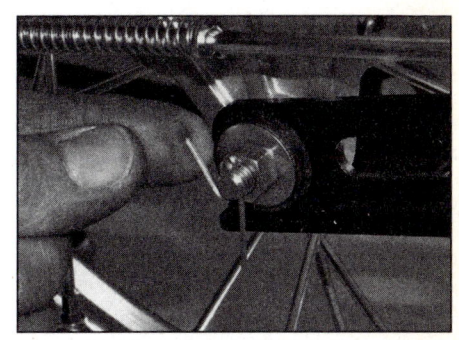

12.16b Fit a new split pin and bend its ends around

the weight of the wheel, or keep the wheel upright. Don't operate the brake lever with the wheel removed.

Note: *Always renew the wheel bearings in sets, never individually. Avoid using a high pressure cleaner on the wheel bearing area.*

Front wheel bearings

1 Remove the wheel (see Section 11). If required remove the disc (see Section 4) to prevent it being damaged or distorted during bearing removal. Support the wheel on wood blocks so that the wheel rim supports the weight of the wheel.

2 Inspect the seals and bearings – check that the bearing inner race turns smoothly and that the outer race is a tight fit in the hub (see *Tools and Workshop Tips* (Section 5) in the Reference Section). **Note:** *Do not remove the*

13.3 Lever out the bearing seals

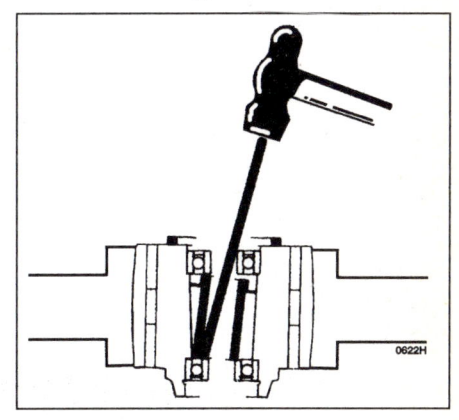

bearings unless they are going to be replaced with new ones.

3 If new components are needed lever out the bearing seal from each side of the hub using a flat-bladed screwdriver or a seal hook **(see illustration)**. Take care not to damage the hub. Discard the seals as new ones must be fitted on reassembly.

4 If the bearings are worn, remove the first one using a metal rod (preferably a brass punch) inserted through the centre of the opposite bearing and locating it on the inner race, pushing the bearing spacer aside to expose it **(see illustration)**. Curve the end of the drift to obtain better purchase if necessary. Strike the drift with a hammer, working evenly around the bearing, to drive it from the hub

13.4a Locate the drift as shown . . .

6•16 Brakes, wheels and final drive

13.4b ... and drive the bearing out

13.5a Locate the puller behind the bearing inner race ...

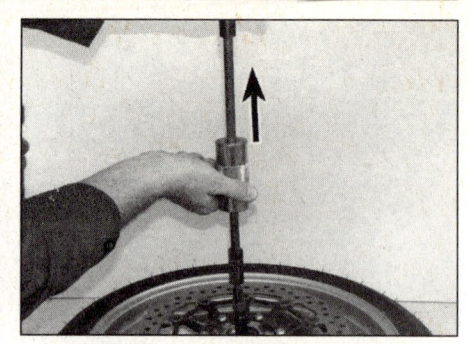

13.5b ... and jar it out using the slide-hammer attachment

(see illustration). The spacer which fits between the bearings will drop free. Turn the wheel over then remove the second bearing using a socket the same size as the inner race fitted onto an extension bar.

5 If the first bearing is difficult to remove using a drift, remove it using an internal expanding puller with slide-hammer attachment – select the correct attachment and locate it behind the inner race of the bearing, then tighten the inner bolt to expand and lock the puller **(see illustration)**. Attach the slide-hammer, hold the wheel firmly down and jar the bearing out **(see illustration)**. Having removed the first bearing remove the spacer that fits between the bearings, then remove the second bearing in the same way, or using a socket and extension as in Step 4.

6 Thoroughly clean the hub area of the wheel with a suitable solvent and inspect the bearing seats for scoring and wear. If the seats are damaged, consult a Honda dealer before reassembling the wheel.

7 Drive the new right-hand bearing squarely into the hub with its marked and sealed side facing out using a driver or suitable socket on the outer race of the bearing (DO NOT drive it via the inner race or the bearing will be ruined) until the bearing seats **(see illustration)**.

8 Turn the wheel over and install the bearing spacer, then drive the other new bearing in using the same method.

9 Fit a new seal into each side of the hub. Press the seals in using your fingers or a suitable driver **(see illustration)**. Level the seals with the rim of the hub using a small block of wood. Apply a smear of grease to the seal lips.

10 Clean the brake disc using acetone or brake system cleaner, then install the wheel (see Section 11).

Rear wheel bearings

11 Remove the wheel (see Section 12). Lift the sprocket coupling out of the hub and remove the spacer and the rubber dampers **(see illustrations)**. Support the wheel on wood blocks so that the wheel rim supports the weight of the wheel.

12 Inspect the bearings in both sides of the hub – check that the bearing inner race turns smoothly and that the outer race is a tight fit in the hub (see *Tools and Workshop Tips* (Section 5) in the Reference section). **Note:** *Do not remove the bearings unless they are going to be replaced with new ones.*

13 Remove and install the bearings using the methods described in Steps 4 to 8 above as required.

14 Check the sprocket coupling/rubber dampers (see Section 17). Check the condition of the hub O-ring and clean it or replace it with a new one if necessary **(see illustration)**. Smear the O-ring

13.7 Using a socket to drive the bearing in

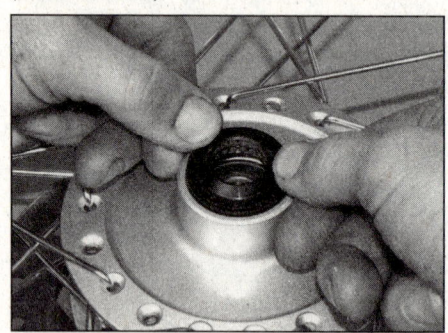

13.9 Press a new seal into each side

13.11a Lift the sprocket coupling off the wheel ...

13.11b ... and remove the spacer ...

13.11c ... and the damper segments

13.14 Fit a new O-ring (arrowed) if necessary

Brakes, wheels and final drive 6•17

13.17 Lever out the bearing seal

13.18 Using a socket to drive the bearing out

13.20 Using a socket to drive the bearing in

13.21 Press the seal into place

with oil. Fit the dampers into the wheel and the spacer into the coupling **(see illustrations 13.11c and b)**. Fit the coupling onto the hub **(see illustration 13.11a)**. Install the wheel (see Section 12).

Sprocket coupling bearing

15 Remove the wheel (see Section 12). Lift the sprocket coupling out of the hub, and remove the spacer **(see illustrations 13.11a and b)**.
16 Inspect the seal and bearing – check that the bearing inner races turn smoothly and that the outer race is a tight fit in the coupling (see *Tools and Workshop Tips (Section 5)* in the Reference Section). **Note:** *Do not remove the bearing unless it is being replaced with a new one.*
17 If new components are needed lever out the bearing seal using a flat-bladed screwdriver or a seal hook **(see illustration)**. Take care not to damage the rim of the coupling. Discard the seal – a new one must be fitted.
18 Support the coupling on blocks of wood, sprocket side down, and drive the bearing

out from the inside using a bearing driver or socket **(see illustration)**.
19 Thoroughly clean the coupling with a suitable solvent and inspect the bearing housing for scoring and wear.
20 Drive the bearing squarely into the hub with its marked and sealed side facing out using a driver or suitable socket on the outer race of the bearing (DO NOT drive it via the inner race or the bearing will be ruined) until the bearing seats (see *Tools and Workshop Tips*) **(see illustration)**.
21 Press the new seal into the coupling **(see illustration)**. Level the seal with the rim of the coupling using a small block of wood. Smear the seal lip with grease.
22 Check the sprocket coupling/rubber dampers (see Section 17). Check the condition of the hub O-ring and clean it or replace it with a new one if necessary **(see illustration 13.14)**. Smear the O-ring with oil. Fit the spacer in the sprocket coupling, then fit the coupling onto the hub **(see illustrations 13.11b and a)**. Install the wheel (see Section 12).

14 Tyres

General information

1 The spoked wheels are designed to take tubed tyres only. Tyre sizes are given in the Specifications at the beginning of this Chapter. Make sure the correct size tube is also fitted, and use a new rim tape when fitting a new tube and/or tyre.
2 Refer to the *Pre-ride checks* listed at the beginning of this manual for tyre maintenance.

Fitting new tyres

3 When selecting new tyres, refer to the tyre information in the Owner's Handbook and on the tyre fitment label stuck to the chaincase or chainguard. Ensure that front and rear tyre types are compatible, the correct size and correct speed rating; if necessary seek advice

6•18 Brakes, wheels and final drive

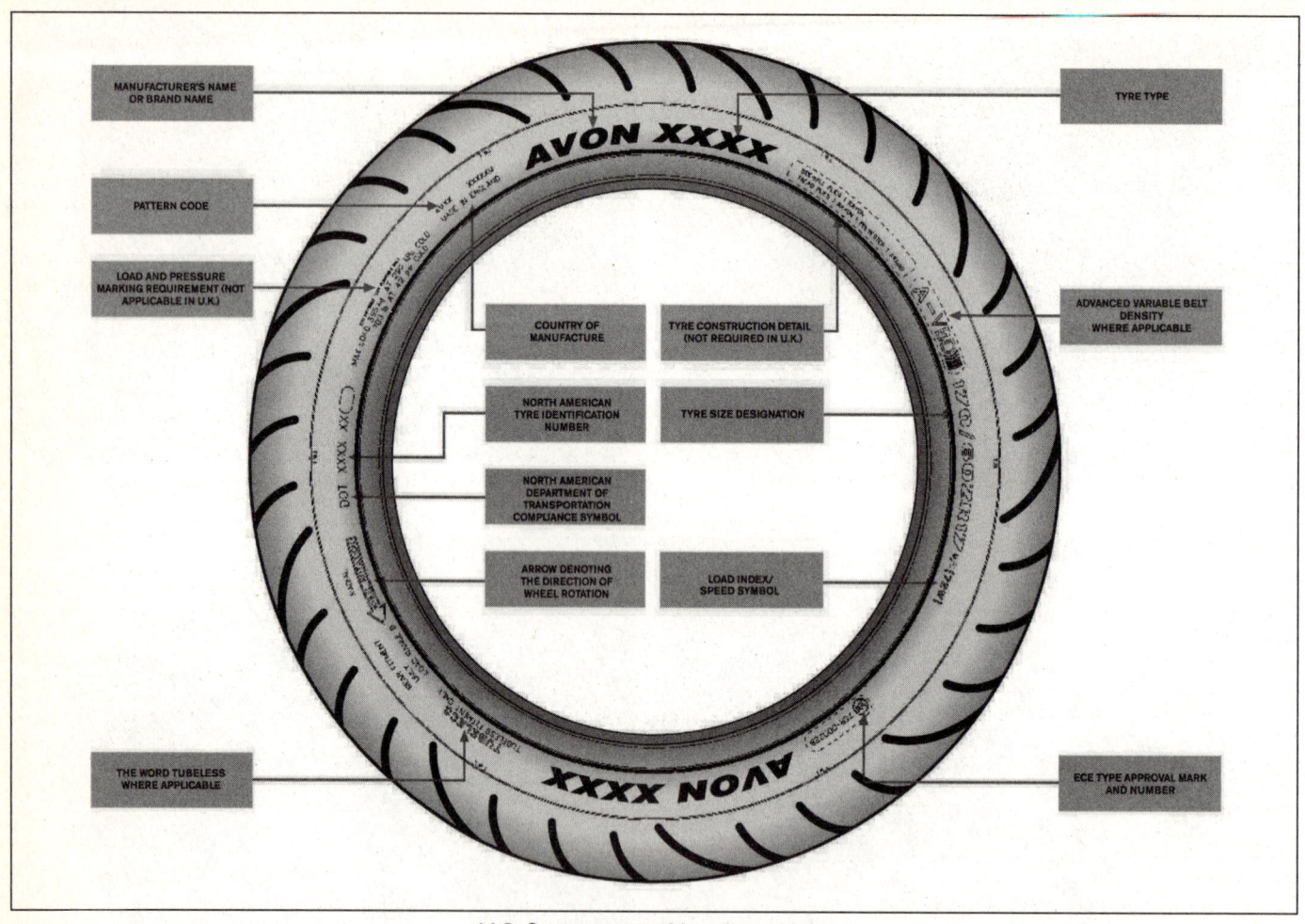

14.3 Common tyre sidewall markings

Labels around the tyre:
- MANUFACTURER'S NAME OR BRAND NAME
- PATTERN CODE
- LOAD AND PRESSURE MARKING REQUIREMENT (NOT APPLICABLE IN U.K.)
- COUNTRY OF MANUFACTURE
- NORTH AMERICAN TYRE IDENTIFICATION NUMBER
- NORTH AMERICAN DEPARTMENT OF TRANSPORTATION COMPLIANCE SYMBOL
- ARROW DENOTING THE DIRECTION OF WHEEL ROTATION
- THE WORD TUBELESS WHERE APPLICABLE
- TYRE TYPE
- TYRE CONSTRUCTION DETAIL (NOT REQUIRED IN U.K.)
- TYRE SIZE DESIGNATION
- LOAD INDEX/ SPEED SYMBOL
- ADVANCED VARIABLE BELT DENSITY WHERE APPLICABLE
- ECE TYPE APPROVAL MARK AND NUMBER

---

from a Honda dealer or tyre fitting specialist **(see illustration)**.

4 It is recommended that tyres are fitted by a tyre specialist rather than attempted in the home workshop. The specialist will be able to balance the wheels after tyre fitting.

5 Note that punctured inner tubes can in some cases be repaired, but only as a temporary measure. If you do repair a tube ride cautiously and at a reduced speed, and replace the tube with a new one as soon as possible.

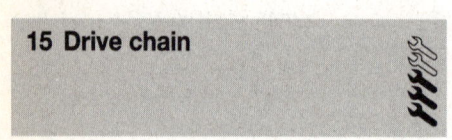

15 Drive chain

Cleaning

1 Refer to Chapter 1, Section 1, for details of routine cleaning with the chain installed on the sprockets.

2 If the chain is extremely dirty remove it from the scooter and soak it in paraffin (kerosene) for approximately five or six minutes, then clean it using a soft brush.

Removal

3 Remove the drive chain case and the front sprocket cover (see Section 16).

4 Support the scooter on its centrestand. Tie the front brake on using a cable-tie or suitable alternative **(see illustration 7.11)**. Locate the joining link near the top of the rear sprocket by rotating the back wheel.

5 Release and remove the clip from the joining link **(see illustration)**. Remove the sideplate, using a small screwdriver to lever it off if necessary **(see illustration)**. Withdraw the joining link from the inside **(see illustration 15.6c)**. Remove the chain from the bike, noting its routing around the swingarm (see

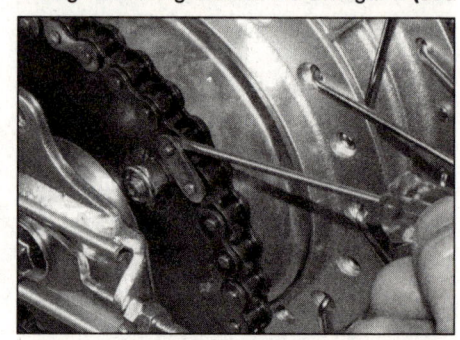

15.5a Remove the joining link clip . . .

15.5b . . . then remove the sideplate and the link

Brakes, wheels and final drive 6•19

15.6a Route the chain around the front sprocket . . .

15.6b . . . and onto the rear sprocket, locating the ends as shown . . .

illustration 15.6a). If the clip distorts when removing it fit a new joining link set.

Installation

6 Route the new chain around the sprockets and swingarm, leaving the ends near the top of the rear sprocket, then fit the joining link through each end of the chain **(see illustrations)**.

7 Fit the sideplate, then slide the clip across the groove in each joining link pin, making sure the closed end points in the direction of normal chain rotation **(see illustrations)**. Make sure the clip has located in the grooves and around the ends of each pin.

8 Install the front sprocket cover and the drive chain case (see Section 16).

9 On completion, adjust and lubricate the chain following the procedures described in Chapter 1, Section 1.

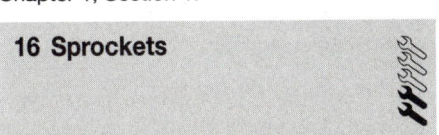

16 Sprockets

Drive chain case

1 Unscrew the four bolts and remove the bottom half of the case first, then the top half, noting how they fit together **(see illustrations)**.

15.6c . . . then fit the joining link from the inside

15.7a Fit the sideplate . . .

15.7b . . . and the clip . . .

15.7c . . . using pliers to seat it in the grooves around the pins

16.1a Drive chain case bolts (arrowed)

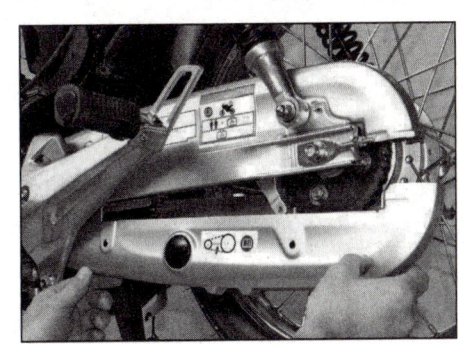

16.1b Remove the bottom half first . . .

16.1c . . . then the top half

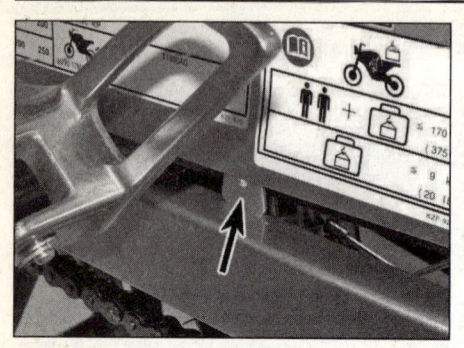

6•20 Brakes, wheels and final drive

16.2a Make sure the top seats over the tab (arrowed) . . .

16.2b . . . and the halves join correctly on the inside

2 Fit the top half of the case first, making sure it locates correctly over the tab **(see illustration)**. Fit the bottom half, making sure it engages correctly with the top half on its inner side **(see illustration)**.

Front sprocket cover

3 Unscrew the two bolts and remove the cover **(see illustrations)**.

Sprocket check

4 Check the wear pattern on both sprockets (see Chapter 1, Section 1). If the sprocket teeth are worn excessively, replace the chain and both sprockets as a set – worn sprockets can ruin a new drive chain and *vice versa*. Whenever the sprockets are inspected, the drive chain should be inspected also (see Chapter 1).

5 Adjust and lubricate the chain following the procedures described in Chapter 1.

Sprocket removal and installation

Front sprocket

6 Remove the front sprocket cover (see Step 3). Tie the front brake on using a cable-tie or suitable alternative **(see illustration 7.11)**.
7 Hold the rear wheel or put the rear brake on and unscrew the sprocket retainer plate bolts **(see illustration)**.
8 If a new drive chain is being fitted, remove the old one now. If not, fully slacken the drive chain as described in Chapter 1. If a new rear sprocket is being fitted, remove the rear wheel now (see Section 12).
9 Turn the sprocket retainer plate to unlock it from the splines then slide it off the shaft **(see illustration)**. Slide the sprocket off the shaft **(see illustration)**.
10 Engage the new sprocket with the chain if not removed, making sure the marked side is facing out, and slide it on the shaft (see

16.3a Unscrew the bolts (arrowed) . . .

16.3b . . . and remove the cover

16.7 Unscrew the bolts (arrowed)

16.9a Remove the retainer plate as described

Brakes, wheels and final drive 6•21

16.9b Draw the sprocket off the shaft and disengage the chain

16.10 Turn the plate in the groove to align the bolt holes

illustration 16.9b). Fit the retainer plate, then turn it in the groove so it is locked in the splines and the bolt holes align **(see illustration)**. Fit the retainer plate bolts and tighten them finger-tight only at this stage.

11 If the rear wheel was removed, change the sprocket now and install the wheel (see Section 12). If the chain was removed, fit it. Take up the slack in the chain.

12 Tighten the retainer plate bolts to the torque setting specified at the beginning of the Chapter.

13 Fit the sprocket cover and drive chain case. Adjust and lubricate the chain following the procedures described in Chapter 1.

Rear sprocket

14 Remove the rear wheel (see Section 12).
15 Unscrew the nuts securing the sprocket to the hub assembly **(see illustration)**. Remove the sprocket, noting which way round it fits.
16 Check the condition of the sprocket studs and make sure they are tight. Replace them all with new ones if any are damaged. The studs can be removed and installed by threading two nuts on and tightening them together – use the bottom nut to unscrew the stud and the top one to tighten it. Clean the stud threads and apply some fresh thread locking compound before fitting them, then tighten them to the torque setting specified at the beginning of the Chapter.

17 Clean the exposed threads on each stud. Fit the sprocket onto the hub with the stamped mark facing out. On 2003 to 2006 models apply some thread locking compound to the nuts. Fit the nuts and tighten them evenly and in a criss-cross sequence to the torque setting specified for your model at the beginning of the Chapter.

18 Install the rear wheel (see Section 12).

17 Rear sprocket coupling/ rubber dampers

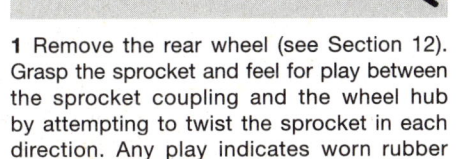

1 Remove the rear wheel (see Section 12). Grasp the sprocket and feel for play between the sprocket coupling and the wheel hub by attempting to twist the sprocket in each direction. Any play indicates worn rubber damper segments.
2 Lift the sprocket coupling off the wheel leaving the rubber dampers in position **(see illustration 13.11a)**. Note the spacer inside the coupling and remove it if it is likely to drop out **(see illustration 13.11b)**. Check the coupling for cracks or any obvious signs of damage.
3 Lift the rubber damper segments from the wheel and check them for cracks, hardening and general deterioration **(see illustration 13.11c)**. Renew them as a set if necessary.

16.15 Rear sprocket nuts (arrowed)

4 Check the condition of the hub O-ring – if it is damaged, deformed or deteriorated replace it with a new one and smear it with oil **(see illustration 13.14)**. Otherwise clean it and smear it with oil.
5 Checking and replacement procedures for the sprocket coupling bearing are in Section 13.
6 Installation is the reverse of removal. Make sure the spacer is still correctly installed in the coupling, or install it if it was removed **(see illustration 13.11b)**.
7 Install the rear wheel (see Section 12).

Notes

Chapter 7
Bodywork

Contents

	Section number		Section number
General information	1	2007-on (fuel injection) models	3
2003 to 2006 (carburettor) models	2		

Degrees of difficulty

| Easy, suitable for novice with little experience | Fairly easy, suitable for beginner with some experience | Fairly difficult, suitable for competent DIY mechanic | Difficult, suitable for experienced DIY mechanic | Very difficult, suitable for expert DIY or professional |

1 General information

Almost all functional components are enclosed by body panels, making removal of the relevant panels a necessary part of many servicing and maintenance procedures.

Before attempting to remove any body panel, study it closely, noting any fasteners and associated fittings. Most panels are retained by screws and inter-locking tabs, and in some places trim clips are used.

To release the trim clips, push the centre of the clip into the body, then draw the body out of the panel. Reset the clip by pulling the centre out of the body. To install the clip, push the body into the hole in the panel, then push the centre into the body.

Once the evident fasteners have been removed, try to remove the panel as described but DO NOT FORCE IT – if it will not release, check that all fasteners have been removed and try again. Where a panel engages another by means of tabs, be careful not to break the tab or its mating slot. Remember that a few moments of patience at this stage will save you a lot of money in replacing broken body panels!

When installing a body panel, check the fasteners and associated fittings removed with it, to be sure of returning everything to its correct place. Ensure all the fasteners are in good condition, including all trim clips and grommets – any that are damaged or deformed should be replaced with new ones before the panel is reassembled. Check also that all mounting brackets are straight and repair or replace them if necessary before attempting to install the panel. Where assistance was required to remove a panel, make sure your assistant is on hand to install it.

Tighten the fasteners securely, but be careful not to overtighten any of them or the panel may break (not always immediately) due to the uneven stress.

HAYNES HiNT *Note that a small amount of lubricant or grease applied to rubber mounting grommets will ease installation and make removal the next time that much easier.*

In the case of damage to the body parts, it is usually necessary to remove the broken component and replace it with a new (or used) one. There are however some shops that specialise in 'plastic welding', so it may be worthwhile seeking the advice of one of these specialists before consigning an expensive component to the bin. Additionally, repair kits can be obtained for repair of small components.

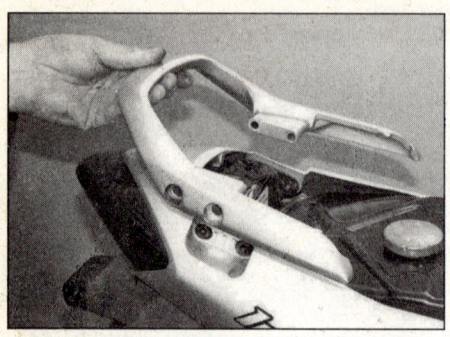

7•2 Bodywork

2.4 Unscrew the bolts and remove the grab-rail

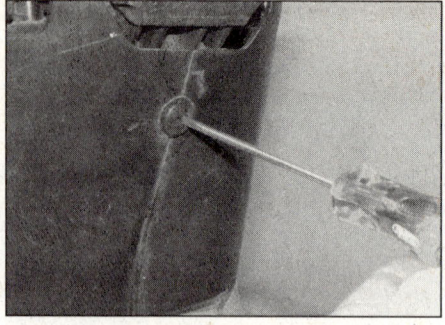

2.9a Press the centre of the trim clip in ...

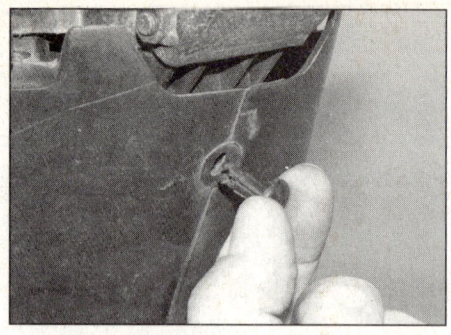

2.9b ... then draw the whole clip out

2 2003 to 2006 (carburettor) models

Seat

1 Unlock the seat and swing it up **(see illustration 3.1)**.
2 Undo the nuts securing the seat to the hinge and remove the seat **(see illustration 3.2)**.
3 Installation is the reverse of removal.

Grab-rail

4 Unscrew the two bolts on each side and remove the rail **(see illustration)**.
5 Installation is the reverse of removal.

Body cover

6 Remove the seat.
7 Remove the grab-rail.
8 Remove the front cover (see below).
9 Release the trim clip at the front **(see illustrations)**.
10 Unscrew the bolt on each side **(see illustration)**.
11 Undo the two screws on each underside **(see illustration)**.
12 Release the joint at the front and release the tab on each side from the rear mudguard, then lift the body cover off.
13 If required undo the tail cover screws and separate the body cover into its component panels.
14 Installation is the reverse of removal. Reset the trim clip by pulling the centre out **(see illustration)**. Fit the clip into the hole then push the centre in to lock it **(see illustration)**.

Storage compartment

15 Remove the seat.
16 Remove the body cover.
17 Remove the battery (see Chapter 8).
18 Disconnect the yellow/red wire bullet connector, the red wire bullet connector, and the three-pin black wiring connector **(see illustration)**.
19 If available fit a hose clamp onto the fuel supply hose close to the fuel valve **(see illustration)**. If not, pinch the hose as you detach it and secure it upright after detaching it so its end is above the fuel tank – if you don't do this the tank will drain itself. Release the hose from the guide. Have some rag to hand, then release the clamp and detach the hose from the valve.
20 Unscrew the two bolts inside the compartment and the two at the back, noting

2.10 Unscrew the bolt (arrowed) on each side ...

2.11 ... and the screws (arrowed) on each underside

2.14a Reset the clip as shown ...

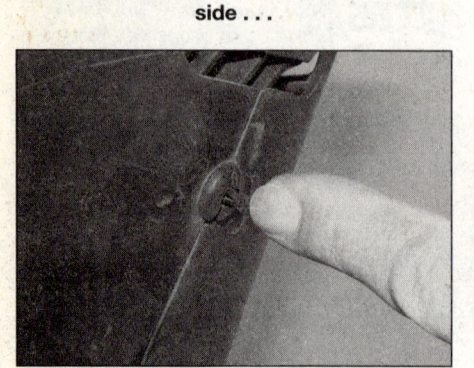

2.14b ... then fit it in the hole and push the centre in

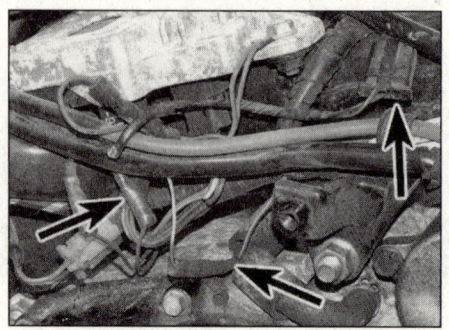

2.18 Disconnect the relevant wiring connectors (arrowed – actual positions will vary)

2.19 Clamp the hose (A) and release it from the guide (B)

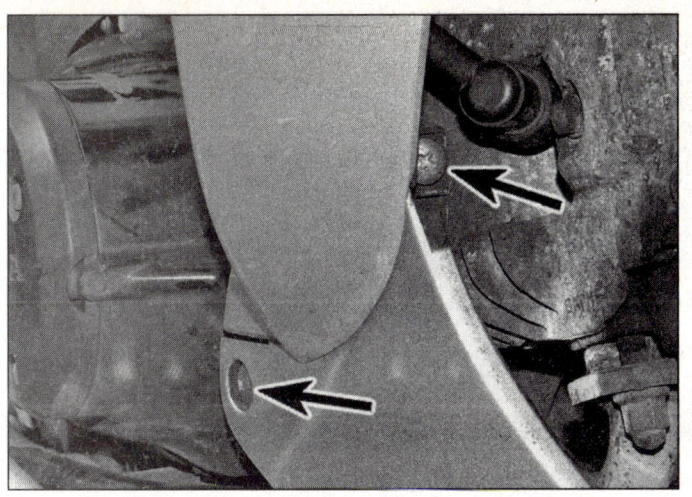

Bodywork 7•3

2.23a Undo the screws (arrowed) on each side . . .

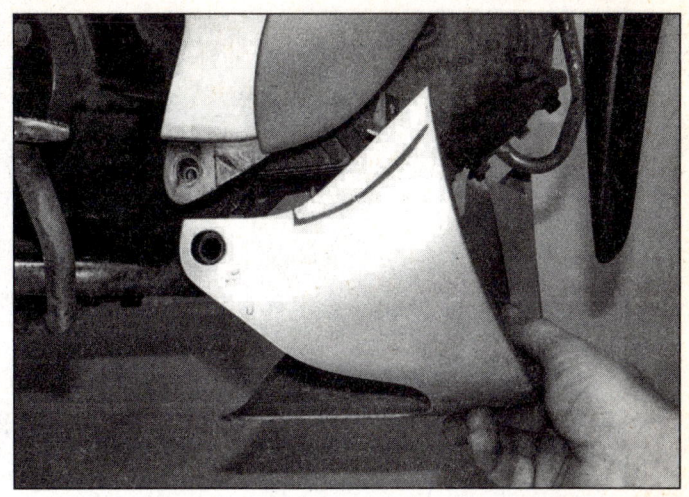

2.23b . . . and remove the bottom cover

the collars in the rubbers **(see illustrations 3.24a and b)**.
21 Lift the storage compartment out, noting the routing of the wiring.
22 Installation is the reverse of removal. Make sure the rubbers are in good condition.

Bottom cover

23 Undo the two screws on each side, noting the collars, and remove the cover **(see illustrations)**.
24 Installation is the reverse of removal.

Centre covers

25 Undo the screw securing the rear centre cover, then draw it back to release its tabs from the front centre cover **(see illustration)**.
26 Undo the three screws securing the front centre cover, then slide it back to release the hooked tabs on each side from the slots **(see illustrations)**.
27 Installation is the reverse of removal.

Top cover

28 Undo the two screws on the rear **(see illustration 3.29a)**.

29 Undo the three screws on the front, noting the washers, and remove the cover, noting the rubber cushions **(see illustrations)**.
30 Installation is the reverse of removal.

Front covers

31 Remove the right-hand front cover first as it overlaps the left-hand one – to remove the left-hand cover you must first remove the right-hand cover.
32 Remove the top cover.
33 Remove the bottom cover.
34 Remove the centre covers.

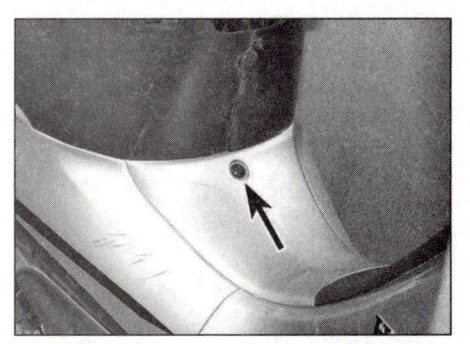

2.25a Undo the screw (arrowed) . . .

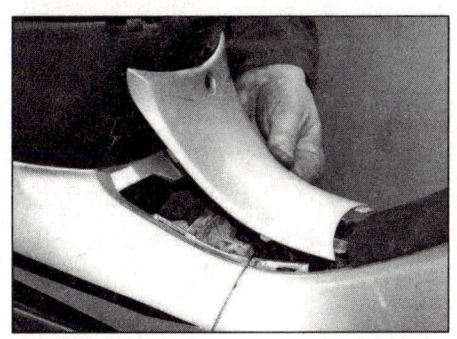

2.25b . . . and remove the rear centre cover

2.26a Undo the screws (arrowed) . . .

2.26b . . . and remove the front centre cover

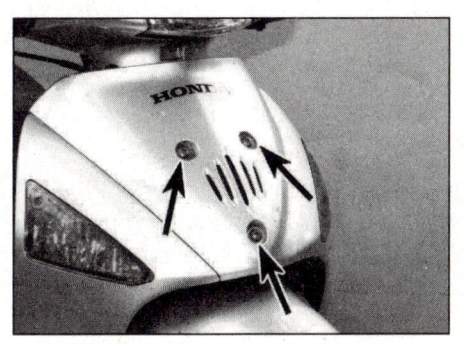

2.29a Undo the screws (arrowed) . . .

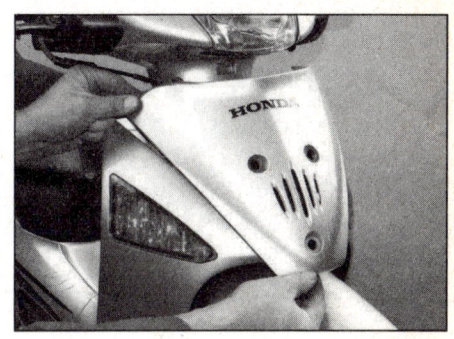

2.29b . . . and remove the top cover

7•4 Bodywork

2.36a Undo the screw and the bolt (arrowed)

2.36b Release the right-hand front cover from the left . . .

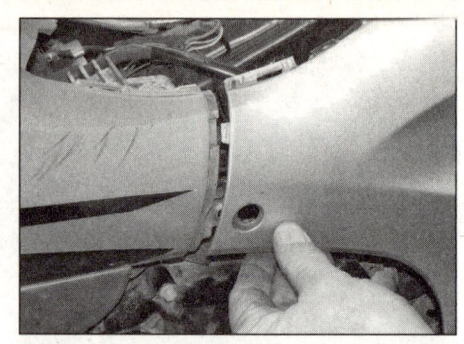

2.36c . . . and free the tabs from the body cover

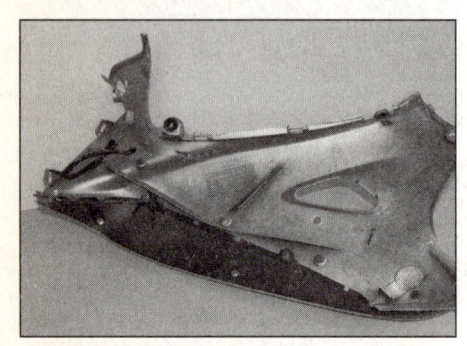

2.37 There are three separate parts to each front cover, joined by screws on the inner side

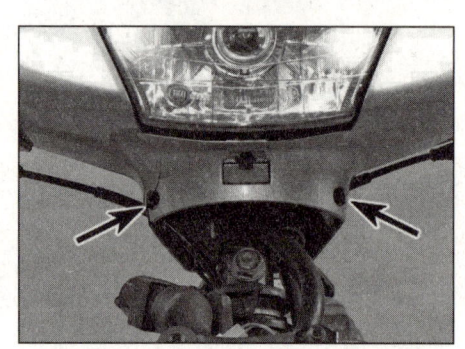

2.45a Undo the screws (arrowed) at the front . .

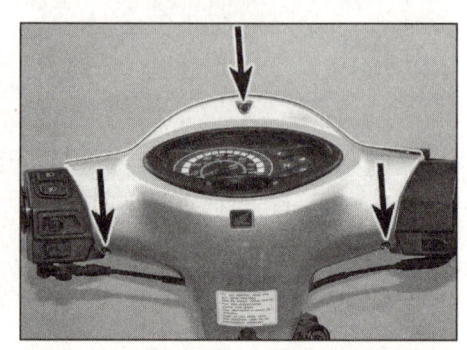

2.45b . . . and the screws (arrowed) on the back

35 Disconnect the turn signal wiring connector.
36 Undo the screw and the bolt, then release and remove the cover **(see illustrations)**.
37 If required undo the screws and separate the cover into its component panels **(see illustration)**. If required remove the turn signal (see Chapter 8).
38 Installation is the reverse of removal.

Mirrors

39 Lift the rubber boot.
40 To remove the mirror unscrew it using the bottom hex **(see illustration 3.45)**.

41 Installation is the reverse of removal.
42 To adjust the position of the mirror hold the bottom hex using one spanner and slacken the locknut using another, turning it clockwise as it has a left-hand thread **(see illustration 3.47)**. Reposition the mirror as required, then hold the bottom hex and tighten the locknut anti-clockwise.

Front handlebar cover

43 Remove the mirrors.
44 Remove the top cover.
45 Undo the two screws in the bottom of the

front cover and the three in the rear cover, then release the front cover from the rear cover at each end, draw the cover forwards and disconnect the headlight wiring connector **(see illustrations)**.
46 Installation is the reverse of removal. Make sure the wiring connector is securely connected, and check the operation of the headlight before riding the scooter.

Rear handlebar cover

47 Remove the front handlebar cover.
48 Release the turn signal relay from its mount and disconnect the instrument cluster

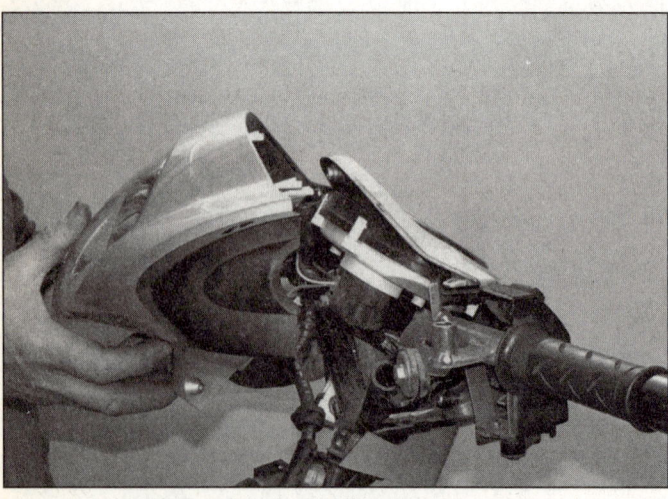

2.45c Release the handlebar front cover . . .

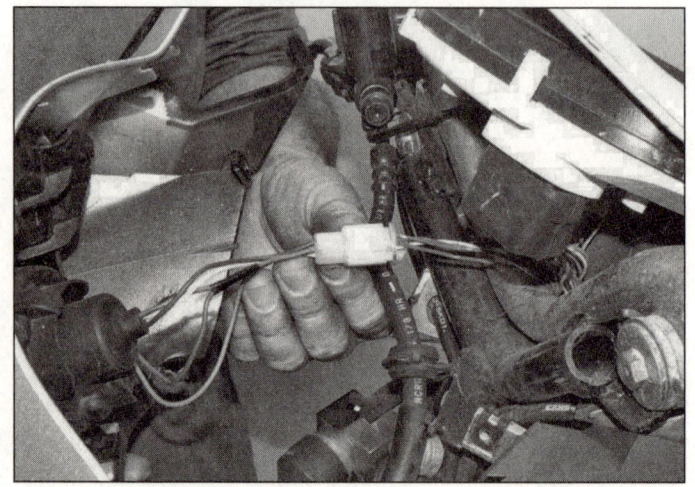

2.45d . . . and disconnect the wiring connector

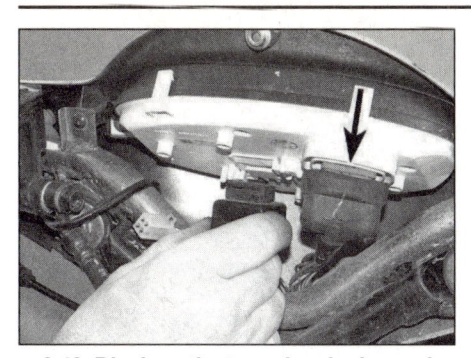

Bodywork 7•5

2.48 Displace the turn signal relay and disconnect the wiring connector (arrowed)

2.49a Undo the screws (arrowed) at the front . . .

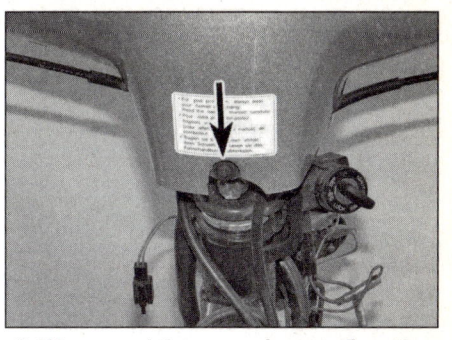

2.49b . . . and the screw (arrowed) on the back of the rear handlebar cover

wiring connector **(see illustration)**. If required remove the instrument cluster (see Chapter 8) – this can be done after removing the cover if preferred.

49 Undo the screws at the front and the one at the rear **(see illustrations)**. Displace the cover and disconnect the handlebar switch wiring connectors **(see illustration 3.54d)**.

50 Refer to Chapter 3A and disconnect the throttle cable, then draw the cover off the cable.

51 Installation is the reverse of removal. Make sure the wiring connectors are correctly and securely connected, and check the operation of all instruments, warning lights and switches before riding the scooter.

Front mudguard

52 Remove the front covers.
53 Remove the front wheel (see Chapter 6).
54 Unscrew the brake hose guide bolt from the rear section of the mudguard **(see illustration 3.57)**.
55 Unscrew the bolts on the underside and remove the rear section **(see illustration 3.58a and b)**.
56 Unscrew the bolts securing the front section, noting the collars and how the right-hand bolt secures the brake hose guide,

then lift it up and manoeuvre it out **(see illustration 3.59a and b)**.
57 Installation is the reverse of removal.

3 2007-on (fuel injection) models

Seat

1 Unlock the seat and swing it up **(see illustration)**.
2 Undo the nuts securing the seat to the hinge and remove the seat **(see illustration)**.

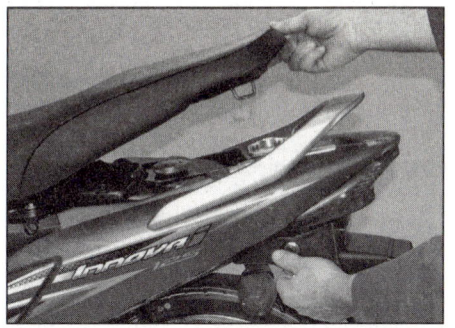

3.1 Unlock the seat and swing the back up

3 Installation is the reverse of removal.

Grab-rail

4 Unlock the seat and swing it up **(see illustration 3.1)**.
5 Unscrew the four bolts and remove the rail **(see illustration)**.
6 Installation is the reverse of removal.

Front body cover

7 Remove the seat.
8 Remove the rear centre cover.
9 Remove the front covers.
10 Unscrew the bolt on each side **(see illustration)**.

3.2 Unscrew the nuts (arrowed) to remove the seat

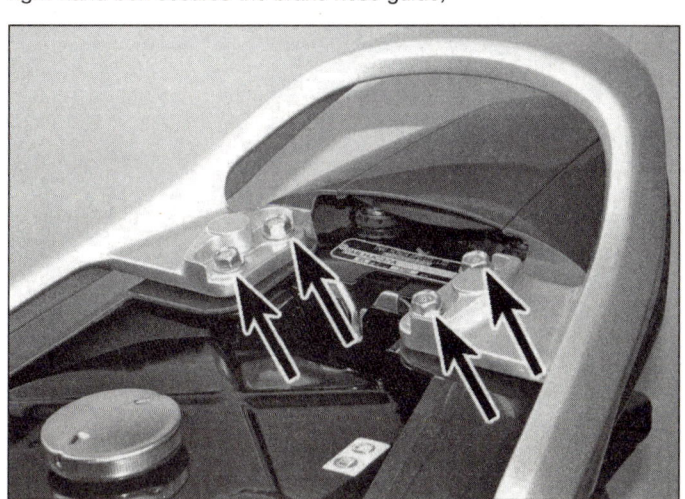

3.5 Unscrew the four bolts (arrowed)

3.10 Unscrew the bolt (arrowed) on each side of the front body cover

7•6 Bodywork

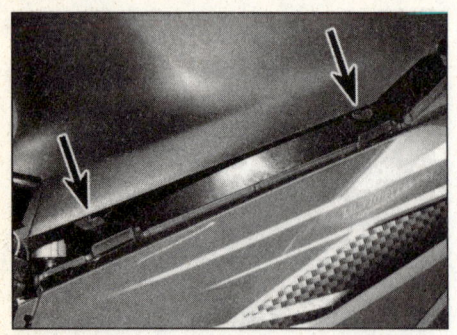

3.11a Release the hooks (arrowed) . . .

3.11b . . . and the tab . . .

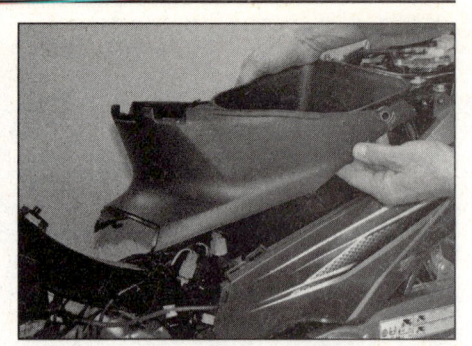

3.11c . . . and remove the front body cover

3.16 Undo the screws (arrowed) . . .

3.17 . . . and remove the rear body cover

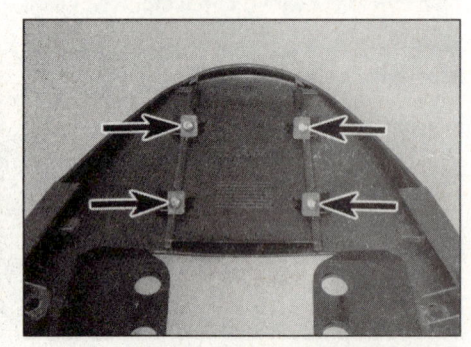

3.18a Undo the screws (arrowed) to separate the sides . . .

3.18b . . . and/or undo the screws (arrowed) to separate the front and rear sections of each side

11 Slide the cover forwards to release the hooks from the slots and the tab at the back then remove the cover (see illustrations).
12 Installation is the reverse of removal – make sure the hooks and the tab engage correctly.

Rear body cover

13 Remove the seat.
14 Remove the grab-rail.
15 Remove the front body cover.
16 Undo the two screws on each underside (see illustration).
17 Carefully lift the body cover off (see illustration).
18 If required undo the screws and separate the body cover into its component panels (see illustrations).
19 Installation is the reverse of removal.

Storage compartment

20 Remove the seat.
21 Remove the body covers.
22 Remove the battery and the starter relay (see Chapter 8).
23 Release the wiring guide from the underside of the compartment on the right.
24 Unscrew the two bolts inside the compartment and the two at the back, noting the collars in the rubbers (see illustrations).
25 Lift the storage compartment out, noting the routing of the wiring.

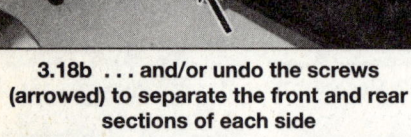

3.24a Unscrew the bolts inside (arrowed) . . .

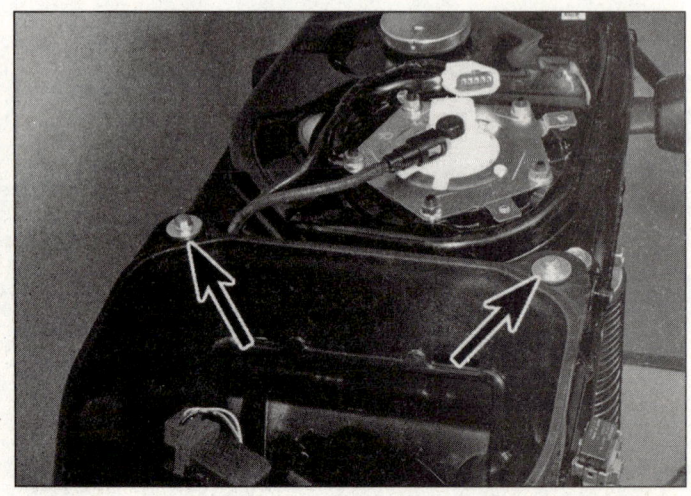

3.24b . . . and the bolts outside of the storage compartment (arrowed)

Bodywork 7•7

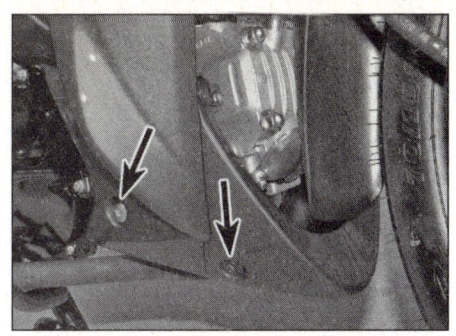

3.27a Undo the screws (arrowed) . . .

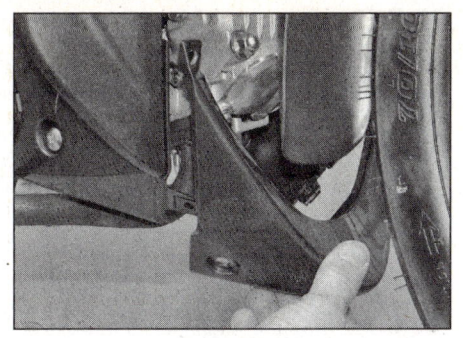

3.27b . . . and remove the bottom cover

3.29a Undo the screws (arrowed) . . .

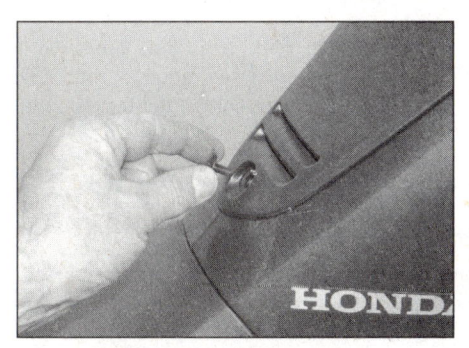

3.29b . . . and the screw . . .

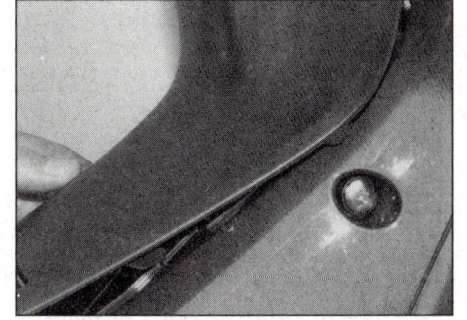

3.29c . . . then release the hooks and remove the front centre cover

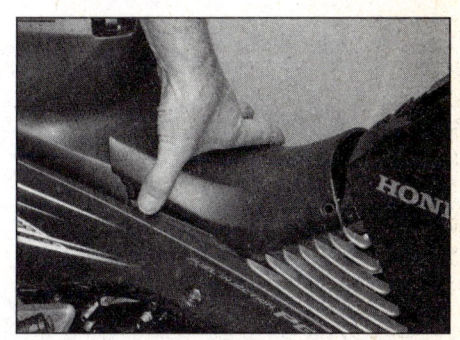

3.31 Undo the screws and remove the rear centre cover

26 Installation is the reverse of removal. Make sure the rubbers are in good condition.

Bottom cover

27 Undo the two screws on each side and remove the cover (see illustrations).
28 Installation is the reverse of removal.

Front centre cover

29 Undo the three screws, then slide the cover back to release the hooked tabs on each side from the slots (see illustrations).
30 Installation is the reverse of removal.

Rear centre cover

31 Undo the three screws, then lift the back of the cover to release its tabs (see illustration).
32 Installation is the reverse of removal.

Top cover

33 Undo the two screws on the rear (see illustration 3.29a).
34 Undo the three screws on the front, then release the tabs and remove the cover (see illustrations).
35 Installation is the reverse of removal.

Front covers

36 Remove the right-hand front cover first as it overlaps the left-hand one – to remove the left-hand cover you must first remove the right-hand cover.
37 Remove the top cover.
38 Remove the bottom cover.
39 Remove the front and rear centre covers.

3.34a Undo the screws (arrowed) . . .

40 Disconnect the turn signal wiring connector (see illustration).

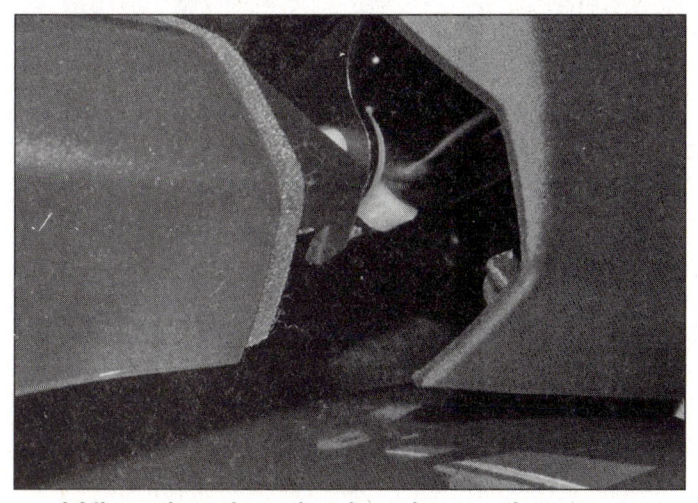

3.34b . . . then release the tabs and remove the top cover

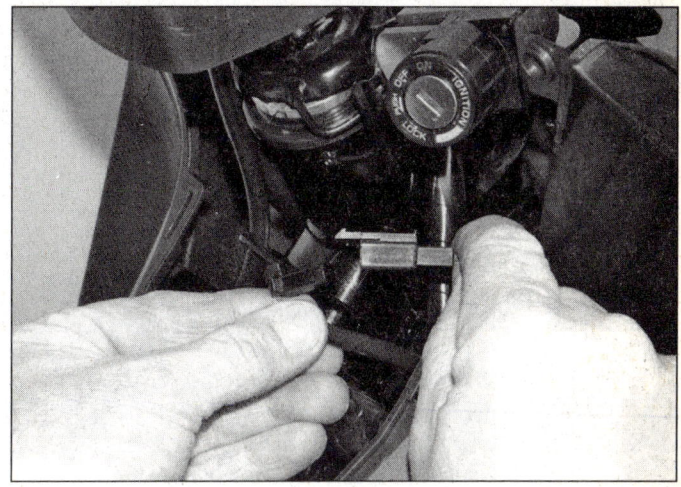

3.40 Disconnect the wiring connector

7•8 Bodywork

3.41a Undo the screws (arrowed) ...

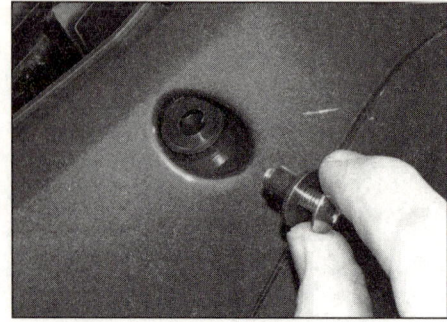

3.41b ... noting the collars ...

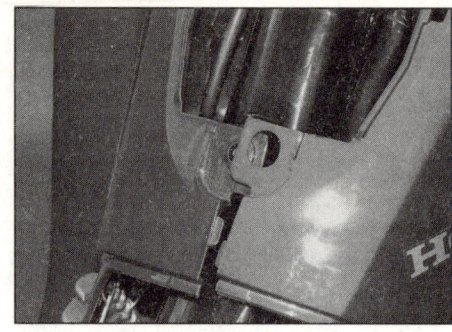

3.41c ... then release ...

41 Undo the three screws, noting the collars with the front screws, then release and remove the cover **(see illustrations)**.

42 If required undo the screws and separate the cover into its component panels **(see illustration)**. If required remove the turn signal (see Chapter 8).

43 Installation is the reverse of removal.

Mirrors

44 Lift the rubber boot.

45 To remove the mirror unscrew it using the bottom hex **(see illustration)**.

46 Installation is the reverse of removal.

47 To adjust the position of the mirror hold the bottom hex using one spanner and slacken the locknut using another, turning it clockwise as it has a left-hand thread **(see illustration)**. Reposition the mirror as required, then hold the bottom hex and tighten the locknut anti-clockwise.

Front handlebar cover

48 Remove the mirrors.

49 Remove the top cover.

3.41d ... and remove the front cover

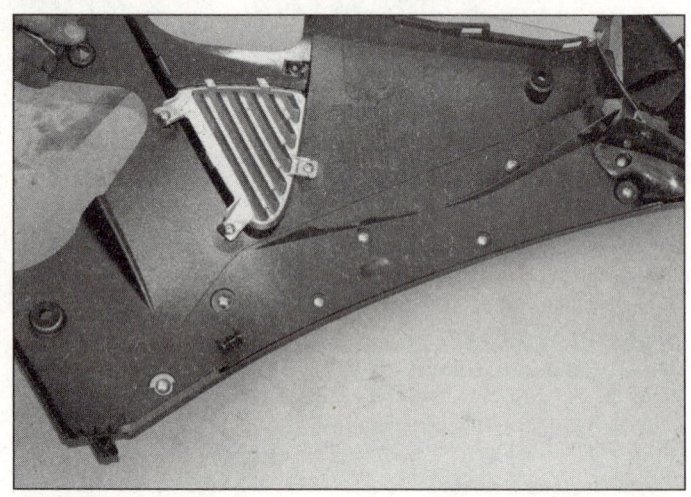

3.42 There are four separate parts to each front cover, joined by screws on the inner side

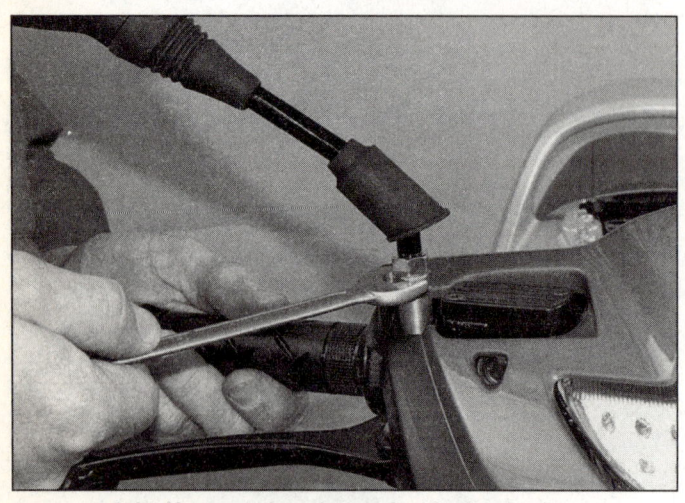

3.45 Unscrew the mirror using the bottom hex

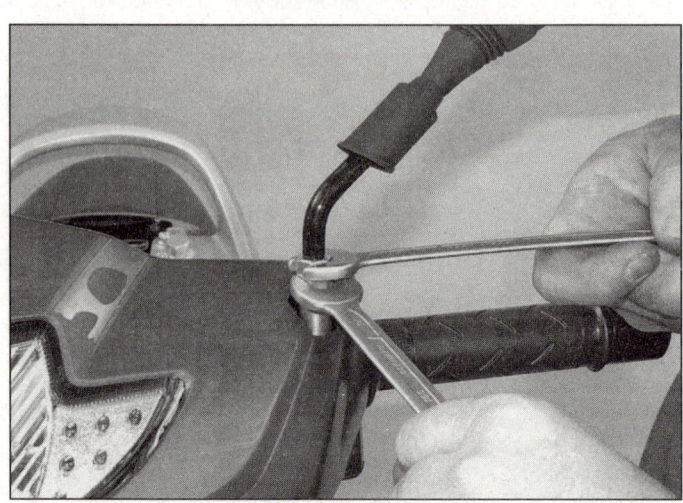

3.47 Counter-hold the bottom hex and slacken the nut

Bodywork 7•9

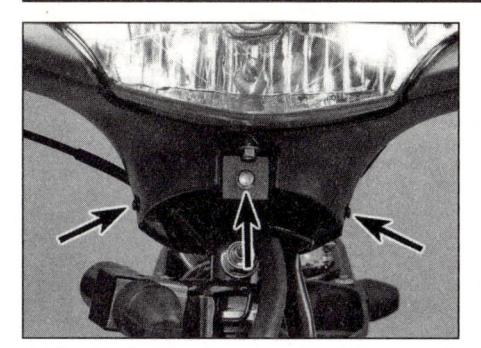

3.50a Undo the screws and bolt (arrowed) at the front . . .

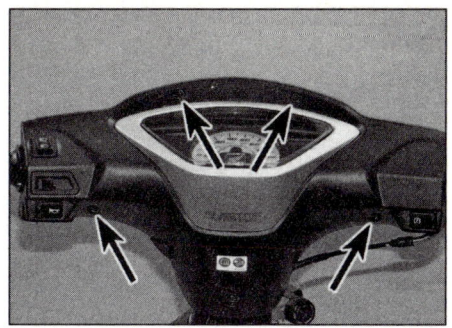

3.50b . . . and the screws (arrowed) on the back

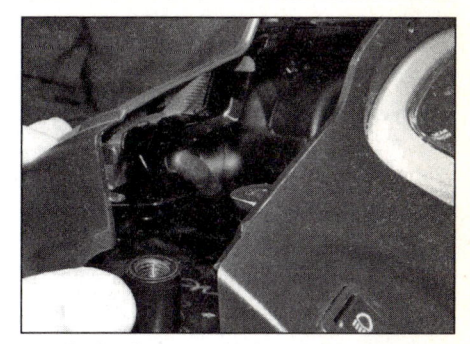

3.50c Release the handlebar front cover . . .

50 Undo the two screws and the bolt in the bottom of the front cover and the four screws in the rear cover, then release the front cover from the rear cover at each end, draw the cover forwards and disconnect the headlight and sidelight wiring connectors **(see illustrations)**. Remove the rubber blanking pieces for safekeeping **(see illustration)**.

51 Installation is the reverse of removal. Make sure the throttle cable is routed through the cut-out in the cover. Make sure the wiring connectors are securely connected, and check the operation of the headlight before riding the scooter.

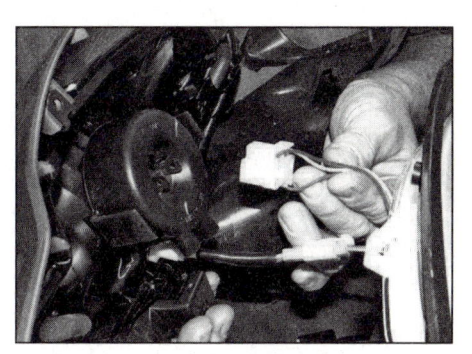

3.50d . . . and disconnect the wiring connectors

3.50e Remove the rubber piece on each side

Rear handlebar cover

52 Remove the front handlebar cover.
53 Undo the screws at the front and the screw at the rear, then displace the cover and release and disconnect the instrument cluster wiring and disconnect the handlebar switch wiring connectors **(see illustrations)**.
54 Installation is the reverse of removal. Make sure the wiring connectors are correctly and securely connected, and check the operation of all instruments, warning lights and switches before riding the scooter.

Front mudguard

55 Remove the front covers.

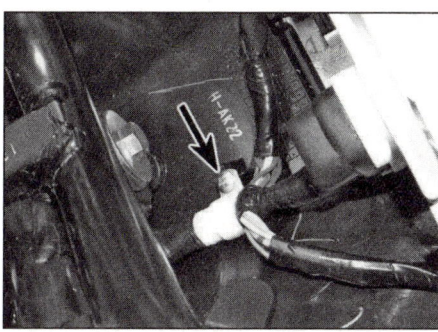

3.53a Undo the screws (arrowed) at the front . .

3.53b . . . and the screw (arrowed) on the back

3.53c Undo the screw (arrowed) to release the wiring

3.53d Disconnect the instrument connector . . .

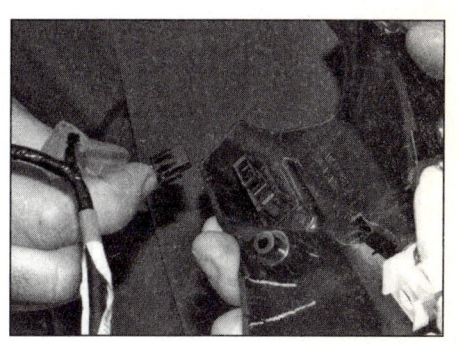

3.53e . . . and the switch connectors

7•10 Bodywork

3.57 Unscrew the bolt (arrowed)

3.58a Unscrew the bolts . . .

3.58b . . . and remove the rear section

3.59a Unscrew the bolts (arrowed) . . .

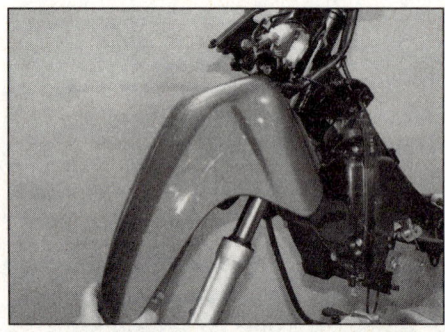

3.59b . . . and remove the front section

56 Remove the front wheel (see Chapter 6).
57 Unscrew the brake hose guide bolt from the rear section of the mudguard **(see illustration)**.
58 Unscrew the bolts on the underside, noting the collars, and remove the rear section **(see illustrations)**.
59 Unscrew the bolts securing the front section, noting the collars and how the right-hand bolt secures the brake hose guide, then lift it up and manoeuvre it out **(see illustrations)**.
60 Installation is the reverse of removal.

Chapter 8
Electrical system

Contents

	Section number
Alternator	28
Battery charging	4
Battery removal, installation and inspection	3
Brake light switches	14
Brake/tail light bulb and licence plate bulb	9
Charging system testing	27
Electrical system fault finding	2
Fuses	5
Gear position switch	22
General information	1
Handlebar switches	20
Headlight	8
Headlight aim	see Chapter 1
Headlight and sidelight bulbs	7
Horn	23
Ignition switch	19

	Section number
Ignition system components	see Chapter 4
Instrument cluster	15
Instrument check	16
Instrument and warning lights	17
Lighting system check	6
Regulator/rectifier and power relay	29
Sidestand switch	21
Speed sensor	18
Starter motor overhaul	26
Starter motor removal and installation	25
Starter relay	24
Tail light	10
Turn signal assemblies	13
Turn signal bulbs	12
Turn signal circuit check	11

Degrees of difficulty

Easy, suitable for novice with little experience	**Fairly easy,** suitable for beginner with some experience	**Fairly difficult,** suitable for competent DIY mechanic	**Difficult,** suitable for experienced DIY mechanic	**Very difficult,** suitable for expert DIY or professional

Specifications

Battery
Capacity ... 12 V, 5 Ah
Voltage
  Fully-charged ... 13.0 to 13.2 V
  Uncharged ... below 12.3 V
Charging rate
  Normal ... 0.5 A for 5 to 10 hrs
  Quick ... 2.5 A for 1 hr

Charging system
Current leakage ... 0.1 mA (max)
Alternator stator coil resistance ... 0.2 to 1.0 ohms
Alternator output
  2003 to 2006 models ... 130 W @ 5000 rpm
  2007-on models ... 150 W @ 5000 rpm
Regulated voltage output ... max. 15.5 V @ 5000 rpm

Starter motor
Brush length
  Standard ... 10 mm
  Service limit (min) ... 3.5 mm

Fuses
Main ... 15 A
Sub ... 10 A

8•2 Electrical system

Bulbs
Headlight	35/35 W
Sidelight	5 W
Brake/tail light	21/5 W
Licence plate light	5 W
Turn signal lights	21 W x 4
Instrument lights	
2003 to 2006 models	
High beam indicator	1.12 W
All others	LED
2007-on models	LED

Torque settings
Alternator rotor nut	64 Nm
Alternator stator bolts	10 Nm

1 General information

All models have a 12 volt electrical system charged by a single-phase alternator with a separate regulator/rectifier.

The regulator maintains the charging system output within the specified range to prevent overcharging, and the rectifier converts the ac (alternating current) output of the alternator to dc (direct current) to power the lights and other electrical systems and components and to charge the battery. The alternator rotor is mounted on the left-hand end of the crankshaft.

The starter motor is mounted on the top of the crankcase. The starting system includes the motor, the battery, the relay and the various wires and switches. Some of the switches are part of a starter safety circuit which prevents the engine from being started if the sidestand is down and the engine is in gear. The system will also cut the engine should the sidestand extend while the engine is running and in gear – see Chapter 1 for further information and checks on the system.

Note: *Keep in mind that electrical parts, once purchased, often cannot be returned. To avoid unnecessary expense, make very sure the faulty component has been positively identified before buying a replacement part.*

2 Electrical system fault finding

1 A typical electrical circuit consists of an electrical component, the switches, relays, etc, related to that component and the wiring and connectors that link the component to the battery and the frame.

2 Before tackling any troublesome electrical circuit, first study the wiring diagram thoroughly to get a complete picture of what makes up that individual circuit. Trouble spots, for instance, can often be narrowed down by noting if other components related to that circuit are operating properly or not. If several components or circuits fail at one time, chances are the fault lies either in the fuse or in a common earth (ground) connection, as several circuits are often routed through the same fuse and earth (ground) connections.

3 Electrical problems often stem from simple causes, such as loose or corroded connections or a blown fuse. Prior to any electrical fault finding, always visually check the condition of the fuse, wires and connections in the problem circuit. Intermittent failures can be especially frustrating, since you can't always duplicate the failure when it's convenient to test. In such situations, a good practice is to clean all connections in the affected circuit, whether or not they appear to be good – where possible use a dedicated electrical cleaning spray along with sandpaper, wire wool or other abrasive material to remove corrosion, and a dedicated electrical protection spray to prevent further problems. All of the connections and wires should also be wiggled to check for looseness which can cause intermittent failure.

4 If you don't have a multimeter it is highly advisable to obtain one – they are not expensive and will enable a full range of electrical tests to be made (see illustration). Go for a modern digital one with LCD display as they are easier to use. A continuity tester and/or test light are useful for certain electrical checks as an alternative, though are limited in their usefulness compared to a multimeter (see illustrations).

Continuity checks

5 The term continuity describes the uninterrupted flow of electricity through an electrical circuit. Continuity can be checked with a multimeter set either to its continuity function (a beep is emitted when continuity is found), or to the resistance (ohms / Ω) function, or with a dedicated continuity tester. Both instruments are powered by an internal battery, therefore the checks are made with the ignition OFF. As a safety precaution, always disconnect the battery negative (-) lead before making continuity checks, particularly if ignition switch checks are being made.

6 If using a multimeter, select the continuity function if it has one, or the resistance (ohms)

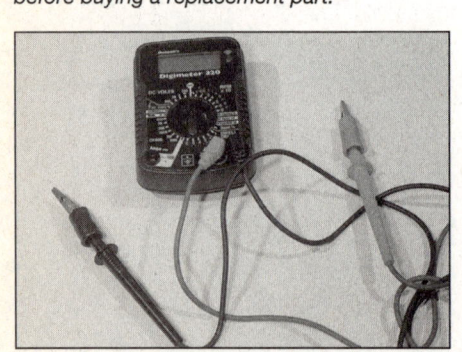

2.4a A digital multimeter can be used for all electrical tests

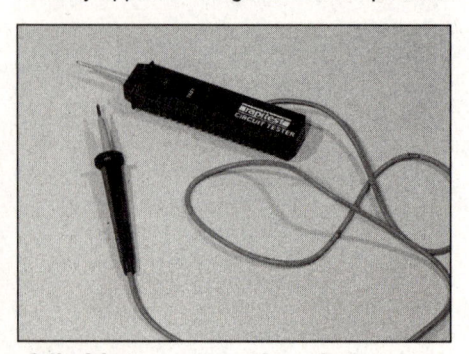

2.4b A battery-powered continuity tester

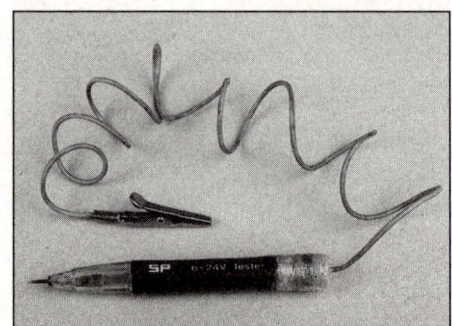

2.4c A simple test light is useful for voltage tests

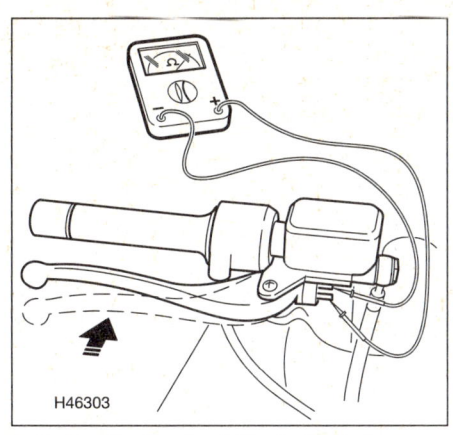

Electrical system 8•3

2.10 Continuity should be indicated across switch terminals when lever is operated

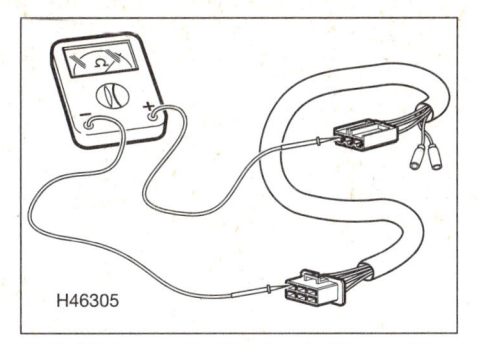

2.12 Wiring continuity check. Connect the meter probes across each end of the same wire

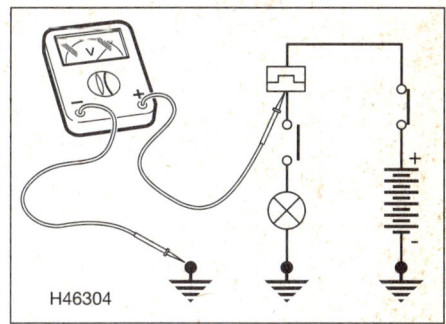

2.15 Voltage check. Connect the meter positive probe to the component and the negative probe to earth

function. Touch the meter probes together and check that a beep is emitted or the meter reads zero, which indicates continuity. If there is no continuity there will be no beep or the meter will show infinite resistance. After using the meter, always switch it OFF to conserve its battery.

7 A continuity tester can be used in the same way – its light should come on or it should beep to indicate continuity in the switch ON position, but should be off or silent in the OFF position.

8 Note that the polarity of the test probes doesn't matter for continuity checks, although care should be taken to follow specific test procedures if a diode or solid-state component is being checked.

Switch continuity checks

9 If a switch is at fault, trace its wiring to the wiring connectors. Separate the connectors and inspect them for security and condition. A build-up of dirt or corrosion here will most likely be the cause of the problem – clean up and apply a water dispersant such as WD40, or alternatively use a dedicated contact cleaner and protection spray.

10 If using a multimeter, select the continuity function if it has one, or the resistance (ohms) function, and connect its probes to the terminals in the connector (see illustration). Simple ON/OFF type switches, such as brake light switches, only have two wires whereas combination

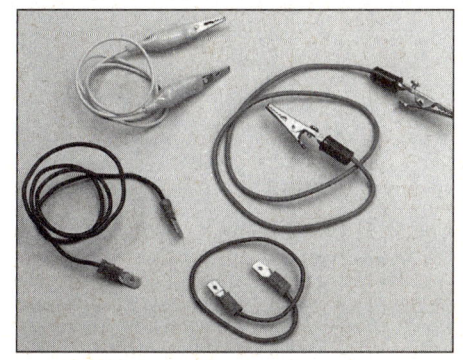

2.23 A selection of insulated jumper wires

switches, like the handlebar switches, have many wires. Study the wiring diagram to ensure that you are connecting to the correct pair of wires. Continuity should be indicated with the switch ON and no continuity with it OFF.

Wiring continuity checks

11 Many electrical faults are caused by damaged wiring, often due to incorrect routing or chaffing on frame components. Loose, wet or corroded wire connectors can also be the cause of electrical problems.

12 A continuity check can be made on a single length of wire by disconnecting it at each end and connecting the meter or continuity tester probes to each end of the wire (see illustration). Continuity (low or no resistance – 0 ohms) should be indicated if the wire is good. If no continuity (high resistance) is shown, suspect a broken wire.

13 To check for continuity to earth in any earth wire connect one probe of your meter or tester to the earth wire terminal in the connector and the other to the frame, engine, or battery earth (-) terminal. Continuity (low or no resistance – 0 ohms) should be indicated if the wire is good. If no continuity (high resistance) is shown, suspect a broken wire or corroded or loose earth point (see below).

Voltage checks

14 A voltage check can determine whether power is reaching a component. Use a multimeter set to the dc voltage scale, or a test light. The test light is the cheaper component, but the meter has the advantage of being able to give a voltage reading.

15 Connect the meter or test light in parallel, i.e. across the load (see illustration).

16 First identify the relevant wiring circuit by referring to the wiring diagram at the end of this manual. If other electrical components share the same power supply (i.e. are fed from the same fuse), take note whether they are working correctly – this is useful information in deciding where to start checking the circuit.

17 If using a meter, check first that the meter leads are plugged into the correct terminals on the meter (red to positive (+), black to negative (-). Set the meter to the dc volts function, where necessary at a range suitable for the battery voltage – 0 to 20 vdc. Connect the meter red probe (+) to the power supply wire and the black probe to a good metal earth (ground) on the scooter's frame or directly to the battery negative terminal. Battery voltage should be shown on the meter with the ignition switch, and if necessary any other relevant switch, ON.

18 If using a test light, connect its positive (+) probe to the power supply terminal and its negative (-) probe to a good earth (ground) on the scooter's frame. With the switch, and if necessary any other relevant switch, ON, the test light should illuminate.

19 If no voltage is indicated, work back towards the fuse continuing to check for voltage. When you reach a point where there is voltage, you know the problem lies between that point and your last check point.

Earth (ground) checks

20 Earth connections are made either directly to the engine or frame via the mounting of the component, or by a separate wire into the earth circuit of the wiring harness. Alternatively a short earth wire is sometimes run from the component directly to the scooter's frame.

21 Corrosion is a common cause of a poor earth connection, as is a loose earth terminal fastener.

22 If total or multiple component failure is experienced, check the security of the main earth lead from the negative (-) terminal of the battery, the earth lead bolted to the engine, and the main earth point(s) on the frame. If corroded, dismantle the connection and clean all surfaces back to bare metal. Remake the connection and prevent further corrosion from forming by smearing battery terminal grease over the connection.

23 To check the earth of a component, use an insulated jumper wire to temporarily bypass its earth connection (see illustration) – connect one end of the jumper wire to the earth terminal or metal body of the component and the other end to the scooter's frame. If the circuit works with the jumper wire installed, the earth circuit is faulty.

24 To check an earth wire first check for corroded or loose connections, then check the wiring for continuity (Step 13) between each connector in the circuit in turn, and then to its earth point, to locate the break.

8•4 Electrical system

3.2 Open the box and remove the toolkit (arrowed)

3.3a Undo the screw (arrowed) ...

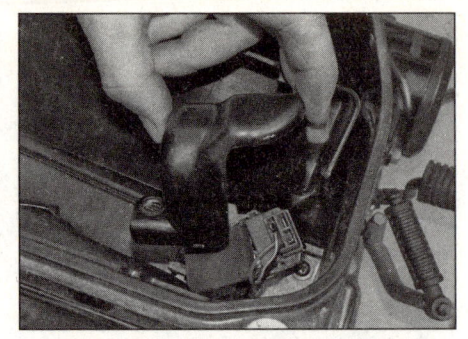

3.3b ... and remove the relay cover ...

3 Battery removal, installation and inspection

Caution: *Be extremely careful when handling or working around the battery. The electrolyte is very caustic and an explosive gas (hydrogen) is given off when the battery is charging.*

Removal and installation

1 Make sure the ignition is switched OFF. Unlock the seat and swing it up.
2 Release the storage box tabs, open the box and remove the toolkit **(see illustration)**.
3 Remove the relay cover and the battery cover **(see illustrations)**.
4 Unscrew the battery negative (–) terminal bolt first and disconnect the lead from the battery **(see illustration)**. Lift up the red insulating cover to access the positive (+) terminal, then unscrew the bolt and disconnect the lead. Lift the battery out **(see illustration)**.
5 On installation, clean the battery terminals and lead ends with a wire brush, fine sandpaper or steel wool. Reconnect the leads, connecting the positive (+) terminal first.

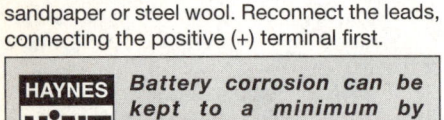

> **HAYNES HiNT** *Battery corrosion can be kept to a minimum by applying a layer of battery terminal grease or petroleum jelly (Vaseline) to the terminals after the leads have been connected. DO NOT use ordinary mineral-based grease.*

3.3c ... then undo the screws (arrowed) ...

3.3d ... and remove the battery cover

6 Fit the battery cover and relay cover **(see illustrations 3.3d, c, b and a)**. Replace the toolkit and close the box.

Inspection

7 The battery fitted to all models covered in this manual is of the maintenance-free (sealed) type, therefore requiring no regular maintenance. However, the following checks should still be performed.
8 Check the battery terminals and leads are tight and free of corrosion. If corrosion is evident, clean the terminals as described above, then protect them from further corrosion (see **Haynes Hint**).
9 Keep the battery case clean to prevent current leakage, which can discharge the battery over a period of time (especially when it sits unused). Wash the outside of the case with a solution of baking soda and water. Rinse the battery thoroughly, then dry it.

10 Look for cracks in the case and replace the battery with a new one if any are found. If acid has been spilled on the frame or battery box, neutralise it with a baking soda and water solution, dry it thoroughly, then touch up any damaged paint.
11 If the scooter sits unused for long periods of time, disconnect the leads from the battery, negative (–) terminal first. Refer to Section 4 and charge the battery once every month to six weeks.
12 Check the condition of the battery by measuring the voltage present at the battery terminals **(see illustration)**. Connect the voltmeter positive (+) probe to the battery positive (+) terminal, and the negative (–) probe to the battery negative (–) terminal. When fully-charged there should be 13.0 to 13.2 volts present. If the voltage falls below 12.3 volts remove the battery (see above), and recharge it as described in Section 4.

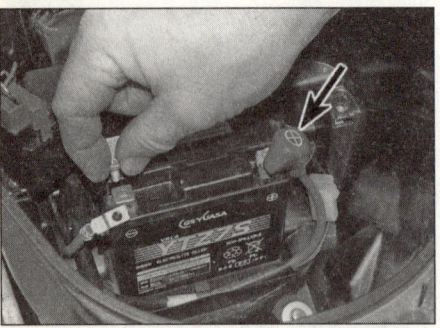

3.4a Disconnect the negative lead first, then disconnect the positive lead (arrowed) ...

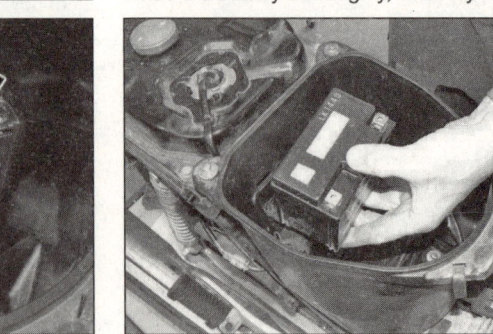

3.4b ... and lift the battery out

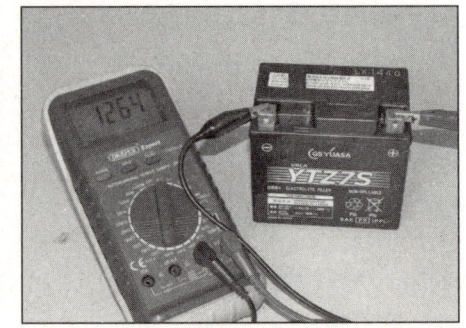

3.12 Checking battery voltage

Electrical system 8•5

4.1 Battery connected to a charger

5.5 Disconnect the wiring connector to access the main fuse (arrowed)

5.6 Open the lid to access the sub fuse

4 Battery charging

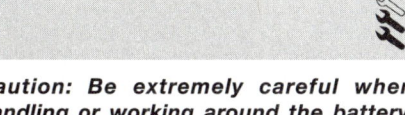

Caution: Be extremely careful when handling or working around the battery. The electrolyte is very caustic and an explosive gas (hydrogen) is given off when the battery is charging.

1 Remove the battery (see Section 3). Connect the charger to the battery, making sure that the positive (+) lead on the charger is connected to the positive (+) terminal on the battery, and the negative (–) lead is connected to the negative (–) terminal **(see illustration)**.
2 Honda recommend that the battery is charged at the normal rate specified at the beginning of the Chapter. A higher 'quick charge' rate that can be used if absolutely necessary is also specified, but note that exceeding this could cause the battery to overheat, buckling the plates and rendering it useless. If a normal domestic charger is used check that after a possible initial peak, the charge rate falls to a safe level. If the battery becomes hot during charging **stop**. Further charging will cause damage. Note that there are many bike-specific chargers available from good suppliers that are designed for the maintenance and recovery of motorcycle/scooter batteries, in particular catering for the requirements of heavily discharged MF batteries. They are not too expensive, and are a worthwhile investment, especially if the scooter is not used over winter. Follow the manufacturer's instructions.
3 If the recharged battery discharges rapidly when left disconnected it is likely that an internal short caused by physical damage or sulphation has occurred. A new battery will be required. A sound item will tend to lose its charge at about 1% per day.
4 Install the battery (see Section 3).
5 If the scooter sits unused for long periods of time, charge the battery once every month to six weeks and leave it disconnected.

5 Fuses

1 The electrical system is protected by two fuses – the main fuse and a sub fuse. The main fuse protects everything all the time – if it blows nothing will work. The sub fuse protects the instrument cluster all the time and all other circuits governed by the ignition switch. The main fuse is housed in the starter relay. The sub fuse is housed in a holder next to the battery.
2 Make sure the ignition is switched OFF. Unlock the seat and swing it up.
3 Release the storage box tabs, open the box and remove the toolkit **(see illustration 3.2)**.
4 Remove the relay cover and the battery cover **(see illustrations 3.3a, b, c and d)**.
5 The main fuse is housed in the starter relay. Disconnect the relay wiring connector to access the fuse **(see illustration)**.
6 The sub fuse is housed in a holder next to the battery. Open the lid of the holder to access the fuse **(see illustration)**.
7 The fuses can be removed and checked visually **(see illustration)**. If you can't pull the fuse out with your fingertips, use a pair of suitable pliers. A blown fuse is easily identified by a break in the element **(see illustration)**. Each fuse is clearly marked with its rating and must only be replaced by a fuse of the correct rating.
8 A spare fuse of each rating is housed in the battery cover **(see illustration)**. If a spare fuse is used, always replace it with a new one so that a spare of each rating is carried on the scooter at all times.

⚠ *Warning: Never put in a fuse of a higher rating or bridge the terminals with any other substitute, however temporary it may be. Serious damage may be done to the circuit, or a fire may start.*

9 If the new fuse blows immediately check the wiring circuit very carefully for evidence of a short-circuit. Look for bare wires and chafed, melted or burned insulation.
10 Occasionally a fuse will blow or cause an open-circuit for no obvious reason. Corrosion of the fuse ends and fusebox terminals may occur and cause poor fuse contact. If this happens, remove the corrosion with a wire brush or emery paper, then spray the fuse end and terminals with electrical contact cleaner.

5.7a Pull the fuse out

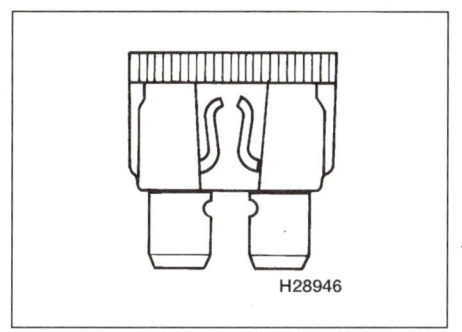

5.7b A blown fuse can be identified by a break in its element

5.8 Spare fuses are clipped into the battery cover

8•6 Electrical system

6 Lighting system check

Note: *Refer to electrical system fault finding in Section 2 and to the wiring diagram for your model at the end of this Chapter.*

1 If a light fails first check the bulb (see relevant Section), and the bulb terminals in the holder. If none of the lights work, check the battery (see Section 3). Low battery voltage indicates either a faulty battery or a defective charging system. Refer to Section 3 for battery checks and Section 27 for charging system tests. If nothing works check the fuses (Section 5) and then the ignition switch. When checking for a blown filament in a bulb, it is advisable to back up a visual check with a continuity test of the filament as it is not always apparent that a bulb has blown. Also make sure all wiring connector terminals are secure.

Caution: *The lighting system on all models runs AC voltage directly from the regulator – when testing the system set your multimeter to the 0 to 20 volts AC range, and make all tests with the engine running at around 5000 rpm.*

Headlight

2 The headlight uses one twin filament bulb. If one or both headlight beams fail to work, first check the bulb (see Section 7). If it is good, the problem lies in the wiring or connectors, or the dimmer switch. Refer to Section 20 for the switch testing procedures, and also to electrical system fault finding (Section 2) and the wiring diagrams at the end of this Chapter.

3 If the bulb is good, refer to Section 7 for access and check there is 11 to 15 volts AC at the blue or white wire terminal (according to beam) in the headlight wiring connector with the connector connected and the engine running. If voltage is present, check for continuity to earth (ground) in the green wire from the wiring connector. If no voltage is indicated, check the wiring and connectors in the circuit. If all is good check the charging system, and particularly the regulator/rectifier.

Tail light/sidelight/licence plate light

4 All these lights work on the same circuit. If one of the lights fails to work, first check the bulb (Section 9 or 7). If the bulb is good, refer to Section 10 or 7 for access and disconnect the wiring connector, and check there is 11 to 15 volts AC at the yellow wire terminal in the connector with the connector connected and the engine running. If voltage is present, check for continuity to earth (ground) in the green wire from the wiring connector. If no voltage is indicated, check the wiring and connectors in the rest of the circuit, referring to electrical system fault finding (Section 2) and the wiring diagrams at the end of this Chapter. Also check between the connector and the bulbholder itself. If all is good check the charging system, and particularly the regulator/rectifier.

Brake light

5 If the brake light fails to work, first check the bulb (Section 9). If it is good refer to Section 10 and disconnect the tail light wiring connector, and check for battery voltage at the green/yellow wire terminal on the loom side of the connector, first with the front brake lever pulled in, then with the rear brake pedal pushed down. If voltage is present with one brake on but not the other, then the switch or its wiring is faulty. If voltage is present in both cases, check for continuity to earth (ground) in the green wire from the wiring connector. If no voltage is indicated, check the wiring and connectors between the brake light and the brake switches, and the ignition switch, then check the switches themselves. Refer to Section 14 for the switch testing procedures, to the electrical system fault finding (Section 2) and to the wiring diagrams at the end of this Chapter.

Turn signals

6 See Section 11.

7 Headlight and sidelight bulbs

Note: *Do not touch the bulb glass as skin acids will shorten the bulb's service life. If the bulb is accidentally touched, it should be wiped carefully when cold with a rag soaked in methylated spirit and dried before fitting.*

Headlight

1 Remove the front handlebar cover (see Chapter 7).
2 On 2003 to 2006 models remove the rubber dust cover **(see illustration)**. Release the bulb retaining clip, noting how it fits **(see illustration)**. Withdraw the bulbholder, noting how the tab locates in the slot **(see illustration)**. Push the bulb in and twist it anti-clockwise to release it from the holder **(see illustration)**.

7.2a Remove the cover . . .

7.2b . . . release the clip . . .

7.2c . . . and remove the bulbholder

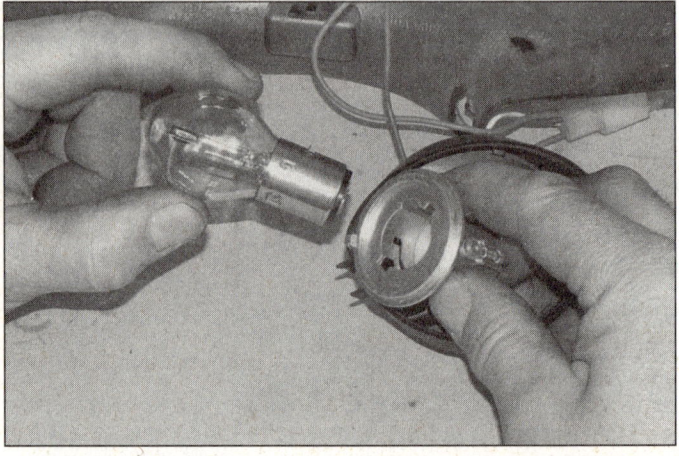

7.2d Push the bulb in and twist anti-clockwise to release it

Electrical system 8•7

7.3a Remove the cover . . .

7.3b . . . release the clip . . .

7.3c . . . and remove the bulb

7.7a Pull the bulbholder out . . .

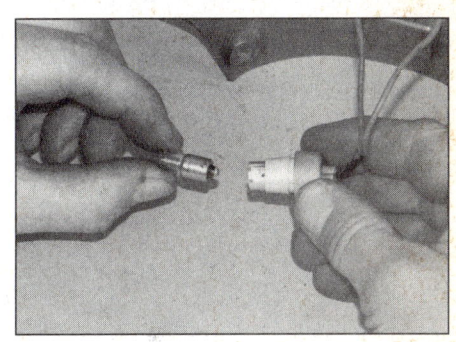

7.7b . . . then push the bulb in and twist anti-clockwise to release it

3 On 2007-on models remove the rubber dust cover **(see illustration)**. Release the bulb retaining clip, noting how it fits **(see illustration)**. Withdraw the bulb, noting how it locates **(see illustration)**.
4 Fit the new bulb in reverse order.
5 Check the operation of the headlight.

Sidelight

6 Remove the front handlebar cover (see Chapter 7).

HAYNES HiNT *Always use a paper towel or dry cloth when handling a new bulb to prevent injury if the bulb should break and to increase bulb life.*

7 On 2003 to 2006 models carefully pull the bulbholder out of the headlight, noting how the recess in the rubber locates over the tab. Push the bulb in and twist it anti-clockwise to release it from the holder **(see illustrations)**.

8 On 2007-on models carefully pull the bulbholder out of the headlight, then pull the bulb out of the holder **(see illustrations)**.
9 Fit the new bulb in reverse order.
10 Check the operation of the sidelight.

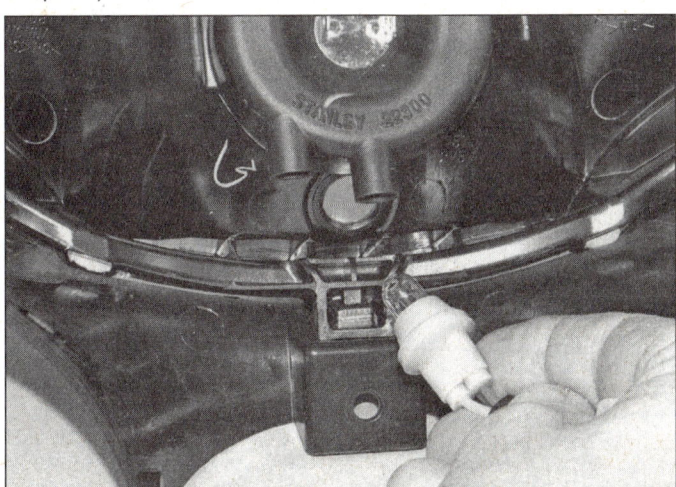

7.8a Pull the bulbholder out . . .

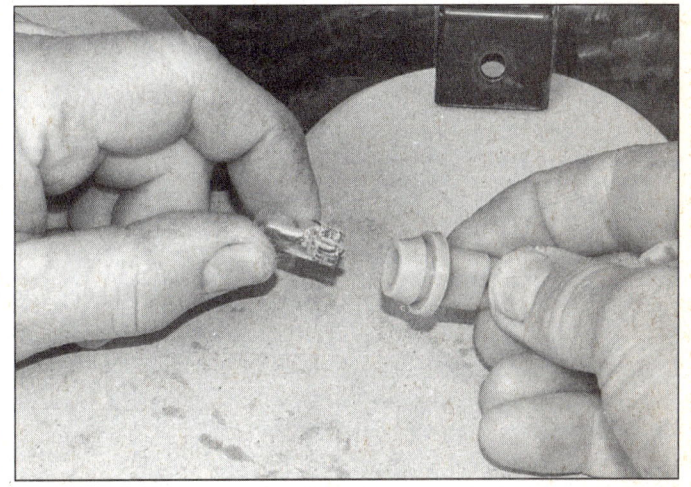

7.8b . . . then pull the bulb out of the holder

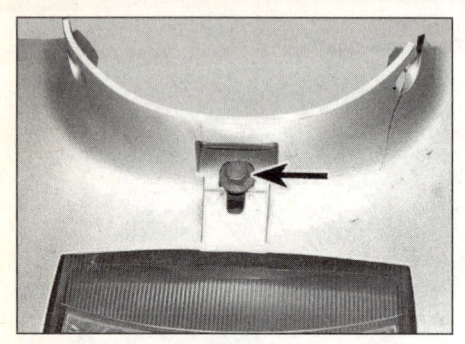

8•8 Electrical system

8.2a Unscrew the bolt (arrowed) . . .

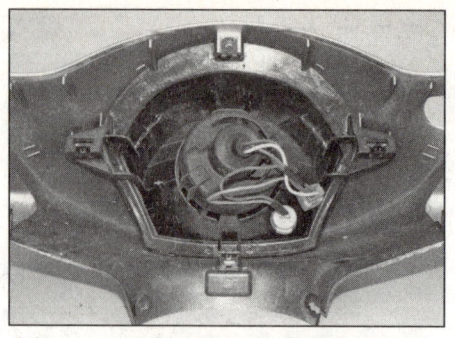

8.2b . . . note how the headlight locates in the cover

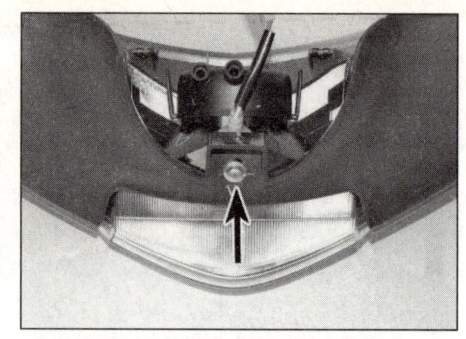

8.3a Unscrew the bolt (arrowed) . . .

8.3b . . . then remove the clips (arrowed)

9.1a Tail light lens screws (arrowed) – 2003 to 2006 models

9.1b Tail light lens screws – 2007-on models

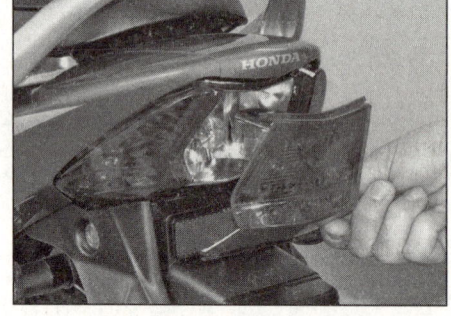

9.1c Remove the lens . . .

9.1d . . . then push the bulb in and twist anti-clockwise to release it

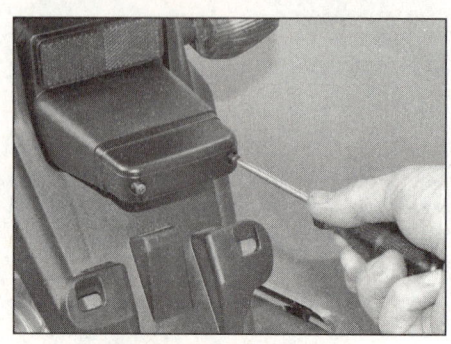

9.3a Undo the screws . . .

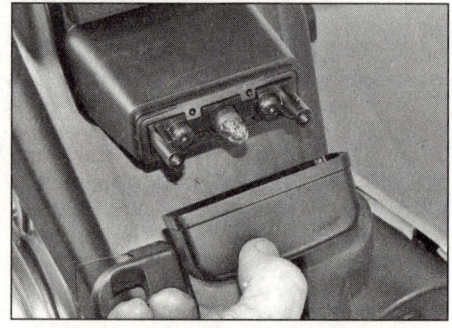

9.3b . . . and remove the cover/lens

8 Headlight

1 Remove the front handlebar cover (see Chapter 7).
2 On 2003 to 2006 models unscrew the adjusting bolt, then lift the headlight out of the cover, noting how it locates **(see illustrations)**.
3 On 2007-on models unscrew the adjusting bolt, then pull the retaining clips off and lift the headlight out of the cover **(see illustrations)**.
4 If required remove the headlight bulb and the sidelight bulbholder (see Section 7).
5 Installation is the reverse of removal. Check the operation of the headlight and sidelight. Check the headlight aim.

9 Brake/tail light bulb and licence plate bulb

Note: *It is a good idea to use a paper towel or dry cloth when handling the new bulb to prevent injury if it breaks, and to increase bulb life.*

Brake/tail light bulb

1 Undo the screws and remove the lens **(see illustrations)**. Carefully push the bulb in and turn it anti-clockwise to release it **(see illustration)**.
2 Fit the new bulb in reverse order. On 2007-on models make sure the seals are in good condition and correctly seated in the groove. Do not over-tighten the screws as it is easy to strip the threads or crack the lens.

Licence plate light bulb

3 Undo the screws and remove the cover/lens **(see illustrations)**.

Electrical system 8•9

4 Pull the bulb out of its socket **(see illustration)**.
5 Fit the new bulb in reverse order. Make sure the seal is correctly seated before fitting the cover/lens **(see illustration)**.

10 Tail light

1 On 2003 to 2006 models remove the body cover (see Chapter 7). Undo the tail light unit bolts and remove the washers, then lift the tail light off the pegs and disconnect the wiring connector **(see illustrations)**.
2 On 2007-on models remove the rear body cover (see Chapter 7). Disconnect the tail light wiring connector, then unscrew the bolts and remove the washers, then lift the tail light off the pegs **(see illustrations)**.
3 Installation is the reverse of removal. Make sure the mounting rubbers are in good condition. Check the operation of the tail and brake lights.

11 Turn signal circuit check

1 Most turn signal problems are the result of a burned out bulb or corroded socket. This is especially true when the turn signals function on one side (although possibly too quickly), but fail to work on the other side. If this is the case, first check the bulbs, the sockets and the wiring connectors. If all the turn signals fail to work, check the relay (Step 2-on). If it is good, the problem lies in the wiring or connectors, or the switch. Refer to Section 20 for the switch testing procedures, and also to the wiring diagrams at the end of this Chapter.
2 To access the relay on 2003 to 2006 models remove the front handlebar cover (see Chapter 7) **(see illustration)**. Displace the relay from its mount and disconnect the wiring connector **(see illustration)**.

9.4 Pull the bulb out of its socket

9.5 Make sure the seal is in place

10.1a Unscrew the bolts (arrowed) . . .

10.1b . . . displace the tail light and disconnect the connector (arrowed)

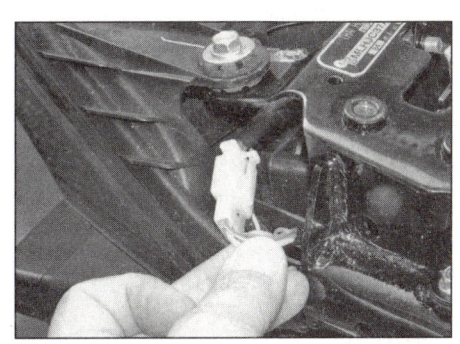

10.2a Disconnect the wiring connector . . .

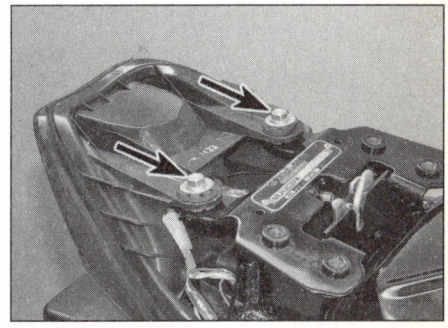

10.2b . . . then unscrew the bolts (arrowed)

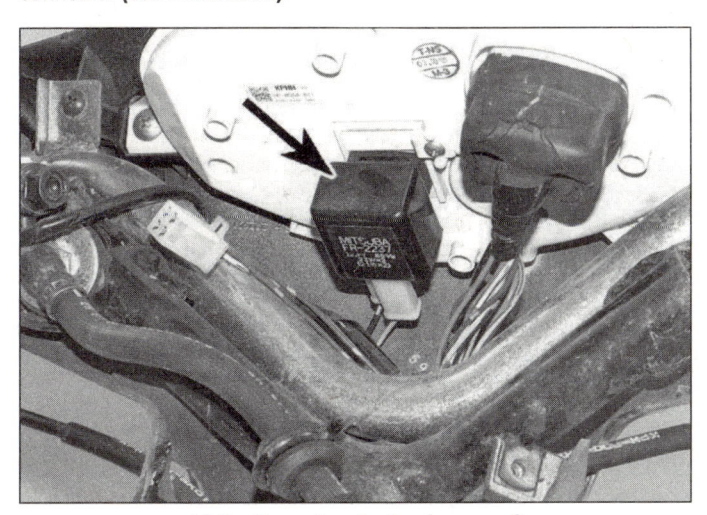

11.2a Turn signal relay (arrowed)

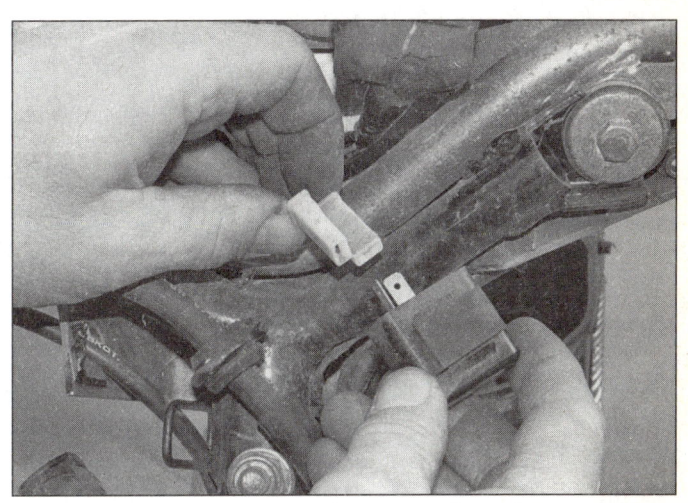

11.2b Displace the relay and disconnect the wiring connector

8•10 Electrical system

11.3a Turn signal relay (arrowed)

11.3b Disconnect the wiring connector

12.2a Undo the screw and remove the lens

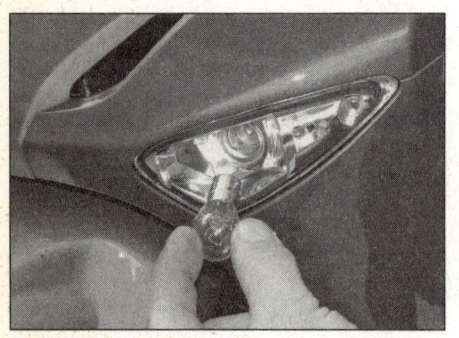

12.2b Push the bulb in and turn it anti-clockwise to release it

12.2c Check the seal

12.2d Make sure the tabs locate correctly

3 To access the relay on 2007-on models remove the rear body cover (see Chapter 7) **(see illustration)**. Disconnect the relay wiring connector **(see illustration)**.

4 Check for battery voltage at the black wire terminal in the connector with the ignition ON. If no voltage is present, check the wiring from the relay to the ignition switch for continuity.

5 If voltage was present, short between the terminals in the connector using a jumper wire. Turn the ignition ON and operate the turn signal switch, first to one side, then the other. If the turn signals come on (they won't flash), the relay is confirmed faulty.

6 If the turn signals do not come on, check the grey wire for continuity to the switch in the handlebar cover. Repair or replace the wiring or connectors as required.

7 If all is good so far, or if the turn signals work on one side but not the other, check the wiring between the switch and the turn signals themselves. Repair or renew the wiring or connectors as necessary.

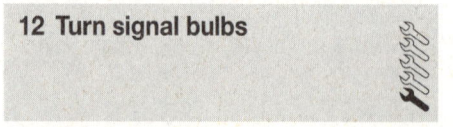

12 Turn signal bulbs

Note: *It is a good idea to use a paper towel or dry cloth when handling the new bulb to prevent injury if the bulb should break and to increase bulb life.*

Front

1 On 2003 to 2006 models undo the lens screws and detach the lens from the housing. Push the bulb into the holder and twist it anti-clockwise to remove it **(see illustration 12.2b)**. Fit the new bulb in reverse order. Make sure the seal is in good condition and correctly seated **(see illustration 12.2c)**. Do not over-tighten it as it is easy to strip the threads or crack the lens.

2 On 2007-on models undo the lens screw and detach the lens from the housing, noting how it fits **(see illustration)**. Push the bulb into the holder and twist it anti-clockwise to remove it **(see illustration)**. Fit the new bulb in reverse order. Make sure the seal is in good condition and correctly seated **(see illustration)**. Locate the lens tabs first then seat the lens and tighten the screw **(see illustration)** – do not over-tighten it as it is easy to strip the threads or crack the lens.

Rear

3 Undo the screw and remove the lens **(see illustration)**. Carefully push the bulb in and turn it anti-clockwise to release it **(see illustration)**.

4 Fit the new bulb in reverse order. Make sure the seal is in good condition and correctly seated **(see illustration)**. Locate the lens tab

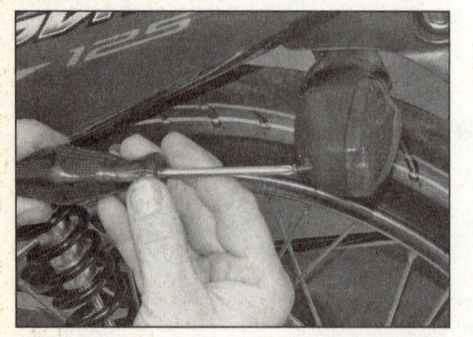

12.3a Undo the screw and remove the lens

12.3b Push the bulb in and turn it anti-clockwise to release it

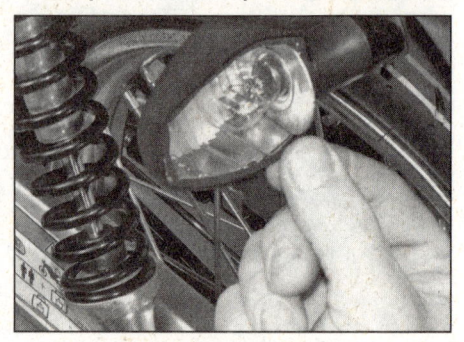

12.4a Check the seal

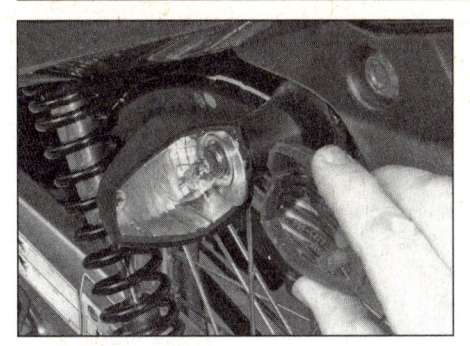

Electrical system 8•11

12.4b Make sure the tab locates correctly

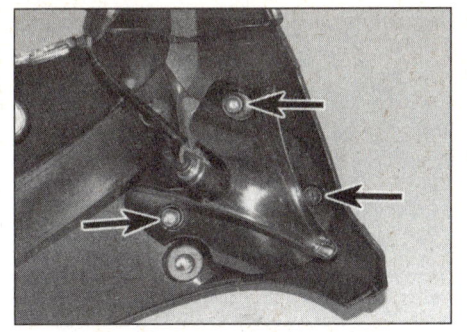

13.3 Undo the screws (arrowed) and remove the cover

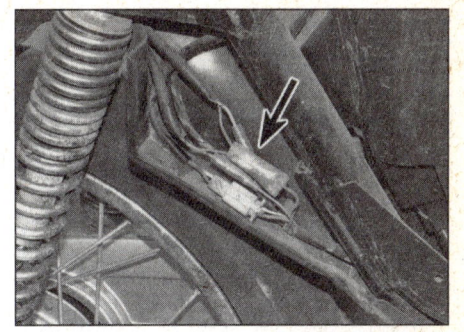

13.7a Rear turn signal wiring connectors (arrowed) – 2003 to 2006 models

first then seat the lens and tighten the screw **(see illustration)** – do not over-tighten it as it is easy to strip the threads or crack the lens.

13 Turn signal assemblies

Front turn signals

1 Remove the front cover(s) as required (see Chapter 7).
2 On 2003 to 2006 models disassemble the front cover panels to access the turn signal screws (see Chapter 7).
3 On 2007-on models remove the turn signal cover **(see illustration)**.
4 Undo the turn signal screws and remove it.
5 Installation is the reverse of removal. Check the operation of the turn signals.

Rear turn signals

6 On 2003 to 2006 models remove the body cover (see Chapter 7). On 2007-on models remove the rear body cover (see Chapter 7).
7 Disconnect the turn signal wiring connectors **(see illustrations)**. Feed the wiring through to the turn signal, noting its routing.
8 Unscrew the nut securing the stem on the inside of the rear mudguard **(see illustration)** – take care not to snag the wiring as you draw it through.
9 Installation is the reverse of removal. Check the operation of the turn signals.

13.7b Rear turn signal wiring connectors (arrowed) – 2007-on models

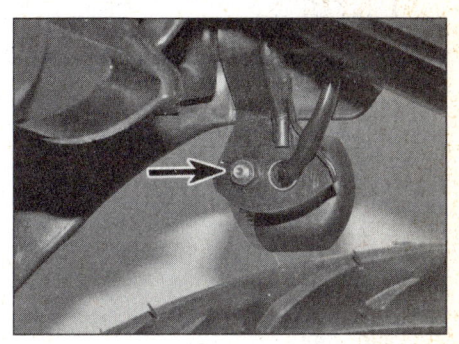

14 Brake light switches

Circuit check

Note: *Refer to electrical system fault finding in Section 2 and to the wiring diagram for your model at the end of this Chapter.*
1 Before checking the switches, and if not already done, check the brake light circuit (see Section 6).
2 The front brake light switch is mounted on the underside of the brake master cylinder – to access it remove the front handlebar cover (see Chapter 7). Disconnect the wiring connectors from the switch **(see illustration)**. Using a continuity tester, connect the probes to the terminals of the switch. With the brake

13.8 Unscrew the nut (arrowed)

lever at rest, there should be no continuity. With the brake lever applied, there should be continuity. If the switch does not behave as described, replace it with a new one.
3 The rear brake light switch is mounted behind the front of the footrest bracket on the right-hand side – to access the wiring connector, on 2003 to 2006 models remove the body cover, and on 2007-on models remove the rear body cover (see Chapter 7). Disconnect the wiring connector **(see illustrations)**. Using a continuity tester, connect the probes to the terminals on the switch side of the connector. With the brake pedal at rest, there should be no continuity. With the brake pedal applied, there should be continuity. If the switch does not behave as described, replace it with a new one, although check first that the spring has not broken and the switch is adjusted correctly (see Chapter 1, Section 10).

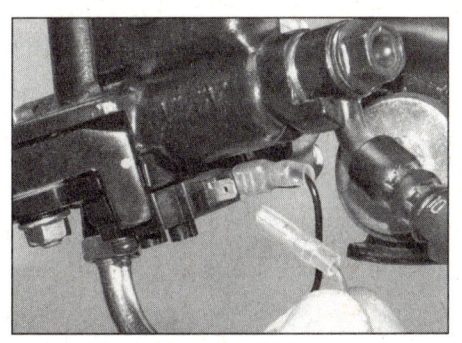

14.2 Disconnect the wiring connectors

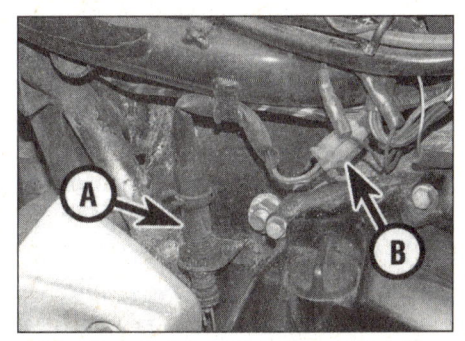

14.3a Rear brake switch (A) and its wiring connector (B) – 2003 to 2006 models

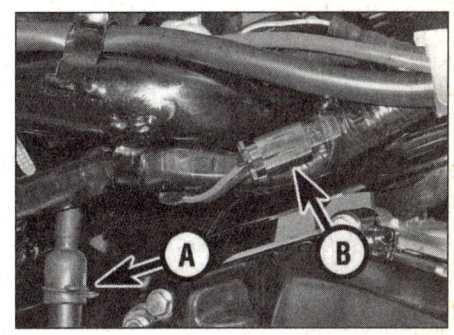

14.3b Rear brake switch (A) and its wiring connector (B) – 2007-on models

8•12 Electrical system

14.6 Undo the screw (arrowed)

14.9a Detach the spring (arrowed) from the pedal ...

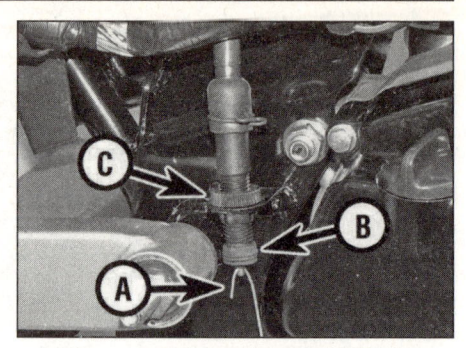

14.9b ... and from the switch (A), then remove the boot (B), hold the nut (C) and unscrew the switch

4 If the switches are good, check for voltage at the black wire terminal on the loom side of the connector with the ignition switch ON – there should be battery voltage. If there's no voltage present, check the wiring between the connector and the ignition switch (see the wiring diagrams at the end of this Chapter). If voltage is present, check the green/yellow wire for continuity to the brake light. Repair or renew the wiring as necessary.

Switch replacement

Front brake lever switch

5 The switch is mounted on the underside of the brake master cylinder – to access it remove the front handlebar cover (see Chapter 7). Disconnect the wiring connectors from the switch **(see illustration 14.2)**.
6 Undo the single screw securing the switch to the master cylinder and remove the switch **(see illustration)**.
7 Installation is the reverse of removal. Make sure the peg on the switch is correctly located in its hole before tightening the screw. The switch isn't adjustable.

Rear brake pedal switch

8 The rear brake light switch is mounted behind the front of the footrest bracket on the right-hand side – to access the wiring connector, on 2003 to 2006 models remove the body cover, and on 2007-on models remove the rear body cover (see Chapter 7). Disconnect the wiring connector and release the wiring from the guide **(see illustration 14.3a or b)**.
9 Detach the bottom of the switch spring from the brake pedal **(see illustration)**. Detach the top of the spring from the switch and remove the rubber boot, then hold the nut and thread the switch out **(see illustration)**. Squeeze the clips on the underside of the nut and draw it out of the bracket.
10 Installation is the reverse of removal. Make sure the brake light is activated just before the rear brake pedal takes effect. If adjustment is necessary, refer to Chapter 1, Section 10.

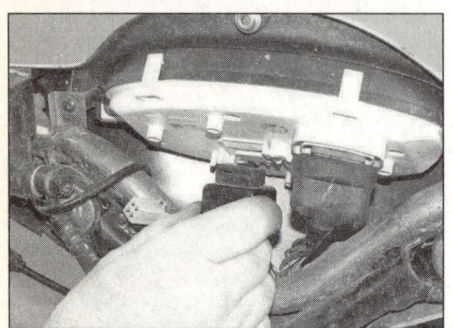

15 Instrument cluster

1 On 2003 to 2006 models remove the front handlebar cover (see Chapter 7). Displace the turn signal relay **(see illustration)**. Disconnect the instrument cluster wiring connector **(see illustration)**. Undo the instrument cluster screws and remove it from the rear cover **(see illustrations)**.
2 On 2007-on models remove the handlebar covers (see Chapter 7). Undo the instrument cluster screws and lift it out of the rear cover **(see illustration)**.
3 Installation is the reverse of removal. Make sure all wiring is correctly routed and all connectors are secure.

16 Instrument check

Note: *Refer to electrical system fault finding in Section 2 and to the wiring diagram for your model at the end of this Chapter.*

15.1a Displace the relay ...

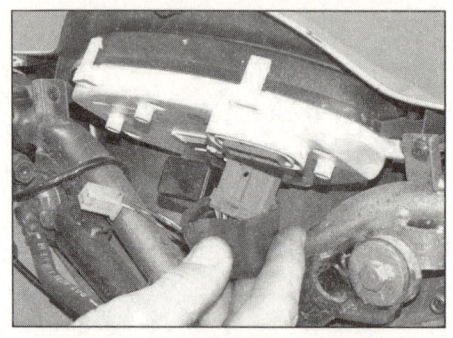

15.1b ... then disconnect the wiring connector

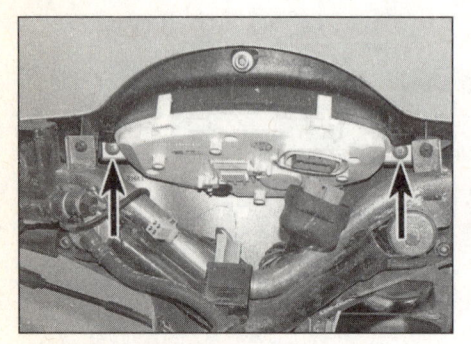

15.1c Undo the screws (arrowed) ...

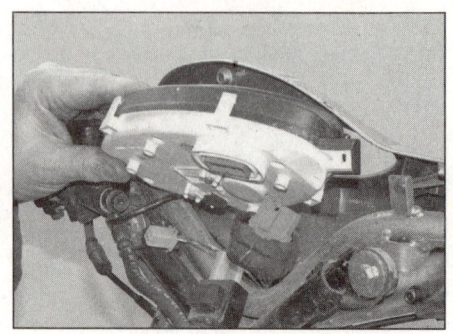

15.1d ... and remove the instruments

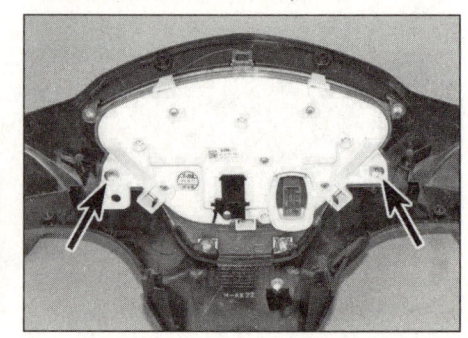

15.2 Undo the screws (arrowed)

Electrical system 8•13

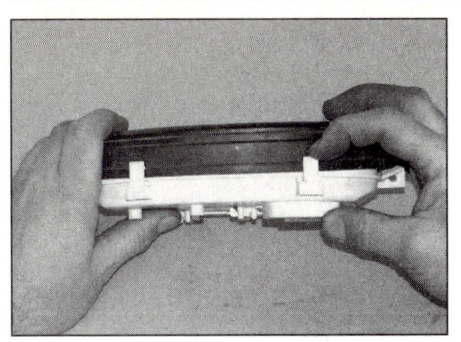

16.9a Release the clips . . .

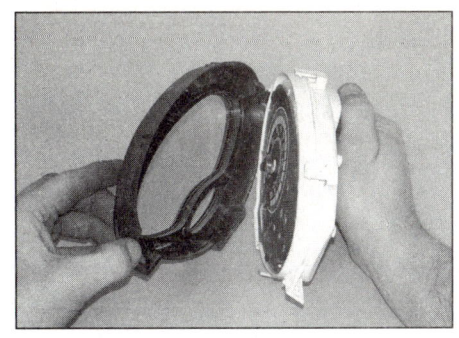

16.9b . . . and remove the cover

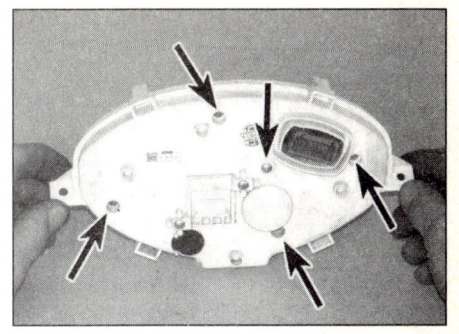

16.9c Undo the screws (arrowed) . . .

Power circuit check

1 If none of the instruments or displays are working, first check the fuses (see Section 5). Next remove the front handlebar cover (see Chapter 7), and check the instrument wiring connector has not come loose.

2 On 2003 to 2006 models disconnect the instrument cluster wiring connector **(see illustration 15.1b)**. Using a voltmeter and connecting the positive (+) probe to the wire specified and the negative (-) probe to a good earth on the frame, check there is battery voltage first at the red wire terminal in the loom side of the wiring connector with the ignition OFF, and then at the black wire terminal in the loom side of the wiring connector with the ignition ON. If there is no voltage in either wire, refer to the wiring diagram and check the wire all the way back from the connector for loose or broken connections or a damaged wire. If there is voltage, check for continuity to earth in the green wire.

3 On 2007-on models remove the rear handlebar cover (see Chapter 7). Using a voltmeter and connecting the positive (+) probe to the wire specified and the negative (-) probe to a good earth on the frame, check there is battery voltage first at the black/red wire terminal in the loom side of the instrument wiring connector with the ignition OFF, and then at the black/blue wire terminal in the loom side of the wiring connector with the ignition ON. If there is no voltage in either wire, refer to the wiring diagram and check the wire all the way back from the connector for loose or broken connections or a damaged wire. If there is voltage, check for continuity to earth in the green wire.

4 If all is good so far, refer to Section 3 and disconnect the battery negative (-) lead, wait a minute, then reconnect it and check the operation of the instruments. If there is still no life, replace the instrument cluster with a new one.

Instrument checks

5 If the speedometer does not work, check the speed sensor (see Section 18).

6 The fuel gauge and level sensor are covered in Chapter 3A or 3B.

7 Referring to Section 2 and to the wiring diagram at the end of this Chapter for your model, check the wiring and connectors between the relevant instrument or LED/bulb and its source for continuity and security.

Instrument replacement

8 Remove the instrument cluster (Section 15). Individual instruments are not available, but the instrument board is available separately from the front cover and housing.

9 On 2003 to 2006 models release the clips and detach the front cover **(see illustrations)**. Undo the screws on the back of the housing and carefully lift the instrument board out **(see illustrations)**.

10 On 2007-on models release the clips and detach the front cover and cover plate **(see illustrations)**. Undo the screws on the back of the housing and carefully lift the instrument board out **(see illustrations)**.

11 Installation is the reverse of removal. Make sure all the retaining clips locate correctly.

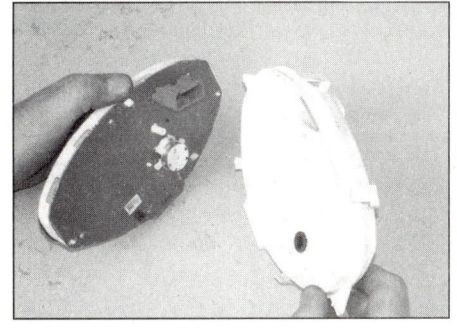

16.9d . . . and lift the instruments out

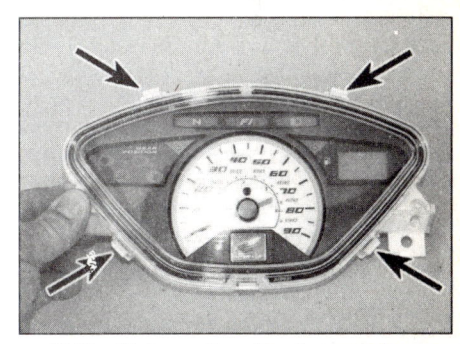

16.10a Release the clips (arrowed) . . .

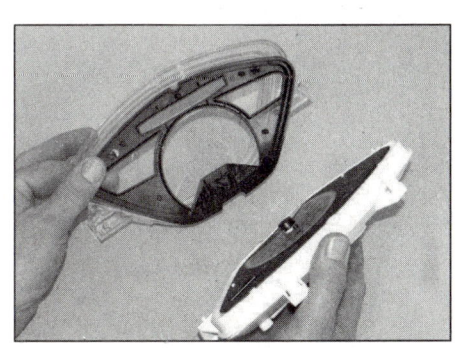

16.10b . . . and remove the cover and the plate

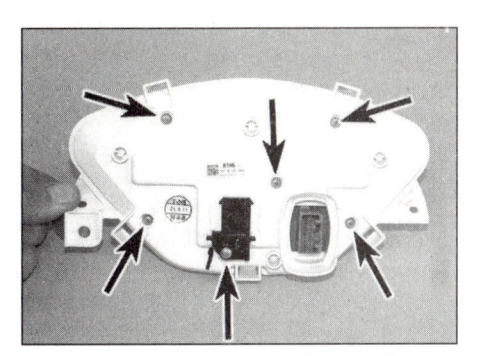

16.10c Undo the screws (arrowed) . . .

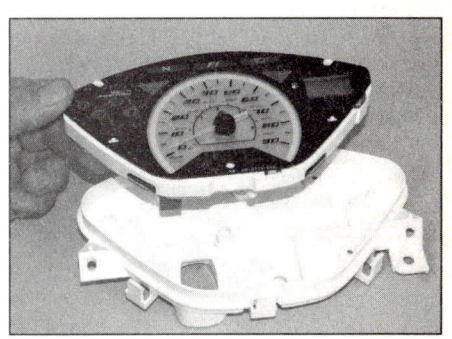

16.10d . . . and lift the instruments out

8•14 Electrical system

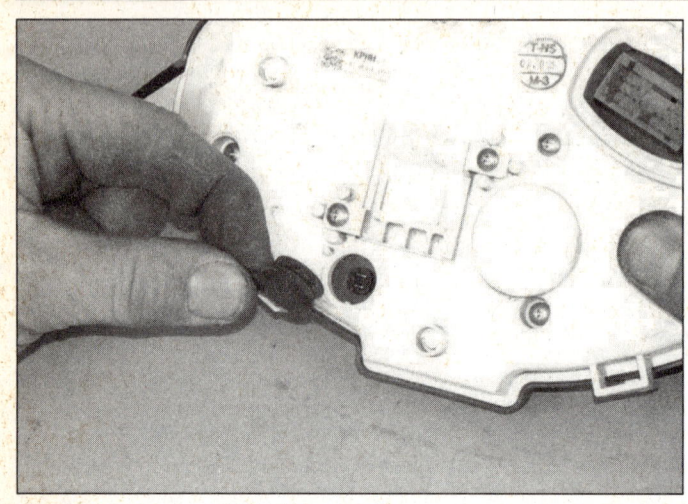

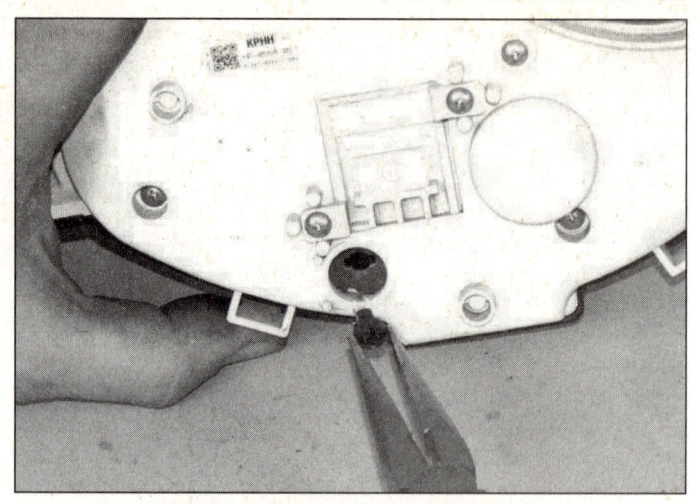

17.1a Remove the cap...

17.1b ...then remove the bulbholder

17 Instrument and warning lights

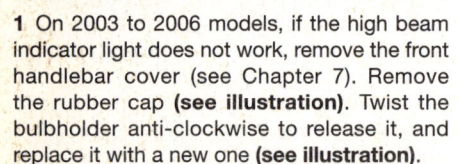

1 On 2003 to 2006 models, if the high beam indicator light does not work, remove the front handlebar cover (see Chapter 7). Remove the rubber cap **(see illustration)**. Twist the bulbholder anti-clockwise to release it, and replace it with a new one **(see illustration)**.
2 On 2003 to 2006 models all other instrument and indicator lights are LEDs, and on 2007-on models all instrument and indicator lights are LEDs. If one fails, and the cause is not due to the source that supplies its signal, and all wiring and connectors between the source and the instrument cluster are good, a new instrument board may have to be fitted – individual LEDs are not available (although an electronics technician may be able to help).

18 Speed sensor

1 If none of the instruments work refer to Section 16. If only the speedometer does not work, check the speed sensor and its circuit as follows:

Check

Note: *Refer to electrical system fault finding in Section 2 and to the wiring diagram for your model at the end of this Chapter.*

2 On 2003 to 2006 models remove the body cover and the front handlebar cover (see Chapter 7). Disconnect the speed sensor wiring connector **(see illustration)**. Disconnect the instrument wiring connector **(see illustration 15.1b)**.

3 On 2007-on models remove the rear body cover and both handlebar covers (see Chapter 7). Disconnect the speed sensor wiring connector **(see illustration)**.
4 Check for continuity first in the white/green wire and then in the pink wire between the speed sensor and instrument wiring connectors. If there is none, there is a break in the wire or a connector. Also check for continuity to earth in the green wire. Also check the wires between the connector and the speed sensor for breaks.
5 If the wiring is good, reconnect the instrument wiring connector (on 2007-on models tie the rear cover to the handlebars to do this). Using a voltmeter and connecting the positive (+) probe to the white/green wire terminal on the loom side of the sensor connector and the negative (-) probe to a good earth on the frame, check there is 5 volts with the ignition ON. If there isn't the instrument cluster is faulty.

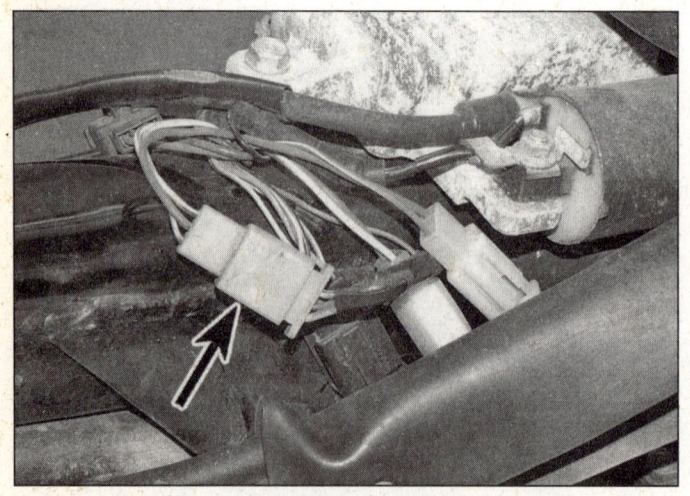

18.2 Speed sensor wiring connector (arrowed) – 2003 to 2006 models

18.3 Speed sensor wiring connector (arrowed) – 2007-on models

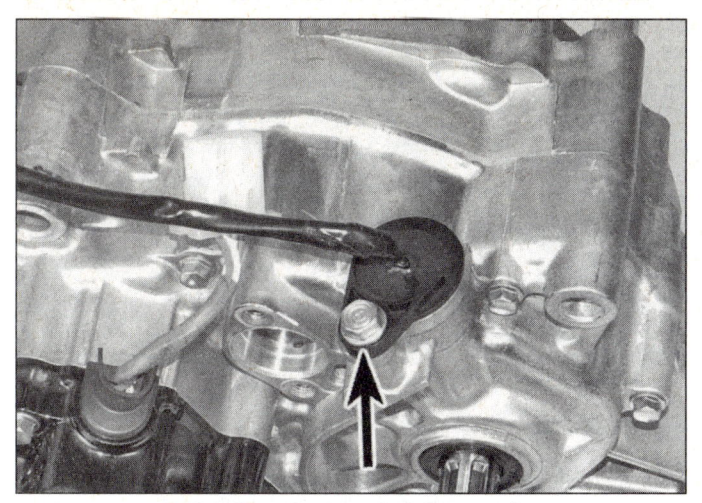

Electrical system 8•15

18.8 Speed sensor bolt (arrowed)

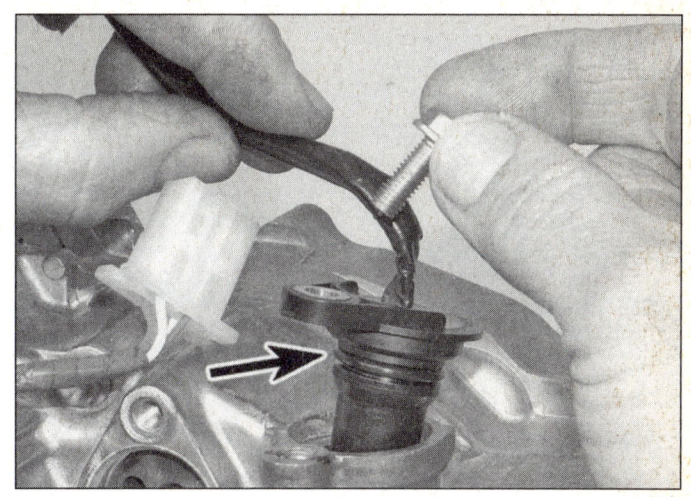

18.9 Lubricate the O-ring (arrowed)

6 If there is the correct voltage, reconnect the sensor wiring connector. Put the scooter on the centrestand, and make sure the transmission is in neutral. Check the voltage between the pink wire (+) and green wire (-) in the wiring connector, with the ignition ON, and turning the rear wheel by hand – a pulsing voltage of 0 to 5 volts should be present. If not, the sensor could be faulty – remove the sensor (see below) and make sure the head is clean and check for damage. If all is good replace the senor with a new one.

Removal and installation

7 Remove the engine (see Chapter 2).
8 Unscrew the bolt and remove the sensor **(see illustration)**.
9 Installation is the reverse of removal. Smear the O-ring with oil **(see illustration)**.

19 Ignition switch

⚠️ **Warning: To prevent the risk of short circuits, disconnect the battery negative (–) lead before making any ignition switch checks.**

1 Before checking the switch, check the fuses (see Section 5).

Check

Note: *Refer to electrical system fault finding in Section 2 and to the wiring diagram for your model at the end of this Chapter.*

2 On 2003 to 2006 models remove the front cover on the right-hand side, and on 2007-on models remove the top cover (see Chapter 7). Disconnect the ignition switch wiring connector(s) **(see illustrations)**.

3 On 2003 to 2006 models, using an ohmmeter or a continuity tester, check there is continuity between the red and red/black wire terminals in the switch side of the connectors with the ignition switch ON, and there is no continuity with it OFF.
4 On 2007-on models, using an ohmmeter or a continuity tester, check there is continuity between the red and black/blue wire terminals in the switch side of the connector with the ignition switch ON, and there is no continuity with it OFF. Repeat the check between the black/red and black wire terminals.
5 If the switch fails the test, replace it with a new one. If the switch is good, check for continuity in each wire and its connectors from the switch connector back to its source.

Removal and installation

6 Remove the steering stem (see Chapter 5).
7 Disconnect the ignition switch wiring connector(s) **(see illustration 19.2a or b)**.

19.2a Ignition switch wiring connectors (arrowed) – 2003 to 2006 models

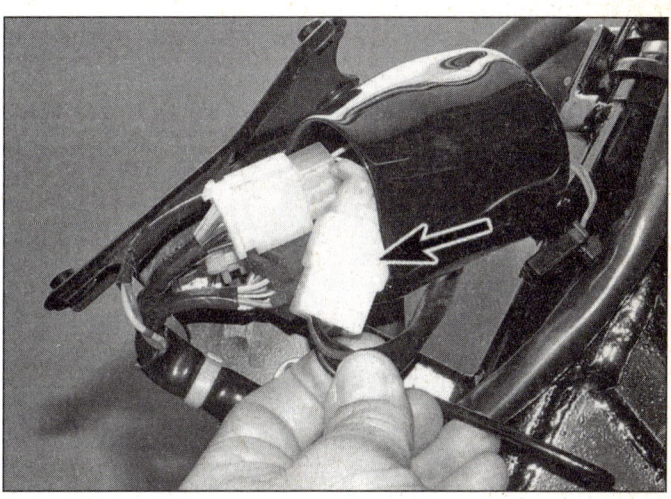

19.2b Ignition switch wiring connector (arrowed) – 2007-on models

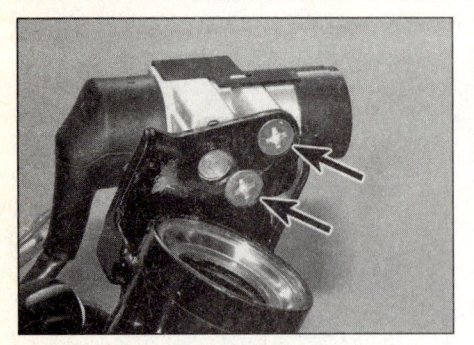

8•16 Electrical system

19.8 Undo the screws (arrowed) and remove the switch

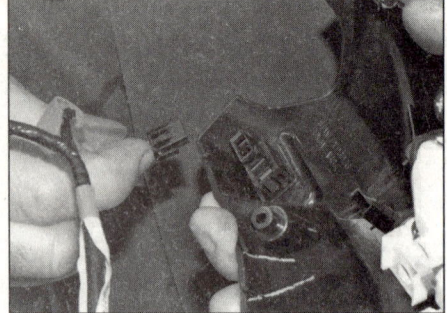

20.4a Disconnect the relevant wiring connector

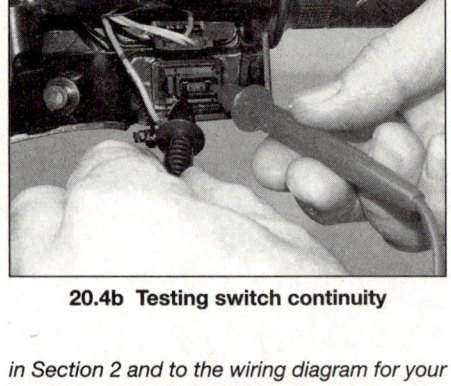

20.4b Testing switch continuity

8 Undo the switch screws and remove the switch **(see illustration)**.
9 Installation is the reverse of removal. Make sure the wiring is securely connected.

20 Handlebar switches

Note: *Refer to electrical system fault finding in Section 2 and to the wiring diagram for your model at the end of this Chapter.*

Check

1 Generally speaking, the switches are reliable and trouble-free. Most troubles, when they do occur, are caused by dirty or corroded contacts, but wear and breakage of internal parts is a possibility that should not be overlooked. If breakage does occur, the switch will have to be replaced with a new one, as individual parts are not available.
2 The switches can be checked for continuity using an ohmmeter or a continuity test light.
3 Remove the front handlebar cover (see Chapter 7). Check access to the switch you need to test, and if necessary also remove the rear handlebar cover.
4 Disconnect the wiring connector from the switch **(see illustration)** (not necessary if the rear cover has been removed). Check for continuity between the terminals of the switch with the switch in the various positions (i.e. switch off – no continuity, switch on – continuity) **(see illustration)** – see the wiring diagrams at the end of this Chapter. Continuity should exist between the terminals connected by a solid line on the diagram when the switch is in the indicated position.
5 If the continuity check indicates a problem exists, replace the switch with a new one.

Removal and installation

6 Remove the front handlebar cover (see Chapter 7). Check access to the switch you need to test, and if necessary also remove the rear handlebar cover. Disconnect the wiring connector from the switch (not necessary if the rear cover has been removed) **(see illustration 20.4a)**.
7 Release the switch tabs and withdraw it from the cover **(see illustration)**.
8 Installation is the reverse of removal. Make sure the switch tabs locate correctly in the cover.
9 Check the operation of the switches before riding the scooter.

21 Sidestand switch

1 The switch prevents the engine starting if the sidestand is down and the engine is in gear, and will stop the engine if the stand is extended while running in gear.

Check

Note: *Refer to Electrical System Fault Finding in Section 2 and to the wiring diagram for your model at the end of this Chapter.*

2 To access the wiring connector, on 2003 to 2006 models remove the body cover, and on 2007-on models remove the rear body cover (see Chapter 7). Disconnect the 3-pin wiring connector with the green/white and green wires **(see illustrations)**.
3 Check the operation of the switch using an ohmmeter or continuity test light. Connect the meter between the terminals on the switch side of the connector. With the sidestand up there should be continuity (zero resistance) between the terminals, and with the stand down there should be no continuity (infinite resistance). If not, replace the switch with a new one.
4 If the switch is good, connect the positive (+) probe of a voltmeter to the green/white wire terminal on the loom side of the connector and the negative (-) probe to a good earth on the frame and check for battery voltage. If there is voltage, check for continuity to earth in the green wire.
5 If the switch is good, check the other components and their wiring and connectors in the starter circuit (see the wiring diagrams at the end of this Chapter). Repair or replace the wiring as required.

Replacement

6 The sidestand switch is mounted on the stand pivot **(see illustration 21.8)**. On 2003 to 2006 models remove the body cover, and on 2007-on models remove the rear body cover (see Chapter 7). On all models remove the front sprocket cover (see Chapter 6).

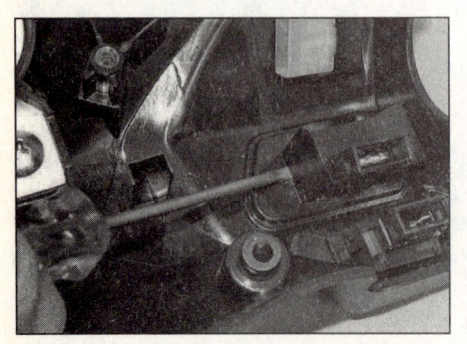

20.7 Press the tabs in to release a switch

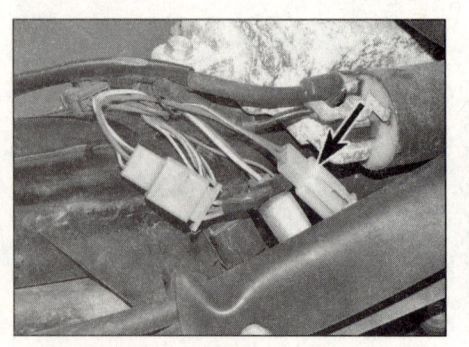

21.2a Sidestand switch wiring connector (arrowed) – 2003 to 2006 models

21.2b Sidestand switch wiring connector (arrowed) – 2007-on models

Electrical system 8•17

21.7 Free the wiring from the clips (arrowed)

21.8 Sidestand switch bolt (arrowed)

7 Disconnect the 3-pin wiring connector with the green/white and green wires **(see illustration 21.2a or b)**. Feed the wiring back to the switch, freeing it from the clips and noting its routing **(see illustration)**.

8 Unscrew the bolt and remove the switch, noting how it locates **(see illustration)**.

9 Fit the new switch onto the sidestand, making sure the pin locates in the hole, and the lug on the stand bracket locates into the cut-out in the switch body. Secure the switch with the bolt.

10 Feed the wiring back to its connector, making sure it is correctly routed and secured by the clips **(see illustration 21.7)**.

11 Reconnect the wiring connector and check the operation of the sidestand switch.

12 Install the sprocket cover and body cover(s).

22 Gear position switch

1 The switch, located in the left-hand side of the transmission casing behind the front sprocket cover, illuminates the neutral and gear position lights in the instrument cluster. The neutral function is also part of the starter safety circuit which prevents the engine from being started if the sidestand is down and the engine is in gear. The system will also cut the engine should the sidestand extend while the engine is running and in gear.

Check

Note: *Refer to Electrical System Fault Finding in Section 2 and to the wiring diagram for your model at the end of this Chapter.*

2 On 2003 to 2006 models remove the body cover, and on 2007-on models remove the rear body cover (see Chapter 7). Check the security of the wiring connector **(see illustrations)**.

3 With the ignition on, go through the gears and check the lights in the instrument cluster.

4 If some work but others don't, on 2003 to 2006 models remove the front handlebar cover and disconnect the instrument wiring connector **(see illustration 15.1b)**, and on 2007-on models remove both handlebar covers (see Chapter 7). Check the relevant individual wire(s) between the switch connector and the instrument wiring connector for continuity.

5 If all the wiring is good, check for continuity between each wire in the switch side of the wiring connector and the crankcase with the gear selected according to the wire colours as follows:

Neutral – light green/red
1st gear – yellow/red
2nd gear – black/blue
3rd gear – white/blue
4th gear – pink

If there is no continuity when there should be in any or all gears, remove the switch and check the contacts on the back of it for wear, and check the contact plunger and spring **(see illustration)**. If anything is obviously worn or damaged replace that part with a new one. If there is nothing obvious the fault is inside the switch, and so it must be replaced with a new one.

6 If the switch is good and all the wiring between it and the instrument are good, the instrument cluster board or one or more of its LEDs is faulty, in which case it must be replaced with a new one – refer to Section 16.

Removal

7 On 2003 to 2006 models remove the body cover, and on 2007-on models remove the rear body cover (see Chapter 7). On all models remove the front sprocket cover (see Chapter 6).

8 Disconnect the switch wiring connector **(see illustration 22.2a or b)**.

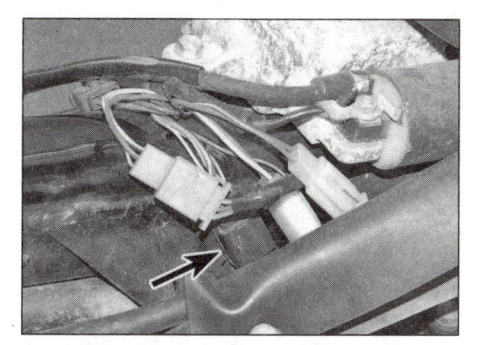

22.2a Gear position switch wiring connector (arrowed) – 2003 to 2006 models

22.2b Gear position switch wiring connector (arrowed) – 2007-on models

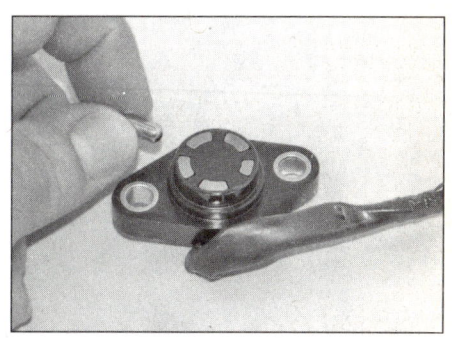

22.5 Check the switch contacts and plunger for wear, and make sure the spring is good

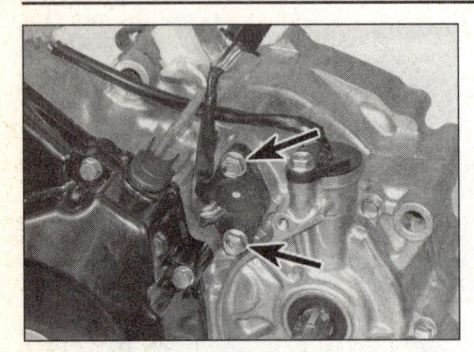

8•18 Electrical system

22.9a Unscrew the bolts (arrowed) and remove the switch . . .

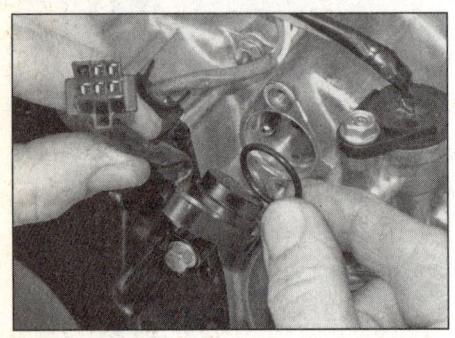

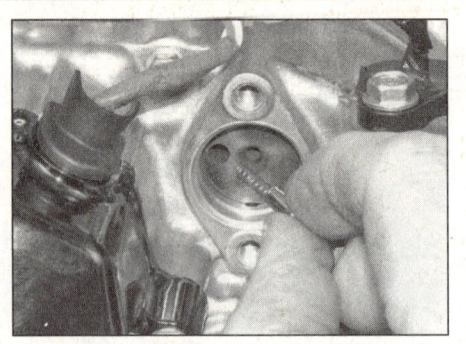

22.9b . . . and the plunger and spring

22.11 Fit the switch using a new O-ring

9 Clean the area around the switch. Unscrew the bolts and pull the switch from the crankcase **(see illustration)**. Note that there is a plunger with a spring behind it in a bore in the end of the selector drum that bears against the switch contacts – take care that they do not drop out as you remove the switch, then remove them for safekeeping **(see illustration)**. Remove the O-ring from the switch – a new one must be used.

Installation

10 Fit the spring and plunger into the offset hole in the end of the selector drum **(see illustration 22.9b)**.

11 Fit the switch using a new O-ring smeared with oil and tighten the bolts **(see illustration)**.
12 Connect the wiring.
13 Check the operation of the switch by going through the gears with the ignition on and checking the lights in the instrument cluster.
14 Install the sprocket cover and body cover(s).

23 Horn

Note: *Refer to Electrical System Fault Finding in Section 2 and to the wiring diagram for your model at the end of this Chapter.*

Check

1 Remove the top cover (see Chapter 7).
2 Disconnect the wiring connectors from the horn **(see illustration)**. Check them for loose wires. Using two jumper wires, apply voltage from a fully-charged 12V battery directly to the terminals on the horn. If the horn doesn't sound, replace it with a new one.
3 If the horn works, check for voltage at the light green wire connector with the ignition ON and the horn button pressed. If voltage is present, check the green wire for continuity to earth.
4 If no voltage was present, remove the front handlebar cover (see Chapter 7), and check the light green wire for continuity between the horn and the horn button. Next check that there is voltage at the black wire to the horn button with the ignition switch ON.
5 If all the wiring and connectors are good, the horn button is faulty (see Section 20).

Replacement

6 Remove the top cover (see Chapter 7).
7 Disconnect the wiring connectors from the horn **(see illustration 23.2)**. Unscrew the bolt and remove the horn.
8 Fit the horn and connect the wiring. Check that it works.

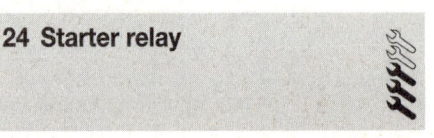

24 Starter relay

Check

1 If the starter circuit is faulty, first check the fuses (see Section 5).
2 The starter relay is located in the storage compartment under the seat. Unlock the seat and swing it up.
3 Release the storage box tabs, open the box and remove the toolkit **(see illustration 3.2)**.
4 Remove the relay cover **(see illustrations 3.3a and b)**.
5 Lift the main terminal cover and unscrew the bolt securing the starter motor lead **(see illustration)**. Position the lead away from the relay terminal. With the transmission in neutral, the ignition switch ON and the sidestand up, press the starter switch. The relay should be heard to click.
6 If the relay doesn't click, switch off the ignition, remove the relay as described below, and test it as follows.

23.2 Horn wiring connectors (A) and mounting bolt (B)

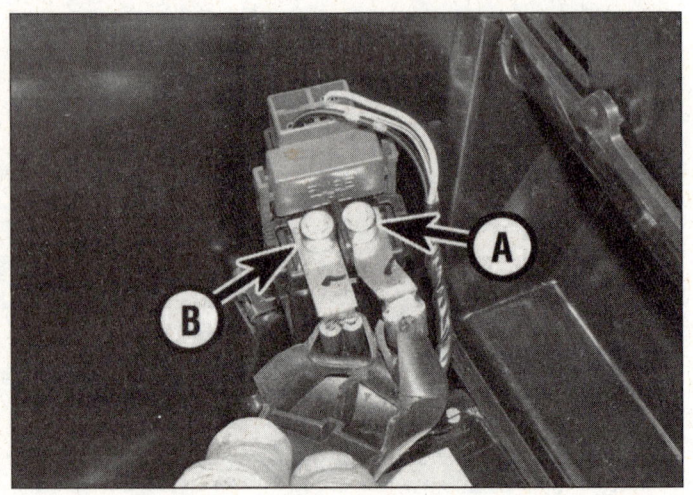

24.5 Lift the rubber cover to access the starter motor lead terminal (A) and battery lead terminal (B)

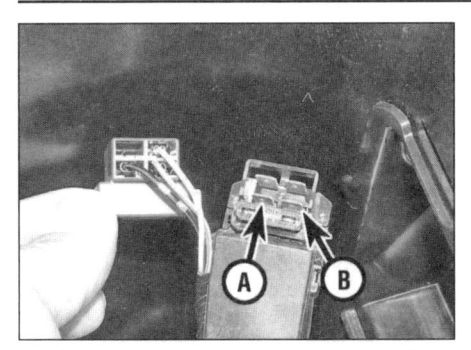

Electrical system 8•19

24.7 Black or black/blue terminal (A), yellow red terminal (B)

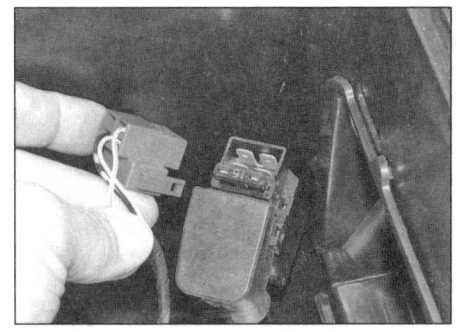

24.13a Disconnect the wiring connector...

24.13b ...then unscrew the lead bolts (arrowed)

7 Set a multimeter to the ohms x 1 scale and connect it across the relay's starter motor and battery lead terminals **(see illustration 24.5)**. There should be no continuity. Using a fully-charged 12 volt battery and two insulated jumper wires, connect the positive (+) terminal of the battery to the black or black/blue (according to model) wire terminal of the relay, and the negative (–) terminal to the yellow/red wire terminal of the relay **(see illustration)**. At this point the relay should be heard to click and the multimeter read 0 ohms (continuity). If this is the case the relay is proved good. If the relay does not click when battery voltage is applied and indicates no continuity (infinite resistance) across its terminals, it is faulty and must be replaced with a new one.

8 If the relay is good, check the security of the main heavy-gauge lead from the battery to the relay. Also check that the terminals and connectors at each end of the lead are tight and corrosion-free.

9 Next check for battery voltage at the black or black/blue wire terminal in the relay wiring connector with the ignition ON. If there is no voltage, check the wiring and connectors from the relay wiring connector to the switch.

10 If voltage is present, check that there is continuity to earth in the yellow/red wire, with the sidestand up and the starter button pressed. If not, check the wiring and connectors between the relay and the button, then between the button and the switch, then check the button and switch (see Sections 20 and 21).

Replacement

11 The starter relay is located in the storage compartment under the seat. Unlock the seat and swing it up.

12 Disconnect the battery, remembering to disconnect the negative (–) terminal first (see Section 3).

13 Disconnect the relay wiring connector **(see illustration)**. Lift the main terminal cover and unscrew the bolts securing the starter motor and battery leads to the relay and detach the leads **(see illustration)**. Remove the relay. If the relay is being replaced with a new one, remove the main fuse from the relay **(see illustration 5.7a)**.

14 Installation is the reverse of removal. Make sure the terminal bolts are securely tightened. Do not forget to fit the main fuse into the relay, if removed. Connect the negative (–) lead last when reconnecting the battery.

25 Starter motor removal and installation

Removal

1 Disconnect the battery negative (–) lead (see Section 3). The starter motor is mounted on the top of the crankcase.

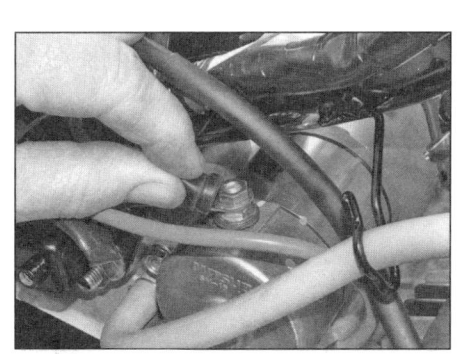

25.3 Pull back the terminal cover then unscrew the nut and detach the lead

25.5a Unscrew the two bolts (arrowed), noting the earth lead...

2 Remove the front cover on the right-hand side (see Chapter 7).

3 Peel back the rubber terminal cover on the starter motor **(see illustration)**. Unscrew the nut securing the starter lead to the motor and detach the lead.

4 On 2007-on models detach the crankcase breather hose **(see illustration)**.

5 Unscrew the two bolts securing the starter motor to the crankcase, noting the earth lead **(see illustration)**. Slide the starter motor out and remove it **(see illustration)**.

6 Remove the O-ring on the end of the starter motor – a new one must be used.

Installation

7 Fit a new O-ring onto the end of the starter

25.4 Release the clamp and detach the hose (arrowed)

25.5b ...and remove the motor

8•20 Electrical system

25.7 Fit a new O-ring and lubricate it

motor, making sure it is seated in its groove **(see illustration)**. Apply a smear of engine oil to the O-ring.
8 Manoeuvre the motor into position and slide it into the crankcase **(see illustration 25.5b)**. Ensure that the starter motor teeth mesh correctly with those of the starter idle/reduction gear. Fit the mounting bolts, not forgetting to secure the earth lead with the front bolt, and tighten them **(see illustration)**.
9 On 2007-on models connect the crankcase breather hose **(see illustration 25.4)**.
10 Connect the starter lead to the motor and secure it with the nut **(see illustration 25.3)**. Fit the rubber cover over the terminal.
11 Connect the battery negative (–) lead (see Section 3). Install the front cover (see Chapter 7).

26 Starter motor overhaul

Check

1 Remove the starter motor (see Section 25). Cover the body in some rag and clamp the motor in a soft-jawed vice – do not over-tighten it.
2 Using a fully-charged 12 volt battery and two insulated jumper wires, connect the positive (+) terminal of the battery to the protruding terminal on the starter motor, and the negative (–) terminal to one of the motor's mounting lugs. At this point the starter motor should spin. If this is the case the motor is proved good, though it is worth overhauling it if you suspect it of not working properly under load. If the motor does not spin, disassemble it for inspection.

Disassembly

3 Remove the starter motor (see Section 25).
4 Note any alignment marks between the main housing and the front and rear covers, or make your own if they aren't clear **(see illustration)**.
5 Unscrew the two long bolts, noting the O-rings, and remove the front cover **(see illustrations)**. Remove the tabbed washer from the cover and slide the washer and shim(s) from the front end of the armature (though they could be stuck to the tabbed washer), noting the number of shims and their correct fitted order **(see illustrations 26.25a and b)**.
6 Hold the rear cover and armature and draw the main housing off **(see illustration)** – it is held in by the attraction of the magnets, so some resistance will be felt Note the sealing ring on each end of the housing.
7 Withdraw the armature from the rear cover **(see illustration 26.23)**. Remove the shim(s) from the rear end of the armature or from in the rear cover noting how many and their correct fitted positions **(see illustration 26.21)**.
8 At this stage check for continuity between the terminal bolt and its brush – there should be continuity (zero resistance). Check for continuity between the terminal bolt and the cover – there should be no continuity (infinite resistance). Also check for continuity between the other brush and the rear cover – there should be continuity (zero resistance). If there is no continuity when there should be or *vice versa*, identify the faulty component and replace it with a new one.
9 On 2003 to 2006 models, unscrew the nut from the terminal bolt and remove the plain washer, the one large and two small insulating washers **(see illustration)**. Lift the brushplate out of the rear cover, noting how it locates, and withdraw the terminal bolt from the cover

25.8 Secure the earth lead with the front bolt

26.4 Note the alignment marks or make your own

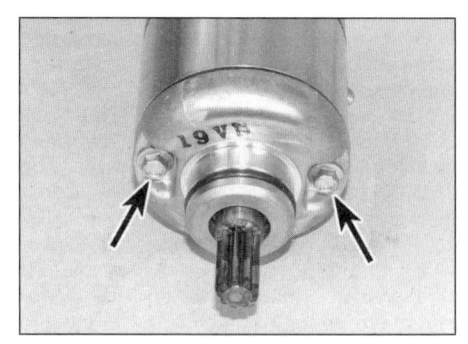

26.5a Unscrew the bolts (arrowed) . . .

26.5b . . . then remove the front cover

26.6 Remove the housing

26.9a Unscrew the nut and remove the plain washer and the large and small insulating washers . . .

Electrical system 8•21

26.9b ... then remove the brushplate

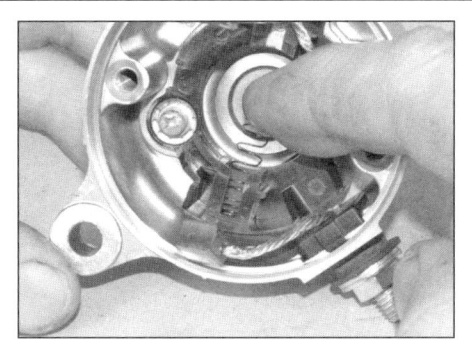

26.10a Slide the brushes out and remove the springs

26.10b Undo the screws and remove the negative brush ...

(see illustration). Remove the O-ring from the bolt and the insulator piece from the bolt or cover.

10 On 2007-on models slide the brushes out of their housings and remove the springs **(see illustration)**. Undo the two screws securing the brushplate, noting how one secures a brush, and remove the washers **(see illustration)**. Lift the brushplate out of the cover **(see illustration)**. Remove the two insulators **(see illustration)**. Unscrew the nut from the terminal bolt and remove the plain washer, the one large and two small insulating washers **(see illustration)**. Withdraw the terminal bolt from the cover, noting how it locates, and remove the O-ring from it **(see illustration)**. Remove the insulator piece from the cover **(see illustration 26.19a)**.

Inspection

11 The parts of the starter motor that are most likely to require attention are the brushes. Measure the length of each brush and compare the results to the length listed in this Chapter's Specifications **(see illustration)**. If either brush is worn beyond the service limit, fit a new set. If the brushes are not worn excessively, nor cracked, chipped, or otherwise damaged, they may be re-used. Check the brush springs for distortion and fatigue. Check the brushplate and insulators for damage.

12 Inspect the commutator bars on the armature for scoring, scratches and discoloration. The commutator can be cleaned and polished with crocus cloth, but do not use sandpaper or emery paper. After cleaning, wipe away any residue with a cloth soaked in electrical system cleaner or denatured alcohol.

13 Using an ohmmeter or a continuity test light, check for continuity between the commutator bars **(see illustration)**. Continuity should exist between each bar and all of the others. Also, check for continuity between the

26.10c ... the brushplate ...

26.10d ... and the insulators

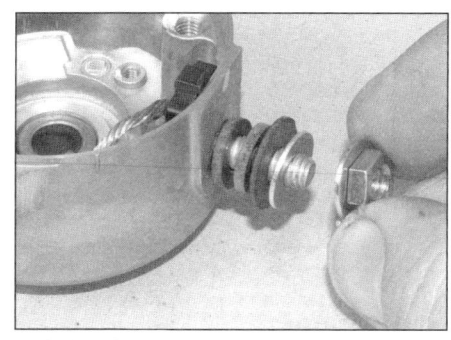

26.10e Unscrew the nut and remove the washers

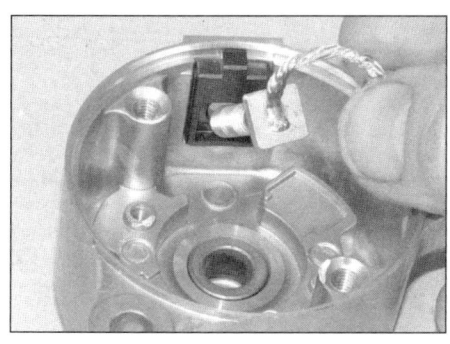

26.10f Remove the terminal bolt

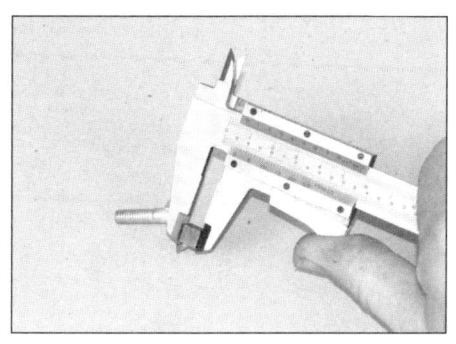

26.11 Measure each brush

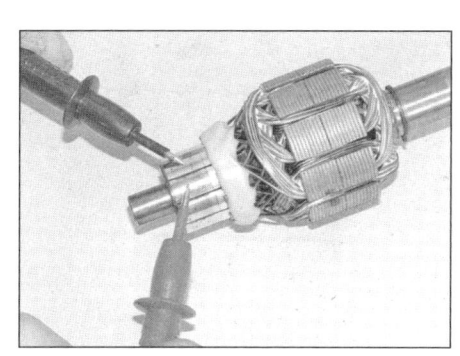

26.13a There should be continuity between the bars ...

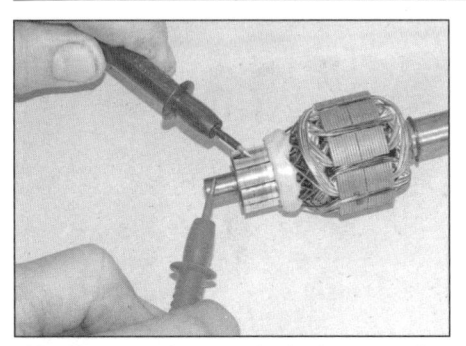

8•22 Electrical system

26.13b ... and no continuity between the bars and the shaft

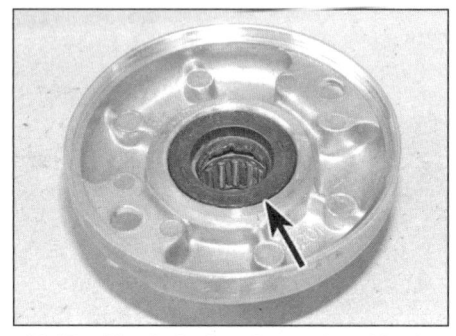

26.15a Check the bearing and seal in the front cover ...

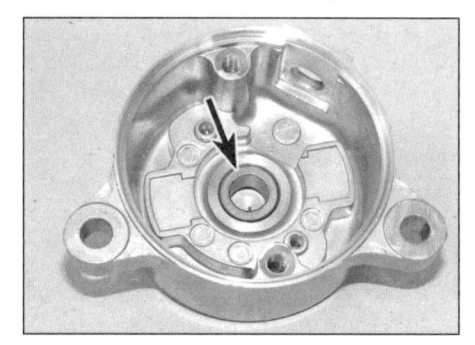

26.15b ... and the bush (arrowed) in the rear cover

26.19a Fit the insulator piece with the tab at the top and the recess facing in

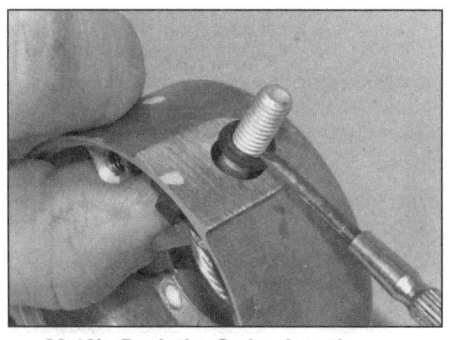

26.19b Push the O-ring into the gap between the bolt and the cover

26.19c Use crocodile clips ...

commutator bars and the armature shaft **(see illustration)**. There should be no continuity (infinite resistance) between the commutator and the shaft. If the checks indicate otherwise, the armature is defective and a new starter motor must be obtained – the armature is not available separately.

14 Check the front end of the armature shaft for worn, cracked, chipped and broken teeth. If the shaft is damaged or worn, a new starter motor must be obtained – the armature is not available separately.

15 Inspect the front and rear covers for signs of cracks or wear. Check the oil seal and the needle bearing in the front cover and the bush in the rear cover for wear and damage – the seal, bearing, bush and covers are not listed as being available separately so if necessary a new starter motor must be fitted **(see illustrations)**.

16 Inspect the magnets in the main housing and the housing itself for cracks.

17 Inspect the insulating washers, O-rings, and sealing rings for signs of damage, deformation and deterioration and replace them with new ones if necessary. Honda specify to use new O-rings and sealing rings whatever the condition of the old ones.

Reassembly

18 On 2003 to 2006 models make sure each brush is correctly located in its housing **(see illustration 26.9b)**. Fit the insulator piece onto the terminal bolt. Insert the terminal bolt through its hole and seat the brushplate in the rear cover, locating the tab in the groove. Fit the O-ring down over the bolt and press it into place between the bolt and the cover **(see illustration 26.19b)**. Slide the small insulating washers onto the terminal bolt, followed by the large insulating washer and the plain washer **(see illustration 26.9a)**. Fit the nut onto the terminal bolt and tighten it.

19 On 2007-on models fit the insulator piece into the rear cover **(see illustration)**. Insert the terminal bolt through its hole **(see illustration 26.10f)**. Fit the O-ring down over the bolt and press it into place between the bolt and the cover **(see illustration)**. Slide the small insulating washers onto the terminal bolt, followed by the large insulating washer and the plain washer **(see illustration 26.10e)**. Fit the nut onto the terminal bolt and tighten it securely. Fit the brush insulators into the rear cover **(see illustration 26.10d)**. Fit the brushplate, making sure it locates correctly, then fit the washers and the screws, not forgetting to secure the brush **(see illustrations 26.10c and b)**. Slide the springs and brushes back into position in their housings **(see illustration 26.10a)**. Push the brushes into the housing and secure them there using crocodile clips or something similar, as shown **(see illustrations)**.

20 At this stage check for continuity between the terminal bolt and the cover – there should be no continuity (infinite resistance). Also check for continuity between the negative brush and the rear cover – there should be continuity (zero resistance). If there is no continuity when there should be or *vice versa*, identify the faulty component and replace it with a new one.

21 Fit the shim(s) onto the rear of the armature shaft **(see illustration)**. Apply a smear of grease to the end of the shaft.

26.19d ... to hold the brushes back

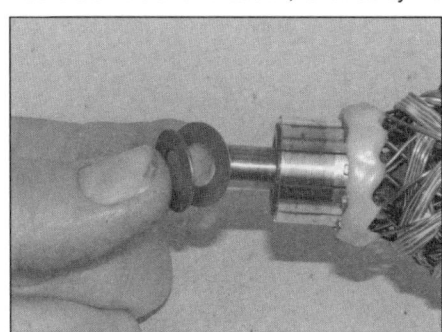

26.21 Fit the shim(s) onto the shaft

Electrical system 8•23

26.23 Fit the armature into the rear cover

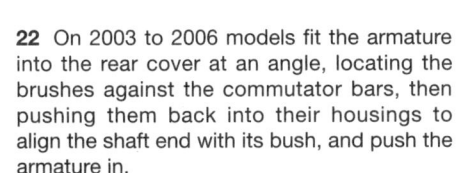

26.24 Fit the sealing rings

26.25a Fit the tabbed washer . . .

22 On 2003 to 2006 models fit the armature into the rear cover at an angle, locating the brushes against the commutator bars, then pushing them back into their housings to align the shaft end with its bush, and push the armature in.

23 On 2007-on models insert the armature into the rear cover so that the shaft end locates in its bush, then release the brushes so they locate against the commutator **(see illustration)**.

24 Fit the sealing rings onto the main housing **(see illustration)**. Grasp both the armature and the rear cover in one hand and hold them together – this will prevent the armature being drawn out by the magnets in the housing. Note however that you should take care not to let the housing be drawn forcibly onto the armature by the magnets. Carefully allow the housing to be drawn onto the armature, making sure the end with the cut-out faces the rear cover, that the cut-out locates over the tab, and the marks between the cover and housing align (Step 4) **(see illustration 26.6)**.

25 Apply a smear of grease to the front cover oil seal lip. Fit the tabbed washer into the cover so that its teeth are correctly located with the cover ribs **(see illustration)**. Slide the shim(s) onto the front end of the armature shaft then fit the washer **(see illustration)**.

26 Slide the front cover into position, aligning the marks **(see illustration 26.5b)**.

27 Check the marks made on removal are correctly aligned then fit the long bolts, not forgetting the O-rings, and tighten them **(see illustration)**.

28 Install the starter motor (see Section 25).

27 Charging system testing

1 If the performance of the charging system is suspect, the system as a whole should be checked first, followed by testing of the individual components. **Note:** *Before beginning the checks, make sure the battery is fully charged and that all system connections are clean and tight.*

2 Checking the output of the charging system and the performance of the various components

26.25b . . . and the shim(s) and washer

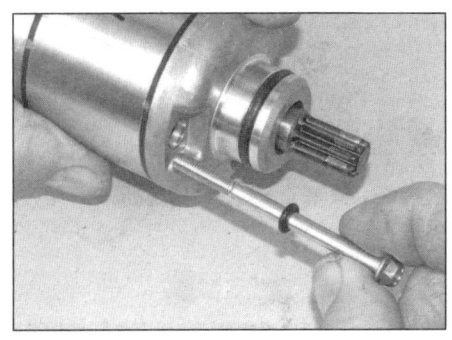

within the charging system requires the use of a multimeter with voltage, current, and resistance checking facilities. If a multimeter is not available, the job of checking the charging system should be left to a Honda dealer.

3 When making the checks, follow the procedures carefully to prevent incorrect connections or short circuits resulting in irreparable damage to electrical system components.

Regulated output test

4 Start the engine and warm it up. Refer to Section 3 to access the battery.

5 To check the regulated (DC) voltage output, allow the engine to idle with the headlight main beam (HI) turned ON. Connect a multimeter set to the 0-20 volts DC scale across the terminals of the battery with the positive (+) meter probe to battery positive (+) terminal and the negative (-) meter probe to battery negative (-) terminal (see Section 3) **(see illustration)**.

6 Slowly increase the engine speed to 5000 rpm and note the reading obtained. Compare the result with the Specification at the beginning of this Chapter. If the regulated voltage output is outside the specification, check the alternator and the regulator (see Sections 28 and 29).

HAYNES HINT *Clues to a faulty regulator are constantly blowing bulbs, with brightness varying considerably with engine speed, and battery overheating.*

26.27 Fit the long bolts with their O-rings and tighten them

Leakage test

Caution: *Always connect an ammeter in series, never in parallel with the battery, otherwise it will be damaged. Do not turn the ignition ON or operate the starter motor when the ammeter is connected – a sudden surge in current will blow the meter's fuse.*

7 Ensure the ignition is OFF, then disconnect the battery negative (-) lead (see Section 3).

8 Set the multimeter to the Amps function – always set the meter to a high amps range initially and then bring it down to the mA (milli Amps) range to avoid blowing the meter's fuse if there is a high current flow in the circuit.

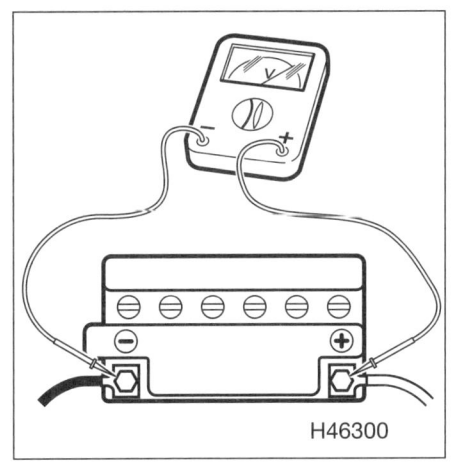

27.5 Checking the charging rate – connect the meter as shown

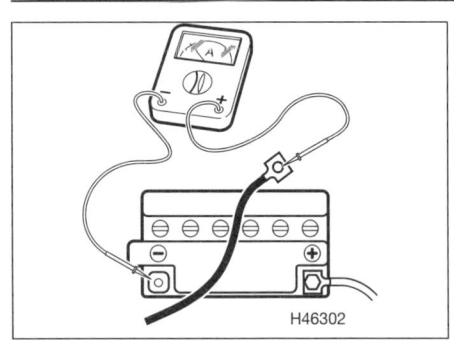

8•24 Electrical system

27.8 Checking the charging system leakage rate – connect the meter as shown

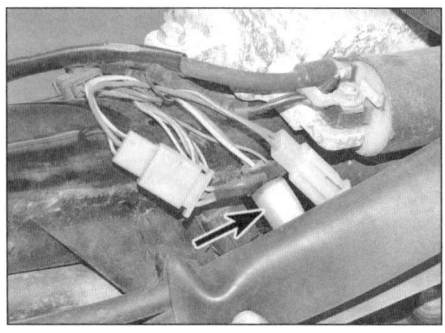

Connect the negative (-) probe of the meter to the battery negative (-) terminal, and positive (+) probe to the disconnected negative (-) lead **(see illustration)**.

9 Battery current leakage should not exceed the maximum limit (see Specifications).

10 If a higher leakage rate is shown there is a short circuit somewhere. Refer to *Wiring Diagrams* at the end of this Chapter and systematically disconnect individual electrical connectors and components until the rate drops, thereby identifying source.

11 Disconnect the meter and reconnect the battery negative (-) lead.

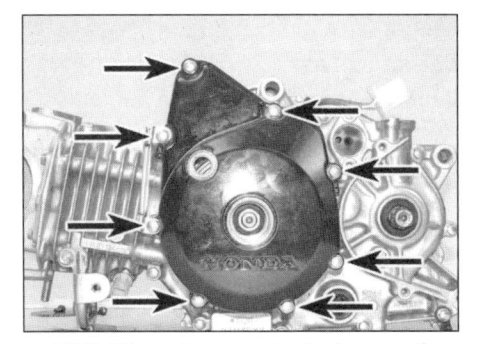

28.7 Alternator cover bolts (arrowed)

28.2a Alternator wiring connector (arrowed) – 2003 to 2006 models

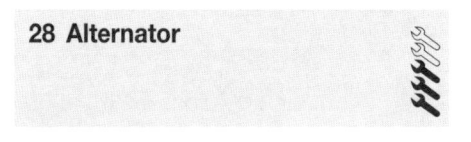

28 Alternator

Check

1 On 2003 to 2006 models remove the body cover, and on 2007-on models remove the rear body cover (see Chapter 7).

2 Trace the alternator wiring from the cover on the left-hand side of the engine and disconnect it at the white wiring connector (2-pin on 2003 to 2006 models and 4-pin on 2007-on models) with the white and green wires **(see illustrations)**. Check the connector terminals for corrosion and security.

3 Using a multimeter set to the ohms x 1 (ohmmeter) scale measure the resistance between the white and green wires on the alternator side of the connector, then check for continuity between the white wire and ground (earth). If the stator coil windings are in good condition the reading should be within the range shown in the Specifications at the start of this Chapter, and there should be no continuity (infinite resistance) between the white wire terminal and ground (earth). If not, the alternator stator coil assembly is at fault and should be replaced with a new one. **Note:** *Before condemning the stator coils, check the fault is not*

28.2b Alternator wiring connector (arrowed) – 2007-on models

due to damaged wiring between the connector and the coils.

Removal

4 Remove the front covers, and on 2003 to 2006 models remove the body cover, and on 2007-on models remove the rear body cover (see Chapter 7).

5 Drain the engine oil (see Chapter 1). Remove the gearchange lever and the front sprocket cover, and if required for better access the rider's footrest assembly (see Chapter 5).

6 Trace the wiring from the alternator cover and disconnect it at the connector(s) **(see illustration 28.2a or b)**.

7 Working in a criss-cross pattern, evenly slacken the alternator cover bolts, noting the positions of the guide and the two shorter bolts **(see illustration)**. Draw the cover off the engine, noting that it will be restrained by the force of the rotor magnets, and be prepared to catch any residual oil. Remove and discard the gasket **(see illustration 28.21a)**. Remove the dowels from either the cover or the crankcase if loose.

8 Draw the idle/reduction gear shaft out of its bore and remove it with the collar and gear **(see illustration)**.

9 To remove the rotor nut it is necessary to stop the rotor from turning using a commercially available rotor strap **(see illustration)**. With the

28.8 Remove the shaft/collar/gear together

28.9 Using a strap to hold the rotor while unscrewing the bolt

Electrical system 8•25

28.10a Thread the puller onto the rotor . . .

28.10b . . . then hold the puller and turn the bolt

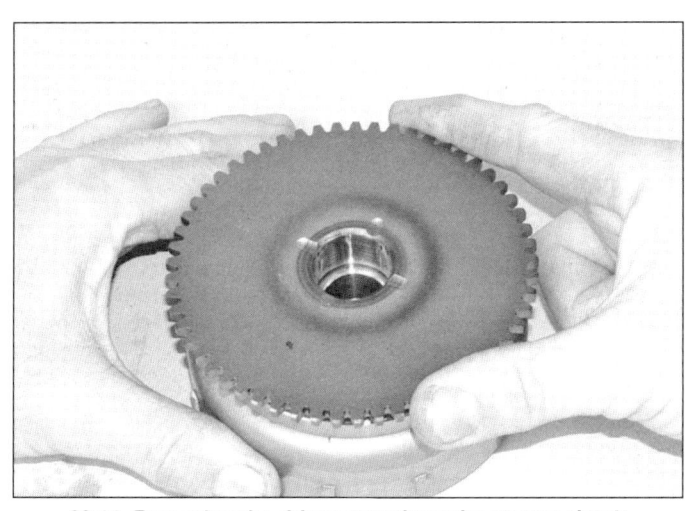

28.11 Removing the driven gear from the starter clutch

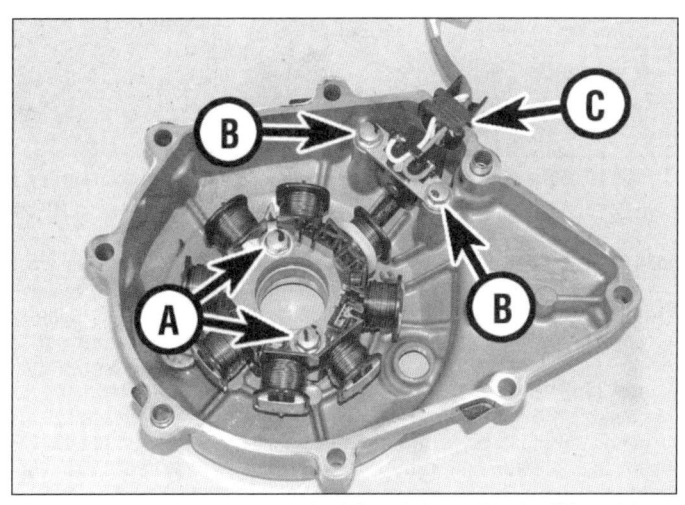

28.12 Unscrew the stator bolts (A) and the coil bolts (B) and free the grommet (C)

rotor held, unscrew the nut and remove the washer. Thread the nut back on until it is flush with the end of the shaft to prevent spread when the puller is tightened.

10 To remove the rotor from the shaft it is necessary to use a rotor puller (Honda part No.07KMC-HE00100, or its commercially available equlvalent with a 30 mm internal thread). Thread the rotor puller onto the centre of the rotor, then counter-hold it using a spanner on the flats and tighten the bolt in its centre until the rotor is displaced from the shaft **(see illustrations)**.

11 Remove the starter driven gear from the starter clutch on the back of the rotor, turning it anti-clockwise as you do **(see illustration)**, or if it did not come away with the rotor, slide it off the crankshaft, followed by the needle bearing **(see illustrations 28.16b and a)**. If required detach the starter clutch from the rotor (see Chapter 2). Remove the Woodruff key from its slot in the crankcase if it is loose **(see illustration 28.15)**.

12 If required unscrew the stator and pulse generator coil bolts and remove them from the cover, noting the wiring guide on 2003 to 2006 models, and how the rubber wiring grommet fits **(see illustration)**.

13 Clean all old sealant and gasket from the cover and crankcase mating surfaces and grommet.

Installation

14 If removed fit the stator and pulse generator coil into the cover, aligning the rubber wiring grommet with the groove, and not forgetting the wiring guide on 2003 to 2006 models **(see illustration 26.12)**. Tighten the bolts to the torque setting specified at the beginning of the Chapter. Apply a suitable sealant to the wiring grommet, then press it into the cut-out in the cover.

15 If removed fit the starter clutch onto the rotor (see Chapter 2). If removed fit the Woodruff key into its slot in the crankshaft **(see illustration)**.

16 Lubricate the flat section of the crankshaft with oil. Slide the needle bearing onto the flat

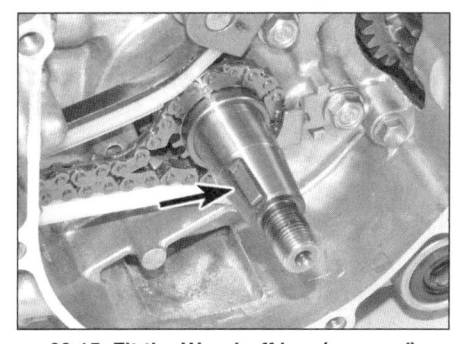

28.15 Fit the Woodruff key (arrowed)

8•26 Electrical system

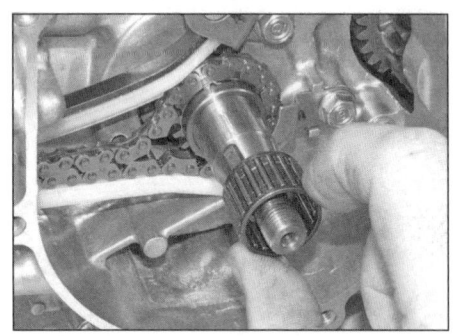

28.16a Slide the bearing onto the shaft . . .

28.16b . . . and the gear onto the bearing

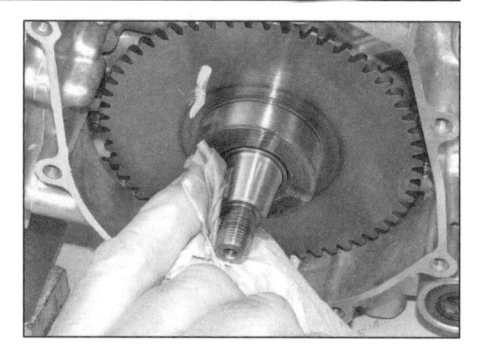

28.17 Make sure the tapered section is completely free of oil and grease

28.18 Slide the rotor onto the shaft

28.19a Lubricate the nut then install it with its washer . . .

28.19b . . . and tighten it to the specified torque

section, then slide the starter driven gear onto the bearing **(see illustrations)**.

17 Clean the tapered end of the crankshaft and the corresponding mating surface on the inside of the rotor with a suitable solvent **(see illustration)**.

18 Make sure that no metal objects have attached themselves to the magnet on the inside of the rotor. Slide the rotor onto the shaft, making sure the groove on the inside of the rotor is aligned with and fits over the Woodruff key **(see illustration)**. Make sure the Woodruff key does not become dislodged when installing the rotor. Turn the starter driven gear clockwise as you look at it to spread the starter clutch rollers and allow the hub to enter.

19 Apply some clean oil to the rotor nut threads and the underside of the head. Fit the nut with its washer and tighten it to the torque setting specified at the beginning of the Chapter, using the method employed on removal to prevent the rotor from turning **(see illustrations)**.

20 Lubricate the idle/reduction gear shaft with clean engine oil, then slide the gear and collar onto it with the smaller pinion facing the inner end of the shaft. Locate the assembly, meshing the small inner gear teeth with those on the driven gear and the larger outer gear teeth with those of the starter motor shaft, and insert the shaft into its bore in the crankcase **(see illustration 28.8)**.

21 Fit the dowels into the crankcase if removed and locate a new gasket onto the dowels **(see illustration)**. Smear a suitable sealant onto the wiring grommet **(see illustration 28.12)**. Install the alternator cover, noting that the rotor magnets will forcibly draw the cover/stator on, making sure it locates onto the dowels **(see illustration)**. Fit the cover bolts, not forgetting the guide, and tighten them evenly in a criss-cross sequence **(see illustration)**.

22 Reconnect the wiring at the connector(s).

29 Regulator/rectifier and power relay

Regulator/rectifier – 2003 to 2006 models

Check

1 Remove the body cover (see Chapter 7).

28.21a Fit the new gasket onto the dowels (arrowed) . . .

28.21b . . . then fit the cover

28.21c Do not forget the guide – 2007-on type shown, earlier type fits with bottom bolt shown

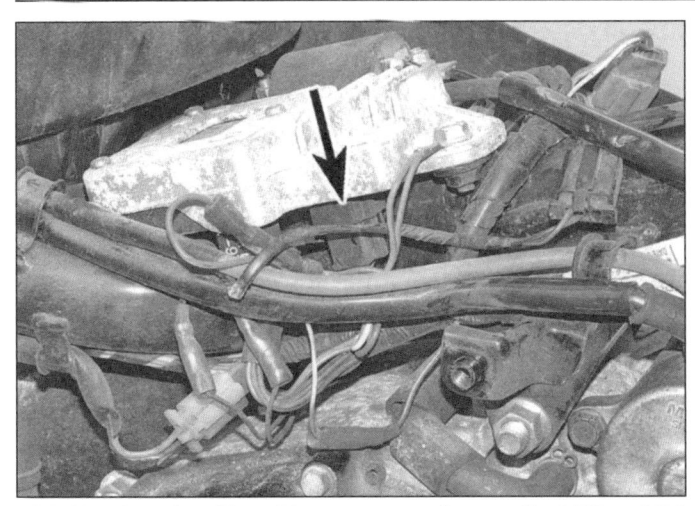

Electrical system 8•27

29.2 Regulator/rectifier wiring connector (arrowed) – 2003 to 2006 models

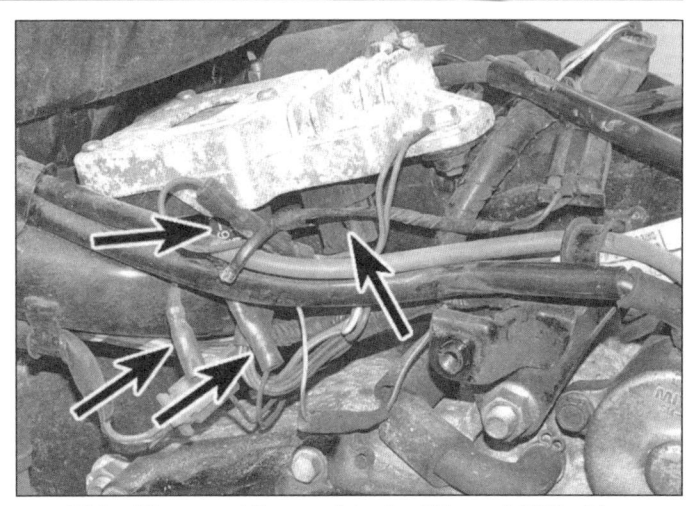

29.9a Disconnect the regulator/rectifier and ECU wiring connectors (arrowed) . . .

2 Disconnect the regulator/rectifier wiring connector **(see illustration)**. Check the connector terminals for corrosion and security.
3 Set the multimeter to the 0-20 DC volts setting. Connect the meter positive (+) probe to the red wire terminal on the loom side of the connector and the negative (–) probe to a suitable ground (earth) and check for voltage. Full battery voltage should be present at all times.
4 Switch the multimeter to the resistance (ohms) scale. Check for continuity between the green wire terminal on the loom side of the connector and ground (earth). There should be continuity in each terminal.
5 Set the multimeter to the ohms x 1 (ohmmeter) scale and measure the resistance between the white and green wire terminals on the loom side of the connector. The reading should be within the range shown in the Specifications for the alternator stator coil at the start of this Chapter, and there should be no continuity (infinite resistance) between the white wire terminal and ground (earth).

6 If the above checks do not provide the expected results check the wiring and connectors between the battery, regulator/rectifier and alternator for shorts, breaks, and loose or corroded terminals (see the wiring diagram at the end of this chapter).
7 If the wiring is good, the regulator/rectifier unit is probably faulty. Honda provide no test data for the unit itself. Take it to a Honda dealer for confirmation of its condition before replacing it with a new one.

> **HAYNES HiNT** *Clues to a faulty regulator are constantly blowing bulbs, with brightness varying considerably with engine speed, and battery overheating.*

Removal and installation

8 Remove the body cover (see Chapter 7).
9 Disconnect the regulator/rectifier and ECU wiring connectors and the two bullet connectors to the ECU **(see illustration)**. Unscrew the two bolts, noting the earth wires, and remove the regulator/rectifier **(see illustration)**. Undo the screws securing the ECU and remove it.
10 Installation is the reverse of removal – do not forget to secure the earth wires. Connect the wiring connectors.

Regulator/rectifier – 2007-on models

Check

11 Remove the rear body cover (see Chapter 7).
12 Disconnect the regulator/rectifier wiring connector **(see illustration)**. Check the connector terminals for corrosion and security.
13 Set the multimeter to the 0-20 DC volts setting. Connect the meter positive (+) probe to the white/red wire terminal on the loom side of the connector and the negative (–) probe to a suitable ground (earth) and check for

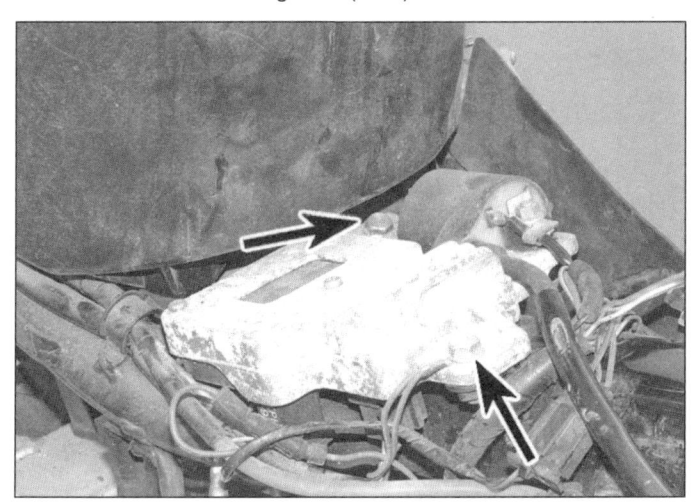

29.9b . . . then unscrew the bolts, noting the earth wires

29.12 Regulator/rectifier wiring connector (arrowed) – 2007-on models

8•28 Electrical system

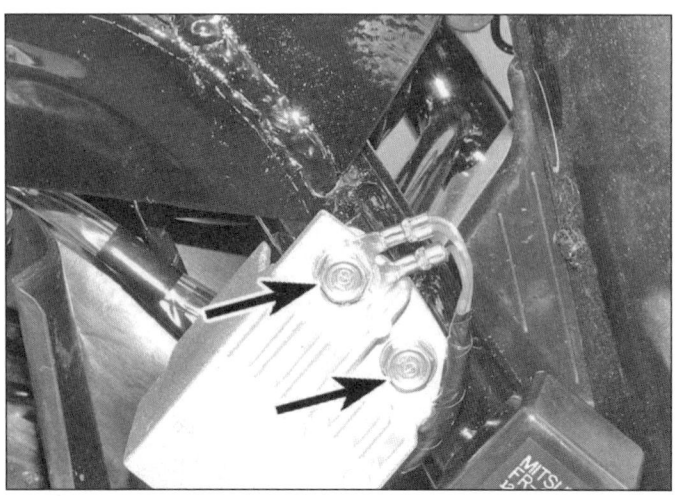

29.21 Regulator/rectifier bolts (arrowed) – note the earth wires

29.24 Power relay

voltage. Full battery voltage should be present at all times.

14 Switch the multimeter to the resistance (ohms) scale. Check for continuity between the green wire terminal on the loom side of the connector and ground (earth). There should be continuity in each terminal.

15 Set the multimeter to the ohms x 1 (ohmmeter) scale and measure the resistance between the white and green wire terminals on the loom side of the connector. The reading should be within the range shown in the Specifications for the alternator stator coil at the start of this Chapter, and there should be no continuity (infinite resistance) between the white wire terminal and ground (earth).

16 Reconnect the wiring connector and check there is battery voltage at the red wire terminal in the connector with the ignition ON, and then at the red/yellow wire terminal with the ignition ON.

17 If there is a problem with the lighting system (either it is weak or bulbs are constantly blowing), set the multimeter to the 0-20 AC volts setting and check there is 11 to 15 volts AC at the yellow wire terminal in the connector with the connector connected and the engine running. If there isn't the regulator/rectifier is faulty. If there is, refer to Section 6 and perform the checks described.

18 If the above checks do not provide the expected results check the wiring and connectors between the battery, regulator/rectifier and alternator for shorts, breaks, and loose or corroded terminals (see the wiring diagram at the end of this chapter). Also check the wiring to the power relay, and check the relay itself (see below).

19 If the wiring and the relay are good, the regulator/rectifier unit is probably faulty. Honda provide no test data for the unit itself. Take it to a Honda dealer for confirmation of its condition before replacing it with a new one.

Removal and installation

20 Remove the rear body cover (see Chapter 7).

21 Disconnect the regulator/rectifier wiring connector **(see illustration 29.12)**. Unscrew the two bolts, noting the earth wires, and remove the regulator/rectifier **(see illustration)**.

22 Installation is the reverse of removal – do not forget to secure the earth wires. Connect the wiring connector.

Power relay (2007-on models only)

23 Remove the rear body cover (see Chapter 7).

24 Remove the relay **(see illustration)**.

25 Test it as follows: set a multimeter to the ohms x 1 scale and connect it across terminals C and D on the relay **(see illustration)**. There should be no continuity (infinite resistance). Using a fully-charged 12 volt battery and two insulated jumper wires, connect the positive (+) terminal of the battery to terminal A, and the negative (–) terminal to terminal B. At this point the relay should be heard to click and the meter read 0 ohms (continuity). If this is the case the relay is good. If the relay does not click when battery voltage is applied and indicates no continuity (infinite resistance) across its terminals, it is faulty and must be replaced with a new one.

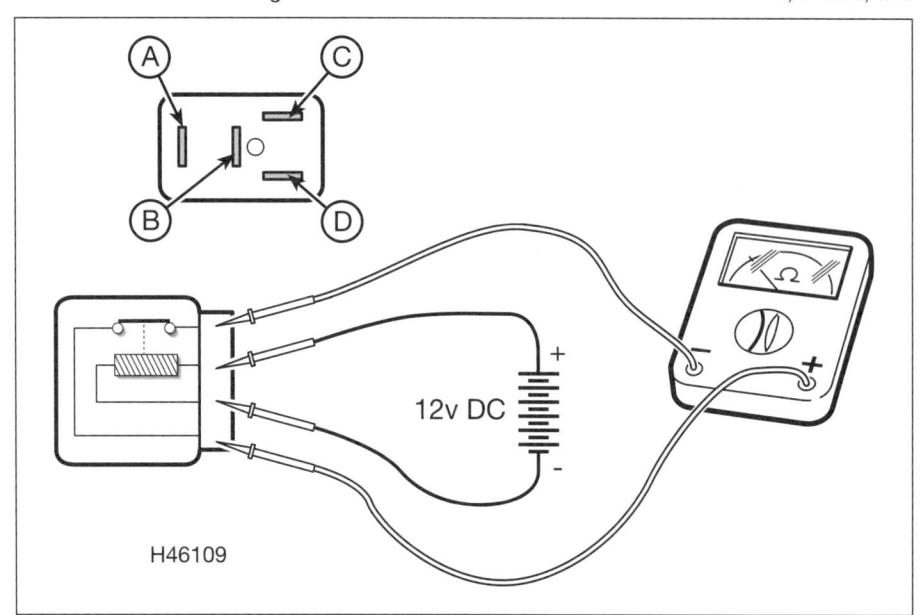

29.25 Power relay test set-up and terminal identification

Wiring diagrams 8•29

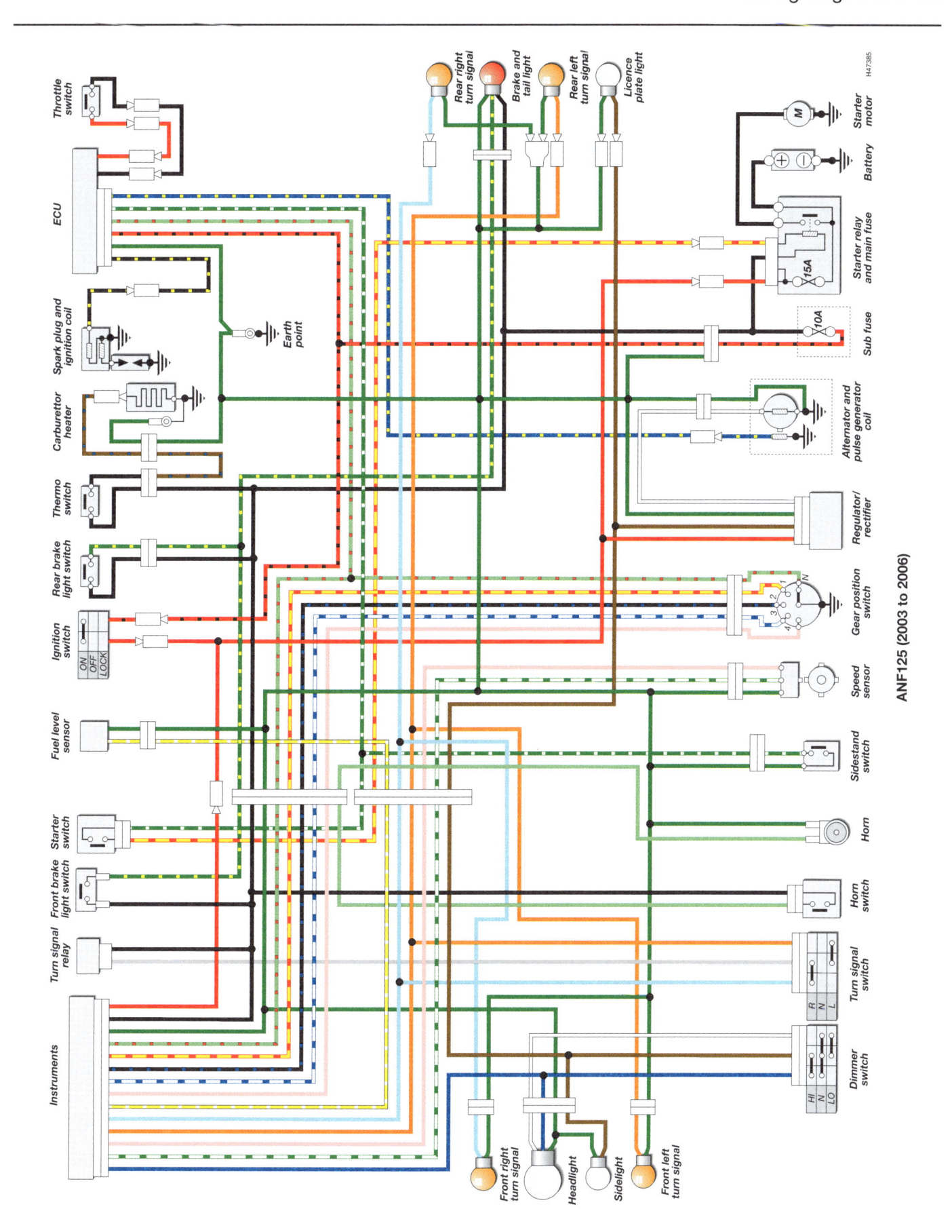

8•30 Wiring diagrams

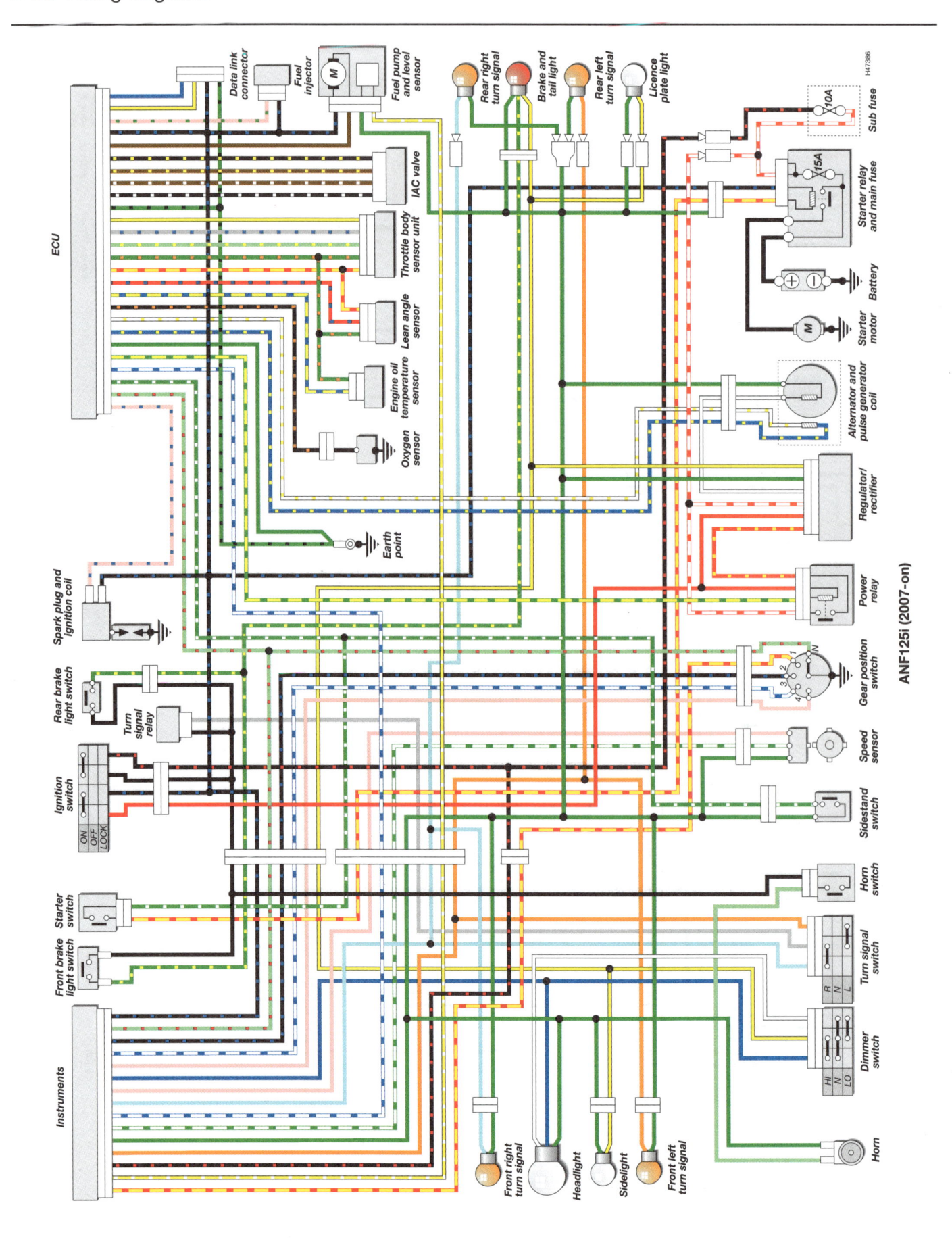

Reference REF•1

Reference

Tools and Workshop Tips — REF•2
- Building up a tool kit and equipping your workshop ● Using tools ● Understanding bearing, seal, fastener and chain sizes and markings ● Repair techniques

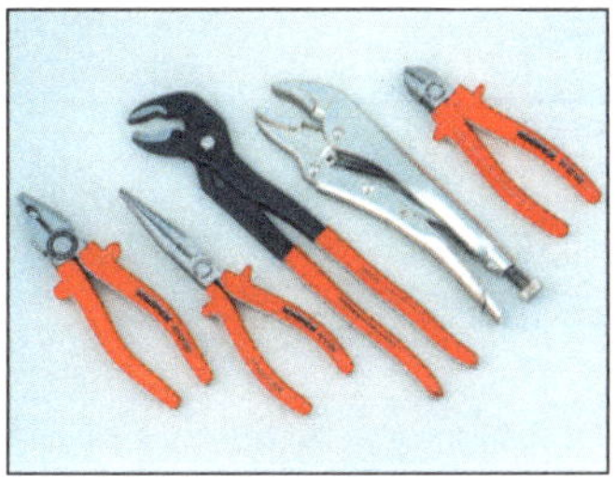

Security — REF•20
- Locks and chains ● U-locks ● Disc locks ● Alarms and immobilisers ● Security marking systems ● Tips on how to prevent bike theft

Lubricants and fluids — REF•23
- Engine oils ● Transmission (gear) oils ● Coolant/anti-freeze ● Fork oils and suspension fluids ● Brake/clutch fluids ● Spray lubes, degreasers and solvents

Conversion Factors — REF•26
34 Nm × 0.738 = 25 lbf ft
- Formulae for conversion of the metric (SI) units used throughout the manual into Imperial measures

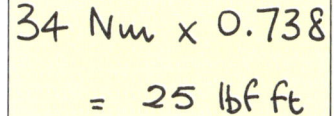

MOT Test Checks — REF•27
- A guide to the UK MOT test ● Which items are tested ● How to prepare your motorcycle for the test and perform a pre-test check

Storage — REF•32
- How to prepare your motorcycle for going into storage and protect essential systems ● How to get the motorcycle back on the road

Fault Finding — REF•35
- Common faults and their likely causes ● Links to main chapters for testing and repair procedures

Technical Terms Explained — REF•44
- Component names, technical terms and common abbreviations explained

Index — REF•48

REF•2 Tools and Workshop Tips

Buying tools

A toolkit is a fundamental requirement for servicing and repairing a motorcycle. Although there will be an initial expense in building up enough tools for servicing, this will soon be offset by the savings made by doing the job yourself. As experience and confidence grow, additional tools can be added to enable the repair and overhaul of the motorcycle. Many of the specialist tools are expensive and not often used so it may be preferable to hire them, or for a group of friends or motorcycle club to join in the purchase.

As a rule, it is better to buy more expensive, good quality tools. Cheaper tools are likely to wear out faster and need to be renewed more often, nullifying the original saving.

> **Warning:** To avoid the risk of a poor quality tool breaking in use, causing injury or damage to the component being worked on, always aim to purchase tools which meet the relevant national safety standards.

The following lists of tools do not represent the manufacturer's service tools, but serve as a guide to help the owner decide which tools are needed for this level of work. In addition, items such as an electric drill, hacksaw, files, soldering iron and a workbench equipped with a vice, may be needed. Although not classed as tools, a selection of bolts, screws, nuts, washers and pieces of tubing always come in useful.

For more information about tools, refer to the Haynes *Motorcycle Workshop Practice Techbook* (Bk. No. 3470).

Manufacturer's service tools

Inevitably certain tasks require the use of a service tool. Where possible an alternative tool or method of approach is recommended, but sometimes there is no option if personal injury or damage to the component is to be avoided. Where required, service tools are referred to in the relevant procedure.

Service tools can usually only be purchased from a motorcycle dealer and are identified by a part number. Some of the commonly-used tools, such as rotor pullers, are available in aftermarket form from mail-order motorcycle tool and accessory suppliers.

Maintenance and minor repair tools

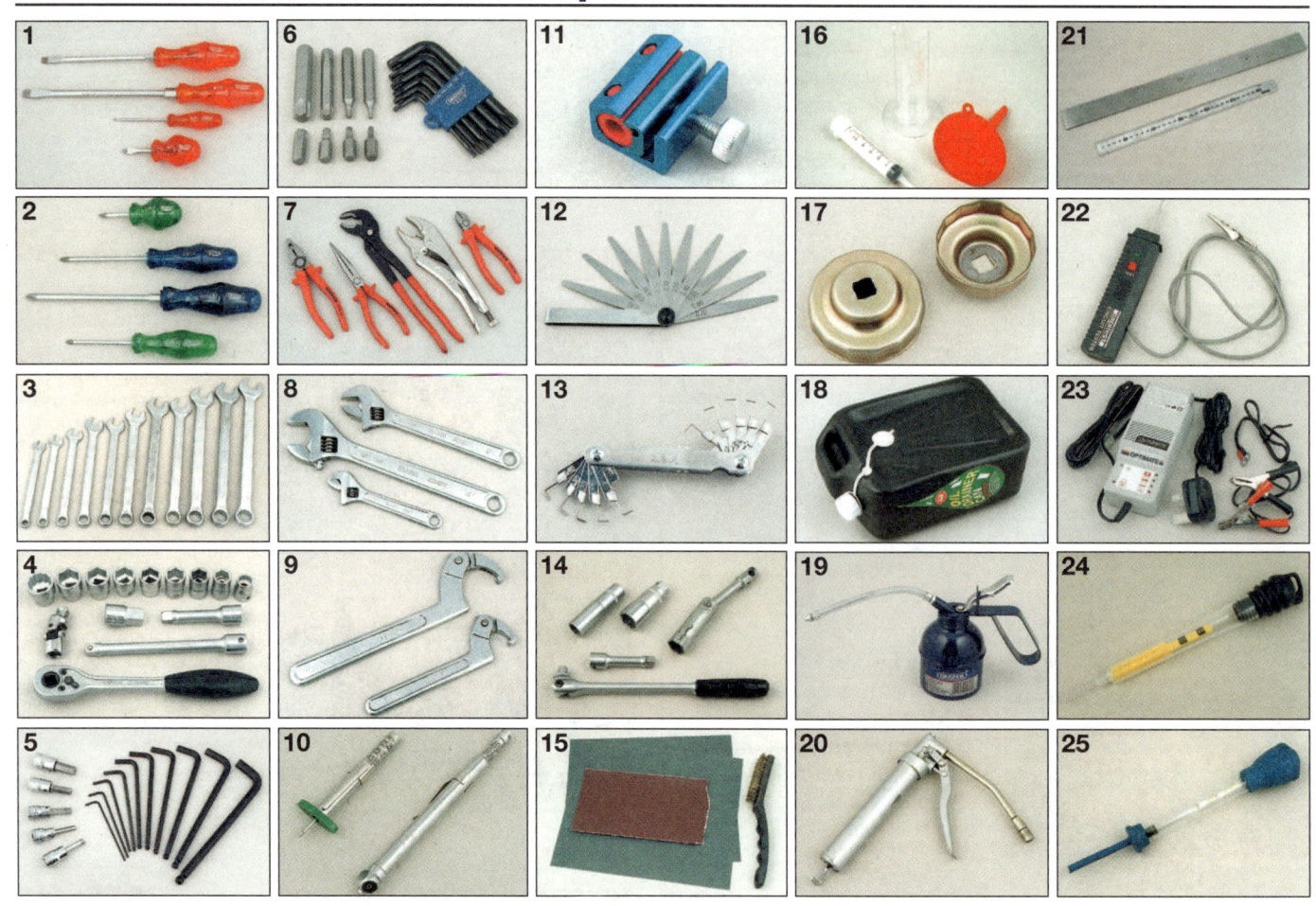

1 Set of flat-bladed screwdrivers
2 Set of Phillips head screwdrivers
3 Combination open-end and ring spanners
4 Socket set (3/8 inch or 1/2 inch drive)
5 Set of Allen keys or bits
6 Set of Torx keys or bits
7 Pliers, cutters and self-locking grips (Mole grips)
8 Adjustable spanners
9 C-spanners
10 Tread depth gauge and tyre pressure gauge
11 Cable oiler clamp
12 Feeler gauges
13 Spark plug gap measuring tool
14 Spark plug spanner or deep plug sockets
15 Wire brush and emery paper
16 Calibrated syringe, measuring vessel and funnel
17 Oil filter adapters
18 Oil drainer can or tray
19 Pump type oil can
20 Grease gun
21 Straight-edge and steel rule
22 Continuity tester
23 Battery charger
24 Hydrometer (for battery specific gravity check)
25 Anti-freeze tester (for liquid-cooled engines)

Tools and Workshop Tips REF•3

Repair and overhaul tools

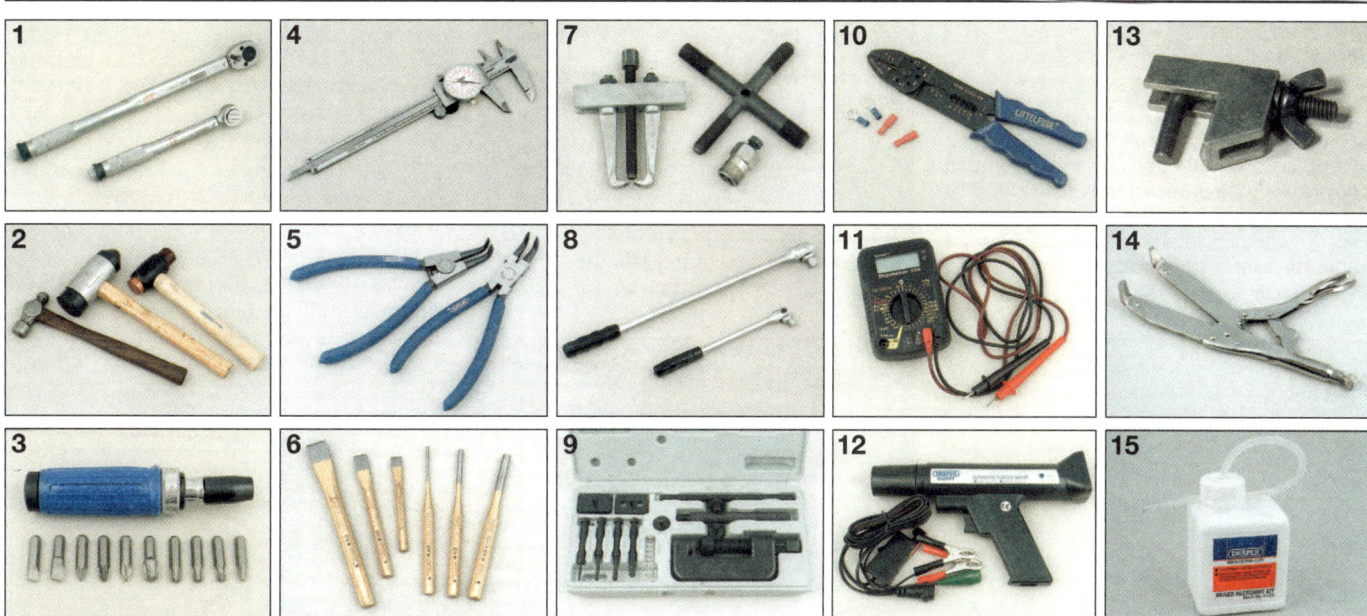

1. Torque wrench (small and mid-ranges)
2. Conventional, plastic or soft-faced hammers
3. Impact driver set
4. Vernier gauge
5. Circlip pliers (internal and external, or combination)
6. Set of cold chisels and punches
7. Selection of pullers
8. Breaker bars
9. Chain breaking/riveting tool set
10. Wire stripper and crimper tool
11. Multimeter (measures amps, volts and ohms)
12. Stroboscope (for dynamic timing checks)
13. Hose clamp (wingnut type shown)
14. Clutch holding tool
15. One-man brake/clutch bleeder kit

Specialist tools

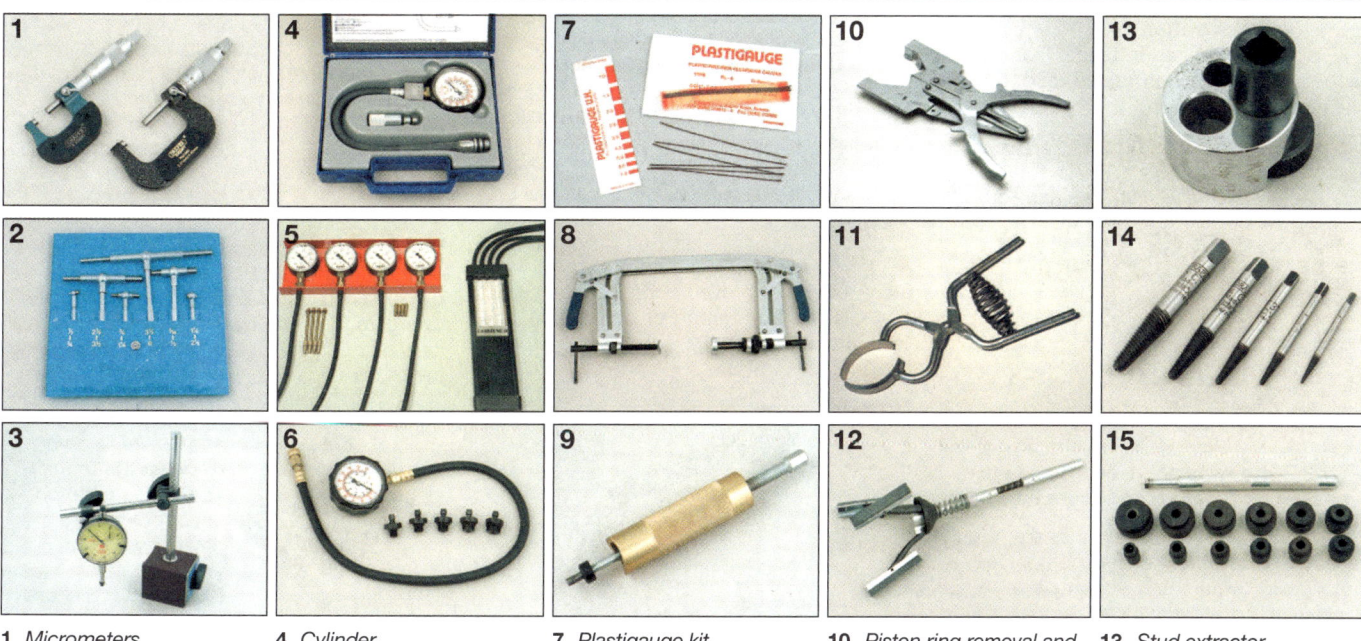

1. Micrometers (external type)
2. Telescoping gauges
3. Dial gauge
4. Cylinder compression gauge
5. Vacuum gauges (left) or manometer (right)
6. Oil pressure gauge
7. Plastigauge kit
8. Valve spring compressor (4-stroke engines)
9. Piston pin drawbolt tool
10. Piston ring removal and installation tool
11. Piston ring clamp
12. Cylinder bore hone (stone type shown)
13. Stud extractor
14. Screw extractor set
15. Bearing driver set

REF•4 Tools and Workshop Tips

1 Workshop equipment and facilities

The workbench

● Work is made much easier by raising the bike up on a ramp - components are much more accessible if raised to waist level. The hydraulic or pneumatic types seen in the dealer's workshop are a sound investment if you undertake a lot of repairs or overhauls **(see illustration 1.1)**.

1.1 Hydraulic motorcycle ramp

● If raised off ground level, the bike must be supported on the ramp to avoid it falling. Most ramps incorporate a front wheel locating clamp which can be adjusted to suit different diameter wheels. When tightening the clamp, take care not to mark the wheel rim or damage the tyre - use wood blocks on each side to prevent this.
● Secure the bike to the ramp using tie-downs **(see illustration 1.2)**. If the bike has only a sidestand, and hence leans at a dangerous angle when raised, support the bike on an auxiliary stand.

1.2 Tie-downs are used around the passenger footrests to secure the bike

● Auxiliary (paddock) stands are widely available from mail order companies or motorcycle dealers and attach either to the wheel axle or swingarm pivot **(see illustration 1.3)**. If the motorcycle has a centrestand, you can support it under the crankcase to prevent it toppling whilst either wheel is removed **(see illustration 1.4)**.

1.3 This auxiliary stand attaches to the swingarm pivot

1.4 Always use a block of wood between the engine and jack head when supporting the engine in this way

Fumes and fire

● Refer to the Safety first! page at the beginning of the manual for full details. Make sure your workshop is equipped with a fire extinguisher suitable for fuel-related fires (Class B fire - flammable liquids) - it is not sufficient to have a water-filled extinguisher.
● Always ensure adequate ventilation is available. Unless an exhaust gas extraction system is available for use, ensure that the engine is run outside of the workshop.
● If working on the fuel system, make sure the workshop is ventilated to avoid a build-up of fumes. This applies equally to fume build-up when charging a battery. Do not smoke or allow anyone else to smoke in the workshop.

Fluids

● If you need to drain fuel from the tank, store it in an approved container marked as suitable for the storage of petrol (gasoline) **(see illustration 1.5)**. Do not store fuel in glass jars or bottles.

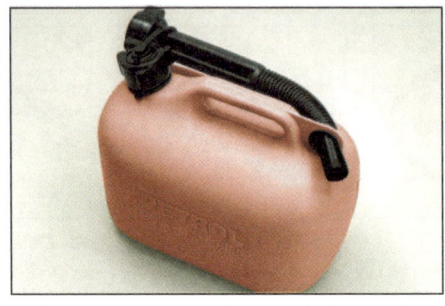

1.5 Use an approved can only for storing petrol (gasoline)

● Use proprietary engine degreasers or solvents which have a high flash-point, such as paraffin (kerosene), for cleaning off oil, grease and dirt - never use petrol (gasoline) for cleaning. Wear rubber gloves when handling solvent and engine degreaser. The fumes from certain solvents can be dangerous - always work in a well-ventilated area.

Dust, eye and hand protection

● Protect your lungs from inhalation of dust particles by wearing a filtering mask over the nose and mouth. Many frictional materials still contain asbestos which is dangerous to your health. Protect your eyes from spouts of liquid and sprung components by wearing a pair of protective goggles **(see illustration 1.6)**.

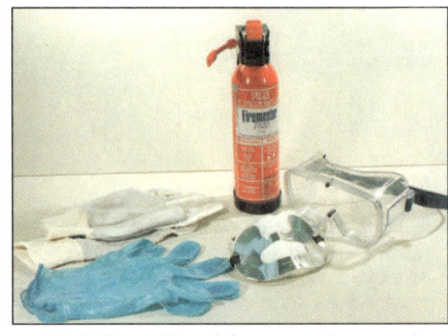

1.6 A fire extinguisher, goggles, mask and protective gloves should be at hand in the workshop

● Protect your hands from contact with solvents, fuel and oils by wearing rubber gloves. Alternatively apply a barrier cream to your hands before starting work. If handling hot components or fluids, wear suitable gloves to protect your hands from scalding and burns.

What to do with old fluids

● Old cleaning solvent, fuel, coolant and oils should not be poured down domestic drains or onto the ground. Package the fluid up in old oil containers, label it accordingly, and take it to a garage or disposal facility. Contact your local authority for location of such sites or ring the oil care hotline.

Note: It is illegal and anti-social to dump oil down the drain. To find the location of your local oil recycling bank in the UK, call 08708 506 506 or visit www.oilbankline.org.uk

In the USA, note that any oil supplier must accept used oil for recycling.

Tools and Workshop Tips REF•5

2 Fasteners - screws, bolts and nuts

Fastener types and applications

Bolts and screws

● Fastener head types are either of hexagonal, Torx or splined design, with internal and external versions of each type **(see illustrations 2.1 and 2.2)**; splined head fasteners are not in common use on motorcycles. The conventional slotted or Phillips head design is used for certain screws. Bolt or screw length is always measured from the underside of the head to the end of the item **(see illustration 2.11)**.

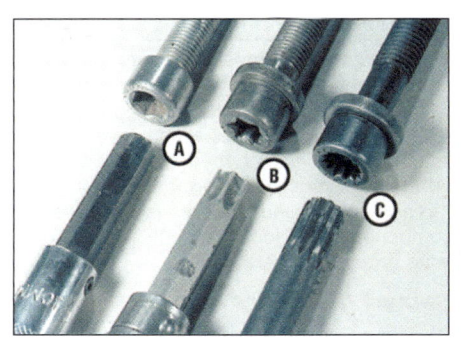

2.1 Internal hexagon/Allen (A), Torx (B) and splined (C) fasteners, with corresponding bits

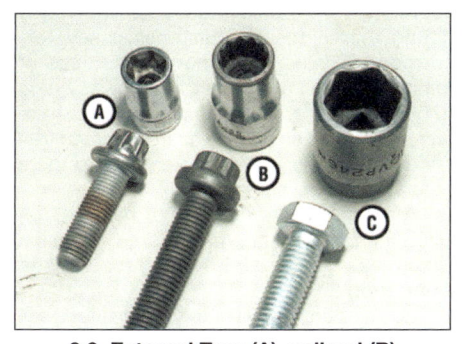

2.2 External Torx (A), splined (B) and hexagon (C) fasteners, with corresponding sockets

● Certain fasteners on the motorcycle have a tensile marking on their heads, the higher the marking the stronger the fastener. High tensile fasteners generally carry a 10 or higher marking. Never replace a high tensile fastener with one of a lower tensile strength.

Washers (see illustration 2.3)

● Plain washers are used between a fastener head and a component to prevent damage to the component or to spread the load when torque is applied. Plain washers can also be used as spacers or shims in certain assemblies. Copper or aluminium plain washers are often used as sealing washers on drain plugs.

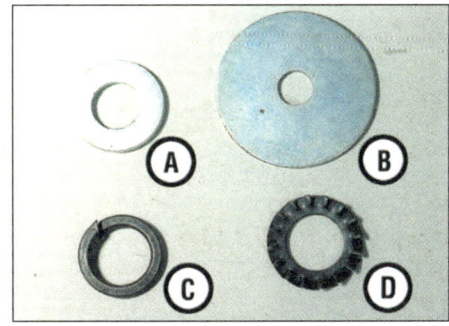

2.3 Plain washer (A), penny washer (B), spring washer (C) and serrated washer (D)

● The split-ring spring washer works by applying axial tension between the fastener head and component. If flattened, it is fatigued and must be renewed. If a plain (flat) washer is used on the fastener, position the spring washer between the fastener and the plain washer.
● Serrated star type washers dig into the fastener and component faces, preventing loosening. They are often used on electrical earth (ground) connections to the frame.
● Cone type washers (sometimes called Belleville) are conical and when tightened apply axial tension between the fastener head and component. They must be installed with the dished side against the component and often carry an OUTSIDE marking on their outer face. If flattened, they are fatigued and must be renewed.
● Tab washers are used to lock plain nuts or bolts on a shaft. A portion of the tab washer is bent up hard against one flat of the nut or bolt to prevent it loosening. Due to the tab washer being deformed in use, a new tab washer should be used every time it is disturbed.
● Wave washers are used to take up endfloat on a shaft. They provide light springing and prevent excessive side-to-side play of a component. Can be found on rocker arm shafts.

Nuts and split pins

● Conventional plain nuts are usually six-sided **(see illustration 2.4)**. They are sized by thread diameter and pitch. High tensile nuts carry a number on one end to denote their tensile strength.

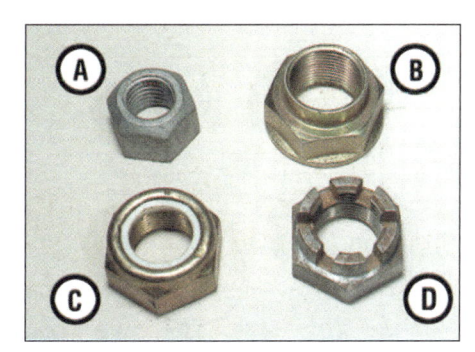

2.4 Plain nut (A), shouldered locknut (B), nylon insert nut (C) and castellated nut (D)

● Self-locking nuts either have a nylon insert, or two spring metal tabs, or a shoulder which is staked into a groove in the shaft - their advantage over conventional plain nuts is a resistance to loosening due to vibration. The nylon insert type can be used a number of times, but must be renewed when the friction of the nylon insert is reduced, ie when the nut spins freely on the shaft. The spring tab type can be reused unless the tabs are damaged. The shouldered type must be renewed every time it is disturbed.
● Split pins (cotter pins) are used to lock a castellated nut to a shaft or to prevent slackening of a plain nut. Common applications are wheel axles and brake torque arms. Because the split pin arms are deformed to lock around the nut a new split pin must always be used on installation - always fit the correct size split pin which will fit snugly in the shaft hole. Make sure the split pin arms are correctly located around the nut **(see illustrations 2.5 and 2.6)**.

2.5 Bend split pin (cotter pin) arms as shown (arrows) to secure a castellated nut

2.6 Bend split pin (cotter pin) arms as shown to secure a plain nut

Caution: If the castellated nut slots do not align with the shaft hole after tightening to the torque setting, tighten the nut until the next slot aligns with the hole - never slacken the nut to align its slot.

● R-pins (shaped like the letter R), or slip pins as they are sometimes called, are sprung and can be reused if they are otherwise in good condition. Always install R-pins with their closed end facing forwards **(see illustration 2.7)**.

REF•6 Tools and Workshop Tips

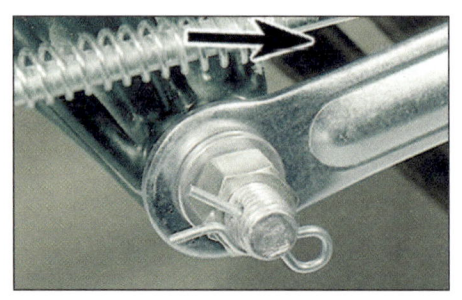

2.7 Correct fitting of R-pin. Arrow indicates forward direction

Circlips (see illustration 2.8)

- Circlips (sometimes called snap-rings) are used to retain components on a shaft or in a housing and have corresponding external or internal ears to permit removal. Parallel-sided (machined) circlips can be installed either way round in their groove, whereas stamped circlips (which have a chamfered edge on one face) must be installed with the chamfer facing away from the direction of thrust load **(see illustration 2.9)**.

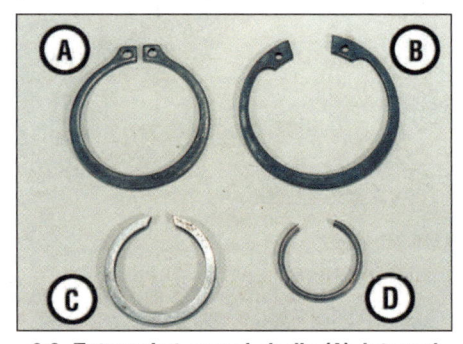

2.8 External stamped circlip (A), internal stamped circlip (B), machined circlip (C) and wire circlip (D)

- Always use circlip pliers to remove and install circlips; expand or compress them just enough to remove them. After installation, rotate the circlip in its groove to ensure it is securely seated. If installing a circlip on a splined shaft, always align its opening with a shaft channel to ensure the circlip ends are well supported and unlikely to catch **(see illustration 2.10)**.

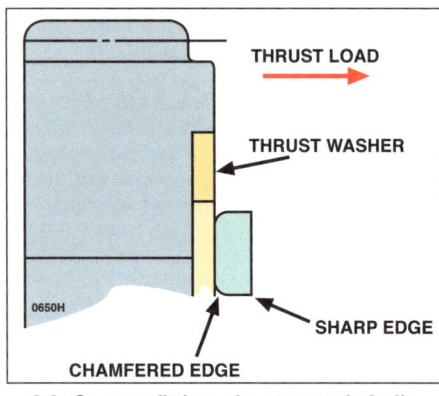

2.9 Correct fitting of a stamped circlip

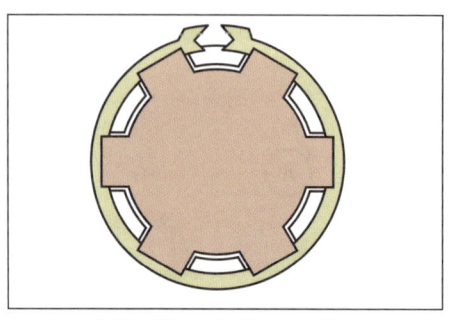

2.10 Align circlip opening with shaft channel

- Circlips can wear due to the thrust of components and become loose in their grooves, with the subsequent danger of becoming dislodged in operation. For this reason, renewal is advised every time a circlip is disturbed.
- Wire circlips are commonly used as piston pin retaining clips. If a removal tang is provided, long-nosed pliers can be used to dislodge them, otherwise careful use of a small flat-bladed screwdriver is necessary. Wire circlips should be renewed every time they are disturbed.

Thread diameter and pitch

- Diameter of a male thread (screw, bolt or stud) is the outside diameter of the threaded portion **(see illustration 2.11)**. Most motorcycle manufacturers use the ISO (International Standards Organisation) metric system expressed in millimetres, eg M6 refers to a 6 mm diameter thread. Sizing is the same for nuts, except that the thread diameter is measured across the valleys of the nut.
- Pitch is the distance between the peaks of the thread **(see illustration 2.11)**. It is expressed in millimetres, thus a common bolt size may be expressed as 6.0 x 1.0 mm (6 mm thread diameter and 1 mm pitch). Generally pitch increases in proportion to thread diameter, although there are always exceptions.
- Thread diameter and pitch are related for conventional fastener applications and the accompanying table can be used as a guide. Additionally, the AF (Across Flats), spanner or socket size dimension of the bolt or nut **(see illustration 2.11)** is linked to thread and pitch specification. Thread pitch can be measured with a thread gauge **(see illustration 2.12)**.

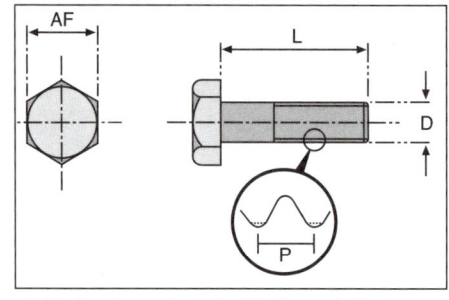

2.11 Fastener length (L), thread diameter (D), thread pitch (P) and head size (AF)

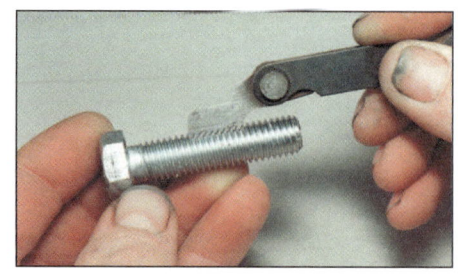

2.12 Using a thread gauge to measure pitch

AF size	Thread diameter x pitch (mm)
8 mm	M5 x 0.8
8 mm	M6 x 1.0
10 mm	M6 x 1.0
12 mm	M8 x 1.25
14 mm	M10 x 1.25
17 mm	M12 x 1.25

- The threads of most fasteners are of the right-hand type, ie they are turned clockwise to tighten and anti-clockwise to loosen. The reverse situation applies to left-hand thread fasteners, which are turned anti-clockwise to tighten and clockwise to loosen. Left-hand threads are used where rotation of a component might loosen a conventional right-hand thread fastener.

Seized fasteners

- Corrosion of external fasteners due to water or reaction between two dissimilar metals can occur over a period of time. It will build up sooner in wet conditions or in countries where salt is used on the roads during the winter. If a fastener is severely corroded it is likely that normal methods of removal will fail and result in its head being ruined. When you attempt removal, the fastener thread should be heard to crack free and unscrew easily - if it doesn't, stop there before damaging something.
- A smart tap on the head of the fastener will often succeed in breaking free corrosion which has occurred in the threads **(see illustration 2.13)**.
- An aerosol penetrating fluid (such as WD-40) applied the night beforehand may work its way down into the thread and ease removal. Depending on the location, you may be able to make up a Plasticine well around the fastener head and fill it with penetrating fluid.

2.13 A sharp tap on the head of a fastener will often break free a corroded thread

Tools and Workshop Tips REF•7

- If you are working on an engine internal component, corrosion will most likely not be a problem due to the well lubricated environment. However, components can be very tight and an impact driver is a useful tool in freeing them **(see illustration 2.14)**.

2.14 Using an impact driver to free a fastener

- Where corrosion has occurred between dissimilar metals (eg steel and aluminium alloy), the application of heat to the fastener head will create a disproportionate expansion rate between the two metals and break the seizure caused by the corrosion. Whether heat can be applied depends on the location of the fastener - any surrounding components likely to be damaged must first be removed **(see illustration 2.15)**. Heat can be applied using a paint stripper heat gun or clothes iron, or by immersing the component in boiling water - wear protective gloves to prevent scalding or burns to the hands.

2.15 Using heat to free a seized fastener

- As a last resort, it is possible to use a hammer and cold chisel to work the fastener head unscrewed **(see illustration 2.16)**. This will damage the fastener, but more importantly extreme care must be taken not to damage the surrounding component.

Caution: Remember that the component being secured is generally of more value than the bolt, nut or screw - when the fastener is freed, do not unscrew it with force, instead work the fastener back and forth when resistance is felt to prevent thread damage.

2.16 Using a hammer and chisel to free a seized fastener

Broken fasteners and damaged heads

- If the shank of a broken bolt or screw is accessible you can grip it with self-locking grips. The knurled wheel type stud extractor tool or self-gripping stud puller tool is particularly useful for removing the long studs which screw into the cylinder mouth surface of the crankcase or bolts and screws from which the head has broken off **(see illustration 2.17)**. Studs can also be removed by locking two nuts together on the threaded end of the stud and using a spanner on the lower nut **(see illustration 2.18)**.

2.17 Using a stud extractor tool to remove a broken crankcase stud

2.18 Two nuts can be locked together to unscrew a stud from a component

- A bolt or screw which has broken off below or level with the casing must be extracted using a screw extractor set. Centre punch the fastener to centralise the drill bit, then drill a hole in the fastener **(see illustration 2.19)**. Select a drill bit which is approximately half to three-quarters the

2.19 When using a screw extractor, first drill a hole in the fastener . . .

diameter of the fastener and drill to a depth which will accommodate the extractor. Use the largest size extractor possible, but avoid leaving too small a wall thickness otherwise the extractor will merely force the fastener walls outwards wedging it in the casing thread.

- If a spiral type extractor is used, thread it anti-clockwise into the fastener. As it is screwed in, it will grip the fastener and unscrew it from the casing **(see illustration 2.20)**.

2.20 . . . then thread the extractor anti-clockwise into the fastener

- If a taper type extractor is used, tap it into the fastener so that it is firmly wedged in place. Unscrew the extractor (anti-clockwise) to draw the fastener out.

> **Warning: Stud extractors are very hard and may break off in the fastener if care is not taken - ask an engineer about spark erosion if this happens.**

- Alternatively, the broken bolt/screw can be drilled out and the hole retapped for an oversize bolt/screw or a diamond-section thread insert. It is essential that the drilling is carried out squarely and to the correct depth, otherwise the casing may be ruined - if in doubt, entrust the work to an engineer.

- Bolts and nuts with rounded corners cause the correct size spanner or socket to slip when force is applied. Of the types of spanner/socket available always use a six-point type rather than an eight or twelve-point type - better grip

REF•8 Tools and Workshop Tips

2.21 Comparison of surface drive ring spanner (left) with 12-point type (right)

is obtained. Surface drive spanners grip the middle of the hex flats, rather than the corners, and are thus good in cases of damaged heads **(see illustration 2.21)**.

● Slotted-head or Phillips-head screws are often damaged by the use of the wrong size screwdriver. Allen-head and Torx-head screws are much less likely to sustain damage. If enough of the screw head is exposed you can use a hacksaw to cut a slot in its head and then use a conventional flat-bladed screwdriver to remove it. Alternatively use a hammer and cold chisel to tap the head of the fastener around to slacken it. Always replace damaged fasteners with new ones, preferably Torx or Allen-head type.

HAYNES HiNT
A dab of valve grinding compound between the screw head and screwdriver tip will often give a good grip.

Thread repair

● Threads (particularly those in aluminium alloy components) can be damaged by overtightening, being assembled with dirt in the threads, or from a component working loose and vibrating. Eventually the thread will fail completely, and it will be impossible to tighten the fastener.

● If a thread is damaged or clogged with old locking compound it can be renovated with a thread repair tool (thread chaser) **(see illustrations 2.22 and 2.23)**; special thread

2.22 A thread repair tool being used to correct an internal thread

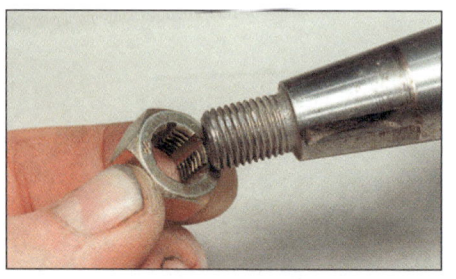

2.23 A thread repair tool being used to correct an external thread

chasers are available for spark plug hole threads. The tool will not cut a new thread, but clean and true the original thread. Make sure that you use the correct diameter and pitch tool. Similarly, external threads can be cleaned up with a die or a thread restorer file **(see illustration 2.24)**.

2.24 Using a thread restorer file

● It is possible to drill out the old thread and retap the component to the next thread size. This will work where there is enough surrounding material and a new bolt or screw can be obtained. Sometimes, however, this is not possible - such as where the bolt/screw passes through another component which must also be suitably modified, also in cases where a spark plug or oil drain plug cannot be obtained in a larger diameter thread size.

● The diamond-section thread insert (often known by its popular trade name of Heli-Coil) is a simple and effective method of renewing the thread and retaining the original size. A kit can be purchased which contains the tap, insert and installing tool **(see illustration 2.25)**. Drill out the damaged thread with the size drill specified **(see illustration 2.26)**. Carefully retap the thread **(see illustration 2.27)**. Install the

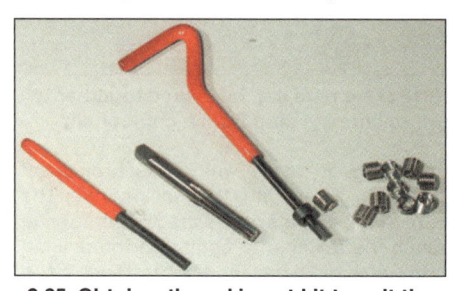

2.25 Obtain a thread insert kit to suit the thread diameter and pitch required

2.26 To install a thread insert, first drill out the original thread . . .

2.27 . . . tap a new thread . . .

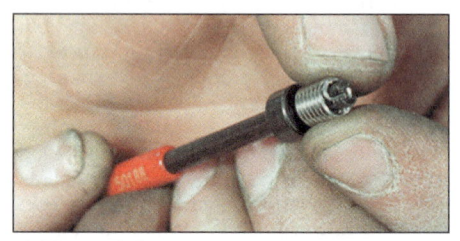

2.28 . . . fit insert on the installing tool . . .

2.29 . . . and thread into the component . . .

2.30 . . . break off the tang when complete

insert on the installing tool and thread it slowly into place using a light downward pressure **(see illustrations 2.28 and 2.29)**. When positioned between a 1/4 and 1/2 turn below the surface withdraw the installing tool and use the break-off tool to press down on the tang, breaking it off **(see illustration 2.30)**.

● There are epoxy thread repair kits on the market which can rebuild stripped internal threads, although this repair should not be used on high load-bearing components.

Tools and Workshop Tips REF•9

Thread locking and sealing compounds

● Locking compounds are used in locations where the fastener is prone to loosening due to vibration or on important safety-related items which might cause loss of control of the motorcycle if they fail. It is also used where important fasteners cannot be secured by other means such as lockwashers or split pins.

● Before applying locking compound, make sure that the threads (internal and external) are clean and dry with all old compound removed. Select a compound to suit the component being secured - a non-permanent general locking and sealing type is suitable for most applications, but a high strength type is needed for permanent fixing of studs in castings. Apply a drop or two of the compound to the first few threads of the fastener, then thread it into place and tighten to the specified torque. Do not apply excessive thread locking compound otherwise the thread may be damaged on subsequent removal.

● Certain fasteners are impregnated with a dry film type coating of locking compound on their threads. Always renew this type of fastener if disturbed.

● Anti-seize compounds, such as copper-based greases, can be applied to protect threads from seizure due to extreme heat and corrosion. A common instance is spark plug threads and exhaust system fasteners.

3 Measuring tools and gauges

Feeler gauges

● Feeler gauges (or blades) are used for measuring small gaps and clearances **(see illustration 3.1)**. They can also be used to measure endfloat (sideplay) of a component on a shaft where access is not possible with a dial gauge.

● Feeler gauge sets should be treated with care and not bent or damaged. They are etched with their size on one face. Keep them clean and very lightly oiled to prevent corrosion build-up.

3.1 Feeler gauges are used for measuring small gaps and clearances - thickness is marked on one face of gauge

● When measuring a clearance, select a gauge which is a light sliding fit between the two components. You may need to use two gauges together to measure the clearance accurately.

Micrometers

● A micrometer is a precision tool capable of measuring to 0.01 or 0.001 of a millimetre. It should always be stored in its case and not in the general toolbox. It must be kept clean and never dropped, otherwise its frame or measuring anvils could be distorted resulting in inaccurate readings.

● External micrometers are used for measuring outside diameters of components and have many more applications than internal micrometers. Micrometers are available in different size ranges, eg 0 to 25 mm, 25 to 50 mm, and upwards in 25 mm steps; some large micrometers have interchangeable anvils to allow a range of measurements to be taken. Generally the largest precision measurement you are likely to take on a motorcycle is the piston diameter.

● Internal micrometers (or bore micrometers) are used for measuring inside diameters, such as valve guides and cylinder bores. Telescoping gauges and small hole gauges are used in conjunction with an external micrometer, whereas the more expensive internal micrometers have their own measuring device.

External micrometer

Note: *The conventional analogue type instrument is described. Although much easier to read, digital micrometers are considerably more expensive.*

● Always check the calibration of the micrometer before use. With the anvils closed (0 to 25 mm type) or set over a test gauge (for the larger types) the scale should read zero **(see illustration 3.2)**; make sure that the anvils (and test piece) are clean first. Any discrepancy can be adjusted by referring to the instructions supplied with the tool. Remember that the micrometer is a precision measuring tool - don't force the anvils closed, use the ratchet (4) on the end of the micrometer to close it. In this way, a measured force is always applied.

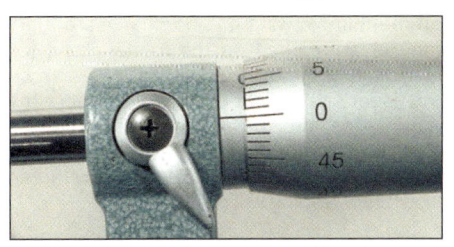

3.2 Check micrometer calibration before use

● To use, first make sure that the item being measured is clean. Place the anvil of the micrometer (1) against the item and use the thimble (2) to bring the spindle (3) lightly into contact with the other side of the item **(see illustration 3.3)**. Don't tighten the thimble down because this will damage the micrometer - instead use the ratchet (4) on the end of the micrometer. The ratchet mechanism applies a measured force preventing damage to the instrument.

● The micrometer is read by referring to the linear scale on the sleeve and the annular scale on the thimble. Read off the sleeve first to obtain the base measurement, then add the fine measurement from the thimble to obtain the overall reading. The linear scale on the sleeve represents the measuring range of the micrometer (eg 0 to 25 mm). The annular scale

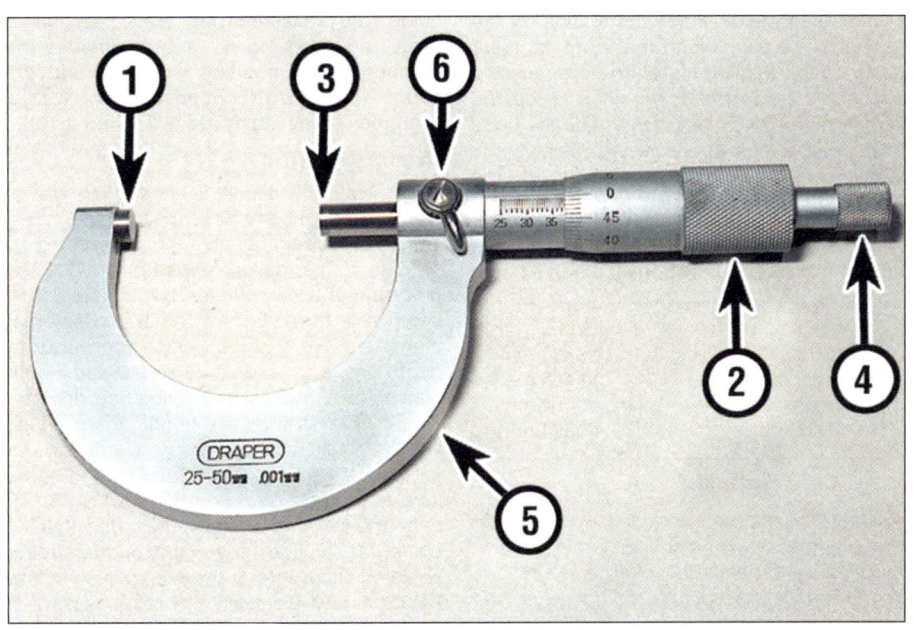

3.3 Micrometer component parts

| 1 Anvil | 3 Spindle | 5 Frame |
| 2 Thimble | 4 Ratchet | 6 Locking lever |

REF•10 Tools and Workshop Tips

on the thimble will be in graduations of 0.01 mm (or as marked on the frame) - one full revolution of the thimble will move 0.5 mm on the linear scale. Take the reading where the datum line on the sleeve intersects the thimble's scale. Always position the eye directly above the scale otherwise an inaccurate reading will result.

In the example shown the item measures 2.95 mm **(see illustration 3.4)**:

Linear scale	2.00 mm
Linear scale	0.50 mm
Annular scale	0.45 mm
Total figure	**2.95 mm**

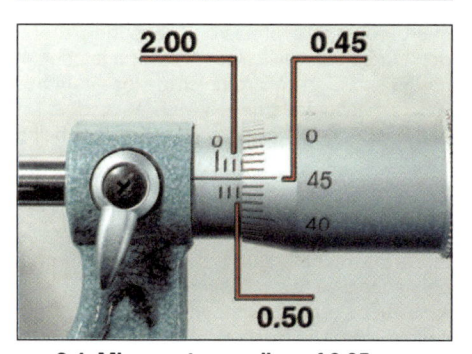

3.4 Micrometer reading of 2.95 mm

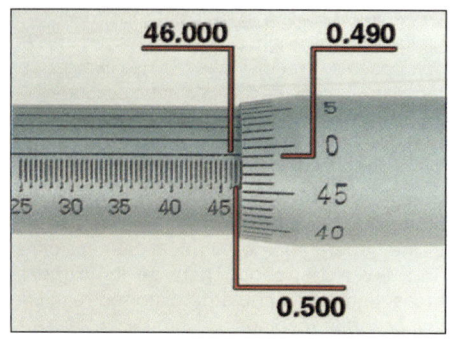

3.5 Micrometer reading of 46.99 mm on linear and annular scales . . .

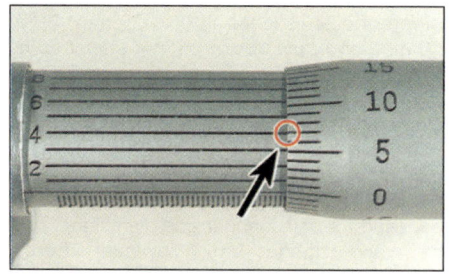

3.6 . . . and 0.004 mm on vernier scale

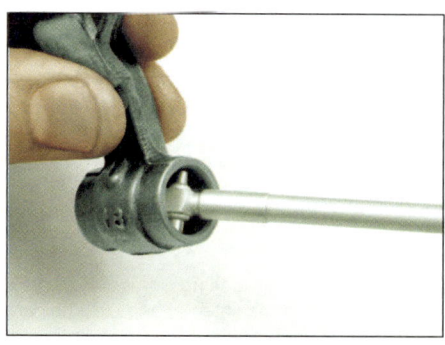

3.7 Expand the telescoping gauge in the bore, lock its position . . .

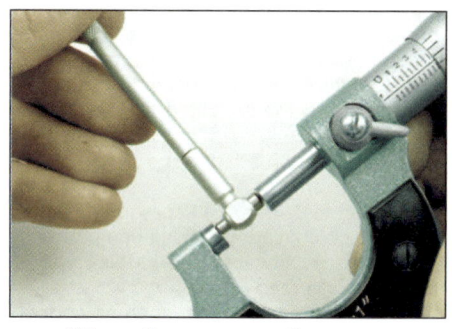

3.8 . . . then measure the gauge with a micrometer

3.9 Expand the small hole gauge in the bore, lock its position . . .

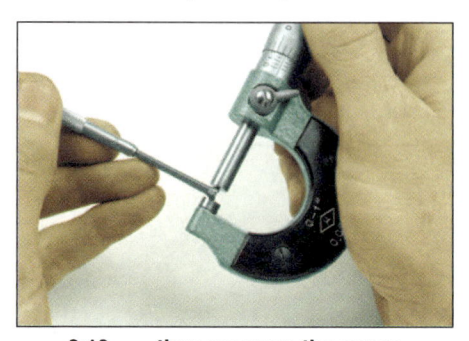

3.10 . . . then measure the gauge with a micrometer

Most micrometers have a locking lever (6) on the frame to hold the setting in place, allowing the item to be removed from the micrometer.
● Some micrometers have a vernier scale on their sleeve, providing an even finer measurement to be taken, in 0.001 increments of a millimetre. Take the sleeve and thimble measurement as described above, then check which graduation on the vernier scale aligns with that of the annular scale on the thimble **Note:** *The eye must be perpendicular to the scale when taking the vernier reading - if necessary rotate the body of the micrometer to ensure this.* Multiply the vernier scale figure by 0.001 and add it to the base and fine measurement figures.

In the example shown the item measures 46.994 mm **(see illustrations 3.5 and 3.6)**:

Linear scale (base)	46.000 mm
Linear scale (base)	00.500 mm
Annular scale (fine)	00.490 mm
Vernier scale	00.004 mm
Total figure	**46.994 mm**

Internal micrometer

● Internal micrometers are available for measuring bore diameters, but are expensive and unlikely to be available for home use. It is suggested that a set of telescoping gauges and small hole gauges, both of which must be used with an external micrometer, will suffice for taking internal measurements on a motorcycle.
● Telescoping gauges can be used to measure internal diameters of components. Select a gauge with the correct size range, make sure its ends are clean and insert it into the bore. Expand the gauge, then lock its position and withdraw it from the bore **(see illustration 3.7)**. Measure across the gauge ends with a micrometer **(see illustration 3.8)**.
● Very small diameter bores (such as valve guides) are measured with a small hole gauge. Once adjusted to a slip-fit inside the component, its position is locked and the gauge withdrawn for measurement with a micrometer **(see illustrations 3.9 and 3.10)**.

Vernier caliper

Note: *The conventional linear and dial gauge type instruments are described. Digital types are easier to read, but are far more expensive.*
● The vernier caliper does not provide the precision of a micrometer, but is versatile in being able to measure internal and external diameters. Some types also incorporate a depth gauge. It is ideal for measuring clutch plate friction material and spring free lengths.
● To use the conventional linear scale vernier, slacken off the vernier clamp screws (1) and set its jaws over (2), or inside (3), the item to be measured **(see illustration 3.11)**. Slide the jaw into contact, using the thumbwheel (4) for fine movement of the sliding scale (5) then tighten the clamp screws (1). Read off the main scale (6) where the zero on the sliding scale (5) intersects it, taking the whole number to the left of the zero; this provides the base measurement. View along the sliding scale and select the division which lines up exactly with any of the divisions on the main scale, noting that the divisions usually represents 0.02 of a millimetre. Add this fine measurement to the base measurement to obtain the total reading.

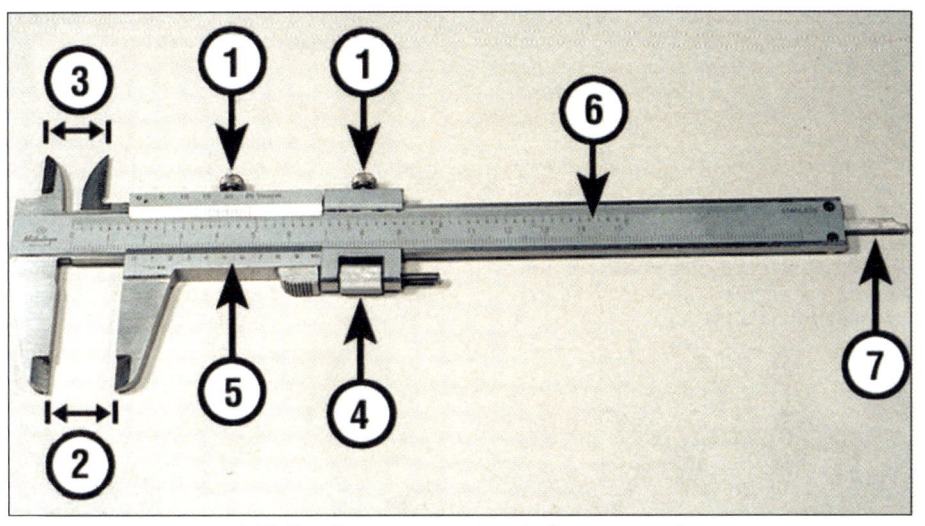

Tools and Workshop Tips   REF•11

3.11 Vernier component parts (linear gauge)

1 Clamp screws
2 External jaws
3 Internal jaws
4 Thumbwheel
5 Sliding scale
6 Main scale
7 Depth gauge

In the example shown the item measures 55.92 mm **(see illustration 3.12)**:

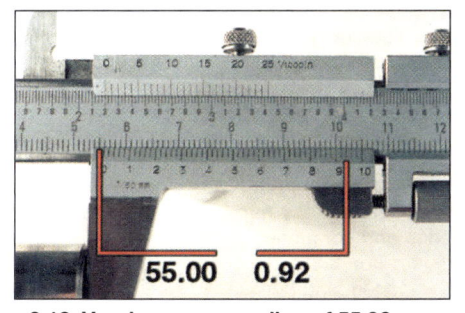

Base measurement	55.00 mm
Fine measurement	00.92 mm
Total figure	**55.92 mm**

3.12 Vernier gauge reading of 55.92 mm

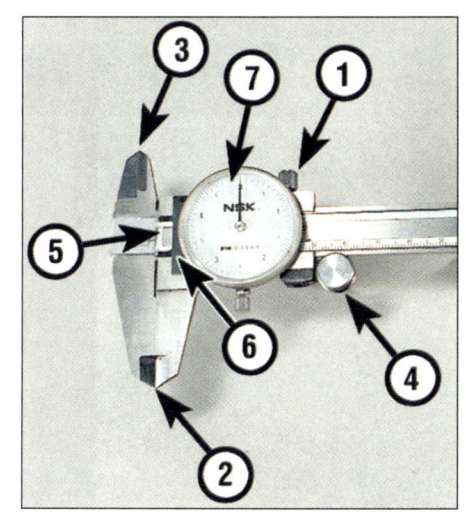

- Some vernier calipers are equipped with a dial gauge for fine measurement. Before use, check that the jaws are clean, then close them fully and check that the dial gauge reads zero. If necessary adjust the gauge ring accordingly. Slacken the vernier clamp screw (1) and set its jaws over (2), or inside (3), the item to be measured **(see illustration 3.13)**. Slide the jaws into contact, using the thumbwheel (4) for fine movement. Read off the main scale (5) where the edge of the sliding scale (6) intersects it, taking the whole number to the left of the zero; this provides the base measurement. Read off the needle position on the dial gauge (7) scale to provide the fine measurement; each division represents 0.05 of a millimetre. Add this fine measurement to the base measurement to obtain the total reading.

In the example shown the item measures 55.95 mm **(see illustration 3.14)**:

Base measurement	55.00 mm
Fine measurement	00.95 mm
Total figure	**55.95 mm**

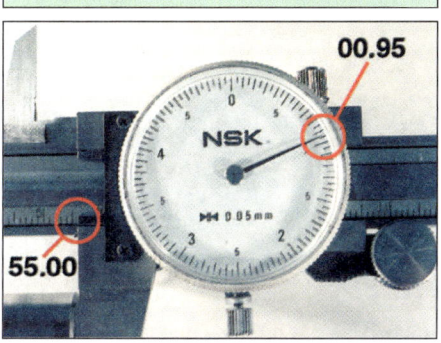

3.13 Vernier component parts (dial gauge)

1 Clamp screw
2 External jaws
3 Internal jaws
4 Thumbwheel
5 Main scale
6 Sliding scale
7 Dial gauge

3.14 Vernier gauge reading of 55.95 mm

Plastigauge

- Plastigauge is a plastic material which can be compressed between two surfaces to measure the oil clearance between them. The width of the compressed Plastigauge is measured against a calibrated scale to determine the clearance.

- Common uses of Plastigauge are for measuring the clearance between crankshaft journal and main bearing inserts, between crankshaft journal and big-end bearing inserts, and between camshaft and bearing surfaces. The following example describes big-end oil clearance measurement.

- Handle the Plastigauge material carefully to prevent distortion. Using a sharp knife, cut a length which corresponds with the width of the bearing being measured and place it carefully across the journal so that it is parallel with the shaft **(see illustration 3.15)**. Carefully install both bearing shells and the connecting rod. Without rotating the rod on the journal tighten its bolts or nuts (as applicable) to the specified torque. The connecting rod and bearings are then disassembled and the crushed Plastigauge examined.

3.15 Plastigauge placed across shaft journal

- Using the scale provided in the Plastigauge kit, measure the width of the material to determine the oil clearance **(see illustration 3.16)**. Always remove all traces of Plastigauge after use using your fingernails.

> **Caution:** *Arriving at the correct clearance demands that the assembly is torqued correctly, according to the settings and sequence (where applicable) provided by the motorcycle manufacturer.*

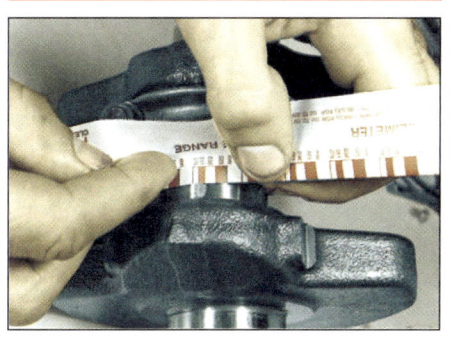

3.16 Measuring the width of the crushed Plastigauge

Tools and Workshop Tips

Dial gauge or DTI (Dial Test Indicator)

● A dial gauge can be used to accurately measure small amounts of movement. Typical uses are measuring shaft runout or shaft endfloat (sideplay) and setting piston position for ignition timing on two-strokes. A dial gauge set usually comes with a range of different probes and adapters and mounting equipment.

● The gauge needle must point to zero when at rest. Rotate the ring around its periphery to zero the gauge.

● Check that the gauge is capable of reading the extent of movement in the work. Most gauges have a small dial set in the face which records whole millimetres of movement as well as the fine scale around the face periphery which is calibrated in 0.01 mm divisions. Read off the small dial first to obtain the base measurement, then add the measurement from the fine scale to obtain the total reading.

In the example shown the gauge reads 1.48 mm (see illustration 3.17):

Base measurement	1.00 mm
Fine measurement	0.48 mm
Total figure	**1.48 mm**

3.17 Dial gauge reading of 1.48 mm

● If measuring shaft runout, the shaft must be supported in vee-blocks and the gauge mounted on a stand perpendicular to the shaft. Rest the tip of the gauge against the centre of the shaft and rotate the shaft slowly whilst watching the gauge reading (see illustration 3.18). Take several measurements along the length of the shaft and record the maximum gauge reading as the amount of runout in the shaft. **Note:** *The reading obtained will be total runout at that point - some manufacturers specify that the runout figure is halved to compare with their specified runout limit.*

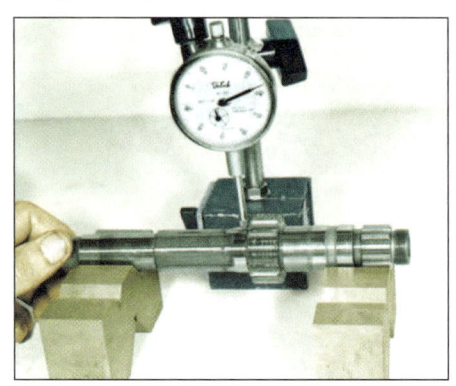

● Endfloat (sideplay) measurement requires that the gauge is mounted securely to the surrounding component with its probe touching the end of the shaft. Using hand pressure, push and pull on the shaft noting the maximum endfloat recorded on the gauge (see illustration 3.19).

3.19 Using a dial gauge to measure shaft endfloat

● A dial gauge with suitable adapters can be used to determine piston position BTDC on two-stroke engines for the purposes of ignition timing. The gauge, adapter and suitable length probe are installed in the place of the spark plug and the gauge zeroed at TDC. If the piston position is specified as 1.14 mm BTDC, rotate the engine back to 2.00 mm BTDC, then slowly forwards to 1.14 mm BTDC.

Cylinder compression gauges

● A compression gauge is used for measuring cylinder compression. Either the rubber-cone type or the threaded adapter type can be used. The latter is preferred to ensure a perfect seal against the cylinder head. A 0 to 300 psi (0 to 20 Bar) type gauge (for petrol/gasoline engines) will be suitable for motorcycles.

● The spark plug is removed and the gauge either held hard against the cylinder head (cone type) or the gauge adapter screwed into the cylinder head (threaded type) (see illustration 3.20). Cylinder compression is measured with the engine turning over, but not running - carry out the compression test as described in *Fault Finding Equipment*. The gauge will hold the reading until manually released.

Oil pressure gauge

● An oil pressure gauge is used for measuring engine oil pressure. Most gauges come with a set of adapters to fit the thread of the take-off point (see illustration 3.21). If the take-off point specified by the motorcycle manufacturer is an external oil pipe union, make sure that the specified replacement union is used to prevent oil starvation.

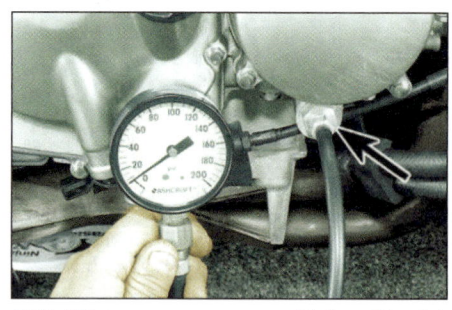

3.21 Oil pressure gauge and take-off point adapter (arrow)

● Oil pressure is measured with the engine running (at a specific rpm) and often the manufacturer will specify pressure limits for a cold and hot engine.

Straight-edge and surface plate

● If checking the gasket face of a component for warpage, place a steel rule or precision straight-edge across the gasket face and measure any gap between the straight-edge and component with feeler gauges (see illustration 3.22). Check diagonally across the component and between mounting holes (see illustration 3.23).

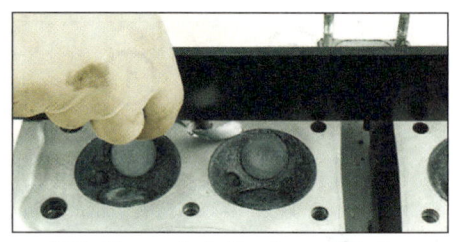

3.22 Use a straight-edge and feeler gauges to check for warpage

3.18 Using a dial gauge to measure shaft runout

3.20 Using a rubber-cone type cylinder compression gauge

3.23 Check for warpage in these directions

Tools and Workshop Tips   REF•13

● Checking individual components for warpage, such as clutch plain (metal) plates, requires a perfectly flat plate or piece or plate glass and feeler gauges.

4 Torque and leverage

What is torque?

● Torque describes the twisting force about a shaft. The amount of torque applied is determined by the distance from the centre of the shaft to the end of the lever and the amount of force being applied to the end of the lever; distance multiplied by force equals torque.

● The manufacturer applies a measured torque to a bolt or nut to ensure that it will not slacken in use and to hold two components securely together without movement in the joint. The actual torque setting depends on the thread size, bolt or nut material and the composition of the components being held.

● Too little torque may cause the fastener to loosen due to vibration, whereas too much torque will distort the joint faces of the component or cause the fastener to shear off. Always stick to the specified torque setting.

Using a torque wrench

● Check the calibration of the torque wrench and make sure it has a suitable range for the job. Torque wrenches are available in Nm (Newton-metres), kgf m (kilograms-force metre), lbf ft (pounds-feet), lbf in (inch-pounds). Do not confuse lbf ft with lbf in.

● Adjust the tool to the desired torque on the scale (see illustration 4.1). If your torque wrench is not calibrated in the units specified, carefully convert the figure (see *Conversion Factors*). A manufacturer sometimes gives a torque setting as a range (8 to 10 Nm) rather than a single figure - in this case set the tool midway between the two settings. The same torque may be expressed as 9 Nm ± 1 Nm. Some torque wrenches have a method of locking the setting so that it isn't inadvertently altered during use.

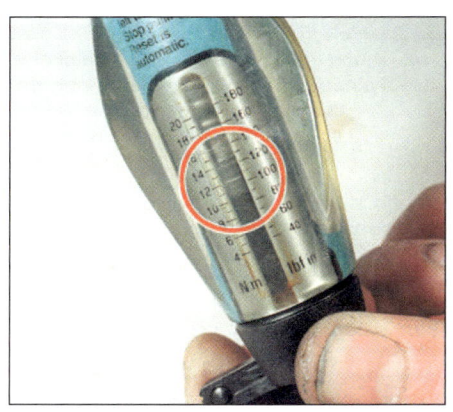

4.1 Set the torque wrench index mark to the setting required, in this case 12 Nm

● Install the bolts/nuts in their correct location and secure them lightly. Their threads must be clean and free of any old locking compound. Unless specified the threads and flange should be dry - oiled threads are necessary in certain circumstances and the manufacturer will take this into account in the specified torque figure. Similarly, the manufacturer may also specify the application of thread-locking compound.

● Tighten the fasteners in the specified sequence until the torque wrench clicks, indicating that the torque setting has been reached. Apply the torque again to double-check the setting. Where different thread diameter fasteners secure the component, as a rule tighten the larger diameter ones first.

● When the torque wrench has been finished with, release the lock (where applicable) and fully back off its setting to zero - do not leave the torque wrench tensioned. Also, do not use a torque wrench for slackening a fastener.

Angle-tightening

● Manufacturers often specify a figure in degrees for final tightening of a fastener. This usually follows tightening to a specific torque setting.

● A degree disc can be set and attached to the socket (see illustration 4.2) or a protractor can be used to mark the angle of movement on the bolt/nut head and the surrounding casting (see illustration 4.3).

4.2 Angle tightening can be accomplished with a torque-angle gauge . . .

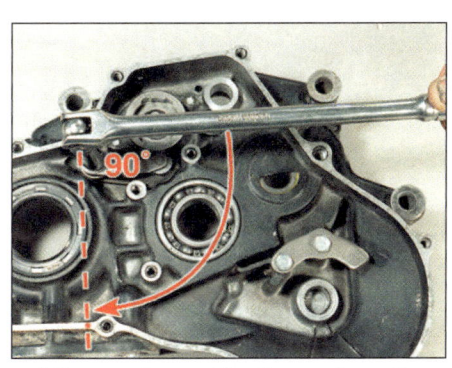

4.3 . . . or by marking the angle on the surrounding component

Loosening sequences

● Where more than one bolt/nut secures a component, loosen each fastener evenly a little at a time. In this way, not all the stress of the joint is held by one fastener and the components are not likely to distort.

● If a tightening sequence is provided, work in the REVERSE of this, but if not, work from the outside in, in a criss-cross sequence (see illustration 4.4).

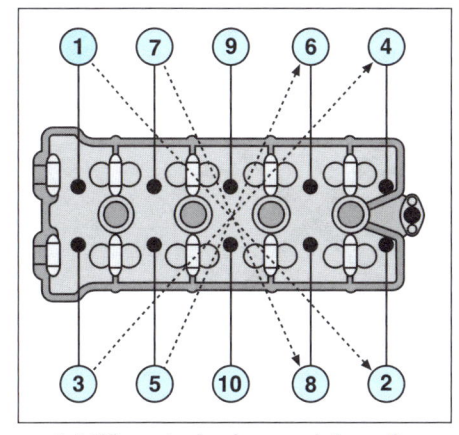

4.4 When slackening, work from the outside inwards

Tightening sequences

● If a component is held by more than one fastener it is important that the retaining bolts/nuts are tightened evenly to prevent uneven stress build-up and distortion of sealing faces. This is especially important on high-compression joints such as the cylinder head.

● A sequence is usually provided by the manufacturer, either in a diagram or actually marked in the casting. If not, always start in the centre and work outwards in a criss-cross pattern (see illustration 4.5). Start off by securing all bolts/nuts finger-tight, then set the torque wrench and tighten each fastener by a small amount in sequence until the final torque is reached. By following this practice,

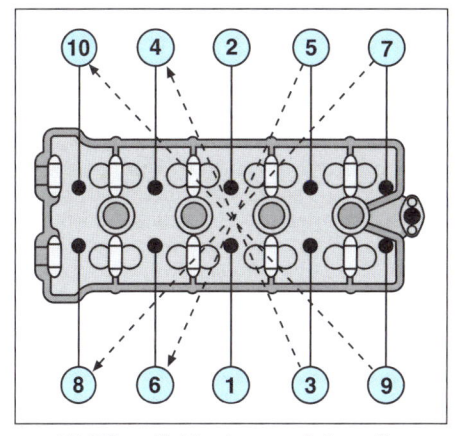

4.5 When tightening, work from the inside outwards

REF•14 Tools and Workshop Tips

the joint will be held evenly and will not be distorted. Important joints, such as the cylinder head and big-end fasteners often have two- or three-stage torque settings.

Applying leverage

● Use tools at the correct angle. Position a socket wrench or spanner on the bolt/nut so that you pull it towards you when loosening. If this can't be done, push the spanner without curling your fingers around it **(see illustration 4.6)** - the spanner may slip or the fastener loosen suddenly, resulting in your fingers being crushed against a component.

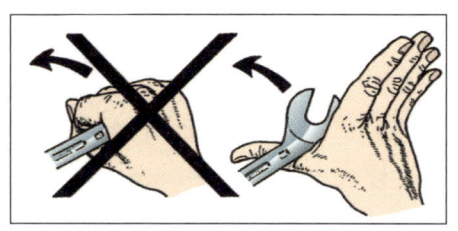

4.6 If you can't pull on the spanner to loosen a fastener, push with your hand open

● Additional leverage is gained by extending the length of the lever. The best way to do this is to use a breaker bar instead of the regular length tool, or to slip a length of tubing over the end of the spanner or socket wrench.
● If additional leverage will not work, the fastener head is either damaged or firmly corroded in place (see *Fasteners*).

5 Bearings

Bearing removal and installation

Drivers and sockets

● Before removing a bearing, always inspect the casing to see which way it must be driven out - some casings will have retaining plates or a cast step. Also check for any identifying markings on the bearing and if installed to a certain depth, measure this at this stage. Some roller bearings are sealed on one side - take note of the original fitted position.
● Bearings can be driven out of a casing using a bearing driver tool (with the correct size head) or a socket of the correct diameter. Select the driver head or socket so that it contacts the outer race of the bearing, not the balls/rollers or inner race. Always support the casing around the bearing housing with wood blocks, otherwise there is a risk of fracture. The bearing is driven out with a few blows on the driver or socket from a heavy mallet. Unless access is severely restricted (as with wheel bearings), a pin-punch is not recommended unless it is moved around the bearing to keep it square in its housing.

● The same equipment can be used to install bearings. Make sure the bearing housing is supported on wood blocks and line up the bearing in its housing. Fit the bearing as noted on removal - generally they are installed with their marked side facing outwards. Tap the bearing squarely into its housing using a driver or socket which bears only on the bearing's outer race - contact with the bearing balls/rollers or inner race will destroy it **(see illustrations 5.1 and 5.2)**.
● Check that the bearing inner race and balls/rollers rotate freely.

5.1 Using a bearing driver against the bearing's outer race

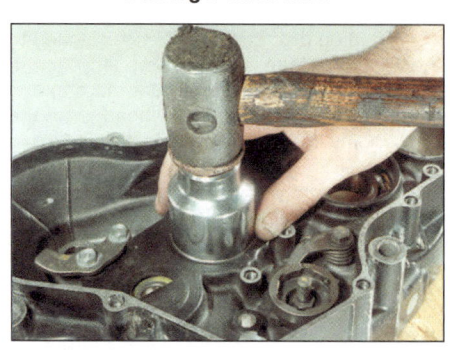

5.2 Using a large socket against the bearing's outer race

Pullers and slide-hammers

● Where a bearing is pressed on a shaft a puller will be required to extract it **(see illustration 5.3)**. Make sure that the puller clamp or legs fit securely behind the bearing and are unlikely to slip out. If pulling a bearing

5.3 This bearing puller clamps behind the bearing and pressure is applied to the shaft end to draw the bearing off

off a gear shaft for example, you may have to locate the puller behind a gear pinion if there is no access to the race and draw the gear pinion off the shaft as well **(see illustration 5.4)**.

Caution: Ensure that the puller's centre bolt locates securely against the end of the shaft and will not slip when pressure is applied. Also ensure that puller does not damage the shaft end.

5.4 Where no access is available to the rear of the bearing, it is sometimes possible to draw off the adjacent component

● Operate the puller so that its centre bolt exerts pressure on the shaft end and draws the bearing off the shaft.
● When installing the bearing on the shaft, tap only on the bearing's inner race - contact with the balls/rollers or outer race with destroy the bearing. Use a socket or length of tubing as a drift which fits over the shaft end **(see illustration 5.5)**.

5.5 When installing a bearing on a shaft use a piece of tubing which bears only on the bearing's inner race

● Where a bearing locates in a blind hole in a casing, it cannot be driven or pulled out as described above. A slide-hammer with knife-edged bearing puller attachment will be required. The puller attachment passes through the bearing and when tightened expands to fit firmly behind the bearing **(see illustration 5.6)**. By operating the slide-hammer part of the tool the bearing is jarred out of its housing **(see illustration 5.7)**.
● It is possible, if the bearing is of reasonable weight, for it to drop out of its housing if the casing is heated as described opposite. If this

Tools and Workshop Tips REF•15

5.6 Expand the bearing puller so that it locks behind the bearing . . .

5.7 . . . attach the slide hammer to the bearing puller

method is attempted, first prepare a work surface which will enable the casing to be tapped face down to help dislodge the bearing - a wood surface is ideal since it will not damage the casing's gasket surface. Wearing protective gloves, tap the heated casing several times against the work surface to dislodge the bearing under its own weight **(see illustration 5.8)**.

5.8 Tapping a casing face down on wood blocks can often dislodge a bearing

● Bearings can be installed in blind holes using the driver or socket method described above.

Drawbolts

● Where a bearing or bush is set in the eye of a component, such as a suspension linkage arm or connecting rod small-end, removal by drift may damage the component. Furthermore, a rubber bushing in a shock absorber eye cannot successfully be driven out of position. If access is available to an engineering press, the task is straightforward. If not, a drawbolt can be fabricated to extract the bearing or bush.

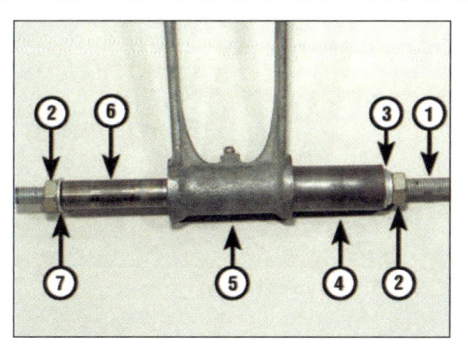

5.9 Drawbolt component parts assembled on a suspension arm

1 Bolt or length of threaded bar
2 Nuts
3 Washer (external diameter greater than tubing internal diameter)
4 Tubing (internal diameter sufficient to accommodate bearing)
5 Suspension arm with bearing
6 Tubing (external diameter slightly smaller than bearing)
7 Washer (external diameter slightly smaller than bearing)

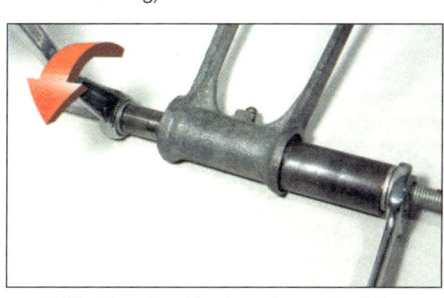

5.10 Drawing the bearing out of the suspension arm

● To extract the bearing/bush you will need a long bolt with nut (or piece of threaded bar with two nuts), a piece of tubing which has an internal diameter larger than the bearing/bush, another piece of tubing which has an external diameter slightly smaller than the bearing/bush, and a selection of washers **(see illustrations 5.9 and 5.10)**. Note that the pieces of tubing must be of the same length, or longer, than the bearing/bush.

● The same kit (without the pieces of tubing) can be used to draw the new bearing/bush back into place **(see illustration 5.11)**.

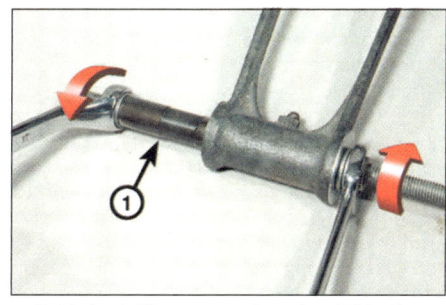

5.11 Installing a new bearing (1) in the suspension arm

Temperature change

● If the bearing's outer race is a light fit in the casing, the aluminium casing can be heated to release its grip on the bearing. Aluminium will expand at a greater rate than the steel bearing outer race. There are several ways to do this, but avoid any localised extreme heat (such as a blow torch) - aluminium alloy has a low melting point.

● Approved methods of heating a casing are using a domestic oven (heated to 100°C) or immersing the casing in boiling water **(see illustration 5.12)**. Low temperature range localised heat sources such as a paint stripper heat gun or clothes iron can also be used **(see illustration 5.13)**. Alternatively, soak a rag in boiling water, wring it out and wrap it around the bearing housing.

> ⚠ **Warning: All of these methods require care in use to prevent scalding and burns to the hands. Wear protective gloves when handling hot components.**

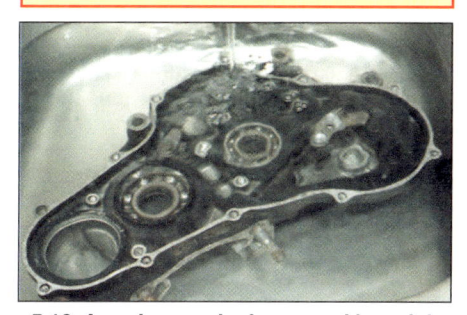

5.12 A casing can be immersed in a sink of boiling water to aid bearing removal

5.13 Using a localised heat source to aid bearing removal

● If heating the whole casing note that plastic components, such as the neutral switch, may suffer - remove them beforehand.

● After heating, remove the bearing as described above. You may find that the expansion is sufficient for the bearing to fall out of the casing under its own weight or with a light tap on the driver or socket.

● If necessary, the casing can be heated to aid bearing installation, and this is sometimes the recommended procedure if the motorcycle manufacturer has designed the housing and bearing fit with this intention.

REF•16 Tools and Workshop Tips

- Installation of bearings can be eased by placing them in a freezer the night before installation. The steel bearing will contract slightly, allowing easy insertion in its housing. This is often useful when installing steering head outer races in the frame.

Bearing types and markings

- Plain shell bearings, ball bearings, needle roller bearings and tapered roller bearings will all be found on motorcycles **(see illustrations 5.14 and 5.15)**. The ball and roller types are usually caged between an inner and outer race, but uncaged variations may be found.

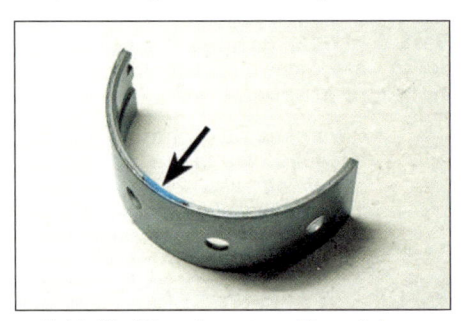

5.14 Shell bearings are either plain or grooved. They are usually identified by colour code (arrow)

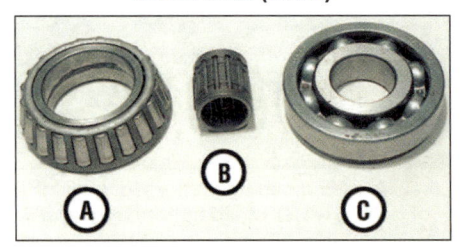

5.15 Tapered roller bearing (A), needle roller bearing (B) and ball journal bearing (C)

- Shell bearings (often called inserts) are usually found at the crankshaft main and connecting rod big-end where they are good at coping with high loads. They are made of a phosphor-bronze material and are impregnated with self-lubricating properties.
- Ball bearings and needle roller bearings consist of a steel inner and outer race with the balls or rollers between the races. They require constant lubrication by oil or grease and are good at coping with axial loads. Taper roller bearings consist of rollers set in a tapered cage set on the inner race; the outer race is separate. They are good at coping with axial loads and prevent movement along the shaft - a typical application is in the steering head.
- Bearing manufacturers produce bearings to ISO size standards and stamp one face of the bearing to indicate its internal and external diameter, load capacity and type **(see illustration 5.16)**.
- Metal bushes are usually of phosphor-bronze material. Rubber bushes are used in suspension mounting eyes. Fibre bushes have also been used in suspension pivots.

5.16 Typical bearing marking

Bearing fault finding

- If a bearing outer race has spun in its housing, the housing material will be damaged. You can use a bearing locking compound to bond the outer race in place if damage is not too severe.
- Shell bearings will fail due to damage of their working surface, as a result of lack of lubrication, corrosion or abrasive particles in the oil **(see illustration 5.17)**. Small particles of dirt in the oil may embed in the bearing material whereas larger particles will score the bearing and shaft journal. If a number of short journeys are made, insufficient heat will be generated to drive off condensation which has built up on the bearings.

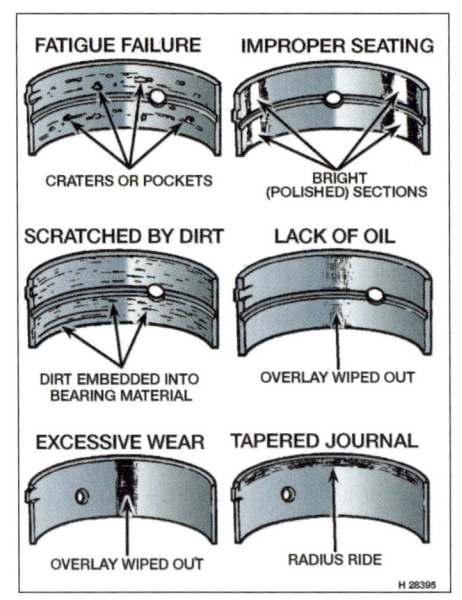

5.17 Typical bearing failures

- Ball and roller bearings will fail due to lack of lubrication or damage to the balls or rollers. Tapered-roller bearings can be damaged by overloading them. Unless the bearing is sealed on both sides, wash it in paraffin (kerosene) to remove all old grease then allow it to dry. Make a visual inspection looking to dented balls or rollers, damaged cages and worn or pitted races **(see illustration 5.18)**.
- A ball bearing can be checked for wear by listening to it when spun. Apply a film of light oil to the bearing and hold it close to the ear - hold the outer race with one hand and spin the inner race with the other hand **(see illustration 5.19)**. The bearing should be almost silent when spun; if it grates or rattles it is worn.

5.18 Example of ball journal bearing with damaged balls and cages

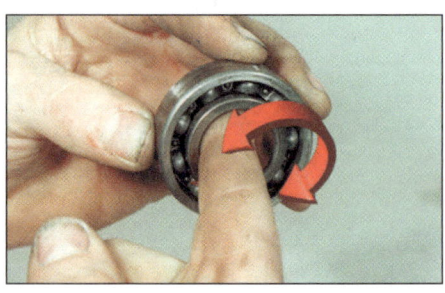

5.19 Hold outer race and listen to inner race when spun

6 Oil seals

Oil seal removal and installation

- Oil seals should be renewed every time a component is dismantled. This is because the seal lips will become set to the sealing surface and will not necessarily reseal.
- Oil seals can be prised out of position using a large flat-bladed screwdriver **(see illustration 6.1)**. In the case of crankcase seals, check first that the seal is not lipped on the inside, preventing its removal with the crankcases joined.

6.1 Prise out oil seals with a large flat-bladed screwdriver

- New seals are usually installed with their marked face (containing the seal reference code) outwards and the spring side towards the fluid being retained. In certain cases, such as a two-stroke engine crankshaft seal, a double lipped seal may be used due to there being fluid or gas on each side of the joint.

Tools and Workshop Tips REF•17

- Use a bearing driver or socket which bears only on the outer hard edge of the seal to install it in the casing - tapping on the inner edge will damage the sealing lip.

Oil seal types and markings

- Oil seals are usually of the single-lipped type. Double-lipped seals are found where a liquid or gas is on both sides of the joint.
- Oil seals can harden and lose their sealing ability if the motorcycle has been in storage for a long period - renewal is the only solution.
- Oil seal manufacturers also conform to the ISO markings for seal size - these are moulded into the outer face of the seal **(see illustration 6.2)**.

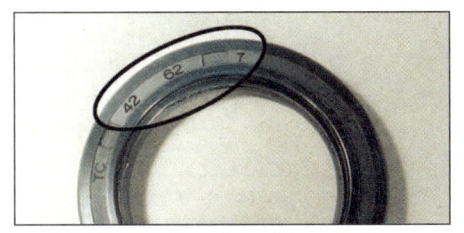

6.2 These oil seal markings indicate inside diameter, outside diameter and seal thickness

7 Gaskets and sealants

Types of gasket and sealant

- Gaskets are used to seal the mating surfaces between components and keep lubricants, fluids, vacuum or pressure contained within the assembly. Aluminium gaskets are sometimes found at the cylinder joints, but most gaskets are paper-based. If the mating surfaces of the components being joined are undamaged the gasket can be installed dry, although a dab of sealant or grease will be useful to hold it in place during assembly.
- RTV (Room Temperature Vulcanising) silicone rubber sealants cure when exposed to moisture in the atmosphere. These sealants are good at filling pits or irregular gasket faces, but will tend to be forced out of the joint under very high torque. They can be used to replace a paper gasket, but first make sure that the width of the paper gasket is not essential to the shimming of internal components. RTV sealants should not be used on components containing petrol (gasoline).
- Non-hardening, semi-hardening and hard setting liquid gasket compounds can be used with a gasket or between a metal-to-metal joint. Select the sealant to suit the application: universal non-hardening sealant can be used on virtually all joints; semi-hardening on joint faces which are rough or damaged; hard setting sealant on joints which require a permanent bond and are subjected to high temperature and pressure. **Note:** *Check first if the paper gasket has a bead of sealant impregnated in its surface before applying additional sealant.*
- When choosing a sealant, make sure it is suitable for the application, particularly if being applied in a high-temperature area or in the vicinity of fuel. Certain manufacturers produce sealants in either clear, silver or black colours to match the finish of the engine. This has a particular application on motorcycles where much of the engine is exposed.
- Do not over-apply sealant. That which is squeezed out on the outside of the joint can be wiped off, whereas an excess of sealant on the inside can break off and clog oilways.

Breaking a sealed joint

- Age, heat, pressure and the use of hard setting sealant can cause two components to stick together so tightly that they are difficult to separate using finger pressure alone. Do not resort to using levers unless there is a pry point provided for this purpose **(see illustration 7.1)** or else the gasket surfaces will be damaged.
- Use a soft-faced hammer **(see illustration 7.2)** or a wood block and conventional hammer to strike the component near the mating surface. Avoid hammering against cast extremities since they may break off. If this method fails, try using a wood wedge between the two components.

Caution: If the joint will not separate, double-check that you have removed all the fasteners.

7.1 If a pry point is provided, apply gently pressure with a flat-bladed screwdriver

7.2 Tap around the joint with a soft-faced mallet if necessary - don't strike cooling fins

Removal of old gasket and sealant

- Paper gaskets will most likely come away complete, leaving only a few traces stuck on

HAYNES HiNT

Most components have one or two hollow locating dowels between the two gasket faces. If a dowel cannot be removed, do not resort to gripping it with pliers - it will almost certainly be distorted. Install a close-fitting socket or Phillips screwdriver into the dowel and then grip the outer edge of the dowel to free it.

the sealing faces of the components. It is imperative that all traces are removed to ensure correct sealing of the new gasket.
- Very carefully scrape all traces of gasket away making sure that the sealing surfaces are not gouged or scored by the scraper **(see illustrations 7.3, 7.4 and 7.5)**. Stubborn deposits can be removed by spraying with an aerosol gasket remover. Final preparation of

7.3 Paper gaskets can be scraped off with a gasket scraper tool . . .

7.4 . . . a knife blade . . .

7.5 . . . or a household scraper

REF•18 Tools and Workshop Tips

7.6 Fine abrasive paper is wrapped around a flat file to clean up the gasket face

7.7 A kitchen scourer can be used on stubborn deposits

8.1 Tighten the chain breaker to push the pin out of the link . . .

8.2 . . . withdraw the pin, remove the tool . . .

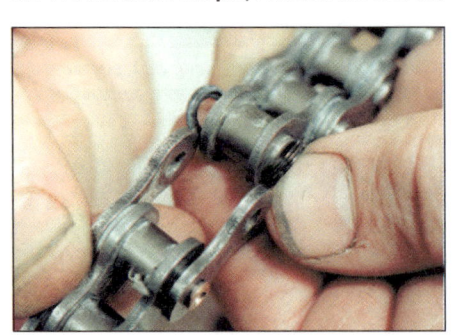

8.3 . . . and separate the chain link

8.4 Insert the new soft link, with O-rings, through the chain ends . . .

8.5 . . . install the O-rings over the pin ends . . .

8.6 . . . followed by the sideplate

8.7 Push the sideplate into position using a clamp

the gasket surface can be made with very fine abrasive paper or a plastic kitchen scourer (see illustrations 7.6 and 7.7).
● Old sealant can be scraped or peeled off components, depending on the type originally used. Note that gasket removal compounds are available to avoid scraping the components clean; make sure the gasket remover suits the type of sealant used.

8 Chains

Breaking and joining final drive chains

● Drive chains for all but small bikes are continuous and do not have a clip-type connecting link. The chain must be broken using a chain breaker tool and the new chain securely riveted together using a new soft rivet-type link. Never use a clip-type connecting link instead of a rivet-type link, except in an emergency. Various chain breaking and riveting tools are available, either as separate tools or combined as illustrated in the accompanying photographs - read the instructions supplied with the tool carefully.

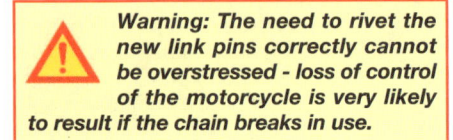

> **Warning:** The need to rivet the new link pins correctly cannot be overstressed - loss of control of the motorcycle is very likely to result if the chain breaks in use.

● Rotate the chain and look for the soft link. The soft link pins look like they have been deeply centre-punched instead of peened over like all the other pins (see illustration 8.9) and its sideplate may be a different colour. Position the soft link midway between the sprockets and assemble the chain breaker tool over one of the soft link pins (see illustration 8.1). Operate the tool to push the pin out through the chain (see illustration 8.2). On an O-ring chain, remove the O-rings (see illustration 8.3). Carry out the same procedure on the other soft link pin.

> **Caution: Certain soft link pins (particularly on the larger chains) may require their ends to be filed or ground off before they can be pressed out using the tool.**

● Check that you have the correct size and strength (standard or heavy duty) new soft link - do not reuse the old link. Look for the size marking on the chain sideplates (see illustration 8.10).
● Position the chain ends so that they are engaged over the rear sprocket. On an O-ring chain, install a new O-ring over each pin of the link and insert the link through the two chain ends (see illustration 8.4). Install a new O-ring over the end of each pin, followed by the sideplate (with the chain manufacturer's marking facing outwards) (see illustrations 8.5 and 8.6). On an unsealed chain, insert the link through the two chain ends, then install the sideplate with the chain manufacturer's marking facing outwards.
● Note that it may not be possible to install the sideplate using finger pressure alone. If using a joining tool, assemble it so that the plates of the tool clamp the link and press the sideplate over the pins (see illustration 8.7). Otherwise, use two small sockets placed over

Tools and Workshop Tips REF•19

8.8 Assemble the chain riveting tool over one pin at a time and tighten it fully

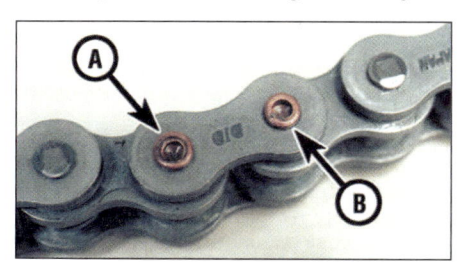

8.9 Pin end correctly riveted (A), pin end unriveted (B)

the rivet ends and two pieces of the wood between a G-clamp. Operate the clamp to press the sideplate over the pins.
● Assemble the joining tool over one pin (following the maker's instructions) and tighten the tool down to spread the pin end securely **(see illustrations 8.8 and 8.9)**. Do the same on the other pin.

> ⚠ **Warning: Check that the pin ends are secure and that there is no danger of the sideplate coming loose. If the pin ends are cracked the soft link must be renewed.**

Final drive chain sizing
● Chains are sized using a three digit number, followed by a suffix to denote the chain type **(see illustration 8.10)**. Chain type is either standard or heavy duty (thicker sideplates), and also unsealed or O-ring/X-ring type.
● The first digit of the number relates to the pitch of the chain, ie the distance from the centre of one pin to the centre of the next pin **(see illustration 8.11)**. Pitch is expressed in eighths of an inch, as follows:

8.10 Typical chain size and type marking

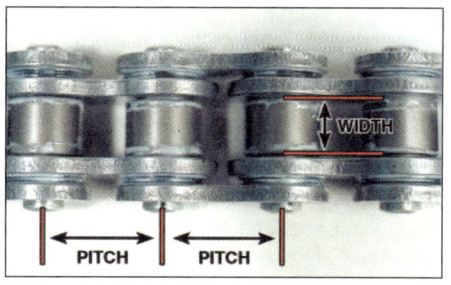

8.11 Chain dimensions

| Sizes commencing with a 4 (eg 428) have a pitch of 1/2 inch (12.7 mm) |
| Sizes commencing with a 5 (eg 520) have a pitch of 5/8 inch (15.9 mm) |
| Sizes commencing with a 6 (eg 630) have a pitch of 3/4 inch (19.1 mm) |

● The second and third digits of the chain size relate to the width of the rollers, again in imperial units, eg the 525 shown has 5/16 inch (7.94 mm) rollers **(see illustration 8.11)**.

9 Hoses

Clamping to prevent flow
● Small-bore flexible hoses can be clamped to prevent fluid flow whilst a component is worked on. Whichever method is used, ensure that the hose material is not permanently distorted or damaged by the clamp.
a) A brake hose clamp available from auto accessory shops **(see illustration 9.1)**.
b) A wingnut type hose clamp **(see illustration 9.2)**.

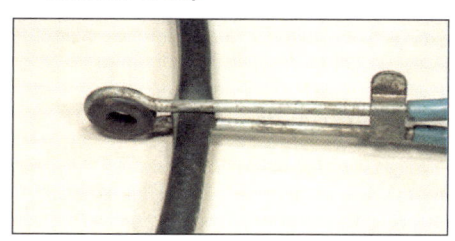

9.1 Hoses can be clamped with an automotive brake hose clamp . . .

9.2 . . . a wingnut type hose clamp . . .

c) Two sockets placed each side of the hose and held with straight-jawed self-locking grips **(see illustration 9.3)**.
d) Thick card each side of the hose held between straight-jawed self-locking grips **(see illustration 9.4)**.

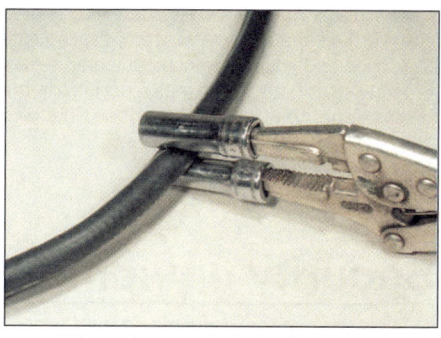

9.3 . . . two sockets and a pair of self-locking grips . . .

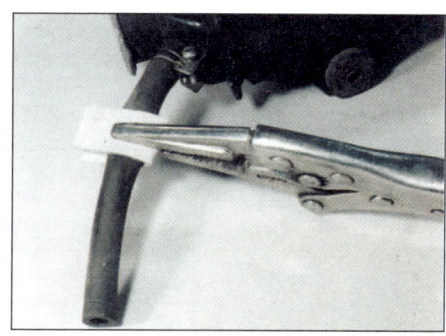

9.4 . . . or thick card and self-locking grips

Freeing and fitting hoses
● Always make sure the hose clamp is moved well clear of the hose end. Grip the hose with your hand and rotate it whilst pulling it off the union. If the hose has hardened due to age and will not move, slit it with a sharp knife and peel its ends off the union **(see illustration 9.5)**.
● Resist the temptation to use grease or soap on the unions to aid installation; although it helps the hose slip over the union it will equally aid the escape of fluid from the joint. It is preferable to soften the hose ends in hot water and wet the inside surface of the hose with water or a fluid which will evaporate.

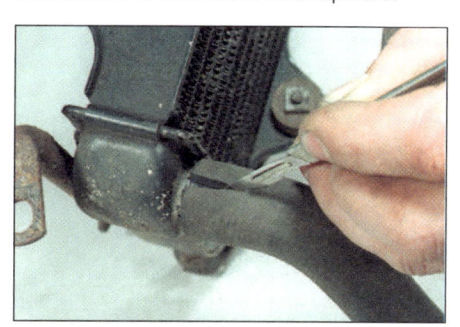

9.5 Cutting a coolant hose free with a sharp knife

REF•20 Security

Introduction

In less time than it takes to read this introduction, a thief could steal your motorcycle. Returning only to find your bike has gone is one of the worst feelings in the world. Even if the motorcycle is insured against theft, once you've got over the initial shock, you will have the inconvenience of dealing with the police and your insurance company.

The motorcycle is an easy target for the professional thief and the joyrider alike and the official figures on motorcycle theft make for depressing reading; on average a motorcycle is stolen every 16 minutes in the UK!

Motorcycle thefts fall into two categories, those stolen 'to order' and those taken by opportunists. The thief stealing to order will be on the look out for a specific make and model and will go to extraordinary lengths to obtain that motorcycle. The opportunist thief on the other hand will look for easy targets which can be stolen with the minimum of effort and risk.

Whilst it is never going to be possible to make your machine 100% secure, it is estimated that around half of all stolen motorcycles are taken by opportunist thieves. Remember that the opportunist thief is always on the look out for the easy option: if there are two similar motorcycles parked side-by-side, they will target the one with the lowest level of security. By taking a few precautions, you can reduce the chances of your motorcycle being stolen.

Security equipment

There are many specialised motorcycle security devices available and the following text summarises their applications and their good and bad points.

Once you have decided on the type of security equipment which best suits your needs, we recommended that you read one of the many equipment tests regularly carried out by the motorcycle press. These tests compare the products from all the major manufacturers and give impartial ratings on their effectiveness, value-for-money and ease of use.

No one item of security equipment can provide complete protection. It is highly recommended that two or more of the items described below are combined to increase the security of your motorcycle (a lock and chain plus an alarm system is just about ideal). The more security measures fitted to the bike, the less likely it is to be stolen.

Lock and chain

Pros: *Very flexible to use; can be used to secure the motorcycle to almost any immovable object. On some locks and chains, the lock can be used on its own as a disc lock (see below).*

Cons: *Can be very heavy and awkward to carry on the motorcycle, although some types will be supplied with a carry bag which can be strapped to the pillion seat.*

● Heavy-duty chains and locks are an excellent security measure **(see illustration 1)**. Whenever the motorcycle is parked, use the lock and chain to secure the machine to a solid, immovable object such as a post or railings. This will prevent the machine from being ridden away or being lifted into the back of a van.

● When fitting the chain, always ensure the chain is routed around the motorcycle frame or swingarm **(see illustrations 2 and 3)**. Never merely pass the chain around one of the wheel rims; a thief may unbolt the wheel and lift the rest of the machine into a van, leaving you with just the wheel! Try to avoid having excess chain free, thus making it difficult to use cutting tools, and keep the chain and lock off the ground to prevent thieves attacking it with a cold chisel. Position the lock so that its lock barrel is facing downwards; this will make it harder for the thief to attack the lock mechanism.

1 Ensure the lock and chain you buy is of good quality and long enough to shackle your bike to a solid object

2 Pass the chain through the bike's frame, rather than just through a wheel . . .

3 . . . and loop it around a solid object

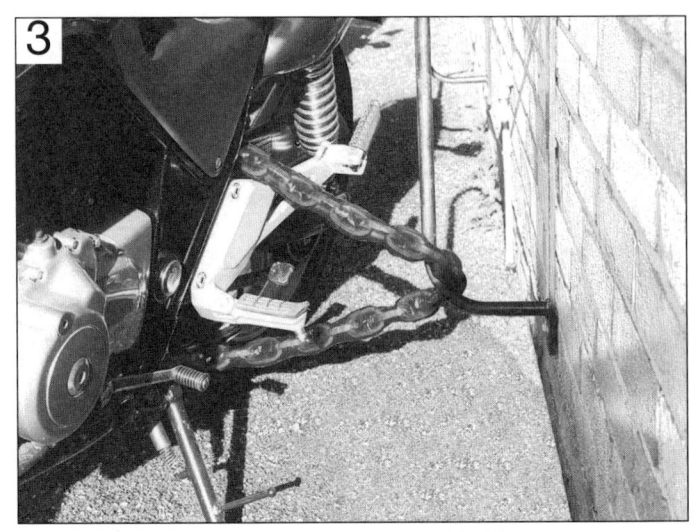

Security REF•21

U-locks

Pros: *Highly effective deterrent which can be used to secure the bike to a post or railings. Most U-locks come with a carrier which allows the lock to be easily carried on the bike.*

Cons: *Not as flexible to use as a lock and chain.*

● These are solid locks which are similar in use to a lock and chain. U-locks are lighter than a lock and chain but not so flexible to use. The length and shape of the lock shackle limit the objects to which the bike can be secured **(see illustration 4)**.

U-locks can be used to secure the bike to a solid object – ensure you purchase one which is long enough

Disc locks

Pros: *Small, light and very easy to carry; most can be stored underneath the seat.*

Cons: *Does not prevent the motorcycle being lifted into a van. Can be very embarrassing if you forget to remove the lock before attempting to ride off!*

● Disc locks are designed to be attached to the front brake disc. The lock passes through one of the holes in the disc and prevents the wheel rotating by jamming against the fork/brake caliper **(see illustration 5)**. Some are equipped with an alarm siren which sounds if the disc lock is moved; this not only acts as a theft deterrent but also as a handy reminder if you try to move the bike with the lock still fitted.

● Combining the disc lock with a length of cable which can be looped around a post or railings provides an additional measure of security **(see illustration 6)**.

A typical disc lock attached through one of the holes in the disc

Alarms and immobilisers

Pros: *Once installed it is completely hassle-free to use. If the system is 'Thatcham' or 'Sold Secure-approved', insurance companies may give you a discount.*

Cons: *Can be expensive to buy and complex to install. No system will prevent the motorcycle from being lifted into a van and taken away.*

● Electronic alarms and immobilisers are available to suit a variety of budgets. There are three different types of system available: pure alarms, pure immobilisers, and the more expensive systems which are combined alarm/immobilisers **(see illustration 7)**.

● An alarm system is designed to emit an audible warning if the motorcycle is being tampered with.

● An immobiliser prevents the motorcycle being started and ridden away by disabling its electrical systems.

● When purchasing an alarm/immobiliser system, check the cost of installing the system unless you are able to do it yourself. If the motorcycle is not used regularly, another consideration is the current drain of the system. All alarm/immobiliser systems are powered by the motorcycle's battery; purchasing a system with a very low current drain could prevent the battery losing its charge whilst the motorcycle is not being used.

A disc lock combined with a security cable provides additional protection

A typical alarm/immobiliser system

Security

Indelible markings can be applied to most areas of the bike – always apply the manufacturer's sticker to warn off thieves

Chemically-etched code numbers can be applied to main body panels . . .

. . . again, always ensure that the kit manufacturer's sticker is applied in a prominent position

Security marking kits

Pros: *Very cheap and effective deterrent. Many insurance companies will give you a discount on your insurance premium if a recognised security marking kit is used on your motorcycle.*

Cons: *Does not prevent the motorcycle being stolen by joyriders.*

● There are many different types of security marking kits available. The idea is to mark as many parts of the motorcycle as possible with a unique security number **(see illustrations 8, 9 and 10)**. A form will be included with the kit to register your personal details and those of the motorcycle with the kit manufacturer. This register is made available to the police to help them trace the rightful owner of any motorcycle or components which they recover should all other forms of identification have been removed. Always apply the warning stickers provided with the kit to deter thieves.

Ground anchors, wheel clamps and security posts

Pros: *An excellent form of security which will deter all but the most determined of thieves.*

Cons: *Awkward to install and can be expensive.*

● Whilst the motorcycle is at home, it is a good idea to attach it securely to the floor or a solid wall, even if it is kept in a securely locked garage. Various types of ground anchors, security posts and wheel clamps are available for this purpose **(see illustration 11)**. These security devices are either bolted to a solid concrete or brick structure or can be cemented into the ground.

Permanent ground anchors provide an excellent level of security when the bike is at home

Security at home

A high percentage of motorcycle thefts are from the owner's home. Here are some things to consider whenever your motorcycle is at home:

✔ Where possible, always keep the motorcycle in a securely locked garage. Never rely solely on the standard lock on the garage door, these are usual hopelessly inadequate. Fit an additional locking mechanism to the door and consider having the garage alarmed. A security light, activated by a movement sensor, is also a good investment.

✔ Always secure the motorcycle to the ground or a wall, even if it is inside a securely locked garage.

✔ Do not regularly leave the motorcycle outside your home, try to keep it out of sight wherever possible. If a garage is not available, fit a motorcycle cover over the bike to disguise its true identity.

✔ It is not uncommon for thieves to follow a motorcyclist home to find out where the bike is kept. They will then return at a later date. Be aware of this whenever you are returning home on your motorcycle. If you suspect you are being followed, do not return home, instead ride to a garage or shop and stop as a precaution.

✔ When selling a motorcycle, do not provide your home address or the location where the bike is normally kept. Arrange to meet the buyer at a location away from your home. Thieves have been known to pose as potential buyers to find out where motorcycles are kept and then return later to steal them.

Security away from the home

As well as fitting security equipment to your motorcycle here are a few general rules to follow whenever you park your motorcycle.

✔ Park in a busy, public place.

✔ Use car parks which incorporate security features, such as CCTV.

✔ At night, park in a well-lit area, preferably directly underneath a street light.

✔ Engage the steering lock.

✔ Secure the motorcycle to a solid, immovable object such as a post or railings with an additional lock. If this is not possible, secure the bike to a friend's motorcycle. Some public parking places provide security loops for motorcycles.

✔ Never leave your helmet or luggage attached to the motorcycle. Take them with you at all times.

Lubricants and fluids REF•23

Lubricants and fluids

A wide range of lubricants, fluids and cleaning agents is available for motor-cycles. This is a guide as to what is available, its applications and properties.

Four-stroke engine oil

● Engine oil is without doubt the most important component of any four-stroke engine. Modern motorcycle engines place a lot of demands on their oil and choosing the right type is essential. Using an unsuitable oil will lead to an increased rate of engine wear and could result in serious engine damage. Before purchasing oil, always check the recommended oil specification given by the manufacturer. The manufacturer will state a recommended 'type or classification' and also a specific 'viscosity' range for engine oil.

● The oil 'type or classification' is identified by its API (American Petroleum Institute) rating. The API rating will be in the form of two letters, e.g. SG. The S identifies the oil as being suitable for use in a petrol (gasoline) engine (S stands for spark ignition) and the second letter, ranging from A to J, identifies the oil's performance rating. The later this letter, the higher the specification of the oil; for example API SG oil exceeds the requirements of API SF oil. **Note:** *On some oils there may also be a second rating consisting of another two letters, the first letter being C, e.g. API SF/CD. This rating indicates the oil is also suitable for use in a diesel engines (the C stands for compression ignition) and is thus of no relevance for motorcycle use.*

● The 'viscosity' of the oil is identified by its SAE (Society of Automotive Engineers) rating. All modern engines require multigrade oils and the SAE rating will consist of two numbers, the first followed by a W, e.g. 10W/40. The first number indicates the viscosity rating of the oil at low temperatures (W stands for winter – tested at –20°C) and the second number represents the viscosity of the oil at high temperatures (tested at 100°C). The lower the number, the thinner the oil. For example an oil with an SAE 10W/40 rating will give better cold starting and running than an SAE 15W/40 oil.

● As well as ensuring the 'type' and 'viscosity' of the oil match the recommendations, another consideration to make when buying engine oil is whether to purchase a standard mineral-based oil, a semi-synthetic oil (also known as a synthetic blend or synthetic-based oil) or a fully-synthetic oil. Although all oils will have a similar rating and viscosity, their cost will vary considerably; mineral-based oils are the cheapest, the fully-synthetic oils the most expensive with the semi-synthetic oils falling somewhere in-between. This decision is very much up to the owner, but it should be noted that modern synthetic oils have far better lubricating and cleaning qualities than traditional mineral-based oils and tend to retain these properties for far longer. Bearing in mind the operating conditions inside a modern, high-revving motorcycle engine it is highly recommended that a fully synthetic oil is used. The extra expense at each service could save you money in the long term by preventing premature engine wear.

● As a final note always ensure that the oil is specifically designed for use in motorcycle engines. Engine oils designed primarily for use in car engines sometimes contain additives or friction modifiers which could cause clutch slip on a motorcycle fitted with a wet-clutch.

Two-stroke engine oil

● Modern two-stroke engines, with their high power outputs, place high demands on their oil. If engine seizure is to be avoided it is essential that a high-quality oil is used. Two-stroke oils differ hugely from four-stroke oils. The oil lubricates only the crankshaft and piston(s) (the transmission has its own lubricating oil) and is used on a total-loss basis where it is burnt completely during the combustion process.

● The Japanese have recently introduced a classification system for two-stroke oils, the JASO rating. This rating is in the form of two letters, either FA, FB or FC – FA is the lowest classification and FC the highest. Ensure the oil being used meets or exceeds the recommended rating specified by the manufacturer.

● As well as ensuring the oil rating matches the recommendation, another consideration to make when buying engine oil is whether to purchase a standard mineral-based oil, a semi-synthetic oil (also known as a synthetic blend or synthetic-based oil) or a fully-synthetic oil. The cost of each type of oil varies considerably; mineral-based oils are the cheapest, the fully-synthetic oils the most expensive with the semi-synthetic oils falling somewhere in-between. This decision is very much up to the owner, but it should be noted that modern synthetic oils have far better lubricating properties and burn cleaner than traditional mineral-based oils. It is therefore recommended that a fully synthetic oil is used. The extra expense could save you money in the long term by preventing premature engine wear, engine performance will be improved, carbon deposits and exhaust smoke will be reduced.

Lubricants and fluids

● Always ensure that the oil is specifically designed for use in an injector system. Many high quality two-stroke oils are designed for competition use and need to be pre-mixed with fuel. These oils are of a much higher viscosity and are not designed to flow through the injector pumps used on road-going two-stroke motorcycles.

Transmission (gear) oil

● On a two-stroke engine, the transmission and clutch are lubricated by their own separate oil bath which must be changed in accordance with the Maintenance Schedule.
● Although the engine and transmission units of most four-strokes use a common lubrication supply, there are some exceptions where the engine and gearbox have separate oil reservoirs and a dry clutch is used.
● Motorcycle manufacturers will either recommend a monograde transmission oil or a four-stroke multigrade engine oil to lubricate the transmission.
● Transmission oils, or gear oils as they are often called, are designed specifically for use in transmission systems. The viscosity of these oils is represented by an SAE number, but the scale of measurement applied is different to that used to grade engine oils. As a rough guide a SAE90 gear oil will be of the same viscosity as an SAE50 engine oil.

Shaft drive oil

● On models equipped with shaft final drive, the shaft drive gears are will have their own oil supply. The manufacturer will state a recommended 'type or classification' and also a specific 'viscosity' range in the same manner as for four-stroke engine oil.
● Gear oil classification is given by the number which follows the API GL (GL standing for gear lubricant) rating, the higher the number, the higher the specification of the oil, e.g. API GL5 oil is a higher specification than API GL4 oil. Ensure the oil meets or exceeds the classification specified and is of the correct viscosity. The viscosity of gear oils is also represented by an SAE number but the scale of measurement used is different to that used to grade engine oils. As a rough guide an SAE90 gear oil will be of the same viscosity as an SAE50 engine oil.
● If the use of an EP (Extreme Pressure) gear oil is specified, ensure the oil purchased is suitable.

Fork oil and suspension fluid

● Conventional telescopic front forks are hydraulic and require fork oil to work. To ensure the forks function correctly, the fork oil must be changed in accordance with the Maintenance Schedule.
● Fork oil is available in a variety of viscosities, identified by their SAE rating; fork oil ratings vary from light (SAE 5) to heavy (SAE 30). When purchasing fork oil, ensure the viscosity rating matches that specified by the manufacturer.
● Some lubricant manufacturers also produce a range of high-quality suspension fluids which are very similar to fork oil but are designed mainly for competition use. These fluids may have a different viscosity rating system which is not to be confused with the SAE rating of normal fork oil. Refer to the manufacturer's instructions if in any doubt.

Brake and clutch fluid

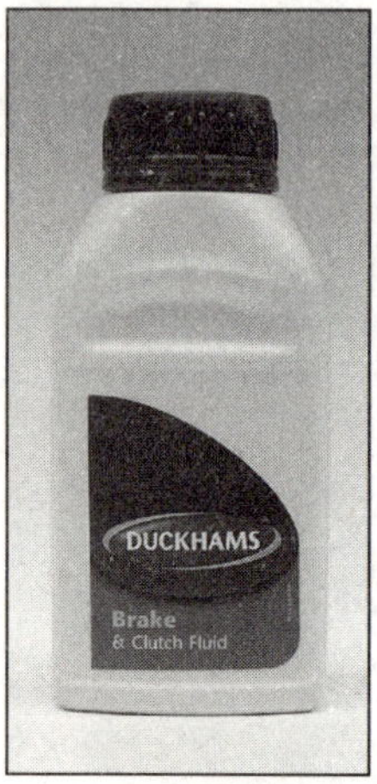

● All disc brake systems and some clutch systems are hydraulically operated. To ensure correct operation, the hydraulic fluid must be changed in accordance with the Maintenance Schedule.
● Brake and clutch fluid is classified by its DOT rating with most motorcycle manufacturers specifying DOT 3 or 4 fluid. Both fluid types are glycol-based and can be mixed together without adverse effect; DOT 4 fluid exceeds the requirements of DOT 3 fluid. Although it is safe to use DOT 4 fluid in a system designed for use with DOT 3 fluid, never use DOT 3 fluid in a system which specifies the use of DOT 4 as this will adversely affect the system's performance. The type required for the system will be marked on the fluid reservoir cap.
● Some manufacturers also produce a DOT 5 hydraulic fluid. DOT 5 hydraulic fluid is silicone-based and is not compatible with the glycol-based DOT 3 and 4 fluids. Never mix DOT 5 fluid with DOT 3 or 4 fluid as this will seriously affect the performance of the hydraulic system.

Coolant/antifreeze

● When purchasing coolant/antifreeze, always ensure it is suitable for use in an aluminium engine and contains corrosion inhibitors to prevent possible blockages of the internal coolant passages of the system. As a general rule, most coolants are designed to be used neat and should not be diluted whereas antifreeze can be mixed with distilled water to provide a coolant solution of the required strength. Refer to the manufacturer's instructions on the bottle.
● Ensure the coolant is changed in accordance with the Maintenance Schedule.

Chain lube

● Chain lube is an aerosol-type spray lubricant specifically designed for use on motorcycle final drive chains. Chain lube has two functions, to minimise friction between the final drive chain and sprockets and to prevent corrosion of the chain. Regular use of a good-quality chain lube will extend the life of the drive chain and sprockets and thus maximise the power being transmitted from the transmission to the rear wheel.
● When using chain lube, always allow some time for the solvents in the lube to evaporate before riding the motorcycle. This will minimise the amount of lube which will

Lubricants and fluids REF•25

'fling' off from the chain when the motorcycle is used. If the motorcycle is equipped with an 'O-ring' chain, ensure the chain lube is labelled as being suitable for use on 'O-ring' chains.

Degreasers and solvents

● There are many different types of solvents and degreasers available to remove the grime and grease which accumulate around the motorcycle during normal use. Degreasers and solvents are usually available as an aerosol-type spray or as a liquid which you apply with a brush. Always closely follow the manufacturer's instructions and wear eye protection during use. Be aware that many solvents are flammable and may give off noxious fumes; take adequate precautions when using them (see Safety First!).

● For general cleaning, use one of the many solvents or degreasers available from most motorcycle accessory shops. These solvents are usually applied then left for a certain time before being washed off with water.

Brake cleaner is a solvent specifically designed to remove all traces of oil, grease and dust from braking system components. Brake cleaner is designed to evaporate quickly and leaves behind no residue.

Carburettor cleaner is an aerosol-type solvent specifically designed to clear carburettor blockages and break down the hard deposits and gum often found inside carburettors during overhaul.

Contact cleaner is an aerosol-type solvent designed for cleaning electrical components. The cleaner will remove all traces of oil and dirt from components such as switch contacts or fouled spark plugs and then dry, leaving behind no residue.

Gasket remover is an aerosol-type solvent designed for removing stubborn gaskets from engine components during overhaul. Gasket remover will minimise the amount of scraping required to remove the gasket and therefore reduce the risk of damage to the mating surface.

Spray lubricants

● Aerosol-based spray lubricants are widely available and are excellent for lubricating lever pivots and exposed cables and switches. Try to use a lubricant which is of the dry-film type as the fluid evaporates, leaving behind a dry-film of lubricant. Lubricants which leave behind an oily residue will attract dust and dirt which will increase the rate of wear of the cable/lever.

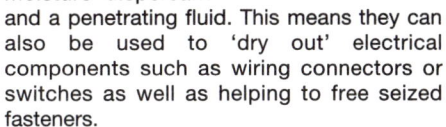

● Most lubricants also act as a moisture dispersant and a penetrating fluid. This means they can also be used to 'dry out' electrical components such as wiring connectors or switches as well as helping to free seized fasteners.

Greases

● Grease is used to lubricate many of the pivot-points. A good-quality multi-purpose grease is suitable for most applications but some manufacturers will specify the use of specialist greases for use on components such as swingarm and suspension linkage bushes. These specialist greases can be purchased from most motorcycle (or car) accessory shops; commonly specified types include molybdenum disulphide grease, lithium-based grease, graphite-based grease, silicone-based grease and high-temperature copper-based grease.

Gasket sealing compounds

● Gasket sealing compounds can be used in conjunction with gaskets, to improve their sealing capabilities, or on their own to seal metal-to-metal joints. Depending on their type, sealing compounds either set hard or stay relatively soft and pliable.

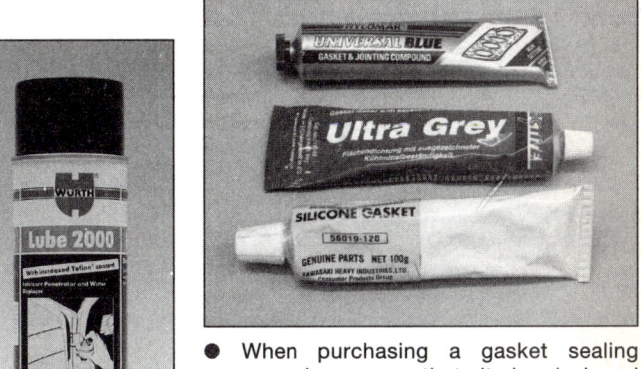

● When purchasing a gasket sealing compound, ensure that it is designed specifically for use on an internal combustion engine. General multi-purpose sealants available from DIY stores may appear visibly similar but they are not designed to withstand the extreme heat or contact with fuel and oil encountered when used on an engine (see 'Tools and Workshop Tips' for further information).

Thread locking compound

● Thread locking compounds are used to secure certain threaded fasteners in position to prevent them from loosening due to vibration. Thread locking compounds can be purchased from most motorcycle (and car) accessory shops. Ensure the threads of the both components are completely clean and dry before sparingly applying the locking compound (see 'Tools and Workshop Tips' for further information).

Fuel additives

● Fuel additives which protect and clean the fuel system components are widely available. These additives are designed to remove all traces of deposits that build up on the carburettors/injectors and prevent wear, helping the fuel system to operate more efficiently. If a fuel additive is being used, check that it is suitable for use with your motorcycle, especially if your motorcycle is equipped with a catalytic converter.

● Octane boosters are also available. These additives are designed to improve the performance of highly-tuned engines being run on normal pump-fuel and are of no real use on standard motorcycles.

Conversion factors

Length (distance)

Inches (in)	x 25.4	= Millimetres (mm)	x 0.0394	= Inches (in)
Feet (ft)	x 0.305	= Metres (m)	x 3.281	= Feet (ft)
Miles	x 1.609	= Kilometres (km)	x 0.621	= Miles

Volume (capacity)

Cubic inches (cu in; in^3)	x 16.387	= Cubic centimetres (cc; cm^3)	x 0.061	= Cubic inches (cu in; in^3)
Imperial pints (Imp pt)	x 0.568	= Litres (l)	x 1.76	= Imperial pints (Imp pt)
Imperial quarts (Imp qt)	x 1.137	= Litres (l)	x 0.88	= Imperial quarts (Imp qt)
Imperial quarts (Imp qt)	x 1.201	= US quarts (US qt)	x 0.833	= Imperial quarts (Imp qt)
US quarts (US qt)	x 0.946	= Litres (l)	x 1.057	= US quarts (US qt)
Imperial gallons (Imp gal)	x 4.546	= Litres (l)	x 0.22	= Imperial gallons (Imp gal)
Imperial gallons (Imp gal)	x 1.201	= US gallons (US gal)	x 0.833	= Imperial gallons (Imp gal)
US gallons (US gal)	x 3.785	= Litres (l)	x 0.264	= US gallons (US gal)

Mass (weight)

Ounces (oz)	x 28.35	= Grams (g)	x 0.035	= Ounces (oz)
Pounds (lb)	x 0.454	= Kilograms (kg)	x 2.205	= Pounds (lb)

Force

Ounces-force (ozf; oz)	x 0.278	= Newtons (N)	x 3.6	= Ounces-force (ozf; oz)
Pounds-force (lbf; lb)	x 4.448	= Newtons (N)	x 0.225	= Pounds-force (lbf; lb)
Newtons (N)	x 0.1	= Kilograms-force (kgf; kg)	x 9.81	= Newtons (N)

Pressure

Pounds-force per square inch (psi; lbf/in^2; lb/in^2)	x 0.070	= Kilograms-force per square centimetre (kgf/cm^2; kg/cm^2)	x 14.223	= Pounds-force per square inch (psi; lbf/in^2; lb/in^2)
Pounds-force per square inch (psi; lbf/in^2; lb/in^2)	x 0.068	= Atmospheres (atm)	x 14.696	= Pounds-force per square inch (psi; lbf/in^2; lb/in^2)
Pounds-force per square inch (psi; lbf/in^2; lb/in^2)	x 0.069	= Bars	x 14.5	= Pounds-force per square inch (psi; lbf/in^2; lb/in^2)
Pounds-force per square inch (psi; lbf/in^2; lb/in^2)	x 6.895	= Kilopascals (kPa)	x 0.145	= Pounds-force per square inch (psi; lbf/in^2; lb/in^2)
Kilopascals (kPa)	x 0.01	= Kilograms-force per square centimetre (kgf/cm^2; kg/cm^2)	x 98.1	= Kilopascals (kPa)
Millibar (mbar)	x 100	= Pascals (Pa)	x 0.01	= Millibar (mbar)
Millibar (mbar)	x 0.0145	= Pounds-force per square inch (psi; lbf/in^2; lb/in^2)	x 68.947	= Millibar (mbar)
Millibar (mbar)	x 0.75	= Millimetres of mercury (mmHg)	x 1.333	= Millibar (mbar)
Millibar (mbar)	x 0.401	= Inches of water (inH$_2$O)	x 2.491	= Millibar (mbar)
Millimetres of mercury (mmHg)	x 0.535	= Inches of water (inH$_2$O)	x 1.868	= Millimetres of mercury (mmHg)
Inches of water (inH$_2$O)	x 0.036	= Pounds-force per square inch (psi; lbf/in^2; lb/in^2)	x 27.68	= Inches of water (inH$_2$O)

Torque (moment of force)

Pounds-force inches (lbf in; lb in)	x 1.152	= Kilograms-force centimetre (kgf cm; kg cm)	x 0.868	= Pounds-force inches (lbf in; lb in)
Pounds-force inches (lbf in; lb in)	x 0.113	= Newton metres (Nm)	x 8.85	= Pounds-force inches (lbf in; lb in)
Pounds-force inches (lbf in; lb in)	x 0.083	= Pounds-force feet (lbf ft; lb ft)	x 12	= Pounds-force inches (lbf in; lb in)
Pounds-force feet (lbf ft; lb ft)	x 0.138	= Kilograms-force metres (kgf m; kg m)	x 7.233	= Pounds-force feet (lbf ft; lb ft)
Pounds-force feet (lbf ft; lb ft)	x 1.356	= Newton metres (Nm)	x 0.738	= Pounds-force feet (lbf ft; lb ft)
Newton metres (Nm)	x 0.102	= Kilograms-force metres (kgf m; kg m)	x 9.804	= Newton metres (Nm)

Power

Horsepower (hp)	x 745.7	= Watts (W)	x 0.0013	= Horsepower (hp)

Velocity (speed)

Miles per hour (miles/hr; mph)	x 1.609	= Kilometres per hour (km/hr; kph)	x 0.621	= Miles per hour (miles/hr; mph)

Fuel consumption*

Miles per gallon (mpg)	x 0.354	= Kilometres per litre (km/l)	x 2.825	= Miles per gallon (mpg)

Temperature

Degrees Fahrenheit = (°C x 1.8) + 32   Degrees Celsius (Degrees Centigrade; °C) = (°F - 32) x 0.56

* *It is common practice to convert from miles per gallon (mpg) to litres/100 kilometres (l/100km), where mpg x l/100 km = 282*

MOT Test Checks REF•27

About the MOT Test

In the UK, all vehicles more than three years old are subject to an annual test to ensure that they meet minimum safety requirements. A current test certificate must be issued before a machine can be used on public roads, and is required before a road fund licence can be issued. Riding without a current test certificate will also invalidate your insurance.

For most owners, the MOT test is an annual cause for anxiety, and this is largely due to owners not being sure what needs to be checked prior to submitting the motorcycle for testing. The simple answer is that a fully roadworthy motorcycle will have no difficulty in passing the test.

This is a guide to getting your motorcycle through the MOT test. Obviously it will not be possible to examine the motorcycle to the same standard as the professional MOT tester, particularly in view of the equipment required for some of the checks. However, working through the following procedures will enable you to identify any problem areas before submitting the motorcycle for the test.

It has only been possible to summarise the test requirements here, based on the regulations in force at the time of printing. Test standards are becoming increasingly stringent, although there are some exemptions for older vehicles. More information about the MOT test can be obtained from the TSO publications, *How Safe is your Motorcycle* and *The MOT Inspection Manual for Motorcycle Testing*.

Many of the checks require that one of the wheels is raised off the ground. If the motorcycle doesn't have a centre stand, note that an auxiliary stand will be required. Additionally, the help of an assistant may prove useful.

Certain exceptions apply to machines under 50 cc, machines without a lighting system, and Classic bikes - if in doubt about any of the requirements listed below seek confirmation from an MOT tester prior to submitting the motorcycle for the test.

Check that the frame number is clearly visible.

Electrical System

Lights, turn signals, horn and reflector

✔ With the ignition on, check the operation of the following electrical components. **Note:** *The electrical components on certain small-capacity machines are powered by the generator, requiring that the engine is run for this check.*

a) *Headlight and tail light.* Check that both illuminate in the low and high beam switch positions.

b) *Position lights.* Check that the front position (or sidelight) and tail light illuminate in this switch position.

c) *Turn signals.* Check that all flash at the correct rate, and that the warning light(s) function correctly. Check that the turn signal switch works correctly.

d) *Hazard warning system (where fitted).* Check that all four turn signals flash in this switch position.

e) *Brake stop light.* Check that the light comes on when the front and rear brakes are independently applied. Models first used on or after 1st April 1986 must have a brake light switch on each brake.

f) *Horn.* Check that the sound is continuous and of reasonable volume.

✔ Check that there is a red reflector on the rear of the machine, either mounted separately or as part of the tail light lens.

✔ Check the condition of the headlight, tail light and turn signal lenses.

Headlight beam height

✔ The MOT tester will perform a headlight beam height check using specialised beam setting equipment **(see illustration 1)**. This equipment will not be available to the home mechanic, but if you suspect that the headlight is incorrectly set or may have been maladjusted in the past, you can perform a rough test as follows.

✔ Position the bike in a straight line facing a brick wall. The bike must be off its stand, upright and with a rider seated. Measure the height from the ground to the centre of the headlight and mark a horizontal line on the wall at this height. Position the motorcycle 3.8 metres from the wall and draw a vertical line up the wall central to the centreline of the motorcycle. Switch to dipped beam and check that the beam pattern falls slightly lower than the horizontal line and to the left of the vertical line **(see illustration 2)**.

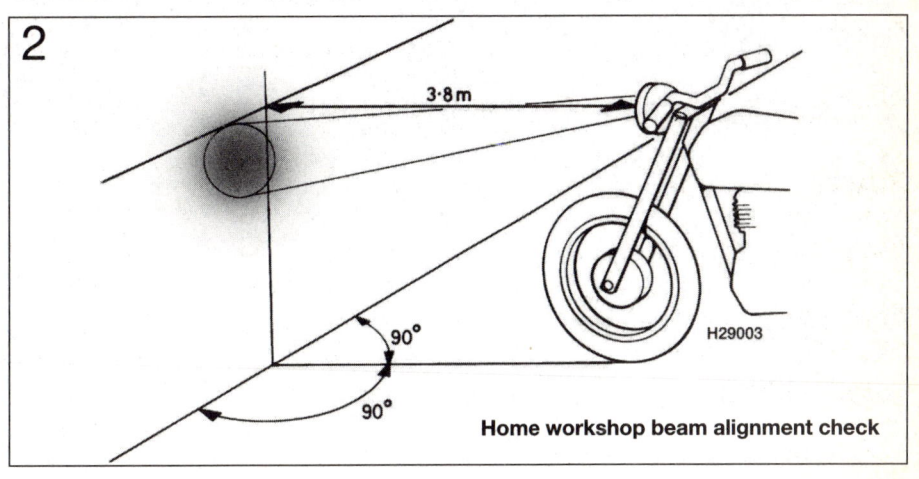

Headlight beam height checking equipment

Home workshop beam alignment check

MOT Test Checks

Exhaust System and Final Drive

Exhaust

✔ Check that the exhaust mountings are secure and that the system does not foul any of the rear suspension components.
✔ Start the motorcycle. When the revs are increased, check that the exhaust is neither holed nor leaking from any of its joints. On a linked system, check that the collector box is not leaking due to corrosion.
✔ Note that the exhaust decibel level ("loudness" of the exhaust) is assessed at the discretion of the tester. If the motorcycle was first used on or after 1st January 1985 the silencer must carry the BSAU 193 stamp, or a marking relating to its make and model, or be of OE (original equipment) manufacture. If the silencer is marked NOT FOR ROAD USE, RACING USE ONLY or similar, it will fail the MOT.

Final drive

✔ On chain or belt drive machines, check that the chain/belt is in good condition and does not have excessive slack. Also check that the sprocket is securely mounted on the rear wheel hub. Check that the chain/belt guard is in place.
✔ On shaft drive bikes, check for oil leaking from the drive unit and fouling the rear tyre.

Steering and Suspension

Steering

✔ With the front wheel raised off the ground, rotate the steering from lock to lock. The handlebar or switches must not contact the fuel tank or be close enough to trap the rider's hand. Problems can be caused by damaged lock stops on the lower yoke and frame, or by the fitting of non-standard handlebars.
✔ When performing the lock to lock check, also ensure that the steering moves freely without drag or notchiness. Steering movement can be impaired by poorly routed cables, or by overtight head bearings or worn bearings. The tester will perform a check of the steering head bearing lower race by mounting the front wheel on a surface plate, then performing a lock to lock check with the weight of the machine on the lower bearing (see illustration 3).
✔ Grasp the fork sliders (lower legs) and attempt to push and pull on the forks (see illustration 4). Any play in the steering head bearings will be felt. Note that in extreme cases, wear of the front fork bushes can be misinterpreted for head bearing play.
✔ Check that the handlebars are securely mounted.
✔ Check that the handlebar grip rubbers are secure. They should by bonded to the bar left end and to the throttle cable pulley on the right end.

Front wheel mounted on a surface plate for steering head bearing lower race check

Front suspension

✔ With the motorcycle off the stand, hold the front brake on and pump the front forks up and down (see illustration 5). Check that they are adequately damped.

Checking the steering head bearings for freeplay

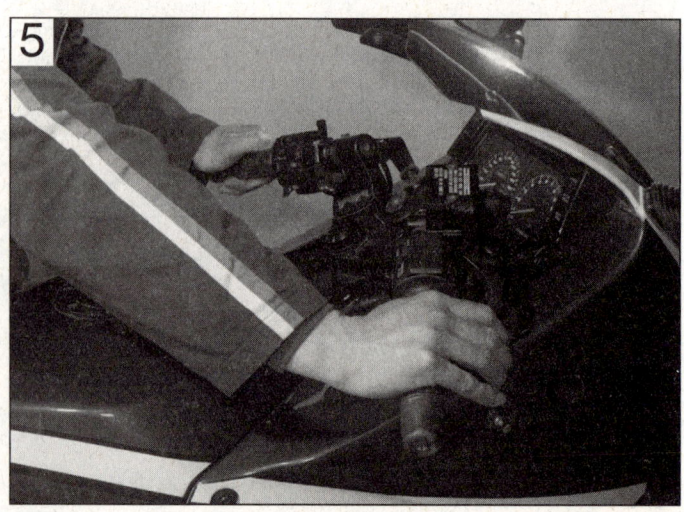

Hold the front brake on and pump the front forks up and down to check operation

MOT Test Checks REF•29

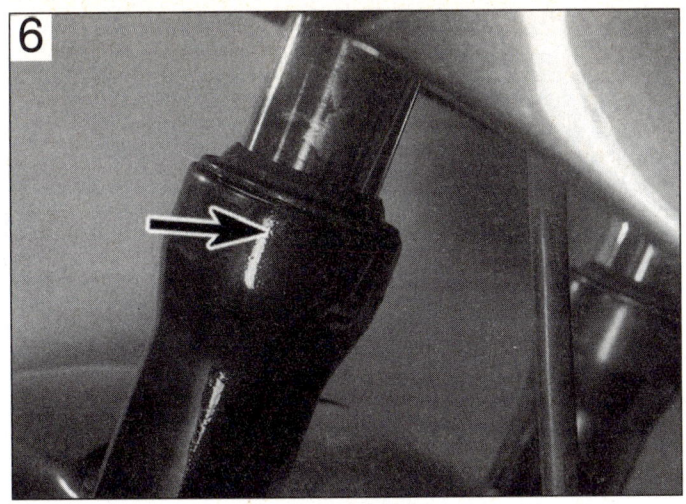

Inspect the area around the fork dust seal for oil leakage (arrow)

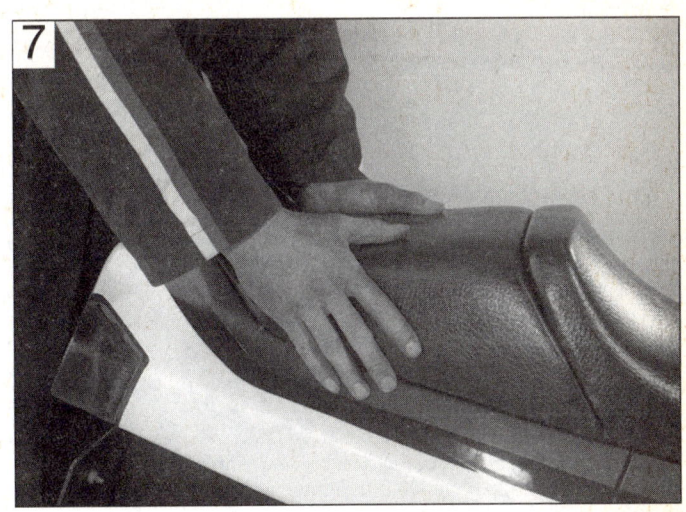

Bounce the rear of the motorcycle to check rear suspension operation

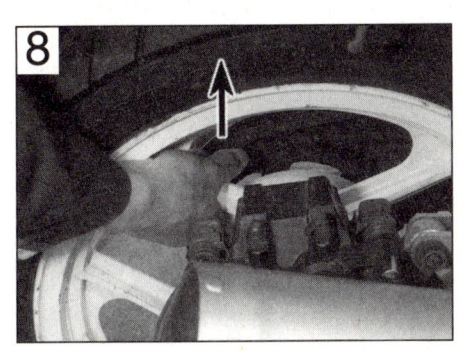

Checking for rear suspension linkage play

✔ Inspect the area above and around the front fork oil seals **(see illustration 6)**. There should be no sign of oil on the fork tube (stanchion) nor leaking down the slider (lower leg). On models so equipped, check that there is no oil leaking from the anti-dive units.
✔ On models with swingarm front suspension, check that there is no freeplay in the linkage when moved from side to side.

Rear suspension

✔ With the motorcycle off the stand and an assistant supporting the motorcycle by its handlebars, bounce the rear suspension **(see illustration 7)**. Check that the suspension components do not foul on any of the cycle parts and check that the shock absorber(s) provide adequate damping.
✔ Visually inspect the shock absorber(s) and check that there is no sign of oil leakage from its damper. This is somewhat restricted on certain single shock models due to the location of the shock absorber.
✔ With the rear wheel raised off the ground, grasp the wheel at the highest point and attempt to pull it up **(see illustration 8)**. Any play in the swingarm pivot or suspension linkage bearings will be felt as movement.
Note: *Do not confuse play with actual suspension movement.* Failure to lubricate suspension linkage bearings can lead to bearing failure **(see illustration 9)**.
✔ With the rear wheel raised off the ground, grasp the swingarm ends and attempt to move the swingarm from side to side and forwards and backwards - any play indicates wear of the swingarm pivot bearings **(see illustration 10)**.

Worn suspension linkage pivots (arrows) are usually the cause of play in the rear suspension

Grasp the swingarm at the ends to check for play in its pivot bearings

REF•30 MOT Test Checks

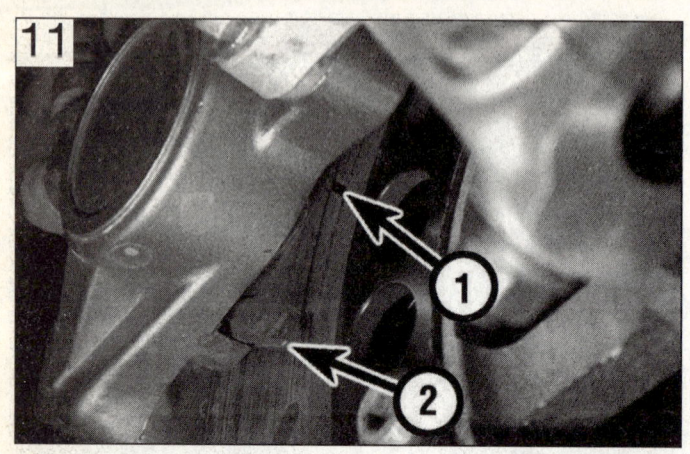

Brake pad wear can usually be viewed without removing the caliper. Most pads have wear indicator grooves (1) and some also have indicator tangs (2)

On drum brakes, check the angle of the operating lever with the brake fully applied. Most drum brakes have a wear indicator pointer and scale.

Brakes, Wheels and Tyres

Brakes

✔ With the wheel raised off the ground, apply the brake then free it off, and check that the wheel is about to revolve freely without brake drag.

✔ On disc brakes, examine the disc itself. Check that it is securely mounted and not cracked.

✔ On disc brakes, view the pad material through the caliper mouth and check that the pads are not worn down beyond the limit **(see illustration 11)**.

✔ On drum brakes, check that when the brake is applied the angle between the operating lever and cable or rod is not too great **(see illustration 12)**. Check also that the operating lever doesn't foul any other components.

✔ On disc brakes, examine the flexible hoses from top to bottom. Have an assistant hold the brake on so that the fluid in the hose is under pressure, and check that there is no sign of fluid leakage, bulges or cracking. If there are any metal brake pipes or unions, check that these are free from corrosion and damage. Where a brake-linked anti-dive system is fitted, check the hoses to the anti-dive in a similar manner.

✔ Check that the rear brake torque arm is secure and that its fasteners are secured by self-locking nuts or castellated nuts with split-pins or R-pins **(see illustration 13)**.

✔ On models with ABS, check that the self-check warning light in the instrument panel works.

✔ The MOT tester will perform a test of the motorcycle's braking efficiency based on a calculation of rider and motorcycle weight. Although this cannot be carried out at home, you can at least ensure that the braking systems are properly maintained. For hydraulic disc brakes, check the fluid level, lever/pedal feel (bleed of air if its spongy) and pad material. For drum brakes, check adjustment, cable or rod operation and shoe lining thickness.

Wheels and tyres

✔ Check the wheel condition. Cast wheels should be free from cracks and if of the built-up design, all fasteners should be secure. Spoked wheels should be checked for broken, corroded, loose or bent spokes.

✔ With the wheel raised off the ground, spin the wheel and visually check that the tyre and wheel run true. Check that the tyre does not foul the suspension or mudguards.

✔ With the wheel raised off the ground, grasp the wheel and attempt to move it about the axle (spindle) **(see illustration 14)**. Any play felt here indicates wheel bearing failure.

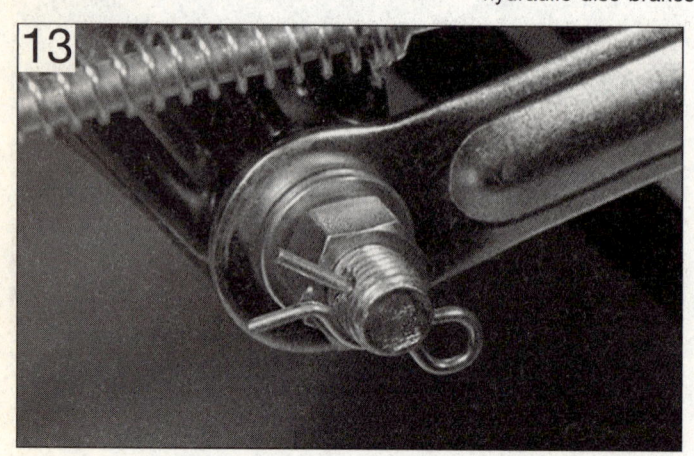

Brake torque arm must be properly secured at both ends

Check for wheel bearing play by trying to move the wheel about the axle (spindle)

MOT Test Checks REF•31

Checking the tyre tread depth

Tyre direction of rotation arrow can be found on tyre sidewall

Castellated type wheel axle (spindle) nut must be secured by a split pin or R-pin

Two straightedges are used to check wheel alignment

✔ Check the tyre tread depth, tread condition and sidewall condition **(see illustration 15)**.
✔ Check the tyre type. Front and rear tyre types must be compatible and be suitable for road use. Tyres marked NOT FOR ROAD USE, COMPETITION USE ONLY or similar, will fail the MOT.

✔ If the tyre sidewall carries a direction of rotation arrow, this must be pointing in the direction of normal wheel rotation **(see illustration 16)**.
✔ Check that the wheel axle (spindle) nuts (where applicable) are properly secured. A self-locking nut or castellated nut with a split-pin or R-pin can be used **(see illustration 17)**.
✔ Wheel alignment is checked with the motorcycle off the stand and a rider seated. With the front wheel pointing straight ahead, two perfectly straight lengths of metal or wood and placed against the sidewalls of both tyres **(see illustration 18)**. The gap each side of the front tyre must be equidistant on both sides. Incorrect wheel alignment may be due to a cocked rear wheel (often as the result of poor chain adjustment) or in extreme cases, a bent frame.

General checks and condition

✔ Check the security of all major fasteners, bodypanels, seat, fairings (where fitted) and mudguards.

✔ Check that the rider and pillion footrests, handlebar levers and brake pedal are securely mounted.

✔ Check for corrosion on the frame or any load-bearing components. If severe, this may affect the structure, particularly under stress.

Sidecars

A motorcycle fitted with a sidecar requires additional checks relating to the stability of the machine and security of attachment and swivel joints, plus specific wheel alignment (toe-in) requirements. Additionally, tyre and lighting requirements differ from conventional motorcycle use. Owners are advised to check MOT test requirements with an official test centre.

Storage

Preparing for storage

Before you start

If repairs or an overhaul is needed, see that this is carried out now rather than left until you want to ride the bike again.

Give the bike a good wash and scrub all dirt from its underside. Make sure the bike dries completely before preparing for storage.

Engine

● Remove the spark plug(s) and lubricate the cylinder bores with approximately a teaspoon of motor oil using a spout-type oil can (**see illustration 1**). Reinstall the spark plug(s). Crank the engine over a couple of times to coat the piston rings and bores with oil. If the bike has a kickstart, use this to turn the engine over. If not, flick the kill switch to the OFF position and crank the engine over on the starter (**see illustration 2**). If the nature on the ignition system prevents the starter operating with the kill switch in the OFF position, remove the spark plugs and fit them back in their caps; ensure that the plugs are earthed (grounded) against the cylinder head when the starter is operated (**see illustration 3**).

Warning: It is important that the plugs are earthed (grounded) away from the spark plug holes otherwise there is a risk of atomised fuel from the cylinders igniting.

HAYNES HINT: *On a single cylinder four-stroke engine, you can seal the combustion chamber completely by positioning the piston at TDC on the compression stroke.*

● Drain the carburettor(s) otherwise there is a risk of jets becoming blocked by gum deposits from the fuel (**see illustration 4**).

● If the bike is going into long-term storage, consider adding a fuel stabiliser to the fuel in the tank. If the tank is drained completely, corrosion of its internal surfaces may occur if left unprotected for a long period. The tank can be treated with a rust preventative especially for this purpose. Alternatively, remove the tank and pour half a litre of motor oil into it, install the filler cap and shake the tank to coat its internals with oil before draining off the excess. The same effect can also be achieved by spraying WD40 or a similar water-dispersant around the inside of the tank via its flexible nozzle.

● Make sure the cooling system contains the correct mix of antifreeze. Antifreeze also contains important corrosion inhibitors.

● The air intakes and exhaust can be sealed off by covering or plugging the openings. Ensure that you do not seal in any condensation; run the engine until it is hot,

1 Squirt a drop of motor oil into each cylinder

2 Flick the kill switch to OFF . . .

3 . . . and ensure that the metal bodies of the plugs (arrows) are earthed against the cylinder head

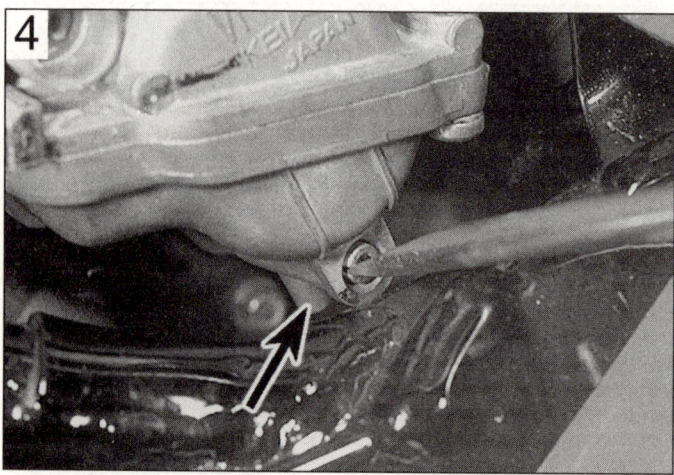

4 Connect a hose to the carburettor float chamber drain stub (arrow) and unscrew the drain screw

Storage   REF•33

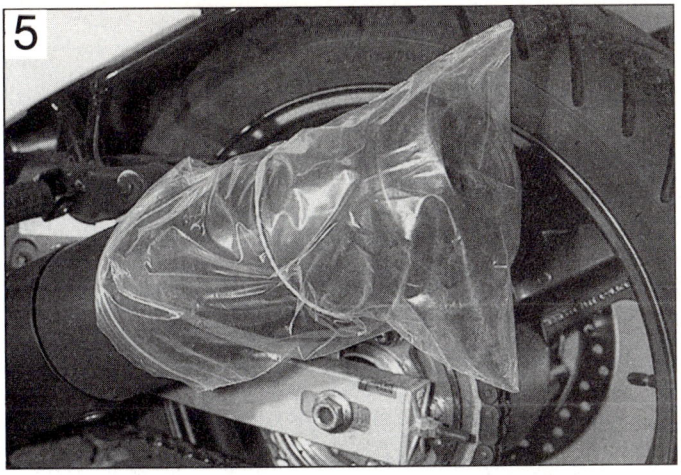

Exhausts can be sealed off with a plastic bag

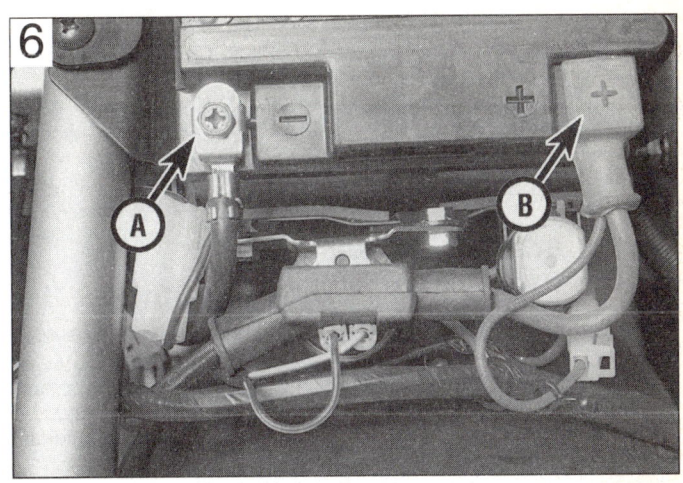

Disconnect the negative lead (A) first, followed by the positive lead (B)

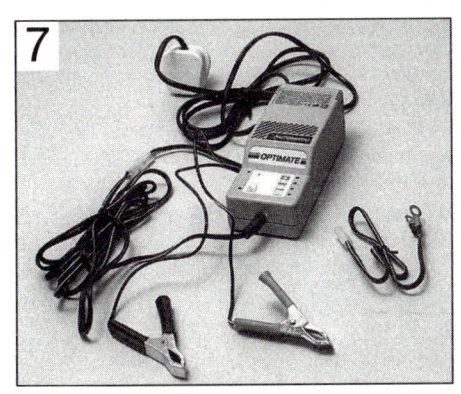

Use a suitable battery charger - this kit also assess battery condition

then switch off and allow to cool. Tape a piece of thick plastic over the silencer end(s) **(see illustration 5)**. Note that some advocate pouring a tablespoon of motor oil into the silencer(s) before sealing them off.

Battery
● Remove it from the bike - in extreme cases of cold the battery may freeze and crack its case **(see illustration 6)**.

● Check the electrolyte level and top up if necessary (conventional refillable batteries). Clean the terminals.
● Store the battery off the motorcycle and away from any sources of fire. Position a wooden block under the battery if it is to sit on the ground.
● Give the battery a trickle charge for a few hours every month **(see illustration 7)**.

Tyres
● Place the bike on its centrestand or an auxiliary stand which will support the motorcycle in an upright position. Position wood blocks under the tyres to keep them off the ground and to provide insulation from damp. If the bike is being put into long-term storage, ideally both tyres should be off the ground; not only will this protect the tyres, but will also ensure that no load is placed on the steering head or wheel bearings.
● Deflate each tyre by 5 to 10 psi, no more or the beads may unseat from the rim, making subsequent inflation difficult on tubeless tyres.

Pivots and controls
● Lubricate all lever, pedal, stand and footrest pivot points. If grease nipples are fitted to the rear suspension components, apply lubricant to the pivots.
● Lubricate all control cables.

Cycle components
● Apply a wax protectant to all painted and plastic components. Wipe off any excess, but don't polish to a shine. Where fitted, clean the screen with soap and water.
● Coat metal parts with Vaseline (petroleum jelly). When applying this to the fork tubes, do not compress the forks otherwise the seals will rot from contact with the Vaseline.
● Apply a vinyl cleaner to the seat.

Storage conditions
● Aim to store the bike in a shed or garage which does not leak and is free from damp.
● Drape an old blanket or bedspread over the bike to protect it from dust and direct contact with sunlight (which will fade paint). This also hides the bike from prying eyes. Beware of tight-fitting plastic covers which may allow condensation to form and settle on the bike.

Getting back on the road

Engine and transmission
● Change the oil and replace the oil filter. If this was done prior to storage, check that the oil hasn't emulsified - a thick whitish substance which occurs through condensation.
● Remove the spark plugs. Using a spout-type oil can, squirt a few drops of oil into the cylinder(s). This will provide initial lubrication as the piston rings and bores comes back into contact. Service the spark plugs, or fit new ones, and install them in the engine.

● Check that the clutch isn't stuck on. The plates can stick together if left standing for some time, preventing clutch operation. Engage a gear and try rocking the bike back and forth with the clutch lever held against the handlebar. If this doesn't work on cable-operated clutches, hold the clutch lever back against the handlebar with a strong elastic band or cable tie for a couple of hours **(see illustration 8)**.
● If the air intakes or silencer end(s) were blocked off, remove the bung or cover used.
● If the fuel tank was coated with a rust

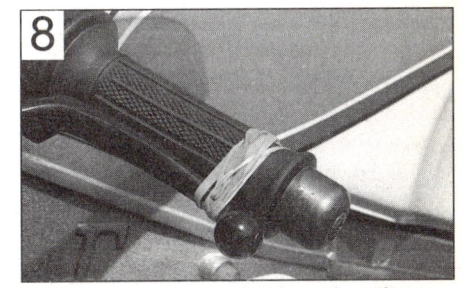

Hold clutch lever back against the handlebar with elastic bands or a cable tie

Storage

preventative, oil or a stabiliser added to the fuel, drain and flush the tank and dispose of the fuel sensibly. If no action was taken with the fuel tank prior to storage, it is advised that the old fuel is disposed of since it will go off over a period of time. Refill the fuel tank with fresh fuel.

Frame and running gear

● Oil all pivot points and cables.
● Check the tyre pressures. They will definitely need inflating if pressures were reduced for storage.
● Lubricate the final drive chain (where applicable).
● Remove any protective coating applied to the fork tubes (stanchions) since this may well destroy the fork seals. If the fork tubes weren't protected and have picked up rust spots, remove them with very fine abrasive paper and refinish with metal polish.
● Check that both brakes operate correctly. Apply each brake hard and check that it's not possible to move the motorcycle forwards, then check that the brake frees off again once released. Brake caliper pistons can stick due to corrosion around the piston head, or on the sliding caliper types, due to corrosion of the slider pins. If the brake doesn't free after repeated operation, take the caliper off for examination. Similarly drum brakes can stick due to a seized operating cam, cable or rod linkage.
● If the motorcycle has been in long-term storage, renew the brake fluid and clutch fluid (where applicable).
● Depending on where the bike has been stored, the wiring, cables and hoses may have been nibbled by rodents. Make a visual check and investigate disturbed wiring loom tape.

Battery

● If the battery has been previously removal and given top up charges it can simply be reconnected. Remember to connect the positive cable first and the negative cable last.
● On conventional refillable batteries, if the battery has not received any attention, remove it from the motorcycle and check its electrolyte level. Top up if necessary then charge the battery. If the battery fails to hold a charge and a visual checks show heavy white sulphation of the plates, the battery is probably defective and must be renewed. This is particularly likely if the battery is old. Confirm battery condition with a specific gravity check.
● On sealed (MF) batteries, if the battery has not received any attention, remove it from the motorcycle and charge it according to the information on the battery case - if the battery fails to hold a charge it must be renewed.

Starting procedure

● If a kickstart is fitted, turn the engine over a couple of times with the ignition OFF to distribute oil around the engine. If no kickstart is fitted, flick the engine kill switch OFF and the ignition ON and crank the engine over a couple of times to work oil around the upper cylinder components. If the nature of the ignition system is such that the starter won't work with the kill switch OFF, remove the spark plugs, fit them back into their caps and earth (ground) their bodies on the cylinder head. Reinstall the spark plugs afterwards.
● Switch the kill switch to RUN, operate the choke and start the engine. If the engine won't start don't continue cranking the engine - not only will this flatten the battery, but the starter motor will overheat. Switch the ignition off and try again later. If the engine refuses to start, go through the fault finding procedures in this manual. **Note:** *If the bike has been in storage for a long time, old fuel or a carburettor blockage may be the problem. Gum deposits in carburettors can block jets - if a carburettor cleaner doesn't prove successful the carburettors must be dismantled for cleaning.*
● Once the engine has started, check that the lights, turn signals and horn work properly.
● Treat the bike gently for the first ride and check all fluid levels on completion. Settle the bike back into the maintenance schedule.

Fault Finding REF•35

This Section provides an easy reference-guide to the more common faults that are likely to afflict your machine. Obviously, the opportunities are almost limitless for faults to occur as a result of obscure failures, and to try and cover all eventualities would require a book. Indeed, a number have been written on the subject.

Successful troubleshooting is not a mysterious 'black art' but the application of a bit of knowledge combined with a systematic and logical approach to the problem. Approach any troubleshooting by first accurately identifying the symptom and then checking through the list of possible causes, starting with the simplest or most obvious and progressing in stages to the most complex.

Take nothing for granted, but above all apply liberal quantities of common sense.

The main symptom of a fault is given in the text as a major heading below which are listed the various systems or areas which may contain the fault. Details of each possible cause for a fault and the remedial action to be taken are given, in brief, in the paragraphs below each heading. Further information should be sought in the relevant Chapter.

1 Engine doesn't start or is difficult to start
- [ ] Starter motor doesn't rotate
- [ ] Starter motor rotates but engine does not turn over
- [ ] Starter works but engine won't turn over (seized)
- [ ] No fuel flow
- [ ] Engine flooded
- [ ] No spark or weak spark
- [ ] Compression low
- [ ] Stalls after starting
- [ ] Rough idle

2 Poor running at low speed
- [ ] Spark weak
- [ ] Fuel/air mixture incorrect
- [ ] Compression low
- [ ] Poor acceleration

3 Poor running or no power at high speed
- [ ] Firing incorrect
- [ ] Fuel/air mixture incorrect
- [ ] Compression low
- [ ] Knocking or pinking
- [ ] Miscellaneous causes

4 Overheating
- [ ] Engine overheats
- [ ] Firing incorrect
- [ ] Fuel/air mixture incorrect
- [ ] Compression too high
- [ ] Engine load excessive
- [ ] Lubrication inadequate
- [ ] Miscellaneous causes

5 Clutch problems
- [ ] Clutch slipping
- [ ] Clutch not disengaging completely

6 Gearchange problems
- [ ] Doesn't go into gear, or lever doesn't return
- [ ] Jumps out of gear
- [ ] Overshifts

7 Abnormal engine noise
- [ ] Knocking or pinking
- [ ] Piston slap or rattling
- [ ] Valve noise
- [ ] Other noise

8 Abnormal driveline noise
- [ ] Clutch noise
- [ ] Transmission noise
- [ ] Driveline noise

9 Abnormal frame and suspension noise
- [ ] Front end noise
- [ ] Shock absorber noise
- [ ] Brake noise

10 Excessive exhaust smoke
- [ ] White smoke
- [ ] Black smoke
- [ ] Brown smoke

11 Poor handling or stability
- [ ] Handlebar hard to turn
- [ ] Handlebar shakes or vibrates excessively
- [ ] Handlebar pulls to one side
- [ ] Poor shock absorbing qualities

12 Braking problems – front disc brake
- [ ] Brakes are ineffective
- [ ] Brake lever pulsates
- [ ] Brakes drag

13 Braking problems – rear drum brake
- [ ] Brakes are ineffective
- [ ] Brake lever pulsates
- [ ] Brakes drag

14 Electrical problems
- [ ] Battery dead or weak
- [ ] Battery overcharged

REF•36 Fault Finding

1 Engine doesn't start or is difficult to start

Starter motor doesn't rotate
- ☐ Fuse blown. Check fuses and starter circuit (Chapter 8).
- ☐ Battery voltage low. Check and recharge battery (Chapter 8).
- ☐ Starter motor defective (Chapter 8). Make sure the wiring to the starter is secure. Make sure the starter relay clicks when the start button is pushed. If the relay clicks, then the fault is in the wiring or motor.
- ☐ Starter relay faulty. Check it (Chapter 8).
- ☐ Starter button on handlebar not contacting. The contacts could be wet, corroded or dirty. Disassemble and clean the switch (Chapter 8).
- ☐ Wiring open or shorted. Check all wiring connections and harnesses to make sure that they are dry, tight and not corroded. Also check for broken or frayed wires that can cause a short to earth.
- ☐ Ignition switch defective. Check the switch according to the procedure in Chapter 8. Replace the switch with a new one if it is defective.
- ☐ Starter safety circuit fault. Check the sidestand and gear position switch and wiring (Chapter 8).

Starter motor rotates but engine does not turn over
- ☐ Starter clutch defective. Inspect and repair or renew (Chapter 2).
- ☐ Damaged starter gears. Inspect for damaged parts (Chapter 2).

Starter works but engine won't turn over (seized)
- ☐ Seized engine caused by one or more internally damaged components. Failure due to wear, abuse or lack of lubrication. Damage can include piston, cylinder, connecting rod, crankshaft and bearings (Chapter 2).

No fuel flow – carburettor models
- ☐ No fuel in tank.
- ☐ Fuel hose pinched – check the hose and its routing.
- ☐ Fuel hose clogged. Remove the fuel hose and carefully blow through it.
- ☐ Fuel tank vent in filler cap blocked. Clean and blow through or replace with a new one.
- ☐ Fuel filter clogged. Fit a new filter (Chapters 1 and 3A).
- ☐ Fuel valve vacuum hose split or detached. Check the hose.
- ☐ Fuel valve diaphragm split. Fit a new valve (Chapter 3A).
- ☐ Float needle valve or carburettor jets clogged. Try draining the float chamber (Chapter 3A). Remove and overhaul the carburettor if draining doesn't solve the problem.

No fuel flow – fuel injection models
- ☐ No fuel in tank.
- ☐ Fuel tank vent in filler cap blocked. Clean and blow through or replace with a new one.
- ☐ Fuel hose pinched – check the hose and its routing.
- ☐ Fuel hose clogged. Remove the fuel hose and carefully blow through it.
- ☐ Fuel pump circuit fault – check all components in the circuit (Chapter 3B).
- ☐ Fuel pump defective – problems could include a faulty pump motor, faulty pressure regulator or blocked filter. In all cases replace the pump with a new one (Chapter 3B).
- ☐ Fuel injection system fault – check for fault codes (Chapter 3B).

Engine flooded
- ☐ On carburettor models the float needle valve could be worn or stuck open. A piece of dirt, rust or other debris can cause the valve to seat improperly, causing excess fuel to be admitted to the float chamber. In this case, the float chamber should be cleaned and the needle valve and seat inspected. If the needle and seat are worn, then the leaking will persist and the parts should be replaced with new ones (Chapter 3A).
- ☐ On fuel injection models the injector could be stuck open, or there could be too much pressure in the system. Check the injector first, then check fuel pressure (Chapter 3B).
- ☐ Starting technique incorrect. Under normal circumstances the machine should start with no throttle, whatever the temperature.

No spark or weak spark
- ☐ Battery voltage low. Check and recharge the battery as necessary (Chapter 8).
- ☐ Spark plug dirty, defective or worn out. Locate reason for fouled plug using the spark plug condition chart on the inside rear cover and follow the plug maintenance procedures (Chapter 1).
- ☐ Spark plug cap or lead faulty. Check condition (Chapter 4).
- ☐ Spark plug cap not making good contact. Make sure that the plug cap fits snugly over the plug end.
- ☐ Electronic control unit (ECU) defective. Check the unit, referring to Chapter 4 for details.
- ☐ Pulse generator coil defective. Check it, referring to Chapter 4 for details.
- ☐ Ignition coil defective. Check the coil, referring to Chapter 4.
- ☐ Wiring shorted or broken. Make sure that all wiring connections are clean, dry and tight. Look for chafed and broken wires (Chapters 4 and 8).

Compression low
- ☐ Spark plug loose (Chapter 1).
- ☐ Cylinder head not sufficiently tightened down. If the cylinder head is suspected of being loose, then there's a chance that the gasket or head is damaged if the problem has persisted for any length of time. The head nuts should be tightened to the proper torque in the correct sequence (Chapter 2).
- ☐ Cylinder and/or piston worn. Excessive wear will cause compression pressure to leak past the rings. This is usually accompanied by worn rings as well. A top-end overhaul is necessary (Chapter 2).
- ☐ Piston rings worn, weak, broken, or sticking. Broken or sticking piston rings usually indicate a lubrication or fuelling problem that causes excess carbon deposits to form on the piston and rings. Top-end overhaul is necessary (Chapter 2).
- ☐ Piston ring-to-groove clearance excessive. This is caused by excessive wear of the piston ring lands. Piston renewal is necessary (Chapter 2).
- ☐ Cylinder head gasket damaged. If the head is allowed to become loose, or if excessive carbon build-up on the piston crown and combustion chamber causes extremely high compression, the head gasket may leak. Retorquing the head is not always sufficient to restore the seal, so gasket renewal is necessary (Chapter 2).
- ☐ Cylinder head warped. This is caused by overheating or improperly tightened head nuts. Machine shop resurfacing or head renewal is necessary (Chapter 2).
- ☐ Incorrect valve clearance. If a valve is not closing completely then engine pressure will leak past the valve. Check and adjust the valve clearances (Chapter 1).
- ☐ Valve not seating properly. This is caused by a bent valve (from over-revving or improper valve adjustment), burned valve or seat (improper combustion) or an accumulation of carbon deposits on the seat (from combustion or lubrication problems). The valves must be cleaned and/or renewed and the seats serviced if possible (Chapter 2).
- ☐ Valve spring broken or weak. Caused by component failure or wear; the springs must be renewed (Chapter 2).

Fault Finding REF•37

1 Engine doesn't start or is difficult to start (continued)

Stalls after starting – carburettor models
- [ ] Carburettor fault (Chapter 3A).
- [ ] Ignition system fault (Chapter 4).
- [ ] Fuel contaminated. The fuel can be contaminated with either dirt or water, or can change chemically if the machine is allowed to sit for several months or more. Drain the tank and carburettor (Chapter 3A).
- [ ] Inlet air leak. Check for loose carburettor-to-intake duct joints (Chapter 3A).

Stalls after starting – fuel injection models
- [ ] Faulty idle air control valve (Chapter 3B).
- [ ] Ignition malfunction (Chapter 4).
- [ ] Fuel injection system fault. Check for fault codes (Chapter 3B).
- [ ] Fuel contaminated. The fuel can be contaminated with either dirt or water, or can change chemically if the machine is allowed to sit for several months or more. Drain the tank and carburettor (Chapter 3B).
- [ ] Inlet air leak. Check for loose throttle body-to-intake duct joint (Chapter 3B).

Rough idle
- [ ] Air filter clogged. Clean or renew the air filter element (Chapter 1).
- [ ] Spark plug fouled, defective or worn out. Refer to Chapter 1 for spark plug maintenance.
- [ ] Ignition malfunction (Chapter 4).
- [ ] Idle speed incorrect (Chapter 1).
- [ ] Carburettor or fuel injection system fault (Chapter 3A or 3B).
- [ ] Fuel contaminated. The fuel can be contaminated with either dirt or water, or can change chemically if the machine is allowed to sit for several months or more. Drain the tank and fuel system components (Chapter 3A or 3B).
- [ ] Intake air leak. Check for loose intake duct joints (Chapter 3A or 3B).

2 Poor running at low speed

Spark weak
- [ ] Battery voltage low. Check and recharge battery (Chapter 8).
- [ ] Spark plug fouled, defective or worn out. Refer to Chapter 1 for spark plug maintenance.
- [ ] Spark plug cap or HT wiring defective. Refer to Chapter 4 for details on the ignition system.
- [ ] Spark plug cap not making contact.
- [ ] Incorrect spark plug. Wrong type, heat range or cap configuration. Check and install correct plug listed in Chapter 1.
- [ ] Electronic control unit (ECU) defective (Chapter 4).
- [ ] Pulse generator coil defective (Chapter 4).
- [ ] Ignition coil defective (Chapter 4).

Fuel/air mixture incorrect – carburettor models
- [ ] Faulty choke (Chapter 3A).
- [ ] Pilot screw out of adjustment (Chapter 3A).
- [ ] Pilot jet or air passage clogged. Remove and clean the carburettor (Chapter 3A).
- [ ] Air hole clogged. Remove carburettor and blow out all passages (Chapter 3A).
- [ ] Air filter clogged, poorly sealed or missing (Chapter 1).
- [ ] Air filter housing poorly sealed. Look for cracks, holes or loose screws and renew or repair defective parts.
- [ ] Carburettor intake duct loose. Check for cracks, breaks, tears or loose fixings.
- [ ] Fuel tank vent in filler cap blocked. Clean and blow through or replace with a new one.

Fuel/air mixture incorrect – fuel injection models
- [ ] Fuel injector clogged or fuel injection system fault (see Chapter 3B).
- [ ] Air filter clogged, poorly sealed or missing (Chapter 1).
- [ ] Air filter housing poorly sealed. Look for cracks, holes or loose clamps and renew or repair defective parts.
- [ ] Intake air leak. Check for loose intake duct joint (Chapter 3B).
- [ ] Faulty idle air control valve (Chapter 3B).
- [ ] Fuel tank vent in filler cap blocked. Clean and blow through or replace with a new one.

Compression low
- [ ] Spark plug loose (Chapter 1).
- [ ] Cylinder head not sufficiently tightened down. If the cylinder head is suspected of being loose, then there's a chance that the gasket or head is damaged if the problem has persisted for any length of time. The head nuts should be tightened to the proper torque in the correct sequence (Chapter 2).
- [ ] Cylinder and/or piston worn. Excessive wear will cause compression pressure to leak past the rings. This is usually accompanied by worn rings as well. A top-end overhaul is necessary (Chapter 2).
- [ ] Piston rings worn, weak, broken, or sticking. Broken or sticking piston rings usually indicate a lubrication or fuelling problem that causes excess carbon deposits to form on the piston and rings. Top-end overhaul is necessary (Chapter 2).
- [ ] Piston ring-to-groove clearance excessive. This is caused by excessive wear of the piston ring lands. Piston renewal is necessary (Chapter 2).
- [ ] Cylinder head gasket damaged. If the head is allowed to become loose, or if excessive carbon build-up on the piston crown and combustion chamber causes extremely high compression, the head gasket may leak. Retorquing the head is not always sufficient to restore the seal, so gasket renewal is necessary (Chapter 2).
- [ ] Cylinder head warped. This is caused by overheating or improperly tightened head nuts. Machine shop resurfacing or head renewal is necessary (Chapter 2).
- [ ] Incorrect valve clearance. If a valve is not closing completely then engine pressure will leak past the valve. Check and adjust the valve clearances (Chapter 1).
- [ ] Valve not seating properly. This is caused by a bent valve (from over-revving or improper valve adjustment), burned valve or seat (improper combustion) or an accumulation of carbon deposits on the seat (from combustion or lubrication problems). The valves must be cleaned and/or renewed and the seats serviced if possible (Chapter 2).
- [ ] Valve spring broken or weak. Caused by component failure or wear; the springs must be renewed (Chapter 2).

Poor acceleration
- [ ] On carburettor models check the choke closes fully. Otherwise overhaul the carburettor (Chapter 3A).
- [ ] On fuel injection models check for fault codes (Chapter 3B).
- [ ] Intake air leak. Check for loose intake duct joint (Chapter 3A or 3B).
- [ ] Timing not advancing. The pulse generator coil or the electronic control unit (ECU) may be defective (Chapter 4).
- [ ] Brakes dragging. On the front disc brake this is usually caused by debris which has entered the brake piston seals – overhaul the caliper. If that doesn't rectify it the master cylinder piston may be sticking. On the rear drum brake this could be caused by no freeplay in brake pedal, shoe return spring broken, or brake arm seized in plate in rear wheel. Refer to Chapter 6.
- [ ] Centrifugal or multi-plate clutch slipping (Chapter 2) – engine speed will rise but road speed won't, accompanied by burnt clutch plate smell. Problem will rapidly get worse.

3 Poor running or no power at high speed

Firing incorrect

- ☐ Air filter clogged. Clean or renew filter (Chapter 1).
- ☐ Spark plug fouled, defective or worn out (Chapter 1).
- ☐ Spark plug cap or HT lead defective. See Chapter 4 for details of the ignition system.
- ☐ Spark plug cap not in good contact (Chapter 4).
- ☐ Incorrect spark plug. Wrong type, heat range or cap configuration. Check and install correct plug listed in Chapter 1.
- ☐ Electronic control unit (ECU) or ignition coil defective (Chapter 4).

Fuel/air mixture incorrect – carburettor models

- ☐ Choke not closing (Chapter 3A).
- ☐ Pilot screw out of adjustment (Chapter 3A).
- ☐ Pilot jet or air passage clogged. Remove and clean the carburettor (Chapter 3A).
- ☐ Air hole clogged. Remove carburettor and blow out all passages (Chapter 3A).
- ☐ Air filter clogged, poorly sealed or missing (Chapter 1).
- ☐ Air filter housing poorly sealed. Look for cracks, holes or loose screws and renew or repair defective parts.
- ☐ Carburettor intake duct loose. Check for cracks, breaks, tears or loose fixings.
- ☐ Fuel tank vent in filler cap blocked. Clean and blow through or replace with a new one.

Fuel/air mixture incorrect – fuel injection models

- ☐ Fuel injector clogged or fuel injection system fault (see Chapter 3B).
- ☐ Air filter clogged, poorly sealed or missing (Chapter 1).
- ☐ Air filter housing poorly sealed. Look for cracks, holes or loose clamps and renew or repair defective parts.
- ☐ Faulty idle air control valve (Chapter 3B).
- ☐ Intake air leak. Check for loose throttle body-to-intake duct joint (Chapter 3B).
- ☐ Fuel tank vent in filler cap blocked. Clean and blow through or replace with a new one.

Compression low

- ☐ Spark plug loose (Chapter 1).
- ☐ Cylinder head not sufficiently tightened down. If the cylinder head is suspected of being loose, then there's a chance that the gasket or head is damaged if the problem has persisted for any length of time. The head nuts should be tightened to the proper torque in the correct sequence (Chapter 2).
- ☐ Cylinder and/or piston worn. Excessive wear will cause compression pressure to leak past the rings. This is usually accompanied by worn rings as well. A top-end overhaul is necessary (Chapter 2).
- ☐ Piston rings worn, weak, broken, or sticking. Broken or sticking piston rings usually indicate a lubrication or fuelling problem that causes excess carbon deposits to form on the piston and rings. Top-end overhaul is necessary (Chapter 2).
- ☐ Piston ring-to-groove clearance excessive. This is caused by excessive wear of the piston ring lands. Piston renewal is necessary (Chapter 2).
- ☐ Cylinder head gasket damaged. If the head is allowed to become loose, or if excessive carbon build-up on the piston crown and combustion chamber causes extremely high compression, the head gasket may leak. Retorquing the head is not always sufficient to restore the seal, so gasket renewal is necessary (Chapter 2).
- ☐ Cylinder head warped. This is caused by overheating or improperly tightened head nuts. Machine shop resurfacing or head renewal is necessary (Chapter 2).
- ☐ Incorrect valve clearance. If a valve is not closing completely then engine pressure will leak past the valve. Check and adjust the valve clearances (Chapter 1).
- ☐ Valve not seating properly. This is caused by a bent valve (from over-revving or improper valve adjustment), burned valve or seat (improper combustion) or an accumulation of carbon deposits on the seat (from combustion or lubrication problems). The valves must be cleaned and/or renewed and the seats serviced if possible (Chapter 2).
- ☐ Valve spring broken or weak. Caused by component failure or wear; the springs must be renewed (Chapter 2).

Knocking or pinking

- ☐ Carbon build-up in combustion chamber. Use of a fuel additive that will dissolve the adhesive bonding the carbon particles to the crown and chamber is the easiest way to remove the build-up. Otherwise, the cylinder head will have to be removed and decarbonised (Chapter 2).
- ☐ Incorrect or poor quality fuel. Old or improper grades of fuel can cause detonation. This causes the piston to rattle, thus the knocking or pinking sound. Drain old fuel and always use the recommended fuel grade.
- ☐ Spark plug heat range incorrect. Uncontrolled detonation indicates the plug heat range is too hot. The plug in effect becomes a glow plug, raising cylinder temperatures. Install the proper heat range plug (Chapter 1).
- ☐ Improper air/fuel mixture. This will cause the cylinder to run hot, which leads to detonation. Clogged carburettor jets, a fuel injection system fault or an air leak can cause this imbalance (Chapter 3A or 3B).

Miscellaneous causes

- ☐ Throttle valve doesn't open fully. Check the action of the twistgrip, and check the cable for kinks and incorrect routing. Adjust the throttle twistgrip freeplay (Chapter 1).
- ☐ Centrifugal or multi-plate clutch slipping (Chapter 2) – engine speed will rise but road speed won't, accompanied by burnt clutch plate smell. Problem will rapidly get worse.
- ☐ Timing not advancing (Chapter 4).
- ☐ Brakes dragging. On the front disc brake this is usually caused by debris which has entered the brake piston seals, or from a warped disc or bent axle. On the rear drum brake, there could be insufficient freeplay or a shoe return spring may have broken. Repair as necessary (Chapter 6).

Fault Finding REF•39

4 Overheating

Firing incorrect
- [ ] Air filter clogged. Clean or renew filter (Chapter 1).
- [ ] Spark plug fouled, defective or worn out (Chapter 1).
- [ ] Spark plug cap or HT lead defective. See Chapter 4 for details of the ignition system.
- [ ] Spark plug cap not in good contact (Chapter 4).
- [ ] Incorrect spark plug. Wrong type, heat range or cap configuration. Check and install correct plug listed in Chapter 1.
- [ ] Electronic control unit (ECU) or ignition coil defective (Chapter 4).

Fuel/air mixture incorrect – carburettor models
- [ ] Pilot screw out of adjustment (Chapter 3A).
- [ ] Fuel jet clogged. Remove and clean the carburettor (Chapter 3A).
- [ ] Fuel tank vent in filler cap blocked. Clean and blow through or replace with a new one.

Fuel/air mixture incorrect – fuel injection models
- [ ] Fuel injector clogged or fuel injection system fault (see Chapter 3B).
- [ ] Fuel tank vent in filler cap blocked. Clean and blow through or replace with a new one.

Compression too high
- [ ] Carbon build-up in combustion chamber. Use of a fuel additive that will dissolve the adhesive bonding the carbon particles to the piston crown and chamber is the easiest way to remove the build-up. Otherwise, the cylinder head will have to be removed and cleaned (Chapter 2).

Engine load excessive
- [ ] Centrifugal or multi-plate clutch slipping (Chapter 2) – engine speed will rise but road speed won't, accompanied by burnt clutch plate smell. Problem will rapidly get worse.
- [ ] Brakes dragging. On the front disc brake this is usually caused by debris which has entered the brake piston seals, or from a warped disc or bent axle. On the rear drum brake there could be insufficient freeplay or a shoe return spring may have broken. Repair as necessary (Chapter 6).

Lubrication inadequate
- [ ] Engine oil level too low. Friction caused by intermittent lack of lubrication or from oil that is overworked can cause overheating. The oil provides a definite cooling function in the engine. Check the oil level (*Pre-ride checks*).
- [ ] Poor quality engine oil or incorrect viscosity or type. Oil is rated not only according to viscosity but also according to type. Some oils are not rated high enough for use in this engine. Check the Specifications section and change to the correct oil (Chapter 1).

5 Clutch problems

Clutch slipping – centrifugal clutch
- [ ] Friction shoes worn. Overhaul the clutch assembly (Chapter 2).
- [ ] Drum worn or warped (Chapter 2).
- [ ] Clutch shoe spring(s) broken or weak. Old or heat-damaged (from slipping clutch) springs should be replaced with new ones (Chapter 2).

Clutch slipping – one-way clutch
- [ ] Rollers, springs or housing worn or damaged. Overhaul the clutch assembly (Chapter 2).

Clutch slipping – multi-plate clutch
- [ ] Friction plates worn or warped. Overhaul the clutch assembly (Chapter 2).
- [ ] Steel plates worn or warped (Chapter 2).
- [ ] Clutch spring(s) broken or weak. Old or heat-damaged (from slipping clutch) springs should be replaced with new ones (Chapter 2).
- [ ] Clutch lifter mechanism defective. Replace any defective parts (Chapter 2).
- [ ] Clutch centre or housing unevenly worn. This causes improper engagement of the plates. Replace the damaged or worn parts (Chapter 2).

Clutch not disengaging completely – centrifugal clutch
- [ ] Clutch shoe(s) seized on posts (Chapter 2).
- [ ] Engine idle speed too high (Chapter 1).

Clutch not disengaging completely – one-way clutch
- [ ] Rollers, springs or housing worn or damaged. Overhaul the clutch assembly (Chapter 2).

Clutch not disengaging completely – multi-plate clutch
- [ ] Clutch plates warped or damaged. This will cause clutch drag, which in turn will cause the machine to creep. Overhaul the clutch assembly (Chapter 2).
- [ ] Clutch spring tension uneven. Usually caused by a sagged or broken spring. Check and replace the spring (Chapter 2).
- [ ] Engine oil deteriorated. Old, thin, worn out oil will not provide proper lubrication for the discs, causing the clutch to drag. Replace the oil and filter (Chapter 1).
- [ ] Engine oil viscosity too high. Using a heavier oil than recommended in Chapter 1 can cause the plates to stick together, putting a drag on the engine. Change to the correct weight oil (Chapter 1).
- [ ] Clutch housing seized on shaft. Lack of lubrication, severe wear or damage can cause the housing to seize on the shaft. Overhaul of the clutch, and perhaps transmission, may be necessary to repair the damage (Chapter 2).
- [ ] Clutch lifter mechanism defective. Worn or damaged release mechanism parts can stick and fail to apply force to the pressure plate. Overhaul the clutch cover components (Chapter 2).
- [ ] Loose clutch centre nut. Causes drum and center misalignment putting a drag on the engine. Engagement adjustment continually varies. Overhaul the clutch assembly (Chapter 2).

Fault Finding

6 Gearchange problems

Doesn't go into gear or lever doesn't return
- [ ] Clutches not disengaging. See Section 5.
- [ ] Selector fork(s) bent or seized. Often caused by dropping the machine or from lack of lubrication. Overhaul the transmission (Chapter 2).
- [ ] Gear(s) stuck on shaft. Most often caused by a lack of lubrication or excessive wear in transmission bearings and bushings. Overhaul the transmission (Chapter 2).
- [ ] Selector drum binding. Caused by lubrication failure or excessive wear. Replace the drum and bearing (Chapter 2).
- [ ] Gearchange lever return spring weak or broken (Chapter 2).
- [ ] Gearchange lever broken. Splines stripped out of lever or shaft, caused by allowing the lever to get loose or from dropping the machine. Replace necessary parts (Chapter 2).
- [ ] Gearchange mechanism stopper arm broken or worn. Full engagement and rotary movement of selector drum results. Replace the arm (Chapter 2).
- [ ] Stopper arm spring broken. Allows arm to float, causing sporadic gearchange operation. Replace spring (Chapter 2).

Jumps out of gear
- [ ] Selector fork(s) worn. Overhaul the transmission (Chapter 2).
- [ ] Gear groove(s) worn. Overhaul the transmission (Chapter 2).
- [ ] Gear dogs or dog slots worn or damaged. The gears should be inspected and replaced. No attempt should be made to service the worn parts.

Overshifts
- [ ] Stopper arm spring weak or broken (Chapter 2).
- [ ] Gearchange shaft return spring post broken or distorted (Chapter 2).

7 Abnormal engine noise

Knocking or pinking
- [ ] Carbon build-up in combustion chamber. Use of a fuel additive that will dissolve the adhesive bonding the carbon particles to the piston crown and chamber is the easiest way to remove the build-up. Otherwise, the cylinder head will have to be removed and decarbonised (Chapter 2).
- [ ] Incorrect or poor quality fuel. Old or improper fuel can cause detonation. This causes the piston to rattle, thus the knocking or pinking sound. Drain the old fuel and always use the recommended grade fuel (Chapter 3A or 3B).
- [ ] Spark plug heat range incorrect. Uncontrolled detonation indicates that the plug heat range is too hot. The plug in effect becomes a glow plug, raising cylinder temperatures. Install the proper heat range plug (Chapter 1).
- [ ] Improper air/fuel mixture. This will cause the engine to run hot and lead to detonation. Clogged jets (carburettor engine) or an air leak can cause this imbalance. See Chapter 3A or 3B.

Piston slap or rattling
- [ ] Cylinder-to-piston clearance excessive. Caused by improper assembly. Inspect and overhaul top-end parts (Chapter 2).
- [ ] Connecting rod bent. Caused by over-revving, trying to start a badly flooded engine or from ingesting a foreign object into the combustion chamber. Replace the damaged parts (Chapter 2).
- [ ] Piston pin or piston pin bore worn or seized from wear or lack of lubrication. Replace damaged parts (Chapter 2).
- [ ] Piston ring(s) worn, broken or sticking. Overhaul the top-end (Chapter 2).
- [ ] Piston seizure damage. Usually from lack of lubrication or overheating. Replace the piston and rebore the cylinder, as necessary (Chapter 2).
- [ ] Connecting rod upper or lower end clearance excessive. Caused by excessive wear or lack of lubrication. Replace worn parts.

Valve noise
- [ ] Incorrect valve clearances. Adjust the clearances by referring to Chapter 1.
- [ ] Valve spring broken or weak. Check and replace weak valve springs (Chapter 2).
- [ ] Camshaft or cylinder head worn or damaged. Lack of lubrication at high rpm is usually the cause of damage. Insufficient oil or failure to change the oil at the recommended intervals are the chief causes (Chapter 2).

Other noise
- [ ] Cylinder head gasket leaking.
- [ ] Exhaust pipe leaking at cylinder head connection. Caused by improper fit of pipe or loose exhaust flange. All exhaust fasteners should be tightened evenly and carefully. Failure to do this will lead to a leak.
- [ ] Crankshaft runout excessive. Caused by a bent crankshaft (from over-revving) or damage from an upper cylinder component failure. Can also be attributed to dropping the machine on either of the crankshaft ends.
- [ ] Engine mounting bolts loose. Tighten all engine mount bolts (Chapter 2).
- [ ] Crankshaft bearings worn (Chapter 2).
- [ ] Cam chain tensioner defective. Replace according to the procedure in Chapter 2.
- [ ] Cam chain, sprockets or guides worn (Chapter 2).

Fault Finding REF•41

8 Abnormal driveline noise

Clutch noise
- ☐ Centrifugal clutch drum or shoes loose (Chapter 2).
- ☐ Multi-plate clutch housing/friction plate clearance excessive (Chapter 2).
- ☐ Loose or damaged multi-plate clutch lifter or pressure plate and/or bolts (Chapter 2).

Transmission noise
- ☐ Bearings worn. Also includes the possibility that the shafts are worn. Overhaul the transmission (Chapter 2).
- ☐ Gears worn or chipped (Chapter 2).
- ☐ Metal chips jammed in gear teeth. Probably pieces from a broken clutch, gear or selector mechanism that were picked up by the gears. This will cause early bearing failure (Chapter 2).
- ☐ Engine oil level too low. Causes a howl from transmission. Also affects engine power and clutch operation (*Pre-ride checks*).

Final drive noise
- ☐ Chain not adjusted properly (Chapter 1).
- ☐ Engine sprocket or rear sprocket loose. Tighten fasteners (Chapters 2 and 6).
- ☐ Sprocket(s) worn. Replace sprocket(s) (Chapter 6).
- ☐ Rear sprocket warped. Replace (Chapter 6).
- ☐ Sprocket coupling worn. Check coupling, dampers and bearing (Chapter 6).

9 Abnormal frame and suspension noise

Front end noise
- ☐ Low fluid level or improper viscosity oil in forks. This can sound like spurting and is usually accompanied by irregular fork action (Chapter 5).
- ☐ Spring weak or broken. Makes a clicking or scraping sound. Fork oil, when drained, will have a lot of metal particles in it (Chapter 5).
- ☐ Steering head bearings loose or damaged. Clicks when braking. Check and adjust or replace as necessary (Chapters 1 and 5).
- ☐ Fork clamp bolts loose. Make sure all fork clamp bolts are tight (Chapter 5).
- ☐ Fork tube bent. Good possibility if machine has been dropped. Replace tube with a new one (Chapter 5).
- ☐ Front axle nut loose. Tighten it to the specified torque (Chapter 6).

Shock absorber noise
- ☐ Fluid level incorrect. Indicates a leak caused by defective seal. Shock will be covered with oil. Replace shocks as a pair (Chapter 5).
- ☐ Defective shock absorber with internal damage. This is in the body of the shock and can't be remedied. The shock must be replaced as a pair (Chapter 5).
- ☐ Bent or damaged shock body. Replace the shocks as a pair (Chapter 5).

Brake noise
- ☐ Squeal caused by dust on front brake pads or rear shoes. Usually found in combination with glazed pads or shoes. Remove for cleaning and inspection (Chapter 6).
- ☐ Contamination of brake pads or shoes due to brake fluid (front pads) or grease (rear shoes). Fit new pads or shoes (Chapter 6).
- ☐ Pads or shoes glazed. Caused by excessive heat from prolonged use or from contamination. Do not use sandpaper, emery cloth, carborundum cloth or any other abrasive to roughen the friction surfaces as abrasives will stay in the material and damage the disc/drum. A very fine flat file can be used, but pad or shoe replacement is best (Chapter 6).
- ☐ Front disc warped. Can cause a chattering, clicking or intermittent squeal. Usually accompanied by a pulsating lever and uneven braking. Replace the disc (Chapter 6).
- ☐ Loose or worn wheel bearings. Check and replace as needed (Chapter 6).

REF•42 Fault Finding

10 Excessive exhaust smoke

White smoke

- ☐ Piston oil ring worn. The ring may be broken or damaged, causing oil from the crankcase to be pulled past the piston into the combustion chamber. Replace the rings with new ones (Chapter 2).
- ☐ Cylinder worn, cracked, or scored. Caused by overheating or oil starvation. The cylinder will have to be rebored and a new piston and rings installed.
- ☐ Valve oil seal damaged or worn. Replace oil seals with new ones (Chapter 2).
- ☐ Valve guide worn. Perform a complete valve job (Chapter 2).
- ☐ Engine oil level too high, which causes the oil to be forced past the rings. Drain oil to the proper level (Chapter 1 and *Pre-ride checks*).
- ☐ Head gasket broken between oil return and cylinder. Causes oil to be pulled into the combustion chamber. Replace the head gasket and check the head for warpage (Chapter 2).
- ☐ Abnormal crankcase pressurisation, which forces oil past the rings. Clogged breather or hose usually the cause (Chapter 1).

Black smoke (rich mixture) – carburettor models

- ☐ Air filter clogged. Clean or renew the element (Chapter 1).
- ☐ Main jet too large or loose. Compare the jet size to the Specifications (Chapter 3A).
- ☐ Choke mechanism faulty (Chapter 3A).
- ☐ Float needle valve held off needle seat. Clean the float chamber and renew the needle if necessary (Chapter 3A).

Black smoke (rich mixture) – fuel injection models

- ☐ Air filter clogged. Clean or renew the element (Chapter 1).
- ☐ Fuel injection system or idle air control valve malfunction (Chapter 3B).
- ☐ Fuel pressure too high. Check the fuel pressure (Chapter 3B).

Brown smoke (lean mixture) – carburettor models

- ☐ Main jet too small or clogged. Lean condition caused by wrong size main jet or by a restricted orifice. Clean float chamber and jets and compare jet size to specifications (Chapter 3A).
- ☐ Fuel flow insufficient. Float needle valve stuck closed due to chemical reaction with old fuel. Restricted fuel hose. Clean hose and float chamber (Chapter 3A).
- ☐ Carburettor clamp or intake duct bolts loose (Chapter 3A).
- ☐ Air filter poorly sealed or not installed (Chapter 1).
- ☐ Ignition timing incorrect (Chapter 4).

Brown smoke (lean mixture) – fuel injection models

- ☐ Fuel pump faulty or pressure regulator stuck open (Chapter 3B).
- ☐ Throttle body clamp or intake duct bolts loose (Chapter 3B).
- ☐ Air filter poorly sealed or not installed (Chapter 1).
- ☐ Fuel injection system malfunction (Chapter 3B).

11 Poor handling or stability

Handlebar hard to turn

- ☐ Steering stem nut or bearing adjuster nut too tight (Chapters 1 and 5).
- ☐ Bearings damaged. Roughness can be felt as the bars are turned from side-to-side. Replace bearings and races (Chapter 5).
- ☐ Races dented or worn. Denting results from wear in only one position (e.g., straight-ahead), from a collision or hitting a pothole or from dropping the machine. Replace races and bearings (Chapter 5).
- ☐ Steering stem lubrication inadequate. Causes are grease getting hard from age or being washed out by high pressure washers. Disassemble steering head and repack bearings (Chapter 5).
- ☐ Steering stem bent. Caused by a collision, hitting a pothole or by dropping the machine. Replace damaged part. Don't try to straighten the steering stem (Chapter 5).
- ☐ Front tyre air pressure too low (*Pre-ride checks*).

Handlebar shakes or vibrates excessively

- ☐ Tyres worn or out of balance (Chapter 6).
- ☐ Swingarm bearings worn. Replace worn bearings by referring to Chapter 5.
- ☐ Rim(s) warped or damaged. Inspect wheels for runout (Chapter 6).
- ☐ Wheel bearings worn – see Chapter 1 for checks. Worn front or rear wheel bearings can cause poor tracking. Worn front bearings will cause wobble. To replace them see Chapter 6.
- ☐ Handlebar bolts loose (Chapter 5).
- ☐ Steering stem or fork clamp bolts loose. Tighten them to the specified torque (Chapter 5).
- ☐ Engine mounting bolts loose. Will cause excessive vibration with increased engine rpm (Chapter 2).

Handlebar pulls to one side

- ☐ Frame bent. Definitely suspect this if the machine has been dropped. May be accompanied by cracking near the bend. Replace the frame.
- ☐ Wheels out of alignment – check the alignment (Chapter 6). Could be caused by improper location of axle spacers (Chapter 6) or from bent steering stem or frame (Chapter 5) or simply failure to observe wheel alignment marks when adjusting the drive chain (Chapter 1)..
- ☐ Swingarm bent or twisted. Caused by age (metal fatigue) or impact damage. Replace the swingarm (Chapter 5).
- ☐ Steering stem bent. Caused by impact damage or by dropping the scooter. Replace the steering stem (Chapter 5).
- ☐ Fork leg bent. Disassemble the forks and replace the damaged parts (Chapter 5).
- ☐ Fork oil level uneven. Check and add or drain as necessary (Chapter 5).

Poor shock absorbing qualities

- ☐ Too hard:
  - a) Fork oil level excessive (Chapter 5).
  - b) Fork oil viscosity too high. Use a lighter oil (see the Specifications in Chapter 5).
  - c) Fork tube bent. Causes a harsh, sticking feeling (Chapter 5).
  - d) Shock shaft or body bent or shock internal damage (Chapter 5).
  - e) Fork internal damage (Chapter 5).
  - f) Tyre pressure too high (*Pre-ride checks*).
- ☐ Too soft:
  - a) Fork or shock oil insufficient and/or leaking (Chapter 5).
  - b) Fork oil level too low (Chapter 5).
  - c) Fork oil viscosity too light (Chapter 5).
  - d) Fork springs weak or broken (Chapter 5).
  - e) Shock internal damage or leakage (Chapter 5).

Fault Finding REF•43

12 Braking problems – front disc brake

Brake is ineffective
- ☐ Air in brake hose. Caused by inattention to master cylinder fluid level (*Pre-ride checks*) or by leakage. Locate problem and bleed brake (Chapter 6).
- ☐ Pads or disc worn (Chapters 1 and 6).
- ☐ Brake fluid leak. Locate problem and rectify (Chapter 6).
- ☐ Contaminated pads. Caused by contamination with oil, grease, brake fluid, etc. Fit new pads. Clean disc thoroughly with brake cleaner (Chapter 6).
- ☐ Brake fluid deteriorated. Fluid is old or contaminated. Drain system, replenish with new fluid and bleed the system (Chapter 6).
- ☐ Master cylinder internal parts worn or damaged causing fluid to bypass – overhaul the master cylinder using rebuild kit (Chapter 6).
- ☐ Master cylinder bore scratched by foreign material or broken spring. Fit new master cylinder (Chapter 6).
- ☐ Disc warped. Fit new disc (Chapter 6).

Brake lever pulsates
- ☐ Disc warped. Fit new disc (Chapter 6).
- ☐ Axle bent. Fit new axle (Chapter 6).
- ☐ Brake caliper bolts loose (Chapter 6).
- ☐ Wheel warped or otherwise damaged (Chapter 6).
- ☐ Wheel bearings damaged or worn (Chapters 1 and 6).

Brake drags
- ☐ Master cylinder piston seized. Caused by wear or damage to piston or cylinder bore (Chapter 6).
- ☐ Lever balky or stuck. Check pivot and lubricate (Chapter 5).
- ☐ Brake caliper piston seized in bore. Caused by wear or ingestion of dirt past deteriorated seal (Chapter 6).
- ☐ Brake pads damaged. Pad material separated from backing plate. Usually caused by faulty manufacturing process or from contact with chemicals. Fit new pads (Chapter 6).
- ☐ Caliper slider pins sticking. Clean the slider pins and apply a smear of silicone grease (Chapter 6).
- ☐ Pads improperly installed (Chapter 6).

13 Braking problems – rear drum brake

Brake is ineffective
- ☐ Pedal freeplay excessive. Check adjustment (Chapter 1).
- ☐ Shoes or drum worn (Chapters 1 and 6).
- ☐ Contaminated shoes. Caused by contamination with oil, grease etc. Fit new shoes. Clean drum thoroughly with brake cleaner (Chapter 6).
- ☐ Brake arm incorrectly positioned, or cam excessively worn (Chapter 6).

Brake pedal pulsates
- ☐ Drum warped. Fit new wheel (Chapter 6).
- ☐ Axle bent. Fit new axle (Chapter 6).

- ☐ Wheel warped or otherwise damaged (Chapter 6).
- ☐ Wheel/hub bearings damaged or worn (Chapter 6).

Brake drags
- ☐ Insufficient pedal freeplay (Chapter 1).
- ☐ Shoe return springs broken (Chapter 6).
- ☐ Pedal balky or stuck. Check pivot and lubricate (Chapter 5).
- ☐ Brake arm or cam binds. Caused by inadequate lubrication or damage (Chapter 6).
- ☐ Brake shoe damaged. Friction material separated from shoe. Usually caused by faulty manufacturing process or from contact with chemicals. Fit new shoes (Chapter 6).
- ☐ Shoes improperly installed or return spring broken (Chapter 6).

14 Electrical problems

Battery dead or weak
- ☐ Battery faulty. Caused by sulfated plates which are shorted through sedimentation or low electrolyte level. Also, broken battery terminal making only occasional contact (Chapter 8).
- ☐ Battery leads making poor contact (Chapter 8).
- ☐ Load excessive. Caused by addition of high wattage lights or other electrical accessories.
- ☐ Ignition switch defective. Switch either grounds (earths) internally or fails to shut off system. Replace the switch (Chapter 8).
- ☐ Regulator/rectifier defective (Chapter 8).

- ☐ Stator coil open or shorted (Chapter 8).
- ☐ Wiring faulty. Wiring grounded (earthed) or connections loose in ignition, charging or lighting circuits (Chapter 8).

Battery overcharged
- ☐ Regulator/rectifier defective. Overcharging is noticed when battery gets excessively warm or boils over (Chapter 8).
- ☐ Battery defective. Replace battery with a new one (Chapter 8).
- ☐ Battery amperage too low, wrong type or size. Install manufacturer's specified amp-hour battery to handle charging load (Chapter 8).

Technical Terms Explained

A

ABS (Anti-lock braking system) A system, usually electronically controlled, that senses incipient wheel lockup during braking and relieves hydraulic pressure at wheel which is about to skid.
Aftermarket Components suitable for the motorcycle, but not produced by the motorcycle manufacturer.
Allen key A hexagonal wrench which fits into a recessed hexagonal hole.
Alternating current (ac) Current produced by an alternator. Requires converting to direct current by a rectifier for charging purposes.
Alternator Converts mechanical energy from the engine into electrical energy to charge the battery and power the electrical system.
Ampere (amp) A unit of measurement for the flow of electrical current. Current = Volts ÷ Ohms.
Ampere-hour (Ah) Measure of battery capacity.
Angle-tightening A torque expressed in degrees. Often follows a conventional tightening torque for cylinder head or main bearing fasteners **(see illustration)**.

Angle-tightening cylinder head bolts

Antifreeze A substance (usually ethylene glycol) mixed with water, and added to the cooling system, to prevent freezing of the coolant in winter. Antifreeze also contains chemicals to inhibit corrosion and the formation of rust and other deposits that would tend to clog the radiator and coolant passages and reduce cooling efficiency.
Anti-dive System attached to the fork lower leg (slider) to prevent fork dive when braking hard.
Anti-seize compound A coating that reduces the risk of seizing on fasteners that are subjected to high temperatures, such as exhaust clamp bolts and nuts.
API American Petroleum Institute. A quality standard for 4-stroke motor oils.
Asbestos A natural fibrous mineral with great heat resistance, commonly used in the composition of brake friction materials. Asbestos is a health hazard and the dust created by brake systems should never be inhaled or ingested.
ATF Automatic Transmission Fluid. Often used in front forks.
ATU Automatic Timing Unit. Mechanical device for advancing the ignition timing on early engines.
ATV All Terrain Vehicle. Often called a Quad.
Axial play Side-to-side movement.
Axle A shaft on which a wheel revolves. Also known as a spindle.

B

Backlash The amount of movement between meshed components when one component is held still. Usually applies to gear teeth.
Ball bearing A bearing consisting of a hardened inner and outer race with hardened steel balls between the two races.
Bearings Used between two working surfaces to prevent wear of the components and a build-up of heat. Four types of bearing are commonly used on motorcycles: plain shell bearings, ball bearings, tapered roller bearings and needle roller bearings.
Bevel gears Used to turn the drive through 90°. Typical applications are shaft final drive and camshaft drive **(see illustration)**.

Bevel gears are used to turn the drive through 90°

BHP Brake Horsepower. The British measurement for engine power output. Power output is now usually expressed in kilowatts (kW).
Bias-belted tyre Similar construction to radial tyre, but with outer belt running at an angle to the wheel rim.
Big-end bearing The bearing in the end of the connecting rod that's attached to the crankshaft.
Bleeding The process of removing air from an hydraulic system via a bleed nipple or bleed screw.
Bottom-end A description of an engine's crankcase components and all components contained there-in.
BTDC Before Top Dead Centre in terms of piston position. Ignition timing is often expressed in terms of degrees or millimetres BTDC.
Bush A cylindrical metal or rubber component used between two moving parts.
Burr Rough edge left on a component after machining or as a result of excessive wear.

C

Cam chain The chain which takes drive from the crankshaft to the camshaft(s).
Canister The main component in an evaporative emission control system (California market only); contains activated charcoal granules to trap vapours from the fuel system rather than allowing them to vent to the atmosphere.
Castellated Resembling the parapets along the top of a castle wall. For example, a castellated wheel axle or spindle nut.
Catalytic converter A device in the exhaust system of some machines which converts certain pollutants in the exhaust gases into less harmful substances.
Charging system Description of the components which charge the battery, ie the alternator, rectifer and regulator.
Circlip A ring-shaped clip used to prevent endwise movement of cylindrical parts and shafts. An internal circlip is installed in a groove in a housing; an external circlip fits into a groove on the outside of a cylindrical piece such as a shaft. Also known as a snap-ring.
Clearance The amount of space between two parts. For example, between a piston and a cylinder, between a bearing and a journal, etc.
Coil spring A spiral of elastic steel found in various sizes throughout a vehicle, for example as a springing medium in the suspension and in the valve train.
Compression Reduction in volume, and increase in pressure and temperature, of a gas, caused by squeezing it into a smaller space.
Compression damping Controls the speed the suspension compresses when hitting a bump.
Compression ratio The relationship between cylinder volume when the piston is at top dead centre and cylinder volume when the piston is at bottom dead centre.
Continuity The uninterrupted path in the flow of electricity. Little or no measurable resistance.
Continuity tester Self-powered bleeper or test light which indicates continuity.
Cp Candlepower. Bulb rating commonly found on US motorcycles.
Crossply tyre Tyre plies arranged in a criss-cross pattern. Usually four or six plies used, hence 4PR or 6PR in tyre size codes.
Cush drive Rubber damper segments fitted between the rear wheel and final drive sprocket to absorb transmission shocks **(see illustration)**.

Cush drive rubbers dampen out transmission shocks

D

Degree disc Calibrated disc for measuring piston position. Expressed in degrees.
Dial gauge Clock-type gauge with adapters for measuring runout and piston position. Expressed in mm or inches.
Diaphragm The rubber membrane in a master cylinder or carburettor which seals the upper chamber.
Diaphragm spring A single sprung plate often used in clutches.
Direct current (dc) Current produced by a dc generator.

Technical Terms Explained REF•45

Decarbonisation The process of removing carbon deposits - typically from the combustion chamber, valves and exhaust port/system.
Detonation Destructive and damaging explosion of fuel/air mixture in combustion chamber instead of controlled burning.
Diode An electrical valve which only allows current to flow in one direction. Commonly used in rectifiers and starter interlock systems.
Disc valve (or rotary valve) A induction system used on some two-stroke engines.
Double-overhead camshaft (DOHC) An engine that uses two overhead camshafts, one for the intake valves and one for the exhaust valves.
Drivebelt A toothed belt used to transmit drive to the rear wheel on some motorcycles. A drivebelt has also been used to drive the camshafts. Drivebelts are usually made of Kevlar.
Driveshaft Any shaft used to transmit motion. Commonly used when referring to the final driveshaft on shaft drive motorcycles.

E

Earth return The return path of an electrical circuit, utilising the motorcycle's frame.
ECU (Electronic Control Unit) A computer which controls (for instance) an ignition system, or an anti-lock braking system.
EGO Exhaust Gas Oxygen sensor. Sometimes called a Lambda sensor.
Electrolyte The fluid in a lead-acid battery.
EMS (Engine Management System) A computer controlled system which manages the fuel injection and the ignition systems in an integrated fashion.
Endfloat The amount of lengthways movement between two parts. As applied to a crankshaft, the distance that the crankshaft can move side-to-side in the crankcase.
Endless chain A chain having no joining link. Common use for cam chains and final drive chains.
EP (Extreme Pressure) Oil type used in locations where high loads are applied, such as between gear teeth.
Evaporative emission control system Describes a charcoal filled canister which stores fuel vapours from the tank rather than allowing them to vent to the atmosphere. Usually only fitted to California models and referred to as an EVAP system.
Expansion chamber Section of two-stroke engine exhaust system so designed to improve engine efficiency and boost power.

F

Feeler blade or gauge A thin strip or blade of hardened steel, ground to an exact thickness, used to check or measure clearances between parts.
Final drive Description of the drive from the transmission to the rear wheel. Usually by chain or shaft, but sometimes by belt.
Firing order The order in which the engine cylinders fire, or deliver their power strokes, beginning with the number one cylinder.
Flooding Term used to describe a high fuel level in the carburettor float chambers, leading to fuel overflow. Also refers to excess fuel in the combustion chamber due to incorrect starting technique.

Free length The no-load state of a component when measured. Clutch, valve and fork spring lengths are measured at rest, without any preload.
Freeplay The amount of travel before any action takes place. The looseness in a linkage, or an assembly of parts, between the initial application of force and actual movement. For example, the distance the rear brake pedal moves before the rear brake is actuated.
Fuel injection The fuel/air mixture is metered electronically and directed into the engine intake ports (indirect injection) or into the cylinders (direct injection). Sensors supply information on engine speed and conditions.
Fuel/air mixture The charge of fuel and air going into the engine. See **Stoichiometric ratio**.
Fuse An electrical device which protects a circuit against accidental overload. The typical fuse contains a soft piece of metal which is calibrated to melt at a predetermined current flow (expressed as amps) and break the circuit.

G

Gap The distance the spark must travel in jumping from the centre electrode to the side electrode in a spark plug. Also refers to the distance between the ignition rotor and the pickup coil in an electronic ignition system.
Gasket Any thin, soft material - usually cork, cardboard, asbestos or soft metal - installed between two metal surfaces to ensure a good seal. For instance, the cylinder head gasket seals the joint between the block and the cylinder head.
Gauge An instrument panel display used to monitor engine conditions. A gauge with a movable pointer on a dial or a fixed scale is an analogue gauge. A gauge with a numerical readout is called a digital gauge.
Gear ratios The drive ratio of a pair of gears in a gearbox, calculated on their number of teeth.
Glaze-busting see **Honing**
Grinding Process for renovating the valve face and valve seat contact area in the cylinder head.
Gudgeon pin The shaft which connects the connecting rod small-end with the piston. Often called a piston pin or wrist pin.

H

Helical gears Gear teeth are slightly curved and produce less gear noise that straight-cut gears. Often used for primary drives.

Installing a Helicoil thread insert in a cylinder head

Helicoil A thread insert repair system. Commonly used as a repair for stripped spark plug threads (see illustration).
Honing A process used to break down the glaze on a cylinder bore (also called glaze-busting). Can also be carried out to roughen a rebored cylinder to aid ring bedding-in.
HT (High Tension) Description of the electrical circuit from the secondary winding of the ignition coil to the spark plug.
Hydraulic A liquid filled system used to transmit pressure from one component to another. Common uses on motorcycles are brakes and clutches.
Hydrometer An instrument for measuring the specific gravity of a lead-acid battery.
Hygroscopic Water absorbing. In motorcycle applications, braking efficiency will be reduced if DOT 3 or 4 hydraulic fluid absorbs water from the air - care must be taken to keep new brake fluid in tightly sealed containers.

I

lbf ft Pounds-force feet. An imperial unit of torque. Sometimes written as ft-lbs.
lbf in Pound-force inch. An imperial unit of torque, applied to components where a very low torque is required. Sometimes written as in-lbs.
IC Abbreviation for Integrated Circuit.
Ignition advance Means of increasing the timing of the spark at higher engine speeds. Done by mechanical means (ATU) on early engines or electronically by the ignition control unit on later engines.
Ignition timing The moment at which the spark plug fires, expressed in the number of crankshaft degrees before the piston reaches the top of its stroke, or in the number of millimetres before the piston reaches the top of its stroke.
Infinity (∞) Description of an open-circuit electrical state, where no continuity exists.
Inverted forks (upside down forks) The sliders or lower legs are held in the yokes and the fork tubes or stanchions are connected to the wheel axle (spindle). Less unsprung weight and stiffer construction than conventional forks.

J

JASO Quality standard for 2-stroke oils.
Joule The unit of electrical energy.
Journal The bearing surface of a shaft.

K

Kickstart Mechanical means of turning the engine over for starting purposes. Only usually fitted to mopeds, small capacity motorcycles and off-road motorcycles.
Kill switch Handebar-mounted switch for emergency ignition cut-out. Cuts the ignition circuit on all models, and additionally prevent starter motor operation on others.
km Symbol for kilometre.
kmh Abbreviation for kilometres per hour.

L

Lambda (λ) sensor A sensor fitted in the exhaust system to measure the exhaust gas oxygen content (excess air factor).

Technical Terms Explained

Lapping see Grinding.
LCD Abbreviation for Liquid Crystal Display.
LED Abbreviation for Light Emitting Diode.
Liner A steel cylinder liner inserted in a aluminium alloy cylinder block.
Locknut A nut used to lock an adjustment nut, or other threaded component, in place.
Lockstops The lugs on the lower triple clamp (yoke) which abut those on the frame, preventing handlebar-to-fuel tank contact.
Lockwasher A form of washer designed to prevent an attaching nut from working loose.
LT Low Tension Description of the electrical circuit from the power supply to the primary winding of the ignition coil.

M

Main bearings The bearings between the crankshaft and crankcase.
Maintenance-free (MF) battery A sealed battery which cannot be topped up.
Manometer Mercury-filled calibrated tubes used to measure intake tract vacuum. Used to synchronise carburettors on multi-cylinder engines.
Micrometer A precision measuring instrument that measures component outside diameters (see illustration).

Tappet shims are measured with a micrometer

MON (Motor Octane Number) A measure of a fuel's resistance to knock.
Monograde oil An oil with a single viscosity, eg SAE80W.
Monoshock A single suspension unit linking the swingarm or suspension linkage to the frame.
mph Abbreviation for miles per hour.
Multigrade oil Having a wide viscosity range (eg 10W40). The W stands for Winter, thus the viscosity ranges from SAE10 when cold to SAE40 when hot.
Multimeter An electrical test instrument with the capability to measure voltage, current and resistance. Some meters also incorporate a continuity tester and buzzer.

N

Needle roller bearing Inner race of caged needle rollers and hardened outer race. Examples of uncaged needle rollers can be found on some engines. Commonly used in rear suspension applications and in two-stroke engines.
Nm Newton metres.
NOx Oxides of Nitrogen. A common toxic pollutant emitted by petrol engines at higher temperatures.

O

Octane The measure of a fuel's resistance to knock.
OE (Original Equipment) Relates to components fitted to a motorcycle as standard or replacement parts supplied by the motorcycle manufacturer.
Ohm The unit of electrical resistance. Ohms = Volts ÷ Current.
Ohmmeter An instrument for measuring electrical resistance.
Oil cooler System for diverting engine oil outside of the engine to a radiator for cooling purposes.
Oil injection A system of two-stroke engine lubrication where oil is pump-fed to the engine in accordance with throttle position.
Open-circuit An electrical condition where there is a break in the flow of electricity - no continuity (high resistance).
O-ring A type of sealing ring made of a special rubber-like material; in use, the O-ring is compressed into a groove to provide the sealing action.
Oversize (OS) Term used for piston and ring size options fitted to a rebored cylinder.
Overhead cam (sohc) engine An engine with single camshaft located on top of the cylinder head.
Overhead valve (ohv) engine An engine with the valves located in the cylinder head, but with the camshaft located in the engine block or crankcase.
Oxygen sensor A device installed in the exhaust system which senses the oxygen content in the exhaust and converts this information into an electric current. Also called a Lambda sensor.

P

Plastigauge A thin strip of plastic thread, available in different sizes, used for measuring clearances. For example, a strip of Plastigauge is laid across a bearing journal. The parts are assembled and dismantled; the width of the crushed strip indicates the clearance between journal and bearing.
Polarity Either negative or positive earth (ground), determined by which battery lead is connected to the frame (earth return). Modern motorcycles are usually negative earth.
Pre-ignition A situation where the fuel/air mixture ignites before the spark plug fires. Often due to a hot spot in the combustion chamber caused by carbon build-up. Engine has a tendency to 'run-on'.
Pre-load (suspension) The amount a spring is compressed when in the unloaded state. Preload can be applied by gas, spacer or mechanical adjuster.
Premix The method of engine lubrication on older two-stroke engines. Engine oil is mixed with the petrol in the fuel tank in a specific ratio. The fuel/oil mix is sometimes referred to as "petroil".
Primary drive Description of the drive from the crankshaft to the clutch. Usually by gear or chain.
PS Pfedestärke - a German interpretation of BHP.
PSI Pounds-force per square inch. Imperial measurement of tyre pressure and cylinder pressure measurement.
PTFE Polytetrafluroethylene. A low friction substance.
Pulse secondary air injection system A process of promoting the burning of excess fuel present in the exhaust gases by routing fresh air into the exhaust ports.

Q

Quartz halogen bulb Tungsten filament surrounded by a halogen gas. Typically used for the headlight (see illustration).

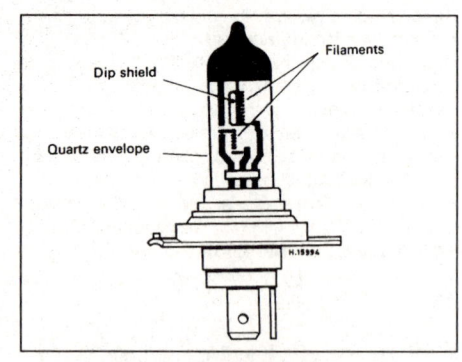

Quartz halogen headlight bulb construction

R

Rack-and-pinion A pinion gear on the end of a shaft that mates with a rack (think of a geared wheel opened up and laid flat). Sometimes used in clutch operating systems.
Radial play Up and down movement about a shaft.
Radial ply tyres Tyre plies run across the tyre (from bead to bead) and around the circumference of the tyre. Less resistant to tread distortion than other tyre types.
Radiator A liquid-to-air heat transfer device designed to reduce the temperature of the coolant in a liquid cooled engine.
Rake A feature of steering geometry - the angle of the steering head in relation to the vertical (see illustration).

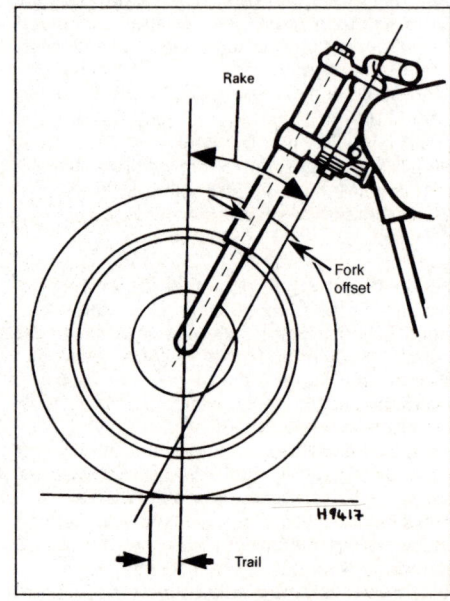

Steering geometry

Technical Terms Explained REF•47

Rebore Providing a new working surface to the cylinder bore by boring out the old surface. Necessitates the use of oversize piston and rings.
Rebound damping A means of controlling the oscillation of a suspension unit spring after it has been compressed. Resists the spring's natural tendency to bounce back after being compressed.
Rectifier Device for converting the ac output of an alternator into dc for battery charging.
Reed valve An induction system commonly used on two-stroke engines.
Regulator Device for maintaining the charging voltage from the generator or alternator within a specified range.
Relay A electrical device used to switch heavy current on and off by using a low current auxiliary circuit.
Resistance Measured in ohms. An electrical component's ability to pass electrical current.
RON (Research Octane Number) A measure of a fuel's resistance to knock.
rpm revolutions per minute.
Runout The amount of wobble (in-and-out movement) of a wheel or shaft as it's rotated. The amount a shaft rotates 'out-of-true'. The out-of-round condition of a rotating part.

S

SAE (Society of Automotive Engineers) A standard for the viscosity of a fluid.
Sealant A liquid or paste used to prevent leakage at a joint. Sometimes used in conjunction with a gasket.
Service limit Term for the point where a component is no longer useable and must be renewed.
Shaft drive A method of transmitting drive from the transmission to the rear wheel.
Shell bearings Plain bearings consisting of two shell halves. Most often used as big-end and main bearings in a four-stroke engine. Often called bearing inserts.
Shim Thin spacer, commonly used to adjust the clearance or relative positions between two parts. For example, shims inserted into or under tappets or followers to control valve clearances. Clearance is adjusted by changing the thickness of the shim.
Short-circuit An electrical condition where current shorts to earth (ground) bypassing the circuit components.
Skimming Process to correct warpage or repair a damaged surface, eg on brake discs or drums.
Slide-hammer A special puller that screws into or hooks onto a component such as a shaft or bearing; a heavy sliding handle on the shaft bottoms against the end of the shaft to knock the component free.
Small-end bearing The bearing in the upper end of the connecting rod at its joint with the gudgeon pin.
Spalling Damage to camshaft lobes or bearing journals shown as pitting of the working surface.
Specific gravity (SG) The state of charge of the electrolyte in a lead-acid battery. A measure of the electrolyte's density compared with water.
Straight-cut gears Common type gear used on gearbox shafts and for oil pump and water pump drives.
Stanchion The inner sliding part of the front forks, held by the yokes. Often called a fork tube.
Stoichiometric ratio The optimum chemical air/fuel ratio for a petrol engine, said to be 14.7 parts of air to 1 part of fuel.
Sulphuric acid The liquid (electrolyte) used in a lead-acid battery. Poisonous and extremely corrosive.
Surface grinding (lapping) Process to correct a warped gasket face, commonly used on cylinder heads.

T

Tapered-roller bearing Tapered inner race of caged needle rollers and separate tapered outer race. Examples of taper roller bearings can be found on steering heads.
Tappet A cylindrical component which transmits motion from the cam to the valve stem, either directly or via a pushrod and rocker arm. Also called a cam follower.
TCS Traction Control System. An electronically-controlled system which senses wheel spin and reduces engine speed accordingly.
TDC Top Dead Centre denotes that the piston is at its highest point in the cylinder.
Thread-locking compound Solution applied to fastener threads to prevent slackening. Select type to suit application.
Thrust washer A washer positioned between two moving components on a shaft. For example, between gear pinions on gearshaft.
Timing chain See **Cam Chain**.
Timing light Stroboscopic lamp for carrying out ignition timing checks with the engine running.
Top-end A description of an engine's cylinder block, head and valve gear components.
Torque Turning or twisting force about a shaft.
Torque setting A prescribed tightness specified by the motorcycle manufacturer to ensure that the bolt or nut is secured correctly. Undertightening can result in the bolt or nut coming loose or a surface not being sealed. Overtightening can result in stripped threads, distortion or damage to the component being retained.
Torx key A six-point wrench.
Tracer A stripe of a second colour applied to a wire insulator to distinguish that wire from another one with the same colour insulator. For example, Br/W is often used to denote a brown insulator with a white tracer.
Trail A feature of steering geometry. Distance from the steering head axis to the tyre's central contact point.
Triple clamps The cast components which extend from the steering head and support the fork stanchions or tubes. Often called fork yokes.
Turbocharger A centrifugal device, driven by exhaust gases, that pressurises the intake air. Normally used to increase the power output from a given engine displacement.
TWI Abbreviation for Tyre Wear Indicator. Indicates the location of the tread depth indicator bars on tyres.

U

Universal joint or U-joint (UJ) A double-pivoted connection for transmitting power from a driving to a driven shaft through an angle. Typically found in shaft drive assemblies.
Unsprung weight Anything not supported by the bike's suspension (ie the wheel, tyres, brakes, final drive and bottom (moving) part of the suspension).

V

Vacuum gauges Clock-type gauges for measuring intake tract vacuum. Used for carburettor synchronisation on multi-cylinder engines.
Valve A device through which the flow of liquid, gas or vacuum may be stopped, started or regulated by a moveable part that opens, shuts or partially obstructs one or more ports or passageways. The intake and exhaust valves in the cylinder head are of the poppet type.
Valve clearance The clearance between the valve tip (the end of the valve stem) and the rocker arm or tappet/follower. The valve clearance is measured when the valve is closed. The correct clearance is important - if too small the valve won't close fully and will burn out, whereas if too large noisy operation will result.
Valve lift The amount a valve is lifted off its seat by the camshaft lobe.
Valve timing The exact setting for the opening and closing of the valves in relation to piston position.
Vernier caliper A precision measuring instrument that measures inside and outside dimensions. Not quite as accurate as a micrometer, but more convenient.
VIN Vehicle Identification Number. Term for the bike's engine and frame numbers.
Viscosity The thickness of a liquid or its resistance to flow.
Volt A unit for expressing electrical "pressure" in a circuit. Volts = current x ohms.

W

Water pump A mechanically-driven device for moving coolant around the engine.
Watt A unit for expressing electrical power. Watts = volts x current.
Wear limit see **Service limit**
Wet liner A liquid-cooled engine design where the pistons run in liners which are directly surrounded by coolant **(see illustration)**.

Wet liner arrangement

Wheelbase Distance from the centre of the front wheel to the centre of the rear wheel.
Wiring harness or loom Describes the electrical wires running the length of the motorcycle and enclosed in tape or plastic sheathing. Wiring coming off the main harness is usually referred to as a sub harness.
Woodruff key A key of semi-circular or square section used to locate a gear to a shaft. Often used to locate the alternator rotor on the crankshaft.
Wrist pin Another name for gudgeon or piston pin.

Index

Note: *References throughout this index are in the form - "Chapter number" • "Page number"*

A

Air filter – 1•9
Air filter housing
 carburettor models – 3A•3
 fuel injection models – 3B•4
Alternator – 8•24

B

Battery – 1•22, 8•1, 8•4, 8•5
Body cover
 carburettor models – 7•2
 fuel injection models – 7•5, 7•6
Bodywork – 7•1 *et seq*
Bottom cover
 carburettor models – 7•3
 fuel injection models – 7•7
Brake (front)
 bleeding and fluid change – 6•9
 caliper – 6•4
 disc – 6•5
 fluid level – 0•14
 hose – 1•17, 6•8
 lever – 5•4
 master cylinder – 6•6
 pads – 1•16, 6•2
 specifications – 6•1
 system check – 1•16
Brake (rear) – 6•11
 pedal freeplay and system check – 1•17
 pedal removal and installation – 5•4
 shoe and drum wear check – 1•16
 specifications – 6•1
Brake light
 bulb – 8•8
 circuit check – 8•6
 switches – 8•11
 unit – 8•9
Bulb
 brake/tail light – 8•8
 headlight – 8•6
 licence plate light – 8•8
 turn signal – 8•10
 wattages – 8•2

C

Cable
 choke – 1•15, 3A•11
 lubrication – 1•20
 throttle – 1•14, 3A•9, 3B•11
Caliper (front brake) – 6•4
Cam chain and blades – 2•15
Cam chain tensioner – 2•11
Camshaft and rocker arms – 2•2, 2•11
Carburettor
 float height check – 3A•8
 heater and thermo switch – 3A•14
 overhaul – 3A•5
 removal and installation – 3A•4
 specifications – 3A•1
 throttle switch – 3A•13
Catalytic converter – 3B•14
Centre cover
 carburettor models – 7•3
 fuel injection models – 7•7
Centrestand – 1•18, 5•5
Chain – 6•18
 cleaning and lubrication – 1•7
 slack – 1•6
 specifications – 6•2
 stretch – 1•8
Chain case – 6•19
Charging (battery) – 8•5
Charging system – 8•1, 8•23
Choke cable – 1•15, 3A•11
Clutch
 adjustment of lifter mechanism – 1•18
 assemblies (removal and installation) – 2•28
 centrifugal clutch – 2•31
 cover – 2•27
 lifter/brake mechanism – 2•37
 multi-plate clutch – 2•34
 specifications – 2•4
Colour code label – 0•9
Compression test – 2•6
Connecting rod – 2•3
Conversion factors – REF•26
Crankcase breather – 1•10
Crankcases – 2•45, 2•46
Crankshaft – 2•4, 2•48
Cylinder block – 2•2, 2•21
Cylinder head – 2•2, 2•16, 2•18

D

Dimensions (model) – 0•9
Disc (front brake) – 6•5
Drive chain – 6•18
 case – 6•19
 cleaning and lubrication – 1•7
 slack – 1•6
 specifications – 6•2
 stretch – 1•8

E

ECU (Electronic Control Unit) – 4•5
Electrical system – 8•1 *et seq*
 battery – 1•22, 8•1, 8•4, 8•5
 brake light switches – 8•11
 brake/tail light – 8•8, 8•9, 8•11
 fault finding – 8•2, REF•43
 fuses – 8•5
 gear position switch – 8•17
 handlebar switches – 8•16
 headlight – 1•20, 8•6, 8•8
 horn – 8•18
 ignition switch – 8•15
 instruments – 8•12
 lighting system – 8•6
 sidestand switch – 8•16
 speed sensor – 8•14
 turn signals – 8•9, 8•10, 8•11
 wiring diagrams – 8•29
Engine
 cam chain and blades – 2•15
 cam chain tensioner – 2•11
 camshaft and rocker arms – 2•11
 compression test – 2•6
 crankcases – 2•45, 2•46
 crankshaft – 2•48
 cylinder block – 2•21
 cylinder head – 2•16, 2•18
 idle speed – 1•15
 oil change – 1•11
 oil filter and strainer – 1•12
 oil level – 0•13
 oil pump – 2•43
 piston – 2•23
 piston rings – 2•25

Index REF•49

removal and installation – 2•7
running-in – 2•56
specifications – 0•9, 1•2, 2•1
starter clutch and gears – 2•26
valve clearances – 1•10
valve covers – 2•10
Engine number – 0•11
EOT (Engine Oil Temperature)
sensor – 3B•8
Exhaust system – 3B•12

F

Fault finding – REF•35 *et seq*
electrical system – 8•2
fuel injection system – 3B•7
ignition system – 4•2
Filter
air – 1•9
engine oil – 1•12
fuel (carburettor models) – 1•14, 3A•2
Footrests – 5•3
Frame – 5•2
Frame number – 0•10
Front brake
bleeding and fluid change – 6•9
caliper – 6•4
disc – 6•5
fluid level – 0•14
hose – 1•17, 6•8
lever – 5•4
master cylinder – 6•6
pads – 1•16, 6•2
specifications – 6•1
system check – 1•16
Front covers
carburettor models – 7•3
fuel injection models – 7•7
Front mudguard
carburettor models – 7•5
fuel injection models – 7•9
Front suspension – 5•6
check – 1•18
fork oil change – 1•19, 5•6
specifications – 5•1
Front wheel – 6•13
Fuel level sensor and gauge
carburettor models – 3A•1, 3A•12
fuel injection models – 3B•1, 3B•13

Fuel system (carburettor models) –
3A•1 *et seq*
carburettor – 3A•4, 3A•5, 3A•8
check – 1•13
fuel filter – 3A•2
fuel tank – 3A•3
fuel valve – 3A•2
idle fuel/air mixture – 3A•4
throttle switch – 3A•13
Fuel system (fuel injection models) –
3B•1 *et seq*
check – 1•14
description – 3B•6
fault diagnosis – 3B•7
fuel injector – 3B•10
fuel pressure check – 3B•2
fuel pump – 3B•3
IACV (Idle Air Control Valve) – 3B•11
sensors – 3B•8
throttle body – 3B•5
Fuses – 8•1, 8•5

G

Gear position switch – 8•17
Gearbox shafts – 2•49, 2•50
Gearchange lever – 5•5
Gearchange mechanism – 2•39
Grab-rail
carburettor models – 7•2
fuel injection models – 7•5

H

Handlebar covers
carburettor models – 7•4
fuel injection models – 7•8, 7•9
Handlebar switches – 8•16
Handlebar weights – 5•2
Handlebars – 5•2
Headlight
aim – 1•20
bulb – 8•6
circuit check – 8•6
unit – 8•8
Horn – 8•18
HT coil – 4•1, 4•2

I

IACV (Idle Air Control Valve) – 3B•11
IAT (Intake Air Temperature) sensor – 3B•9
Idle fuel/air mixture – 3A•4
Idle speed – 1•15
Ignition switch – 8•15
Ignition system
coil – 4•1, 4•2
ECU (Electronic Control Unit) – 4•5
pulse generator coil – 4•4
spark plug – 1•8
system check – 4•2
timing – 4•5
Injector (fuel) – 3B•10
Instruments – 8•12, 8•14

K

Kickstart – 2•41
lever – 5•5
specifications – 2•5

L

Lean angle sensor – 3B•9
Legal checks – 0•15
Licence plate light
bulb – 8•8
circuit check – 8•6
Lighting system – 8•6
Lubricants – 1•2
Lubricants and fluids (general) –
REF•23 *et seq*
Lubrication (pivots and cables) – 1•20

M

Maintenance and servicing – 1•1 *et seq*
schedule – 1•3
specifications – 1•2
MAP (Manifold Absolute Pressure)
sensor – 3B•8
Master cylinder (front brake) – 6•6
Mirrors
carburettor models – 7•4
fuel injection models – 7•8
Model development – 0•9
MOT test checks – REF•27 *et seq*

Index

O

Oil (engine)
 change – 1•11
 filter and strainer – 1•12
 level – 0•13
Oil (front forks) – 5•1
Oil pump – 2•3, 2•43
Oxygen sensor – 3B•9

P

Pads (front brake) – 1•16, 6•2
PAIR (Pulse secondary Air) system – 3A•11
 check – 1•21
Piston – 2•3, 2•23
Piston rings – 2•3, 2•25
Power relay – 8•28
Pre-ride checks – 0•13 et seq
Pressure
 fuel (injection models) – 3B•2
 tyre – 0•15
Pulse generator coil – 4•1, 4•4
Pump
 fuel – 3B•3
 oil – 2•43

R

Rear brake – 6•11
 pedal freeplay and system check – 1•17
 shoe and drum wear check – 1•16
Rear suspension
 check – 1•18, 1•19
 shock absorbers – 5•12
 swingarm – 5•13
Rear wheel – 6•14
Regulator/rectifier – 8•26
Relay
 power – 8•28
 starter – 8•18
 turn signal – 8•9
Running-in procedure – 2•56

S

Safety – 0•12, 0•15
Seat
 carburettor models – 7•2
 fuel injection models – 7•5
Security – REF•20 et seq
Selector drum and forks – 2•4, 2•54
Sensor unit – 3B•8
Service schedule – 1•3
Shoes (rear brake) – 1•16, 6•12
Sidelight bulb – 8•6, 8•7
Sidestand – 1•18, 5•5
Sidestand switch – 8•16
Spark plug – 1•8
Speed sensor – 8•14
Sprocket coupling – 6•21
 bearing – 6•17
 rubber dampers – 6•21
Sprockets (drive chain) – 6•19
 wear check – 1•8
Stands – 1•18
Starter clutch – 2•4, 2•26
Starter motor – 8•1, 8•19, 8•20
Starter relay – 8•18
Steering head bearings – 5•11
 adjustment – 1•21
 check – 1•20
 lubrication – 1•21
Steering stem – 5•10
Storage advice – REF•32 et seq
Storage compartment
 carburettor models – 7•2
 fuel injection models – 7•6
Suspension
 check – 1•18
 front forks – 5•6
 rear shock absorbers – 5•12
 specifications – 5•1
 swingarm – 5•13

T

Tail light
 bulb – 8•8
 circuit check – 8•6
 unit – 8•9

Tank (fuel)
 carburettor models – 3A•3
 fuel injection models – 3B•2
Timing (ignition) – 4•5
Throttle body – 3B•5
Throttle cable – 1•14
 carburettor models – 3A•9
 fuel injection models – 3B•11
Throttle switch – 3A•13
Tools and Workshop Tips – REF•2 et seq
Top cover
 carburettor models – 7•3
 fuel injection models – 7•7
Torque settings – 1•2, 2•6, 3A•1, 3B•1, 4•1, 5•1, 6•2, 8•2
TP (Throttle Position) sensor – 3B•9
Transmission
 shafts – 2•49, 2•50
 specifications – 2•5
Turn signals – 8•11
 bulbs – 8•2, 8•10
 circuit check and relay – 8•9
Tyres – 6•17
 checks – 1•19
 pressures and tread depth – 0•15
 sizes – 0•9, 6•2

V

Valve clearances – 1•2, 1•9
Valve covers – 2•10
Valve (fuel) – 3A•2
Valves – 2•2
VIN (Vehicle Identification Number) – 0•10

W

Weight – 0•9
Wheel
 alignment – 6•12
 bearings – 1•19, 6•15
 checks – 1•19• 6•12
 removal and installation – 6•13, 6•14
 specifications – 6•1
Wiring diagrams – 8•29

Haynes Motorcycle Manuals – The Complete List

Title	Book No
APRILIA RS50 (99 - 06) & RS125 (93 - 06)	4298
Aprilia RSV1000 Mille (98 - 03)	♦ 4255
Aprilia SR50	4755
BMW 2-valve Twins (70 - 96)	♦ 0249
BMW F650	♦ 4761
BMW K100 & 75 2-valve Models (83 - 96)	♦ 1373
BMW R850, 1100 & 1150 4-valve Twins (93 - 04)	♦ 3466
BMW R1200 (04 - 06)	♦ 4598
BSA Bantam (48 - 71)	0117
BSA Unit Singles (58 - 72)	0127
BSA Pre-unit Singles (54 - 61)	0326
BSA A7 & A10 Twins (47 - 62)	0121
BSA A50 & A65 Twins (62 - 73)	0155
Chinese Scooters	4768
DUCATI 600, 620, 750 and 900 2-valve V-Twins (91 - 05)	♦ 3290
Ducati MK III & Desmo Singles (69 - 76)	◊ 0445
Ducati 748, 916 & 996 4-valve V-Twins (94 - 01)	♦ 3756
GILERA Runner, DNA, Ice & SKP/Stalker (97 - 07)	4163
HARLEY-DAVIDSON Sportsters (70 - 08)	♦ 2534
Harley-Davidson Shovelhead and Evolution Big Twins (70 - 99)	♦ 2536
Harley-Davidson Twin Cam 88 (99 - 03)	♦ 2478
HONDA NB, ND, NP & NS50 Melody (81 - 85)	◊ 0622
Honda NE/NB50 Vision & SA50 Vision Met-in (85 - 95)	◊ 1278
Honda MB, MBX, MT & MTX50 (80 - 93)	0731
Honda C50, C70 & C90 (67 - 03)	0324
Honda XR80/100R & CRF80/100F (85 - 04)	2218
Honda XL/XR 80, 100, 125, 185 & 200 2-valve Models (78 - 87)	0566
Honda H100 & H100S Singles (80 - 92)	◊ 0734
Honda CB/CD125T & CM125C Twins (77 - 88)	◊ 0571
Honda CG125 (76 - 07)	0433
Honda NS125 (86 - 93)	3056
Honda CBR125R (04 - 07)	4620
Honda MBX/MTX125 & MTX200 (83 - 93)	◊ 1132
Honda CD/CM185 200T & CM250C 2-valve Twins (77 - 85)	0572
Honda XL/XR 250 & 500 (78 - 84)	0567
Honda XR250L, XR250R & XR400R (86 - 03)	2219
Honda CB250 & CB400N Super Dreams (78 - 84)	0540
Honda CR Motocross Bikes (86 - 01)	2222
Honda CRF250 & CRF450 (02 - 06)	2630
Honda CBR400RR Fours (88 - 99)	◊ ♦ 3552
Honda VFR400 (NC30) & RVF400 (NC35) V-Fours (89 - 98)	◊ ♦ 3496
Honda CB500 (93 - 02) & CBF500 03 - 08	♦ 3753
Honda CB400 & CB550 Fours (73 - 77)	0262
Honda CX/GL500 & 650 V-Twins (78 - 86)	0442
Honda CBX550 Four (82 - 86)	0940
Honda XL600R & XR600R (83 - 08)	♦ 2183
Honda XL600/650V Transalp & XRV750 Africa Twin (87 to 07)	♦ 3919
Honda CBR600F1 & 1000F Fours (87 - 96)	♦ 1730
Honda CBR600F2 & F3 Fours (91 - 98)	♦ 2070
Honda CBR600F4 (99 - 06)	♦ 3911
Honda CB600F Hornet & CBF600 (98 - 06)	◊ ♦ 3915
Honda CBR600RR (03 - 06)	♦ 4590
Honda CB650 sohc Fours (78 - 84)	0665
Honda NTV600 Revere, NTV650 and NT650V Deauville (88 - 05)	◊ ♦ 3243
Honda Shadow VT600 & 750 (USA) (88 - 03)	2312
Honda CB750 sohc Four (69 - 79)	0131
Honda V45/65 Sabre & Magna (82 - 88)	0820
Honda VFR750 & 700 V-Fours (86 - 97)	♦ 2101
Honda VFR800 V-Fours (97 - 01)	♦ 3703
Honda VFR800 V-Tec V-Fours (02 - 05)	♦ 4196
Honda CB750 & CB900 dohc Fours (78 - 84)	0535
Honda VTR1000 (FireStorm, Super Hawk) & XL1000V (Varadero) (97 - 08)	♦ 3744
Honda CBR900RR FireBlade (92 - 99)	♦ 2161
Honda CBR900RR FireBlade (00 - 03)	♦ 4060
Honda CBR1000RR Fireblade (04 - 07)	♦ 4604
Honda CBR1100XX Super Blackbird (97 - 07)	♦ 3901
Honda ST1100 Pan European V-Fours (90 - 02)	♦ 3384
Honda Shadow VT1100 (USA) (85 - 98)	2313
Honda GL1000 Gold Wing (75 - 79)	0309

Title	Book No
Honda GL1100 Gold Wing (79 - 81)	0669
Honda Gold Wing 1200 (USA) (84 - 87)	2199
Honda Gold Wing 1500 (USA) (88 - 00)	2225
KAWASAKI AE/AR 50 & 80 (81 - 95)	1007
Kawasaki KC, KE & KH100 (75 - 99)	1371
Kawasaki KMX125 & 200 (86 - 02)	◊ 3046
Kawasaki 250, 350 & 400 Triples (72 - 79)	0134
Kawasaki 400 & 440 Twins (74 - 81)	0281
Kawasaki 400, 500 & 550 Fours (79 - 91)	0910
Kawasaki EN450 & 500 Twins (Ltd/Vulcan) (85 - 07)	2053
Kawasaki EX500 (GPZ500S) & ER500 (ER-5) (87 - 08)	♦ 2052
Kawasaki ZX600 (ZZ-R600 & Ninja ZX-6) (90 - 06)	♦ 2146
Kawasaki ZX-6R Ninja Fours (95 - 02)	♦ 3541
Kawasaki ZX-6R (03 - 06)	♦ 4742
Kawasaki 600 (GPZ600R, GPX600R, Ninja 600R & RX) & ZX750 (GPX750R, Ninja 750R)	♦ 1780
Kawasaki 650 Four (76 - 78)	0373
Kawasaki Vulcan 700/750 & 800 (85 - 04)	2457
Kawasaki 750 Air-cooled Fours (80 - 91)	0574
Kawasaki ZR550 & 750 Zephyr Fours (90 - 97)	♦ 3382
Kawasaki Z750 & Z1000 (03 - 08)	♦ 4762
Kawasaki ZX750 (Ninja ZX-7 & ZXR750) Fours (89 - 96)	♦ 2054
Kawasaki Ninja ZX-7R & ZX-9R (94 - 04)	♦ 3721
Kawasaki 900 & 1000 Fours (73 - 77)	0222
Kawasaki ZX900, 1000 & 1100 Liquid-cooled Fours (83 - 97)	♦ 1681
KTM EXC Enduro & SX Motocross (00 - 07)	♦ 4629
MOTO GUZZI 750, 850 & 1000 V-Twins (74 - 78)	0339
MZ ETZ Models (81 - 95)	◊ 1680
NORTON 500, 600, 650 & 750 Twins (57 - 70)	0187
Norton Commando (68 - 77)	0125
PEUGEOT Speedfight, Trekker & Vivacity Scooters (96 - 08)	◊ 3920
PIAGGIO (Vespa) Scooters (91 - 06)	3492
SUZUKI GT, ZR & TS50 (77 - 90)	◊ 0799
Suzuki TS50X (84 - 00)	◊ 1599
Suzuki 100, 125, 185 & 250 Air-cooled Trail bikes (79 - 89)	0797
Suzuki GP100 & 125 Singles (78 - 93)	◊ 0576
Suzuki GS, GN, GZ & DR125 Singles (82 - 05)	◊ 0888
Suzuki GSX-R600/750 (06 - 09)	♦ 4790
Suzuki 250 & 350 Twins (68 - 78)	0120
Suzuki GT250X7, GT200X5 & SB200 Twins (78 - 83)	◊ 0469
Suzuki GS/GSX250, 400 & 450 Twins (79 - 85)	0736
Suzuki GS500 Twin (89 - 06)	♦ 3238
Suzuki GS550 (77 - 82) & GS750 Fours (76 - 79)	0363
Suzuki GS/GSX550 4-valve Fours (83 - 88)	1133
Suzuki SV650 & SV650S (99 - 08)	♦ 3912
Suzuki GSX-R600 & 750 (96 - 00)	♦ 3553
Suzuki GSX-R600 (01 - 03), GSX-R750 (00 - 03) & GSX-R1000 (01 - 02)	♦ 3986
Suzuki GSX-R600/750 (04 - 05) & GSX-R1000 (03 - 06)	♦ 4382
Suzuki GSF600, 650 & 1200 Bandit Fours (95 - 06)	♦ 3367
Suzuki Intruder, Marauder, Volusia & Boulevard (85 - 06)	♦ 2618
Suzuki GS850 Fours (78 - 88)	0536
Suzuki GS1000 Four (77 - 79)	0484
Suzuki GSX-R750, GSX-R1100 (85 - 92), GSX600F, GSX750F, GSX1100F (Katana) Fours	♦ 2055
Suzuki GSX600/750F & GSX750 (98 - 02)	♦ 3987
Suzuki GS/GSX1000, 1100 & 1150 4-valve Fours (79 - 88)	0737
Suzuki TL1000S/R & DL1000 V-Strom (97 - 04)	♦ 4083
Suzuki GSF650/1250 (05 - 09)	♦ 4798
Suzuki GSX1300R Hayabusa (99 - 04)	♦ 4184
Suzuki GSX1400 (02 - 07)	♦ 4758
TRIUMPH Tiger Cub & Terrier (52 - 68)	0414
Triumph 350 & 500 Unit Twins (58 - 73)	0137
Triumph Pre-Unit Twins (47 - 62)	0251
Triumph 650 & 750 2-valve Unit Twins (63 - 83)	0122
Triumph Trident & BSA Rocket 3 (69 - 75)	0136
Triumph Bonneville (01 - 07)	♦ 4364
Triumph Daytona, Speed Triple, Sprint & Tiger (97 - 05)	♦ 3755
Triumph Triples and Fours (carburettor engines) (91 - 04)	♦ 2162
VESPA P/PX125, 150 & 200 Scooters (78 - 06)	0707
Vespa Scooters (59 - 78)	0126
YAMAHA DT50 & 80 Trail Bikes (78 - 95)	◊ 0800
Yamaha T50 & 80 Townmate (83 - 95)	◊ 1247

Title	Book No
Yamaha YB100 Singles (73 - 91)	◊ 0474
Yamaha RS/RXS100 & 125 Singles (74 - 95)	0331
Yamaha RD & DT125LC (82 - 95)	◊ 0887
Yamaha TZR125 (87 - 93) & DT125R (88 - 07)	◊ 1655
Yamaha TY50, 80, 125 & 175 (74 - 84)	◊ 0464
Yamaha XT & SR125 (82 - 03)	◊ 1021
Yamaha YBR125	4797
Yamaha Trail Bikes (81 - 00)	2350
Yamaha 2-stroke Motocross Bikes 1986 - 2006	2662
Yamaha YZ & WR 4-stroke Motocross Bikes (98 - 08)	2689
Yamaha 250 & 350 Twins (70 - 79)	0040
Yamaha XS250, 360 & 400 sohc Twins (75 - 84)	0378
Yamaha RD250 & 350LC Twins (80 - 82)	0803
Yamaha RD350 YPVS Twins (83 - 95)	1158
Yamaha RD400 Twin (75 - 79)	0333
Yamaha XT, TT & SR500 Singles (75 - 83)	0342
Yamaha XZ550 Vision V-Twins (82 - 85)	0821
Yamaha FJ, FZ, XJ & YX600 Radian (84 - 92)	2100
Yamaha XJ600S (Diversion, Seca II) & XJ600N Fours (92 - 03)	♦ 2145
Yamaha YZF600R Thundercat & FZS600 Fazer (96 - 03)	♦ 3702
Yamaha FZ-6 Fazer (04 - 07)	♦ 4751
Yamaha YZF-R6 (99 - 02)	♦ 3900
Yamaha YZF-R6 (03 - 05)	♦ 4601
Yamaha 650 Twins (70 - 83)	0341
Yamaha XJ650 & 750 Fours (80 - 84)	0738
Yamaha XS750 & 850 Triples (76 - 85)	0340
Yamaha TDM850, TRX850 & XTZ750 (89 - 99)	◊ 3540
Yamaha YZF750R & YZF1000R Thunderace (93 - 00)	♦ 3720
Yamaha FZR600, 750 & 1000 Fours (87 - 96)	♦ 2056
Yamaha XV (Virago) V-Twins (81 - 03)	♦ 0802
Yamaha XVS650 & 1100 Drag Star/V-Star (97 - 05)	♦ 4195
Yamaha XJ900F Fours (83 - 94)	♦ 3239
Yamaha XJ900S Diversion (94 - 01)	♦ 3739
Yamaha YZF-R1 (98 - 03)	♦ 3754
Yamaha YZF-R1 (04 - 06)	♦ 4605
Yamaha FZS1000 Fazer (01 - 05)	♦ 4287
Yamaha FJ1100 & 1200 Fours (84 - 96)	♦ 2057
Yamaha XJR1200 & 1300 (95 - 06)	♦ 3981
Yamaha V-Max (85 - 03)	♦ 4072
ATVs	
Honda ATC70, 90, 110, 185 & 200 (71 - 85)	0565
Honda Rancher, Recon & TRX250EX ATVs	2553
Honda TRX300 Shaft Drive ATVs (88 - 00)	2125
Honda Foreman (95 - 07)	2465
Honda TRX300EX, TRX400EX & TRX450R/ER ATVs (93 - 06)	2318
Kawasaki Bayou 220/250/300 & Prairie 300 ATVs (86 - 03)	2351
Polaris ATVs (85 - 97)	2302
Polaris ATVs (98 - 06)	2508
Yamaha YFS200 Blaster ATV (88 - 06)	2317
Yamaha YFB250 Timberwolf ATVs (92 - 00)	2217
Yamaha YFM350 & YFM400 (ER and Big Bear) ATVs (87 - 03)	2126
Yamaha Banshee and Warrior ATVs (87 - 03)	2314
Yamaha Kodiak and Grizzly ATVs (93 - 05)	2567
ATV Basics	10450
TECHBOOK SERIES	
Twist and Go (automatic transmission) Scooters Service and Repair Manual	4082
Motorcycle Basics TechBook (2nd Edition)	3515
Motorcycle Electrical TechBook (3rd Edition)	3471
Motorcycle Fuel Systems TechBook	3514
Motorcycle Maintenance TechBook	4071
Motorcycle Modifying	4272
Motorcycle Workshop Practice TechBook (2nd Edition)	3470

◊ = not available in the USA   ♦ = Superbike

The manuals on this page are available through good motorcycle dealers and accessory shops.
In case of difficulty, contact: **Haynes Publishing**
(UK) **+44 1963 442030**   (USA) **+1 805 498 6703**
(SV) **+46 18 124016**
(Australia/New Zealand) **+61 3 9763 8100**

MCL24.08/09

Preserving Our Motoring Heritage

< The Model J Duesenberg Derham Tourster. Only eight of these magnificent cars were ever built – this is the only example to be found outside the United States of America

Almost every car you've ever loved, loathed or desired is gathered under one roof at the Haynes Motor Museum. Over 300 immaculately presented cars and motorbikes represent every aspect of our motoring heritage, from elegant reminders of bygone days, such as the superb Model J Duesenberg to curiosities like the bug-eyed BMW Isetta. There are also many old friends and flames. Perhaps you remember the 1959 Ford Popular that you did your courting in? The magnificent 'Red Collection' is a spectacle of classic sports cars including AC, Alfa Romeo, Austin Healey, Ferrari, Lamborghini, Maserati, MG, Riley, Porsche and Triumph.

A Perfect Day Out

Each and every vehicle at the Haynes Motor Museum has played its part in the history and culture of Motoring. Today, they make a wonderful spectacle and a great day out for all the family. Bring the kids, bring Mum and Dad, but above all bring your camera to capture those golden memories for ever. You will also find an impressive array of motoring memorabilia, a comfortable 70 seat video cinema and one of the most extensive transport book shops in Britain. The Pit Stop Cafe serves everything from a cup of tea to wholesome, home-made meals or, if you prefer, you can enjoy the large picnic area nestled in the beautiful rural surroundings of Somerset.

> John Haynes O.B.E., Founder and Chairman of the museum at the wheel of a Haynes Light 12.

< The 1936 490cc sohc-engined International Norton – well known for its racing success

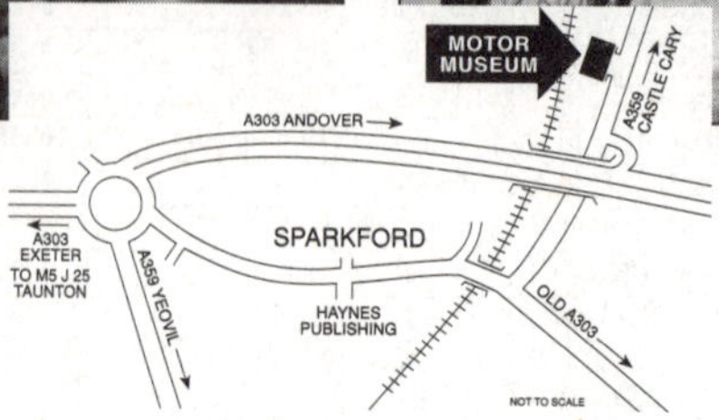

The Museum is situated on the A359 Yeovil to Frome road at Sparkford, just off the A303 in Somerset. It is about 40 miles south of Bristol, and 25 minutes drive from the M5 intersection at Taunton.
Open 9.30am - 5.30pm (10.00am - 4.00pm Winter) 7 days a week, *except Christmas Day, Boxing Day and New Years Day*
Special rates available for schools, coach parties and outings Charitable Trust No. 292048